Modeling and Profiling Taxpayer Behavior and Compliance

Bouchra Alj
Faculty of Legal, Economic, and Social Sciences of Mohammedia, Hassan II University, Casablanca, Morocco

Lhoussaine Alla
Sidi Mohamed Ben Abdellah University, Morocco

Badr Bentalha
Sidi Mohamed Ben Abdellah University, Morocco

IGI Global
Scientific Publishing
Publishing Tomorrow's Research Today

Vice President of Editorial	Melissa Wagner
Director of Acquisitions	Mikaela Felty
Director of Book Development	Jocelynn Hessler
Production Manager	Mike Brehm
Cover Design	Phillip Shickler

Published in the United States of America by
IGI Global Scientific Publishing
701 East Chocolate Avenue
Hershey, PA, 17033, USA
Tel: 717-533-8845
Fax: 717-533-7115
Website: https://www.igi-global.com E-mail: cust@igi-global.com

Library of Congress Cataloging-in-Publication Data

Names: Alj, Bouchra editor | Alla, Lhoussaine, 1969- editor | Bentalha, Badr, 1985- editor
Title: Modeling and profiling taxpayer behavior and compliance / edited by Bouchra Alj, Lhoussaine Alla, Badr Bentalha.
Description: Hershey, PA : IGI Global Scientific Publishing, [2025] | Includes bibliographical references and index. | Summary: "The objective of this book is to establish itself as a fundamental reference work in the field of tax compliance. To this end, it offers an exhaustive and multifaceted examination of the factors that shape taxpayers' behavior, both at the individual and collective levels. The book employs a multidisciplinary approach, encompassing economic, sociological, psychological, legal, technological, and other perspectives"-- Provided by publisher.
Identifiers: LCCN 2025000130 (print) | LCCN 2025000131 (ebook) | ISBN 9798337304229 hardcover | ISBN 9798337304236 paperback | ISBN 9798337304243 ebook
Subjects: LCSH: Taxpayer compliance--Case studies | Taxpayers--Attitudes--Case studies | Taxation--Public opinion--Case studies
Classification: LCC HJ2319 .M63 2025 (print) | LCC HJ2319 (ebook) | DDC 336.2/91--dc23/eng/20250314
LC record available at https://lccn.loc.gov/2025000130
LC ebook record available at https://lccn.loc.gov/2025000131
British Cataloguing in Publication Data
A Cataloguing in Publication record for this book is available from the British Library.

Table of Contents

Detailed Table of Contents

This chapter is exploratory in nature. Its aim is to establish a better understanding of tax morality based on psychosociological determinants. It is based on a qualitative study of 17 Moroccan doctors working in the liberal professions. The main results reveal various determinants, classified into two categories: psychological and social. These results confirm that personal values play a crucial role in understanding tax morality. In addition, the perception of inequalities in the tax system and the fear of sanctions also influence their tax morality. In addition, empathy for the beneficiaries of tax-financed public services and a sense of community reinforce commitment to tax compliance. The contributions of this research may be useful to public authorities, health professionals, researchers, as well as stakeholders involved in local and regional development.

This paper determines the key values of fiscal awareness by using a wide range of variables, mainly related to personal values, political ideology and cultural factors. After the introduction, the theoretical framework reviews key literature and define the fiscal awareness in relation to the tax morale and the fiscal ethics. The following sections introduce the methodology and examine the results of a questionnaire filled by 562 University students, analysing the variables that might have an impact on fiscal awareness. This paper contributes to the literature on tax morale analysing the influence of political ideology together with other variables. The influence of political ideology is thoroughly examined, aiming to ascertain whether students with liberal ideology would show a higher level of fiscal awareness than those with a conservative ideology. Results show that honesty and tax fairness foster higher levels of fiscal awareness. Political ideology prevails over other factors, like tax education, when explaining high levels of fiscal awareness.

The purpose of this study is to examine the importance of tax mentality and spatial difference elements emphasized within the framework of Schmölders' fiscal psychology theory on an empirical level through Turkish taxpayers residing in European countries. To achieve this objective, field research was conducted in the capitals of Germany, Austria, Belgium, the Netherlands, and France, where Turkish taxpayers predominantly reside. Data were collected through face-to-face interviews with 700 taxpayers residing in these countries and earning personal income. After conducting relevant preliminary tests, the data were analyzed using mediator variable and moderator variable analyses, as well as cross-tabulation analyses, in line with the study's purpose. The findings demonstrated that spatial difference acts as both a mediator and a moderator variable, empirically validating Schmölders' theory.

In order to improve taxpayers' civic participation and tax compliance, this research examines the complex connections between tax solidarity, tax morality, and civic obligation. The study illustrates how these elements combine to affect people's feeling of civic duty by examining the functions of tax morality as an ethical issue and tax solidarity as a social ideal. According to the research, encouraging a feeling of community around tax payments can greatly increase compliance rates by establishing a moral duty to support the common good. Additionally, the study finds that tax morality plays a significant mediating role in this connection, highlighting the necessity of public awareness efforts and ethical education to preserve the moral aspects of taxes. These findings have ramifications for legislators and public officials, who are urged to put policies into place that support openness, involvement of the community, and moral responsibility in taxation. In the end, the study urges greater investigation into socioeconomic and cultural elements that could influence taxpayer behavior.

Tax minimization remains a critical concern for all taxpayers, particularly for businesses. To reduce this burden, various accounting techniques can be employed within the framework of "creative accounting." While the relationship between taxation and creative accounting has been extensively studied in developed countries to better understand taxpayer behavior, such research is largely lacking in developing nations. In this context, the objective of this article is to explore the extent to which creative accounting techniques can be considered explanatory factors of taxpayer behavior in Morocco. Through a survey conducted with 50 companies, the study finds that 92% of respondents use creative accounting techniques to minimize their taxes liabilities. The most commonly employed techniques include depreciation (or amortization) and expense spreading. The findings of this study offer valuable theoretical and managerial implications for both academics and policymakers.

This investigation explores the complex connections that exist within business contexts among compliance for tax, civic duty, and social responsibility of corporates (CSR). The investigation's conclusions demonstrate the ability of CSR programs to influence moral behavior by manifesting a excellent optimistic correlation among them and people's feeling of social responsibility. Also, the investigation depicts a clear connection among CSR and compliance for tax, highlighting how moral company conduct encourages compliance with tax laws. It is also manifested how the Sense for Civics Duty mediates the association among CSR and compliance for tax, providing insight into the ways in which moral principles influence compliance practices. The investigation's theoretical ramifications advance knowledge of the conceptual frameworks underlying civic responsibility, social responsibility of corporates, and adherence to legal obligations. Policymakers are urged to create laws that encourage moral behavior and social responsibility, and corporations are advised to incorporate CSR activities.

This chapter examines tax administration systems that utilizes artificial intelligence (AI) technologies including predictive analytics and natural language processing across multiple nations such as the United States, Europe, Australia, and India. These tools improve tax efficiency by reducing administrative costs and ensuring accurate compliance. However, the implementation of AI introduces critical ethical concerns regarding algorithmic fairness, data privacy, and equitable outcomes. These challenges can be addressed through explainable AI (XAI), ethical standards, and robust regulatory frameworks. The chapter describes the differences between AI adoption in developed nations and less developed countries alongside recommendations for local use and worldwide teamwork. Tax systems that use AI technology to serve more people become more transparent as governments learn how to handle its disadvantages. Furthermore, the chapter outlines upcoming trends like blockchain and quantum computing and presents clear steps tax authorities should take to use AI responsibly in tax operations.

Tax evasion poses significant challenges to governments, undermining revenue collection and trust in public institutions. E-Government platforms, leveraging advanced digital tools and data analytics, offer a promising solution to address this issue by enabling efficient monitoring and profiling of taxpayer behavior. This study explores the role of E-Government systems in mitigating tax evasion through the behavioral profiling of non-compliant taxpayers. By integrating machine learning algorithms and anomaly detection techniques, the research identifies patterns of non-compliance and develops predictive models for early detection of evasion risks. Furthermore, the study examines the psychological and socio-economic factors influencing taxpayer behavior, emphasizing the role of trust, transparency, and system usability in fostering voluntary compliance. The findings underscore the importance of data-driven policy interventions and ethical considerations in behavioral profiling, offering a robust framework for enhancing tax compliance and promoting fiscal transparency.

The e-tax portal/system is a web-based tax filling and payment system designed to reduce cumbersome manual processes, cut evasion and help boost domestic revenue collection. The system is also used for payment of public services and other remittances. Usability of the e-tax portals is key for the public to find it easy to use. The heuristic evaluation (HE) method is used for the usability evaluations. The data collected were analyzed based on the ten Nielsen usability heuristics. The results showed that this method of assessment is effective in pointing out various usability issues in e-government services specifically e-tax portal interface. A usable e-tax portal decreases training cost, support, and maintenance costs. The paper also provides general recommendations on how to develop and manage more usable websites.

This chapter seeks to highlight and evaluate the use of 10-K filings as a methodology to effectively measure corporate tax behavior at publicly traded, American corporations. The chapter delivers examples of how to utilize sections of the 10-K filing (including textual analyses strategy and example of application to recent presidential policy) to evaluate tax behavior in the context of federal regulation. Utilization of both qualitative narrative and quantitative metrics found in the 10-K filing leads to more substantive and meaningful analyses of the corporate tax conduct that impacts the direction of the global economy.

Preface

1. GENERAL OVERVIEW OF THE TOPIC

In an economic context characterized by recurrent crises and increasing pressure on public finances, the issue of tax compliance emerges as a critical concern. The book Modeling and Profiling Taxpayer Behavior and Compliance seeks to examine contemporary challenges associated with tax compliance through the lens of taxpayer behavior. Tax compliance extends beyond the mere adherence to legal obligations; rather, it is shaped by a complex interplay of economic, psychological, sociological, cultural, institutional, legal, political, and technological factors. Despite this multifaceted nature, there remains a dearth of integrated approaches that effectively connect these dimensions to the decision-making processes underlying compliance or non-compliance with fiscal duties.

The primary objective of this book is thus to investigate the principal challenges of tax compliance by focusing on taxpayer behavior. It aims to address this gap by offering a comprehensive analysis of the factors influencing individuals' and businesses' adherence to tax obligations. The chapters draw upon rigorous and innovative theoretical studies, methodologically robust and reliable empirical research, and pioneering experimental methods to elucidate fiscal behavior and promote greater compliance with tax responsibilities.

2. OBJECTIVES OF THE COLLECTIVE BOOK

The primary objective of this book is to enhance trust between taxpayers and tax authorities by raising public awareness of the stakes involved in tax compliance and the repercussions of non-compliance. By providing practical tools and recommendations for policymakers, the work aspires to foster the development of fairer and more effective tax policies. It seeks to establish itself as a foundational reference within the field of fiscal studies. To this end, it offers a comprehensive and multidimensional examination of the factors shaping taxpayer behavior, both at the individual and collective levels. Adopting a multidisciplinary approach, the book integrates economic, sociological, psychological, legal, technological, and other perspectives. Its central aim is to facilitate constructive dialogue and exchange regarding fiscal behavior and strategies to enhance adherence to tax obligations. In doing so, it transcends the predominantly economic, conventional analyses that have historically dominated the field, aiming instead for a more nuanced understanding of the complex interactions that influence the tax-related decisions of individuals and businesses.

Furthermore, the book endeavors to provide an international perspective, drawing on case studies from diverse regions worldwide to enable comparative analysis and the identification of global trends while respecting local specificities. This international dimension enriches the analysis by incorporating a variety of contexts, which is essential for a sophisticated understanding of fiscal dynamics. Beyond analysis, the work aims to educate and sensitize taxpayers to the importance of complying with tax obligations. Its goal is to strengthen trust between taxpayers and tax authorities by emphasizing the legal and financial implications of non-compliance, particularly by clarifying procedures and elucidating the rationale behind tax requirements. This promotes improved communication and fosters a more transparent and constructive relationship between the two parties.

Ultimately, this book proposes a holistic approach, blending theoretical insights with practical tools and recommendations tailored for policymakers and tax experts. It establishes a framework for preventing fraud, enhancing compliance practices, and designing tax policies that are both more equitable and efficient.

3. SYNTHESIS OF CONTRIBUTIONS

The contributions assembled in this book draw upon rigorous theoretical studies and innovative empirical research to elucidate the motivations underlying fiscal behaviors. Additionally, the book presents international case studies, enabling the identification of global trends while respecting local particularities. Aimed at a broad audience—including researchers, tax professionals, policymakers, and students—this work provides a valuable interdisciplinary perspective on fiscal behaviors, thereby enhancing the understanding of contemporary tax dynamics.

The principal themes addressed in each chapter are summarized below:

Chapter 1: Determinants of the Compliant Behavior of the Taxpayer: Bibliometric and Prospective Approach

This contribution seeks to identify the primary determinants of taxpayers' fiscal behavior through a bibliometric and prospective analysis, aiming to better anticipate shifts in fiscal conduct within a complex tax environment. Employing a methodological approach that integrates bibliometric analysis with qualitative foresight, the study catalogs key theoretical, methodological, and empirical gaps in the existing literature and offers recommendations to refine tax policies and enforcement strategies.

Chapter 2: Fiscal Feelings: Behavioral & Neuroeconomic Insights on Tax Compliance

By examining the influence of emotions, cognitive biases, and social preferences on fiscal behavior, this chapter investigates how neuroscience and behavioral psychology illuminate taxpayers' decision-making processes. Through an interdisciplinary methodological framework grounded in neuroeconomics and behavioral economics, the research concludes that emotions and cognitive biases play a pivotal role in tax compliance, substantiated by practical examples illustrating how these factors can be leveraged for effective taxation.

Chapter 3: The Psychosociological Determinants of Tax Morality in Morocco: The Case of Liberal Professions

This chapter aims to explore the psychosociological determinants of tax morality in Morocco, with a specific focus on liberal professions. It addresses the research question: What factors influence tax morality in this particular context? Through a qualitative study involving 17 Moroccan doctors in private practice, the empirical findings reveal that tax morality is shaped by several key factors, including personal values, perceptions of tax inequity, and fear of sanctions. Furthermore, the analysis highlights the significant role of empathy and a sense of community belonging in fostering tax compliance. These insights offer a valuable contribution to understanding the psychosociological dynamics underpinning adherence to fiscal obligations within this professional group.

Chapter 4: Political Ideology and Individual Values as Key Determinants of Fiscal Awareness

This study examines the impact of political ideology and personal values on fiscal awareness. Utilizing logistic regression analysis, the authors demonstrate that values such as honesty and tax equity positively enhance taxpayers' fiscal awareness. Political ideology emerges as a significant determinant, with findings indicating that students aligned with liberal ideologies exhibit higher levels of fiscal awareness compared to peers with differing ideological orientations.

Chapter 5: The Relationship Between Taxpayers' Perceptions and Attitudes Toward Taxation: The Mediator and Moderator Effects of Spatial Diversity

Exploring the role of fiscal perceptions and spatial diversity in tax compliance, this chapter addresses the question: To what extent do spatial differences influence taxpayers' attitudes toward taxation? Based on an empirical study of 700 Turkish taxpayers residing in five European countries, and employing a rigorous analysis of mediation and moderation factors, the research establishes that spatial diversity serves dual roles as both a moderator and mediator. These findings reinforce Schmölders' psychological tax theory, underscoring the importance of spatial contexts in shaping fiscal behaviors.

Chapter 6: Effect of Tax Solidarity on the Taxpayer's Sense of Civic Duty by Mediation of Tax Morality in the Horn of Africa

This study investigates the impact of tax solidarity on taxpayers' sense of civic duty, with tax morality and compliance as mediating variables. Through a qualitative analysis of moral and social dynamics, the results indicate that tax solidarity strengthens civic duty by leveraging tax morality. The research highlights its potential as an effective lever for promoting community engagement and transparency within tax systems.

Chapter 7: Examining Creative Accounting as an Explanatory Factor of Taxpayer Behavior: Evidence from Morocco

This chapter assesses the extent to which creative accounting techniques influence the fiscal behavior of Moroccan firms, an underexplored area in developing economies compared to well-documented advanced economy contexts. Drawing on a survey of Moroccan enterprises, the study reveals that a majority of respondents employ practices such as amortization and expense spreading to reduce tax liabilities. These findings shed light on strategies adopted under fiscal pressure, offering both theoretical and managerial implications, and enriching the understanding of fiscal dynamics in emerging economies while suggesting avenues for tailoring tax policies to these realities.

Chapter 8: Moroccan Taxpayers' Perception of Tax Amnesties

This chapter examines Moroccan taxpayers' perceptions of tax amnesties, exploring their effects on compliance and trust in the tax system. It addresses the question: What are the effects of amnesties on taxpayer compliance and trust in the fiscal system? Through extensive documentary research and interviews with taxpayers, the authors demonstrate that amnesties are perceived as a "win-win" mechanism benefiting both the state and taxpayers. However, they emphasize a critical condition for their efficacy: the necessity of deterrent sanctions to ensure sustained fiscal discipline.

Chapter 9: Effective Communication and Awareness Campaigns as Tools for Enhancing Tax Compliance: Insights and Strategies

This chapter analyzes the influence of communication and awareness campaigns on tax compliance. Based on a qualitative study involving interviews with experts and taxpayers, the authors find that transparency and targeted campaigns significantly bolster taxpayers' trust in tax authorities, thereby reducing tax evasion behaviors.

Chapter 10: Corporate Social Responsibility Effect on Tax Compliance by Mediation of Sense of Civic Duty in the Horn of Africa

This chapter examines the role of corporate social responsibility (CSR) in promoting tax compliance, analyzing its influence on taxpayers' sense of civic duty. The findings reveal that CSR enhances civic duty, which acts as a mediator in the tax compliance process.

Chapter 11: Artificial Intelligence in Tax Compliance: Transforming Taxpayer Behavior and System Efficiency

This chapter explores the impact of artificial intelligence (AI) on fiscal behavior and tax system efficiency, framing AI as a transformative factor in tax compliance. Through a methodological approach combining comparative analysis and international case studies, the authors demonstrate that AI enhances fraud detection capabilities and improves taxpayer experience while optimizing administrative processes. However, this integration raises significant ethical challenges, particularly regarding data privacy and equity in policy enforcement, necessitating deeper reflection on normative frameworks and governance mechanisms.

Chapter 12: The Role of E-Government in Mitigating Tax Evasion: Behavioral Profiling of Non-Compliant Taxpayers

This chapter analyzes how e-government platforms reduce tax evasion through behavioral profiling and identifies the most effective digital tools. Leveraging predictive models and psychological factors, the authors highlight e-government systems as a key mechanism for improving evasion risk detection and enhancing transparency.

Chapter 13: Usability of E-Government Service for Taxpayers in Ethiopia: The Case of the E-Tax System

Within a broader reflection on technological determinants of tax administration modernization in emerging contexts, this chapter evaluates the usability of Ethiopia's electronic tax filing system. It explores the central question: How can user experience be improved to increase system adoption? Using a heuristic evaluation based on Nielsen's usability criteria, the study demonstrates that enhancing the user interface significantly reduces training costs while boosting the operational efficiency of the tax portal.

Chapter 14: Utilizing 10-K Filings to Profile American Corporate Tax Conduct: A Methodological Proposal

This final chapter proposes an innovative methodology for analyzing U.S. corporate fiscal behavior using 10-K annual reports to assess tax conduct. Combining in-depth textual analysis with quantitative metrics derived from these filings, the study underscores the value of 10-K reports as a robust and reliable analytical framework for decoding corporate fiscal behavior. It offers a complementary perspective to traditional profiling models, highlighting the potential of narrative and financial data to refine understanding of tax optimization or evasion strategies, while inviting nuanced exploration of the interplay between organizational transparency and tax compliance.

4. TARGET AUDIENCE OF THE BOOK

This book establishes itself as an essential reference, offering a comprehensive analysis of the economic, psychological, sociological, and cultural factors influencing the compliance of individuals and businesses. By adopting a multidisciplinary approach, it seeks to enrich the discourse on tax compliance, moving beyond traditional economic analyses.

The book is intended for a diverse audience, encompassing both academic experts and general readers interested in taxation and behavioral economics, including:

- Researchers and Academics: They will find in this book an invaluable resource for understanding the factors that shape fiscal behavior, as well as the underlying theories and analytical approaches.
- Tax Professionals: Tax inspectors, tax lawyers, consultants, auditors, accountants, and other specialists aiming to deepen their understanding of taxpayer behavior to facilitate legal compliance.
- Policymakers and Legislators: Governments, tax policy officials, and regulators who can leverage insights into taxpayer behavior to refine public policies and enhance adherence to tax obligations.

- Entrepreneurs and Business Leaders: Those seeking to better grasp their companies' tax obligations and how to comply with them to avoid penalties.
- Students: Individuals studying economics, law, sociology, or psychology who wish to expand their knowledge of taxation and behavior will benefit from its exceptional interdisciplinary perspective.

The book also holds appeal for the broader public, including taxpayers and citizens concerned with fiscal matters. It demystifies complex tax issues, enabling readers to understand why and how individuals and entities comply—or fail to comply—with their tax obligations.

5. CONCLUSION AND PERSPECTIVES

The book Modeling and Profiling Taxpayer Behavior and Compliance offers a multidimensional analysis of the determinants of tax compliance, skillfully integrating innovative theoretical, empirical, and methodological approaches. It explores fiscal behaviors through four primary axes:

- Psychosocial Factors: Emotions, cognitive biases, tax morality, political ideology, and personal values.
- Contextual Influences: Spatial diversity, tax solidarity, and perceptions of tax amnesties.
- Technological Tools: Artificial intelligence (AI), big data, and e-government for fraud detection and compliance enhancement.
- Institutional Strategies: Transparent communication, corporate social responsibility (CSR), and creative accounting.

Case studies from diverse regions (USA, Morocco, Spain, Turkey, Ethiopia, Australia, the United Kingdom, etc.) enrich the analysis by providing both local and global perspectives.

The book's key contributions manifest across three levels:

- Theoretical: It broadens analytical frameworks beyond economics, incorporating neuroeconomics, social psychology, and sociology, while integrating concepts such as "tax morality," "fiscal awareness," "tax solidarity," and the impact of cognitive biases.
- Methodological: It employs a variety of approaches (bibliometric analyses, qualitative studies, logistic regressions, PRISMA systematic reviews, heuristic evaluations) and leverages hybrid data sources (surveys, interviews, 10-K reports, behavioral data).
- Empirical: The studies validate the influence of emotions and personal values on tax compliance, the contributions of AI to fraud detection, and the role of transparent communication and e-government platforms in promoting compliant taxpayer behavior.

Nevertheless, certain limitations emerge. Theoretically, fragmentation across disciplines and the absence of integrative models tailored to specific cultural contexts are noted. Methodologically, biases in qualitative studies and challenges to generalizability persist. Empirically, ethical concerns surrounding AI (algorithmic biases, data privacy) and inconsistencies in some findings are evident.

The book opens promising avenues for future research. It calls for the development of unified models integrating behavioral economics, neuroscience, and sociology; further exploration of taxpayer-state trust dynamics in developing countries; and long-term evaluations of technological tools' effectiveness. Mixed-method approaches combining qualitative and quantitative analyses, alongside randomized experiments, are also recommended to better capture the complexity of taxpayer behavior vis-à-vis tax compliance.

In conclusion, this book bridges disciplines and methodologies to shed light on fiscal behaviors. Its limitations pave the way for future research to refine public policies, particularly in an era of increasing digitalization and global crises. It stands as a vital resource for researchers, practitioners, and policy-makers committed to fostering behaviors conducive to sustainable tax compliance.

Bouchra Alj
Faculty of Legal, Economic, and Social Sciences of Mohammedia, Hassan II University, Casablanca, Morocco

Lhoussaine Alla
Sidi Mohamed Ben Abdellah University, Morocco

Badr Bentalha
Sidi Mohamed Ben Abdellah University, Morocco

Chapter 1
Determinant of the Compliant Behavior of the Taxpayer: Bibliometric and Prospective Approach

Lhoussaine Alla
https://orcid.org/0000-0002-7238-1792
Sidi Mohamed Ben Abdellah University, Morocco

Bouchra Alj
https://orcid.org/0000-0002-7856-3044
Hassan II University, Casablanca, Morocco

Mourad Aarabe
https://orcid.org/0009-0003-9772-6683
Sidi Mohamed Ben Abdellah University, Morocco

Majda El Agy
Cady Ayad University, Marrakech, Morocco

Badr Bentalha
https://orcid.org/0000-0003-1339-542X
Sidi Mohamed Ben Abdellah University, Morocco

Naoual Bouhtati
Sidi Mohamed Ben Abdellah University, Morocco

ABSTRACT

Tax compliance, a key issue for governments, requires a better understanding of the determinants of taxpayers' behaviour. This research, using a bibliometric and prospective approach, explores these factors in a context marked by the complexity of tax systems, globalization and the rise of digital technologies. The objective is to optimize tax collection and promote fiscal citizenship through holistic approaches such as tax nudges and artificial intelligence. The study identifies theoretical (often one-dimensional research), methodological (lack of reliable data, selection bias) and empirical (few analyses of specific fiscal policies in the long term) gaps. The question is: what are the main determinants of tax compliance according to the literature, and how can they be analyzed to anticipate future developments? By combining bibliometric analysis and qualitative prospective, the study offers recommendations for improving tax policies and control strategies.

INTRODUCTION

Understanding the determinants of taxpayers' tax behaviour is critically important in a global context of increasing fiscal challenges. As Alm & Torgler (2024) point out, tax compliance has become a major issue for governments, particularly in an environment characterized by the digitalization of the economy

DOI: 10.4018/979-8-3373-0422-9.ch001

and the emergence of new forms of transactions (Adelakun et al., 2024). Recent OECD estimates (2024) indicate that tax losses due to non-compliance represent between 20% and 30% of potential revenues in many countries.

Tax compliance is a critical issue for governments around the world, as it directly influences their ability to finance essential public services. Research on the determinants of taxpayer compliance is therefore critically important, especially in a context where tax evasion and fraud pose major challenges to tax administrations. The latter are under increasing pressure to optimize tax collection in the face of complex tax systems, globalization and the emergence of digital technologies such as cryptocurrencies (Adelakun et al., 2024). Understanding the factors that influence tax compliance allows for more effective and equitable tax policies, while promoting greater tax civility.

The issue of tax compliance is at the heart of a functioning and fair society. Governments around the world depend on steady tax revenues to fund essential public services, from health care and education to infrastructure and social protection programs. Understanding the multiple factors that influence taxpayers' behaviour is therefore not only an academic quest, but also a key element of effective governance. This research explores the determinants of compliant tax behaviour using a combined bibliometric and prospective approach to provide a comprehensive and prospective analysis of this crucial issue. The urgency of this issue is underlined by the current context, characterized by increasing pressure on tax administrations to optimize collection in the face of complex tax systems, globalization and rapid evolution of digital technologies, cryptocurrencies (OECD, 2024). These developments present both challenges and opportunities, requiring ongoing analysis and adaptation of existing models to integrate more holistic and intelligent approaches such as tax incentives ("nudges") and artificial intelligence (Muehlbacher & Hartl, 2023).

Tax compliance, in its simplest form, refers to the fulfilment by individuals and businesses of their legal obligations to report their income and pay their taxes accurately and on time. This includes not only compliance with the letter of the law, but also a broader sense of fiscal morality, reflecting the will to contribute equitably to the common good (Dahlan et al., 2024). Conversely, non-compliance ranges from involuntary errors to deliberate tax fraud and evasion, each with different implications for public finances (Slemrod & Yitzhaki, 2023). Our goal is to understand the factors that promote voluntary compliance, thereby fostering a culture of tax civility.

Tax compliance is defined as the voluntary fulfilment by taxpayers of their tax obligations (Slemrod, 2019; Alm, 2023). The determinants of compliance include all economic, psychological, social and institutional factors that influence fiscal behaviour (Dahlan et al., 2024). The bibliometric approach allows for a systematic analysis of existing scientific literature (López-Lozano & Pérez-López, 2023), while the prospective approach aims to anticipate future developments in tax behaviour (Kirchler & Gangl, 2023).

Despite extensive research on tax compliance, there are still significant gaps in our understanding of this complex phenomenon. Traditional models, often based on rational choice theory, often fail to capture the full spectrum of influences on taxpayer behaviour (Alm, 2023). While economic factors such as income levels and perceived cost of non-compliance undoubtedly play a role, the integration of psychological, social and behavioural factors remains incomplete (O'shaughnessy, 2014; Ben Othman et al., 2024). The influence of cognitive biases, social norms (Reddy et al., 2024) and trust in tax administration (Williams, 2020) deserves further exploration. Methodologically, existing empirical studies often face limitations related to data availability and selection biases (De Neve, Imbert, & Spinnewijn, 2024). In addition, the application of advanced quantitative methods such as machine learning and network analysis remains limited (López-Lozano & Pérez-López, 2023). Empirically, there is a lack of comparative research between different countries and cultural contexts (Hashimzade & Myles, 2023; López-Laborda & Rodrigo, 2023), which hinders the development of universally applicable models.

Previous research has often addressed tax compliance in a one-dimensional way, neglecting the complexity of the determinants that influence this behaviour. Identified gaps include:

- **Theoretical gaps:** Existing models, often based on the theory of rational choice, do not fully capture the complexity of taxpayers' behaviour. The integration of psychological, social and behavioural factors remains partial (Dahlan et al., 2024).
- **Methodological gaps:** Empirical studies often suffer from methodological limitations, particularly with regard to the available data and selection biases. The use of sophisticated quantitative methods, such as machine learning, is still limited (Al-Asfour & McGee, 2024; Surugiu et al., 2025).
- **Empirical gaps:** There is a lack of comparative research across countries and cultural contexts, as well as a need for rigorous empirical studies on the impact of specific tax policies on compliance (López-Lozano & Pérez-López, 2023).

This research aims to contribute significantly to the existing literature by providing an integrated conceptual model of the determinants of tax compliance, identifying key research gaps and future research avenues, and by providing practical recommendations to policy makers for improving tax compliance. Forward-looking analysis will also help anticipate future trends and challenges, thus informing the development of responsive and effective fiscal policies and control strategies in a rapidly changing world.

In light of the above shortcomings, our central research problem is as follows: What are the main determinants of compliant tax behaviour identified in the literature? How can these determinants be identified and prospectively analysed to anticipate developments in the field of tax compliance?

To clarify this question, we propose the following sub-questions:

- What are the economic factors (income, cost of non-compliance, equity perception, etc.) that most influence tax compliance?
- What is the role of psycho-sociological factors (trust, social norms, risk aversion, moral obligation, etc.) in tax compliance?
- How do the intentions of taxpayers translate into concrete behaviour? What are the mediating factors?
- What is the impact of the characteristics of the tax administration (efficiency, transparency, fairness, quality of service, etc.) on compliance?
- How do new technologies (cryptocurrencies, online platforms, data analysis, etc.) influence taxpayer behaviour and tax control strategies (Adelakun et al., 2024; Gupta & Keen, 2024)?
- What are the prospects for changes in taxpayers' behaviour in the medium and long term (Kirchler & Gangl, 2023)? How will these changes affect fiscal policy and control (Slemrod, 2019; Alm, 2023)?

Methodologically, this research uses a mixed approach. First, a comprehensive bibliometric analysis will be conducted using databases such as Web of Science and Scopus, mapping trends in existing research, identifying key themes and authors, and highlighting gaps in the literature (Batrancea, Nichita, Olsen, & Kogler, 2024). This analysis will be followed by a qualitative thematic analysis of the most cited articles, deepening the nuances of the determinants identified. Finally, a prospective analysis, based on both literature review and potentially expert interviews, will explore potential future scenarios of taxpayer behaviour and the effectiveness of evolving tax policies. Forward-looking modelling techniques, such as scenario planning and sensitivity analysis, may be used to assess the impact of various factors on future compliance levels.

The chapter's structure is reflected in a theoretical and conceptual framework, followed by a methodological approach and then an analysis and discussion of the results.

1. THEORETICAL AND CONCEPTUAL FRAMEWORK

To provide a theoretical and conceptual insight into our research, we will address the conceptual approach and state of the art in research on the issue to understand our analysis.

1.1. Conceptual Lighting

Taxpayer Compliant Behavior

Tax compliance refers to the voluntary fulfilment by taxpayers (businesses and individuals) of their tax obligations, including accurate reporting of their income and timely payment of taxes (Slemrod, 2019; Alm, 2023). This implies not only compliance with tax laws, but also a moral dimension, where taxpayers feel responsible for contributing to the common good (Dahlan et al., 2024), through its n commitment not only legal but also moral towards the common good (Dahlan et al., 2024).

Compliance behaviour refers to all actions and decisions of taxpayers regarding the fulfilment or breach of their tax obligations. Compliance behaviour can be influenced by a variety of factors, including economic, psychological and social elements (O'shaughnessy, 2014). This behaviour refers to all actions taken by taxpayers to comply with tax laws. These are behaviours that go beyond avoidance of sanctions to include proactive contribution to tax obligations (Ben Othman et al., 2024).

Determinant of the Compliant Behavior of the Taxpayer

Determinants include all factors that influence a taxpayer's decision to comply with or not with their tax obligations (Tehulu & Dinberu, 2014). This includes such things as economic incentives, social standards, trust in the tax administration, and perceptions of fairness in the tax system (Reddy et al., 2024). The determinants of this behaviour include economic (income, cost of non-compliance), psycho-sociological (confidence, social standards) and institutional (efficiency of tax administration) factors (Williams, 2020).

To this end, Batrancea et al. (2012) present a mapping of the determinants of compliant taxpayer behaviour, divided into five main areas: Business, Industry, Sociological, Economic and Psychological (Figure 1). Each category lists specific factors that influence tax compliance, such as type of business, competition, inflation, and psychological aspects such as confidence and fears.

Figure 1. Determinant of the Compliant Behavior of the Taxpayer (Batrancea et al., 2012)

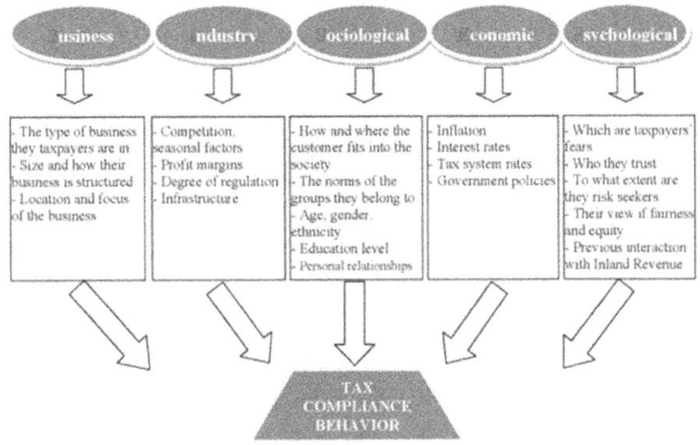

This structured approach allows us to understand the complexity of taxpayers' behaviour by analysing the influences of different domains, through systemic analysis. In this regard, Randlane (2015) presents a model of tax compliance as a system, highlighting the complex relationship between the taxpayer, his environment, economic, socio-political and personal factors (Figure 2).

Figure 2. A Model of tax compliance as a system (Randlane, 2015)

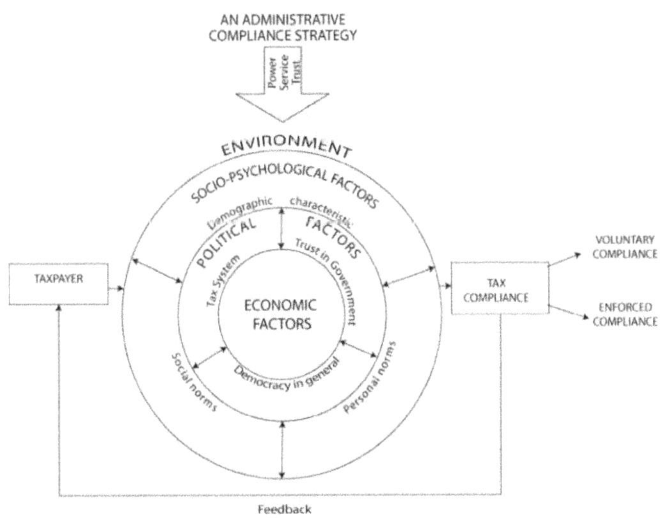

This visual representation demonstrates in a structured and interconnected way how these various elements interact to influence tax compliance, both voluntary and mandatory, as well as enforcement mechanisms.

This systemic approach allows us to understand tax compliance in its entirety by integrating the multiple dimensions that contribute to it. By viewing the taxpayer as an actor within a complex tax ecosystem, this approach highlights the crucial importance of interactions between economic, socio-political and personal factors in shaping compliant behavior. Indeed, the integration of trust in government, social norms, demographic factors and policy considerations into the tax compliance process provides a holistic and nuanced view of this dynamic.

1.2. State of the Art

As shown in our literature review, the state of the art on determinants of taxpayers' behaviour summarizes the main factors that influence their tax compliance with respect to the various dimensions above (Figure 1). Based on a series of recent empirical studies, the synthesis (Table 1) reveals a variety of factors influencing tax compliance. First, sociological determinants such as social standards, trust in government, procedural justice, and social capital play a crucial role in taxpayers' decision to comply. Second, economic determinants such as income level, tax rate, audit likelihood and sanctions also impact tax compliance. In addition, from a psychological perspective, risk aversion, the perception of fairness in the tax system, fiscal sophistication, and fiscal morality influence taxpayers' decision-making. Finally, business and industry determinants such as company size, sector of activity, ownership structure, and competition may also affect tax compliance.

Table 1. State of the art on determinants of compliant behaviour of taxpayers (Authors)

Dteterminant		Principle	References
Sociological	**Social standards**	The influence of peer behaviour and perception of tax evasion in the community.	Wenzel (2005); Kirchler et al; (2010); Pickhardt & Prinz (2014).
	Confidence in government	The level of confidence in institutions and the perception of fair use of tax revenues.	Kirchgässner (2011). Hashimzade et al; (2013); Schneider & Torgler (2007).
	Procedural justice	The perception of fairness in tax procedures and treatment by the tax administration	Murphy. (2003); Bin (2020); Gobena & Van Dijke (2017).
	Social capital	Civic engagement and participation in community life.	Alm & Gomez (2008); Hasan et al. (2017) ; Yong & Martin (2017)
Economic	**Income level**	The impact of taxpayers' income on their compliance propensity.	Piketty, T. (2014) ; Durham et a. (2014) ; Alhempi et al. (2014)
	Tax rate	The influence of the level of taxation on compliance behaviour.	Fullerton & Metcalf (2002) ; Mas'ud et al. (2014); Freire-Serén & Panadés (2013).
	Audit probability	The perception of risk to be controlled by the tax administration.	Ritsatos (2014); Chan & Song (2021) ; Kasper & Alm (2022)
	Sanctions	The impact of sanctions in case of non-compliance.	Kleven et al. (2011); Doran (2009) ; Rahmayanti & Prihatiningtias (2020)
Psychological	**Risk aversion**	The influence of risk aversion on the decision to comply or not.	Eisenhauer (2008); Engström et al. (2015) ; Khodamipour & Pourheydari (2024)
	Perception of equity	The sense of fairness in the tax system.	Mei Tan & Chin-Fatt (2000). Oladipo et al. (2022); Fajriana et al. (2023)
	Fiscal sophistication	The level of understanding of the tax system.	Reck & Bomare (2022); Borrego (2015); Drumbl (2013)
	Tax morality	Personal values and beliefs about paying taxes.	Khaerunnisa et al. (2016); Devano et al. (20224; Lis (2015)
Business/Industry	**Size of the company**	The impact of company size on tax compliance.	Fauziati & Kassim (2018) ; Akinboade (2015) ; Webley (2004)
	Business sector	Differences in tax behaviour between sectors.	Lignier & Evans (2012); Akhand (2018) ; Lignier et al. (2014)
	Ownership structure	The influence of ownership structure (public, private, family) on compliance.	Rakayana et al. (2021); Shaharuddin et al. (2012); Annuar et al. (2014)
	Competition	The impact of competition on incentives for tax evasion.	Damayanti & Matasik (2021) ; Yimam et al. (2023) ; Casagrande et al. (2015)

In summary, these determinants interact in complex ways to influence the behaviour of compliant taxpayers. Understanding these factors is crucial to designing effective tax policies and promoting tax compliance in modern companies.

This theoretical and conceptual framework highlights the complexity of the determinants of taxpayers' compliance behaviour. By integrating economic, psychological and social perspectives, this research aims to enrich the understanding of tax behaviours and provide practical recommendations for improving tax compliance.

We will now move on to the methodological framing and bibliometric and qualitative analysis of our study.

2. METHODOLOGY

2.1. Methodological Approach

To address the above issue, we have opted for a mixed, hybrid and reflexive methodological approach, combining bibliometric analysis and qualitative analysis, in order to better understand the complexity of fiscal behaviour:

- ***Bibliometric analysis:*** A systematic review of the scientific literature (Zou and Vu, 2019) on tax compliance determinants will be conducted using bibliographic databases (Web of Science, Scopus, etc.). The analysis will identify dominant research themes, gaps and emerging trends. Via VOSviewer and Bibliometrix R-package, this step seeks to map the intellectual landscape of tax compliance research and identify dominant and emerging research streams (Aria & Cuccurullo, 2017).
- ***Qualitative analysis:*** Based on the results of the bibliometric study, a more in-depth analysis (Miles and Huberman, 2003) will focus on a highly representative sample of the most cited references through a qualitative thematic analysis to deepen understanding of the determinants of taxpayer behavior in tax compliance. This step involves content analysis (titles, summaries and keywords), identification of emerging trends and classification of determinants (economic, psycho-sociological, institutional and technological).
- ***Prospective analysis:*** A qualitative thematic analysis will be carried out on the basis of literature and possible interviews with experts (tax administrators, researchers, taxpayers). This analysis will help identify possible scenarios for changing taxpayers' behaviour and the effectiveness of tax policies. Prospective modelling (e.g. scenarios, sensitivity analysis) can be used to explore the impacts of different factors on tax compliance.

2.2. Selection Process

In order to implement such a methodological approach, we have adopted a rigorous reference selection process in accordance with the following approach (Preferred Reporting Items for Systematic Reviews and Meta-Analyses (PRISMA):

Table 2. Reference selection process (Authors)

Phase 1	**Refined research equation**	("Tax compliance" OR "Taxpayer behavior") AND ("Determinants" OR "Factors") AND ("Economic" OR "Psychological" OR "Social")	250 references
Phase 2	**Initial selection of databases**	Web of Science- Scopus – JSTOR - ScienceDirect	
Phase 3	**Reference selection inclusion filters**	– Scientific papers (articles, systematic reviews). – Publications in English. – Period 2010-2024. – Fields: social sciences, economics, management.	–
Phase 4	**Reference selection exclusion filters**	– Government reports. – Conference papers. – Articles not peer reviewed. – Non-academic publications.	–
Phase 5	**Reference selection scrubber filters**	– Filtering by title and keywords	150
		– Reading the abstracts	90
		– Open access articles	29
Phase 6	**Refined research equation**	– Open access articles	29

This selection process provides a systematic, transparent and rigorous approach to building a high-quality body of research on the determinants of tax behaviour (Page et al., 2021).

3. BIBLIOMETRIC ANALYSIS

3.1. Overview

3.1.1. Main Information

As summarised in Figure 3 below, the bibliometric analysis of our research theme, covering the period 1989-2024, reveals a substantial scientific corpus of 676 documents, published in 303 different sources. Research in this field involves 1410 researchers, with a marked preference for collaborative work (2.68 co-authors per paper on average) and a moderate international dimension (25.3% of international co-authors). The scientific impact is notable with 18.52 average citations per document. Although the field has a solid theoretical basis (28,363 references) and a significant thematic diversity (1,477 keywords), the negative annual growth rate (-1.91%) suggests a possible slowdown in research on this topic.

Figure 3. Summary of bibliometric research data (Bibliometrix (R) output)

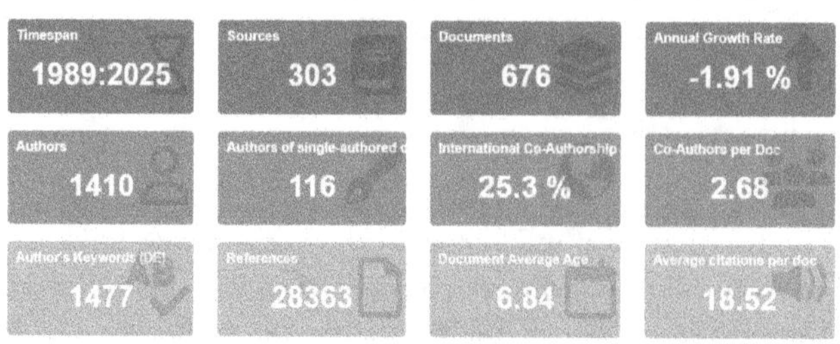

This analysis reveals a mature, well-established field of research with strong collaboration between researchers, but which could benefit from greater internationalization. The slight decline in growth may suggest a need for new approaches or issues.

3.1.2. Annual Scientific Production

In terms of the temporal evolution of publications, bibliometric analysis of scientific production on the determinants of taxpayers' tax behaviour reveals three distinct phases (Figure 4): a period of relative stability (1990-2010) with a low scientific output, followed by a moderate growth phase (2010-2015), and then a significant acceleration in publications (2015-2022) reaching a peak of more than 60 articles annually. This trend reflects the growing importance of understanding tax behaviour in contemporary academic research, probably stimulated by the challenges of fiscal modernization and tax compliance.

Figure 4. Publication time trends (Bibliometrix (R) output)

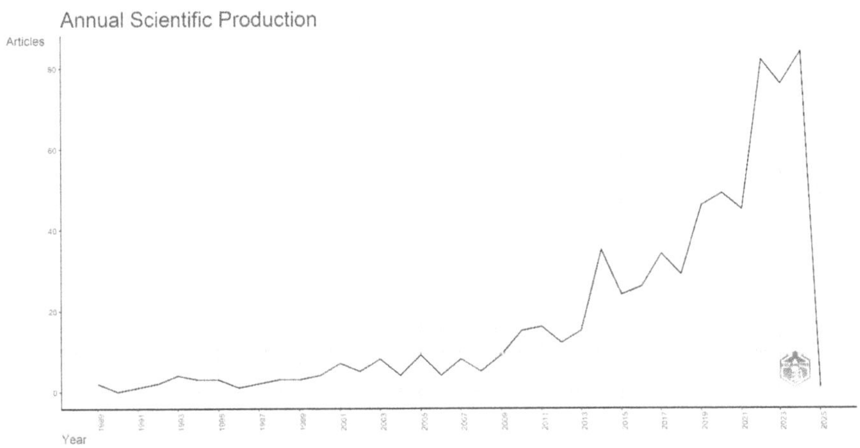

This reflects the growing importance of understanding taxpayers' behaviour in a context of modernizing tax systems and combating tax evasion.

3.1.3. Average Quotes Per Year

As for the analysis in terms of average citations per year (Figure 5), the bibliometric analysis reveals a significant fluctuation in the interest in tax compliance, measured by the average number of citations per year. Interest peaked around 2005, followed by a gradual decline until 2012. A slight recovery is visible around 2013, before a further decline until 2024.

Figure 5. Average reference citations per year (Bibliometrix (R) output)

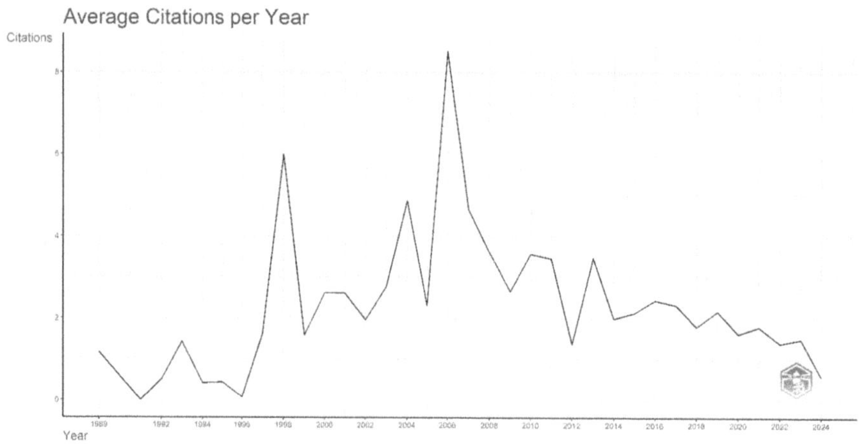

These variations suggest changes in the intensity of research on this topic, possibly influenced by socio-economic factors or legislative developments. Further investigation is needed to identify the causes of these fluctuations and their correlation with specific events.

3.1.4. Most Relevant Sources

Analysis of the most relevant sources reveals a concentration of tax compliance publications in economic and economic psychology journals (Figure 6). The Journal of Economic Psychology is clearly in the lead with 35 articles, followed by the eJournal of Tax Research and the Journal of Economic Behavior and Organization. This predominance highlights the importance of psychological and behavioural factors in understanding the determinants of tax compliance.

Figure 6. Most relevant sources (Bibliometrix (R) output)

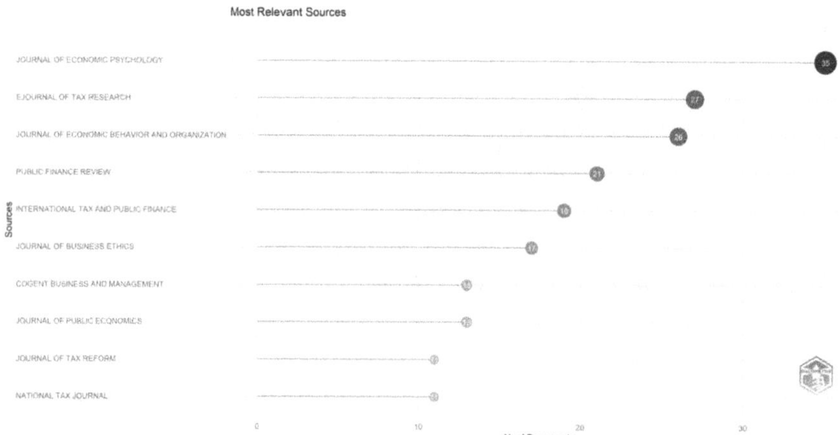

The presence of journals focusing on public finance and business ethics also indicates the interest in the public and ethical dimensions of this issue. The lower contribution of tax law journals such as the National Tax Journal and the Journal of Tax Reform suggests a research perspective that focuses primarily on behavioural aspects rather than legal aspects of tax compliance.

3.2. Authors

3.2.1. Most Relevant Authors

Bibliometric analysis reveals a concentration of research within a relatively small group of authors (Figure 7). Kirchler E. is the most prolific author in this field with 29 publications indexed in Scopus. ALM J follows with a significant contribution of 20 publications. A second group of authors (Torgler B, Farrar J, Muehlbacher S, Hauptman L, Kasper M, Kogler C, Santoro F and Gangl K) produced between 7 and 10 publications each. This distribution suggests a core of researchers who lead research on tax compliance behaviour, with Kirchler E. and ALM J playing a particularly influential role. The smaller output of the second group may indicate emerging researchers or researchers with a more specialized focus within this broader research topic.

Figure 7. Most Relevant Authors (Bibliometrix (R) output)

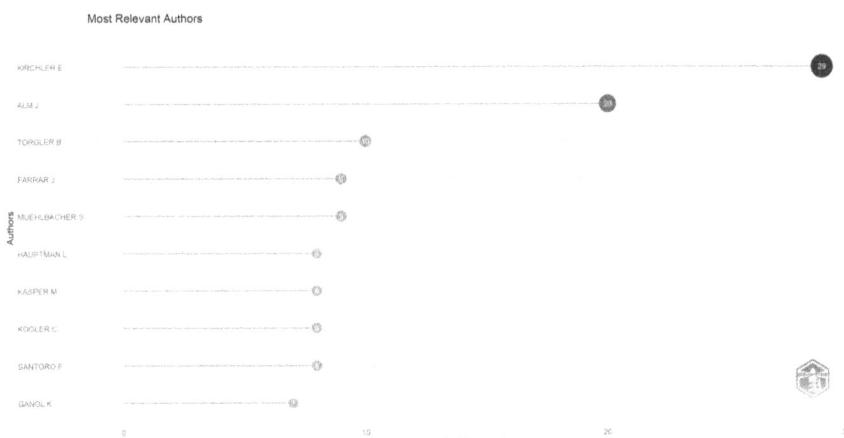

A more in-depth analysis of the networks of co-authors and citation patterns would allow for a more nuanced understanding of the relationships between these authors and the overall structure of the research field.

3.2.2. Most Relevant Affiliations

The bibliometric analysis reveals a concentration of research on taxpayers' tax compliance behaviour within a select group of institutions (Figure 8). The University of Vienna has a much higher scientific output (62 articles) than other institutions, suggesting a leading role in this field. The University Utara

Malaysia and the Universitas Indonesia also contribute substantially with 21 and 17 articles respectively. The remaining institutions have a more moderate level of research activity, with 11 to 15 articles. This distribution indicates the potential existence of research clusters and collaborations, particularly in Malaysia, given the presence of two Malaysian universities among the main contributors. The predominance of the University of Vienna justifies a more in-depth analysis to understand its specific research focus on tax compliance.

Figure 8. Most Relevant Affiliations (Bibliometrix (R) output)

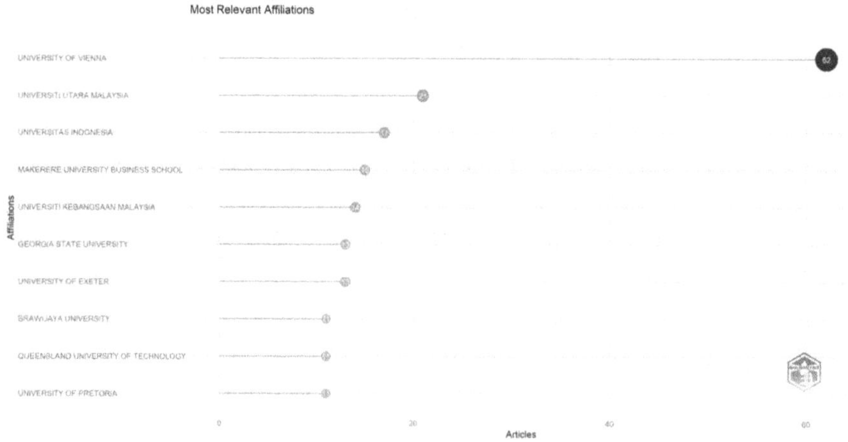

Overall, the analysis highlights key institutions that drive scientific discourse in this area and provides a starting point for identifying potential research partnerships and exploring thematic concentrations.

3.2.3. Most Globally Cited References

Bibliometric analysis of the most cited references worldwide on taxpayers' tax compliance behaviour highlights a concentration of citations around a few key publications (Table 3). The article in ALM J. (2006) in the Journal of Economic Psychology clearly dominates with 528 total citations, although its normalized influence (TC per Year Normalized) is less than other more recent publications. This underlines the importance of considering both the total number of citations and the time-based dynamics of publications. Several articles by ALM J. are among the most cited, confirming the significant influence of this author in the field. The themes covered in the most influential publications, such as Journal of Business Ethics, Law & Policy, American Journal of Political Science, and Management Science, suggest a multidisciplinary approach to the issue, integrating economic perspectives, psychological, legal and managerial. The presence of recent articles, notably those by BOTT K.M. (2019), DE NEVE J-E (2021) and SARAGIH A.H. (2023), attests to the dynamism of research and the emergence of new investigative leads, such as artificial intelligence applied to tax law.

Table 3. Most Globally Cited References (Bibliometrix (R) output)

Paper	DOI	Total Citations	TC per Year	Normalized TC
ALM J, 2006, J ECON PSYCHOL	10.1016/j.joep.2005.09.002	528	27.79	3.26
ALM J, 2011, J BUS ETHICS	10.1007/s10551-011-0761-9	285	20.36	5.91
FELD LP, 2007, LAW POLICY	10.1111/j.1467-9930.2007.00248.x	352	19.56	4.21
SCHOLZ JT, 1998, AM J POLIT SCI	10.2307/2991764	470	17.41	2.91
BOTT KM, 2020, MANAGE SCI	10.1287/mnsc.2019.3390	96	16.00	7.37
CASTRO L, 2015, J ECON BEHAV ORGAN	10.1016/j.jebo.2015.04.002	135	13.50	6.33
DE NEVE J-E, 2021, J POLIT ECON	10.1086/713096	51	12.75	7.13
WAHL I, 2010, LAW POLICY	10.1111/j.1467-9930.2010.00327.x	185	12.33	3.45
KASTLUNGER B, 2013, J ECON PSYCHOL	10.1016/j.joep.2012.11.007	146	12.17	3.50
BOBEK DD, 2013, J BUS ETHICS	10.1007/s10551-012-1390-7	146	12.17	3.50
JIMENEZ P, 2016, ADV ACCOUNT	10.1016/j.adiac.2016.07.001	104	11.56	4.74
WENZEL M, 2004, J ECON PSYCHOL	10.1016/S0167-4870(02)00168-X	233	11.10	2.28
MUEHLBACHER S, 2011, EUR J LAW ECON	10.1007/s10657-011-9236-9	147	10.50	3.05
SARAGIH AH, 2023, ARTIF INTELL LAW	10.1007/s10506-022-09321-y	21	10.50	7.06
ALM J, 2010, J ECON PSYCHOL	10.1016/j.joep.2010.03.018	156	10.40	2.91
LAGO-PEÑAS I, 2010, EUR J POLIT ECON	10.1016/j.ejpoleco.2010.06.003	155	10.33	2.89
TRAXLER C, 2010, EUR J POLIT ECON	10.1016/j.ejpoleco.2009.11.001	155	10.33	2.89
ALMUNIA M, 2018, AM ECON J ECON POLICY	10.1257/pol.20160229	71	10.14	5.67
GÓRECKI MA, 2021, J BUS ETHICS	10.1007/s10551-020-04502-8	37	9.25	5.17
SLEMROD J, 2017, J PUBLIC ECON	10.1016/j.jpubeco.2017.02.010	73	9.13	3.93
HASHIMZADE N, 2013, J ECON SURV	10.1111/j.1467-6419.2012.00733.x	108	9.00	2.59
HALLSWORTH M, 2014, OXF REV ECON POLICY	10.1093/oxrep/gru034	98	8.91	4.47
KUBICK TR, 2017, J ACCOUNT ECON	10.1016/j.jacceco.2016.09.005	68	8.50	3.66
DULLECK U, 2016, J PUBLIC ECON	10.1016/j.jpubeco.2015.12.007	75	8.33	3.42
INASIUS F, 2019, INT J PUBLIC ADM	10.1080/01900692.2018.1464578	50	8.33	3.84

Finally, the importance given to public economics (Journal of Public Economics) and political economy (European Journal of Political Economy) confirms the relevance of these disciplines for understanding tax compliance behaviour.

3.3. Social Structure

3.3.1. Countries' Collaboration World Map

The international collaborative map on contributory behaviour (Figure 9) shows a strong centrality of the US and Western Europe, with many bilateral links between these regions, indicating intense scientific collaboration. North America and Western Europe dominate research output. Participation from other regions (Asia, Africa, South America) is less important, suggesting less frequent collaborations. The strength of the links indicates the intensity of collaboration, revealing closer relations between some countries.

Figure 9. Countries' Collaboration World Map (Bibliometrix (R) output)

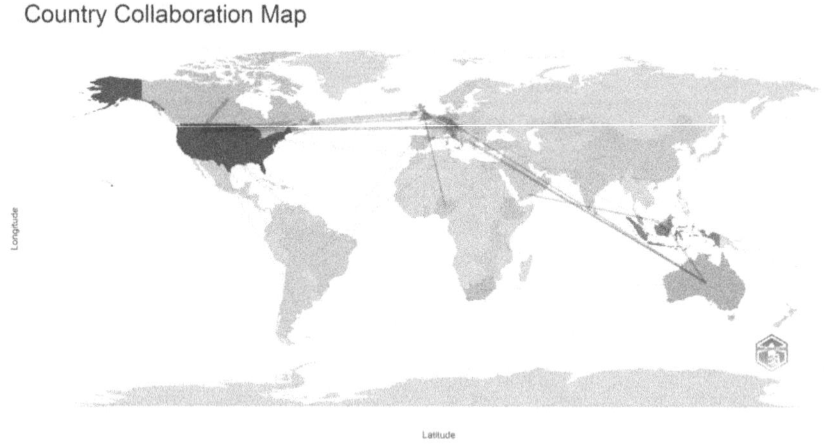

This geographical heterogeneity highlights an imbalance in research. International collaboration is needed to gain a better overall understanding. Analysis of social networks could provide further insight into these observations. The study highlights geographical disparities in research. Greater collaboration is essential if knowledge is to be disseminated equitably. Further analysis is needed.

3.3.2. Corresponding Author's Countries

Figure 10 shows the geographical distribution of the main authors (corresponding authors) of publications on contributory behaviour, distinguishing between publications from a single country (SCP) and from international collaborations (MCP). We find that Indonesia and the USA dominate the total number of publications, with Indonesia having a majority of SCP publications, while the USA shows a balance between SCP and MCP. The UK, Italy and Malaysia follow, with a significant proportion of SCP publications. Germany and Austria show a similar number of publications, with a higher proportion of SCP publications for Germany. However, the remaining countries (South Africa, Netherlands, Australia, Canada, Georgia, Korea, Spain, China, Nigeria, Romania, Croatia, Uganda, Ethiopia) show a lower number of publications, and a predominance of PCS publications. This suggests that these countries are less involved in international collaborative research on the subject.

In summary, the geographical distribution is uneven, with a high concentration in some developed countries (US, UK, Indonesia) and a more modest participation of developing and emerging countries, mostly in non-collaborative publications. This highlights the need for increased international collaboration for better geographic representation and a more comprehensive understanding of contributory behaviour.

Figure 10. Corresponding Author's Countries (Bibliometrix (R) output)

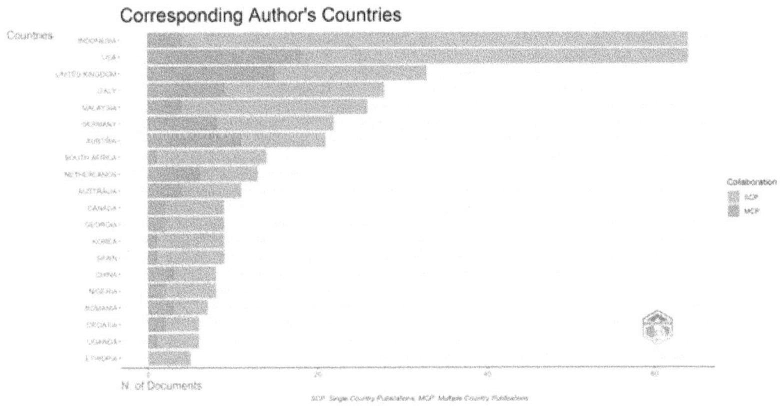

3.4. Thematic Clusters

3.4.1. Thematic Clustering by Coupling

The thematic clustering analysis by linkage reveals three main clusters of tax compliance research (Figure 11). The first cluster (group 1) focuses on social norms, suggesting that the influence of social context and collective perceptions plays an important role in taxpayers' behaviour. The second cluster (group 2), the most important in terms of frequency (107), focuses on the "slippery slope framework" concept, indicating an interest in the dynamics of tax evasion and the mechanisms that can lead to an escalation of non-compliant behaviour. Finally, the third cluster (group 3) explores tax morality, highlighting the importance of individual values and beliefs in deciding whether or not to comply with tax obligations.

Figure 11. Thematic Clustering by Coupling (Bibliometrix (R) output)

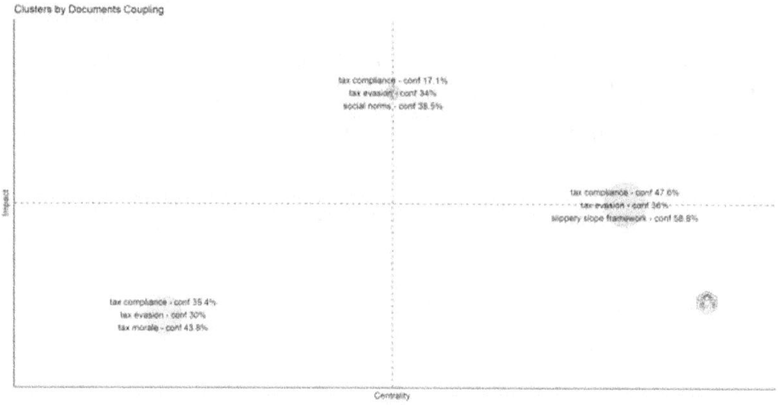

The relatively similar centrality and impact of the three clusters reflects a diversified and balanced research on the different determinants of tax compliance, although group 2, which focuses on the slippery slope, seems to be slightly more prominent in the literature.

3.4.2. Full Coupling of Co-occurrence Network

The analysis of the co-occurrence network (Figure 12) reveals a multidisciplinary structure of tax behaviour research. Distinct clusters emerge, articulated around tax administration ("tax reform", "policy maker"), compliance ("compliance cost"), economic aspects ("income", "vat"), and psycho-sociological factors ("trust", "authority", "tax fairness"). The proximity of these to "tax morality" and "tax literacy" suggests the influence of social norms and understanding of tax rules. Smaller clusters focus on methodologies ("laboratory experiments") and specific categories of taxpayers ("smes"). The presence of geographical names ("china", "nigeria") indicates international comparative analyses.

Figure 12. Full Coupling of Co-occurrence Network (VOSviewer output)

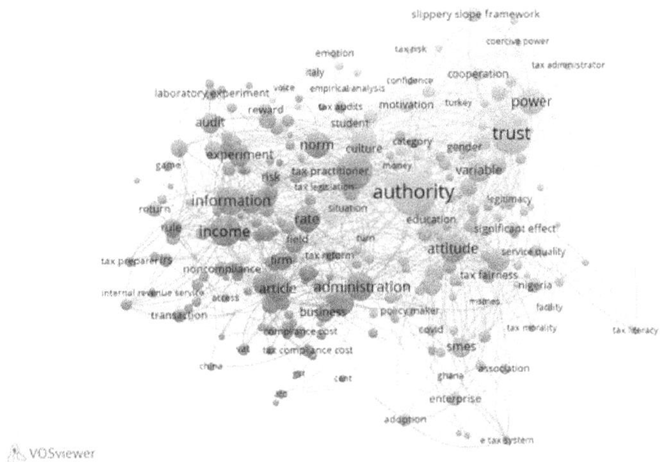

This thematic mapping highlights the complexity of fiscal behaviour, requiring an integrative approach, and highlights potential research leads in the network's poorly connected areas.

3.4.3. Thematic Map of Co-occurrence Network

Bibliometric analysis in the form of a thematic map of co-occurrence (figure 13) highlights significant trends in taxpayer behaviour research, reflecting both relevance (centrality) and level of development (density) research themes, structured in four main thematic clusters:

- ***The "Motor Themes" cluster***, which brings together the most central and developed themes, highlighting the importance of tax compliance, tax evasion, and related factors such as outlook theory, tax audit, and tax complexity. These themes are the core of current research.
- ***The "Niche Themes" cluster***, which identifies less central but nevertheless developed topics, suggesting more specialized research areas, such as tax regulatory frameworks and the impact of technologies (artificial intelligence). These themes could represent promising research niches.
- ***The "Basic Themes" cluster***, which brings together central but less developed themes, indicating important research areas requiring further development. The classic themes here are field experiments and property taxes.
- ***The cluster "Emerging or Declining Themes"***, which shows both uncentral and undeveloped themes. These themes, like discontinuous regression analysis, could be considered as emerging or declining approaches, requiring further exploration to determine their potential.

Figure 13. Thematic Map of Co-occurrence Network (VOSviewer output)

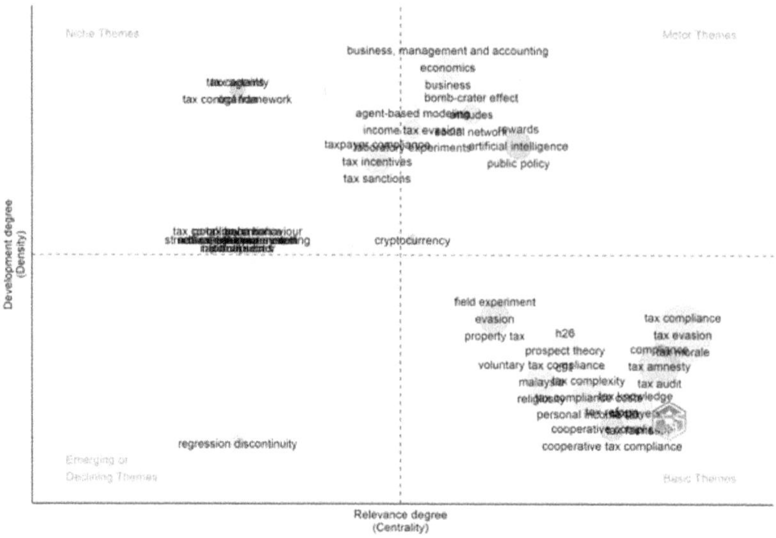

In summary, this bibliometric analysis allows to identify the main research axes and emerging themes in the study of taxpayers' behavior. It highlights the need to deepen certain key areas while exploring new research perspectives. The analysis suggests a shift in research towards a more multidisciplinary approach integrating concepts from behavioural economics, artificial intelligence and social sciences.

3.4.4. Factorial Analysis

The concept map in Figure 14 visualizes a factor analysis of the relationships between different concepts related to taxpayer behaviour, in the form of a triangular representation revealing the three main factors structuring the research field:

- ***The first factor (Cooperation and Trust)***, which opposes a pole of confidence (tax cooperation, trust in the tax administration, procedural justice, ...) and a pole of mistrust (corruption, frequent audits, ...). This factor suggests a latent dimension representing the quality of the taxpayer-tax administration relationship, where trust and perception of justice contribute to greater cooperation. A high burden on this factor indicates a significant influence of these aspects on fiscal behaviour.
- ***The second factor (Evasion and Economic Rationality)***, which contrasts tax evasion strategies and the economic rationality of taxpayers with aspects related to fiscal education and transparency of the system. This factor reflects a dimension related to the decision-making of taxpayers in relation to the incentives for evasion and control mechanisms. A high load on this factor suggests an importance of economic considerations and risk perceptions in tax behaviour.
- ***The 3rd factor (Experimentation and Fiscal Policy)***, which opposes the use of experimental methods in economics to study tax behaviour to concepts more directly related to fiscal policy. This factor represents a dimension related to the methodological approach and the influence of

public policies on taxpayers' behaviour. A high load on this factor highlights the importance of empirical research and assessment of tax policies.

Figure 14. Factorial Analysis of Co-occurrence Network (Bibliometrix (R) output)

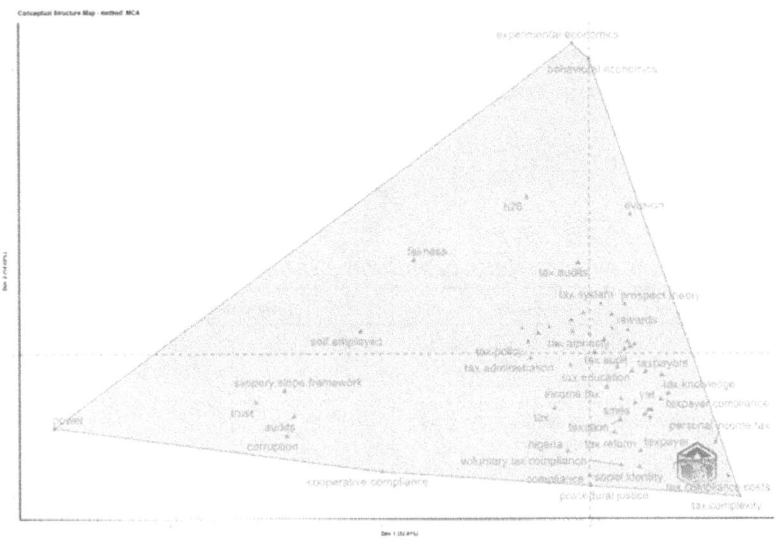

The non-orthogonality of factors reveals complex interactions. The analysis suggests a multidimensional approach to understanding tax compliance, integrating institutional, psychological and political aspects. Additional analyses are needed for a comprehensive interpretation. The study highlights the need for integrated theoretical and methodological approaches to understand the complexity of contributory behaviour.

4. PROSPECTIVE QUALITATIVE ANALYSIS

4.1. Qualitative Thematic Analysis

The thematic qualitative analysis of the determinants of taxpayers' behaviour in tax compliance, presented in Table 4, highlights several key dimensions: sociological, economic, psychological and business/ industry. Each of these dimensions offers unique insights into the factors influencing tax compliance.

- **Sociological dimension:** Social standards and community pressure, as well as fiscal morality, significantly influence compliance. High confidence in the tax administration and a positive perception of tax fairness promote compliance.

continued on following page

Table 4. Continued

- **Economic dimension:** The level of income affects the collection of tax rates and compliance costs. Taxpayers may reject compliance if the benefits received are insufficient in relation to the costs.
- **Psychological Dimension:** Risk aversion and equity perception play a crucial role. Taxpayers who perceive a high audit risk are more likely to comply, as are those who believe the tax system is fair.
- **Business/Industry Dimension:** Company size and oversight can increase compliance, while competition can encourage non-compliant behaviour, although industry standards put pressure on compliance.

Table 4. Summary of the determinants of tax compliance (Authors)

Dimensions		– Determinants	– Dimensions		– Determinants
Sociological	**Social standards**	– Social standards and social pressure – Confidence in the tax administration – Perception of tax fairness – Fiscal morality and ethical commitment – Psychological costs associated with non-compliance	– Psychological	**– Risk aversion**	– Risk aversion and compliance – Perception of risk associated with tax evasion – Influence of potential penalties – Impact on reporting decisions – Proactive behaviour in the face of tax risks
	Confidence in government	– Confidence in the tax administration – Perceived tax legitimacy – Communication and transparency – Satisfaction with public services – Social standards and community pressure	–	**– Perception of equity**	– Positive perception of tax fairness – Influence on tax morality – Impact on tax behaviour – Reciprocity and trust in the tax system – Effects on voluntary compliance
	Procedural justice	– Perceived fairness in tax treatment – Transparency of tax processes – Fair application of tax rules – Perception of procedural justice – Impact of social standards	–	**– Fiscal sophistication**	– Understanding the tax system – Tax sophistication of taxpayers – Impact of advanced technologies – Reduction of tax errors – Increased awareness of tax obligations
	Social capital	– Social relations and community engagement – Collective standards and social pressure – Social media and information sharing – Cooperation between taxpayers – Impact of AI systems on community engagement	–	**– Tax morality**	– Influence of personal morality – Role of ethical values – Impact of perceived morality – Social standards and community pressure – Psychological consequences of tax evasion
Economic	**Income level**	– Perception of tax fairness – Costs and benefits received – Attitudes toward compliance – Influence of social standards – Variability of tax behaviour	– Business/Industry	**– Size of the company**	– Resources available for compliance – Increased oversight by tax authorities – Perceptions of responsibility – Complexity of tax obligations – Impact on risk perception
	Tax rate	– Collection of tax rates – Costs and benefits of compliance – Impact on moral behaviour – Reactions to public services – Psychological effects of tax rates	–	**– Business sector**	– Sectoral social standards – Compliance expectations – Sectoral economic environment – Resources for compliance – Impact of technologies on compliance
	Audit probability	– Audit risk perception – Compliance incentive – Influence of technological tools – Psychological costs associated with non-compliance – Impact of social interactions	–	**– Ownership structure**	– Influence on tax decisions – Attitudes toward tax compliance – Dynamics of collective and family ownership – Impact on commitment to the tax system – Agency issues and tax management
	Sanctions	– Collection of sanctions – Proportionality of penalties – Clarity and knowledge of sanctions – Effectiveness of sanction mechanisms – Psychological impact of sanctions	–	**– Competition**	– Competitive pressure and non-compliant behaviour – Competition-influenced tax strategies – Sectoral social standards – Impact of compliance costs – Technology and transparency

Promoting transparency, fairness and tax education is essential to improving compliance, thereby building trust between the tax administration and taxpayers.

To better manage the relationship between the tax administration and taxpayers, it is essential to promote transparency and fairness in the tax system, educate taxpayers about their obligations and build confidence in the tax administration. By integrating these elements, it is possible to encourage more compliant and responsible tax behaviour.

4.2. Discussion of Results

The state of the art above presents an exhaustive synthesis of the determinants of taxpayers' behaviour in tax compliance, organized according to sociological, economic, psychological and business/industry dimensions. These dimensions provide a multidimensional perspective, essential to understanding the factors influencing the relationship between the tax administration and taxpayers. This analysis also highlights the need for multidisciplinary approaches to optimize tax compliance strategies.

To assess the relevance of these findings, we will discuss them in conjunction with recent and relevant work on the issue. Indeed, overall, the results in Table 4 confirm that tax compliance is not only an economic phenomenon but also a multidimensional process influenced by sociological, psychological and structural factors. Kirchler et al. (2010) highlight that tax compliance decisions are based on a mix of economic incentives (costs and benefits), social norms and psychological attitudes. For example, moral tax, perceived fairness and trust in institutions play a central role in the decision to comply (Schneider & Torgler, 2007). In addition, modern tools such as advanced technologies are increasingly influencing tax behaviour by reducing errors and increasing transparency, as noted by Borrego (2015) and Reck & Bomare (2022). These developments call for a more proactive management of the relationship between tax authorities and taxpayers, with an emphasis on fairness, transparency and communication.

With regard to the sociological dimension, and concerning the axis «Social standards and community pressure», studies confirm the fundamental role of social norms, the perception of tax fairness in tax compliance, in terms of perceptions of social standards. (Wenzel, 2005) and share capital (Alm & Gomez, 2008). For the "Trust and legitimacy of tax institutions" axis, it appears that trust in tax administrations is particularly important to encourage voluntary compliance, in terms of procedural fairness and transparency (Murphy, 2003). On the "implication of sectoral social standards", the work of Damayanti & Matasik (2021) demonstrates that social standards vary across sectors, which may explain differences in levels of compliance between industries.

The economic dimension, highlighting perceptions of costs and benefits, tax rates and income levels as major economic determinants. The "tax rate and perceived equity" component, the observation that high tax rates, if they are perceived as unfair, can encourage tax evasion is confirmed in terms of the level of tax rates (Ma'ud et al., 2014) and justice and fairness (Freire-Serén & Panadés, 2013). On the "perceived costs and benefits" side, the perception of compliance costs as prohibitive leads to tax evasion strategies (Lignier & Evans, 2012), while clear benefits such as quality public services, may motivate taxpayers to comply (Fullerton & Metcalf, 2002). For the income level component, Reck & Bomare (2022) confirm its correlation with tax compliance, to the extent that low or medium incomes favour it, while high incomes favour tax evasion or avoidance.

With regard to the psychological dimension, many aspects such as fiscal morality, risk aversion and the perception of sanctions significantly influence fiscal behaviour. First, the scientific community confirms the importance of the fiscal and personal ethics component in this area, particularly through personal ethical values and perceived tax morality (Devano et al., 2024) and community pressure (Kirchler et al., 2010). As for the "risk aversion and sanctions" component, the risk aversion combined with a perception of penalties as proportionate and effective promotes voluntary compliance by the taxpayer, but as soon as excessive sanctions can generate more sophisticated evasion behaviors (Eisenhauer, 2008; Doran, 2009). Finally, in the area of "perception of procedural justice", Gobena & Van Dijke (2017) highlighted the importance of fair and transparent management by tax authorities.

Finally, in the Business/Industry dimension, we found that company characteristics such as size, ownership structure and sector of activity influence tax compliance. This is confirmed by (Webley, 2004; Lignier et al., 2014; Annuar et al., 2014) in the area of "business size and tax complexity" where small and medium-sized enterprises often perceive tax obligations as complex and costly, This reduces their compliance. For the "ownership structure" component, Rakayana et al. (2021 found that family-owned or collectively owned businesses often have lower tax compliance due to specific internal dynamics. Finally, for the "competition" axis, Casagrande et al. (2015) argued that competitive pressure can encourage companies to adopt non-compliant behaviour, whereas strict sector regulation and regular audits can reduce such behaviour.

4.3. Modelling Test

Based on the above state of the art, we can propose a formalization test of the analysis model, highlighting the possible causal links between the different dimensions of tax compliance determinants and the taxpayer's behavior, via the following Figure 15:

Figure 15. Outline of the analysis model (Authors)

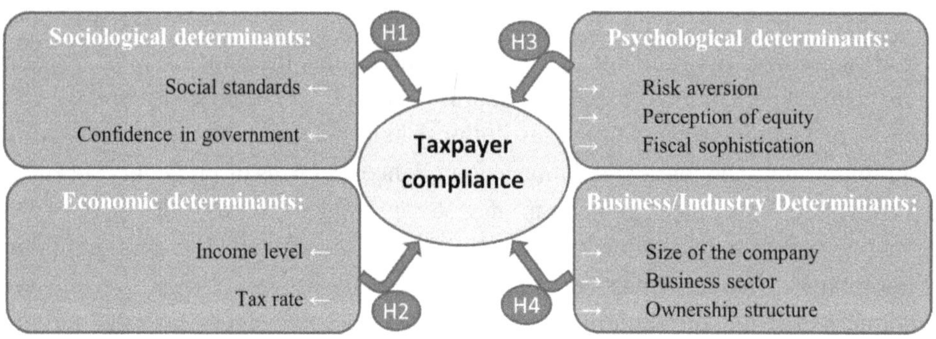

We propose a formalization of the main assumptions above to illustrate the causal links between the dimensions of tax compliance determinants and the taxpayer's behaviour:

- ***Assumption H1:*** The higher social standards, confidence in government institutions, procedural justice and social capital, the more positive the tax compliance behavior.
- ***Assumption H2:*** The more economic incentives (such as fair tax rates and dissuasive sanctions) are aligned, the more compliant the taxpayer is.
- ***Assumption H3:*** The more taxpayers perceive the tax system as fair and adopt strong moral values, the more their tax compliance behaviour is strengthened.

- ***Assumption H4:*** The more the Business/Industry characteristics (such as company size and sector regulation) promote transparency, the more tax compliance behavior is observed.

These assumptions demonstrate that tax compliance results from complex interactions between sociological, economic, psychological and sector-specific dimensions. Each dimension acts as a lever or brake on fiscal behaviour, highlighting the need for a multidimensional approach to promote compliance.

4.4. Prospective Approach and Future Research Leads

The prospective analysis of taxpayers' behaviour in tax compliance is based on a preventive and anticipatory management of factors influencing this behaviour. By identifying and acting on compliance history, the tax administration can establish a lasting relationship of trust with taxpayers, fostering voluntary adherence to their tax obligations.

The tax administration can encourage voluntary compliance by implementing appropriate policies and strategies:

- ***Enhancing transparency and fairness*** through clear and accessible communication with taxpayers to reduce uncertainty, More transparency in the use of tax revenues for public service financing to increase the perceived legitimacy of the tax system, and more fairness and efficiency of the tax system to gain both trust and taxpayer buy-in.
- ***Better educate taxpayers*** through more tax education and literacy programs, digital tools and online services to simplify tax procedures and reduce errors.
- ***Adopt differentiated management***, by a segmented approach by taxpayer profiles and past behavior, and by supporting good faith contributors through offering alternative and conciliatory solutions to taxpayers in difficulty.

Proactive management relies on the use of data and behavioural approaches to anticipate taxpayer behaviour:

- ***Data analysis and prediction***, by using tax data and artificial intelligence tools to identify risk profiles of non-taxcompliance, as well as the implementation of predictive algorithms to detect sectors or groups most likely to develop non-compliant behaviors.
- ***Tax incentives***, by applying behavioural incentives (nudges) to encourage tax compliance.
- ***Dispute prevention***, which promotes the preventive resolution of tax disputes through mediation mechanisms or early agreements, reducing tensions between the administration and taxpayers.

Understanding taxpayer behaviour and promoting tax compliance requires a multi-dimensional, proactive approach. By acting on the sociological, economic, psychological and business/industry dimensions, the tax administration can promote voluntary and sustainable membership through:

- Transparency and fairness of the tax system;
- Education and support for taxpayers;
- Proactive management based on data and behaviors.

By developing a relationship of trust and adopting a preventive posture, the tax administration can not only reduce tax evasion but also promote a culture of responsible and shared compliance.

CONCLUSION AND PERSPECTIVES

The determinants of taxpayer behaviour in tax compliance are multiple and interconnected. Effective management of the relationship between tax authorities and taxpayers requires a thorough understanding of these factors. By fostering trust, ensuring transparent communication, and establishing positive social standards, the tax compliance rate can be improved. In addition, special attention should be paid to the economic and psychological perceptions that influence individuals' and companies' tax decisions.

This research aims to contribute to the existing literature by proposing an integrated analysis of the determinants of tax compliance and anticipating their future developments, as suggested by De Neve et al. (2024) and Muehlbacher & Hartl (2023).

By integrating these theoretical and empirical perspectives, our study aims to develop an integrated conceptual model of the determinants of tax compliance. This model will serve as a basis for anticipating future changes in fiscal behaviour, taking into account technological and societal changes.

After a theoretical framework and a descriptive bibliometric analysis, our study presented an in-depth thematic analysis of the determinants of taxpayers' behavior in tax compliance, organized according to sociological, economic, psychological, and Business/Industry. These dimensions provide a multidimensional perspective, essential to understanding the factors influencing the relationship between the tax administration and taxpayers. This analysis also highlights the need for multidisciplinary approaches to optimize tax compliance strategies.

- To improve the relationship between the tax administration and taxpayers, it is essential to:
- Enhance transparency and procedural justice (Murphy, 2003).
- Simplify tax obligations to reduce compliance costs (Lignier et al., 2014)
- Promote tax policies that are perceived as fair and proportionate (Mas'ud et al., 2014).
- Encourage community cooperation and positive social standards (Wenzel, 2005).
- Educate taxpayers about their tax obligations and the benefits associated with compliance (Mei Tan & Chin Fatt, 2000).

In conclusion, a balanced strategy that combines fairness, transparency and positive incentives is essential to strengthen tax compliance and build trust between taxpayers and the tax administration.

REFERENCES

Adelakun, B. O., Nembe, J. K., Oguejiofor, B. B., Akpuokwe, C. U., & Bakare, S. S.Beatrice Oyinkansola AdelakunJoseph Kuba NembeBisola Beatrice OguejioforChidiogo Uzoamaka AkpuokweSeun Solomon Bakare. (2024). Legal frameworks and tax compliance in the digital economy: A finance perspective. *Engineering Science & Technology Journal, 5*(3), 844–853. DOI: 10.51594/estj.v5i3.922

Akhand, Z. (2018). The influence of the corporate sector on the effectiveness of tax compliance instruments. In *Advances in taxation* (Vol. 25, pp. 119–146). Emerald Publishing Limited. DOI: 10.1108/S1058-749720180000025006

Akinboade, O. A. (2015). Correlates of tax compliance of small and medium size businesses in Cameroon. *Managing global transitions, 13*(4), 389-413.

Al-Asfour, F., & McGee, R. W. (2024). Tax Evasion and Tax Compliance: What Have We Learned from the 100 Most Cited Studies? In R.W. McGee & J. Shopovski (Eds.), The Ethics of Tax Evasion, Volume 2: New Perspectives in Theory and Practice. Springer.

Alhempi, R. R., Ardiansyah, I., Kusumastuti, S. Y., & Endri, E. (2020). Tax compliance in income tax payments. *International Journal of Innovation. Creativity and Change, 13*(1), 356–374.

Alm, J. (2023). Tax Compliance Technology, Trust, and Inequality in a Post-Pandemic World. *eJTR, 21*, 152.

Alm, J., Cherry, T., Jones, M., & McKee, M. (2010). Taxpayer information assistance services and tax compliance behavior. *Journal of Economic Psychology, 31*(4), 577–586. DOI: 10.1016/j.joep.2010.03.018

Alm, J., & Gomez, J. L. (2008). Social capital and tax morale in Spain. *Economic Analysis and Policy, 38*(1), 73–87. DOI: 10.1016/S0313-5926(08)50007-5

Alm, J., & Torgler, B. (2006). Culture differences and tax morale in the United States and in Europe. *Journal of Economic Psychology, 27*(2), 224–246. DOI: 10.1016/j.joep.2005.09.002

Alm, J., & Torgler, B. (2011). Do ethics matter? Tax compliance and morality. *Journal of Business Ethics, 101*(4), 635–651. DOI: 10.1007/s10551-011-0761-9

Almunia, M., & Lopez-Rodriguez, D. (2018). Under the radar: The effects of monitoring firms on tax compliance. *American Economic Journal. Economic Policy, 10*(1), 1–38. DOI: 10.1257/pol.20160229

Annuar, H. A., Salihu, I. A., & Obid, S. N. S. (2014). Corporate ownership, governance and tax avoidance: An interactive effects. *Procedia: Social and Behavioral Sciences, 164*, 150–160. DOI: 10.1016/j.sbspro.2014.11.063

Batrancea, L. M., Nichita, R., & Batrancea, I. (2012). Understanding The Determinants Of Tax Compliance Behavior As A Prerequisite For Increasing Public Levies. *USV Annals of Economics and Public Administration, 12*, 201–210.

Ben Othman, H., Hussainey, K., & Moumen, N. (2024). The influence of cultural tightness–looseness, religiosity, and the institutional environment on tax evasion behaviour: A cross-country study. *European Financial Management, 30*(1), 346–374. DOI: 10.1111/eufm.12420

Bin, F. (2020). À l'ombre du positivisme: quelle place pour une doctrine de la justice fiscale propre aux juristes fiscalistes (XIXe-XXe siècle)?.

Bobek, D. D., Hageman, A. M., & Kelliher, C. F. (2013). Analyzing the role of social norms in tax compliance behavior. *Journal of Business Ethics*, *115*(3), 451–468. DOI: 10.1007/s10551-012-1390-7

Borrego, A. C. D. C. (2015). Tax compliance and tax complexity in Portugal: essays on the perception of tax professionals.

Bott, K. M., Cappelen, A. W., Sørensen, E. Ø., & Tungodden, B. (2020). You've got mail: A randomized field experiment on tax evasion. *Management Science*, *66*(7), 2801–2819. DOI: 10.1287/mnsc.2019.3390

Casagrande, A., Di Cagno, D., Pandimiglio, A., & Spallone, M. (2015). The effect of competition on tax compliance: The role of audit rules and shame. *Journal of Behavioral and Experimental Economics*, *59*, 96–110. DOI: 10.1016/j.socec.2015.08.006

Castro, L., & Scartascini, C. (2015). Tax compliance and enforcement in the pampas evidence from a field experiment. *Journal of Economic Behavior & Organization*, *116*, 65–82. DOI: 10.1016/j.jebo.2015.04.002

Chan, S. H., & Song, Q. (2021). Implications of tax audit risk, consequences, aggressive behavior and ethics for compliance. *International Journal of Accounting & Information Management*, *29*(5), 823–847. DOI: 10.1108/IJAIM-09-2021-0183

Dahlan, A., Chandrarin, G., & Triatmanto, B. (2024). *Understanding Tax Morale: A Critical Review of Its Impact on Compliance and Policy*. KnE Social Sciences.

Damayanti, T. W., & Matasik, A. L. (2021). Market competition, fairness and tax compliance: The formal sector's perspective. *Journal of International Students*, *14*(1).

De Neve, J. E., Imbert, C., & Spinnewijn, J. (2024). How to improve tax compliance? Evidence from population-wide experiments in Belgium. *Journal of Political Economy*, *132*(1), 85–128.

De Neve, J. E., Imbert, C., Spinnewijn, J., Tsankova, T., & Luts, M. (2021). How to improve tax compliance? Evidence from population-wide experiments in Belgium. *Journal of Political Economy*, *129*(5), 1425–1463. DOI: 10.1086/713096

Devano, S., Mulyani, S., Winarningsih, S., & Ghani, E. (2024). Tax amnesty and taxpayer morality in predicting taxpayer compliance. *International Journal of Applied Economics. Finance and Accounting*, *18*(1), 98–106.

Devos, K. (2013). *Factors influencing individual taxpayer compliance behaviour*. Springer Science & Business Media.

Doran, M. (2009). Tax penalties and tax compliance. *Harvard Journal on Legislation*, *46*, 111.

Drumbl, M. L. (2013). Those Who Know, Those Who Don't, and Those Who Know Better: Balancing Complexity, Sophistication, and Accuracy on Tax Returns. *Pitt. Tax Rev.*, *11*(1), 113. DOI: 10.5195/taxreview.2013.23

Dulleck, U., Fooken, J., Newton, C., Ristl, A., Schaffner, M., & Torgler, B. (2016). Tax compliance and psychic costs: Behavioral experimental evidence using a physiological marker. *Journal of Public Economics*, *134*, 9–18. DOI: 10.1016/j.jpubeco.2015.12.007

Durham, Y., Manly, T. S., & Ritsema, C. (2014). The effects of income source, context, and income level on tax compliance decisions in a dynamic experiment. *Journal of Economic Psychology*, *40*, 220–233. DOI: 10.1016/j.joep.2012.09.012

Eisenhauer, J. G. (2008). Ethical preferences, risk aversion, and taxpayer behavior. *Journal of Socio-Economics*, *37*(1), 45–63. DOI: 10.1016/j.socec.2007.01.030

Engström, P., Nordblom, K., Ohlsson, H., & Persson, A. (2015). Tax compliance and loss aversion. *American Economic Journal. Economic Policy*, *7*(4), 132–164. DOI: 10.1257/pol.20130134

Fajriana, N., Irianto, G., & Andayani, W. (2023). The role of tax fairness and taxpayer trust in building voluntary compliance in MSME taxpayers. *International Journal of Business and Society*, *24*(1), 478–487. DOI: 10.33736/ijbs.5629.2023

Fauziati, P., & Kassim, A. A. M. (2018). The effect of business characteristics on tax compliance costs. *Advanced Science Letters*, *24*(6), 4377–4379. DOI: 10.1166/asl.2018.11608

Feld, L. P., & Frey, B. S. (2007). Tax compliance as the result of a psychological tax contract: The role of incentives and responsive regulation. *Law & Policy*, *29*(1), 102–120. DOI: 10.1111/j.1467-9930.2007.00248.x

Freire-Serén, M. J., & Panadés, J. (2013). Do higher tax rates encourage/discourage tax compliance? *Modern Economy*, *4*(12), 809–817. DOI: 10.4236/me.2013.412086

Fullerton, D., & Metcalf, G. E. (2002). Tax incidence. *Handbook of public economics*, *4*, 1787-1872.

Gobena, L. B., & Van Dijke, M. (2017). Fear and caring: Procedural justice, trust, and collective identification as antecedents of voluntary tax compliance. *Journal of Economic Psychology*, *62*, 1–16. DOI: 10.1016/j.joep.2017.05.005

Górecki, M. A., & Letki, N. (2021). Social norms moderate the effect of tax system on tax evasion: Evidence from a large-scale survey experiment. *Journal of Business Ethics*, *172*(4), 727–746. DOI: 10.1007/s10551-020-04502-8

Gupta, S., & Keen, M. (2024). Digital transformation and tax administration. IMF Working Paper Series, WP/24/15.

Hallsworth, M. (2014). The use of field experiments to increase tax compliance. *Oxford Review of Economic Policy*, *30*(4), 658–679. DOI: 10.1093/oxrep/gru034

Hasan, I., Hoi, C. K., Wu, Q., & Zhang, H. (2017). Does social capital matter in corporate decisions? Evidence from corporate tax avoidance. *Journal of Accounting Research*, *55*(3), 629–668. DOI: 10.1111/1475-679X.12159

Hashimzade, N., & Myles, G. D. (2023). A comparative analysis of tax compliance across OECD countries. *International Tax and Public Finance*, *30*(2), 367–396.

Hashimzade, N., Myles, G. D., & Tran-Nam, B. (2013). Applications of behavioural economics to tax evasion. *Journal of Economic Surveys*, *27*(5), 941–977. DOI: 10.1111/j.1467-6419.2012.00733.x

Inasius, F. (2019). Factors influencing SME tax compliance: Evidence from Indonesia. *International Journal of Public Administration*, *42*(5), 367–379. DOI: 10.1080/01900692.2018.1464578

Jimenez, P., & Iyer, G. S. (2016). Tax compliance in a social setting: The influence of social norms, trust in government, and perceived fairness on taxpayer compliance. *Advances in Accounting*, *34*, 17–26. DOI: 10.1016/j.adiac.2016.07.001

Kasper, M., & Alm, J. (2022). Audits, audit effectiveness, and post-audit tax compliance. *Journal of Economic Behavior & Organization*, *195*, 87–102. DOI: 10.1016/j.jebo.2022.01.003

Kastlunger, B., Lozza, E., Kirchler, E., & Schabmann, A. (2013). Powerful authorities and trusting citizens: The Slippery Slope Framework and tax compliance in Italy. *Journal of Economic Psychology*, *34*, 36–45. DOI: 10.1016/j.joep.2012.11.007

Khaerunnisa, I., Wiratno, A., & Luthan, E. (2016). The effect of tax morality, tax culture, and good governance to taxpayers compliance. *The Accounting Journal of BINANIAGA*, *1*(1), 267759.

Khodamipour, A., & Pourheydari, O. (2024). Investigating the effect of attitude, risk aversion and loss aversion of tax payers on tax compliance considering the moderating role of personality type (case study of tax payers of Kerman city). *Journal of Tax Research*, *32*(61), 87–132. DOI: 10.61186/taxjournal.32.61.87

Kirchgässner, G. (2011). Tax morale, tax evasion and the shadow economy. In *Handbook on the shadow economy*. Edward Elgar Publishing. DOI: 10.4337/9780857930880.00019

Kirchler, E., & Gangl, K. (2023). Future trends in tax compliance: A prospective analysis. *Behavioural Public Policy*, *7*(2), 252–276.

Kirchler, E., Muehlbacher, S., Kastlunger, B., & Wahl, I. (2010). Why pay taxes? A review of tax compliance decisions. *Developing alternative frameworks for explaining tax compliance, 59*.

Kleven, H. J., Knudsen, M. B., Kreiner, C. T., Pedersen, S., & Saez, E. (2011). Unwilling or unable to cheat? Evidence from a tax audit experiment in Denmark. *Econometrica*, *79*(3), 651–692. DOI: 10.3982/ECTA9113

Kubick, T. R., Lockhart, G. B., Mills, L. F., & Robinson, J. R. (2017). IRS and corporate taxpayer effects of geographic proximity. *Journal of Accounting and Economics*, *63*(2-3), 428–453. DOI: 10.1016/j.jacceco.2016.09.005

Lago-Peñas, I., & Lago-Peñas, S. (2010). The determinants of tax morale in comparative perspective: Evidence from European countries. *european. European Journal of Political Economy*, *26*(4), 441–453. DOI: 10.1016/j.ejpoleco.2010.06.003

Lignier, P., & Evans, C. (2012). The rise and rise of tax compliance costs for the small business sector in Australia. In *Australian Tax Forum* (Vol. 27, No. 3, pp. 615-672). Sydney, NSW: Tax Institute.

Lignier, P., Evans, C., & Tran-Nam, B. (2014). Tangled up in tape: The continuing tax compliance plight of the small and medium enterprise business sector. *Austl.SSRN*, *29*, 217. DOI: 10.2139/ssrn.2479153

Lisi, G. (2015). Tax morale, tax compliance and the optimal tax policy. *Economic Analysis and Policy*, *45*, 27–32. DOI: 10.1016/j.eap.2014.12.004

López-Laborda, J., & Rodrigo, F. (2023). Tax compliance in developing countries: Evidence and policy implications. *World Development*, *161*, 106089.

López-Lozano, M. A., & Pérez-López, C. (2023). Tax compliance determinants: A systematic literature review using bibliometric analysis. *Economic Analysis and Policy*, *77*, 584–601.

Mas'ud, A., Aliyu, A. A., Gambo, E. M. J., Al-Qudah, A. A., & Al Sharari, N. (2014). Tax rate and tax compliance in Africa. *European Journal of Accounting Auditing and Finance Research*, *2*(3), 22–30.

Mei Tan, L., & Chin-Fatt, C. (2000). The impact of tax knowledge on the perceptions of tax fairness and attitudes towards compliance. *Asian Review of Accounting*, *8*(1), 44–58. DOI: 10.1108/eb060720

Muehlbacher, S., & Hartl, B. (2023). The role of artificial intelligence in tax compliance: Opportunities and challenges. *Journal of Tax Administration*, *9*(1), 22–45.

Muehlbacher, S., Kirchler, E., & Schwarzenberger, H. (2011). Voluntary versus enforced tax compliance: Empirical evidence for the "slippery slope" framework. *European Journal of Law and Economics*, *32*(1), 89–97. DOI: 10.1007/s10657-011-9236-9

Murphy, K. (2003). Procedural justice and tax compliance. [Australian Council of Social Service]. *The Australian Journal of Social Issues*, *38*(3). Advance online publication. DOI: 10.1002/j.1839-4655.2003.tb01151.x

O'shaughnessy, D. B. (2014). Tax compliance determinants: A proposed model for cross-country analysis.

OECD. (2024). *Tax Administration 3.0: The Digital Transformation of Tax Administration*. OECD Publishing.

Oladipo, O. A., Nwanji, T. I., Eluycla, F. D., Godo, B., & Adegboyegun, A. E. (2022). Impact of tax fairness and tax knowledge on tax compliance behavior of listed manufacturing companies in Nigeria. *Problems and Perspectives in Management*, *20*(1), 41–48. DOI: 10.21511/ppm.20(1).2022.04

Pickhardt, M., & Prinz, A. (2014). Behavioral dynamics of tax evasion–A survey. *Journal of Economic Psychology*, *40*, 1–19. DOI: 10.1016/j.joep.2013.08.006

Piketty, T. (2014). *Capital in the twenty-first century*. Trans. Arthur Goldhammer/Belknap. DOI: 10.4159/9780674369542

Rahmayanti, N. P., & Prihatiningtias, Y. W. (2020). Effect of tax penalties, tax audit, and taxpayers awareness on corporate taxpayers' compliance moderated by compliance intentions. *International Journal of Research in Business and Social Science (2147-4478)*, *9*(2), 118-124.

Rakayana, W., Sudarma, M., & Rosidi, R. (2021). The structure of company ownership and tax avoidance in Indonesia. *International Research Journal of Management. IT and Social Sciences*, *8*(3), 296–305.

Randlane, K. (2015). Tax Compliance as a System: Mapping the Field. *International Journal of Public Administration*, *39*(7), 515–525. DOI: 10.1080/01900692.2015.1028636

Reck, D., & Bomare, J. (2022). Different from you and me: Tax enforcement and sophisticated tax evasion by the wealthy. *LSE Public Policy Review*, *2*(4), 6. DOI: 10.31389/lseppr.71

Reddy, D., Moodley, A., & Olugbara, O. (2024). Factors informing tax compliance: A meta-analytical study. *Suid-Afrikaanse Tydskrif vir Ekonomiese en Bestuurswetenskappe*, *27*(1), 11. DOI: 10.4102/sajems.v27i1.5738

Ritsatos, T. (2014). Tax evasion and compliance; from the neo classical paradigm to behavioural economics, a review. *Journal of Accounting & Organizational Change*, *10*(2), 244–262. DOI: 10.1108/JAOC-07-2012-0059

Saragih, A. H., Reyhani, Q., Setyowati, M. S., & Hendrawan, A. (2023). The potential of an artificial intelligence (AI) application for the tax administration system's modernization: The case of Indonesia. *Artificial Intelligence and Law*, *31*(3), 491–514. DOI: 10.1007/s10506-022-09321-y

Schneider, F., & Torgler, B. (2007). *The impact of tax morale and institutional quality on the shadow economy* (No. 0702). Working Paper.

Scholz, J. T., & Lubell, M. (1998). Trust and taxpaying: Testing the heuristic approach to collective action. *American Journal of Political Science*, *42*(2), 398–417. DOI: 10.2307/2991764

Shaharuddin, N. S., Palil, M. R., Ramli, R., & Maelah, R. (2012). Sole Proprietorship and Tax Compliance Intention in Self-Assessment System: A Theory of Planned Behavior Approach. *International Journal of Business. Economics and Law*, *1*(6), 34–42.

Slemrod, J. (2019). Tax compliance and enforcement. *Journal of Economic Literature*, *57*(4), 904–954. DOI: 10.1257/jel.20181437

Slemrod, J., Collins, B., Hoopes, J. L., Reck, D., & Sebastiani, M. (2017). Does credit-card information reporting improve small-business tax compliance? *Journal of Public Economics*, *149*, 1–19. DOI: 10.1016/j.jpubeco.2017.02.010

Slemrod, J., & Yitzhaki, S. (2023). Tax avoidance, evasion, and administration. In *Handbook of Public Economics* (Vol. 3, pp. 1423-1470).

Surugiu, M. R., Vasile, V., Surugiu, C., Mazilescu, C. R., Panait, M. C., & Bunduchi, E. (2025). Tax Compliance Pattern Analysis: A Survey-Based Approach. *International Journal of Financial Studies*, *13*(1), 14. DOI: 10.3390/ijfs13010014

Tehulu, T. A., & Dinberu, Y. D. (2014). Determinants of tax compliance behavior in Ethiopia: The case of Bahir Dar city taxpayers. *Journal of Economics and Sustainable Development*, *5*(15), 268–280.

Traxler, C. (2010). Social norms and conditional cooperative taxpayers. *European Journal of Political Economy*, *26*(1), 89–103. DOI: 10.1016/j.ejpoleco.2009.11.001

Wahl, I., Kastlunger, B., & Kirchler, E. (2010). Trust in authorities and power to enforce tax compliance: An empirical analysis of the "slippery slope framework". *Law & Policy*, *32*(4), 383–406. DOI: 10.1111/j.1467-9930.2010.00327.x

Webley, P. (2004). Tax compliance by businesses. *New perspectives on economic crime*, 95-126.

Wenzel, M. (2004). An analysis of norm processes in tax compliance. *Journal of Economic Psychology, 25*(2), 213–228. DOI: 10.1016/S0167-4870(02)00168-X

Wenzel, M. (2005). Misperceptions of social norms about tax compliance: From theory to intervention. *Journal of Economic Psychology, 26*(6), 862–883. DOI: 10.1016/j.joep.2005.02.002

Williams, C. (2020). Evaluating public administration approaches towards tax non-compliance in Europe. *Administrative Sciences, 10*(3), 43. DOI: 10.3390/admsci10030043

Yimam, S., Asmare, F., & Moore, M. (2023). *Does Competition from the Informal Sector Reduce Tax Compliance in the Formal Sector?* Evidence from Ethiopia.

Yong, S., & Martin, F. (2017). Tax compliance of ethnic minority immigrant entrepreneurs: A social capital perspective. *eJTR, 15*, 51.

Chapter 2
Fiscal Feelings:
Behavioral and Neuroeconomic Insights on Tax Compliance

Ashlesha Khedekar
https://orcid.org/0000-0001-9020-9091
Symbiosis International University, India

Maithilee Umranikar
https://orcid.org/0009-0002-0990-9379
Symbiosis School of Economics, Symbiosis International University, India

ABSTRACT

Tax compliance is a behavior which is not driven only by the threats of penalties and punishments, but one which tends to be influenced by the economic and societal factors in the taxpayer's environment as well as the taxpayer's own psychology. To understand any human behavior, an interdisciplinary approach is preferred as behavior is acknowledged to be the result of the complex interaction of internal aspects of being human like emotions, cognitive processes along with factors from the external environment like social norms and uncertainty. This chapter aims to provide a comprehensive and interdisciplinary explanation of tax compliance behavior based on the theories grounded in behavioral economics and which encompass the influence of emotions, cognitive biases, social preferences and neuroscience. The empirical evidence from behavioral and neuroeconomic research discussed provides a more nuanced and comprehensive understanding of a taxpayer's decision making process and provides examples that can be used by tax administrations in any country to improve tax compliance behavior.

INTRODUCTION

Successful collection of tax revenue depends on taxpayers' willingness to cooperate with tax authorities and comply with tax rules. Some economics models emphasize that taxpayers make strategic, financially motivated compliance decisions because they are rational. We believe this argument assumes a narrow view of human behavior. Complex tax codes are hard for lay people to understand and comply with. Behavioral economics assumes tax payers are boundedly rational and use the dual process model (Kahneman, 2011) while making decisions. They involuntarily use heuristics which are decision short-

DOI: 10.4018/979-8-3373-0422-9.ch002

cuts constructed by automatic, cognitive, psychological processes which include but are not limited to emotions, memory, associative reasoning and reference dependence. The automatic tendency to use heuristic-based decision making has resulted in deviations from what neo classical theories predict for behavior in the real world (Thaler,1990; Tversky & Thaler, 1990; Rabin & Thaler, 2001). Departures from rationality emerge both in judgments (beliefs) and choices (Ritsatos, 2014; Hashimzade et al.,2012) and are captured in the prospect theory of decision making under risk introduced by Kahneman and Tversky (1979). This field combines insights from economics and psychology providing a better explanation of behavioral puzzles like the tax compliance puzzle - *the effects of audits on voluntary compliance rates*. Existing literature on tax compliance highlights the significance of non-economic factors such as attitudes toward taxes, personal, social and national norms, perceived fairness (Dumre & Shrestha, 2023; James, 2016; Bornman, 2015; Engida & Baisa, 2014; Bărbuţă-Mişu, 2011) trust (Faizal et al., 2017; Bornman 2015) and positive emotional experiences with tax authorities (Enachescu et al.,2019) in tax compliance behavior. Alm and Torgler (2006) and Cummings et al. (2009) showed that tax morale is also an important factor in reducing tax evasion and increasing voluntary tax compliance. Attempts to understand any human behavior require an interdisciplinary approach as behavior is the result of the complex interaction of internal aspects of being human like emotions, cognitive processes combined with factors from the external environment like social norms and uncertainty (Macintyre et al., 2023; Barrett, 2017).

In this chapter, we propose to address the question of how neural mechanisms shape tax compliance behavior across taxpayer profiles based on insights from neuroeconomic studies in order to enhance the behavioral perspective on voluntary tax compliance. The role of emotions in prediction and decision making is highlighted in the discussion to add a robust scientific dimension to deviation from rational theory. Neuroeconomics methods combine behavioral experiments with neuroimaging techniques to record and investigate the physiological and neural underpinnings of concepts described in behavioral economics literature. It aims to provide a biologically-based account of human behavior that can be applied in social sciences (Rangel et al., 2008). A neuroscientific understanding of voluntary tax compliance behavior can contribute to shaping policies and systems in an advantageous and cost-effective manner (Chorvat, 2007).

Neuroscience has provided valuable insights for the field of behavioral economics by reshaping prevailing psychological theories that inform economic models. Advances in neuroscience have facilitated the direct measurement of brain activity, enabling the study of thoughts, feelings, and cognitive processes. Techniques such as brain imaging allow researchers to infer the mechanisms underlying mental states and gain a strong scientific foundation to challenge established assumptions regarding the relationship between the mind and human behavior. Neuroscience highlights two critical limitations of the neoclassical approach. First, much of human behavior is driven by "automatic" cognitive processes, which operate faster than conscious deliberation and often occur without awareness or intentional effort (Bargh & Chartrand 1999). These automatic processes evolved to address problems of evolutionary significance such as survival and do not necessarily conform to the normative axioms of logical inference and rational choice. Second, human behavior is profoundly influenced by emotional and affective systems (LeDoux, 1996) which are essential for survival and daily functioning. Emotional experiences and subjective perceptions should be taken into consideration when designing policies to promote compliance.

THEORETICAL FRAMEWORK

The Allingham-Sandmo (A-S) model (1972) has traditionally been regarded as the standard model of tax compliance or evasion. In this model, tax compliance depends primarily on the perceived probability of detection, the tax rate and the penalty for evasion. A rising probability of being detected and an increasing fine rate reduce the expected payoff from evading taxes, thus making tax evasion relatively less attractive Yitzhaki (1974). Many limitations to this approach have been documented because of the complexity involved in the real context of tax compliance. Research indicates that many individuals are honest tax payers and consistently avoid tax evasion, even when the risk of detection is low (Elffers, 2000). Alm and Torgler (2011) argue that the neoclassical approach to tax compliance behavior is not robust enough to predict behavior accurately because they overlook sociological and psychological factors - such as attitudes, beliefs, norms, perceptions, and motivations.

Furthermore, conventional approaches towards enhancing taxpayer compliance - such as audits, legislative and administrative reforms are costly to enforce. Context-specific, behaviorally informed messaging presents an immediate, low-cost alternative to overcoming non-compliance. Interventions grounded in behavioral insights assist individuals and businesses in better processing information, making decisions, and submitting accurate and timely tax declarations, while simultaneously enabling tax administration officials to enhance the effectiveness of their operations (Dalton et al., 2021). Behavioral economics examines the impact of psychological, social, and cultural factors on an individual's economic decision-making. Some of the main concepts used in policy nudges are described in detail below.

Prospect theory (Kahneman & Tversky, 1979) is a behavioral choice theory that predicts decision-making under conditions of risk and uncertainty. It predicts that individuals will be risk-averse when faced with gains but will become risk-seeking when faced with losses. It assumes that people use heuristics or decision short cuts based on emotions or memory recall to predict outcome probability rather than analytical thinking. Although this shortcut allows for quick prioritization and processing large amounts of information it results in systematic involuntary cognitive biases which deviate from rationality in judgment. Loss aversion and risk aversion are key factors in predicting risky financial decisions such as tax non-compliance or avoidance wherein the risk is being caught and penalized. Therefore, Prospect theory has been frequently applied in tax research (Dhami & al-Nowaihi, 2007, Yaniv, 1999) to explain phenomena such as withholding. Taxpayers who are under withheld and face the prospect of additional payments are more likely to engage in tax evasion than those who are over withheld and expect a tax refund. The theory also predicts that framing of choices influences behavior. The limitation of Prospect theory in the context of tax compliance is that it ignores the influence of non-economic factors involved such as trust and social norms on the compliance decision.

Rashid et al. (2022) examined the differential effects of various forms of power on the cognitive and affective attitudes (resistance, capitulation, and commitment) of individual taxpayers in Malaysia. The study found that harsh or coercive power, manifested through enforcement, has a more pronounced impact on cognitive defiance than on negative emotional responses. Conversely, soft power, particularly persuasive and reward-based power, exerts a greater influence on taxpayers' emotional deference than on their cognitive deference.

Figure 1. Types of Tax compliance vs. Tax Authority Strategies (Rashid et al., 2022)

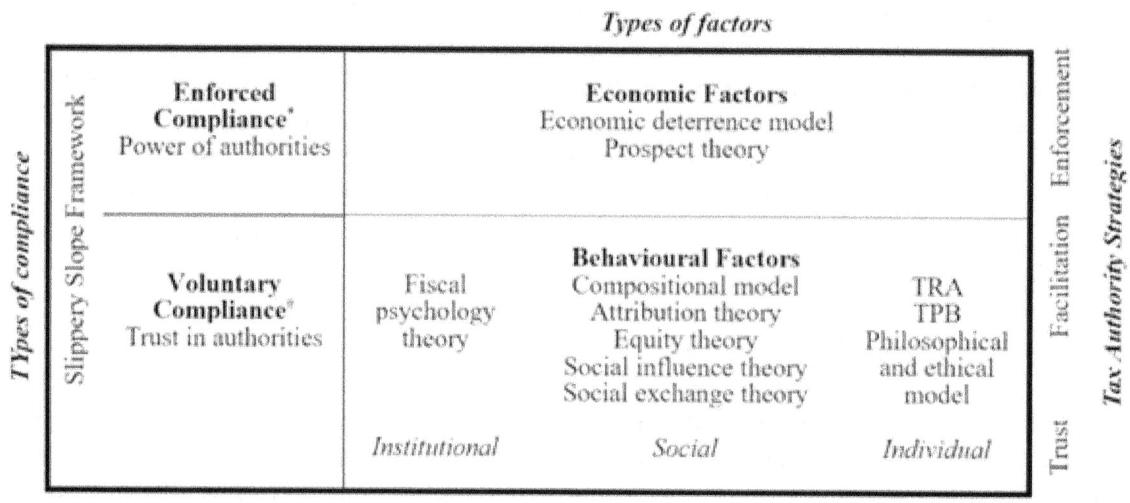

As illustrated in Figure 1, although the economic perspective plays a crucial role in explaining enforced tax compliance, when tax authorities compel compliance through sanctions taxpayers do not comply voluntarily; rather, they seek to avoid the costs associated with detection and penalties, which often exceed the actual tax liability. In contrast, the institutional perspective offers insight into voluntary tax compliance. This behavior aligns with Prospect theory which predicts that in the context of tax decisions, taxpayers' choices may be influenced not only by objective financial consequences but also by the framing of these choices in terms of gains or losses. As a result, taxpayers are likely to be more concerned with potential losses, such as penalties or legal sanctions, than with financial gains associated with non-compliance. This perspective neglects the broader social preference aspects of trust, fairness and social norms.

Figure 2. Slippery Slope framework (Kirchler, Hoelzl, and Wahl, 2008)

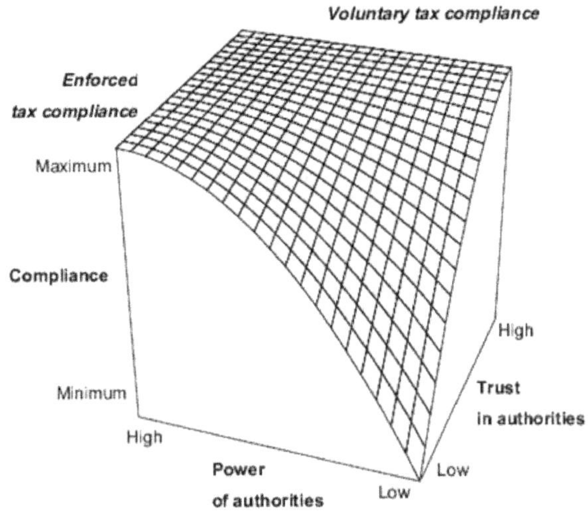

Discriminatory behaviors exhibited due to social preferences are reflected in altruism and reciprocity as a response to perceptions of inequity and unfairness. A substantial percentage of people are motivated by other-regarding preferences, such as fairness and reciprocity (Fehr, 2009). Specific social preferences are a result of different social norms within a variety of cultures. Perceptions of trustworthiness and fairness of government institutions are influenced by social norms and will impact an individual's behavior when interacting with rules enacted by these institutions. The anticipation of punishment driven by social preferences has been shown to strongly increase cooperation in public goods and contract enforcement games. Costly punishments were found to correlate positively with higher cooperation in norms as well as contractual obligations (Fehr & Gachter, 2002). The "slippery slope" framework (Figure 2) proposed by Kirchler et al. (2008) posits that two key dimensions - trust in authorities and the power of authorities - shape tax compliance. Trust in authorities is defined as the belief that tax authorities act benevolently and in the public interest, while the power of authorities refers to taxpayers' perception of the ability of tax officers to detect and punish tax evasion. Both dimensions promote tax compliance: voluntary compliance is driven by trust and enforced compliance is driven by the perceived power of authorities. If taxpayers try to evade detection and avoid paying taxes, it creates an antagonistic environment, where taxpayers comply more when they perceive the authorities as powerful (Hofmann et al., 2017). Such compliance is called *enforced compliance*, where individuals pay taxes due to *fear* of penalties. In contrast, *trust* in authority fosters a "service and customer" mentality wherein authorities are seen as transparent, helpful, and honest, creating a "synergistic atmosphere" where both taxpayers and authorities collaborate with high trust. This leads to *voluntary compliance*, where individuals fulfill their tax duties without coercion. Voluntary compliance by an individual is a function of the combination of their social preferences, social norms in their environment. Conforming behaviors are perceived as "signals" to convey compliance and reinforce community belonging which provides a sense of safety (Akerlof & Kranton, 2000). Conformity includes aligning one's attitude, opinion or behavior to those of others in the group. This behavior aligns the self-image to the public image which creates a positive psychological experience for the individual. In addition to the psychological benefits of compliance, people who accurately identify, value, and cooperate with in-group members enjoy numerous physical benefits that are associated with belonging to the group, thus making compliance largely voluntary.

The highest levels of tax compliance, irrespective of its nature, occur under conditions of both high trust and high power. Gangl et al. (2015) further conceptualized the dynamics of interplay between power and trust by distinguishing between coercive and legitimate power and between reason-based and implicit trust. Legitimate power, when exercised transparently, fairly, and consistently, fosters taxpayer trust based on reasoned judgment. This trust, in turn, strengthens the relationship between taxpayers and authorities, potentially encouraging greater voluntary compliance. In contrast, the negative association between coercive power and implicit trust suggests that an over-reliance on punitive measures can undermine individuals' natural inclination to trust authorities. Such an approach may strain the relationship between taxpayers and authorities, leading to increased resistance and non-compliance. This approach is limited by the exclusion of the financial or economic aspect of tax compliance.

Further, moral factors such as intrinsic motivation, altruism, reciprocity, and fairness may affect the tax compliance decision. People may be willing to sacrifice resources to help others, or to establish fairness or justice. Tax morale encompasses these factors which may intrinsically motivate individuals to pay taxes without any enforcement (Torgler, 2003) and feel shame or guilt in cases of tax evasion (Dulleck et al.,2016; Coricelli et al., 2010). Research shows a significant correlation between tax morale and tax compliance (Ali et al., 2014). In high income countries, higher tax rates, strong enforcement, and public trust in Government and institutions, facilitated by higher tax morale among taxpayers has resulted in higher tax compliance. In emerging and developing economies, tax authorities face the challenges of lower tax compliance, high tax evasion and mistrust of government institutions.

Azmi and Daud (2024) suggest that taxpayer behavior should be understood as existing along a spectrum, ranging from complete compliance to total non-compliance, rather than being confined to the traditional binary framework of compliance versus non-compliance. They argue for recognizing the possibility of varying degrees of compliance, where taxpayer behavior may involve a combination of both compliant and non-compliant actions. For instance, a taxpayer might fully declare both principal and part-time income but exaggerate their tax deductions. Conversely, another taxpayer may accurately report their total income and taxable expenses but fail to submit their tax return on time or pay the due amount by the deadline. The dynamic interaction between compliance and non-compliance is inherently fluid and difficult to quantify. But this theory does not consider the cognitive psychological aspect of behavior. In practice, it can be challenging to precisely determine the degree of compliance or non-compliance exhibited by a taxpayer. Both societal and individual-level factors are integral to understanding taxpayers' attitudes and beliefs regarding compliance decisions (Smart, 2012).

These theories highlight the fact that tax compliance is a behavior which is not driven only by the threats of penalties and punishments, it is shaped and influenced by economic, psychological, cultural, societal factors within the taxpayer's environment (Ostrom, 2010). We propose that the theories discussed are limited by the absence of the neuroscientific background of behavior. Tax compliant behavior is the result of the evaluations and predictions made by the brain with regards to risk and reward not only in an economic context but also in the contexts of trust, fairness and compliance. Behavior depends significantly on these predictions. In order to achieve an enhanced profile of taxpayers, authorities should also consider the neural effects of economic consequences of tax avoidance, social preferences and perceptions regarding trust in authorities.

METHODOLOGY

Based on the theoretical underpinnings, the current study proposes a conceptual framework to refine a behavioral taxpayer profile which incorporates findings from neuroeconomic studies as shown in Figure 3. The model is based on the review of behavioral field experiments and neuroeconomic lab experiments on trust, fairness, biases and risk. Neural responses to potential outcomes are automatic and affective (emotion based). They influence the prediction of risk-reward outcomes for economic and behavioral choices in the context of uncertainty and therefore should be incorporated into taxpayer profiling. The model suggests the framework from the perspective of enhancing voluntary tax compliance which is the more cost-effective outcome for tax authorities.

Figure 3. Proposed Conceptual Model (Authors contribution)

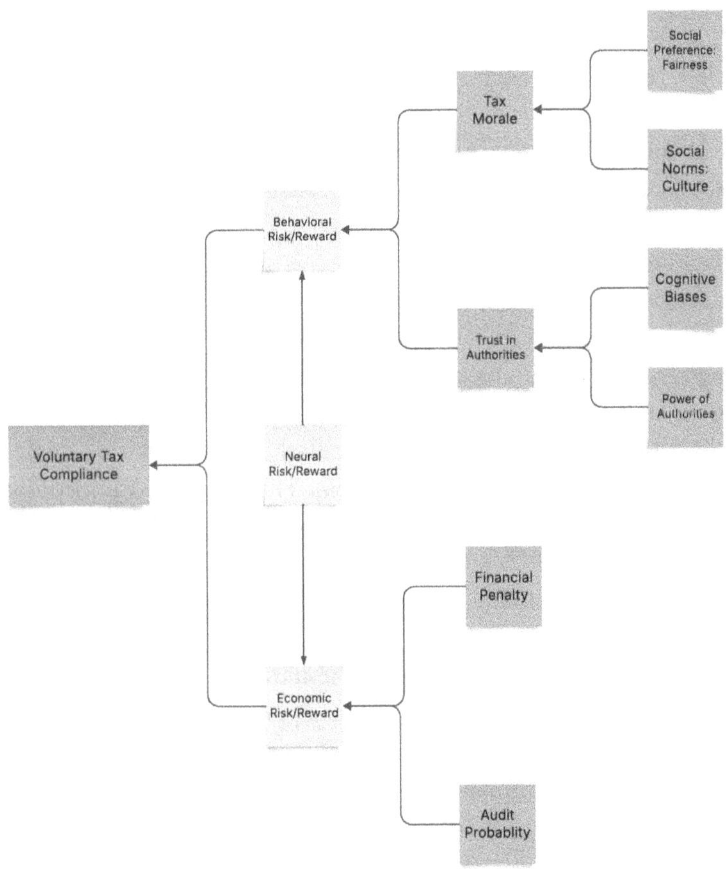

EMPIRICAL INSIGHTS

Emotions & Cognitive Biases

People systematically show the same distinctive idiosyncrasies in reasoning and judgment (Kahneman, 2011; Shafir & LeBoeuf, 2002). These similar judgment processes appear to be a result of the neural connections in the brain which are the same in most, healthy human brains. Korteling et al. (2018) proposed a *neural network* perspective to explain this ubiquitous phenomenon wherein "human decision making is determined by the basic design characteristics of neural information processing". Processes work together rather than in isolation, collectively leading to distorted information processing. Specifically, biased attention, biased processing of emotional stimuli, biased thoughts and rumination, and biased memory processes (Jiang,2024). The prefrontal cortex (PFC) is responsible for executive functions including planning, decision-making, working memory, and problem-solving and the hippocampus which stores memories and records associations. This communication occurs via sensory inputs of an initial stimuli that are interpreted as information which is sent to the PFC which determines the additional required information and retrieves complementary information from the hippocampus (Wang, 2008). This process generates a preferred decision (Saberi et al., 2019).

The neuroscientific understanding of emotion is that it is "proposed to reflect the discrete response to an external or internal event that entails a range of synchronized features including subjective experience, expression, bodily response and action tendencies" (Phelps, 2009). Barrett (2017) proposed a theory of "constructed emotion" which explains how the brain constructs feelings in a given moment based on sensory inputs and argues the automatic nature of this process means that total rationality is not possible. Damasio's perspective (2009) is that emotion "includes mechanisms of drives and motivations as well as those of reward and punishment, which are the fundamental constituents of the emotion machinery" therefore their role in modifying the decision process is significant. Emotion-related brain areas (Figure 4) include the amygdala which is particularly associated with negative emotions of fear, anger and anxiety, arousal and the flight or fight response. The presence of uncertainty in the environment induces a "fear" response elicited by the amygdala (Trepel et al., 2005). The fear response activates the ventromedial prefrontal cortex (vmPFC) whose function is to mediate decision making by allowing for cautious deliberative processes by linking together working memory and emotional systems (Damasio, 1994). Positive emotions associated with positive outcomes activate the nucleus accumbens (NAcc) which is involved in emotional processing, motivation and reinforcement learning involving rewards and pleasure as well as the ventral tegmental area which is a part of the reward circuitry in the brain which releases dopamine which signals rewards and reward predicting cues (Fernández-Espejo, 2000; Yoo et al., 2016; Wang & Cui, 2018).

Figure 4. Brain regions associated with emotions

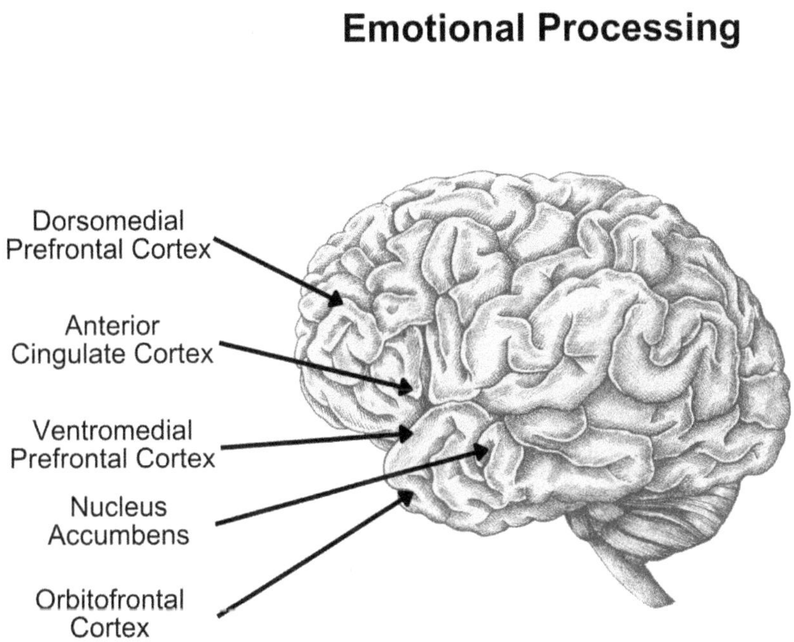

Figure 5. Brain regions associated with rewards processing

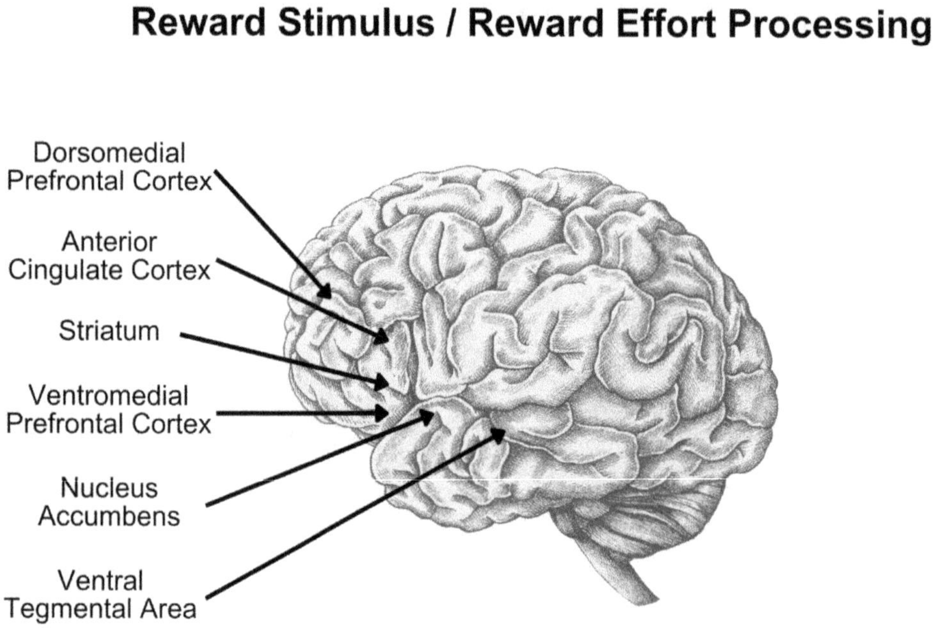

Behavioral interventions for voluntary tax compliance which use simple messages and personal attention reduce uncertainty and elicit positive emotions encouraging voluntary compliance. Compliance can also be influenced by taxpayers' willingness to avoid negative emotions (shame, regret, guilt). Publicly displaying tax evaders increases compliance more than only monetary sanctions (Batrancea & Nichita, 2012). Using simple images alongside messages, as tested in Rwanda, improved taxpayer understanding and compliance (Mascagni et al., 2017).

In Colombia, in-person visits proved more effective than emails or letters in motivating delinquent taxpayers. The likelihood of making a payment increased with different methods: 8.5percent for letters, 17 percent for emails, and 88 percent for personal visits. The probability of paying off the full debt also rose: 6 percent for letters, 13 percent for emails, and 65 percent for visits. Payments as a share of debt were 7 percent for letters, 15 percent for emails, and 73 percent for personal visits. (Ortega & Scartascini., 2015).

In the UK, simplified letters to improve tax compliance among doctors and dentists clearly outlining required actions, resulted in a 15 to 30 percent higher response rate compared to other messaging approaches (Behavioural Insights Team, 2012).

Van Dijk et al. (2020) found that prefilled returns with accurate information led to the highest compliance rates (69.9 percent) and returns with underestimated liabilities had the lowest compliance rates (41.3 percent).

Letters announcing either a certain audit or a 50 percent probability of an audit, resulted in taxpayers reporting higher income (Kleven et al., 2011). Messages that increase the perceived probability of punishment not only has a positive impact on compliance but also on the filing compliance of delinquent taxpayers (Meiselman, 2018).

Emotions, Risk, and Uncertainty

Emotions or affective states result in feelings in our physical body. Homeostasis ensures that these feelings will automatically self-regulate towards balance, influencing behavior in the process. According to the Somatic marker hypothesis (Damasio, 1994) emotions trigger somatic markers, which are 'body and brain' related responses that guide behavior in an advantageous direction i.e. people tend to choose the outcomes associated with positive, anticipated emotions. Thus, in order to maintain mental stability, resolving uncertainty is one of the primary jobs of the brain. Neuroimaging studies suggest that there is strong path dependence in the brain's reaction to economic quantities like likelihood or risk (Weber & Johnson, 2009). In studies of risky choice, activation in the right anterior insula increased which is thought to play a key role in combining signals from the body with factors related to balance, pleasure, and motivation. Risk preference was found to correlate with activity in the parietal cortex (Huettel et al., 2006). This insular activation may reflect the region's presumed role in representing somatic states that can be used to simulate the potential negative consequences of actions i.e. loss (Damasio, 1996).

When considering the effect of outcomes of risky decisions, both gains and losses evoke activation in similar regions, including the striatum which is involved in decision making and reward processing, the midbrain which functions as relay system for sensory input and stores dopamine neurons, the vmPFC and the ACC which is involved in motivation control including reward (Figure 5) and effort prediction as well as decision making in uncertainty. The results of these studies suggest that the brain values risky gambles by evaluating their expected reward and risk. Activation increased with potential gain but decreased with potential loss (Tom et al. 2007). Consistent with the assumptions of Prospect theory, activation in these regions is more sensitive to the magnitude of loss than that of gain (Trepel et al., 2005).

Behavioral research has found that anticipation of uncertain monetary gains elicits positive arousal, whereas anticipation of uncertain monetary losses elicits negative arousal – even before outcomes are revealed (Samanez-Larkin et al., 2007). There is also neuroscientific evidence that brain regions activated by anticipated monetary gains and losses are the same as those activated by automatic emotional reactions. The NAcc shows proportional activation during anticipation of monetary gains (Breiter et al., 2001; Knutson et al., 2001), and this activation correlates with positive aroused affect (Bjork et al., 2004; Knutson et al., 2005). Lo et al. (2005) found that loss-avoidance circuits involve the amygdala and anterior insula. Anticipation of financial outcomes involving uncertain large losses is likely to elicit negative arousal and activate the anterior insula while gain anticipation shows greater activation in the NAcc (Knutson & Greer, 2008). The anticipatory affect model (Knutson & Greer, 2008) attempts to link activity in deep brain circuits to affective experience and ultimately choice. The model posits that "uncertainty elicits increased aroused affect, while potential gains versus losses elicit positive versus negative affect" wherein positive arousal (e.g., feelings like excitement) evokes neural activity in the NAcc and potential losses elicit negative arousal (e.g., feelings like anxiety) as well as correlated neural activity in the anterior insula. If positive arousal increases, uncertain gains should appear more prominent, which should lead people to choose the risky option. Alternatively, if negative arousal increases, uncertain losses should appear more prominent, which should lead people to become risk averse. An fMRI study that used neural activity to predict financial risk taking showed that anticipatory NAcc activity predicted increased financial risk taking, whereas anticipatory anterior insula activity predicted decreased financial risk taking. Results showed that NAcc activation preceded both risky choices and risk-seeking mistakes, anterior insula activation preceded both riskless choices and risk-aversion mistakes (Paulus et al., 2003; Kuhnen and Knutson, 2005).

The process of learning which behaviors to repeat, and which to discontinue is dependent on signals from midbrain dopamine neurons. Dopamine neurons compute reward prediction errors and transmit this signal to various brain regions, significantly to the striatum (Rothenhoefer et al., 2017; Montague et al., 1996). Reward prediction errors measure the gap between the reward you expect and the reward you actually get. Dopamine signals in the brain take into account both how likely a reward is and how big it might be. An increase in uncertainty can slow down learning, reduce automatic body responses, and reduce the strength of dopamine signals that reflect these prediction errors (Rothenhoefer et al., 2017). This dopaminergic system is associated with reward-based learning which reinforces behavioral patterns based on past gains (Valentin & O'Doherty, 2009). Many behavioral patterns that are considered irrational in financial decision making are consistent with reward-based learning where previous choices are positively reinforced; they are more likely to be repeated if they were followed by a gain in the past (Miendlarzewska et al., 2019; Pine et al., 2010; Breiter et al., 2001).

Behavioral interventions framing outcomes as rewards or punishments or emphasizing the probability (risk) of an audit encourage tax compliance. In Costa Rica, making punishment salient, mentioning potential sanctions a taxpayer could be subject to, including shop closure, audit, or online publication of names encouraged compliance. The income tax filing rate rose by 20 percentage points within five weeks. Additionally, filing rates increased by another two percentage points for individuals who received a message that included examples of third-party information (Dalton et al., 2021).

In Poland, 'hard-tone' messages were more effective than 'soft-tone' messages. Similarly in Latvia, the most effective message adopted a harder tone, emphasizing the deliberate choice to avoid compliance. This approach resulted in a 9.4percent greater improvement in compliance compared to a social norms message, which highlighted the increasing number of taxpayers filing by the deadline each year (Behavioral Insights Team, 2012).

In Bangladesh, an intervention that informed firms that their compliance details would be shared with others resulted in a 17 percent increase in VAT payments. An SMS message threatening to publicly disclose the names of non-compliant firms online led to a significant increase in tax filings (Brockmeyer et al., 2016; Chetty et al., 2014).

In Denmark, firms with a guaranteed audit were nearly twice as likely to comply compared to those with a 50 percent audit probability (Kleven et al., 2011).

Use of third-party information, emphasizing that reports from clients, suppliers, and financial service providers could be used to validate a non-compliers sales and spending (Dalton et al., 2021).

Providing tangible rewards for tax payments can enhance the intrinsic motivation of citizens, while also generating positive externalities for the surrounding community. In Argentina, winners of the "Good Taxpayer Award" lottery were granted the opportunity to receive a sidewalk construction or renovation project. The prospect of winning this lottery effectively incentivized short-term tax compliance. 86 percent of lottery participants settled their tax obligations on time, 89 percent paid within three months, and 99 percent within six months. A 3 percentage point increase in on-time payments led to a 21 percent decrease in delayed payments (Carrillo et al., 2017).

Tax refund time has been recognized as a key opportunity for low- and moderate-income consumers to save for unexpected expenses. Grinstein-Weiss et al. (2017) found that simply presenting savings as one of the available options in the choice architecture was not enough to boost savings deposits. However, placing strong emphasis on saving and making the process "frictionless" by offering a simple, one-click decision significantly increased savings allocations.

Emotions, Social Preferences and Trust

The social context for tax compliant or evading behavior is particularly significant for tax authorities in developing countries as the cognitive perceptions and neural activity associated with trustworthiness, fairness and reciprocity influence compliance behavior.

Figure 6 and Figure 7 depict the brain regions activated in behavioral expression of fairness and social preferences respectively. Neuroscientific studies on the evaluation of fairness use the behavior exhibited in economic games as a metric. These studies have shown that the ACC, the brain region responsible for decision making in uncertain situations and emotional regulation, shows activation when facing unfair offers. The anterior insula (AI) has also shown activation in trials wherein unfair offers were rejected. This activity may be related to the degree of emotional resentment of unfair offers. Both the right DLP-FC and vlPFC are involved in the cognitive control of impulse to reject unfair offers. The right DLPFC activity is seen as crucial for the behavioral implementation of fairness motives i.e. rejection of unfair offers (Koenigs et al., 2007). With regards to possible punishment, the brain regions activated are the lateral orbitofrontal cortex (OFC) known to be involved in emotional processing and controlling behavior specifically with regards to rewards and punishments and the DLPFC. The right DLPFC was involved in impulse control for temptation to violate the norm and stronger activation was observed in the right DLPFC and the left OFC during a punishment game indicating a stronger increase in norm compliance when faced with punishment threat (Knoch et al. 2008; Spitzer et al., 2007). Further, research suggests that conformity activates brain signals similar to those used in reinforcement learning (Shestakova et al., 2013; Kim et al., 2012; Campbell-Meiklejohn et al., 2010; Klucharev et al., 2009).

Studies on cooperation use economic games like the Ultimatum game and the Dictator game or their variations. Brain regions showing activation in these studies include the ventral striatum, ventral tegmental area, the NAcc and the vmPFC. The ventral striatum shows activation when a person experienced mutual cooperation (Rilling et al. 2002). Tabibnia & Murphy (2007) found that the fairness of a bargaining offer also activated the ventral striatum, which plays a key role in processing rewards and emotions. The behavioral hypothesis that social preferences are similar to preferences for one's own rewards in terms of neural activation is also supported by these studies.

Social preferences also influence the decision of whether to trust. In behavioral economics trust is assumed to mean reciprocal cooperation. The inherent assumption is that trust is earned not given, but whether to trust can only be known after taking the risk to trust, so a risky choice inherently exists in trusting, and it affects the decision to trust (Bohnet et al., 2008). It is significant to point out here that the brain appears to make a distinction between monetary risk taking and risk in social trust (Kirsh et al., 2005). Bohnet and Zeckhauser (2004) coined the term "betrayal aversion" to refer to this social aspect of risk. Betrayal aversion and the preference for reciprocity were found to impact the decision to repay trust (Bohnet et al., 2008). Neuroscience studies support this behavioral theory by shedding light on the innate role of the PFC in the creation and maintenance of trust. This region of the brain is intricately involved in the assessment of the intentions and reliability of others (Zak, 2017 HBR). It was found that conditional trust selectively activated the ventral tegmental area which is linked to the evaluation of expected and realized reward (Krueger et al.,2007) indicating that reciprocal trust is perceived by the brain as an earned reward.

Figure 6. Brain regions involved in evaluation of fairness

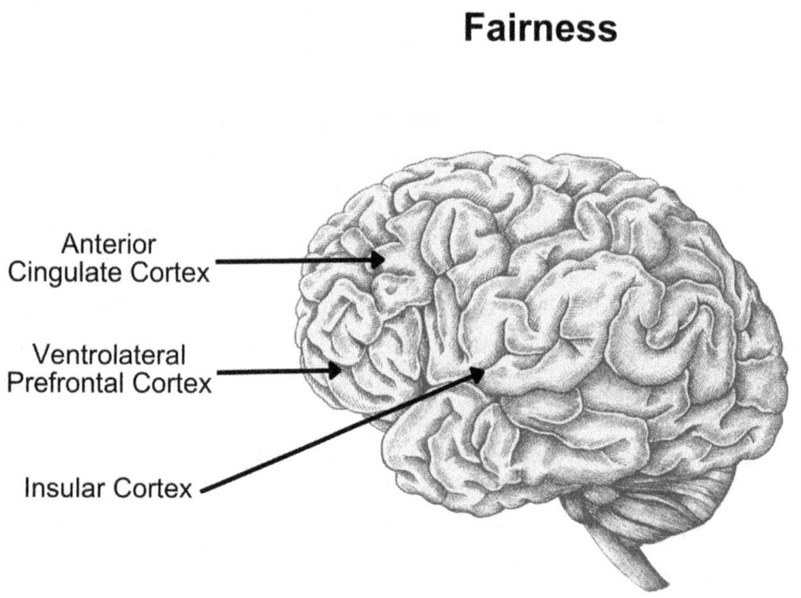

Figure 7. Brain regions involved in judgement of social preference

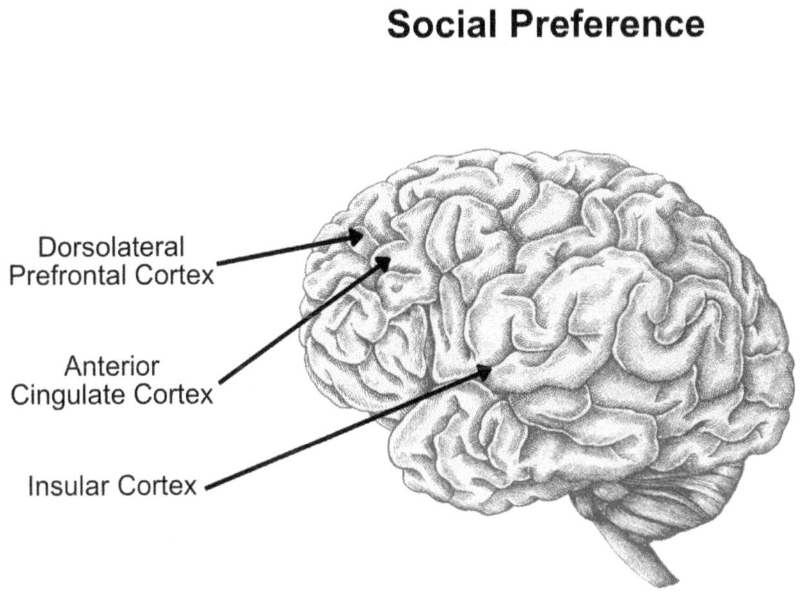

The use of social preference and transparency encourages tax morale and trust. Studies suggest that when taxpayers feel involved, they are more likely to comply (Torgler, 2004). Social proof, a choice frame which emphasizes behavior adopted by the majority, plays a powerful role in compliance behavior. Framing non-compliance as a deliberate choice, rather than a mere oversight in the message, can also increase compliance by reminding taxpayers of their desire to be good citizens (Ritov & Baron, 1990).

A UK field experiment showed that referencing the average compliance rate increased tax payments. Additionally, taxpayers are more likely to pay if they believe others are contributing fairly, suggesting that highlighting others' compliance can improve adherence (Bazart & Bonein, 2014). In Guatemala, a message highlighting the deviation of the recipient's behavior from the majority of taxpayers regarding compliance, increased compliance (Dalton et al., 2021).

Framing of explanations of deployment of tax revenue also affects compliance (Druckman, 2001). Sniderman and Theriaults (1999) found that individuals' support varies if government spending for the poor is framed as enhancing the chance that poor people can get ahead as opposed to resulting in higher taxes.

Ali et al. (2014) found that in Tanzania, Uganda, Kenya, and South Africa, the level of public goods provision has a significant, positive relationship with tax compliance (Sjoberg et al., 2019). In Rwanda, emphasizing the role of taxes in funding public goods like education and healthcare led to sustained tax compliance (Mascagni et al., 2017). In the DRC, enforcement of tax payments correlated with greater public participation in town hall meetings and demand for accountability (Weigel, 2018).

Evidence from Latin America shows that taxpayers who were given vignettes about high government performance in the provision of public goods like school supplies were more tax compliant (Ortega et al., 2016). In Uruguay, sharing audit statistics and penalties with firms boosted compliance, while in Chile, notifying firms of monitoring and potential audits increased VAT payments (Bergolo et al., 2017; Pomeranz, 2015; Kleven et al., 2011). Experimental evidence from Mexico showed that respondents who were reminded that their tax money is spent on security (the most salient public good in the country) show the highest increase in tax compliance, compared to other messages (Flores-Macías, 2018).

In Indonesia, distribution of a behaviorally-informed calendar providing clear information on procedures and public benefits from tax revenue saw a 3 percent increase in tax revenue, raising compliance to 25 percent compared to the control group. The modest implementation cost was only USD 3 per participant, and the revenue-to-cost ratio was 36 (Suharnoko et al., 2020).

PRACTICAL APPLICATIONS

Increased digitalization and analytical tools have significantly increased the efficiency and effectiveness of tax administration (OECD,2020). As online transactions are now a part of most people's natural experience, tax authorities will be required to provide an online interface for taxpayers not only to make payments but also to answer queries, make calculations and solve any problems and provide services like e-filing, e-payment, online self-service tools and online live chats for targeted help. These developments are also making it easier for taxpayers to understand and to meet their obligations. The behavioral insights discussed can be leveraged to design the user interface intentionally while maintaining critical attributes of transparency and trustworthiness. The potential consolidation of a large amount of personal financial data inherent in tax computation can raise issues of trust regarding data privacy. It is imperative to justify collection of certain data and explain how and where it would be used and how it would be protected both legally and practically (OECD,2020).

Interactions between taxpayers and tax authorities have a number of touchpoints through which customer communication, interaction and facilitation of engagements is managed. These are critical to the smooth running of tax administration. Touchpoints include face-to face interactions, phone calls, multifunction websites, e-services, and business management systems (OECD,2022). Tax authorities have an opportunity to behaviorally design each touch point to optimize the required effects. The positive correlation between psychic stress and tax compliance, underscores the importance of moral sentiment in tax compliance (Dulleck et al., 2016). Further, accumulating evidence suggests that barriers can discourage participation out of proportion to the magnitude of the costs they impose (Bertrand et al., 2006).

Behaviorally designed digital measures to improve tax compliance reduce the physical and cognitive effort of taxpayers making compliance easier. Measures can be designed to trigger positive emotions, rewards and trust such as the use of personalised communication in emails and texts as well as through taxpayer portals and web chats.

Web-based applications can be designed to use the native features of the relevant devices (such as cameras, reading of QR codes and biometrics) to make verification easier. Pre-filling tax returns by creating pre populated fields within the tax form, uses the default bias advantageously making the tax filing process easier as well as reduces the scope for errors (Fonseca & Grimshaw, 2017).

Self-service channels can be supported by real time assistance (such as Chat bots) supported by artificial intelligence while options for human interaction remain available and are transparent and easily accessible. The Virtual Assistant tool based on AI was used with the objective of advancing towards a quality information provision system as well as facilitating the understanding of complex regulations. Relevant information is provided about registration and rectification of invoices, tax obligations, tax rate, exemptions and deductions. The Virtual Assistant autocompletes questions with the necessary information to obtain the sought answer. Using a well-designed chatbot can enhance transparency and trust among taxpayers (OECD, 2022).

Providing a clear and graphically pleasant menu on the website makes the experience less burdening and facilitates compliance. The clarity of menus reduces phone call enquiries and emails, reducing time and money spent on responding. Ambiguous design and complicated menus have the opposite effect. Bright colors used to highlight important information disorients users who ignore the information. Unfriendly website design adds to perceived complexity reducing trust and compliance (Batrancea & Nichita, 2012).

Ethical Considerations

The ethical considerations for research in behavioral sciences largely address the protection of human rights. Any unethical practices will compromise society at large via the methods used and have real implications on research findings (Reese & Fremouw, 1984). Ethical considerations must include respecting the dignity of the human participants and their environment; avoiding exploitation of participants and their communities and protecting those with diminished autonomy. Authorities should be mindful of the consequences of their research, and any potential conflict of interest of diverse groups of participants, communities, and society (Kucirkova et al., 2019). While implementing nudges and interventions in policy decisions ethical guidelines should emphasize transparency, stakeholder involvement, risk mitigation, fairness and accountability.

The biological data collected from non-invasive devices used in neuroscientific studies can be combined with generative artificial intelligence technologies which engage with deep-learning models to adapt and create new knowledge based on this data. In the future, behavioral science will be required to make use of generative AI to design powerful and personalized interventions. Ethical considerations will need to encompass aspects like helping participants understand how the AI technology will be used, to what extent is it ethical to extrapolate brain activity from other biological data such as facial micro-expressions, posture and biometrics, which should require explicit consent from research participants. In addition, adequate human oversight would be required. There is also evidence that humans may respond differently to behavioral interventions provided by AI as opposed to those provided by humans (Lavery et al., 2024).

CONCLUSION

When outcomes are uncertain, the brain uses a risk-reward outcome framework and predicts gains or losses. Risk and uncertainty elicit affective responses. Fear of probable punishment or financial loss motivates avoidance behavior while potential rewards motivate approach behavior. As suggested by the neuroeconomic evidence, this neural framework processes financial and social outcomes in the same manner. Dopamine is released when the reward is received which creates a feedback loop for reward prediction, encouraging repetition of the behavior. The behavioral evidence from economically developed and developing countries shows that the behavior of a significant proportion of taxpayers is based on the neural risk-reward framework. Behavior is motivated towards rewards like trust, social norms, fairness and away from punishment, financial and social loss. A neural understanding of tax compliance will aid tax authorities in profiling compliant and non-compliant taxpayers, sustaining compliance as well as nudging non-compliant taxpayers towards compliance by leveraging behaviorally designed messages, communication and interfaces.

The empirical evidence discussed has been collected from W.E.I.R.D., Latam and Asian countries emphasizing the universal application of behaviorally designed measures for enhancing voluntary tax compliance, particularly for their cost effectiveness. But these designs should not be used as templates. Policies and interventions will be effective only in the cultural and economic context of a specific country. The use of reward and punishment nudges incorporating social norms and preferences should be tested before adoption in mass communication and policy.

Future research efforts in neuroeconomics and tax behavior should be aligned to developments in the field of artificial intelligence (AI) to be useful and applicable for tax authorities as they will need to adapt to digital communication and interfaces in the near future. AI agents can resolve customer queries, reducing response times and minimizing the need for human interaction. Future expectations of developments in AI point to AI powered chatbots and humanoids for customer interaction, designed on agentic AI models for decision making. Future research can be directed towards exploring the neural effects of interacting with AI bots for both simple and complicated tax transactions on both trust and fairness. Another aspect which can be explored is neural differences when interacting with humans and chatbots on willingness to comply and cooperate. It is also anticipated that AI will drive hyper-personalization of digital interactions. It would be beneficial to explore whether hyper-personalization positively affects compliance and trust. Research specifically directed towards studying the neuroscientific and behavioral effects of AI on digital communication as well as consequent tax behavior of real taxpayers would add significant value to tax revenue collections.

REFERENCES

Akerlof, G., & Kranton, R. (2000). Economics and identity. *The Quarterly Journal of Economics*, *115*(3), 715–753. DOI: 10.1162/003355300554881

Ali, M., Fjeldstad, O. H., & Sjursen, I. H. (2014). To pay or not to pay? Citizens' attitudes toward taxation in Kenya, Tanzania, Uganda, and South Africa. *World Development*, *64*, 828–842. DOI: 10.1016/j.worlddev.2014.07.006

Allingham, M. G., & Sandmo, A. (1972). Income tax evasion: A theoretical analysis. *Journal of Public Economics*, *1*(3–4), 323–338. DOI: 10.1016/0047-2727(72)90010-2

Alm, J., & Torgler, B. (2006). Culture differences and tax morale in the United States and in Europe. *Journal of Economic Psychology*, *27*(2), 224–246. DOI: 10.1016/j.joep.2005.09.002

Alm, J., & Torgler, B. (2011). Do ethics matter? Tax compliance and morality. *Journal of Business Ethics*, *101*(4), 635–651. DOI: 10.1007/s10551-011-0761-9

Azmi, D. A. W. M., & Daud, S. A. M. M. (2024). Reconceptualizing tax compliance behavior: A theoretical matrix approach. *Accounting and Finance Research*, *13*(1), 1–67.

Bărbuţă-Mişu, N. (2011). A review of factors for tax compliance. *Annals of Dunărea de Jos University. Fascicle I: Economics and Applied Informatics*.

Bargh, J. A., & Chartrand, T. L. (1999). The unbearable automaticity of being. *The American Psychologist*, *54*(7), 462–479. DOI: 10.1037/0003-066X.54.7.462

Barrett, L. F. (2017). The theory of constructed emotion: An active inference account of interoception and categorization. *Social Cognitive and Affective Neuroscience*, *12*(1), 1–23. DOI: 10.1093/scan/nsx060 PMID: 27798257

Bătrâncea, L., & Nichita, R.-A. (2012). Tax non-compliance behavior in the light of tax law complexity and the relationship between authorities and taxpayers. *Scientific Annals of Alexandru Ioan Cuza University of Iasi - Economic Series, 59*(1), 97–106.

Bazart, C., & Bonein, A. (2014). Reciprocal relationships in tax compliance decisions. *Journal of Economic Psychology*, *40*, 83–102. DOI: 10.1016/j.joep.2012.10.002

Behavioural Insights Team, Cabinet Office, UK. (2012). *Applying behavioural insights to reduce fraud, error and debt.*

Bergolo, M., Ceni, R., Cruces, G., Giaccobasso, M., & Perez-Truglia, R. (2017). Tax audits as scarecrows: Evidence from Uruguay. *NBER Working Paper No. 23631.*

Bertrand, M., & Shafir, E. (2006). Behavioral Economics and Marketing in Aid of Decision Making Among the Poor. *Journal of Public Policy & Marketing*, *25*(1), 8–23. Advance online publication. DOI: 10.1509/jppm.25.1.8

Bjork, J. M., Knutson, B., Fong, G. W., Caggiano, D. M., Bennett, S. M., & Hommer, D. W. (2004). Incentive-elicited brain activation in adolescents: Similarities and differences from young adults. *The Journal of Neuroscience : The Official Journal of the Society for Neuroscience, 24*(8), 1793–1802. DOI: 10.1523/JNEUROSCI.4862-03.2004 PMID: 14985419

Bohnet, I., Greig, F., Herrmann, B., & Zeckhauser, R. (2008). Betrayal aversion: Evidence from Brazil, China, Oman, Switzerland, Turkey, and the United States. *The American Economic Review, 98*(1), 294–310. DOI: 10.1257/aer.98.1.294

Bohnet, I., & Zeckhauser, R. (2004). Trust, risk, and betrayal. *Journal of Economic Behavior & Organization, 55*(4), 467–484. DOI: 10.1016/j.jebo.2003.11.004

Bornman, M. (2015). The determinants and measurement of trust in tax authorities as a factor influencing tax compliance behaviour. *Journal of Economic and Financial Sciences, 8*(3), 772–789. DOI: 10.4102/jef.v8i3.121

Breiter, H. C., Aharon, I., Kahneman, D., Dale, A., & Shizgal, P. (2001). Functional imaging of neural responses to expectancy and experience of monetary gains and losses. *Neuron, 30*(2), 619–639. DOI: 10.1016/S0896-6273(01)00303-8 PMID: 11395019

Brockmeyer, A., Hernandez, M., Kettle, S., & Smith, S. (2016). Casting the tax net wider: Experimental evidence from Costa Rica. *World Bank Policy Research Working Paper* No. 7850. https://hdl.handle.net/10986/25167

Campbell-Meiklejohn, D. K., Bach, D. R., Roepstorff, A., Dolan, R. J., & Frith, C. D. (2010). How the opinion of others affects our valuation of objects. *Current Biology, 20*(12), 1165–1170. DOI: 10.1016/j.cub.2010.04.055 PMID: 20619815

Carrillo, P. E., Castro, E., & Scartascini, C. (2017, April). Do rewards work? Evidence from the randomization of public works. *Inter-American Development Bank (IDB) Working Paper Series* No. 794.

Chetty, R., Mobarak, M., & Singhal, M. (2014, August). Increasing tax compliance through social recognition. *International Growth Centre Policy Brief* No. 14/0658.

Chorvat, T. (2007). Tax Compliance and the Neuroeconomics of Intertemporal Substitution. *National Tax Journal, 60*(3). The University of Chicago Press Journals. DOI: 10.17310/ntj.2007.3.15

Coricelli, G., Joffily, M., Montmarquette, C., & Villeval, M. C. (2010). Cheating, emotions, and rationality: An experiment on tax evasion. *Experimental Economics, 13*(2), 226–247. DOI: 10.1007/s10683-010-9237-5

Cummings, R. G., Martinez-Vazquez, J., McKee, M., & Torgler, B. (2009). Tax morale affects tax compliance: Evidence from surveys and an artefactual field experiment. *Journal of Economic Behavior & Organization, 70*(3), 447–457. DOI: 10.1016/j.jebo.2008.02.010

Dalton, A. G., Manning, L. A., Jamison, J. C., Sen, I. K., Karver, J. G., Nunez, C., Jorge, L., Guedes, L. P., Estevez, M., & Serrana, B. (2021). *Behavioral insights for tax compliance*. World Bank Group.

Damasio, A. (2009). Neuroscience and the emergence of neuroeconomics. In Glimcher, P. W., Camerer, C. F., Fehr, E., & Poldrack, R. A. (Eds.), *Neuroeconomics: Decision making and the brain* (pp. 209–217). Academic Press. DOI: 10.1016/B978-0-12-374176-9.00014-2

Damasio, A. R. (1994). *Descartes' error: Emotion, reason, and the human brain*. Putnam.

Damasio, A. R. (1996). The somatic marker hypothesis and the possible functions of the prefrontal cortex. *Philosophical Transactions of the Royal Society of London. Series B, Biological Sciences, 351*(1346), 1413–1420. DOI: 10.1098/rstb.1996.0125 PMID: 8941953

Dhami, S., & al-Nowaihi, A. (2007). Why do people pay taxes? Prospect theory versus expected utility theory. *Journal of Economic Behavior & Organization, 64*(1), 171–192. DOI: 10.1016/j.jebo.2006.08.006

Druckman, J. N. (2001). The implications of framing effects for citizen competence. *Political Behavior, 23*(3), 225–256. DOI: 10.1023/A:1015006907312

Dulleck, U., Fooken, J., Newton, C., Ristl, A., Schaffner, M., & Torgler, B. (2016). Tax compliance and psychic costs: Behavioral experimental evidence using a physiological marker. *Journal of Public Economics, 134*, 9–18. DOI: 10.1016/j.jpubeco.2015.12.007

Dumre, D. P., & Shrestha, L. M. (2023). Factors influencing tax compliance behavior among the industries of Butwal Industrial Estate. *The Lumbini Journal of Business and Economics, XI*(2), 1–20. DOI: 10.3126/ljbe.v11i2.64720

Elffers, H. (2000). But taxpayers do cooperate! In A. Biel, M. Snyder, T. R. Tyler, & M. van Vugt (Eds.), *Cooperation in modern society: Promoting the welfare of communities, states, and organizations* (pp. 184–194). Taylor & Francis Group.

Enachescu, J., Olsen, J., Kogler, C., Zeelenberg, M., Breugelmans, S. M., & Kirchler, E. (2019). The role of emotions in tax compliance behavior: A mixed-methods approach. *Journal of Economic Psychology, 74*, 102194. Advance online publication. DOI: 10.1016/j.joep.2019.102194

Engida, T. G., & Baisa, G. A. (2014). Factors influencing taxpayers' compliance with the tax system: An empirical study in Mekelle City, Ethiopia. *eJournal of Tax Research, 12*(2), 433–452.

Faizal, S., Palil, M., Maelah, R., & Ramli, R. (2017). Power and trust as factors influencing tax compliance behavior in Malaysia. *Asian Journal of Accounting and Governance, 8*, 79–85. DOI: 10.17576/AJAG-2017-08-07

Fehr, E. (2009). Social preferences and the brain. In Glimcher, P. W., Camerer, C. F., Fehr, E., & Poldrack, R. A. (Eds.), *Neuroeconomics: Decision making and the brain* (pp. 215–232). Academic Press. DOI: 10.1016/B978-0-12-374176-9.00015-4

Fehr, E., & Gächter, S. (2002). Altruistic punishment in humans. *Nature, 415*(6868), 137–140. DOI: 10.1038/415137a PMID: 11805825

Fernández-Espejo, E. (2000). Cómo funciona el nucleus accumbens? [How does the nucleus accumbens function?]. *Revista de Neurología, 30*(9), 845–849. DOI: 10.33588/rn.3009.99617 PMID: 10870199

Flores-Macías, G. A. (2018). Building support for taxation in developing countries: Experimental evidence from Mexico. *World Development, 105*, 13–24. DOI: 10.1016/j.worlddev.2017.12.014

Fonseca, M. A., & Grimshaw, S. B. (2017). Do behavioral nudges in prepopulated tax forms affect compliance? Experimental evidence with real taxpayers. *Journal of Public Policy & Marketing, 36*(2), 213–226. DOI: 10.1509/jppm.15.128

Gangl, K., Hofmann, E., & Kirchler, E. (2015). Tax authorities' interaction with taxpayers: A conception of compliance in social dilemmas by power and trust. *New Ideas in Psychology, 37*, 13–23. DOI: 10.1016/j.newideapsych.2014.12.001 PMID: 25859096

Grinstein-Weiss, M., Cryder, C., Despard, M. R., Perantie, D. C., Oliphant, J. E., & Ariely, D. (2017, October 1). The Role of Choice Architecture in Promoting Saving at Tax Time: Evidence from a Large–Scale Field Experiment. *Behavioral Science & Policy, 3*(2), 21-38. Sage Journals. DOI: 10.1177/237946151700300203

Hashimzade N., Myles G.D. and Tran-Nam B. (2012). 'Application of behavioural economics to tax evasion'. *Journal of Economic Surveys*, Online Version, .DOI: 10.1111/j.1467-6419.2012.00733.x

Hofmann, E., Voracek, M., Bock, C., & Kirchler, E. (2017). Tax compliance across socio demographic categories: Meta-analyses of survey studies in 111 countries. *Journal of Economic Psychology, 62*, 63–71. DOI: 10.1016/j.joep.2017.06.005

Huettel, S., Stowe, C., Gordon, E., Warner, B., & Platt, M. (2006). Neural signatures of economic preferences for risk and ambiguity. *Neuron, 49*(5), 765–775. DOI: 10.1016/j.neuron.2006.01.024 PMID: 16504951

James, S. (2016). The Importance of Fairness in Tax Policy: Behavioral Economics and the UK Experience. [IJABE]. *International Journal of Applied Behavioral Economics, 3*(1), 1–12. DOI: 10.4018/ijabe.2014010101

Jiang, Y. (2024). A theory of the neural mechanisms underlying negative cognitive bias in major depression. *Frontiers in Psychiatry, 15*, 1348474. DOI: 10.3389/fpsyt.2024.1348474 PMID: 38532986

Kahneman, D. (2011). *Thinking, fast and slow*. Farrar, Straus and Giroux.

Kahneman, D., & Tversky, A. (1979). Prospect Theory: An Analysis of Decision under Risk. *Econometrica, 47*(2), 263–291. DOI: 10.2307/1914185

Kim, B. R., Liss, A., Rao, M., Singer, Z., & Compton, R. J. (2012). Social deviance activates the brain's error-monitoring system. *Cognitive, Affective & Behavioral Neuroscience, 12*(1), 65–73. DOI: 10.3758/s13415-011-0067-5 PMID: 22038705

Kirchler, E., Hoelzl, E., & Wahl, I. (2008). Enforced versus voluntary tax compliance: The "slippery slope" framework. *Journal of Economic Psychology, 29*(2), 210–225. DOI: 10.1016/j.joep.2007.05.004

Kirsch, P., Esslinger, C., Chen, Q., Mier, D., Lis, S., Siddhanti, S., Gruppe, H., Mattay, V. S., Gallhofer, B., & Meyer-Lindenberg, A. (2005). Oxytocin modulates neural circuitry for social cognition and fear in humans. *The Journal of Neuroscience : The Official Journal of the Society for Neuroscience, 25*(49), 11489–11493. DOI: 10.1523/JNEUROSCI.3984-05.2005 PMID: 16339042

Kleven, H. J., Knudsen, M. B., Kreiner, C. T., Pedersen, S., & Saez, E. (2011). Unwilling or unable to cheat? Evidence from a tax audit experiment in Denmark. *Econometrica*, *79*(3), 651–692. DOI: 10.3982/ECTA9113

Klucharev, V., Hytönen, K., Rijpkema, M., Smidts, A., & Fernández, G. (2009). Reinforcement learning signal predicts social conformity. *Neuron*, *61*(1), 140–151. DOI: 10.1016/j.neuron.2008.11.027 PMID: 19146819

Knoch, D., Nitsche, M. A., Fischbacher, U., Eisenegger, C., Pascual-Leone, A., & Fehr, E. (2008). Studying the neurobiology of social interaction with transcranial direct current stimulation: The example of punishing unfairness. *Cerebral Cortex (New York, N.Y.)*, *18*(9), 1987–1990. DOI: 10.1093/cercor/bhm237 PMID: 18158325

Knutson, B., Adams, C. M., Fong, G. W., & Hommer, D. (2001). Anticipation of increasing monetary reward selectively recruits nucleus accumbens. *The Journal of Neuroscience : The Official Journal of the Society for Neuroscience*, *21*(16), RC159. Advance online publication. DOI: 10.1523/JNEUROSCI.21-16-j0002.2001 PMID: 11459880

Knutson, B., & Greer, S. M. (2008). Anticipatory affect: Neural correlates and consequences for choice. *Philosophical Transactions of the Royal Society of London. Series B, Biological Sciences*, *363*(1511), 3771–3786. DOI: 10.1098/rstb.2008.0155 PMID: 18829428

Knutson, B., Taylor, J., Kaufman, M., Peterson, R., & Glover, G. (2005). Distributed neural representation of expected value. *The Journal of Neuroscience : The Official Journal of the Society for Neuroscience*, *25*(19), 4806–4812. DOI: 10.1523/JNEUROSCI.0642-05.2005 PMID: 15888656

Koenigs, M., Young, L., Adolphs, R., Tranel, D., Cushman, F., Hauser, M., & Damasio, A. (2007). Damage to the prefrontal cortex increases utilitarian moral judgements. *Nature*, *446*(7138), 908–911. DOI: 10.1038/nature05631 PMID: 17377536

Korteling, J. E., Brouwer, A. M., & Toet, A. (2018). A Neural Network Framework for Cognitive Bias. *Frontiers in Psychology*, *9*, 1561. DOI: 10.3389/fpsyg.2018.01561 PMID: 30233451

Krueger, F., McCabe, K., Moll, J., Kriegeskorte, N., Zahn, R., Strenziok, M., Heinecke, A., & Grafman, J. (2007). Neural correlates of trust. *Proceedings of the National Academy of Sciences of the United States of America*, *104*(50), 20084–20089. DOI: 10.1073/pnas.0710103104 PMID: 18056800

Kucirkova, N., Landoni, M., Murgia, E., & Pera, M. S. (2019). Theo Huibers University of Twente Enschede, The Netherlands twc huibers@ utwente. Nl.

Kuhnen, C. M., & Knutson, B. (2005). The neural basis of financial risk taking. *Neuron*, *47*(5), 763–770. DOI: 10.1016/j.neuron.2005.08.008 PMID: 16129404

Lavery, T. J., Mahieu, V., Emmer de Albuequerque Green, C., Bol, E., Nohlen, H., Zafiroglu, A., Perriam, J., & Varazzani, C. (2024). Neuro-Nudging and Predictive Models:Adaptive Ethics for Behavioural Science in a Changing World. In Samson, A. (Ed.), *The Behavioral Economics Guide 2024* (pp. 100–108).

LeDoux, J. (1996). Emotional networks and motor control: A fearful view. *Progress in Brain Research*, *107*, 437–446. DOI: 10.1016/S0079-6123(08)61880-4 PMID: 8782535

Lo, A., Repin, D., & Steenbarger, B. (2005). Fear and Greed in Financial Markets: A Clinical Study of Day-Traders. *The American Economic Review*, *95*(2), 352–359. DOI: 10.1257/000282805774670095

Macintyre, A., Chan, H. F., Schaffner, M., & Torgler, B. (2023). National pride and tax compliance: A laboratory experiment using a physiological marker (No. 2021-07). *CREMA Working Paper.*

Mascagni, G., Nell, C., & Monkam, N. (2017). *One Size Does Not Fit All: A Field Experiment on the Drivers of Tax Compliance and Delivery Methods in Rwanda.* ICTD Working Paper 58.https://www.ictd.ac/publication/ictd-wp58/

Meiselman, B. (2018). Ghostbusting in Detroit: Evidence on nonfilers from a controlled field experiment. *Journal of Public Economics*, *158*, 180–193. DOI: 10.1016/j.jpubeco.2018.01.005

Miendlarzewska, E. A., Kometer, M., & Preuschoff, K. (2019). Neurofinance. *Organizational Research Methods*, *22*(1), 196–222. DOI: 10.1177/1094428117730891

Montague, P. R., Dayan, P., & Sejnowski, T. J. (1996). A framework for mesencephalic dopamine systems based on predictive Hebbian learning. *The Journal of Neuroscience : The Official Journal of the Society for Neuroscience*, *16*(5), 1936–1947. DOI: 10.1523/JNEUROSCI.16-05-01936.1996 PMID: 8774460

OECD. (2020), Tax Administration 3.0: The Digital Transformation of Tax Administration, OECD,Paris. https://www.oecd.org/tax/forum-on-tax-administration/publications-and-products/tax-administration-3-0-the-digital-transformation-of-tax-administration.htm

OECD. (2022), Digital Transformation Maturity Model, OECD, Paris. www.oecd.org/tax/forum-on-tax-administration/publications-and-products/digital-transformation-maturity-model.htm

Ortega, D., Ronconi, L., & Sanguinetti, P. (2016). Reciprocity and Willingness to Pay Taxes: Evidence from a Survey Experiment in Latin America. *Economía (Washington, D.C.)*, *16*(2), 55–88. DOI: 10.31389/eco.78

Ortega, D., & Scartascini, C. (2015, November). Don't Blame the Messenger: A Field Experiment on Delivery Methods for Increasing Tax Compliance. IDB Working Paper No. IDB-WP-627. DOI: 10.18235/0000204

Ostrom, E. (2010). Beyond markets and states: Polycentric governance of complex economic systems. *The American Economic Review*, *100*(3), 641–672. DOI: 10.1257/aer.100.3.641

Paulus, M., Rogalsky, C., Simmons, A., Feinstein, J., & Stein, M. B. (2003). Increased activation in the right insula during risk-taking decision making is related to harm avoidance and neuroticism. *NeuroImage*, *19*(4), 1439–1448. DOI: 10.1016/S1053-8119(03)00251-9

Phelps, E. (2009). The study of emotion in Neuroeconomics.

Glimcher, P., Camerer, C., Fehr, E., & Poldrack, R. (2009). *Neuroeconomics: Decision making and The Brain.* Academic Press., DOI: 10.1016/B978-0-12-374176-9.00016-6

Pine, A., Shiner, T., Seymour, B., & Dolan, R. J. (2010). Dopamine, time, and impulsivity in humans. *The Journal of Neuroscience : The Official Journal of the Society for Neuroscience*, *30*(26), 8888–8896. DOI: 10.1523/JNEUROSCI.6028-09.2010

Pomeranz, D. (2015). No Taxation without Information: Deterrence and Self-Enforcement in the Value Added Tax. *The American Economic Review, 105*(8), 2539–2569. https://www.nber.org/papers/w19199 DOI: 10.1257/aer.20130393

Rabin, M., & Thaler, R. H. (2001). Anomalies: Risk Aversion. *The Journal of Economic Perspectives, 15*(1), 219–232. DOI: 10.1257/jep.15.1.219

Rangel, A., Camerer, C., & Montague, P. (2008). A framework for studying the neurobiology of value-based decision making. *Nature Reviews. Neuroscience, 9*(7), 545–556. DOI: 10.1038/nrn2357

Rashid, S. F. A., Ramli, R., Palil, M. R., & Amir, A. M. (2022). The influence of power of tax administrator on cognitive and affective tax attitude in Malaysia. *Asian Journal of Accounting and Governance, 17*, 59–74.

Reese, H. W., & Fremouw, W. J. (1984). Normal and normative ethics in behavioral sciences. *The American Psychologist, 39*(8), 863–876. DOI: 10.1037/0003-066X.39.8.863

Rilling, J., Gutman, D., Zeh, T., Pagnoni, G., Berns, G., & Kilts, C. (2002). A neural basis for social cooperation. *Neuron, 35*(2), 395–405. DOI: 10.1016/S0896-6273(02)00755-9

Ritov, I., & Baron, J. (1990). Reluctance to vaccinate: Omission bias and ambiguity. [Wiley Online Library.]. *Journal of Behavioral Decision Making, 3*(4), 263–277.DOI: 10.1002/bdm.3960030404

Ritsatos, T. (2014). Tax evasion and compliance; from the neo classical paradigm to behavioural economics, a review. *Journal of Accounting & Organizational Change, 10*(2), 244–262. DOI: 10.1108/JAOC-07-2012-0059

Rothenhoefer, K., Costa, V., Bartolo, R., Vicario-Feliciano, R., Murray, E., & Averbeck, B. (2017). Effects of Ventral Striatum Lesions on Stimulus-Based versus Action-Based Reinforcement Learning. *The Journal of Neuroscience : The Official Journal of the Society for Neuroscience, 37*(29), 6902–6914. DOI: 10.1523/JNEUROSCI.0631-17.2017

Saberi Moghadam, S., Samsami Khodadad, F., & Khazaeinezhad, V. (2019). An Algorithmic Model of Decision Making in the Human Brain. *Basic and Clinical Neuroscience, 10*(5), 443–449. DOI: 10.32598/bcn.9.10.395

Samanez-Larkin, G., Gibbs, S., Khanna, K., Nielsen, L., Carstensen, L., & Knutson, B. (2007). Anticipation of monetary gain but not loss in healthy older adults. *Nature Neuroscience, 10*(6), 787–791. DOI: 10.1038/nn1894

Shafir, E., & LeBoeuf, R. (2002). Rationality. *Annual Review of Psychology, 53*(1), 491–517. DOI: 10.1146/annurev.psych.53.100901.135213

Shestakova, A., Rieskamp, J., Tugin, S., Ossadtchi, A., Krutitskaya, J., & Klucharev, V. (2013). Electrophysiological precursors of social conformity. *Social Cognitive and Affective Neuroscience, 8*(7), 756–763. DOI: 10.1093/scan/nss064

Sjoberg, F., Mellon, J., Peixoto, T., Hemker, J., & Tsai, L. (2019, May). Voice and Punishment: A Global Survey Experiment on Tax Morale. Policy Research Working Paper; No. 8855, World Bank. https://hdl.handle.net/10986/31713

Smart, M. (2012). The application of the theory of planned behaviour and structural equation modelling in tax compliance behaviour: a New Zealand study.

Sniderman, P. M., & Theriault, S. M. (1999). The Dynamics of Political Argument and the Logic of Issue Framing. Paper presented at the annual meeting of the Midwest Political Science Association, Chicago, IL, 15-17.

Spitzer, M., Fischbacher, U., Herrnberger, B., Grön, G., & Fehr, E. (2007). The neural signature of social norm compliance. *Neuron, 56*(1), 185–196. DOI: 10.1016/j.neuron.2007.09.011

Suharnoko, B., Castaneda, N., Jorge, L., Chairunissa, T., Farid, M., Poerwanto, J., & Wirapati, B. (2020). *Applying Behavioral Insights to Promote SME Tax Compliance in Indonesia: Activity Report*. World Bank Documents and Reports.

Tabibnia, G., & Lieberman, M. (2007). Fairness and cooperation are rewarding: Evidence from social cognitive neuroscience. *Annals of the New York Academy of Sciences, 1118*(1), 90–101. DOI: 10.1196/annals.1412.001

Thaler, R. (1990). Anomalies: Saving, Fungibility, and Mental Accounts. *The Journal of Economic Perspectives, 4*(1), 193–205. DOI: 10.1257/jep.4.1.193

Tom, S., Fox, C., Trepel, C., & Poldrack, R. (2007). The neural basis of loss aversion in decision-making under risk. *Science, 315*(5811), 515–518. DOI: 10.1126/science.1134239

Torgler, B. (2003). Tax Morale in Transition Countries. *Post-Communist Economies, 15*(3), 357–381. DOI: 10.1080/1463137032000139052

Torgler, B. (2004). Cross-Culture Comparison of Tax Morale and Tax Compliance: Evidence from Costa Rica and Switzerland. [Sage Journals.]. *International Journal of Comparative Sociology, 45*(1-2), 17–43. DOI: 10.1177/0020715204048309

Trepel, C., Fox, C., & Poldrack, R. (2005). Prospect theory on the brain? Toward a cognitive neuroscience of decision under risk. *Brain Research. Cognitive Brain Research, 23*(1), 34–50. DOI: 10.1016/j.cogbrainres.2005.01.016

Tversky, A., & Thaler, R. (1990). Anomalies: Preference Reversals. *The Journal of Economic Perspectives, 4*(2), 201–211. DOI: 10.1257/jep.4.2.201

Valentin, V., & O'Doherty, J. (2009). Overlapping prediction errors in dorsal striatum during instrumental learning with juice and money reward in the human brain. *Journal of Neurophysiology, 102*(6), 3384–3391. DOI: 10.1152/jn.91195.2008

van Dijk, W. W., Goslinga, S., Terwel, B. W., & van Dijk, E. (2020). How choice architecture can promote and undermine tax compliance: Testing the effects of prepopulated tax returns and accuracy confirmation. *Journal of Behavioral and Experimental Economics, 87*, 101574. Advance online publication. DOI: 10.1016/j.socec.2020.101574

Wang, J., & Cui, S. (2018). Associative memory cells and their working principle in the brain. *F1000 Research, 7*, 108. DOI: 10.12688/f1000research.13665.1

Wang, X. (2008). Decision making in recurrent neuronal circuits. *Neuron*, *60*(2), 215–234. DOI: 10.1016/j.neuron.2008.09.034

Weber, E., & Johnson, E. (2009). *Decisions under uncertainty: Psychological, Economic and Neuro-economic explanations of Risk Preference. Glimcher, P., Camerer, C., Fehr, E., Poldrack, Rl. (2009). Neuroeconomics: Decision making and The Brain*. Academic Press.

Weigel, J. (2018). Building State and Citizen: How Tax Collection in Congo Engenders Citizen Engagement with the State. Working Paper.

Yaniv, G. (1999). Tax Compliance and Advance Tax Payments: A Prospect Theory Analysis. [University of Chicago Press.]. *National Tax Journal*, *52*(4), 753–764.DOI: 10.1086/NTJ41789428

Yitzhaki, S. (1974). A note on income tax evasion: A theoretical analysis. *Journal of Public Economics*, *3*(2), 201–202. DOI: 10.1016/0047-2727(74)90037-1

Yoo, J., Zell, V., Gutierrez-Reed, N., Wu, J., Ressler, R., Shenasa, M., Johnson, A., Fife, K., Faget, L., & Hnasko, T. (2016). Ventral tegmental area glutamate neurons co-release GABA and promote positive reinforcement. *Nature Communications*, *7*(1), 13697. DOI: 10.1038/ncomms13697

Zak, P. (2017). The neuroscience of trust. *Harvard Business Review*, *95*(1), 84–90.

Chapter 3
The Psychosociological Determinants of Tax Morality in Morocco:
The Case of Liberal Professions

Bouchra Alj
https://orcid.org/0000-0002-7856-3044
Hassan II University, Casablanca, Morocco

Majda El Agy
Cadi Ayyad University, Marrakech, Morocco

Lhoussain Alla
https://orcid.org/0000-0002-7238-1792
Sidi Mohammed Ben Abdellah University, Morocco

ABSTRACT

This chapter is exploratory in nature. Its aim is to establish a better understanding of tax morality based on psychosociological determinants. It is based on a qualitative study of 17 Moroccan doctors working in the liberal professions. The main results reveal various determinants, classified into two categories: psychological and social. These results confirm that personal values play a crucial role in understanding tax morality. In addition, the perception of inequalities in the tax system and the fear of sanctions also influence their tax morality. In addition, empathy for the beneficiaries of tax-financed public services and a sense of community reinforce commitment to tax compliance. The contributions of this research may be useful to public authorities, health professionals, researchers, as well as stakeholders involved in local and regional development.

1. INTRODUCTION

In many developing economies, the mobilization of fiscal resources is a central issue for financing development projects and guaranteeing macroeconomic stability. However, high levels of tax evasion and avoidance considerably hamper these efforts, compromising the ability of states to mobilize the

DOI: 10.4018/979-8-3373-0422-9.ch003

domestic resources needed to finance public policies (OECD, 2022). This problem, amplified by a lack of fiscal civic-mindedness and widespread informal practices, highlights the need to explore the psychosociological factors influencing taxpayers' fiscal morality.

In Morocco, as in other emerging economies, tax reforms are aimed at modernizing tax administration and promoting greater transparency and fairness. Despite these initiatives, the challenges of broadening the tax base and combating tax evasion persist. These issues cannot be dissociated from taxpayers' attitudes and behaviors, which are influenced by their perceptions of tax fairness, their trust in institutions and the social norms to which they conform (Macintyre and Torgler, 2024).

This chapter focuses specifically on the psychosociological determinants of tax morality in Morocco, a concept that goes beyond mere legal compliance to encompass taxpayers' intrinsic motivations for complying with their tax obligations. It highlights factors such as personal values, social norms, perceptions of justice and empathy towards the beneficiaries of public services, while taking into account the specificities of the Moroccan context, marked by significant socio-economic and cultural diversity.

This study focused specifically on private practitioners, a key sub-group of healthcare professionals. According to the 2023 health map, Morocco has a total of 30,643 doctors, 15,394 of whom work in the private sector. Unlike public-sector doctors, these liberal professionals have direct responsibility for tax returns, placing them at the heart of the interaction between the often complex tax obligations and exacting ethical standards that govern their profession. These specific features, combined with their geographical and socio-economic diversity - between urban and rural areas - make them a particularly relevant group for analyzing the psychosociological dynamics of tax morality.

The central question guiding this study is: How do socio-psychological determinants influence the fiscal morality of doctors in Morocco? The aim is to analyze the psychosociological determinants influencing tax morality in Morocco, and to contribute to a better understanding of the levers that can be mobilized to strengthen tax compliance in the country.

2. LITERATURE REVIEW

2.1. Concept of Tax Morality

The term “morality,” derived from the Latin “moralitas,” is defined by the dictionary of the French academy as “character” or “characteristic.” It denotes a set of rules and principles intended to guide human behavior according to the fundamental distinction between good and evil. The dictionary also defines morality as “the character of an action considered from the moral point of view”, that is, the inner conscience that dictates actions to be performed or avoided. This concept possesses a universal ethical dimension and is frequently characterized as the “moral law” inherent in every individual, an inner voice that functions as a compass, guiding behavior in accordance with socially accepted norms. In a similar vein, the Collins English Dictionary accentuates this dimension by defining morality as “the observance of conventionally accepted standards of ethical behavior based on a sense of right and wrong in accord with conscience”. These definitions converge on the common idea that morality represents an ethical ideal that structures interactions between individuals and society.

In the context of taxation, this notion is referred to as “tax morality”, a concept that, despite its historical roots, has received surprisingly limited attention in the academic literature on tax compliance. During the 1960s, scholars from the prominent Cologne School of Psychology proposed integrating behavioral perspectives into economic analysis to bridge the gap between economics and social psychology. Specifically, Schmölders (1960) and Strümpel (1969) underscored the significance of behavioral factors in taxpayers' decisions, conceptualizing tax morality as "the attitude of individuals towards their tax obligations, intimately linked to their sense of duty."The term "duty" inherently implies a connection with morality.

This definition of tax morality aligns with the concept of "taxpayer ethics", as introduced by Song and Yarbrough (1978). Song and Yarbrough define "taxpayer ethics" as "the norms of behavior dictating the relationship between citizens, as taxpayers, and government". This concept expanded the perspective by integrating relational dimensions, particularly trust in the state, and paved the way for exploring the ethical motivations linked to compliance with tax obligations.

The conceptualization of tax morality has undergone a gradual evolution, marked by an increasing emphasis on the intrinsic motivations that drive taxpayers to fulfill their tax obligations.Researchers such as Frey (1997), Torgler (2011), and others (e.g., Braithwaite and Ahmed, 2005; Bilgin, 2014) have demonstrated that this morality is founded on internalized ethical perceptions and moral norms. Consequently, the act of paying taxes becomes a morally just action that aligns with a set of values that transcend mere economic incentives.In contrast, low tax morality has been associated with a growing tendency to engage in tax evasion (Torgler, 2011). When taxpayers exhibit low tax morality, they demonstrate a reduced inclination to comply with the established rules and a heightened propensity to evade their tax obligations (Oberholzer, 2008). Moral norms, when internalized, function as behavioral benchmarks, and any deviation from these norms engenders "moral costs", such as guilt or shame (Wenzel, 2004).

The conceptualization of tax morality has undergone a gradual evolution, marked by an increasing emphasis on the intrinsic motivations that drive taxpayers to fulfill their tax obligations.Researchers such as Frey (1997), Torgler (2011), and others (e.g., Braithwaite and Ahmed, 2005; Bilgin, 2014) have demonstrated that this morality is founded on internalized ethical perceptions and moral norms. Consequently, the act of paying taxes becomes a morally just action that aligns with a set of values that transcend mere economic incentives. In contrast, low tax morality has been associated with a growing tendency to engage in tax evasion (Torgler, 2011).When taxpayers exhibit low tax morality, they demonstrate a reduced inclination to comply with the established rules and a heightened propensity to evade their tax obligations (Oberholzer, 2008). Moral norms, when internalized, function as behavioral benchmarks, and any deviation from these norms engenders "moral costs", such as guilt or shame (Wenzel, 2004).

Accordingly, researchers such as Luttmer and Singhal (2014) have described fiscal morality as an "umbrella term that encompasses all non-monetary motivations and factors beyond the scope of the standard expected utility model" (Luttmer and Singhal, 2014). These motivations include, among others, an intrinsic willingness to pay taxes or the negative emotions, such as guilt or shame, felt in the event of non-compliance. This perspective aligns with that of Young *et al.* (2016), who conceptualize moral behavior as an intrinsic motivation to uphold ethical principles, irrespective of external constraints.

Milesi and Alberici (2018) have further enriched the understanding of tax morality by incorporating psychological and social dimensions, arguing that an individual's moral obligation should prompt them to comply with their conscience, regardless of the personal costs and the probability of success.Moral obligation refers to an individual's internal motivation to commit to ethical standards of behavior, which primarily impact human behavior through self-imposed restrictions.

The establishment of this concept is pivotal in comprehending the intricacies of moral obligation and its implications for behavioral outcomes.

2.2. Psycho Sociological Determinants of Tax Morality

The concept's origins can be traced to the 1960s, initially proposed by Schmölders (1960) and Strümpel (1969). However, it is often considered to be a pioneering work in the field of tax behavior research, with Allingham and Sandmo (1972) serving as a seminal publication. Building upon Becker's (1968) crime model, Allingham and Sandmo developed a simplified economic model. In this model, taxpayers, guided by purely selfish rationality, determine their declared income through a cost-benefit analysis. This reasoning is based on an assessment of the potential gains associated with noncompliance and the losses associated with the probability of detection and the severity of sanctions (Alexander and Balavac-Orlic, 2022). Inspired by this model, tax authorities have introduced deterrent measures, such as tax audits and investigations, accompanied by enhanced sanctions against recalcitrant taxpayers, to enforce tax compliance (Sikay et al., 2022).

Nonetheless, Allingham and Sandmo's model, while representing a substantial advancement in the study of tax behavior, has been subject to considerable criticism. According to Barile et al. (2024), this theoretical framework grapples with explaining why a significant proportion of taxpayers comply with their tax obligations despite low detection rates.Other works have criticized the model's inability to account for the diversity of factors that determine tax morality. While rational neoclassical approaches, predicated on cost-benefit calculations such as increased audit probabilities or harsher penalties, have a demonstrable impact on tax morality (Feld and Larsen, 2012; Slemrod, 2024; Alm, 2019), they are insufficient, in and of themselves, to explain taxpayers' decisions.

A substantial body of research, including contributions from Alm (1991), Barone and Mocetti (2011), Brink and Porcano (2016), Feld and Frey (2002), Torgler et al. (2011), and McKerchar et al. (2013), has demonstrated that tax morality is influenced by a multitude of factors that extend beyond the realm of economic rationality.Non-pecuniary motivations have been shown to play a fundamental role in understanding tax behavior (Torgler, 2001, 2011). Torgler (2011) describes tax morality as a “black box”, a metaphor that illustrates the richness and complexity of the factors that shape it, as well as the subtle and sometimes opaque interactions between these elements.

Among the non-pecuniary determinants that influence tax behavior, personality traits and intrinsic motivations, peer influence, social norms, trust in institutions, and perceptions of tax fairness are of particular significance.

2.2.1. Personality Traits and Intrinsic Motivations

Early theoretical studies on this issue have identified various factors that influence individuals' willingness to submit taxes effectively. These factors include individual honesty (Gordon, 1989), feelings of guilt and shame (Erard and Feinstein, 1994; Andreoni et al., 1998), and the psychic cost of evasion (Thomas, 2015).

Luttmer and Singhal (2014), Dwenger et al. (2016), and Bergolo et al. (2020) underscore motivations such as pride, positive self-image, honesty, and a sense of civic duty as having a significant influence on tax morality. These outcomes align with the theory of Deci and Ryan (1980), which underscores the significance of personal values and the intrinsic satisfaction derived from actions perceived as honest. In this perspective, individuals act not to attain external rewards, but rather to uphold their moral integrity.

This perspective has been further advanced by recent studies, such as that of Owusu et al. (2021). Their study, employing the Big Five model, demonstrates that three distinct traits — namely, agreeableness, conscientiousness, and openness to experience - exhibit a positive and statistically significant association with fiscal morality. These traits foster intrinsic motivation to pay taxes, independent of external pressures such as deterrent policies. For instance, individuals who are characterized as agreeable, with traits such as honesty, altruism, and cooperation, exhibit a strong inclination to fulfill their tax obligations. This inclination is driven by intrinsic values and high personal standards rather than external constraints. Conversely, moral emotions such as guilt, associated with transgressing moral standards, and shame, linked to the preservation of self-image, impose a psychological cost on non-compliance. These emotions thus reinforce fiscal morality by deterring evasive behavior. Empathy, in its affective and cognitive dimensions, has been shown to reduce the inclination to evade taxes by enhancing individuals' sensitivity to the social ramifications of such actions.

However, the experimental study by Jacquemet et al. (2017) calls these conclusions into question. In the laboratory, they observed that affective and cognitive empathy, as well as the public dimension of morality (propensity to shame and submission to the norm), strongly influence compliance decisions. Conversely, guilt had no significant effect. These findings challenge the prevailing notion of a universal intrinsic tax morality, suggesting that the personality traits and emotions studied account for only a portion of the observed behavior, leaving 85% of decisions unexplained. This limitation casts doubt on the concept of an "innate" or universal tax morality.

2.2.2. Peer Influence and Social Norms

Beyond personality traits and intrinsic motivations, peer influence and social norms play a decisive role in shaping tax morality. Contrary to a view of the individual as an isolated agent, social theories highlight the impact of collective interactions on tax behavior.

According to social influence theory (Kelman, 1958) and Bandura's social learning theory (1977), an individual's decisions are shaped by their social environment, be it peers, family, or colleagues. These influences, whether explicit or implicit, play a crucial role in shaping fiscal attitudes. Peer influence, defined as the pressure exerted by the immediate social circle (Jackson and Milliron, 1986; Bobek et al., 2013), has been shown to influence tax choices, with individuals tending to conform to behaviors perceived as normative within their group (Sussman& Gifford, 2013).

The seminal contributions of Bénabou and Tirole (2011), Castro and Scartascini (2015), and Alm et al. (2017) have illuminated the dynamics of collective influence, demonstrating that when compliance behaviors prevail, they can engender virtuous cycles that reinforce collective tax morality. Specifically, when taxpayers observe that their peers are adhering to tax obligations, they are more inclined to adopt a similar stance, thereby establishing a virtuous cycle in which collective morality fosters individual morality (Cummings et al., 2009; Alm and McKee, 2004). Conversely, a pervasive perception of fraud can lead to a weakening of conformity, as individuals adjust their behavior to that of others to avoid perceived dissonance (Bosco and Mittone, 1997).

Social norms, whether personal (derived from one's own values) or injunctive (dictated by society), also reinforce tax morality by providing a frame of reference.Researchers such as Frey (1997) and Kirchler (2007) have demonstrated that tax evasion can generate moral discomfort in individuals who transgress these norms. In a similar vein, Bobek et al. (2013) have demonstrated that norms perceived as widely accepted promote compliance. Conversely, Bazart and Bonein (2017) have sounded a note of caution, warning of the perverse effects of disseminating information about fraud, which can induce a false perception of widespread fraud.

However, the influence of peers is not universally beneficial. Some studies, including those by Abdixhiku et al. (2018) and Bidin and Sinnasamy (2018), demonstrate that exposure to tax evasion behaviors within one's social network can increase the probability of adopting similar practices.This negative influence has also been observed in other contexts, such as Zakat payments (Bidin et al., 2009), where non-compliant behaviors can be amplified by peers.

Finally, the seminal work of Bosco and Mittone (1997) offers crucial insight into the mechanisms of social reciprocity, demonstrating how perceptions of fairness influence the adherence to fiscal norms. Their research indicates that when individuals perceive a lack of fairness in the actions of others, they are less inclined to adhere to fiscal norms. Conversely, when individuals become aware that their actions may adversely affect collective well-being, they are less likely to engage in fraudulent behavior. This dynamic underscores the notion that tax behavior is not solely influenced by social norms and pressures but also by sensitivity to interpersonal consequences.

2.2.3. Trust in Institutions

The extant literature on tax morality reveals that trust in public institutions and perceptions of corruption are among the most influential determinants of tax behavior. These factors, often interconnected, shape the relationship between citizens and the state, influencing their commitment to their tax obligations.

The social contract, as conceptualized by Torgler (2001) and Luttmer and Singhal (2014), serves as a foundational framework for understanding this relationship. This contract is predicated on a logic of reciprocal exchange, whereby citizens fulfill their tax obligations in exchange for public goods and quality services.When a government is perceived as efficient and legitimate, this reciprocity is reinforced, thereby encouraging taxpayers to comply voluntarily. Feld & Frey (2002) and Frey & Meier (2004) underscore the significance of this perception, demonstrating that trust in public institutions fosters an environment conducive to tax compliance.

At the core of this dynamic is the concept of vertical trust, defined as the conviction that the state acts with transparency, fairness and efficiency. Feld and Frey (2010) underscore that this trust is founded on transparency in the utilization of tax revenues. Citizens are more inclined to comply when they perceive that their contributions are used efficiently and serve legitimate collective objectives. This dynamic, characterized by the intertwining of transparency and efficiency in public management, fosters a virtuous cycle that reinforces fiscal morality. By ensuring that taxpayers' contributions are not in vain, this cycle contributes to the development of a robust social contract between the state and its citizens.

However, when this trust deteriorates, whether due to the mismanagement of public resources or the implementation of inappropriate policies, the feeling of reciprocity weakens. According to Timmons and Garfias (2015), such a situation weakens the social contract and justifies, in the eyes of taxpayers, tax evasion behavior.In the absence of legitimate and fair management, some taxpayers rationalize their noncompliance by believing that the state is not honoring its own implicit obligations.

Trust in judicial and administrative institutions is also a determining factor in tax morality. Feld & Frey (2002) and Torgler et al. (2011) demonstrate that institutions perceived as fair and reliable encourage citizens to adopt compliant behavior, as they guarantee fair application of tax rules and appropriate sanctions. Conversely, perceptions of unfairness or bias can erode this trust, prompting individuals to rationalize tax evasion (Andreoni et al., 1998).

Corruption is a significant impediment to the establishment of trust and reciprocal relationships, eroding perceptions of justice and compliance with tax obligations when it is perceived as widespread (Levin & Satarov, 2000; Bird et al., 2008). In such contexts, taxpayers rationalize their tax noncompliance by attributing heightened distrust to public institutions, perceived as inefficient (Bird et al., 2008). Empirical studies substantiate these observations. In sub-Saharan Africa, for instance, Ali et al. (2014) and Bol et al. (2019) have found that corruption, manifesting as extortion of bribes or embezzlement of public funds, erodes trust in tax administration and reduces taxpayers' propensity to pay their taxes. From a more global perspective, Litina and Palivos (2016) identify a significant correlation between the perception of government corruption and tax evasion in 45 countries. Jahnke and Weisser (2019) go further, pointing out that corruption has more than just economic consequences; it also undermines the morale of citizens, who perceive their fiscal efforts as pointless in an environment marked by mismanagement and injustice.

The study's findings underscore the pivotal role that citizens' perceptions of corruption and trust in public institutions play in shaping their views on the legitimacy and effectiveness of the state. The researchers emphasize that transparent and efficient institutions, by reinforcing the principles of reciprocity and taxpayer commitment, can foster a robust social contract, thereby reducing the incidence of tax noncompliance. Conversely, corruption and mismanagement, they argue, erode this social contract, leading to a breakdown in citizens' trust in public institutions and, ultimately, contributing to increased tax noncompliance.

2.2.4. Perception of Tax Fairness

The concept of tax fairness is founded on robust theoretical underpinnings, underscoring its pivotal role in shaping tax systems and its impact on tax morality. Adams & Freedman's (1976) theory of fairness serves as a seminal starting point in this examination. According to this theory, individuals evaluate the relative fairness of their tax contributions and the benefits they receive in comparison to those of other members of society. This subjective evaluation significantly influences their stance on tax obligations.

Andreoni et al. (1998) have further enriched this theoretical framework by exploring the practical dimensions of tax fairness and its impact on taxpayers' behavior, demonstrating that perceptions of fairness, whether horizontal (between taxpayers) or vertical (between different income levels), directly influence tax compliance decisions.A negative perception of tax fairness, for example, when citizens judge that their contributions are not fair or that government benefits are insufficient, can lead to an increase in tax evasion.

Empirical research has corroborated these theoretical principles by examining their practical implications. Feld and Frey (2010), for instance, emphasize that the legitimacy of tax policies hinges significantly on their perceived fairness. When taxpayers perceive a system as fair and transparent, they are more inclined to voluntarily comply with their tax obligations. In a similar vein, Kirchler (2007) and Torgler (2003) have demonstrated that perceived fairness reinforces trust in tax institutions, which in turn encourages greater taxpayer cooperation.

Horizontal equity, in particular, has been identified as a significant factor in this regard. Through laboratory experiments, Fortin et al. (2007) demonstrated that taxpayers are less inclined to comply when they perceive disparities in the tax treatment of their peers that are considered unjustified. This dynamic is further substantiated by the findings of Bazart and Bonein (2014), who emphasize that perceived inequity, whether stemming from a lack of progressivity or from divergent treatment, fosters increased tolerance for tax evasion.

Furthermore, Castañeda's (2024) research underscores the pivotal role of individual perceptions of fairness in tax behavior, demonstrating that taxpayers who are sensitive to injustice are more inclined to morally justify acts of tax evasion. These findings are consistent with the conclusions of Alkhatib et al. (2019), who assert that tax fairness is not merely an economic concern but a significant catalyst for influencing behavior.

This comprehensive review underscores the intricate web of psychosocial factors that shape tax morality, defying conventional frameworks rooted in economic rationality.The extant literature underscores the continued relevance of incentive-based approaches (e.g., the Allingham and Sandmo model) within the broader context of tax behavior, though their capacity to fully explicate its intricacies remains constrained.

The literature indicates that personality traits and intrinsic motivations play a crucial role in shaping tax morality.Concepts such as honesty, guilt, shame and the inner satisfaction derived from compliance highlight the importance of individual factors.Concurrently, the influence of peers and social norms, whether personal or injunctive, demonstrates the impact of collective dynamics.These social interactions, reinforced by perceptions of compliance or fraud within groups, shape the propensity of individuals to comply with their tax obligations.

Another salient factor pertains to the level of trust citizens have in public institutions. Perceptions of government transparency, legitimacy and efficiency have been demonstrated to exert a profound influence on taxpayers' behavior. When citizens perceive that their tax contributions are being utilized fairly and efficiently, their inclination towards tax morality is likely to be reinforced.

A critical yet often overlooked facet is the complexity of tax systems. Recent studies (Hashimzade et al. 2013; Abeler and Jäger, 2015) have demonstrated that the complexity of tax regulations and limited access to clear information can lead to a decline in tax morality, even among taxpayers inclined to comply. This complexity functions as a cognitive barrier, generating confusion and mistrust, and thereby undermining intrinsic motivation to comply (Bhargava and Manoli, 2015). Conversely, policies aimed at simplifying.

Another aspect, no less important, deserves further attention: the complexity of tax systems. Recent studies (Hashimzade et al., 2013; Abeler and Jäger, 2015; Bhargava and Manoli, 2015) show that the complexity of tax regulations and a lack of access to clear information can reduce tax morality, even among taxpayers motivated to comply. This complexity acts as a cognitive barrier, generating confusion and mistrust, and can thus undermine intrinsic motivation to comply with the rules. Conversely, policies aimed at simplifying tax obligations and improving transparency strengthen tax morality by reducing informational friction and encouraging citizens' trust in the system.

3. METHODOLOGY

3.1. Operational Framework of the Research

This section presents the methodological approach adopted for this study. To address the research question, a qualitative study was conducted among liberal professions, particularly Moroccan doctors. The choice of this category as the research field was motivated by several factors. On the one hand, doctors are among the well-established liberal professions, and their activity is often visible in the socioeconomic fabric. According to the health map published by the Ministry of Health and Social Protection in 2023, Morocco has a total of 15,394 doctors operating in the liberal sector. Their tax practices may reflect trends specific to these professions.

On the other hand, doctors are subject to strict ethical standards in their professional practice. Therefore, analyzing their tax morality can reveal how these standards influence their tax behavior and compliance with tax obligations. Finally, Moroccan doctors practice in various contexts, ranging from large cities to rural areas. This diversity allows for the exploration of how different socio-economic environments influence tax morality.

3.2. Data Collection Method

In Morocco, there are no databases capable of providing sufficient information to delineate the research sample. Therefore, considerable investigative work was required to find the cases that best correspond to the central question of this chapter. Thus, the sample was identified based on the recommendations of previously interviewed individuals or through acquaintances in the medical field (snowball sampling technique). During the first interview, mutual trust was established with the interviewed doctor, who then provided the contact details of another doctor who had set up their practice in the same sector.

In terms of sample size, given the exploratory nature of the research, seventeen (17) doctors operating in the liberal professions sector were selected. Furthermore, the theoretical saturation method was adopted. Thus, data collection continued until new interviews no longer provided additional information.

Data collection was carried out through semi-structured individual interviews to directly engage the interviewees and ensure that the questions were fully understood. Indeed, this tool is effective for capturing the behaviors and concerns of the actors (Usunier, Easterby-Smith, and Thorpe, 1993). The guide is organized into four themes addressed during the interview. First, the initial theme concerns general information about the interviewed doctors and their practices.Next, the second theme deals with the perception of tax morality. The third theme examines the psychological determinants of tax morality. Finally, the fourth theme addresses the social determinants of tax morality.

3.3. Data Processing and Analysis Techniques

The technical means used are audio recording and note-taking. This recording allows for the preservation of the entirety of the expressed opinions, making the discursive data exhaustive, without worrying about the risk of missing information (Thiétart, 1999). Note-taking allows for focusing on conducting the interview (prompting, listening, etc.), thus requiring "sagacity and liveliness on the part of the researcher (Baumard, 1999; p.236).

The interviews conducted with the concerned individuals were fully transcribed to allow for proper analysis. The transcription enabled the coding of empirical data. The exploitation of these interviews was carried out through vertical and horizontal thematic analysis, as well as using the qualitative analysis software "QSR Nvivo12".

4. RESEARCH RESULTS

According to Miles and Huberman (2003), qualitative data analysis requires rigor at every stage of the analysis. Thus, this research first presents the characteristics of the physicians who participated in this study. Then, the results will be presented.

4.1. Characteristics of the Selected Sample

To ensure confidentiality, the identification of the interviewees will not be disclosed. To facilitate reading, a code has been assigned to each case. This approach will have no impact on the data analysis. The characteristics of the selected sample are reported in Figure 1 below.

Figure 1 shows that the sample consists of 9 women and 8 men. This distribution highlights a certain gender equality among the physicians of different specialties who were interviewed. All the interviewed physicians are individuals. Their ages range from 29 to 75 years old. Additionally, all the interviewees practice individually in a medical office and are subject to income tax related to professional income.

Figure 1. Description of the study sample

Case	Specialty	Gender	Age	City	Years of Experience	Interview Duration
D1*	Nephrologist	F**	47	Rabat	15	40 minutes
D2	Ophthalmologist	M***	36	Marrakech	5	28 minutes
D3	Gastroenterologist	F	32	Marrakech	2	30 minutes
D4	Pediatrics and Neuropediatrics	M	68	Rabat	33	35 minutes
D5	General Practitioner	M	38	Khemisset	2	30 minutes
D6	Cardiologist	F	58	Rabat	6	35 minutes
D7	Endocrinologist-Diabetologist	F	45	Marrakech	11	20 minutes
D8	Gynecologist and Obstetrician	F	42	Rabat	9	40 minutes
D9	Orthopedic Traumatologist	M	48	Mohammedia	15	40 minutes
D10	Dentist	M	31	Marrakech	2	20 minutes
D11	Dermatologist	F	30	Marrakech	2	25 minutes
D12	Allergist	M	75	Casablanca	40	30 minutes
D13	General Practitioner	M	65	Marrakech	18	20 minutes
D14	Dermatologist	F	31	Marrakech	2	29 minutes
D15	Orthodontist	F	54	Rabat	27	40 minutes
D16	Dermatologist	F	29	Marrakech	2	26 minutes
D17	Cardiologist	M	64	Marrakech	12	26 minutes

*Note. *Doctor **Female *** Male*

The tax base is determined according to the real net result regime or the simplified net result regime. The tax rate varies from 0% to 38% depending on the income brackets achieved. The number of years of experience ranges from 2 to 40 years.

4.2. The Perception of Fiscal Morality

Fiscal morality is a concept that is often misunderstood and misinterpreted, particularly among some of the doctors interviewed: *"I've never heard of this concept"* (Doctor 3).

"This is the first time I've heard of this concept" (Doctor 16). In the course of the semi-structured interviews, it became apparent that several of them are not precisely familiar with the definition of fiscal morality. They tend to confuse it with the simple act of paying their taxes to the tax authorities.

However, fiscal morality goes far beyond the payment of taxes. It includes a set of ethical and responsible behaviors with regard to tax obligations, such as transparency in income declaration, honesty in tax deductions and compliance with current tax laws (Figure 2). A better understanding of tax morality is crucial to promoting a culture of tax compliance and responsibility within the medical profession.

Figure 2. Perceptions of tax morality

List of verbatims on the perception of tax morality.	
"Fiscal morality is a little like medical ethics: paying taxes consciously, respecting the rules in place [...] It means respecting one's tax obligations while demanding fair and equitable rules [...] Fiscal morality is also a question of reciprocity: if citizens pay their taxes, the State must use them fairly, rationally and transparently".	**D4**
"As a doctor, I associate fiscal morality with a form of professional ethics. Just as I am honest with my patients, I think it's right to be transparent with the tax authorities.	**D8**
"Tax morality, for me, means being honest in your tax declarations".	**D17**
"Tax morality could thus be likened to a kind of social contribution ethic [...] for this morality to be effective, citizens must have confidence in the State and in the fair use of their contributions".	**D6**

Although definitions of tax morality vary from doctor to doctor, they converge on a central idea that represents an intrinsic motivation to comply with tax rules. Thus, for the purposes of this chapter, the chosen definition of fiscal morality refers to an intrinsic motivation and ethical duty to comply with tax obligations in order to contribute to the financing of public goods. Founded on values such as honesty, solidarity and a sense of duty, it is conditioned by the perception of transparency, equity and justice in the management of public funds. This interplay between taxpayers' moral conscience and their trust in the State embodies a delicate balance, influencing their voluntary adherence to the tax system.

4.3. Psychosociological Determinants of Tax Morality

4.3.1. Psychological Determinants of Tax Morality

The psychosociological determinants of tax morality play a crucial role in understanding doctors' behavior towards their tax obligations. These determinants include several factors presented in Figure 3.

According to this figure, doctors emphasize that personal norms and values are the main factors influencing their fiscal morality. They highlight specific values such as responsibility or a sense of duty, honesty, faith, fear of punishment and self-determination. These aspects are frequently mentioned in interviewees' statements (Table3). Thus, honesty and a sense of duty are fundamental values that motivate doctors to comply with tax obligations.

Faith plays a crucial role in reinforcing morality. Thus, contributing to the common good is a moral obligation, prompting doctors to respect tax laws as an act of faith and service to the community.

Figure 3. Psychological determinants of tax morality

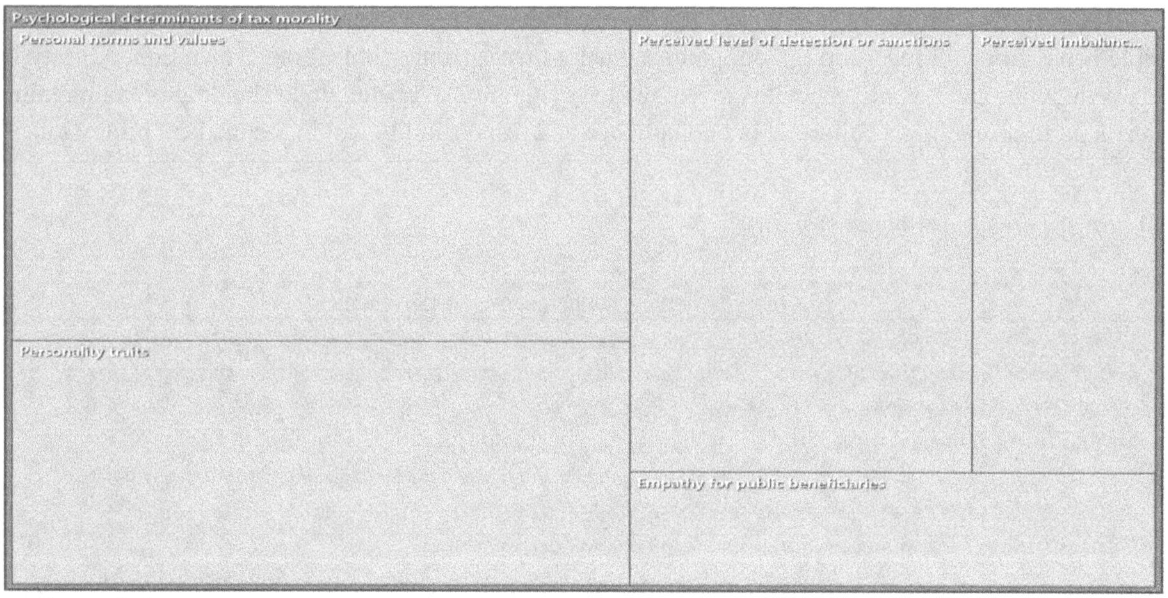

Source: *Authors*

Importantly, empathy for the beneficiaries of tax-financed public services, as well as the perception of an imbalance between tax rights and obligations, also influence tax morality. For some respondents, these two elements are of particular importance, as shown in figure 3 above.

These statements show that empathy and a sense of belonging play a decisive role in doctors' tax morality. These elements reinforce their commitment to meeting their tax obligations, linking them directly to tangible benefits for the community and for themselves.

As far as personality traits are concerned, the doctors interviewed consider compliance with tax obligations a duty and a source of civic pride. However, they feel that tax evasion provokes feelings of guilt, frustration and betrayal of their values.

In this same context, the research results highlight the perceived level of detection or sanction in terms of tax morality. Indeed, fear and apprehension of state-imposed sanctions encourage doctors to comply with their tax obligations. Thus, fear of sanctions may indeed be a motivating factor for some doctors. For others, however, compliance with tax regulations is based on deeper ethical and moral principles.

Figure 4. Psychological determinants of tax morality

List of verbatim psychological determinants of tax morality	
Religious values and ethics	
"I think respect for rules and responsibility play a big role".	D1
"I would say honesty, professional ethics and a sense of duty. As a doctor, I'm used to respecting strict rules. I think this also applies to tax obligations".	D8
"My personal values are guided by my faith and my professional ethics. In Islam, it's important to contribute to the common good".	D9
Empathy for the beneficiaries of public services	
"A lot of empathy, of course. Tax-funded services are essential, especially in healthcare. Everyone benefits in one way or another, and I'm well aware of the positive impact this has on people's lives."	D1
"There's always a sense of empathy for those who use the services funded".	D17
Sense of belonging	
"It's a source of pride to participate in social development, but it would be even more of an incentive to see the concrete counterpart of taxes for these social categories."	D2
"A sense of belonging is always present among those who benefit from the services funded."	D10
Civic duty and pride	
"I feel a moral and civic duty, but also a frustration at the lack of transparency and the sometimes opaque management of funds".	D15
"If you don't pay your taxes, you're guilty...It's more a duty than anything else, and it's a source of pride, I feel at ease, because I've done	D13
Fear of sanctions	
"Fear of sanctions plays an important role in their compliance with tax obligations, especially those who are not guided by a moral conscience or an understanding of the role of taxes in national solidarity."	D9
"Sincerely, I declare what I earn to avoid sanctions".	D16
"At the end of the exemption period, I will ensure that my taxes are paid correctly and on time, to avoid penalties and unnecessary administrative complications".	D5
Self-determination	
"I think that the fear of sanctions may play a role for some, but that's not what should be the basis for respecting the rules. For me, it's more a question of principle: do the right thing, be in order, and be able to sleep soundly".	D1
"Fear can be a deterrent for some people, but for me, it's more a question of principles and personal convictions".	D9

4.3.2. Sociological Determinants of Fiscal Morality

The research results also reveal several social factors influencing the tax morality of the doctors interviewed. First of all, as shown in Figure 5 below, respondents emphasize the inequity and unfairness of the Moroccan tax system. Indeed, the perception of injustice and inequalities between different sectors have a negative impact on the tax behavior of the doctors interviewed.

Figure 5. Social determinants of tax morality

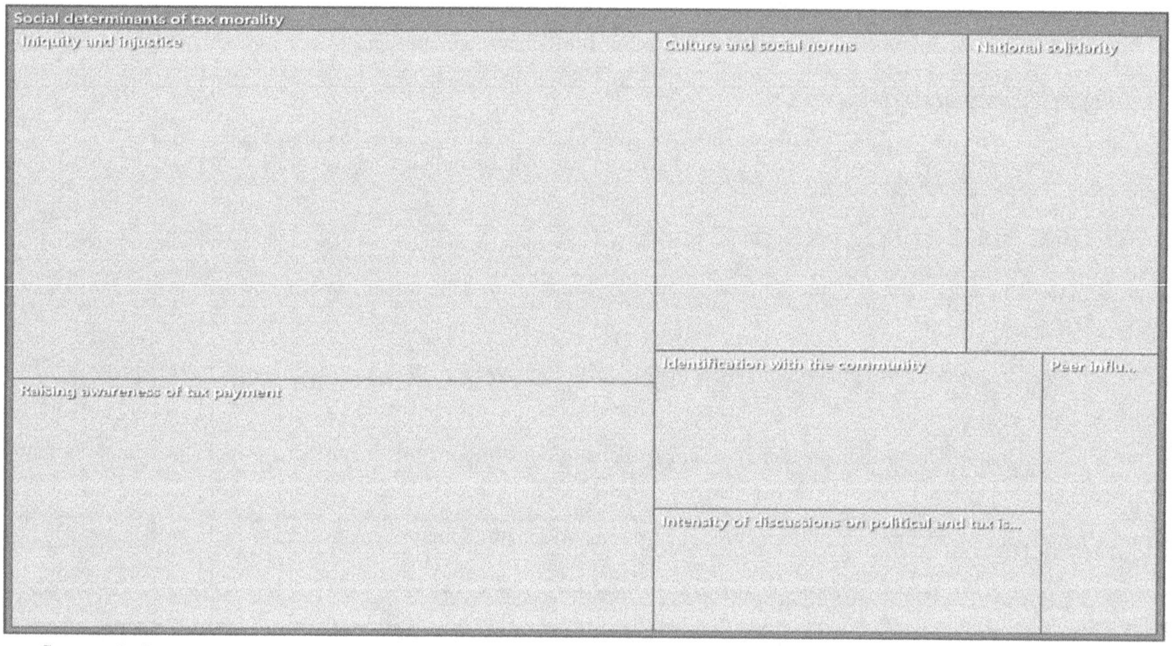

Source: *Authors*

Secondly, it is interesting to note that awareness of tax payment, as well as tax culture and education, are also social determinants of tax morality in the Moroccan context. In terms of culture and social norms, the results show that Moroccan culture does not encourage compliance with tax obligations. This is evident in the statements of several interviewees (Figure 6). Although Moroccans are known for their solidarity, they see paying taxes as a burden imposed by the state.

Interviewees' statements show that the perception of the transparency of tax-financed public services and trust in institutions play a crucial role in doctors' tax morality. These elements reinforce their commitment to meeting their tax obligations, linking them directly to tangible benefits for the community and for themselves.

Figure 6. Social determinants of tax morality

List of verbatim psychological determinants of tax morality	
Iniquity and unfairness of the tax system	
"Honestly, I think the system is far from perfect. There are loopholes, inequalities, and some people are more comfortable escaping them".	D1
"There are people who earn more, but don't pay and don't declare their income. The worst thing is that these people are well known. We are not equal".	D6
"Doctors are being short-changed. We are charged the highest rate of IR, almost double that applied to other professions."	D2
Tax awareness and education	
"Awareness-raising always plays an important role. The state needs to communicate the importance of taxes through the media".	D17
"It is crucial to better educate citizens on the importance of paying taxes and how this can benefit society as a whole. A better understanding of tax implications can lead to more responsible behavior and a greater willingness to comply with the law."	D7
"In our Moroccan culture, paying taxes is often perceived as a constraint rather than a voluntary or civic act. Many people see it as a necessary evil, with phrases often heard such as: We pay because we have no choice, otherwise we'll be in trouble".	D8
Confidence in institutions	
"[...] there are also those who pay to be on the safe side and not get into trouble with the taxman, even if they don't trust the system".	D8
"[...] However, others choose to evade their taxes because of a lack of confidence in the system, the impression that taxes are excessive, particularly in the face of informality [...] Perceived corruption, the absence of tangible results in public services, and the complexity of administrative procedures also contribute to discouraging compliance with tax obligations."	D9
Reputation	
"[...] I pay my taxes mainly for my reputation and the reputation of my firm, which are my main motivation".	D5
"The reputation of my firm is paramount, which is why I make sure I'm always in good standing with my taxes".	D14
Perception of transparency	
"If we knew clearly how each dirham was spent, it would change a lot of things. Then the government would have to visibly improve public services. When you see concrete results, it's easier to pay your taxes with a smile".	D1
"It is imperative to improve transparency by publishing regular reports on the use of public funds. Communication on the destination of taxes must be clear and comprehensible to the population".	D4
Peer influence	
"Yes, we often talk about it. These discussions reinforce my belief in the need for a fairer, more transparent tax system".	D9
"I have regular discussions about taxation, especially with my colleagues in the medical field [...] These exchanges help me better understand tax developments and adjust my behavior accordingly".	D8

Reputation has a strong influence on tax behavior. Doctors wish to maintain an image of respectability and integrity, which motivates them to comply with tax obligations to avoid any damage to their reputation.

In addition, it is interesting to note that the influence of peers, as well as the intensity of discussions on political and fiscal issues with family, friends and colleagues and national solidarity, also condition tax morality. However, compared with the social determinants mentioned above, these factors were of minor importance to the doctors interviewed.

5. DISCUSSION

The results of this analysis will be discussed in light of previous work. This comparison will provide a better understanding of tax behavior in Morocco. From the analysis, it emerges that the doctors interviewed expressed varied feelings about tax morality.

5.1. Personal Standards and Values

5.1.1. Religious Values and Ethics

Religious teachings often include principles of honesty (Deci& Ryan, 1980; Gordon, 1989, Rosa, 2024), responsibility (Jestin, 2020)and faith that can encourage doctors to meet their tax obligations. These values are often transmitted from an early age through family and school education. These basic principles are then reinforced throughout doctors' professional training. As a result, doctors are aware of the importance of their actions and their impact on society. This awareness is reflected in their fiscal behavior, where they see paying taxes as an extension of their duty. Furthermore, doctors are accustomed to following strict rules in their daily practice. This habit of respecting medical protocols is transposed to their tax behavior. By following the same principles of rigor and respect for rules, doctors are more inclined to comply with tax laws.

5.1.2. Empathy Towards Public Services Beneficiaries

Empathy towards the beneficiaries of public services plays an essential role in tax morality. When citizens feel empathy with those who benefit from public services, they are more inclined to perceive paying taxes as a moral duty and a positive contribution to society. This empathy encourages responsible fiscal behavior. Recent studies show that empathy, both affective and cognitive, plays a significant role in tax behavior (Jacquemet et al., 2017, Yoo& Jang, 2019). Thus, individuals with strong affective and cognitive empathy are less prone to tax evasion.

5.1.3. Sense of Belonging

A sense of belonging plays an indispensable role in tax morality (Horodnic, 2018, Fonseca Corona, 2024). When taxpayers feel part of their community, they are more inclined to contribute positively to its well-being. This sense of belonging strengthens the willingness to comply with tax obligations (Jacquemet et al., 2017). It also creates an emotional and social bond that motivates taxpayers to act responsibly.

5.1.4. Duty and Civic Pride

Paying taxes is often seen as a civic duty, on a par with voting. Compliance with this obligation strengthens the bond between the taxpayer and the state (El Ghazali and Benkendil, 2020, Rosa, 2024). Moreover, civic pride is the sense of satisfaction and dignity that a doctor feels by actively participating in the life of his community and fulfilling his duties as a citizen. Thus, civic pride and fiscal morality are two interconnected concepts that underline the importance of citizens' active and responsible participation in society (Jestin, 2020).

5.1.5. Fear of Sanctions and Self-Determination

Fear of sanctions is a determining factor in doctors' tax compliance (Lambert, 2007). Tax sanctions, whether financial or administrative, act as a powerful deterrent against tax evasion (El Harchi and El Bennissi, 2024). Sanctions can include fines, interest on arrears, or even prosecution, creating a strong incentive for doctors to declare their income correctly and pay their taxes on time. However, it should not be forgotten that some doctors are also intrinsically motivated. They act out of personal choice and a desire to conform to their own ethical standards, rather than out of fear of external sanctions. These doctors are characterized by self-determination. They are motivated by an intrinsic desire to comply with tax rules, not out of fear of sanctions, but out of a personal commitment to ethics and morality.

5.2. Trust in Institutions

Trust in public institutions is a fundamental element of tax morality (Torgler, 2001, Feld & Frey, 2002,Luttmer&Singhal, 2014). Indeed, when taxpayers have confidence in these institutions, they are more inclined to comply voluntarily with their tax obligations. This trust is based on the perception that institutions are fair, transparent and efficient in their use of public funds. As a result, it fosters a climate of cooperation between citizens and government, which is essential for the smooth running of the state and the implementation of public policies. The work of Feld & Frey (2002) and Frey & Meier (2004) underlines the importance of this perception, showing that trust in public institutions creates a climate conducive to compliance with tax rules.

5.3. Reputation

Reputation plays an important role in the tax behavior of some of the taxpayers we interviewed. For them, paying taxes is not only a legal obligation but also a way of maintaining a good social and professional image. Companies, in particular, can be very sensitive to their tax reputation (Jestin, 2020). A good reputation can attract investors, business partners and customers, while a bad reputation can have negative consequences for business.

5.4. Perceived Transparency of Public Institutions

Transparency enables taxpayers to see how their taxes are being used, which in turn boosts confidence in public institutions (Lecourt, 2022). Indeed, when the Moroccan state is open about its spending, citizens are more inclined to believe that their contributions are being used appropriately. In addition, transparent management of public funds (Jestin, 2020) reduces opportunities for corruption and mismanagement. By making financial information accessible and understandable, it becomes more difficult for individuals to embezzle funds without being detected.

5.5. Perception of the Fairness and Justice of the Tax System

The doctors interviewed perceive the Moroccan tax system as unfair and inequitable. This perception of unfairness negatively influences their tax behavior. These perceptions may lead to lower tax compliance, as doctors feel unfairly treated compared to other professions. On the other hand, a system perceived as fair and equitable (Kirchler, 2007, Feld & Frey, 2010) reinforces citizens' willingness to comply with tax obligations (Rosa, 2024). In 2019, the Economic, Social and Environmental Council noted improvements in tax fairness in Morocco, particularly in terms of improved reception, speed in handling claims, and simplification of steps and procedures.

5.6. Tax Awareness and Education

Tax awareness and education play a crucial role in society. By better understanding the importance of taxes, citizens can change their perception and strengthen their sense of fiscal responsibility. In this context, Chan (2000) found that cultural differences, such as religion, respect for authority and family upbringing, strongly influence taxpayers' attitudes towards taxes. For example, he notes that Chinese taxpayers tend to respect tax laws more than American taxpayers. This is partly explained by an upbringing that emphasizes respect for authorities and laws. By contrast, American culture values freedom of thought, and the right to disobedience and encourages dialogue with the authorities.

Another important sociological determinant that emerges from this study and which influences tax compliance is the level of education. Indeed, the higher the level of education, the more likely taxpayers are to comply with tax laws (Chan *et al.,* 2000).

5.7. Peer Influence

Interactions with peers who value tax morality can reinforce positive behaviors (Bénabou & Tirole, 2011; Castro &Scartascini, 2015; Alm *et al.,* 2017). In addition, the exchange of ideas about the importance of paying taxes can reinforce the belief that such actions are beneficial to the community. Furthermore, in some contexts, tax non-compliance behaviors can be socially sanctioned. Indeed, taxpayers who fail to meet their tax obligations may be criticized by their peers, which can deter fraudulent behavior.

CONCLUSION

The tax morality of Moroccan doctors is influenced by a complex combination of psychosociological factors. Personal norms and values reinforce tax compliance. In addition, trust in institutions, reputation, transparency of public services, peer influence and the equity and fairness of the tax system also influence tax morality. Tax awareness and education also have an impact on tax behavior.

The benefits of this research for stakeholders are manifold. Initially, it enables policy-makers to understand the psychosociological factors that influence doctors' tax morality, which can help design more effective and equitable tax policies. Indeed, by taking into account personal values and perceptions of inequality, policies can be adjusted to reinforce trust in the tax system and encourage compliance. Next, for tax authorities, transparency and fairness in public services are essential to improving tax morality. Thus, tax authorities can use this information to develop communication and awareness-raising strategies that highlight the importance of transparency and fairness, as well as the benefits of taxes for society. In addition, healthcare professionals can benefit from educational programs and continuing training on tax morality and tax obligations. This can help them to better understand the importance of their role in financing public services and to adopt fiscally responsible behaviors. This study also paves the way for future research into other determinants of tax morality.

This study has certain limitations. At first, it is based on a small sample of doctors, which may not be representative of the medical population as a whole. In addition, doctors' responses may be influenced by social or personal biases, which may affect the reliability of the results. Moreover, the results are specific to the Moroccan context and may not be generalizable to other contexts.

The results of this research have several practical implications. First of all, it is essential to raise awareness and educate citizens about the importance of taxes and their positive impact on society. In addition, effective communication campaigns can help change negative perceptions and encourage responsible tax behavior. It is crucial to put in place concrete measures to support these initiatives and ensure their long-term success.

In addition, improving the transparency of the tax system and ensuring the fair application of tax laws can reduce feelings of injustice and boost taxpayers' confidence. Showing in concrete terms how taxes are used to finance public services can also motivate citizens to meet their tax obligations.

The study focuses on the socio-psychological determinants of tax morality. However, it would be relevant to also explore institutional determinants, such as tax policies, administrative structures and governance mechanisms, to obtain a more in-depth view. In addition, it would be interesting to conduct longitudinal studies to observe the evolution of tax morality over time and the impact of tax reforms. In addition, testing the effectiveness of different interventions, such as the inclusion of chartered accountants in such research, could provide valuable insights into tax practices and the challenges faced by stakeholders.

REFERENCES

Abdixhiku, L., Pugh, G., & Hashi, I. (2018). Business tax evasion in transition economies: A cross-country panel investigation. *European Journal of Comparative Economics, 15*(1), 11–36.

Abeler, J., & Jäger, S. (2015). Complex tax incentives. *American Economic Journal. Economic Policy, 7*(3), 1–28. DOI: 10.1257/pol.20130137

Adams, J. S., & Freedman, S. (1976). Equity theory revisited: Comments and annotated bibliography. *Advances in Experimental Social Psychology, 9*, 43–90. DOI: 10.1016/S0065-2601(08)60058-1

Alexander, P., & Balavac-Orlic, M. (2022). Tax morale: Framing and fairness. *Economic Systems, 46*(1), 100936. DOI: 10.1016/j.ecosys.2021.100936

Ali, M., Fjeldstad, O. H., & Sjursen, I. H. (2014). To pay or not to pay? Citizens' attitudes toward taxation in Kenya, Tanzania, Uganda, and South Africa. *World Development, 64*, 828–842. DOI: 10.1016/j.worlddev.2014.07.006

Alkhatib, A. A., Abdul-Jabbar, H., Abuamria, F., & Rahhal, A. (2019). The effects of social influence factors on income tax evasion among the Palestinian SMEs. *International Journal of Advanced Science and Technology, 28*(17), 690–700.

Allingham, M., & Sandmo, A. (1972). Income tax evasion: A theoretical analysis. *Journal of Public Economics, 1*(3/4), 323–338. DOI: 10.1016/0047-2727(72)90010-2

Alm, J. (1991). A perspective on the experimental analysis of taxpayer reporting. *The Accounting Review, 66*(3), 577–593.

Alm, J. (2019). What motivates tax compliance? *Journal of Economic Surveys, 33*(2), 353–388. DOI: 10.1111/joes.12272

Alm, J., & McKee, M. (2004). Tax compliance as a coordination game. *Journal of Economic Behavior & Organization, 54*(3), 297–312. DOI: 10.1016/j.jebo.2003.02.003

Andreoni, J., Erard, B., & Feinstein, J. (1998). Tax compliance. *Journal of Economic Literature, 36*, 818–860.

Bandura, A. (1977). *Social learning theory.* General Learning Press.

Barile, S., Saviano, M., & Polese, F. (2024). Rethinking fiscal policies: A systemic perspective. *Journal of Systemic Fiscal Studies, 5*(1), 45–63.

Barone, G., & Mocetti, S. (2011). Tax morale and public spending inefficiency. International Tax and Public Finance, 18, 724-749.Bazart, C., &Bonein, A. (2014). Reciprocal relationships in tax compliance decisions. *Journal of Economic Psychology, 40*, 83–102.

Baumard, P. (1997). *Constructivisme et processus de la recherche: l'émergence d'une posture épistémologique chez le chercheur. Cahiers de recherche LAREGO.* Université de Versailles St Quentin.

Bazart, C., & Bonein, A. (2017). La force du symbole: Sommes-nous prêts à punir les fraudeurs? *Revue Économique (Paris), 68*(5), 829–841. DOI: 10.3917/reco.pr3.0092

Bénabou, R., & Tirole, J. (2011). Identity, morals, and taboos: Beliefs as assets. *The Quarterly Journal of Economics, 126*(2), 805–855. DOI: 10.1093/qje/qjr002 PMID: 22073409

Bergolo, M. L., Leites, M., Perez-Truglia, R., & Strehl, M. (2020). *What makes a tax evader? (No. w28235).* National Bureau of Economic Research. DOI: 10.3386/w28235

Bhargava, S., & Manoli, D. (2015). Psychological frictions and the incomplete take-up of social benefits: Evidence from an IRS field experiment. *The American Economic Review, 105*(11), 3489–3529. DOI: 10.1257/aer.20121493

Bidin, Z., Idris, K. M., & Shamsudin, F. M. (2009). Predicting compliance intention on zakah on employment income in Malaysia: An application of reasoned action theory. *JurnalPengurusan, 28*(July), 85–102.

Bidin, Z., & Sinnasamy, P. (2018). Excise duty compliance behavior in Malaysia. *The International Journal of Accounting, 3*(13), 106–116.

Bilgin, C. (2014). Determinants of tax morale in Spain and Turkey: an empirical analysis. European Journal of government and economics, 3(1), 60-74.

Bird, R. M., Martinez-Vazquez, J., & Torgler, B. (2008). Tax effort in developing countries and high-income countries: The impact of corruption, voice and accountability. *Economic Analysis and Policy, 38*(1), 55–71. DOI: 10.1016/S0313-5926(08)50006-3

Bobek, D. D., Hageman, A. M., & Kelliher, C. F. (2013). Analyzing the role of social norms in tax compliance behavior. *Journal of Business Ethics, 115*(3), 451–468. DOI: 10.1007/s10551-012-1390-7

Boly, A., Konte, M., & Shimeles, A. (2019). *Corruption and tax morale in Africa. Maastricht Economic and Social Research Institute on Innovation and Technology*. UNU-MERIT.

Bosco, L., & Mittone, L. (1997). Tax evasion and moral constraints: Some experimental evidence. *Kyklos, 50*(3), 297–324. DOI: 10.1111/1467-6435.00018

Braithwaite, V., & Ahmed, E. (2005). A threat to tax morale: The case of Australian higher education policy. *Journal of Economic Psychology, 26*(4), 523–540. DOI: 10.1016/j.joep.2004.08.003

Brink, W. D., & Porcano, T. M. (2016). The impact of culture and economic structure on tax morale and tax evasion: A country-level analysis using SEM. In *Advances in taxation* (Vol. 23, pp. 87–123). Emerald Group Publishing Limited.

Castañeda, N. (2024). Fairness and tax morale in developing countries. *Studies in Comparative International Development, 59*(1), 113–137. DOI: 10.1007/s12116-023-09394-z PMID: 37360793

Castro, L., & Scartascini, C. (2015). Tax compliance and enforcement in the pampas evidence from a field experiment. *Journal of Economic Behavior & Organization, 116*, 65–82. DOI: 10.1016/j.jebo.2015.04.002

Chan, C. W., Troutman, C. S., & O'Bryan, D. (2000). An expanded model of taxpayercompliance: Empiricalevidencefrom the United States and Hong Kong. *Journal of International Accounting, Auditing & Taxation, 9*(2), 83–103. DOI: 10.1016/S1061-9518(00)00027-6

ConseilÉconomique. Social et Environnemental. (2019). Le Nouveau Modèle de Développement du Maroc: Contribution du Conseil Économique, Social et Environnemental. Rabat.

Cummings, R. G., Martinez-Vazquez, J., McKee, M., & Torgler, B. (2009). Tax morale affects tax compliance: Evidence from surveys and an artefactual field experiment. *Journal of Economic Behavior & Organization*, *70*(3), 447–457. DOI: 10.1016/j.jebo.2008.02.010

Deci, E. L., & Ryan, R. M. (1980). The empirical exploration of intrinsic motivational processes. In Berkowitz, L. (Ed.), Advances in Experimental Social Psychology: Vol. 13. *Academic Press* (pp. 39–80). DOI: 10.1016/S0065-2601(08)60130-6

Dwenger, N., Kleven, H., Rasul, I., & Rincke, J. (2016). Extrinsic and intrinsic motivations for tax compliance: Evidence from a field experiment in Germany. *American Economic Journal. Economic Policy*, *8*(3), 203–232. DOI: 10.1257/pol.20150083

El Ghazali, M., &Benkendil, H. (2020). Civisme fiscal: Comment peut-on instaurer un climat de confiance entre l'administration fiscale et le contribuable ? International Journal of Accounting, Finance, Auditing, Management and Economics, 1(2).

El Harchi, A., & El Bennissi, L. (2024). Réflexions autour de l'articulation des sanctions dans la répressionfiscale: uneapproche comparative entre la France et le Maroc. International Journal of Accounting, Finance, Auditing, Management and Economics.

Erard, B., & Feinstein, J. (1994). Honesty and evasion in the tax compliance game. *The RAND Journal of Economics*, *25*(1), 1–19. DOI: 10.2307/2555850

Feld, L. P., & Frey, B. S. (2002). Trust breeds trust: How taxpayers are treated. *Economics of Governance*, *3*(2), 87–99. DOI: 10.1007/s101010100032

Feld, L. P., & Frey, B. S. (2010). Tax evasion and the psychological tax contract. Developing alternative frameworks for explaining tax compliance, 59, 74.

Feld, L. P., & Larsen, C. (2012). Self-perceptions, government policies and tax compliance in Germany. *International Tax and Public Finance*, *19*(1), 78–103. DOI: 10.1007/s10797-011-9196-6

Fonseca Corona, F. J. (2024). Tax morale: A global scopingreviewfrom the cultural approach to economics. *International Review of Economics*, *71*(2), 343–365. DOI: 10.1007/s12232-024-00446-x

Fortin, B., Lacroix, G., & Villeval, M. C. (2007). Tax evasion and social interactions. *Journal of Public Economics*, *91*(11-12), 2089–2112. DOI: 10.1016/j.jpubeco.2007.03.005

Frey, B. (1997). A constitution for knaves crowds out civic virtues. *Economic Journal (London)*, *107*(443), 1043–1053. DOI: 10.1111/j.1468-0297.1997.tb00006.x

Frey, B. S., & Meier, S. (2004). Pro-social behavior in a natural setting. *Journal of Economic Behavior & Organization*, *54*(1), 65–88. DOI: 10.1016/j.jebo.2003.10.001

Gordon, J. (1989). Individual morality and reputation costs as deterrents to tax evasion. *European Economic Review*, *33*(4), 797–805. DOI: 10.1016/0014-2921(89)90026-3

Hashimzade, N., Myles, G. D., & Tran-Nam, B. (2013). Applications of behavioural economics to tax evasion. *Journal of Economic Surveys*, *27*(5), 941–977. DOI: 10.1111/j.1467-6419.2012.00733.x

Horodnic, I. A. (2018). Tax morale and institutional theory: A systematic review. *The International Journal of Sociology and Social Policy*, *38*(9/10), 868–886. DOI: 10.1108/IJSSP-03-2018-0039

Jackson, B. R., & Milliron, V. C. (1986). Tax compliance research: Findings, problems, and prospects. *Journal of Accounting Literature*, *5*(1), 125–165.

Jacquemet, N., Luchini, S., Malézieux, A., & Shogren, J. F. (2017). L'évasion fiscale est-elle un trait de personnalité? Une évaluation empirique des déterminants psychologiques de la «morale fiscale». *Revue Économique (Paris)*, *68*(5), 809–828. DOI: 10.3917/reco.pr3.0091

Jahnke, B., & Weisser, R. A. (2019). How does petty corruption affect tax morale in Sub-Saharan Africa? *European Journal of Political Economy*, *60*, 101751. DOI: 10.1016/j.ejpoleco.2018.09.003

Jestin, K. (2020). De la perception du concept de Responsabilité Sociétale de l'Entreprise (RSE) a sa transposition dans le domaine fiscal. Revue européenne et internationale de droit fiscal, (1), 129-144.

Kelman, H. C. (1958). Compliance, identification, and internalization three processes of attitude change. *The Journal of Conflict Resolution*, *2*(1), 51–60. DOI: 10.1177/002200275800200106

Kirchler, E. (2007). *The economic psychology of tax behavior*. Cambridge University Press. DOI: 10.1017/CBO9780511628238

Lago, I., & Lago-Peñas, S. (2010). The determinants of tax morale in comparative perspective: Evidence from European countries. *European Journal of Political Economy*, *26*(4), 441–453. DOI: 10.1016/j.ejpoleco.2010.06.003

Lambert, T. (Ed.). (2007). *Les sanctions pénales fiscales* (p. 173). L'Harmattan.

Lecourt, B. (2022). Transparence fiscale: Directive no 2021/2101 du 24 novembre 2021 sur la publication d'informations relatives à l'impôt sur les revenus des sociétés. [Journal des Sociétés]. *Revue des Sociétés*, (02), 119.

Levin, M., & Satarov, G. (2000). Corruption and institutions in Russia. *European Journal of Political Economy*, *16*(1), 113–132. DOI: 10.1016/S0176-2680(99)00050-6

Litina, A., & Palivos, T. (2016). Corruption, tax evasion and social values. *Journal of Economic Behavior & Organization*, *124*, 164–177. DOI: 10.1016/j.jebo.2015.09.017

Luttmer, E. F., & Singhal, M. (2014). Tax morale. *The Journal of Economic Perspectives*, *28*(4), 149–168. DOI: 10.1257/jep.28.4.149

Macintyre, A., &Torgler, B. (2024). Neuroscience and Tax Compliance. The Ethics of Tax Evasion, 2.

McKerchar, M., Bloomquist, K., & Pope, J. (2013). Indicators of tax morale: an exploratory study. eJTR, 11, 5.

Milesi, P., & Alberici, A. I. (2018). Pluralistic morality and collective action: The role of moral foundations. *Group Processes & Intergroup Relations*, *21*(2), 235–256. DOI: 10.1177/1368430216675707

Oberholzer, R. (2008). Attitudes of South African taxpayers towards taxation: A pilot study. *Account. Bus. Public Interest*, *7*(1), 46–52.

OECD. (2022). *Tax Morale II: Building Trust between Tax Administrations and Large Businesses*. OECD Publishing., DOI: 10.1787/7587f25c-

Owusu, G. M. Y., Bart-Plange, M.-A., Koomson, T. A. A., & Arthur, M. (2022). The effect of personality traits and tax morale on tax evasion intention. *Journal of Financial Crime*, *29*(1), 272–292. DOI: 10.1108/JFC-02-2021-0026

Rosa, A. (2024). *Civisme fiscal vs éthique fiscale: Quel (s) devoir (s) du contribuable? Saad, N. (2011). Fairness perceptions and compliance behavior: Taxpayers' judgments in self-assessment environments*. University of Canterbury.

Saad, N. (2012). Perceptions of tax fairness and tax compliance behavior: A comparative study. [UKM Journal of Management]. *Jurnal Pengurusan*, *36*, 89–100.

Schmölders, G. (1970). Survey research in public finance: A behavioral approach to fiscal theory. *Public Finance*, *25*(2), 300–306.

Sikayu, S. H., Rahmat, M., & Chan, A. N. (2022). Fairness, transparency and attitude towards tax evasion amongst owners of SMEs [IJSMS]. *International Journal of Service Management and Sustainability*, *7*(1), 185–206. DOI: 10.24191/ijsms.v7i1.17786

Slemrod, J. (2024). What taxpayers, governments and tax economists do–and what they should do. *Fiscal Studies*, *45*(1), 7–19. DOI: 10.1111/1475-5890.12324

Song, Y., & Yarbrough, T. E. (1978). Tax Ethics and Taxpayer Attitudes: A Survey. *Public Administration Review*, *38*(5), 442–452. DOI: 10.2307/975503

Strümpel, B. (1969). The Contribution of Survey Research to Public Finance. In Peacock, A. T. (Ed.), *Quantitative Analysis in Public Finance* (pp. 13–32). Praeger.

Sussman, R., & Gifford, R. (2013). Be the change you want to see: Modeling food composting in public places. *Environment and Behavior*, *45*(3), 323–343. DOI: 10.1177/0013916511431274

Timmons, J. F., & Garfias, F. (2015). Revealed corruption, taxation, and fiscal accountability: Evidence from Brazil. *World Development*, *70*, 13–27. DOI: 10.1016/j.worlddev.2014.12.011

Torgler, B. (2001). Is tax evasion never justifiable? *Journal of Public Finance and Public Choice*, *19*(2-3), 143–167. DOI: 10.1332/251569201X15668905707203

Torgler, B. (2003). To evade or not: That is the question. *Journal of Socio-Economics*, *32*(3), 283–302. DOI: 10.1016/S1053-5357(03)00040-4

Torgler, B. (2011). Tax morale and compliance.Review of evidence and case studies for Europe. World Bank policy research working paper series, 5922.

Usunier, J. C., Easterby-Smith, M., & Thorpe, R. (1993). *Introduction à la recherche en gestion*. Economica.

Wenzel, M. (2004). An analysis of norm processes in tax compliance. *Journal of Economic Psychology*, *25*(2), 213–228. DOI: 10.1016/S0167-4870(02)00168-X

Yoo, C., & Jang, W. (2019). Social empathy for society beyond the social work profession: A contextual understanding of poverty and attitudes towards government interventions. *Sociétés*, *145*(3), 25–36. DOI: 10.3917/soc.145.0025

Young, A., Lei, L., Wong, B., & Kwok, B. (2016). Individual tax compliance in China: a review. International Journal of Law and management, 58(5), 562-574.

Chapter 4
Political Ideology and Individual Values as Key Determinants of Fiscal Awareness

Gloria Alarcon-Garcia
https://orcid.org/0000-0003-1177-6026
University of Murcia, Spain

Alicia Martinez-Serrano
https://orcid.org/0000-0002-8478-2753
University of Murcia, Spain

ABSTRACT

This paper determines the key values of fiscal awareness by using a wide range of variables, mainly related to personal values, political ideology and cultural factors. After the introduction, the theoretical framework reviews key literature and define the fiscal awareness in relation to the tax morale and the fiscal ethics. The following sections introduce the methodology and examine the results of a questionnaire filled by 562 University students, analysing the variables that might have an impact on fiscal awareness. This paper contributes to the literature on tax morale analysing the influence of political ideology together with other variables. The influence of political ideology is thoroughly examined, aiming to ascertain whether students with liberal ideology would show a higher level of fiscal awareness than those with a conservative ideology. Results show that honesty and tax fairness foster higher levels of fiscal awareness. Political ideology prevails over other factors, like tax education, when explaining high levels of fiscal awareness.

1. INTRODUCTION

For several decades, the study of tax compliance has generated an extensive literature. Early research focused on the identification of the economic determinants of tax evasion (Clotfelter 1983; Klepper & Nagin 1989; Feinstein 1991). Thereafter, research interest areas included the psychosocial factors that might have an impact on tax noncompliance (Pommerehne & Weck-Hannemann 1996; Alm, McClelland & Schulze 1999; Feld & Tyran 2002; Torgler 2003b). Numerous studies identified factors related to

DOI: 10.4018/979-8-3373-0422-9.ch004

culture, institutions, trust in government, psychosocial aspects and even globalization, as determinants of tax morale (Alm, Jackson & Mckee 1992; Torgler 2003a; Torgler & Schneider 2005; Murphy 2004; Kirchler & Wahl 2010; Richardson 2008; Hoffmann, Hoelzl & Kirchler 2008; Hammar, Jagers, & Nordblom 2009). Despite the depth and breadth of this academic output, there continues to be a growing interest in understanding how psychosocial factors influence taxpayers' fiscal behaviour.

The main objective of this chapter is to provide new evidence on the psychosocial factors that influence tax compliance. Emphasis is placed on how political ideology and personal values, such as honesty, solidarity and perceptions of tax fairness, are some key determinants of tax morale. The results were obtained through a survey of Spanish university students. Our study adds further evidence that taxpayers' socio-cultural and individual ideologies and values, influence tax compliance. The influence of political ideology is thoroughly examined, aiming to ascertain whether Spanish students with a conservative or right-wing ideology would show a lower level of tax awareness than those with liberal or left-wing ideological beliefs.

Another important aspect of this study relates to the concept of fiscal awareness. In addressing the concept of fiscal awareness, we must, first of all, highlight its close relationship with tax ethics and tax morale. Tax ethics, tax morale and fiscal awareness have traditionally been used to refer to the same concept. All three have been applied to the set of attitudes and behaviours of the taxpayer when complying with the tax authorities, however, there are nuances of meaning that need to be explored in greater depth and which we will work on, in this study.

This chapter first discusses the theoretical framework and reviews the literature that proves that the political-institutional environment, where the relationships between the administration and the taxpayers operate, provides some key aspects shaping fiscal awareness. Next section describes the methodology and the survey, defines the fiscal awareness concept in relation to the tax morale and the fiscal ethics, as well as the explanatory variables used in the model, supporting and contrasting our results with other results obtained by previous studies. The following part of this chapter introduces the econometric analysis of the survey and the results. By using a discrete choice model, this study aims to ascertain if personal values, political ideology or tax knowledge, among others, influence fiscal awareness. And finally, last section shows the main conclusions.

Having established the objectives and scope of this study, the following section presents the theoretical framework and reviews the relevant literature that supports our analysis and provide a solid foundation for this research.

2. THEORETICAL FRAMEWORK

The terms 'ethics' and 'morals' have been applied and used in the tax compliance literature. Vogel (1974) defined 'tax ethics' as the attitude and behaviour of the taxpayer necessary to comply with his tax obligations in the sense of filing his tax return properly, accurately and legally.

On the other hand, at the beginning of the 21st century, 'tax morale' is beginning to be considered in the work on tax compliance as an endogenous rather than exogenous variable, due to its relevance for the study of tax compliance (Torgler, 2002b, 2002a). How is the concept of 'tax morale' or 'tax morale' defined? For Schmölders (1965), tax morale is the attitude of a group or the totality of taxpayers towards the fulfilment of their fiscal duties, being thus rooted in the mentality of the population towards the tax authorities and in their social conscience, in their recognition of the duty to contribute and in their acceptance of the fiscal sovereignty of the State. It is the result of the simultaneous action of several causes: subjective tax pressure, unjustified tax discrimination, the feeling of fiscal injustice, the distancing from community objectives and, of course, the ineffectiveness of tax control (García, 1975). Kirchler (1997) defined tax morale as disagreeing with tax evasion; while for Fernández (2006), the notion of tax morale is not only the fact of disagreeing with tax evasion, but also the fact of disagreeing with tax evasion.

The notion of tax morale is primarily related to the propensity to evade or comply with the established tax system or specific levies within it.

According to this approach, tax morale refers to individuals' attitudes towards tax payment (Antequera & Florensa, 2008), relating to the concept of civic duty motivation (Hofmann, Hoelzl, & Kirchler, 2008) and being considered a reasonable explanation for why tax compliance rates are so high (Brink & Porcano, 2016; María-Dolores, Alarcón, & Garre, 2010). This concept refers to how the principles of fiscal ethics take a specific form in a given society at a particular point in time (Alarcón et al., 2012).

Subsequently, a more rigorous and precise concept than tax morality emerged: "fiscal awareness," which is the term used in this study. Tax awareness is described as the individual perception of each citizen regarding fiscal ethics and the tax morality of the society in which they live, leading to the voluntary fulfilment of their tax obligations (Alarcón et al., 2012; Alarcón et al., 2015).

The formation of fiscal awareness involves the assumption that there are a series of justificatory criteria for the collective financing of public and common needs, beyond specific fiscal options and models (Delgado et al., 2005). Those with a high level of fiscal awareness will voluntarily pay their taxes, regardless of what others do, what the group's collective morality considers appropriate, or the opportunities available for tax fraud (Alarcón et al., 2015).

Thus, tax compliance encompasses both the term "fiscal awareness"—based on an individual's identification with their own personal values—and the term "tax moral"—the correlation between individual values and socially accepted values—since it may depend on internal factors, whether related to taxpayers (values and/or knowledge) or to regulations (laws, social norms, ideology, etc.).

There are some criteria to groups the factors into categories that shape tax compliance (Horodnic, 2018) as formal institutions, informal institutions and socio-demographic characteristics and personal values. In our opinion Fiscal awareness is shaped by the principles and values that form part of fiscal morale and fiscal ethics, but also by other factors (Alarcón, 2018; Alarcón et al., 2015; Alarcón & Tipke, 2007):

a) Internal factors: principles, ideologies, and values of each individual, as well as principles related to taxation.
b) Psychosocial factors: satisfaction with the efficiency of the administration in managing tax revenue and trust in tax authorities, among others
c) Technical factors: technical elements related to the facts and subjects involved in the tax process
d) Demographic factors or determinants.

In the literature review we are about to reference, we will adhere to the use of the terms fiscal ethic, tax moral, or tax compliance as employed by the authors in their works.

The first studies on tax morale (Schmölders 1960; Allingham & Sandmo 1972; Becker 1968; and Arrow & Lind 1970) reached the same conclusion: there is some inconsistency between high tax compliance and the rational behaviour taxpayers should exhibit, according to the expected utility theory. If all individuals modelled their behaviour in line with the classical assumptions, the "rational" decision would lead to a positive share of evaded income. However, as the results obtained by Alm, Jackson &

Mckee (1992) show, not all taxpayers are tax evaders; actually, there is a great share of individuals that are determined to pay taxes.

Randlane (2015) focuses on defining key terms related to tax compliance, as well as mapping and systematising the determinants of tax compliance. It proposes a way to develop an administrative strategy for tax compliance. The novelty of the study lies in approaching tax compliance as a systemic whole. This approach can serve as a basis for tax authorities to develop comprehensive administrative strategies.

Brizi, Giacomantonio, Schumpe and Mannetti (2015) argue that economic factors such as audit fees and penalties have shown inconsistent effects on tax payment, suggesting that they are not sufficient to explain tax compliance. The results of the studies analysed by the authors support the relationship between social value orientation and measures of tax compliance. Furthermore, the results provided evidence of a causal effect of social value orientation on the intention not to comply with taxes. These results prompted further research on the psychosocial factors that might have an impact on tax noncompliance. Ciziceno and Pizzuto (2022) analyse whether life satisfaction is one of the psychological aspects that affect tax morale. Using longitudinal data from the World Values Survey, they show that people who are more satisfied with their lives, have higher tax morale.

Jayawardane (2015) examines the influence of psychological factors on tax compliance decisions. Among the 'tax compliance variables' analysed by various researchers, this study includes those related to psychological factors, which stand out for their value for tax compliance decisions. In addition, it introduces the main contributions that have attempted to explain the obvious agreements and disagreements between the evidence on taxpayers' reaction to tax compliance through psychological factors.

Gangl and Torgler (2020) discuss how and why the wealthy differ from less well-off taxpayers due to specific and interrelated political, social and psychological conditions. According to these authors understanding the psychological mechanisms that determine the tax compliance of the wealthy can provide insights for policies to better integrate the wealthy into the tax system. This study proposes new policy approaches to increase tax compliance and tax morale among the wealthy.

The relationship between political power and citizenship is one of the factors that most affect voluntary tax compliance. In fact, this variable offers some of the most consistent results from empirical research: Individuals who support democracy are more likely to show willingness to comply with their taxes (Torgler 2003; Torgler & Schneider 2007; Marcelo Leonardo 2011). Lozza et al. (2013) found that left-leaning taxpayers expressed higher levels of voluntary cooperation and showed reactance to the coercive power of authorities, whereas right-leaning taxpayers expressed higher levels of enforced tax compliance and were more averse to tax evasion with increased trust in authorities and institutions. Wahlund (1992) studied the factors that affected individual tax compliance and found that Swedish taxpayers who supported conservative parties were more prone to evasion than other voters. In the Jaime-Castillo and Sáez-Lozano (2016) study, multilevel models are estimated to test the effect of socio-economic status and political ideology on individual preferences. The findings show that both self-interest motivations and political ideology are important factors in explaining these preferences. Results show that as direct taxation increases, left-wing parties strengthen their ability to mobilise their voters to pursue redistributive interests, while right-wing voters increase their resistance to taxing the rich.

Marcelo Leonardo (2011) found some interesting facts: individuals living in democratic countries show a positive relationship between trust on institutions and upholding democratic values on tax morale; there is a negative relationship between conservative ideology and tax morale; and no relationship is found between upholding post-materialist values and tax morale.

Pommerehne & Weck-Hannemann (1996) concluded that the higher the direct political control, the lower the level of tax evasion. Alm, McClelland & Schulze (1999), together with Feld & Tyran (2002), proved that voting on tax issues has a positive impact on tax compliance. Torgler (2003b) argued that the more direct the democracy (tax issues are voted by taxpayers in Switzerland), the higher the level of tax compliance. Frey and Torgler (2006, 2007) highlighted other determinants of tax morale, such as quality of political institutions based on political stability, effectiveness of governments and fight against corruption. There are also studies that state the relationship between tax behaviour and the sense of belonging to the country of residence (Konrad & Qari 2012).

Social capital is a recently developed concept used as an explanatory variable for studying a wide range of phenomena, including the creation of human capital, the effectiveness of democratic institutions, economic development, or, more broadly, as a resource for solving collective action problems (Herreros & De Francisco, 2001). It refers to certain characteristics of social organization, such as social trust, norms, and social networks, which can enhance societal efficiency by facilitating coordinated actions (Putnam, 2001, 2011).

Social capital is a subjective phenomenon composed of a set of values and attitudes held by citizens, which influence or determine how they relate to one another (Brehm & Rahn, 1997; Newton, 1997). Bourdieu (2001) defines it as the sum of actual or potential resources linked to the possession of a durable network of more or less institutionalised relationships of mutual acquaintance and recognition, or, in other words, to membership of a group.

When individuals who comply with their tax obligations observe that many others evade these obligations or only partially fulfil them, or when they feel they are treated unfairly compared to others, the sense of relative injustice tends to strongly drive the growth of tax fraud (Lagares, 1991). Therefore, although it is extremely difficult to estimate the proportion of tax evaders (Elster, 1991), if an individual believes that most other taxpayers are honest, their willingness to pay taxes will increase. Conversely, if they perceive that the majority are tax evaders, their intrinsic motivation to comply with taxation will decline (Alarcón et al., 2009; Antequera & Florensa, 2008; Aquino, 2008; Arias, 2008; Elster, 1991; Gächter, 2007; Goksu & Sahpaz, 2015; Torgler, 2005b).

It is unlikely that a citizen will fully comply with their tax obligations if tax evasion is widespread in the society in which they live (Castañeda, 2015). Consequently, the perception that others evade taxes further encourages non-compliance (De Miguel & De Miguel, 2001). Empirical evidence generally suggests that when individuals trust that others obey the law, tax morale tends to increase significantly (Bedoya & Vásconez, 2010; Torgler, 2005b). In contrast, perceiving high levels of tax evasion (Frey & Torgler, 2007; Kaplan & Reckers, 1985) or suspecting that others are engaging in tax evasion (Molero & Pujol, 2012) tends to increase an individual's likelihood of evading taxes.

In this line of research, Feld & Frey (2002, 2007) examined how Swiss tax authorities treat taxpayers. They concluded that taxpayers living in the cantons with more decentralized powers were treated with more respect by the Public Administration, which affected their perception of fairness. Trust is therefore reciprocal: the more the government trust citizens, the more citizens trust the government. Alm & Torgler (2006) agreed on this when analysing perceived fairness, trust in the government and the exchange between government and taxpayers. Barone & Mocetti (2011) studied the connection between effectiveness of the government and tax morale.

Trust has been another key aspect to understand tax morale. Relationships of trust between the public and the administration are necessary for the conditional cooperation to occur. The theory of the "slippery slope" framework developed by Kirchler, Hoelzl, & Wahl (2008) supports this theory. It underlines two key values to obtain taxpayers' compliance: trust and power. In the "slippery slope" framework, Kirchler, Hoelzl, & Wahl (2008) distinguish between enforced and voluntary tax compliance depending on the power attributed to authorities and trust in them.

Ciziceno and Pizzuto (2022) also provide evidence on the role of trust in government and people's cultural orientation in the relationship between life satisfaction and tax morale. According to these authors, implementing alternative policies that directly or indirectly increase tax morale could be politically relevant, given that the prosecution of tax evasion is imperfect.

The results of the study by Ho Fai Chan, Mohammad Wangsit Supriyadi and Benno Torgler in 2017 indicate that while vertical trust matters, horizontal trust in the form of generalised trust is not linked to fiscal morale. However, they identify cross-country differences that merit further exploration. They also show that uncertainty in generalised trust, in contrast to uncertainty in vertical trust, is negatively correlated with fiscal morale, and they provide evidence that generalised trust varies under different conditions of vertical governance.

The literature has also underlined conditional cooperation as another key determinant of tax morale, in other words, the impact of others' attitude on individual tax morale. Frey & Meier (2004), Heldt (2005) and Shang & Croson (2005) concluded that the greater the expected cooperation, the higher the willingness to pay taxes and the social commitment. Likewise, Frey & Torgler (2006, 2007) showed that conditional cooperation is a key factor of tax morale.

Other authors focused on the cultural and geographical aspects that may influence taxpaying behaviour. Comparative analyses on tax morale across European countries have been carried out from the very beginning of tax studies (Strümpel 1969; Torgler 2003a; Alm & Torgler 2006; Weck, Pommerehne & Frey 1984; Frey & Weck-Hannemann 1984; Frey & Torgler 2006, 2007). Pampel, Andrighetto and Steinmo (2019) point to the importance of culture-based attitudes and institutionally structured rules for taxes and benefits through a unique set of multi-country experiments and multi-site attitude surveys in Italy, the United Kingdom, the United States and Sweden. They analyse the influence of institutional settings and three attitude scales measuring pro-redistributive ideology, fiscal responsibility and perceived government competence, finding varied and inconsistent country-specific effects. Marandu, Mbekomize and Ifezue (2015) review the factors that determine tax compliance from a social marketing perspective. The data were drawn from 18 empirical studies published between 1985 and 2012 from different parts of the world. The analysis shows that attitudinal, normative and subjective control variables are good predictors of tax compliance

Citizen participation related to tax compliance is another point of interest. In this sense, all the work on tax compliance that has considered participation analyzing the differences between residing and not residing in a given region with a direct or semi-direct democracy system, and these have dealt mostly with Switzerland or the United States. In a direct democracy, taxpayers know that the public services they enjoy are worth the taxes they pay, which means they are paying their taxes honestly (Feld and Frey, 2002). Thus, according to empirical evidence, there is a positive relationship between direct democracy and tax morality (Feld and Tyran, 2002; Torgler et al., 2010), with tax evasion being higher in purely representative systems than in systems with direct or semi-direct democracy (Feld and Kirchgässner, 2000).

However, the fact that most studies focus on this type of democratic system has meant that the participation of individual citizens has been neglected, since they have only considered whether or not there are opportunities to participate actively, but not whether individuals actually participate. It has also meant limiting the study to countries or regions where this type of democracy exists, or limiting the study to the mere correlation between the variables direct democracy and tax compliance. Moreover, these studies have not considered the differences that may exist between men and women in tax compliance.

Citizen participation is associated with certain characteristics that lead to citizens who are involved in different participatory settings showing a greater sense of the values of democracy, greater trust in public institutions, greater tolerance of civic attitudes and greater social responsibility. For all these reasons, it would seem reasonable to think that the most participative individuals have a greater fiscal awareness than others. However, the studies that focus on this are very limited. Citizens have mechanisms for participation, such as public meetings or citizen assemblies, neighborhood and communal meetings, citizens' juries, oral interventions in public sessions of government bodies or participatory budgets, among others (Goma and Font, 2001). Only in the last of these participatory mechanisms has its effect been studied, with the studies concluding that, in the regions examined, tax revenues are higher in those places where participatory budget processes occur (Beuermann and Amelina, 2014; Biderman and Silva, 2007; Cabannes, 2015).

Similarly, the literature on tax compliance shows the trend that men and women do not have similar predispositions and tolerances to tax fraud. Men tend to have lower levels of tax compliance than women (Dulleck et al., 2016), so they would tend to evade taxes more than women (Vera and Grijalva, 2014). In general, women are significantly more disinterested or altruistic (Feingold, 1983), show greater aversion to risk (Bohnet, 2007), are more honest (Torgler, 2002c) and show higher tax morals than men (María-Dolores, Alarcón, and Garre, 2010; Martinez-Vazquez and Torgler, 2009); while men believe they have better opportunities to defraud the Treasury (De Juan and Truyols, 1993). Beyond the biological differences between men and women, there are studies that consider other characteristics. Thus, for example, Ashby and Webley (2010) conclude that it is not necessarily the fact of being a man or woman that influences tax compliance but rather having a stereotypically masculine or feminine job. Another study conducted in the same year sought to distinguish between psychological, social, and biological sex with respect to fiscal behavior, and the results suggested that women's greater tax compliance compared to men could be better explained by differences in socialization, self-image, and femininity-masculinity traits, rather than by prenatal hormonal differences (Kastlunger, Dressler, Kirchler, Mittone, and Voracek, 2010). López-Luzuriaga and Scartascini (2023) reaffirms that women are typically more di ligent in paying their taxes than men. However if we put together fiscal awareness and educaction, according to the study by Alarcón, Ayala, and Quiñones (2013), gender presents an interesting interaction with level of education: the higher the level of education, the greater the fiscal awareness, but the effect is greater for men than for women in primary school, is equal for both in secondary school, and is greater for university women.

Collecting individual participant data from 70 papers that use laboratory experiments to examine individual tax evasion behavior (or "Tax Evasion Games"), in order to use meta-analysis to estimate the impacts of different public policy, experimental design and individual level variables on tax evasion choices, Alm and Malézieux (2021) concludes that the sociodemographic factors of the subjects, as gender differences, income, occupation, or risk attitude affect tax compliance.

Cizeno and Pituzzo (2022) using longitudinal data from the World Value Survey, shows that people more satisfied with their own life show higher tax morale. They also provide evidence on the roles played by confidence in government and people's cultural orientation in shaping the relationship between life satisfaction and tax morale.

After the review of the theoretical framework and the analysis of the literature, in the following section we present the methodology and the analysis of the main variables that might have an impact on fiscal awareness and the relationships between them.

3. METHODOLOGY

Most empirical studies have used laboratory experiments or survey methodology to examine the factors mentioned in the theoretical framework. Even though these methods have some disadvantages, surveys allow researchers to investigate a wide range of variables. We selected the survey data approach, using a sample of Spanish university students. The selection of a student sample has another advantage: some socioeconomic and demographic factors, like age and education, do not need to be considered. Acording to some authors, the use of students could bias the results, as the participants show higher levels of education attainment and intelligence quotient than average (Frey and Torgler 2007). Additionally, university students usually belong to well-off families and their age bracket is more limited (Fehr, Fishbacher & Gächter 2002). Nevertheless, Alm, Bloomquist & Mckee (2015) find that the behavioural patterns of subjects in the laboratory conform to those of individuals making a similar decision in naturally occurring settings. We also find that the behavioural responses of students are largely the same as those of nonstudents in identical experiments even if the experiment is about tax evasion.

We conducted a survey addressed to university students on their opinions on tax fraud, tax fairness, solidarity, honesty, corruption, political ideology and tax education, among others. Specifically, the survey used for this analysis is an adaptation of the survey developed and used by the Fiscal Observatory of the University of Murcia since 2006, FOSUM. This Observatory has been conducting annual surveys on tax attitudes and behaviour since 2006, both nationally, regionally and academically, and several studies have been published based on these surveys (Alarcón et al., 2012; 2021; 2022). We have used microdata from a questionnaire carried out by means of a discretionary or judgmental sample completed -anonymously- between the academic years 2010/2011 by a total of 562 young students of the Spanish Tax System course at the Faculty of Economics and Business of the University of Murcia. It was anonymous and confidential and filled on line. All the survey items used in this study are explained in following sections.

Firstly, the variables that might have an impact on tax morale and the relationships between them were analysed. Secondly, a multiple regression model was applied to identify the explanatory variables affecting tax morale. The econometric model explains the behaviour of the dependent variable based on a series of independent variables and a perturbation term. The dependent variable (tax morale) in our model is qualitative or categorical. It takes two values: 0 in the presence of the variable and 1 in its absence. Given the inconsistency of a linear regression model in these cases, we chose a binary logistic regression model, by using a logistic function in the model estimation. The model implementation and the analysis of results are explained in next section.

4. ANALYSIS OF RESULTS

4.1. Analysis of Fiscal Awareness Through the Survey Items

We are working at this chapter from the fiscal awareness concept rather than from tax morale or fiscal ethic. When addressing the concept of fiscal awareness, we need, first, to highlight its close relation to fiscal ethics and tax morale. The three terms: fiscal ethics, tax morale and fiscal awareness, have traditionally been used to refer to the same concept. All three have been applied to the set of attitudes and behaviors of the taxpayer when complying with the tax authorities. Yet there are shades of meaning which need to be gone into.

Morale can be defined as having to do with human actions as regards their goodness, while ethics deals with moral and human obligations. Awareness is a wider concept, covering reflexive knowledge. When applied to the field of tax, tax morale refers to the actions of the taxpayer as regards the Inland Revenue. The human obligations dealt with by ethics are those which have to do with complying with the tax authorities. The reflexive knowledge which is alluded to under the term awareness would imply knowledge of both revenue and expense within the tax world, from a perspective of correct fiscal compliance. Professor Tipke (2002) defines tax ethics as the theory which studies the morality of actions in tax matters performed by public, legislative, executive and legal powers, as well as by the taxpaying citizen. Higuera Udías (1982) uses the terms fiscal ethics and fiscal moral indistinctively and Rodríguez Duplá (2001) identifies ethics with moral philosophy. Álvarez García and Herrera Molina (2004) focus on the term fiscal ethics, which is addressed from various angles: ethics of the Administration; ethics of the legislator; ethics of the taxpayer; ethics of judges and even ethics of the tax consultant.

Most empirical papers on tax morale carried out up to 2003, regarded tax morale as an exogenous variable. From that moment on, tax morale started to be used as an endogenous variable because it was relevant to determine compliance levels (Torgler & Murphy 2004). Several items from different surveys, such as the European Values Survey or the World Values Survey, have been used to measure tax morale. The most used item in previous research has been *Tell whether you think it can always be justified (10), never be justified (1), or something in between: ... cheating on tax if you have a chance* (Torgler 2003d 2012; Alm & Torgler 2006; Alm et al 2006; Martínez-Vázquez & Torgler 2009; Torgler & Schneider 2009; Lago-Peñas & Lago-Peñas 2010). Some authors considered that the *(un)willingness to cheat* is the variable for measuring tax morale, which has not been exempt from criticism (Alm et al 2006; Torgler 2004; Frey & Torgler 2007; Martínez-Vázquez & Torgler 2009).

Tolerance towards tax evasion is the most obvious consequence of low levels of tax awareness, which is why it has been traditionally used to measure tax morale. Following these studies, we used one item on the justification of tax fraud. Nevertheless, we consider that using a single-item measurement is insufficient. We agree with Alm & Torgler (2006) and Torgler (2012) that tax morale is a multidimensional concept that requires a multi-item measurement tool. Using a single variable in this context is disadvantageous compared to multi-item indexes (Lewis 1982; Jackson & Milliron 1986). For instance, a single-item measurement may hamper the adequate assessment of some aspects, as well as being adversely affected by random errors. Additionally, a multi-item index has the advantage that errors tend to average, which results in more reliability. Compared to a single-item measurement, a multi-item probability index is also more reliable because the common information is collected. A multi-item tool also increases validity and accuracy, providing a more representative sample and reducing the variability of data (Torgler et al 2010). Consequently, this paper also examines the relationships between individual values and tax morale, introducing a new variable for the gap between the public good and the individual interest.

Fiscal awareness means the prioritization of the public good, which is a legal asset that must be ensured more than the individual interest. This concept has been used in other studies (Alarcón-García, De Pablos & Garre 2009; Alarcón-García, Beyaert & De Pablos 2012; Alarcón-García & Ayala 2013). And it is directly related to the fact that tax fraud is considered a misdemeanour (Song & Yarbrough 1978; Vogel 1974), which hinders voluntary compliance (Kirchler 1998). That is why we introduced the following item as a proxy variable in the assessment of Fiscal awareness: *Which of these two actions do you consider more reprehensible: somebody failing to pay €6,000 to the Treasury or you being stolen*

€100?. This is an indirect question where individuals had to choose between social benefit and the protection of their personal assets. In doing it, respondents revealed their ethical priorities and the extent to which they realized that failing to pay the Treasury is stealing from the public good. Our variable assesses the level of awareness based on the value taxpayers assign to public revenues and household income. This allowed us to find out whether the individual was self-interested or had internalized that taxation is important for us all, and if they knew that a particular theft only affects one citizen and tax cheating affects us all.

The following items were used: a) the item on the justification of tax fraud, selecting the individuals who thought tax noncompliance is not justified (59.1 per cent); and b) the item related to the most reprehensible action, selecting, among those individuals who did not justify tax fraud, those who thought tax evasion is more reprehensible. In total, 21.4 per cent did not justify tax evasion and thought tax cheating is the most reprehensible action.

4.2. Analysis of the Explanatory Variables

This section analyses the main explanatory or independent variables included in the econometric model developed in next section. Other studies are mentioned and the results of each one of these variables and their relationship to tax morale are explained.

This study focuses on a specific, homogeneous population sample: university students. This homogeneity in the sample selection has the advantage that some socioeconomic and demographic factors do not need to be considered: age, being between 20 and 25 years old; economic background, as most of them receive no income; or educational attainment, for they are all university students. Nevertheless, we do consider some other aspects like parental income, given the significant impact of economic variables on tax morale, as proved by Alm, Jackson & McKee (1992), who found a positive relationship, although a negative relationship was pointed out by Slemrod (1985) and Ali et al (2001).

As to the remaining variables, we highlighted those that are directly related to individual values, such as solidarity, honesty, tax fairness, political ideology and tax education.

As for political ideology, Prieto et al. (2006) showed how political ideas influence fiscal morale. Marcelo (2011) carried out a thorough study on ideology, beliefs and tax morale, where the relationships between tax fraud and political leanings were explained. The relationship between political power and citizenship is one of the factors that most affect voluntary tax compliance. Wahlund (1992) studied the factors that affected individual tax compliance and found that Swedish taxpayers who supported conservative parties were more prone to evasion than other voters.

In this survey, students were asked about the political leaning they were most identified with (left or right). And there was a third option for those who were not interested in politics. 35.4 per cent of total respondents showed a right-wing ideology, 31.5 per cent a left-wing leaning, and the rest answered they were not interested in politics. The influence of political ideology is thoroughly examined, aiming to ascertain whether Spanish students with liberal or left-wing ideological beliefs would show a higher level of tax morale than those with a conservative or right-wing ideology. Firstly, we conducted the analysis of the variable by implementing it in the model as a value taking two values: 1 if the respondent chose a right-wing ideology and 0 if they chose left-wing leaning or show no interest in politics. And secondly, the variable takes value 1 if the respondent chose a left-wing ideology and 0 if they chose right-wing leaning or show no interest in politics. Of the tax-aware students, 72.1 per cent chose a left-wing leaning or showed no interest in politics and only 27.9 per cent were more identified with a right-wing ideology.

The variables solidarity and honesty are individual values and should be regarded as key intrinsic values of fiscal awareness. There are few previous studies analysing their influence on tax morale. Porcano supported that honesty was a personal value (Porcano 1988) and Erard & Feinstein (2004) used it to bridge the gap between the economic literature and the psychological and sociological literature on tax compliance. Molero & Pujol (2012) underlined that these variables have a positive impact on tax morale, even though other variables (e.g., the perception of others' tax cheating and the quality of social services) have a greater impact. Torgler (2003a) examines lack of honesty and affirms that it is a key aspect to higher levels of tax noncompliance.

On the other hand, honesty is measured by the following item: *Imagine you found a wallet with €1,000 and the owner's ID in it. Which of these actions is more in keeping with what you would do? 1) Return the wallet and the money (you give it back personally, take it to the police station, mail it...); 2) You don't return it and keep everything for yourself, or 3) You keep the money and return the wallet and ID (you take it to the police station, mail it, etc.).* The share of honest students who chose option 1) is 82.4 per cent.

Solidarity is also assessed by the item on willingness to donate to NGOs. The item was: *Would you be prepared to contribute to an NGO by giving money?* Results show that 32.5 per cent of students were willing to collaborate with NGOs, and 40.5 per cent of tax-aware respondents showed solidarity.

Another key determinant of tax compliance is justice. A number of studies proved the strong relationship between perceived tax fairness and tax compliance. Taxpayers' perception of justice determines voluntary compliance (Andreoni et al 1998; Kirchler 2007), and they use perceived unfairness as a way for justifying noncompliance (Falkinger 1988).

Likewise, perceived tax fairness can be regarded either as the balanced relationship between taxes paid and services enjoyed, or as the perceived justice in the procedures and reactions to noncompliance (Hofmann et al 2008). It may also be classified as distributive, procedural and retributive justice (Wenzel 2006). The concept of tax fairness used throughout this work is the general fairness of the tax system. Perceived tax fairness is assessed by the following item: *Do you consider taxes in your country fair?* Out of the total of participants, 57 per cent considered taxes unfair.

As for the demographic variables, the literature largely shows that gender influences tax morale. In most cases, it was reported that women are more likely to comply with taxation (Torgler & Valev, 2006). Some psychological research suggested that women are more compliant than men (Tittle 1980). Andreoni & Vesterlund (2001), along with Eckel and Grossman (2001) provided empirical research supporting that gender has an impact on charitable giving. Torgler (2003c) and Martínez-Vázquez & Torgler (2009) also found higher levels of tax morale and compliance in women in most cases. Still other analyses showed that Spanish women are more tolerant of tax noncompliance than men, except for women in higher income brackets (Alarcón-García, Beyaert & De Pablos 2012).

Although results show higher levels of tax morale in women than men (62.1 per cent of tax-aware students were women), the econometric analysis conducted in this paper did not find a relationship between gender and fiscal awareness.

The relationship between education level and fiscal awareness can be seen from two viewpoints. On the one hand, the higher the level of educational attainment, the greater the likelihood of having a good knowledge of taxes and social goods and services, which may lead to higher levels of tax compliance. On the other hand, according to the literature, the higher the level of educational attainment the greater the amount of information available to commit fraud (Torgler & Schneider 2005). Likewise, tax-related attitudes mainly depend on the perceived use of the revenues collected, which is another aspect related to tax knowledge (Kirchler et al 2008).

Focusing on a population with a similar education level, this paper intends to determine the extent of tax education received by the students. The objective is to find out if they have ever taken a specific taxation-related course or received any tax training or civic education, which has been recently implemented in most of the countries under study.

The research was extended to test the hypothesis that there is a positive relationship between tax education and tax morale, as supported by Lewis (1982), Roberts et al. (1994), Spicer & Lundstedt (1976), Kirchler (1998), Tyler (2001), Job & Reinhart (2003), Blumenthal & Christian (2004), and Wenzel (2006).

In our survey, 63.1 per cent of students had not received any tax training, whereas 40.1 per cent of tax-aware students had.

The relationship between income and tax morale has been widely discussed in the literature but the results are not conclusive. Some authors (Slemrod 1985; Ali, Cecil et al 2001) found a negative relationship between income and tax morale; others reported a positive one (Alm et al 1992); and Feinstein (1991) saw no connection.

The variable of parental income was considered in our survey because most students do not receive any income, therefore they were asked about their monthly household income.

Once the explanatory variables have been identified and described, in next section, we proceed with the formulation and estimation of the regression model employed to empirically assess the influence of these variables on fiscal awareness.

4.3. Econometric Estimation: Logistic Regression Model

A multiple regression model was used to identify the variables influencing fiscal awareness. This enabled us to explain the behaviour of a dependent variable Y based on a series of independent variables and a perturbation term u.

$$Y = f(\beta_1 + \beta_2 X_2 + \beta_3 X_3 \ldots\ldots + \beta_k X_k) + u$$

The dependent variable Y is fiscal awareness. It is a qualitative or categorical binary variable that takes two values: 1 in the presence of the variable and 0 in its absence. The independent variables (solidarity, honesty, tax fairness, perceived level of corruption, gender, parental income, political ideology) included in the model by vector Xi were selected after the analysis described in the previous section.

The models containing qualitative endogenous variables are also known as discrete choice models. Given the inconsistency of linear regression models in these cases, a generalization of the linear probability model is developed, where f is the function used in the model estimation.

By employing a Logit model where function f is the logistic function:

$$f(x) = \frac{\exp(x)}{1 + \exp(x)}$$

In probability terms:

$$E[Y] = P(Y=1) = f(\beta_1 + \beta_2 X_2 + \beta_3 X_3 \ldots\ldots + \beta_k X_k)$$

Therefore, in the Logit model:

$$E[Y] = P(Y=1) = \frac{\exp(\beta_1 + \beta_2 X_2 + \beta_3 X_3 \ldots\ldots + \beta_k X_k)}{1 + \exp(\beta_1 + \beta_2 X_2 + \beta_3 X_3 \ldots\ldots + \beta_k X_k)}$$

These nonlinear models do not permit to directly interpret the estimations of the parameters β. However, if their sign is positive, the increases in the associated variable cause increases in the probability P(Y = 1). On the contrary, if the sign is negative, an increase in the variable causes a decrease in the probability of the dependent variable being 1.

Table 1 and table 2 show the results of the binary logistic regression model following a Logit model that represents the highest R squared. Both tables show the coefficients, their standard errors, the Wald test statistic with p-values, and the exponential coefficient (also known as odds ratio).

Table 1. Logistic Regression Results (including Right-Wing Ideology)

	B	Std. Error	Wald	Sig.	Odds Ratio
Gender (Female)	0.182	0.207	0.776	0.378	1.200
Family income	-0.204	0.196	1.078	0.299	0.816
Solidarity	0.109	0.197	0.303	0.582	1.115
Tax Fairness	0.632	0.195	10.462	0.001	1.881
Corruption	-0.025	0.247	0.010	0.920	0.976
Honesty	0.630	0.222	8.056	0.005	1.878
Tax Education	0.173	0.242	0.509	0.476	1.188
Right- Wing Ideology	-0.388	0.209	3.456	0.063	0.679
Constant	-1.544	0.346	19.869	0.000	0.213

Source: Own elaboration

Table 2. Logistic Regression Results (Including Left-Wing Ideology)

	B	Std. Error	Wald	Sig.	Odds Ratio
Gender (Female)	0.245	0.207	1.402	0.236	1.277
Family income	-0.238	0.195	1.484	0.223	0.788
Solidarity	0.068	0.198	0.120	0.730	1.071
Tax Fairness	0.609	0.197	9.582	0.002	1.839
Corruption	-0.019	0.247	0.006	0.938	0.981
Honesty	0.646	0.222	8.439	0.004	1.908
Tax Education	0.404	0.204	3,924	0.048	1.498
Right- Wing Ideology	0.166	0.242	0.473	0.492	1.181
Constant	-1.814	0.350	26.822	0.000	0.163

Source: Own elaboration

Table 1 includes the analysis of the variable political ideology by implementing it in the model as a value taking two values: 1 if the respondent chose a right-wing ideology and 0 if they chose left-wing leaning or show no interest in politics. In table 2 the variable takes value 1 if the respondent chose a left-wing ideology and 0 if they chose right-wing leaning or show no interest in politics.

At a five per cent significance level, the variables of honesty and tax fairness are significant with the positive sign of the parameter, which implies a positive relationship with the dependent variable. Tax fairness holds the highest level of statistical significance in determining tax awareness.

All of them show an odds-ratio higher than 1, which indicates that an increase in the variable raises the likelihood of fiscal awareness. Political ideology also influences fiscal awareness, but the sign of the parameter is negative in table 1 which leads to a lower likelihood of fiscal awareness in students with a right-wing political ideology. In table 2 the sign is positive which means higher likelihood of tax awareness in students with a left-wing political ideology.

On the other hand, the signs are the expected ones in the analysis of the parameter estimation. There is a positive sign in variables like solidarity, honesty, gender (female), perceived tax fairness and tax education, which means a positive impact on higher levels of fiscal awareness. Nevertheless, there is a negative sign in the following variables: perceived corruption, family income, and political ideology (right-wing leaning), indicating a lower probability of tax awareness, although only the latter is significant in the regression analysis, but at a 10 per cent significance level.

The results obtained offer significant insights, which are further examined in the concluding section, where we synthesize key contributions and suggest directions for future studies.

5. DISCUSSION

Results show that values such as honesty and tax fairness influence the probability of higher levels of fiscal awareness in Spanish university students. In this work, honesty, fair taxation and political ideology prevail over other factors like tax education when explaining high levels of fiscal awareness. In this respect, our sample is made up by students with some tax training, which is why this is not a determining factor and shows no significance in relation with fiscal awareness. However, other studies with general population samples did obtain a positive correlation (Lewis, 1982; Roberts et al., 1994; Spicer & Lundstedt, 1976; Kirchler, 1998; Tyler, 2001; Job & Reinhart, 2003; Blumenthal & Christian, 2004; and Wenzel, 2006).

As pointed out in previous research (Wahlund, 1992; Prieto et al. (2006), Marcelo Leonardo, 2011, Lozza et al. 2013), political ideology proved significant and lower probability of fiscal awareness occurs in right-leaning individuals. The results indicate that a conservative political ideology is associated with lower fiscal awareness, which may be linked to skepticism toward government intervention and a stronger emphasis on individual economic freedom. In contrast, those with left-leaning ideologies tend to exhibit higher fiscal awareness, likely due to a greater acceptance of taxation as a tool for social redistribution.

In the Spanish political context, conservative or right-wing ideologies are traditionally represented by parties such as the *Partido Popular* (PP) and, more recently, *Vox*. These political groups tend to advocate for lower taxes and reduced government intervention, which may influence their supporters' attitudes toward fiscal responsibility. On the other hand, left-wing ideologies, represented by parties like the *Partido Socialista Obrero Español* (PSOE), *Sumar* and *Unidas Podemos*, emphasize social welfare, wealth redistribution, and the importance of progressive taxation to fund public services. This ideological divide can shape perceptions of taxation, with conservative-leaning individuals potentially viewing taxes as an excessive burden, while left-leaning individuals may see them as a necessary tool for social cohesion and economic equality.

The results of our work show that most students identify with a conservative ideology, although it is necessary to highlight the time when the survey was conducted. The dates might be the reason why the right-leaning ideology is the predominant one, as it was then when the economic crisis in Spain was at its peak. The mainstream centre-left party ruling at that moment, *Partido Socialista Obrero Español* (PSOE), lost the 2011 general elections, and the conservative *Partido Popular* (PP) obtained most of the votes. PSOE was rejected by a large part of the population, as it was the ruling party when the crisis worsened, and Spain was on the edge of a bailout. The serious economic crisis had a political cost in Spain as well as in other South European countries (Bosco & Verney 2012).

The high share (33.1%) of students showing no interest in politics is to be underlined. These data match those of the Spanish Centre for Sociological Research (CIS), where the Spanish population's interest in politics is examined: 37.5% of women and 20% of men define themselves as apolitical.

The young people's political stance has been traditionally heterogeneous, but there exists a general trend towards the lack of interest, as they show boredom, irritation or indifference towards politics and distrust in politicians (Megías, 2006). The students of our sample exhibit more political indifference than the rest of the population. This reflects the changes affecting the Spanish young: unemployment rate over 50% and high levels of spreading corruption in the political sphere. The result is the increasing distrust in politicians and a great political indifference, leading to the deterioration of the democracy. Since the Spanish transition from the dictatorship to the democracy under the government of the mainstream centre party Union of the Democratic Centre (UCD), the moderate conservative party (PP) and the socialist party (PSOE) have been alternating the power. The rest of the political options included the following parties: United Left (IU), the nationalist parties mainly from the Basque Country (Basque Nationalist Party) and Catalonia (Convergence and Union, and Republican Left), and the new parties with both centre-right ideology (Union, Progress and Democracy, and Citizens) and left-leaning ideology (Podemos). The new parties were founded in the last decade and some of them received enormous citizen support, due to the general disappointment caused by the corruption, the economic crisis and the need for a political regeneration.

6. CONCLUSIONS

The review of literature shows that voluntary tax compliance is shaped by psychosocial and ethical aspects, such as conditional cooperation, and by institutional and cultural factors, such as the tolerance for tax fraud, and using fiscal awareness as an endogenous variable. However, this study examines the values influencing fiscal awareness, considering it as an exogenous variable of voluntary compliance and as a factor that is independent from the attitude towards fiscal fraud.

Results highlight that, of the total number of tax-conscious students, 62.4 per cent were women, 33.9 per cent showed solidarity, and 47.9 per cent thought taxation is fair. On the other hand, 80.6 per cent perceived high levels of corruption, and 92.5 per cent thought fight against fraud is barely effective. Moreover, 77.6 per cent showed honesty, and 27.9 per cent chose a right-wing political leaning. Results pointed out that honesty and tax fairness are key determinants in the likelihood of students showing higher levels of fiscal awareness. Likewise, political ideology proved significant but with a negative sign in the coefficient, which indicates a lower probability of fiscal awareness in right-leaning individuals. Regarding the gender variable, although results show higher levels of tax morale in women than men (62.1 per cent of tax-aware students were women), the econometric analysis conducted in this paper did not find a relationship between gender and fiscal awareness.

In summary, results show that young university students are very concerned about the fight against fraud and perceive high levels of corruption in Spain. In addition, students show high levels of solidarity and honesty which leads to high fiscal awareness rates in this group, even though the survey was conducted at the peak of the economic crisis. Regarding key determinants, honesty and tax fairness proved significant variables in the likelihood of high fiscal awareness rate. Political ideology also influences fiscal awareness, furthermore, results showed that a conservative political ideology involves lower probability of fiscal awareness. In this paper, honesty, fair taxation and political ideology prevail over other factors like tax education when explaining high levels of fiscal awareness.

The econometric analysis conducted in this study demonstrates that the variable tax fairness holds the highest level of statistical significance in determining tax awareness. When citizens perceive the tax system as fair, they are more likely to comply voluntarily, contributing to greater tax revenue and more sustainable public finances. Consequently, it is essential for governments to design and implement fair fiscal systems that foster trust and a sense of equity among taxpayers. By enhancing the perception of fiscal justice, policymakers can improve tax compliance.

These insights have important implications for policymakers and educators aiming to improve tax morale and compliance. First, tax education programs should not only focus on technical knowledge—such as how the tax system functions—but also incorporate ethical and civic dimensions that emphasize the role of taxation in maintaining public goods and social equity. Programs could include discussions on tax fairness, social responsibility, and the long-term consequences of tax evasion to reinforce the moral obligation of tax compliance. Second, policymakers should consider how ideological perceptions shape attitudes toward taxation. Public communication campaigns designed to enhance tax morale should address ideological skepticism directly, highlighting the tangible benefits of taxation in ways that resonate with different political perspectives.

Despite these compelling findings, this study has certain limitations that must be acknowledged. The analysis is based on a sample of university students in Spain, which restricts the generalizability of the conclusions. University students may have different attitudes toward taxation compared to the general population due to factors such as lower income levels, exposure to academic discussions on political and economic issues, and limited direct experience with tax obligations. Although the results are biased by the limitations of an all-undergraduate sample, the main conclusions drawn are consistent with previous research in other countries (Wahlund, 1992; Prieto et al. (2006), Marcelo Leonardo, 2011, Lozza et al. 2013). Nevertheless, future research will expand the sample to include a more diverse demographic representation, both within Spain and in other countries, to examine whether these patterns hold across different socio-economic and cultural contexts. This would provide a more comprehensive understanding of the relationship between political ideology and fiscal awareness in a broader global framework.

REFERENCES

Alarcón, G., Mayor, J. M., & Ayala, E. A. (2021). La participación ciudadana y el pago voluntario de los impuestos. *Obets*, *16*(2), 227–244. DOI: 10.14198/OBETS2021.16.2.01

Alarcón, G., Mayor, J. M., & Quintanilla, C. M. (2022). Conciencia fiscal y presupuestos participativos: Un estudio exploratorio. *Revista Española de Investigaciones Sociológicas*, *177*(177), 69–88. DOI: 10.5477/cis/reis.177.69

Alarcón, G., & Tipke, K. (2007). La Conciencia Fiscal. In Serrano, F. (Ed.), *La Conciencia Fiscal y el Marketing Tributario en las Haciendas Locales* (pp. 45–66). Editorial Civitas.

Alarcón-García, G., & Ayala, E. (2013). Trust in Spanish Governments: Antecedents and Consequences. *Economic Analysis and Policy. Australian Economic Association*, *43*(2), 135–152.

Alarcón-García, G., & Ayala, E. A. (2013). Trust in Spanish Governments: Antecedents and Consequences. *Economic Analysis and Policy*, *43*(2), 177–193. DOI: 10.1016/S0313-5926(13)50017-8

Alarcón-García, G., Beyaert, A., & De Pablos, L. (2012). Fiscal awareness: a study of female versus male attitudes towards tax fraud in Spain. In Pickhardt, M., & Prinz, A. (Eds.), *Tax Evasion and the Shadow Economy* (pp. 61–86). Edward Elgar. DOI: 10.4337/9781781006740.00012

Alarcón-García, G., Dc Pablos, L., & Garre, E. (2009). Análisis del comportamiento de los individuos ante el fraude fiscal. Resultados obtenidos a partir de la Encuesta del Observatorio Fiscal de la Universidad de Murcia. *Revista Principios*, *13*, 55–84.

Ali, M. M., Cecil, H. W., & Knoblett, J. A. (2001). The Effects of Tax Rates and Enforcement Policies on Taxpayer Compliance: A Study of Sclf-Employcd Taxpayers. *Atlantic Economic Journal*, *29*(2), 186–202. DOI: 10.1007/BF02299137

Allingham, M., & Sandmo, A. (1972). Income tax evasion: A theoretical analysis. *Journal of Public Economics*, *1*(3-4), 323–338. DOI: 10.1016/0047-2727(72)90010-2

Alm, J., Bloomquist, K., & Mckee, M. (2015). On the external validity of laboratory tax compliance experiments?*Economic Inquiry*, *53*(2), 1170–1186. DOI: 10.1111/ecin.12196

Alm, J., Jackson, B., & Mckee, M. (1992). Estimating the determinants of taxpayer compliance with experimental data. *National Tax Journal*, *45*(1), 107–114. DOI: 10.1086/NTJ41788949

Alm, J., & Malézieux, A. (2021). 40 years of tax evasion games: A meta-analysis. *Experimental Economics*, *2021*(24), 699–750. DOI: 10.1007/s10683-020-09679-3

Alm, J., Martínez-Vázquez, J., & Torgler, B. (2006). Russian attitudes toward paying taxes before, during, and after the transition. *International Journal of Social Economics*, *33*(12), 832–857. DOI: 10.1108/03068290610714670

Alm, J., McClelland, G. H., & Schulze, W. D. (1992). Why do people pay taxes? *Journal of Public Economics*, *48*(1), 21–48. DOI: 10.1016/0047-2727(92)90040-M

Alm, J., McClelland, G. H., & Schulze, W. D. (1999). Changing the social norm of tax compliance by voting. *Kyklos*, *48*(2), 141–171. DOI: 10.1111/j.1467-6435.1999.tb01440.x

Alm, J., & Torgler, B. (2006). Culture differences and tax morale in the United States and in Europe. *Journal of Economic Psychology*, *27*(2), 224–246. DOI: 10.1016/j.joep.2005.09.002

Álvarez García, S., & Herrera Molina, P. M. (2004). *Ética Fiscal, Documentos de trabajo del Instituto de Estudios Fiscales, nº 10*. Ministerio de Economía y Hacienda.

Andreoni, J., Erard, B., & Feinstein, J. (1998). Tax Compliance. *Journal of Economic Literature*, *36*, 818–860.

Andreoni, J., & Vesterlund, L. (2001). Which Is the Fair Sex? Gender Differences in Altruism. *The Quarterly Journal of Economics*, *116*(1), 293–31. DOI: 10.1162/003355301556419

Antequera, G., & Florensa, M. (2008). Determinantes de la Moral Tributaria en la Provincia de Buenos Aires. *Serie Anales de La Asociación de Economía Política*, (Noviembre), 1–15.

Aquino, M. Á. (2008). *La evasión fiscal: Origen y medidas de acción para combatirla*. Instituto de Estudios Fiscales. DOC. N.º 13/08. Madrid.

Arias, R. J. (2008). Comentarios sobre "Determinantes de la Moral Tributaria en la Provincia de Buenos Aires", de Germán Antequera y Marcelo Florensa. *Serie Anales de La Asociación de Economía Política*, (Noviembre), 16–20.

Ashby, J., & Webley, P. (2010). The existence of distinct occupational taxpaying cultures in Australia. *Australian Tax Forum*, 25(1), 29–55.

Barone, G., & Mocetti, S. (2011). With a little help from abroad: The effect of lowskilled immigration on the female labour supply. *Labour Economics*, *18*(5), 664–675. DOI: 10.1016/j.labeco.2011.01.010

Becker, G. (1968). Crime and punishment: An economic approach. *Journal of Political Economy*, *76*(2), 169–217. DOI: 10.1086/259394

Bedoya, A., & Vásconez, B. (2010). Entendiendo la Moral Tributaria en Ecuador. *Fiscalidad.Revista Institucional Del Servicio de Rentas Internas*, *5*, 91–132.

Beuermann, D. W., & Amelina, M. (2014). Does Participatory Budgeting Improve Decentralized Public Service Delivery? *Inter-American Development Bank Working Paper Series* No. IDB-WP-547.

Biderman, C., & Da Silva, G. P. (2007). *Estimating the Impact of Participatory Budget on Observed Outcomes. Comunicación presentada en el 35 Encontro Nacional de Economia*. Recif.

Blumenthal, M., & Christian, C. (2004). Tax preparers. In Aaron, H. H., & Selmrod, J. (Eds.), *The crisis in tax administration* (pp. 201–299). Brookings Institution Press.

Bohnet, I. (2007). Why Women and Men Trust Others. In B. S. Frey y A. Stutzer (Eds.), *Economics and psychology: A promising new cross-disciplinary field*. London: CESifo Seminar Series. DOI: 10.7551/mitpress/2604.003.0008

Bosco, A., & Verney, S. (2012). Electoral Epidemic: The Political Cost of Economic Crisis in Southern Europe 2010-11. *South European Society & Politics*, *17*(2), 129–154. DOI: 10.1080/13608746.2012.747272

Bourdieu, P. (2001). El capital social. Apuntes provisionales. *Zona Abierta*, (94/95), 83–87.

Brehm, J. & Rahn, W. (1997). Individual-Level Evidence for the Causes and Consequences of Social Capital. *American Journal o f Political Science, 41*(3), 999–1023.

Brink, W. D., & Porcano, T. M. (2016). The Impact of Culture and Economic Structure on Tax Morale and Tax Evasion: A Country-Level Analysis Using SEM. In J. Hasseldine (Ed.), *Advances in Taxation (Advances in Taxation, Volume 23)* (pp. 87–123). Emerald Group Publishing Limited. DOI: 10.1108/S1058-749720160000023004

Brizi, A., Giacomantonio, M., Schumpe, B. M., & Mannetti, L. (2015). Intention to pay taxes or to avoid them: The impact of social value orientation. *Journal of Economic Psychology*, *50*, 22–31. DOI: 10.1016/j.joep.2015.06.005

Cabannes, Y. (2015). The impact of participatory budgeting on basic services: Municipal practices and evidence from the field. *Environment and Urbanization*, *27*(1), 257–284. DOI: 10.1177/0956247815572297

Castañeda, V. M. (2015). La moral tributaria en América Latina y la corrupción como uno de sus determinantes. *Revista Mexicana de Ciencias Politicas y Sociales*, *60*(224), 103–132. DOI: 10.1016/S0185-1918(15)30005-2

Chan, H. F., Supriyadi, M. W., & Torgler, B. (2017). Trust and tax morale. In Eric M. Uslaner (ed.). *The Oxford Handbook of Social and Political Trust*. Oxford Handbooks online Oxford Academic. DOI: 10.1093/oxfordhb/9780190274801.013.23

Ciziceno, M., & Pizzuto, P. (2022). Life satisfaction and tax morale: The role of trust in government and cultural orientation. *Journal of Behavioral and Experimental Economics*, *97*, 101824. DOI: 10.1016/j.socec.2021.101824

Clotfelter (1983) .Tax Evasion and Tax Rate: An Analysis of Individual Return. *The Review of Economic and Statistics*, 65 (3), 363-373.

De Juan, A., & Truyols, M. A. (1993). Predisposición, habilidad y oportunidad de los contribuyentes hacia el fraude fiscal. *Cuadernos de Actualidad*, (1), 27–36.

De Miguel, I., & De Miguel, A. (2001). *Los españoles y los impuestos*. Centro de Investigaciones Sociológicas.

Delgado, M. L., Fernández-Cuartero, M., Maldonado, A., Roldán, C., & Valdenebro, M. L. (2005). *La Educación Fiscal en España*. Instituto de Estudios Fiscales. DOC. N.º 29/05. Madrid.

Dulleck, U., Fooken, J., Newton, C., Ristl, A., Schaffner, M., & Torgler, B. (2016). Tax Compliance and Psychic Costs: Behavioral Experimental Evidence Using a Physiological Marker. *Journal of Public Economics*, *134*, 9–18. DOI: 10.1016/j.jpubeco.2015.12.007

Eckel, C. C., & Grossman, P. J. (2001). Chivalry and Solidarity in Ultimatum Games. *Economic Inquiry*, *39*(2), 171–188. DOI: 10.1111/j.1465-7295.2001.tb00059.x

Elster, J. (1991). *El cemento de la sociedad. Las paradojas del orden social*. Gedisa Editorial.

Erard, B., & Feinstein, J. S. (1994). Honesty and evasion in the tax compliance game. *The RAND Journal of Economics*, *25*(1), 1–19. DOI: 10.2307/2555850

Falkinger, J. (1988). Tax Evasion and Equity: A Theoretical Analysis. *Public Finance*, *43*, 388–395.

Fehr, E., Fischbacher, U., & Gächter, S. (2002). Strong reciprocity, human cooperation and the Enforcement of Social Norms. *Human Nature (Hawthorne, N.Y.)*, *13*(1), 1–25. DOI: 10.1007/s12110-002-1012-7 PMID: 26192593

Feingold, A. (1983). Happiness, unselfishness, and popularity. *The Journal of Psychology*, *115*(1), 3–5. DOI: 10.1080/00223980.1983.9923590

Feinstein, J. S. (1991). An econometric analysis of income tax evasion and its detection. *The RAND Journal of Economics*, *22*(1), 22–50. DOI: 10.2307/2601005

Feld, L., & Tyran, J. R. (2002). Tax evasion and voting: An experimental analysis. *Kyklos*, *55*(2), 197–222. DOI: 10.1111/1467-6435.00183

Feld, L. P., & Frey, B. S. (2002). Trust breeds trust: How taxpayers are treated. *Economics of Governance*, *3*(2), 87–99. DOI: 10.1007/s101010100032

Feld, L. P., & Frey, B. S. (2007). Tax Compliance as the Result of a Psychological Tax Contract: The Role of Incentives and Responsive Regulation. *Law & Policy*, *29*(1), 102–120. DOI: 10.1111/j.1467-9930.2007.00248.x

Feld, L. P., & Kirchgässner, G. (2000). Direct Democracy, Political Culture, and the Outcome of Economic Policy: A Report on the Swiss Experience. *European Journal of Political Economy*, *16*(2), 287–306. DOI: 10.1016/S0176-2680(00)00003-3

Fernández, J. J. (2006). *Sociología de la Hacienda Pública*. Ministerio de Economía y Hacienda. Instituto de Estudios Fiscales.

Frey, B., & Meier, S. (2004). Social comparisons and pro-social behaviour. Testing conditional cooperation in a field experiment. *The American Economic Review*, *94*(5), 1717–1722. DOI: 10.1257/0002828043052187

Frey, B., & Torgler, B. (2007). Tax Morale and Conditional Cooperation. *Journal of Comparative Economics*, *35*(1), 136–159. DOI: 10.1016/j.jce.2006.10.006

Frey, B. S., & Weck-Hanneman, H. (1984). The hidden economy as an unobserved variable. *European Economic Review*, *26*(1-2), 33–53. DOI: 10.1016/0014-2921(84)90020-5

Gächter, S. (2007). Conditional Cooperation: Behavioral Regularities from the Lab and the Field and Their Policy Implications. In B. S. Frey y A. Stutzer (Eds.), *Economics and psychology: A promising new cross-disciplinary field* (pp. 19–50). London: CESifo Seminar Series.

Gangl, K., & Torgler, B. (2020). How to achieve tax compliance by the wealthy: A review of the literature and agenda for policy. *Social Issues and Policy Review*, *14*(1), 108–151. DOI: 10.1111/sipr.12065

García, J. (1975). Crítica popular al sistema tributario español. *Hacienda Pública Española*, (34), 55–99.

Goksu, G. G., & Sahpaz, K. I. (2015). Comparison of Tax Morale of Turkish and Spanish Higher Education Students: The Samples of Sakarya University and the University of Zaragoza. *Procedia: Social and Behavioral Sciences*, *186*, 222–230. DOI: 10.1016/j.sbspro.2015.04.027

Gomà, R., & Font, J. (2001). La democracia local: Un mapa de experiencias participativas. En J. Font (Ed.), *Ciudadanos y decisiones públicas* (pp. 61–91). Barcelona: Editorial Ariel, S.A.

Hammar, H., Jagers, S. C., & Nordblom, K. (2009). Perceived tax evasion and the importance of trust. *Journal of Socio-Economics*, *38*(2), 238–245. DOI: 10.1016/j.socec.2008.07.003

Heldt, T. (2005) Conditional Cooperation in the Field: Cross-Country Skiers? Behaviour in Sweden, unpublished manuscript, Uppsala University.

Herreros, F., & De Francisco, A. (2001). Introducción: El capital social como programa de investigación. *Zona Abierta*, (94/95), 1–46.

Higueras Udía, G. (1982). *Ética fiscal* (Biblioteca de Autores, C., Ed.).

Hoffmann, H., Hoelzl, E., & Kirchler, E. (2008). Preconditions of Voluntary Tax Compliance: Knowledge and Evaluation of Taxation, Norms, Fairness, and Motivation to Cooperate. *Zeitschrift für Psychologie*, *216*(4), 209–217. DOI: 10.1027/0044-3409.216.4.209 PMID: 22428111

Horodnic, I. A. (2018). Tax morale and institutional theory: a systematic review IJSSP 38,9/10 www .emeraldinsight.com/0144-333X.htm

Jackson, B. R., & Milliron, V. C. (1986). Tax compliance research: Findings, problems, and prospects. *Journal of Accounting Literature*, *5*, 125–166.

Jaime-Castillo, A. M., & Sáez-Lozano, J. L. (2016). Preferences for tax schemes in OECD countries, self-interest and ideology. *International Political Science Review*, *37*(1), 81–98. DOI: 10.1177/0192512114539716

Jayawardane, D. (2015). Psychological factors affect tax compliance. A review paper. *International Journal of Arts and Commerce*, *4*(6), 131–141.

Job, J., & Reinhart, M. (2003). Trusting the tax office: Does Putnam.s thesis relate to tax., *Australian Journal of Social Issues*, 38(3), 307-334.

Kaplan, S. E., & Reckers, P. M. J. (1985). A Study of Tax Evasion Judgments. *National Tax Journal*, *38*(1), 97–102. DOI: 10.1086/NTJ41791998

Kastlunger, B., Dressler, S. G., Kirchler, E., Mittone, L., & Voracek, M. (2010). Sex differences in tax compliance: Differentiating between demographic sex, gender-role orientation, and prenatal masculinization (2D:4D). *Journal of Economic Psychology*, *31*(4), 542–552. DOI: 10.1016/j.joep.2010.03.015

Keppler, S., & Nagin, D. (1989). The anatomy of tax evasion. *Journal o f Law. Economics and Organization*, *5*(1), 1–24.

Kirchler, E. (1997). The burden of new taxes: Acceptance of taxes as a function of affectedness and egoistic versus altruistic orientation. *Journal of Socio-Economics*, *26*(4), 421–437. DOI: 10.1016/ S1053-5357(97)90005-6

Kirchler, E. (1998). Differential representations of taxes: Analysis of free associations and judgments of five employment groups. *Journal of Socio-Economics, 27*(1), 117–131. DOI: 10.1016/S1053-5357(99)80080-8

Kirchler, E. (2007). *The Economic Psychology of Tax Behaviour*. Cambridge University Press. DOI: 10.1017/CBO9780511628238

Kirchler, E., Hoelzl, E., & Wahl, I. (2008). Enforced versus voluntary tax compliance: The slippery slope framework. *Journal of Economic Psychology, 29*(2), 210–225. DOI: 10.1016/j.joep.2007.05.004

Kirchler, E., & Wahl, I. (2010). Tax Compliance Inventory: TAX-I Voluntary tax compliance, enforced tax compliance, tax avoidance, and tax evasión. *Journal of Economic Psychology, 31*(3), 331–346. DOI: 10.1016/j.joep.2010.01.002 PMID: 20502612

Konrad, K. A., & Qari, S. (2012). The last refuge of a scoundrel? patriotism and tax compliance. *Economica, 79*(315), 516–533. DOI: 10.1111/j.1468-0335.2011.00900.x

Lagares, M. J. (1991). Fraude fiscal y aceptación social del sistema tributario. *Moneda y Crédito, 192*, 127–162.

Lago-Peñas, I., & Lago-Peñas, S. (2010). The determinants of tax morale in comparative perspective: Evidence from European countries. *European Journal of Political Economy, 26*(4), 441–453. DOI: 10.1016/j.ejpoleco.2010.06.003

Lewis, A. (1982). *The Psychology of Taxation*. Martin Robertson.

López-Luzuriaga, A., & Scartascini, C. (2023) Willing but Unable to Pay? The Role of Gender in Tax Compliance, IDB Working Paper Series; 1330.

Lozza, E., Kastlunger, B., Tagliabue, S., & Kirchler, E. (2013). The relationship between political ideology and attitudes toward tax compliance: The case of Italian taxpayers. *Journal of Social and Political Psychology, 1*(1), 51–73. DOI: 10.5964/jspp.v1i1.108

Marandu, E. E., Mbekomize, C. J., & Ifezue, A. N. (2015). Determinants of tax compliance: A review of factors and conceptualizations. *International Journal of Economics and Finance, 7*(9), 207–218. DOI: 10.5539/ijef.v7n9p207

Marcelo Leonardo, G. (2011). *Politics, and tax morale. The rol of trust, values and beliefs, in shaping individual attitudes towards tax compliance*. Georgia State University.

María-Dolores, R., Alarcón, G., & Garre, M. E. (2010). Tax morale in Spain: A study into some of its principal determinants. *Journal of Economic Issues, 44*(4), 855–876. DOI: 10.2753/JEI0021-3624440401

Martínez-Vázquez, J., & Torgler, B. (2009). The evolution of tax morale in modern Spain. *Journal of Economic Issues, 43*(1), 1–28. DOI: 10.2753/JEI0021-3624430101

Megías E. (2006). El discurso de los jóvenes sobre la política. *Temas para el debate,* 138 (6), 29-32.

Molero, J. C., & Pujol, F. (2012). Walking inside the potential tax evader's mind: Tax morale does matter. *Journal of Business Ethics, 105*(2), 151–162. DOI: 10.1007/s10551-011-0955-1

Murphy, K. (2004). The role of trust in nurturing compliance: A study of accused tax avoiders. *Law and Human Behavior*, *28*(2), 187–209. DOI: 10.1023/B:LAHU.0000022322.94776.ca PMID: 15141778

Newton, K. (1997). Social Capital and Democracy. *The American Behavioral Scientist*, *40*(5), 575–586. DOI: 10.1177/0002764297040005004

Pampel, F., Andrighetto, G., & Steinmo, S. (2019). How institutions and attitudes shape tax compliance: A cross-national experiment and survey. *Social Forces*, *97*(3), 1337–1364. DOI: 10.1093/sf/soy083

Pommerehne, W., & Weck-Hannemann, H. (1996). Tax rates, tax administration and income tax evasion in Switzerland. *Public Choice*, *88*(1-2), 161–170. DOI: 10.1007/BF00130416

Porcano, T. M. (1988). Correlates of tax evasion. *Journal of Economic Psychology*, *9*(1), 47–67. DOI: 10.1016/0167-4870(88)90031-1

Prieto, J., Sanzo, M. J., & Suárez, J. (2006). Análisis económico de la actitud hacia el fraude fiscal en España. *Hacienda Pública Española*, *177*, 107–128.

Putnam, R. D. (2001). La comunidad próspera. El capital social y la vida pública. *Zona Abierta*, (94/95), 89–104.

Putnam, R. D. (2011). *Para que la democracia funcione: las tradiciones cívicas en la Italia moderna*. Centro de Investigaciones Sociológicas.

Richardson, G. (2008). The Relationship between Culture and Tax Evasion across Countries: Additional Evidence and Extensions. *Journal of International Accounting, Auditing & Taxation*, *17*(2), 67–78. DOI: 10.1016/j.intaccaudtax.2008.07.002

Roberts, M. L., Hite, P. A., & Bradley, C. F. (1994). Understanding attitudes toward progressive taxation. *Public Opinion Quarterly*, *58*(2), 165–190. DOI: 10.1086/269417

Rodríguez Duplà, L. (2001). *Ética* (Biblioteca de Autores, C., Ed.).

Schmölders, G. (1960). Survey Research in Public Finance: A Behavioural Approach to Fiscal Theory. *Public Finance*, *25*, 300–306.

Schmölders, G. (1965). Lo Irracional en la Hacienda Pública. In *Problemas de Psicología Financiera* (pp. 3–149). Editorial de Derecho Financiero.

Shang, J., & Croson, R. (2005). *Field experiment in charitable contribution: The impact of social influence on the voluntary provision of public goods*. University of Pennsylvania.

Slemrod, J. B. (1985). An empirical test for tax evasion. *The Review of Economics and Statistics*, *67*(2), 232–267. DOI: 10.2307/1924722

Song, Y., & Yarbrough, T. E. (1978). Tax Ethics and Taxpayer Attitudes: A Survey. *Public Administration Review*, *38*(5), 442–452. DOI: 10.2307/975503

Spicer, M. W., & Lundstedt, S. B. (1976). Understanding tax evasion. *Public Finance*, *31*, 295–305.

Strümpel, B. (1969). The contribution of survey research to public finance. In Peacock, A. T. (Ed.), *Quantitative Analysis in Public Finance* (pp. 14–32). Praeger Publishers.

Tipke, K. (2002). *Moral tributaria del Estado y de los contribuyentes* (Pons, M., Ed.).

Tittle, C. (1980). *Sanctions and Social Deviance: The Question of Deterrence*. Praeger Publishers.

Torgler, B. (2002a). Direct Democracy Matters: Tax Morale and Political Participation. *Proceedings. Annual Conference on Taxation and Minutes of the Annual Meeting of the National Tax Association, 95*, 50–59.

Torgler, B. (2002b). *Preaching Matters: Tax Morale and Religiosity*. WWZ-Discussion Paper 02/03, Basel: WWZ.

Torgler, B. (2002c). Vertical and Exchange Equity in a Tax Morale Experiment. WWZ-Discussion Paper 02/02, Basel: WWZ.

Torgler, B. (2003a). Direct Democracy Matters: Tax Morale and Political Participation. *National Tax Association Papers and Proceedings, 95*, 50–59.

Torgler, B. (2003b). Does culture matter? Tax morale in an east–west German comparison. *Finanz-Archiv, 59*(4), 504–528. DOI: 10.1628/0015221032500856

Torgler, B. (2003c). Tax morale: theory and empirical analysis of tax compliance, PhD Thesis, University of Basel, Faculty of Business and Economics.

Torgler, B. (2003d). To evade taxes or not: That is the question. *Journal of Socio-Economics, 32*(3), 283–302. DOI: 10.1016/S1053-5357(03)00040-4

Torgler, B. (2004). Moral suasion: An alternative tax policy strategy? Evidence from a controlled field experiment in Switzerland. *Economics of Governance, 5*(3), 235–253. DOI: 10.1007/s10101-004-0077-7

Torgler, B. (2005a). Tax morale and direct democracy. *European Journal of Political Economy, 21*(2), 525–531. DOI: 10.1016/j.ejpoleco.2004.08.002

Torgler, B. (2005b). Tax Morale in Latin America. *Public Choice, 122*(1-2), 133–157. DOI: 10.1007/s11127-005-5790-4

Torgler, B., & Murphy, K. (2004). Tax Morale in Australia: What Factors Shape It and Has It Changed Over Time? *Journal of Australian Taxation, 7*, 298–335.

Torgler, B., Schaffner, M., & Macintyre, A. (2010). Tax compliance, tax morale, and governance quality. In Alm, J., Martinez-Vazquez, J., & Torgler, B. (Eds.), *Developing Alternative Frameworks for Explaining Tax Compliance* (pp. 56–73). Routledge.

Torgler, B., & Schneider, F. (2005). Attitudes Towards Paying Taxes in Austria: An Empirical Analysis. *Empirica, 32*(2), 231–250. DOI: 10.1007/s10663-004-8328-y

Torgler, B., & Schneider, F. (2007). Shadow Economy, Tax Morale, Governance and Institutional Quality: A Panel Analysis. QUT School of Economics and Finance Working/Discussion Paper 210, February 2007.

Torgler, B., & Schneider, F. (2009). The Impact of Tax Morale and Institutional Quality on the Shadow Economy. *Journal of Economic Psychology, 30*(2), 228–245. DOI: 10.1016/j.joep.2008.08.004

Torgler, B., & Valev, N. (2006). Women and Illegal Activities: Gender Differences and Women.s Willingness to Comply over Time. *CREMA Working Paper* 15.

Tyler, T. R. (2001). Public trust and confidence in legal authorities: What do majority and minority group members want from the law and legal institutions? *Behavioral Sciences & the Law*, *19*(2), 215–235. DOI: 10.1002/bsl.438 PMID: 11385699

Vera, P., & Grijalva, D. (2014). Motivación Intrínseca y Cooperación Condicional en el Pago de Impuestos: Una perspectiva Experimental. *Fiscalidad.Revista Institucional Del Servicio de Rentas Internas*, *9*, 52–94.

Vogel, J. (1974). Taxation and public opinion in Sweden: An interpretation of recent survey data. *National Tax Journal*, *27*(4), 499–513. DOI: 10.1086/NTJ41861983

Wahlund, R. (1992). Tax changes and economic behavior: The case of tax evasion. *Journal of Economic Psychology*, *13*(4), 657–677. DOI: 10.1016/0167-4870(92)90017-2

Weck, H., Pommerehne, W. W., & Frey, B. S. (1984). *Schattenwirtschaft*. Franz Vahlen.

Wenzel, M. (2006). A letter from the tax office: Compliance effects of informational and interpersonal justice. *Social Justice Research*, *19*(3), 345–364. DOI: 10.1007/s11211-006-0011-y

APPENDIX

Main Questionnaire Items

Q1. What are you studying?
Q2. Is your father or mother originally from a country other than that specified above?
Q3. Sex
Q4. Have you taken any subjects covering taxation as part of your university studies?
Q5. In your opinion, why do we have to pay taxes?
1. So we can all have access to the same public services and the same social benefits
2. To promote the redistribution of wealth and income
3. Because we are obliged by law to pay taxes
Q6. Do you consider the taxes paid in your country to be fair?
Q7. In your opinion, which of these actions is more objectionable?
1. Someone who fails to pay €6,000 to the tax authorities
2. Someone who steals €100 from you
Q16. Using a scale from 1 to 10, state to what extent you agree or disagree with the following statements (1 = totally disagree and 10 = totally agree)
Q16.1 Fraud does not harm anyone and this justifies tax fraud
Q16.2 Too much is paid to the state and this justifies tax fraud
Q16.3 Those who have the most do not pay as much as they should, and this justifies tax fraud by those less fortunate
Q16.4 The existence of unpunished tax evaders encourages fraud by honest people
Q16.5 Tax fraud cannot be justified on any grounds
Q16.6 The public services provided are not worth what is paid and this justifies tax fraud
Q16.7 Tax evasion is closely tied to a lack of honesty and public spirit
Q16.8 Mishandling of public funds by corrupt politicians encourages people to commit fraud
Q17. Do you think the population in your region is tolerant of tax fraud? Rate the level of tolerance from 0 to 10 (0 = not tolerant at all, 10 = entirely tolerant)
Q18. Do you think your family is tolerant of tax fraud? Rate the level of tolerance from 0 to 10 (0 = not tolerant at all, 10 = entirely tolerant)
Q19. Rate the effectiveness of the tax authorities in fighting fraud from 1 to 5, where 1 = not effective at all and 5 = highly effective
Q29. Would you be prepared to contribute to an NGO by giving money?
Q33. Please indicate on a scale of 1 to 10 how far you agree with the following statements (0 = totally disagree and 10 = entirely agree)
Q33.1. In central (state) government, the level of corruption is low
Q33.2. In local (municipal) government, the level of corruption is low
Q33.3. In regional (between central and local) government, the level of corruption is low]

Q34. Please indicate which of the following ideologies you identify most closely with (mark one option only) 1: Left-wing ideology 2: Right-wing ideology 3: I am not interested in politics

Q35. Please indicate on a scale of 1 to 10 how far you agree with the following statements (0 = totally disagree, 10 = entirely agree)

Q35.1. In the region where I live, people tolerate the submerged economy

Q35.2. My family tolerates the submerged economy

Q36. Were you taught Civics as a subject at primary or secondary school?

Q37. In the course of your school or university education were you taught about citizens' duties to contribute to public spending through taxes?

Q37B. Was this included in the core Civics syllabus within the school curriculum?

Q37C. Was it included with other core subjects (social sciences, history, mathematics, etc.)?

Q37D. Was the topic dealt with as an extra-curricular activity or non-curricular education (talks, visits to the tax authorities, fairs, etc.)?

Q37E. Has any teacher of a subject other than taxation ever made any reference to the importance, meaning and scope of taxation at any time during your university studies?

Q43. Please indicate the monthly income of your family unit (approximately)

Chapter 5
The Relationship Between Taxpayers' Perceptions and Attitudes Toward Taxation:
The Mediator and Moderator Effects of Spatial Diversity

Esra Doğan
https://orcid.org/0000-0002-9886-4186
Eskisehir Osmangazi University, Turkey

ABSTRACT

The purpose of this study is to examine the importance of tax mentality and spatial difference elements emphasized within the framework of Schmölders' fiscal psychology theory on an empirical level through Turkish taxpayers residing in European countries. To achieve this objective, field research was conducted in the capitals of Germany, Austria, Belgium, the Netherlands, and France, where Turkish taxpayers predominantly reside. Data were collected through face-to-face interviews with 700 taxpayers residing in these countries and earning personal income. After conducting relevant preliminary tests, the data were analyzed using mediator variable and moderator variable analyses, as well as cross-tabulation analyses, in line with the study's purpose. The findings demonstrated that spatial difference acts as both a mediator and a moderator variable, empirically validating Schmölders' theory.

INTRODUCTION

Considering the proportion of taxes levied on personal income within total tax revenues and especially within GDP, the collection rate of these taxes has become a critical issue for the state budget and the national economy. Indeed, income policies implemented by both OECD countries and others involve regulations and measures at national and international levels aimed at ensuring tax compliance.

DOI: 10.4018/979-8-3373-0422-9.ch005

Parallel to this empirical reality, the scientific literature has expanded its scope to assess the status of tax compliance processes empirically and to provide policy recommendations.

Some of the regulations and measures for tax compliance are directed at the administration, which is one party to the taxation process, while others are targeted at taxpayers, the other party. While the administrative aspects can be regulated by the relevant authorities, the taxpayer-related aspects are relatively less controllable. This is because numerous factors, which could be decisive for tax compliance and are beyond the control of the administration, come into play. This taxpayer-related aspect has, since the 20th century, fostered the development of fields such as fiscal psychology and fiscal sociology in the scientific literature. Within this context, studies examining empirical cases in different samples have enriched the relevant literature based on models developed by various scholars.

This study, within the framework of the relevant literature, conducts an inquiry into the approaches of taxpayers toward taxation, focusing on the context of tax perceptions and attitudes. The study draws on the perspective of Günter Schmölders, a pioneer in the development of fiscal psychology, and one of its three fundamental problematics. Additionally, Schmölders' emphasis on spatial differences, as highlighted in his fiscal psychology approach and presented through the following excerpt (Schmölders, 1959: 341-342), forms the central problematic of this study:

> [...]*The main task of fiscal psychology remains, however, to analyze the direct resistance to direct taxation of individuals and nations according to their general 'tax mentality.' Such tax mentality can be shown to differ widely between different peoples of Europe. Whereas, in the Latin world, the word tax means something felt as an 'imposition' upon the citizens (impôt, imposto, impuesto), the German word, Steuer, means 'support,' and the Scandinavian, skat, the common treasure destined for common purposes. On the basis of such different national tax mentalities, which are closely connected with the citizens' community-mindedness in general, individual tax-mindedness develops by personal experiences. Confronted with the obligation to pay, the taxpayer feels inclined to a certain degree of resistance, leading to evasion, tax-dodging, or even to open revolt, like M. Poujade and his followers in France.*

On the other hand, the empirical focus of this study differentiates itself from examples in the relevant literature by examining Turkish taxpayers residing in European countries (Germany, Austria, Belgium, the Netherlands, and France) and earning personal income. This study aims to contribute to the fiscal psychology literature by empirically analyzing and comparatively examining the perceptions, attitudes, and motivations of these taxpayers toward taxation in the context of spatial differences. Accordingly, the study presents the relevant literature, the empirical analysis sections, and ultimately the evaluation and conclusions in sequence.

THEORETICAL BACKGROUND

The issue of tax compliance is as old as taxation itself. Although tax compliance has long been a subject of concern, scientific studies on the topic date back to the early 20th century. From a historical perspective, studies conducted in the 1940s (Eaton, 1937) focused more on tax compliance costs (Martin, 1944) rather than tax compliance itself. These studies primarily aimed to identify compliance costs (Svanoe, 1944). In the 1950s and 1960s, along with research on compliance costs, studies directly related to tax compliance began to increase. It is believed that the theory of tax compliance began with Becker's (1968) economic model of crime. However, Becker's model left the concept of crime open-ended and did not specifically address tax compliance. Based on Becker's model, the first study to apply this framework to tax compliance was conducted by Allingham and Sandmo (1972), which is considered a pioneering work in tax compliance theory.

Indeed, in the literature, taxpayer-based studies first emerged in the 1960s through the Cologne School of Tax Psychology, established by German scholars. The primary aim of this school was to build a bridge between economics and social psychology, arguing that economic phenomena could not be fully explained by the traditional neoclassical perspective alone. In this context, they treated tax morale as a behavioral pattern related to tax compliance (Alm & Torgler, 2006:228). However, these tax compliance studies primarily focused on differences arising from taxpayers' employment types and tax administrations, limiting their scope to regional comparisons.

Contrary to the Cologne School of Tax Psychology, some studies approached taxpayer behavior through a purely economic perspective, formulating models within a formal economic framework. One of the first of these was the study by Michael Allingham and Agnar Sandmo, titled "Income Tax Evasion: A Theoretical Analysis." The model developed in this study assumes that taxpayer behavior varies depending on variables such as the probability of detection when there is a discrepancy between declared income and actual income, and the magnitude of penalties (Allingham & Sandmo, 1972:324). However, subsequent studies in the literature demonstrated that the Allingham-Sandmo model was insufficient and that tax penalties, which form the model's fundamental assumption, were not effective deterrents for tax compliance (Torgler, 2003).

Furthermore, this model was tested for New Zealand by Norman Gemmell, who replaced the "probability of detection" variable with "the likelihood of implementing delayed tax payments." Unlike the Allingham-Sandmo model, Gemmell's study found that partial rather than complete tax evasion still had an impact on tax compliance (Gemmell, 2016). Although Gemmell improved the Allingham-Sandmo model, his approach remained limited to economic factors.

Taxpayer-based studies have examined the relationship between tax morale and economic constraints in two different contexts: one limited to economic factors and another incorporating non-economic factors. These studies share a common ground in reducing tax morale to tax compliance and taxpayer psychology. However, tax morale, as a social phenomenon, is often analyzed at the individual level through technical methods without questioning its broader societal nature.

This issue was articulated by Lars Feld and Bruno Frey, who stated that "...in many studies, tax morale is treated as a black box without discussion, and without considering how it emerges or persists. It is generally regarded as an unexplained effect within the taxpayer's decision-making process, particularly in empirical studies of tax evasion behavior. The fundamental problem is identifying the factors that lead to the emergence and persistence of tax morale." (Feld & Frey, 2002:3).

Following this perspective, Feld and Frey investigated the impact of political participation rights on tax evasion behavior. They equated high political participation with high tax morale. Their study explained the relationship between political participation and tax morale through the concept of a "psychological contract" between taxpayers and tax authorities. Building upon Feld and Frey's approach, Alm and Torgler (2006) conducted a study examining the impact of cultural factors on tax morale, concluding that tax morale varies across countries with different cultural dynamics (Alm & Torgler, 2006).

As a result, two distinct approaches have emerged in tax compliance theory: the economic approach (rational choice theory) and the psychological approach (theory of moral sentiments). The economic approach attempts to explain tax compliance through quantitative factors such as penalties, audit rates, and tax collection/assessment mechanisms. Meanwhile, the psychological approach, while acknowledging the validity of the economic approach, critiques it for overlooking the role of human psychology and behavior in tax compliance.

LITERATURE REVIEW

When studies on tax perceptions and attitudes in the literature are examined, it is observed that they are generally evaluated within the conceptual framework of tax compliance. Tax compliance is used as an umbrella concept, encompassing various empirical studies with different samples within a sub-conceptual framework, such as tax evasion, tax avoidance, and the motivations affecting the taxation process. However, the methodologies used in these studies vary significantly. While there are studies in the scientific literature where the variables within the scope of the issue are used as mediating or moderating variables (Kant & Adula, 2024), such studies remain quite limited specifically within the tax compliance literature in the context of tax perception and tax attitude. In this regard, the current empirical literature on tax perception and tax attitude, including these limited studies, is presented in a comparative manner.

Firstly, examining studies on tax perception reveals that many studies (Gitaru, 2017; Kwok & Yip, 2018; Mascagni & Santoro, 2018; Mbilla et al., 2020; Teega, 2008; Trawule et al., 2022) have concluded that tax perception plays a critical role in tax compliance. For instance, studies examining the relationship between taxpayer perception and tax compliance in Greece with SMEs (Kaplanoglu et al., 2016), Italy (Elena, Alberto, & Giuseppe, n.d.), and Malaysia (Sritharan & Salawati, 2019) have found this relationship to be significant and positive. Similarly, in the case of Pakistan (Latif et al., 2023), it was found that a positive perception of the tax system positively affects tax compliance, with demographic factors not being decisive. In a study on the Spanish sample (Garcia et al., 2015), the gender factor was specifically examined in relation to perceptions of the tax system and tax evasion, and it was found that this factor did not have a directly significant effect. However, it was observed that housewives within the female group had a higher level of negative perception. Additionally, studies from various countries (Vietnam, India, Malaysia, Uganda, Kenya) (Gayathri & Jayakumar, 2016; Geetha & Sekar, 2012; Kijjambu & Mwesigye, 2024; Kiring'a et al., 2017; Kumar & Gupta, 2017; Le et al., 2021; Simuyu & Jagongo, 2019; Zakaria et al., 2009) have identified a significant and positive relationship between tax compliance and perceptions of electronic taxation. Conversely, some studies focusing on Nigeria and Türkiye (Mustapha, 2013; Mamta, 2012; Olatunji & Ayodele, 2017; Ozgen & Turan, 2007) have used perceptions of electronic taxation as a dependent variable.

A limited number of studies have also examined whether taxpayer perception acts as a mediating variable. For example, a study on Vietnam (Nguyen et al., 2021) found that psychological factors (emotion and trust) directly and indirectly affect tax compliance, with taxpayer perception acting as a mediating variable in this relationship. Similarly, a study on Indonesia (Febrian & Islami, 2020) revealed that gender and trust in the government significantly affect tax compliance, with taxpayer perception (justice) also serving as a mediating variable in this relationship.

On the other hand, a small number of studies have found no significant relationship between taxpayer perception and tax compliance. For instance, a study on Nigeria (Aronmwan & Eragbhe, 2015) reported no significant effect of taxpayer perception on tax compliance, although tax attitude was found to have a significant impact. Similarly, a study on Egypt (Engida & Baisa, 2014) concluded that taxpayer perception had no significant effect on tax avoidance. Another study on Indonesia (Hakki et al., 2023) investigating the relationship between perceptions of the moral dimension of money and taxpayer perception found no significant relationship, nor did it identify religious motivation as a moderating factor in this context.

Secondly, when studies on tax attitudes are examined, it is evident that there is a wide range of studies involving various samples. However, these studies tend to be broader in scope, encompassing tax perception as well. Some of these studies examine the relationship between taxpayer perception and taxpayer attitude, while others explore the combined effect of both variables on tax compliance. In studies that examine the effect of taxpayer attitude on taxpayer perception, a limited number of studies have found that taxpayer attitude significantly influences taxpayer perception, as demonstrated in a study on Malaysia (Pui et al., 2017). In contrast, studies investigating the effect of taxpayer perception on taxpayer attitude have covered more diverse country samples. For example, studies on Vietnam (Oanh et al., 2021), India (Ramkumar et al., 2023), Indonesia (Ratnawati & Darmanto, 2023), and 36 African countries (Boly et al., 2021) have found significant effects of taxpayer perception on taxpayer attitude. However, a study on Ghana (Razak & Adafula, 2013) reported no significant effect of taxpayer perception on taxpayer attitude. In studies examining the effects of both variables on tax compliance, differences in country samples and diverse results are noted. For instance, studies on Nigeria (Azaka, 2022; Vincent, 2021) concluded that both tax attitude and taxpayer perception (tax justice) significantly affect tax compliance. However, other studies (Ogungbade et al., 2021) found no significant effect of taxpayer perception on tax evasion, while identifying taxpayer attitude as a moderating variable in the relationship between taxpayer awareness and tax evasion.

On the other hand, studies specifically examining taxpayer attitudes hold a more comprehensive place in the literature. In studies conducted in Nigeria (Alabede, Ariffin, & Idris, 2011), Indonesia (Manan, 2021), and Malaysia (Safian & Ngah, 2020), a significant and positive relationship between taxpayer attitudes and tax compliance has been identified. Similarly, studies on Jordan and Kenya (Simuyu & Jagongo, 2019; Ondara et al., 2016; Maisiba & Atambo, 2016; Al-Debei et al., 2015) have found a significant relationship between taxpayer attitudes towards electronic tax systems and tax compliance. Additionally, a different study on Indonesia (Aristantia et al., 2022) revealed that tax motivation, alongside taxpayer attitudes, plays a determining role in tax compliance. Moreover, studies conducted in Uganda (Night & Bananuka, 2020) and Vietnam (Do et al., 2022) confirmed the significant relationship between taxpayer attitudes and tax compliance, while also demonstrating that the electronic tax system acts as a mediating variable, strengthening this relationship. A study on Nigeria (Otekunrin et al., 2021) found a significant relationship between the electronic tax system and tax compliance, with taxpayer attitudes acting as a mediating variable in addition to other factors. However, studies examining the Indonesian sample have reached different conclusions. In one study (Utama et al., 2022), tax motivation (religion) was found to significantly impact tax attitudes, and tax attitudes, in turn, significantly influenced tax compliance. The study also investigated the moderating role of electronic taxation (e-filing) but found it to be insignificant. Conversely, another study (Hidayat et al., 2022) found that both tax motivation (religion) and tax attitudes significantly affected tax compliance, with electronic taxation (e-filing) acting as a moderating variable in this relationship.

In more extensive studies, factors determining taxpayer attitude have been examined. For instance, studies on Germany (Bruns et al., 2023) identified moral motivation as a determinant of taxpayer attitude toward tax compliance, while studies on Brazil, Russia, India, and China (McGee et al., 2022) explored the effect of religious motivation on taxpayer attitude. A study on Iran (Khodamipour & Pourheydari, 2024) concluded that taxpayer attitude significantly influences tax compliance, with tax motivation as a determinant and personality type as a moderating variable. n a study on Nigerian SMEs (Haruna et al., 2023), a significant relationship was found between tax practices (forensic accounting) and taxpayer attitudes. Similarly, a study on the Nepalese sample (Dhakal, 2024) determined that the tax system and tax practices were key factors influencing tax attitudes. In a study examining the tax compliance attitudes of businesses in North America (Judd et al., 2023), larger businesses were found to have a more confrontational attitude. Meanwhile, in the Latin American sample (Yepes & Gergerlioğlu, 2022), demographic factors were identified as influential in the relationship between tax awareness and tax attitude. Likewise, in the Spanish sample (García et al., 2012), gender was found to be a key determinant in this relationship. A more comprehensive study using the World Values Survey (Pardisi & McGee, 2020), which covers more than 80 countries, examined the relationship between income level and taxpayer attitude. The findings varied across countries, with culture playing a fundamental role in these differences, alongside demographic factors and variations in tax motivation.

As seen in the studies within the literature, tax compliance in the context of tax perception and tax attitude is examined across various samples influenced by spatial differences. Moreover, while different findings have been obtained within similar samples, similar findings have also been observed across different samples. Although there are no empirical studies directly examining this variable within the relevant problem context, some studies (Garcia et al., 2020) have found that spatial factors have a significant impact as a variable. Based on these findings, this study aims to contribute to the literature by comparatively analyzing the tax perceptions and tax attitudes of taxpayers with similar socio-cultural backgrounds but residing in different spatial environments. This approach seeks to directly observe the impact of spatial differences.

RESEARCH DESING AND METHODOLOGY

In line with the aim of the study, cognitive consistency and cognitive dissonance theories have been considered to conduct an evaluation based on fiscal psychology. Within this framework, taxpayers' perceptions and attitudes toward taxation are comparatively examined to investigate tax awareness. Perception is generally defined as a sensory experience interpreted by an individual and can be distorted by processes such as interests, projection, selective exposure, reference points, expectations, and biases (Gordon, 1999, p. 16). Attitude, on the other hand, is defined as a behavior observed as a tendency to act in a certain way toward persons, situations, institutions, or societal processes, believed to reflect a fundamental value or belief. Unlike perception, attitude involves judgment and behavioral inclination (Gordon, 1999, p. 765). Thus, unlike perception, attitude entails judgment and behavioral tendencies. Accordingly, the problem based on fiscal psychology is addressed in terms of both perception and attitude within the context of cognitive consistency at the cognitive level.

The empirical testing of the theory was conducted through a survey-based field study. The survey instrument was developed based on previous literature (Tekin et al., 2018; Doğan et al., 2019). The survey used a 5-point Likert Scale and included demographic questions as well as questions aimed at examining taxpayers' perceptions and attitudes regarding the tax system and tax applications. The validity (KMO = 0.774 > 0.6, Bartlett's Test significance = 0.000) and reliability (Alpha = 0.84) of the survey were first tested through a pilot study and subsequently applied to the entire sample.

The sample size of the study considered the density of Turkish taxpayers residing in the capitals of selected countries. Accordingly, face-to-face interviews were conducted with approximately 700 participants in the capitals of five countries: Germany, Austria, Belgium, the Netherlands, and France. However, 688 of these survey forms were deemed usable.

Within this scope, the hypotheses to be tested in the study are categorized into three main hypotheses, which are further divided into sub-hypotheses i) The relationship between tax perception and tax attitude; ii) The mediating/moderating effect of spatial differences in the relationship between tax perception and tax attitude; iii) The mediating/moderating effect of spatial differences in the relationship between tax perception, tax attitude, and tax compliance motivation. These hypotheses are systematically categorized and presented as follows.

Table 1.

H1	There is a significant relationship between tax perception and tax attitude.
H2	There is a mediating/moderating effect of spatial difference on the relationship between tax perception and tax attitude.
H2.1	Spatial difference has a mediating effect on the relationship between tax perception and tax attitude.
H.2.2	Spatial difference has a moderating effect on the relationship between tax perception and tax attitude.
H3	There is a mediating/moderating effect of spatial difference on the relationship between tax compliance motivation and the relationship between tax perception and tax attitude.
H.3.1	Spatial difference has a mediating effect on the relationship between tax compliance motivation and tax perception.
H.3.1.1	Spatial difference has a mediating effect on the relationship between tax compliance motivation (morality) and tax perception.
H.3.1.2	Spatial difference has a mediating effect on the relationship between tax compliance motivation (compulsion) and tax perception.
H.3.1.3	Spatial difference has a mediating effect on the relationship between tax compliance motivation (citizenship consciousness) and tax perception.
H.3.1.4	Spatial difference has a mediating effect on the relationship between tax compliance motivation (religion) and tax perception.
H.3.2	Spatial difference has a mediating effect on the relationship between tax compliance motivation and tax attitude.
H.3.2.1	Spatial difference has a mediating effect on the relationship between tax compliance motivation (morality) and tax attitude.
H.3.2.2	Spatial difference has a mediating effect on the relationship between tax compliance motivation (compulsion) and tax attitude.
H.3.2.3	Spatial difference has a mediating effect on the relationship between tax compliance motivation (citizenship consciousness) and tax attitude.
H.3.2.4	Spatial difference has a mediating effect on the relationship between tax compliance motivation (religion) and tax attitude.
H.3.3	Spatial difference has a moderating effect on the relationship between tax compliance motivation and tax perception.
H.3.3.1	Spatial difference has a moderating effect on the relationship between tax compliance motivation (morality) and tax perception.
H.3.3.2	Spatial difference has a moderating effect on the relationship between tax compliance motivation (compulsion) and tax perception.
H.3.3.3	Spatial difference has a moderating effect on the relationship between tax compliance motivation (citizenship consciousness) and tax perception.
H.3.3.4	Spatial difference has a moderating effect on the relationship between tax compliance motivation (religion) and tax perception.
H.3.4	Spatial difference has a moderating effect on the relationship between tax compliance motivation and tax attitude.

continued on following page

Table 1. Continued

H.3.4.1	Spatial difference has a moderating effect on the relationship between tax compliance motivation (morality) and tax attitude.
H.3.4.2	Spatial difference has a moderating effect on the relationship between tax compliance motivation (compulsion) and tax attitude.
H.3.4.3	Spatial difference has a moderating effect on the relationship between tax compliance motivation (citizenship consciousness) and tax attitude.
H.3.4.4	Spatial difference has a moderating effect on the relationship between tax compliance motivation (religion) and tax attitude.

In testing these hypotheses, tax perception, tax attitude, and tax motivation are treated as the main variables. The spatial effect is examined in the model as both a mediating and moderating variable. Additionally, analyses related to mediating and moderating variables are further detailed through cross-tabulation analyses.

FINDINGS

The analyses aimed at testing the hypotheses formulated in line with the purpose of the study are presented categorically. Additionally, the variables of tax perception and tax attitude are categorized and examined within the context of the tax system and tax applications. Accordingly, four main variables are identified: perception of the tax system (P.S.), perception of tax applications (P.A.), attitude toward the tax system (A.S.), and attitude toward tax applications (A.A.).

In this context, the existence of the relationship between tax perception and tax attitude, which forms the basis for conducting the analyses, was first tested through a regression analysis (Table 2) below. The results indicate a significant relationship between the relevant variables ($p = 0.000 < 0.05$).

Table 2. Regression Analysis Between Tax Perception and Tax Attitude

Model		Unstandardized Coefficients		Standardized Coefficients	t	Sig.	95,0% Confidence Interval for B	
		B	Std. Error	Beta			Lower Bound	Upper Bound
Dep. Var. A.S	(Constant)	2,424	0,121		20,075	0,000	2,187	2,661
	P.S	0,259	0,039	,247	6,660	0,000	0,182	0,335
Dep. Var. A.A.	(Constant)	2,029	0,086		23,655	0,000	1,860	2,197
	P.A	0,359	0,032	,397	11,282	0,000	0,297	0,422

COMPARISON OF TAXPAYER PERCEPTIONS AND ATTITUDES BY COUNTRY

When comparing taxpayers' perceptions of the tax system across countries, it is observed that the level of indecision among taxpayers is quite high (40% and above). Additionally, taxpayers with a positive perception of the tax system are at the highest level in Germany, while France differs significantly from the other countries. Accordingly, taxpayers in France have a predominantly negative perception of the tax system (50%), and those with a positive perception are at the lowest level (12.5%).

Table 3. Perception of the Tax System by Country

Perception of the Tax System		Country					Total
		Germany	**Austria**	**Belgium**	**Netherlands**	**France**	**Total**
Disagree (Negative)	Count	32	14	36	44	56	182
	% within P.S.	17,6%	7,7%	19,8%	24,2%	30,8%	100,0%
	% within Country	22,9%	14,6%	23,1%	23,9%	50,0%	26,5%
Neutral	Count	56	52	72	106	42	328
	% within P.S.	17,1%	15,9%	22,0%	32,3%	12,8%	100,0%
	% within Country	40,0%	54,2%	46,2%	57,6%	37,5%	47,7%
Agree (Positive)	Count	52	30	48	34	14	178
	% within P.S.	29,2%	16,9%	27,0%	19,1%	7,9%	100,0%
	% within Country	37,1%	31,3%	30,8%	18,5%	12,5%	25,9%
Total	Count	140	96	156	184	112	688
	% within P.S.	20,3%	14,0%	22,7%	26,7%	16,3%	100,0%
	% within Country	100,0%	100,0%	100,0%	100,0%	100,0%	100,0%

When comparing taxpayers' perceptions of tax applications across countries, it is observed that taxpayers predominantly have negative perceptions (38% and above), while their level of indecision is also quite high (32% and above). Taxpayers with negative perceptions are at the highest levels in Belgium (55.1%) and Austria (54.2%), while they are at the lowest level in the Netherlands (38%).

Table 4. Perception of the Tax Applications by Country

Perception of the Tax Applications		Country					Total
		Germany	**Austria**	**Belgium**	**Netherlands**	**France**	**Total**
Disagree (Negative)	Count	64	52	86	70	54	326
	% within P.A.	19,6%	16,0%	26,4%	21,5%	16,6%	100,0%
	% within Country	45,7%	54,2%	55,1%	38,0%	48,2%	47,4%
Neutral	Count	66	36	50	88	44	284
	% within P.A.	23,2%	12,7%	17,6%	31,0%	15,5%	100,0%
	% within Country	47,1%	37,5%	32,1%	47,8%	39,3%	41,3%
Agree (Positive)	Count	10	8	20	26	14	78
	% within P.A.	12,8%	10,3%	25,6%	33,3%	17,9%	100,0%
	% within Country	7,1%	8,3%	12,8%	14,1%	12,5%	11,3%

continued on following page

Table 4. Continued

Perception of the Tax Applications		Country					Total
		Germany	Austria	Belgium	Netherlands	France	Total
Total	Count	140	96	156	184	112	688
	% within P.A.	20,3%	14,0%	22,7%	26,7%	16,3%	100,0%
	% within Country	100,0%	100,0%	100,0%	100,0%	100,0%	100,0%

When comparing taxpayers' attitudes toward tax applications across countries, it is observed that taxpayers are largely indecisive (47% and above). Taxpayers in the Netherlands differ from those in other countries, with indecisiveness reaching the highest level at 65.2%, which cannot be overlooked, while those with positive attitudes are at the lowest level at 15.2%.

Table 5. Attitude towards the Tax Applications by Country

Attitude towards the Tax Applications		Country					Total
		Germany	Austria	Belgium	Netherlands	France	Total
Disagree (Negative)	Count	42	14	40	36	34	166
	% within A.A.	25,3%	8,4%	24,1%	21,7%	20,5%	100,0%
	% within Country	30,4%	14,6%	25,6%	19,6%	30,9%	24,3%
Neutral	Count	66	54	80	120	58	378
	% within A.A.	17,5%	14,3%	21,2%	31,7%	15,3%	100,0%
	% within Country	47,8%	56,3%	51,3%	65,2%	52,7%	55,3%
Agree (Positive)	Count	30	28	36	28	18	140
	% within A.A.	21,4%	20,0%	25,7%	20,0%	12,9%	100,0%
	% within Country	21,7%	29,2%	23,1%	15,2%	16,4%	20,5%
Total	Count	138	96	156	184	110	684
	% within A.A.	20,2%	14,0%	22,8%	26,9%	16,1%	100,0%
	% within Country	100,0%	100,0%	100,0%	100,0%	100,0%	100,0%

When comparing taxpayers' attitudes toward the tax system across countries, it is observed that the level of indecision is quite high (32% and above). However, there are significant differences in indecision levels among the countries. In this context, the proportion of indecisive taxpayers is noticeably the highest in the Netherlands (54.3%), where the proportion of taxpayers with a positive attitude is also the lowest (21.7%). In France, where the level of indecision is the lowest (32.7%), the proportion of taxpayers with a negative attitude is at its highest (29.1%). In Belgium, while the level of indecision is relatively low (39.7%), the proportion of taxpayers with a positive attitude is the highest (46.2%).

Table 6. Attitude towards The Tax System by Country

Attitude towards The Tax System		Country					Total
		Germany	Austria	Belgium	Netherlands	France	Total
Disagree (Negative)	Count	24	16	22	44	32	138
	% within A.S.	17,4%	11,6%	15,9%	31,9%	23,2%	100,0%
	% within Country	17,4%	16,7%	14,1%	23,9%	29,1%	20,2%
Neutral	Count	64	46	62	100	36	308
	% within A.S.	20,8%	14,9%	20,1%	32,5%	11,7%	100,0%
	% within Country	46,4%	47,9%	39,7%	54,3%	32,7%	45,0%
Agree (Positive)	Count	50	34	72	40	42	238
	% within A.S.	21,0%	14,3%	30,3%	16,8%	17,6%	100,0%
	% within Country	36,2%	35,4%	46,2%	21,7%	38,2%	34,8%
Total	Count	138	96	156	184	110	684
	% within A.S.	20,2%	14,0%	22,8%	26,9%	16,1%	100,0%
	% within Country	100,0%	100,0%	100,0%	100,0%	100,0%	100,0%

In this context, when taxpayers' perceptions and attitudes toward the tax system and applications are evaluated as a whole, significant differences are observed across countries. While taxpayers in Germany exhibit a high level of positive perception toward the tax system, taxpayers in France demonstrate the highest levels of negative perceptions and attitudes toward the tax system. Negative perceptions of tax applications are most prominent in Austria and Belgium, with Belgium also having the highest level of positive attitudes toward the tax system. In contrast, taxpayers in the Netherlands display the lowest levels of positive attitudes toward both the tax system and applications, while their negative perceptions of tax applications are the lowest. Thus, differences exist in taxpayers' perceptions and attitudes both within and across countries, and these differences become even more pronounced when considered in terms of the tax system and applications.

THE MEDIATOR AND MODERATOR ROLE OF COUNTRIES IN THE RELATIONSHIP BETWEEN TAXPAYER PERCEPTIONS AND ATTITUDES

When examining whether a country serves as a mediator in the relationship between a taxpayer's perception of the tax system and their attitude, it was initially found that the perception of the tax system has a significant effect on the country ($p<0.05$). However, when examining the effect of the country on the taxpayer's attitude toward taxes, it was concluded that this effect is not significant ($0.425>0.05$). Therefore, it can be seen that the country does not act as a mediator in the relationship between the taxpayer's perception of the tax system and their attitude.

Table 7. The Mediatör Analysis of the Country in the Relationship Between P.S. & A.S

MODEL			coeff	se	t	p	LLCI	ULCI
Outcome Variable	Country	constant	3,978	0,174	22,925	0,000	3,637	4,318
		P.S.	-0,313	0,056	-5,614	0,000	-0,423	-0,204
	A.S.	constant	2,509	0,161	15,609	0,000	2,193	2,825
		P.S.	0,252	0,040	6,342	0,000	0,174	0,330
		Country	-0,021	0,027	-0,798	0,425	-0,074	0,031

When examining whether a country serves as a mediator in the relationship between a taxpayer's perception of tax applications and their attitude, it was found that both the perception of tax pappli-cations on the country (p=0.08>0.05) and the effect of the country on the taxpayer's attitude toward taxes (p=0.07>0.05) are not significant. Therefore, it can be concluded that the country does not act as a mediator in the relationship between the taxpayer's perception of tax applications and their attitude.

Table 8. The Mediatör Analysis of the Country in the Relationship Between P.A. & A.A

MODEL			coeff	se	t	p	LLCI	ULCI
Outcome Variable	Country	constant	2,80	0,15	18,27	0,00	2,50	3,10
		P.A.	0,10	0,06	1,75	0,08	-0,01	0,21
	A.A.	constant	2,14	0,10	20,44	0,00	1,93	2,34
		P.A.	0,36	0,03	11,39	0,00	0,30	0,43
		Country	-0,04	0,02	-1,79	0,07	-0,08	0,00

When examining whether a country serves as a moderating variable in the relationship between a taxpayer's perception of the tax system and their attitude, it was found that the combined effect of tax perception and the country on the tax attitude (Int_1) is borderline but significant (p=0.051). Accordingly, it can be said that the country acts as a moderating variable in this relationship, positively contributing to and strengthening the relationship (coeff=0.055>0).

Table 9. The Moderator Analysis of the Country in the Relationship Between P.S. & A.S

MODEL			coeff	se	t	p	LLCI	ULCI
		constant	**2,994**	**0,295**	**10,141**	**0,000**	**2,415**	**3,574**
Y	A.S.	P.S.	0,089	0,092	0,964	0,335	-0,092	0,270
X	P.S.	Country	-0,180	0,085	-2,110	0,035	-0,347	-0,013
W	Country	Int_1	0,055	0,028	1,958	0,051	0,000	0,110

When examining whether a country serves as a moderating variable in the relationship between a taxpayer's perception of tax applications and their attitude, it was found that the combined effect of tax perception and the country on tax attitude (Int_1) is significant (p=0.022<0.05). Therefore, in this relationship, the country is a moderating variable and positively contributes to strengthening the rela-tionship (coeff=0.055>0).

Table 10. The Moderator Analysis of the Country in the Relationship Between P.A. & A.A

MODEL			**coeff**	**se**	**t**	**p**	**LLCI**	**ULCI**
		constant	**2,571**	**0,217**	**11,874**	**0,000**	**2,146**	**2,996**
Y	A.A.	P.A.	0,190	0,082	2,307	0,021	0,028	0,351
X	P.A.	Country	-0,177	0,064	-2,760	0,006	-0,303	-0,051
W	Country	Int_1	0,055	0,024	2,293	0,022	0,008	0,102

The roles of countries as mediating and moderating variables in the relationship between taxpayer motivation and taxpayer perceptions and attitudes toward the tax system and applications have been examined. As a result of this analysis, it was first determined that the country acts as a mediating variable only in the relationship between taxpayer motivation for paying taxes and the perception of the tax system. Therefore, the country is not a mediating variable in the relationships between taxpayer motivation for paying taxes and attitudes toward the tax system, perceptions of tax applications, or attitudes toward tax applications. Moreover, when the country is a mediating variable, taxpayer motivation related to religion, obligation, and perception is involved, but not citizenship awareness.

Second, it was found that the country acts as a moderating variable only in the relationship between one type of taxpayer motivation (obligation) and the perception of the tax system, the attitude toward the tax system, the perception of tax applications, and the attitude toward tax applications. Therefore, there is no moderating role of the country in the relationship between motivation related to religion, morality, or citizenship awareness and the perceptions and attitudes toward the tax system and applications.

In this context, data related to the mediating variable role are presented first. When examining whether the country acts as a mediating variable in the relationship between taxpayer motivation for paying taxes and the perception of the tax system, it was found that both taxpayer motivation for paying taxes and the country have significant effects on the country's perception of the tax system ($p=0,00<0,05$). Thus, it was concluded that the country is a mediating variable in the relationship between taxpayer motivation for paying taxes and the perception of the tax system.

Table 11. The Mediatör Analysis of the Country in the Relationship Between P.S. & Motivation

MODEL		**X**	**coeff**	**se**	**t**	**p**	**LLCI**	**ULCI**
Outcome Variable	Country	constant	3,59	0,17	20,53	0,00	3,25	3,93
		Religion	-0,34	0,11	-3,26	0,00	-0,55	-0,14
	P.S.	constant	2,77	0,14	19,21	0,00	2,49	3,05
		Religion	0,37	0,07	5,33	0,00	0,23	0,50
		Country	-0,12	0,02	-5,02	0,00	-0,17	-0,08
Outcome Variable	Country	constant	3,71	0,16	23,84	0,00	3,40	4,02
		Obligation	-0,48	0,11	-4,53	0,00	-0,69	-0,27
	P.S.	constant	2,82	0,14	20,61	0,00	2,55	3,09
		Obligation	0,37	0,07	5,24	0,00	0,23	0,50
		Country	-0,12	0,02	-4,65	0,00	-0,16	-0,07

continued on following page

Table 11. Continued

MODEL		X	coeff	se	t	p	LLCI	ULCI
Outcome Variable	Country	constant	3,58	0,18	19,75	0,00	3,23	3,94
		Morality	-0,33	0,11	-3,05	0,00	-0,54	-0,12
	P.S.	constant	2,81	0,15	19,07	0,00	2,52	3,10
		Morality	0,34	0,07	4,89	0,00	0,20	0,48
		Country	-0,13	0,02	-5,21	0,00	-0,18	-0,08

Secondly, data related to the moderating variable role are presented. When examining whether the country acts as a moderating variable in the relationships between taxpayer motivation for paying taxes (obligation) and perceptions and attitudes toward the tax system and applications, it was found that the combined effect of taxpayer motivation for paying taxes and the country on tax perception and attitude is significant (Int_1) (p=0.006<0.05; p=0.002<0.005; p=0.000<0.005; p=0.023<0.05). Therefore, in these relationships, the country acts as a moderating variable, positively contributing to and strengthening the relationships (coeff=0.149>0; coeff=0.178>0; coeff=0.214>0; coeff=0.130>0).

Table 12. The Moderator Analysis of the Country in the Relationship Between P.S.-P.A.-A.A.-A.S. & Motivation

MODEL		X	coeff	se	t	p	LLCI	ULCI
		constant	**3,397**	**0,250**	**13,618**	**0,000**	**2,908**	**3,887**
Y	P.S.	Obligation	-0,065	0,171	-0,381	0,703	-0,401	0,270
X	Obligation	Country	-0,309	0,075	-4,153	0,000	-0,456	-0,163
W	Country	Int_1	0,149	0,054	2,755	0,006	0,043	0,254
MODEL		constant	3,334	0,260	12,848	0,000	2,824	3,843
Y	P.A.	Obligation	-0,675	0,178	-3,796	0,000	-1,023	-0,326
X	Obligation	Country	-0,194	0,078	-2,509	0,012	-0,347	-0,042
W	Country	Int_1	0,178	0,056	3,173	0,002	0,068	0,288
MODEL		constant	3,384	0,232	14,584	0,000	2,928	3,840
Y	A.A.	Obligation	-0,332	0,159	-2,092	0,037	-0,644	-0,020
X	Obligation	Country	-0,285	0,069	-4,115	0,000	-0,421	-0,149
W	Country	Int_1	0,214	0,050	4,270	0,000	0,116	0,313
MODEL		constant	3,119	0,264	11,822	0,000	2,601	3,637
Y	A.S.	Obligation	0,098	0,181	0,540	0,590	-0,257	0,452
X	Obligation	Country	-0,194	0,079	-2,466	0,014	-0,349	-0,040
W	Country	Int_1	0,130	0,057	2,286	0,023	0,018	0,242

DISCUSSION

The study, which compares the relationships between taxpayer perceptions, attitudes, and tax motivations across different countries, concludes that spatial differences have a significant impact that cannot be overlooked. In this context, the first analysis focused on the relationship between taxpayers' perceptions and attitudes, revealing that taxpayer perception significantly affects taxpayer attitude. Therefore, H1 hypothesis is accepted. The results obtained are similar to those found in the literature for samples from Vietnam (Oanh et al., 2021), India (Ramkumar et al., 2023), Indonesia (Ratnawati & Darmanto, 2023), and 36 African countries (Boly et al., 2021), while differing from the findings for the Ghana sample (Razak & Adafula, 2013).

Secondly, the level of inter-country differences in the relationship between taxpayers' perceptions and attitudes was examined. Through cross-tabulation analyses, it was determined that there were significant differences between countries, and these differences became more pronounced as the relationship between variables was further detailed. Based on this result, the role of the country in the relationship between taxpayer perception and attitude was analyzed in terms of whether it acted as a mediator or moderator. It was concluded that spatial differences did not significantly impact the relationship as a mediator, but they did have a significant moderating effect, strengthening the relationship. As a result, the H2.1 hypothesis was rejected, and the H2.2 hypothesis was accepted.

Based on the findings and previous literature, the impact of spatial differences was further examined through the relationship between taxpayers' tax payment motivations and tax perception and attitude. Initially, it was found that spatial differences acted as a mediator in the relationship between religious, moral, and obligation motivations and perceptions of the tax system. As a result, H3.1.1, H3.1.2 and H3.1.4 hypotheses were accepted, while the H3.1.3 hypothesis was rejected. These findings are supported by the cross-tabulation analyses (Appendix 1). Specifically, taxpayers motivated by religion show significant indecisiveness in their perceptions of the tax system in Germany (Table 13), Austria (Table 14), and the Netherlands (Table 16), while in Belgium (Table 15), they show positive perceptions, and in France (Table 17), taxpayer perception is nearly equally distributed between indecisive, positive, and negative. Taxpayers motivated by morality and obligation only exhibit positive perceptions of the tax system in Germany (Table 13, Table 18), whereas in other countries (Table 14, Table 15, Table 16, Table 17, Table 19, Table 20, Table 21, Table 22), indecisiveness prevails, and both positive and negative perceptions are present.

On the other hand, it was found that spatial differences did not have a significant mediating effect in the relationship between these motivations and tax attitude, so H.3.2 hypotheses were rejected.

Secondly, only the obligation motivation showed that spatial differences moderated the relationships between tax perception and attitude, as well as the relationship between moral motivation and tax perception. Other motivations such as religion and citizenship awareness did not have an effect in the relationships between tax perception and attitude. Therefore, the H3.3.1, H3.3.2 and H3.4.2 hypotheses were accepted, while H3.3.3, H3.3.4, H3.4.1, H3.4.3 and H3.4.4 hypotheses were rejected. These results are also examined through cross-tabulation analyses (Appendix 2).

- As previously mentioned, taxpayer perception of the tax system is only positive in Germany, while in other countries, there is a high level of indecisiveness and diversity in positive and negative taxpayer rates.

- Taxpayer perceptions of tax applications are significantly negative across all countries, but indecisiveness levels and the proportions of those with positive perceptions vary considerably.
- Taxpayer attitudes toward the tax system are generally positive across all countries. However, in Austria, the indecisiveness level is significantly high, and in other countries, the proportion of taxpayers with negative attitudes varies.
- Taxpayer attitudes toward tax applications are predominantly indecisive in all countries, with significant variation in indecisiveness levels and the proportions of positive and negative attitudes.

The details of the differences between countries are presented below:

- In Germany (Table 18, Table 23), the perception (41.7%) and attitude (54.2%) toward the tax system are positive, while the perception of tax applications (54.2%) is negative, and the attitude is indecisive (45.8%) with a notable level of negativity (37.5%).
- In Austria (Table 19, Table 24), the perception (54.8%) and attitude (41.9%) toward the tax system are predominantly indecisive, but also significantly positive (29% and 41.9%). However, the perception of tax applications is largely negative (61.3%), while the attitude is mostly indecisive (64.5%) and notably positive (29%).
- In Belgium (Table 20, Table 25), the perception (34.9%) and attitude (48.8%) toward the tax system are significantly positive, while the perception of tax applications is largely negative (65.1%), but the attitude is indecisive (58.1%).
- In the Netherlands (Table 21, Table 26), both perception and attitude toward the tax system are significantly indecisive (50% and 33.3%), but also notably positive (41.7% and 50%). However, the perception of tax applications is negative (45.8%), while the attitude is indecisive (62.5%) but positive (33.3%).
- In France (Table 22, Table 27), taxpayer perception of the tax system shows indecisiveness (54.5%) and negativity (27.3%), while the attitude is largely positive (81.8%). Similarly, the perception of tax applications is negative (45.5%), but the attitude is indecisive (72.7%) and positive (27.5%).

Ultimately, the results regarding the impact of spatial differences on the relationship between taxpayers' motivations for paying taxes, tax perception, and attitude align with previous studies in the literature, such as the meaningful relationship between religion and attitude (Hidayat et al., 2022; McGee et al., 2022; Utama et al., 2022), morality and attitude (Bruns et al., 2023), and generally the relationship between taxation motivations and attitude (Khodamipour & Pourheydari, 2024). However, these results differ from other studies in the literature, particularly those that use spatial differences as a mediator and moderator (Al-Zaqeba & Al-Rashdan, 2020; Do et al., 2022; Febrian & Islami, 2020; Hakki et al., 2023; Hidayat et al., 2022; Khodamipour & Pourheydari, 2024; Nguyen et al., 2021; Night & Bananuka, 2020; Otekunrin et al., 2021; Utama et al., 2022).

CONCLUSION

Implications of the Study

In countries with a high concentration of Turkish nationals, such as Germany, Austria, Belgium, the Netherlands, and France, taxes on personal income are categorized based on whether the individual is a resident or non-resident. Accordingly, in all of these countries, the taxation practice is such that residents are taxed on all income earned globally, while non-residents are only taxed on income earned within the respective country. Additionally, in all of these countries, a progressive taxation method is applied to personal income, with tax brackets and rates varying across countries. Furthermore, in all of these countries, the rate of personal income tax, both as a percentage of GDP (8%-12%) and total tax revenues (22%-28%), is significantly higher than that of Türkiye (2% and 11%, respectively) (OECD, 2024). This situation makes it crucial to consider the tax compliance level of Turkish nationals residing in these countries.

In this study, the tax compliance level of Turkish nationals living in European countries has been examined from the perspective of Schmölders' theory of fiscal psychology. Thus, the importance of the tax mentality and spatial differences emphasized by Schmölders' theory has been empirically tested and confirmed based on the tax perception, attitude, and motivation of the five countries. In line with this, based on the findings from the literature and this study, it is suggested that tax policies, especially those directly related to taxpayers, should prioritize country-specific regulations and applications. Additionally, international regulations should be shaped through scientific evaluations and recommendations, ensuring that these country-specific differences are not overlooked.

Limitations of the Study and Recommendations for Future Study

The main limitation of this field-based study is the sample size and the fact that the sample is limited to taxpayers who earn personal income. Although the sample size is sufficient and reliable for statistical evaluation, expanding the sample to include other European countries where Turkish nationals reside would enhance the representativeness of the empirical findings. Therefore, future studies could involve a larger sample and include other taxable sources of income (such as corporate tax) to further develop the research.

REFERENCES

Al-Debei, M. M., Akroush, M. N., & Ashouri, M. I. (2015). Consumer attitudes towards online shopping: The effects of trust, perceived benefits, and perceived web quality. *Internet Research, 25*(5), 707–733. DOI: 10.1108/IntR-05-2014-0146

Al-Zaqeba, M. A. A., & Al-Rashdan, M. T. (2020). Extension of the TPB in tax compliance behavior: The role of moral intensity and customs tax. *International Journal of Scientific and Technology Research, 9*(4), 227–232.

Alabede, J. O., Ariffin, Z. Z., & Idris, K. (2011). Individual taxpayers" attitude and compliance behaviour in Nigeria: The moderating role of financial condition and risk preference. *Journal of Accounting and Taxation, 3*(6), 91–104.

Allingham, M. G., & Sandmo, A. (1972). Income Tax Evasion: A Theoretical Analysis. *Journal of Public Economics, 1*(3-4), 323–338. DOI: 10.1016/0047-2727(72)90010-2

Alm, J., & Torgler, B. (2006). Culture Differences and Tax Morale in the United States and in Europe. *Journal of Economic Psychology, 27*(2), 224–246. DOI: 10.1016/j.joep.2005.09.002

Aristantia, S. E., Yuniarni, R. K., & Junjunan, M. I. (2022). The Effect of Taxation Rational Attitude, Religiusity, and Ethics on Taxpayer Compliance. *Journal of Accounting* [JAEF]. *Entrepreneurship and Financial Technology, 4*(1), 1–14.

Aronmwan, E., & Eragbhe, E. (2015, May). Taxpayers income, taxpayers attributes and personal income tax compliance. *African Journal of Management Sciences, 1*, 95–111.

Azaka, L. (2022). Tax Knowledge, Tax Attıtude, And Perceptıon Of Tax Faırness As Predıctors Of Tax Complıance Among Tech Workers In Lagos State, Nıgerıa. *Afrıcan Journal For The Psychologıcal Studıes Of Socıal Issues, 25*(2).

Boly, A., Konte, M., & Shimeles, A. (2021). Corruption perception and attitude towards taxation in Africa. *Journal of African Economies, 30*(Supplement_1), i140–i157. DOI: 10.1093/jae/ejab024

Bruns, C., Fochmann, M., Mohr, P. N., & Torgler, B. (2023). Multidimensional tax compliance attitude. *Freie Universität Berlin, School of Business & Economics Discussion Paper*, (2023/7).

Dhakal, B. (2024). Impact of attitude variables, Tax rate and perceptions of government fairness on Tax Compliance.

Do, H. T. H., Mac, Y. T. H., Van Tran, H. T., & Nguyen, T. T. L. (2022). The impact of attitude towards an e-tax system on tax compliance of Vietnamese enterprises: Adoption of an e-tax system as a mediator.

Doğan, E., Tekin, A., & Çelikay, F. (2019). Mükelleflerin Vergiye Bakışında Yargı Yetisi Sorunsalı: Kant Perspektifinden Mekânsal Farklılık Temelli Bir Değerlendirme. *Mehmet Akif Ersoy Üniversitesi İktisadi ve İdari Bilimler Fakültesi Dergisi, 6*(3), 702–720. DOI: 10.30798/makuiibf.597471

Eaton, G.M. (1937). "Organizations for Compliance with Taxing Statutes". Tax Mag, No 15.

Elena, D. A., Alberto, D. B. M., & Giuseppe, S. (n.d.). *Tax Evasion, government size and taxpayers perceptions on public goods provision, evidence from italian regions.*

Engida, T. G., & Baisa, G. A. (2014). Factors Influencing t axpayers" compliance with the tax system: An empirical study in Mekelle City, Ethiopia. *Journal of Tax Research, 12*(2), 433–453.

Febrian, Y. B., & Islami, I. N. (2020). Gender, trust, and tax compliance: The mediating effect of fairness perception. [Journal of Applied Accounting and Finance]. *JAAF, 4*(2), 131–145. DOI: 10.33021/jaaf.v4i2.1244

Feld, L. P. ve Frey, B.S. (2002), "Trust Breeds Trust: How Taxpayers are Treated", Cesifo Working Paper Series, 2-18.

García, A. G. Beyaert Stevens, A & De Pablos Escobar, L. (2012) 'Fiscal Awareness: a study of the female attitude towards fraud in Spain' in Michael Pickhardt, and Aloys Prinz (ed.) Tax Evasion and the Shadow Economy, Publisher (if book): Edward Elgar, pp. 61-86.

García, A. G., Buendía Azorín, J. D., & Sánchez de la Vega, M. M. (2020): Shadow Economy and National Culture: A Spatial Approach, Hacienda Pública Española / Review of Public Economics, 232-(1/2020), pp. 53-74 DOI: 10.7866/HPE-RPE.20.1.3

García, A. G., Quiñones, E., & Sánchez-Meca, J. (2015). How can being a housewife influence women's fiscal awareness? The case of Spain. Anales de Psicología/Annals of Psychology, 31(3), 952-961. ISSN 0212-9728.

Gayathri P, Jayakumar K (2016) A Study on Tax Payer's Perception Towards EFiling of Income Tax Returns. International Journal of Trend in Research and Development 32-38.

Geetha, R., & Sekar, M. (2012). E-Filing of Income Tax: Awareness and Satisfaction level of individual tax payer. *Research Journal of Management Science, 1*, 6–11.

Gemmell, N. (2016). *An Allingham-Sandmo Tax Compliance Model with Imperfect Enforcement. Chair in Public Finance*. Victoria Business School.

Gitaru, K. (2017). The effect of taxpayer education on tax compliance in Kenya. Munich Personal RePEc Archive, 2(80344), 12–23. https://mpra.ub.unimuenchen.de/id/eprint/80344

Hakki, T. W., Simanungkalit, J., & Siat, M. (2023). The Antecedents Of Tax Evasion Perception With A Religiousity As Moderation. *Kajian Akuntansi, 24*(2), 325–335. DOI: 10.29313/kajian_akuntansi.v24i2.2526

Haruna, H. T., Ibrahim, A. S., Yusuf, A. U., & Ardo, A. M. (2023). The impact of forensic accounting on tax payer attitude and compliance towards tax evasion within smes in the north east nigeria. *Journal of Business Management and Accounting, 13*(1), 79–105. DOI: 10.32890/jbma2023.13.1.4

Hidayat, K., Utama, M. S., Nimran, U., & Prasetya, A. (2022). The effect of attitude and religiosity on tax compliant intention moderated by the utilization of e-Filing. *Journal of Financial Services Marketing*, •••, 1.

Judd, H. W., McGuire, S. T., Weaver, C. D., & Xia, J. (2023). Check Your Attitude: An Examination of Companies' Attitude Toward Tax Enforcement. *Available atSSRN* 4322643. DOI: 10.2139/ssrn.4322643

Kant, S., & Adula, M. (2024). AI Learning and Work Attitude Mediation Between Reward and Organizational Support in Ethiopia. In Gomathi Sankar, J., & David, A. (Eds.), *Generative AI for Transformational Management* (pp. 109–136). IGI Global., DOI: 10.4018/979-8-3693-5578-7.ch005

Kant, S., & Adula, M. (2024). Mediated by AI-Based Generative Re-Enforcement Learning and Work Attitude: Are Intrinsic Rewards Transforming Employee Perceived Organizational Support? In Gomathi Sankar, J., & David, A. (Eds.), *Generative AI for Transformational Management* (pp. 83–108). IGI Global., DOI: 10.4018/979-8-3693-5578-7.ch004

Kaplanoglou, G., Rapanos, V. T., & Daskalakis, N. (2016). Tax compliance behaviour during the crisis : The case of Greek SMEs. *European Journal of Law and Economics*, *42*(3), 405–444. DOI: 10.1007/s10657-016-9547-y

Khodamipour, A., & Pourheydari, O. (2024). Investigating the effect of attitude, risk aversion and loss aversion of tax payers on tax compliance considering the moderating role of personality type (case study of tax payers of Kerman city). *Journal of Tax Research*, *32*(61), 87–132. DOI: 10.61186/taxjournal.32.61.87

Kijjambu, F. N., & Mwesigye, B. (2024). Taxpayer Perception and Income Tax Filing Compliance among Small Taxpayers in Mbarara City. *American Journal of Finance*, *10*(1), 89–110. DOI: 10.47672/ajf.1896

Kiring'a, S.E., Jagongo, A., Kiio, J.M., Njuguna, I.M., Muguongo, G.K., Nganyi, M.S., & Sei, M.J., KaraniGichimu, C., Macharia, I., Mwangi, M. and Qiao, Y. (2017). Impact of online tax filing on tax compliance among small and medium enterprises (MSE) in Kibwezi Sub-County in Kenya. *International Journal of Current Research*, *9*(4), 45196–45206.

Kumar, S., & Gupta, S. (2017). A study on income tax payers perception towards electronic filing. *Journal of Internet Banking and Commerce*, *22*(S7), 1.

Kwok, B. Y. S., & Yip, R. W. Y. (2018). Is Tax Education Good or Evil for Boosting Tax Compliance? Evidence from Hong Kong. *Asian Economic Journal*, *32*(4), 359–386. DOI: 10.1111/asej.12163

Latif, F., Jabeen, M., & Jabeen, M. (2023). The Impact of Tax Knowledge, Tax System Complexity and Tax Fairness Perception on Compliance Behavior of a Taxpayer in KPK:-. *International Journal of Business and Management Sciences*, *4*(4), 19–40.

LE, H. T. D., BUI, M. T., & NGUYEN, G. T. C. (2021). Factors affecting electronic tax compliance of small and medium enterprises in Vietnam. *The Journal of Asian Finance, Economics and Business*, *8*(1), 823–832.

Maisiba, J. G., & Atambo, W. (2016). Effects of electronic tax system on the revenue collection efficiency of Kenya Revenue Authority. *Imperial Journal of Interdisciplinary Research*, *2*(4), 815–827.

Mamta, B. (2012). Taxpayers' perception of E-File adoption: An empirical investigation. *Journal of Management Research*, *5*, 1–16.

Manan, S. (2021). The Influence of Nationalism Attitude, Institutional Perception, and Trust in Willing to Pay Tax. *Golden Ratio of Taxation Studies, 1*(2).

Martin, W. J. (1944). Costs of Tax Administration: Expenses of Compliance. *The Bulletin of the National Tax Association*, *29*(6), 162–167. DOI: 10.1086/bullnattax41787304

Mascagni, G., & Santoro, F. (2018). ICTD Research in Brief: Why is tax education important for compliance?: Summary of African Tax Administration. ICTD Working Papers, 23.

Mbilla, A. S. E., Abiire, M. A., Atindaana, P. A., & Ayimpoya, R. N. (2020). Tax Education and Tax Compliance In Ghana. Researchjournali's. *Journal of Accountancy*, *28*(1), 1–22.

McGee, R. W., Petrides, Y., & Zhou, J. (2022). Attitude toward tax evasion in Brazil, Russia, India and China (BRIC). *Philosophy. Economics and Law Review*, *2*(2), 70–84.

Mustapha, B. (2013). The impact of perceived ease of use and perceived usefulness on an online tax system. *International Journal of Advanced Research*, *1*(4), 1–18.

Nguyen, V. M. H., Nguyen, V. T. B., Nguyen-Cuu, D., Nguyen, V. T. T., Ngoc, P. L., Ngoc Ngo, T. T., & Tran-Nam, B. (2021). The effects of emotion, trust and perception on tax compliance: empirical evidence from vietnam. In *Advances in Taxation* (pp. 111–134). Emerald Publishing Limited. DOI: 10.1108/S1058-749720210000029010

Night, S., & Bananuka, J. (2020). The mediating role of adoption of an electronic tax system in the relationship between attitude towards electronic tax system and tax compliance. *Journal of Economics, Finance and Administrative Science*, *25*(49), 73–88. DOI: 10.1108/JEFAS-07-2018-0066

Oanh, T. T. K., LE THUY, N. T., VAN SONG, N. G. U. Y. E. N., MAC THI HAI, Y. E. N., HANG, N. T., & HUONG, N. T. T. (2021). Assessing perception and attitude of supporting of enterprises regarding the continued application of E-Tax In Vietnam. *Journal of Contemporary Issues in Business and Government*, *27*(3), 216–227.

OECD data. (2024). Tax on Personel Income Indicators. https://www.oecd.org/en/data/indicators/tax-on-personal-income.html?oecdcontrol-3422f520c2-var8=PC_GDP&oecdcontrol-38c744bfa4-var1=OAVG%7COECD%7CAUT%7CBEL%7CDEU%7CFRA%7CNLD%7CTUR

Ogungbade, O. I., Enitan, A., & Adekoya, A. C. (2021). Tax Awareness, Taxpayers" Perceptions and Attitudes and Tax Evasion in Informal Sector of Ekiti State, Nigeria. *International Journal of Financial Research*, *12*(5), 24–40. DOI: 10.5430/ijfr.v12n5p24

Olatunji, O. C., & Ayodele, K. B. (2017). *Impact of information technology on tax administration in the southwest*. DOI: 10.14738/abr.59.3549

Ondara, T. G., Kimani, M., & Kwasira, J. (2016). Influence of online tax filing on tax compliance among small and medium enterprises in Nakuru town, Kenya. *IOSR Journal of Business and Management*, *18*(10), 82–92. DOI: 10.9790/487X-1810028292

Otekunrin, A. O., Nwanji, T. I., Eluyela, D. F., Inegbedion, H., & Eleda, T. (2021). E-tax system effectiveness in reducing tax evasion in Nigeria. *Problems and Perspectives in Management*, *19*(4), 175–185. DOI: 10.21511/ppm.19(4).2021.15

Ozgen, F. B., & Turan, A. H. (2007). Usage and adoption of online tax filing and payment system in tax management: An empirical assessment with Technology Acceptance Model (TAM) in Turkey. *9th International Scientific Conference, Management Horizons: Visions and Challenges*, Vytautas Magnus University, Kaunas, September 27-28, 2007, Lithuania. DOI: 10.1057/ejis.2010.63

Pardisi, A., & McGee, R. W. (2020, October). The Relationship between Income Level and Attitude toward Tax Evasion: An Empirical Study. In *International Academy of Business and Public Administration Disciplines Fall Conference* (Vol. 17, No. 4, pp. 128-138).

Pui, Y. C., Moorthy, K., & Choo, K. S. W. (2017). Taxpayers" perceptions on tax evasion behaviour: An empirical study in Malaysia. *Journal of Law and Management, 59*(3), 413–429. DOI: 10.1108/IJLMA-02-2016-0022

Ramkumar, G., Kalimuthu, L. P., Selvaraj, A. P., Shankarii, S., & Rajasekaran, K. K. (2023). A structural equation modelling approach towards taxpayers' perceptions on goods and services tax in India. *International Journal of Professional Business Review, 8*(4), e02166–e02166. DOI: 10.26668/business-review/2023.v8i4.2166

Ratnawati, A. T., & Darmanto, S. (2023). Role of attitude and intention on the relationship between perceived ease of use, perceived usefulness, trust, and e-tax system behavior. [GBFR]. *Global Business & Finance Review, 28*(7), 89–104. DOI: 10.17549/gbfr.2023.28.7.89

Razak, A. A., & Adafula, C. J. (2013, September). Evaluating taxpayers " attitude and its influ ence on tax compliance decisions in Tamale, Ghana. *Journal of Accounting and Taxation, 5*(3), 48–57. DOI: 10.5897/JAT2013.0120

Safian, N., & Ngah, N. (2020, October). The Influence Of Attıtude Towards Tax Complıance Behavıour Among Cıvıl Servants In Selangor. In *Proceedıng: 3rd Internatıonal Conference On Global Busıness And Socıal Scıence 2020 (3RD ICGBSS 2020)* (p. 44).

Schmölders, G. (1959). Fiscal psychology: A new branch of public finance. *National Tax Journal, 12*(4), 340–345. DOI: 10.1086/NTJ41790780

Simuyu, K. E., & Jagongo, A. (2019). Impact of online tax filing on tax compliance among small and medium enterprises in Kibwezi Sub-county in Kenya. *International Journal of Current Research, 9*(1), 45196–45206.

Sritharan, N., & Salawati, S. (2019). Economic factors impact on individual taxpayers" tax compliance behaviour in Malaysia. Nternational Journal of Academic Research in Accounting. *Finance and Management Sciences, 9*(2), 172–182. DOI: 10.6007/IJARAFMS/v9-i2/6166

Svanoe, H. T. (1944). "Cost to Life Insurance Companies of Tax Compliance in Information at the Source". *Proceedings of the Annual Conference on Taxation under the Auspices of the National Tax Association 37.*

Teega, S. (2008). The Effect of Tax Education on Tax Compliance in Uganda: A Case Study of Kampala Central Tax District. Uganda Martyrs University. https://ir.umu.ac.ug/xmlui/handle/20.500.12280/972

Tekin, A., Doğan, E., & Çelikay, F. (2018). Vergi Ahlakı Kavramsallaştırmasına Yönelik Bir Değerlendirme: Eskişehir-Kütahya Örneği. *Maliye Dergisi*, *175*, 228–252.

Torgler, B. (2003). To Evade Taxes or Not to Evade: That is the Question. *Journal of Socio-Economics*, *32*(3), 283–302. DOI: 10.1016/S1053-5357(03)00040-4

Trawule, A. Y., Gadzo, S. G., Kportorgbi, H. K., & Sam-Quarm, R. (2022). Tax education and fear-appealing messages: A grease or sand in the wheels of tax compliance? *Cogent Business & Management*, *9*(1), 2049436. Advance online publication. DOI: 10.1080/23311975.2022.2049436

Utama, M. S., Nimran, U., Hidayat, K., & Prasetya, A. (2022). Effect of religiosity, perceived risk, and attitude on tax compliant intention moderated by e-filing. *International Journal of Financial Studies*, *10*(1), 8. DOI: 10.3390/ijfs10010008

Vincent, O. (2021). Assessing SMEs tax non-compliance behaviour in Sub-Saharan Africa (SSA): An insight from Nigeria. *Cogent Business & Management*, *8*(1), 1938930. DOI: 10.1080/23311975.2021.1938930

Yepes-López, G. A., & Gergerlioğlu, U. (2022). Tax Education and the Attitude of University Students Towards Tax Consciousness: The Case of University of Externado (Colombia). *Journal of Tax Reform*, *8*(1), 69–87. DOI: 10.15826/jtr.2022.8.1.109

Zakaria, Z., Hussin, Z. H., Zakaria, Z., Noordin, N. B., Sawal, M. Z. H. B. M., Saad, S. F. B. M., & Kamil, S. B. O. (2009). E-Filing System Practiced by Inland Revenue Board (IRB): Perception towards Malaysian Taxpayers/Systeme De Depot Electronique Applique Par Inland Revenue Board (Irb): Perception Des Contribuables De Malaisie. *Cross-Cultural Communication*, *5*(4), 10.

APPENDIX 1

Table 13. Cross-tabulation analysis of the Relationship between Perception of the Tax System & Motivation for Germany

Perception of the Tax System		The motivation for paying taxes being religion			The motivation for paying taxes being morality		
		No	Yes	Total	No	Yes	Total
Disagree (Negative)	Count	16	16	32	18	14	32
	% within P.S.	50,0%	50,0%	100,0%	56,3%	43,8%	100,0%
	% within Country	30,8%	18,6%	23,2%	34,6%	16,3%	23,2%
Neutral	Count	20	36	56	30	26	56
	% within P.S.	35,7%	64,3%	100,0%	53,6%	46,4%	100,0%
	% within Country	38,5%	41,9%	40,6%	57,7%	30,2%	40,6%
Agree (Positive)	Count	16	34	50	4	46	50
	% within P.S.	32,0%	68,0%	100,0%	8,0%	92,0%	100,0%
	% within Country	30,8%	39,5%	36,2%	7,7%	53,5%	36,2%
Total	Count	52	86	138	52	86	138
	% within P.S.	37,7%	62,3%	100,0%	37,7%	62,3%	100,0%
	% within Country	100,0%	100,0%	100,0%	100,0%	100,0%	100,0%

Table 14. Cross-tabulation analysis of the Relationship between Perception of the Tax System & Motivation for Austria

Perception of the Tax System		The motivation for paying taxes being religion			The motivation for paying taxes being morality		
		No	Yes	Total	No	Yes	Total
Disagree (Negative)	Count	10	4	14	12	2	14
	% within P.S	71,4%	28,6%	100,0%	85,7%	14,3%	100,0%
	% within Country	26,3%	6,9%	14,6%	30,0%	3,6%	14,6%
Neutral	Count	20	32	52	18	34	52
	% within P.S	38,5%	61,5%	100,0%	34,6%	65,4%	100,0%
	% within Country	52,6%	55,2%	54,2%	45,0%	60,7%	54,2%

continued on following page

Table 14. Continued

Perception of the Tax System		The motivation for paying taxes being religion			The motivation for paying taxes being morality		
		No	Yes	Total	No	Yes	Total
Agree (Positive)	Count	8	22	30	10	20	30
	% within P.S	26,7%	73,3%	100,0%	33,3%	66,7%	100,0%
	% within Country	21,1%	37,9%	31,3%	25,0%	35,7%	31,3%
Total	Count	38	58	96	40	56	96
	% within P.S	39,6%	60,4%	100,0%	41,7%	58,3%	100,0%
	% within Country	100,0%	100,0%	100,0%	100,0%	100,0%	100,0%

Table 15. Cross-tabulation analysis of the Relationship between Perception of the Tax System & Motivation for Belgium

Perception of the Tax System		The motivation for paying taxes being religion			The motivation for paying taxes being morality		
		No	Yes	Total	No	Yes	Total
Disagree (Negative)	Count	16	20	36	8	28	36
	% within P.S	44,4%	55,6%	100,0%	22,2%	77,8%	100,0%
	% within Country	27,6%	20,4%	23,1%	28,6%	21,9%	23,1%
Neutral	Count	36	36	72	16	56	72
	% within P.S	50,0%	50,0%	100,0%	22,2%	77,8%	100,0%
	% within Country	62,1%	36,7%	46,2%	57,1%	43,8%	46,2%
Agree (Positive)	Count	6	42	48	4	44	48
	% within P.S	12,5%	87,5%	100,0%	8,3%	91,7%	100,0%
	% within Country	10,3%	42,9%	30,8%	14,3%	34,4%	30,8%
Total	Count	58	98	156	28	128	156
	% within P.S	37,2%	62,8%	100,0%	17,9%	82,1%	100,0%
	% within Country	100,0%	100,0%	100,0%	100,0%	100,0%	100,0%

Table 16. Cross-tabulation analysis of the Relationship between Perception of the Tax System & Motivation for Netherlands

Perception of the Tax System		**The motivation for paying taxes being religion**			**The motivation for paying taxes being morality**		
		No	**Yes**	**Total**	**No**	**Yes**	**Total**
Disagree (Negative)	Count	10	34	44	10	34	44
	% within P.S	22,7%	77,3%	100,0%	22,7%	77,3%	100,0%
	% within Country	17,9%	26,6%	23,9%	15,2%	28,8%	23,9%
Neutral	Count	36	70	106	44	62	106
	% within P.S	34,0%	66,0%	100,0%	41,5%	58,5%	100,0%
	% within Country	64,3%	54,7%	57,6%	66,7%	52,5%	57,6%
Agree (Positive)	Count	10	24	34	12	22	34
	% within P.S	29,4%	70,6%	100,0%	35,3%	64,7%	100,0%
	% within Country	17,9%	18,8%	18,5%	18,2%	18,6%	18,5%
Total	Count	56	128	184	66	118	184
	% within P.S	30,4%	69,6%	100,0%	35,9%	64,1%	100,0%
	% within Country	100,0%	100,0%	100,0%	100,0%	100,0%	100,0%

Table 17. Cross-tabulation analysis of the Relationship between Perception of the Tax System & Motivation for France

Perception of the Tax System		**The motivation for paying taxes being religion**			**The motivation for paying taxes being morality**		
		No	**Yes**	**Total**	**No**	**Yes**	**Total**
Disagree (Negative)	Count	44	10	54	42	14	56
	% within P.S	81,5%	18,5%	100,0%	75,0%	25,0%	100,0%
	% within Country	56,4%	31,3%	49,1%	58,3%	35,0%	50,0%
Neutral	Count	30	12	42	22	20	42
	% within P.S	71,4%	28,6%	100,0%	52,4%	47,6%	100,0%
	% within Country	38,5%	37,5%	38,2%	30,6%	50,0%	37,5%
Agree (Positive)	Count	4	10	14	8	6	14
	% within P.S	28,6%	71,4%	100,0%	57,1%	42,9%	100,0%
	% within Country	5,1%	31,3%	12,7%	11,1%	15,0%	12,5%

continued on following page

Table 17. Continued

Perception of the Tax System		The motivation for paying taxes being religion			The motivation for paying taxes being morality		
		No	Yes	Total	No	Yes	Total
Total	Count	78	32	110	72	40	112
	% within P.S	70,9%	29,1%	100,0%	64,3%	35,7%	100,0%
	% within Country	100,0%	100,0%	100,0%	100,0%	100,0%	100,0%

APPENDIX 2

Table 18. Cross-tabulation analysis of the Relationship between Perception of the Tax System-Tax Applications& Motivation for Germany

Perception of the Tax System and Tax Applications		Perception of the Tax System			Perception of the Tax Applications		
		The motivation for paying taxes being obligation					
		No	Yes	Total	No	Yes	Total
Disagree (Negative)	Count	18	14	32	36	26	62
	% within P.S.	56,3%	43,8%	100,0%	58,1%	41,9%	100,0%
	% within Country	20,0%	29,2%	23,2%	40,0%	54,2%	44,9%
Neutral	Count	42	14	56	46	20	66
	% within P.S.	75,0%	25,0%	100,0%	69,7%	30,3%	100,0%
	% within Country	46,7%	29,2%	40,6%	51,1%	41,7%	47,8%
Agree (Positive)	Count	30	20	50	8	2	10
	% within P.S.	93,8%	62,5%	156,3%	80,0%	20,0%	100,0%
	% within Country	33,3%	41,7%	36,2%	8,9%	4,2%	7,2%
Total	Count	90	48	138	90	48	138
	% within P.S.	65,2%	34,8%	100,0%	65,2%	34,8%	100,0%
	% within Country	100,0%	100,0%	100,0%	100,0%	100,0%	100,0%

Table 19. Cross-tabulation analysis of the Relationship between Perception of the Tax System-Tax Applications& Motivation for Austria

Perception of the Tax System and Tax Applications		Perception of the Tax Ssytem			Perception of the Tax Applications		
		The motivation for paying taxes being obligation					
		No	Yes	Total	No	Yes	Total
Disagree (Negative)	Count	4	10	14	14	38	52
	% within P.S.	28,6%	71,4%	100,0%	26,9%	73,1%	100,0%
	% within Country	11,8%	16,1%	14,6%	41,2%	61,3%	54,2%
Neutral	Count	18	34	52	16	20	36
	% within P.S.	34,6%	65,4%	100,0%	44,4%	55,6%	100,0%
	% within Country	52,9%	54,8%	54,2%	47,1%	32,3%	37,5%
Agree (Positive)	Count	10	14	24	4	4	8
	% within P.S.	41,6%	58,4%	100,0%	50,0%	50,0%	100,0%
	% within Country	35,3%	29,0%	31,3%	11,8%	6,5%	8,3%
Total	Count	34	62	96	34	62	96
	% within P.S.	35,4%	64,6%	100,0%	35,4%	64,6%	100,0%
	% within Country	100,0%	100,0%	100,0%	100,0%	100,0%	100,0%

Table 20. Cross-tabulation analysis of the Relationship between Perception of the Tax System-Tax Applications& Motivation for Belgium

Perception of the Tax System and Tax Applications		Perception of the Tax Ssytem			Perception of the Tax Applications		
		The motivation for paying taxes being obligation					
		No	Yes	Total	No	Yes	Total
Disagree (Negative)	Count	20	16	36	30	56	86
	% within P.S.	55,6%	44,4%	100,0%	34,9%	65,1%	100,0%
	% within Country	28,6%	18,6%	23,1%	42,9%	65,1%	55,1%
Neutral	Count	32	40	72	28	22	50
	% within P.S.	44,4%	55,6%	100,0%	56,0%	44,0%	100,0%
	% within Country	45,7%	46,5%	46,2%	40,0%	25,6%	32,1%
Agree (Positive)	Count	18	30	48	12	8	20
	% within P.S.	37,5%	62,5%	100,0%	60,0%	40,0%	100,0%
	% within Country	25,7%	34,9%	30,8%	17,1%	9,3%	12,8%
Total	Count	70	86	156	70	86	156
	% within P.S.	44,9%	55,1%	100,0%	44,9%	55,1%	100,0%
	% within Country	100,0%	100,0%	100,0%	100,0%	100,0%	100,0%

Table 21. Cross-tabulation analysis of the Relationship between Perception of the Tax System-Tax Applications & Motivation for Netherlands

Perception of the Tax System and Tax Applications		Perception of the Tax Ssytem			Perception of the Tax Applications		
		The motivation for paying taxes being obligation					
		No	Yes	Total	No	Yes	Total
Disagree (Negative)	Count	38	4	42	46	22	68
	% within P.S.	90,5%	9,5%	100,0%	67,6%	32,4%	100,0%
	% within Country	28,4%	8,3%	23,1%	34,3%	45,8%	37,4%
Neutral	Count	82	24	106	76	12	88
	% within P.S.	77,4%	22,6%	100,0%	86,4%	13,6%	100,0%
	% within Country	61,2%	50,0%	58,2%	56,7%	25,0%	48,4%
Agree (Positive)	Count	14	20	34	12	14	26
	% within P.S.	41,2%	58,8%	100,0%	46,2%	53,8%	100,0%
	% within Country	10,4%	41,7%	18,7%	9,0%	29,2%	14,3%
Total	Count	134	48	182	134	48	182
	% within P.S.	73,6%	26,4%	100,0%	73,6%	26,4%	100,0%
	% within Country	100,0%	100,0%	100,0%	100,0%	100,0%	100,0%

Table 22. Cross-tabulation analysis of the Relationship between Perception of the Tax System-Tax Applications & Motivation for France

Perception of the Tax System and Tax Applications		Perception of the Tax System			Perception of the Tax Applications		
		The motivation for paying taxes being obligation					
		No	Yes	Total	No	Yes	Total
Disagree (Negative)	Count	48	6	54	42	10	52
	% within P.S.	88,9%	11,1%	100,0%	80,8%	19,2%	100,0%
	% within Country	54,5%	27,3%	49,1%	47,7%	45,5%	47,3%
Neutral	Count	30	12	42	36	8	44
	% within P.S.	71,4%	28,6%	100,0%	81,8%	18,2%	100,0%
	% within Country	34,1%	54,5%	38,2%	40,9%	36,4%	40,0%
Agree (Positive)	Count	10	4	14	10	4	14
	% within P.S.	71,4%	28,6%	100,0%	71,4%	28,6%	100,0%
	% within Country	11,4%	18,2%	12,7%	11,4%	18,2%	12,7%
Total	Count	88	22	110	88	22	110
	% within P.S.	80,0%	20,0%	100,0%	80,0%	20,0%	100,0%
	% within Country	100,0%	100,0%	100,0%	100,0%	100,0%	100,0%

Table 23. Cross-tabulation analysis of the Relationship between Attitudes towards the Tax System-Tax Applications& Motivation for Germany

Attitudes towards the Tax System and Tax Applications		Attitudes towards the Tax System			Attitudes towards the Tax Applications		
		The motivation for paying taxes being obligation					
		No	Yes	Total	No	Yes	Total
Disagree (Negative)	Count	20	4	24	24	18	42
	% within A.S.	83,3%	16,7%	100,0%	57,1%	42,9%	100,0%
	% within Country	22,2%	8,3%	17,4%	26,7%	37,5%	30,4%
Neutral	Count	46	18	64	44	22	66
	% within A.S.	71,9%	28,1%	100,0%	66,7%	33,3%	100,0%
	% within Country	51,1%	37,5%	46,4%	48,9%	45,8%	47,8%
Agree (Positive)	Count	24	26	50	22	8	30
	% within A.S.	48,0%	52,0%	100,0%	73,3%	26,7%	100,0%
	% within Country	26,7%	54,2%	36,2%	24,4%	16,7%	21,7%
Total	Count	90	48	138	90	48	138
	% within A.S.	65,2%	34,8%	100,0%	65,2%	34,8%	100,0%
	% within Country	100,0%	100,0%	100,0%	100,0%	100,0%	100,0%

Table 24. Cross-tabulation analysis of the Relationship between Attitudes towards the Tax System-Tax Applications& Motivation for Austria

Attitudes towards the Tax System and Tax Applications		Attitudes towards the Tax System			Attitudes towards the Tax Applications		
		The motivation for paying taxes being obligation					
		No	Yes	Total	No	Yes	Total
Disagree (Negative)	Count	6	10	16	10	4	14
	% within A.S.	37,5%	62,5%	100,0%	71,4%	28,6%	100,0%
	% within Country	17,6%	16,1%	16,7%	29,4%	6,5%	14,6%
Neutral	Count	20	26	46	14	40	54
	% within A.S.	43,5%	56,5%	100,0%	25,9%	74,1%	100,0%
	% within Country	58,8%	41,9%	47,9%	41,2%	64,5%	56,3%
Agree (Positive)	Count	8	26	34	10	18	28
	% within A.S.	23,5%	76,5%	100,0%	35,7%	64,3%	100,0%
	% within Country	23,5%	41,9%	35,4%	29,4%	29,0%	29,2%
Total	Count	34	62	96	34	62	96
	% within A.S.	35,4%	64,6%	100,0%	35,4%	64,6%	100,0%
	% within Country	100,0%	100,0%	100,0%	100,0%	100,0%	100,0%

Table 25. Cross-tabulation analysis of the Relationship between Attitudes towards the Tax System-Tax Applications& Motivation for Belgium

Attitudes towards the Tax System and Tax Applications		Attitudes towards the Tax System			Attitudes towards the Tax Applications		
		The motivation for paying taxes being obligation					
		No	Yes	Total	No	Yes	Total
Disagree (Negative)	Count	12	10	22	22	18	40
	% within A.S.	54,5%	45,5%	100,0%	55,0%	45,0%	100,0%
	% within Country	17,1%	11,6%	14,1%	31,4%	20,9%	25,6%
Neutral	Count	28	34	62	30	50	80
	% within A.S.	45,2%	54,8%	100,0%	37,5%	62,5%	100,0%
	% within Country	40,0%	39,5%	39,7%	42,9%	58,1%	51,3%
Agree (Positive)	Count	30	42	72	18	18	36
	% within A.S.	41,7%	58,3%	100,0%	50,0%	50,0%	100,0%
	% within Country	42,9%	48,8%	46,2%	25,7%	20,9%	23,1%
Total	Count	70	86	156	70	86	156
	% within A.S.	44,9%	55,1%	100,0%	44,9%	55,1%	100,0%
	% within Country	100,0%	100,0%	100,0%	100,0%	100,0%	100,0%

Table 26. Cross-tabulation analysis of the Relationship between Attitudes towards the Tax System-Tax Applications & Motivation for Netherlands

Attitudes towards the Tax System and Tax Applications		Attitudes towards the Tax System			Attitudes towards the Tax Applications		
		The motivation for paying taxes being obligation					
		No	Yes	Total	No	Yes	Total
Disagree (Negative)	Count	36	6	42	34	2	36
	% within A.S.	85,7%	14,3%	100,0%	94,4%	5,6%	100,0%
	% within Country	26,9%	12,5%	23,1%	25,4%	4,2%	19,8%
Neutral	Count	82	18	100	90	30	120
	% within A.S.	82,0%	18,0%	100,0%	75,0%	25,0%	100,0%
	% within Country	61,2%	37,5%	54,9%	67,2%	62,5%	65,9%
gree (Positive)	Count	16	24	40	10	16	26
	% within A.S.	40,0%	60,0%	100,0%	38,5%	61,5%	100,0%
	% within Country	11,9%	50,0%	22,0%	7,5%	33,3%	14,3%
Total	Count	134	48	182	134	48	182
	% within A.S.	73,6%	26,4%	100,0%	73,6%	26,4%	100,0%
	% within Country	100,0%	100,0%	100,0%	100,0%	100,0%	100,0%

Table 27. Cross-tabulation analysis of the Relationship between Attitudes towards the Tax System-Tax Applications & Motivation for France

Attitudes towards the Tax System and Tax Applications		Attitudes towards the Tax System			Attitudes towards the Tax Applications		
		The motivation for paying taxes being obligation					
		No	Yes	Total	No	Yes	Total
Disagree (Negative)	Count	30	2	32	34	0	34
	% within A.S.	93,8%	6,3%	100,0%	100,0%	0,0%	100,0%
	% within Country	34,1%	9,1%	29,1%	38,6%	0,0%	30,9%
Neutral	Count	34	2	36	42	16	58
	% within A.S.	94,4%	5,6%	100,0%	72,4%	27,6%	100,0%
	% within Country	38,6%	9,1%	32,7%	47,7%	72,7%	52,7%
Agree (Positive)	Count	24	18	42	12	6	18
	% within A.S.	57,1%	42,9%	100,0%	66,7%	33,3%	100,0%
	% within Country	27,3%	81,8%	38,2%	13,6%	27,3%	16,4%
Total	Count	88	22	110	88	22	110
	% within A.S.	80,0%	20,0%	100,0%	80,0%	20,0%	100,0%
	% within Country	100,0%	100,0%	100,0%	100,0%	100,0%	100,0%

Chapter 6

Effect of Tax Solidarity on the Taxpayer's Sense of Civic Duty by Mediation of Tax Morality in the Horn of Africa

Tamire Ashuro
Bule Hora University, Ethiopia

Shashi Kant
https://orcid.org/0000-0003-4722-5736
Bule Hora University, Ethiopia

Zerihun Kinde Alemu
Ethiopian Civil Service University, Ethiopia

Gebre Sorsa Takaro
https://orcid.org/0000-0003-0846-2894
Ethiopian Civil Service University, Ethiopia

ABSTRACT

In order to improve taxpayers' civic participation and tax compliance, this research examines the complex connections between tax solidarity, tax morality, and civic obligation. The study illustrates how these elements combine to affect people's feeling of civic duty by examining the functions of tax morality as an ethical issue and tax solidarity as a social ideal. According to the research, encouraging a feeling of community around tax payments can greatly increase compliance rates by establishing a moral duty to support the common good. Additionally, the study finds that tax morality plays a significant mediating role in this connection, highlighting the necessity of public awareness efforts and ethical education to preserve the moral aspects of taxes. These findings have ramifications for legislators and public officials, who are urged to put policies into place that support openness, involvement of the community, and moral responsibility in taxation. In the end, the study urges greater investigation into socioeconomic and cultural elements that could influence taxpayer behavior.

DOI: 10.4018/979-8-3373-0422-9.ch006

STUDY BACKGROUND

Influence tax systems must include together tax solidarity and a feeling of civic responsibility among taxpayers, particularly in emerging nations like the Eastern part of Africa. Understanding the association among tax compliance and civic duty is crucial as global economies grow more and more reliant on steady income streams for public goods and services (Amelio et al., 2024; Greggi et al., 2024). Tax solidarity manifests the shared responsibility of citizens to pay taxes to the administration, acknowledging that these involvements are indispensable for infrastructure improvement and communal wellbeing. The implication of nurturing a culture of tax compliance founded on civic responsibility cannot be emphasized as economies throughout the world strive to augment their tax systems in the face of issues like economic disparity and public discontent (Cascavilla, 2023). Communal contract theories, which place an emphasis on reciprocal duties among citizens and their administrations, are where the idea of tax solidarity first emerged. As per to this association, people are more willing to pay their taxes when they believe their involvements benefit society (Guyo et al., 2024). Cultural, communal, and institutional settings have a substantial influence on taxpayer conduct, as per to empirical investigation that has examined a variety of elements that influence tax morality (Cascavilla et al., 2024). As per to studies, those who have a strong feeling of belonging and confidence in administration agencies typically have greater tax morale, which in turn leads to higher compliance. Establishing successful tax cultures is made more difficult in the Eastern part of Africa by particular difficulties, such as political unpredictability, widespread informality, and a lack of faith in administration institutions (Stetsenko & Nishcheretov, 2021).

The Eastern part of Africa faces substantial challenges in taxation, exacerbated by political instability and widespread informality. For instance, Somalia's reliance on clan-founded taxation illustrates how informal systems can overshadow formal administration revenue, creating gaps in state funding (Cascavilla, 2023). In Ethiopia, high levels of corruption have led to public distrust; citizens often perceive taxes as benefiting elites rather than funding indispensable services. To augment practical relevance, case studies should be integrated (Guo & Gong, 2024). For a case study, Kenya's success with the iTax system demonstrates how digitalization can streamline tax processes and augment compliance. By leveraging mobile technology, Kenya has augmented revenue and transparency, serving as a model for neighboring economies. Also, fostering partnerships among administrations and technology firms can facilitate the implementation of digital tax solutions. Real-world applications of these strategies can be seen in Tanzania, where efforts to formalize the informal economy through registration campaigns have begun to yield results (Amelio et al., 2024; Greggi et al., 2024). By combining technology, community engagement, and robust governance, economies in the Eastern part of Africa can build more influence tax systems that augment public trust and augment civic responsibility.

Inadequate tax administration, pervasive corruption, and a lack of taxpayer education are real obstacles to augmenting tax solidarity in the Eastern part of Africa (Guo & Gong, 2024). These elements eventually undermine compliance attempts by making taxpayers feel less civically obligated. As well, current empirical investigation frequently ignores the unique sociopolitical circumstances of the Eastern part of Africa, leaving gaps in our understanding of how indigenous dynamics influence civic duty as well tax morality. By offering a thorough examination of the influence of tax solidarity on taxpayers' sense of civic responsibility, mediated by tax morality in the Eastern part of Africa, this chapter seeks to close these gaps. The investigation will clarify the complex associations among these ideas and provide insights into how tax laws might be changed to augment compliance by fusing theoretical frameworks with actual evidence. The main issue that motivates this investigation is: ***"How does tax solidarity in-***

fluence the taxpayer's sense of civic duty through the mediation of tax morality in the Eastern part of Africa, and what strategies can be implemented to strengthen these inter associations in the region's unique socio-political landscape?"

CHAPTER JUSTIFICATION

The Eastern part of Africa, the cover country, has a diverse tax system shaped by historical heritage and socioeconomic dynamics. Historically, colonial regimes have introduced a tax system in which income priorities often ignored public wellbeing and civic participation. After independence, many economies with all troops sought to reform these systems due to political instability, conflict, and inadequate institutional executive (Cascavilla, 2023). Key issues with indigenous tax systems include high levels of informality, low response metrics, and limited management capabilities. The informal sector, which constitutes an important part of the economy, escapes official taxation by receiving state revenue. Also, common corruption and low managers further destroy taxpayer trust and civil obligations, complicating efforts to develop tax culture. Recent reforms aim to expand the tax base, augment compliance and augment public engagement in tax issues. As well, these efforts often face resistance due to the incorporated sociopolitical issues and the lack of indigenous research dealing with the country's own context (Amelio et al., 2024; Greggi et al., 2024).

Theoretical models of tax behavior often fall short in fragile or informal economies, as they may not account for the complexities of communal norms and trust in governance. The limited application of these models in the Eastern part of Africa highlights the need for more region-specific research to understas well taxpayer motivations and the influence of tax solidarity on civic duty, particularly in settings with substantial informal economic activity. The imposition in the Eastern part of Africa is influenced by a mixture of historical heritage, socio-economic conditions and cultural practices (Sandu, 2022). Traditional tax systems, often established in colonial times, had trouble evolving in the face of political instability and continuous conflicts. Informal institutions such as clans and religious taxation play an important function in indigenous management. Clans fund public services and impose taxes to maintain communal order, but religious institutions can gather adequate paths or zakats to strengthen cultural norms, a main concern for community wells (Guyo et al., 2024). Corruption has a serious influence on tax morale in the region. If taxpayers perceive involvements to be sucked up by corrupt officials, their desire to adhere to decreases. This erosion of trust creates a cycle of low compliance and reducing the provision of public services, which further contributes to the perception of corruption. Citizens often believe that taxes are not transferred to public benefits, which leads to a wide evasion of taxes and the culture of distrust in the administration (Guo & Gong, 2024; Sandu, 2022). Digitalization becomes an important factor in augmenting tax collection. Electronic management and mobile payment platform initiatives optimize tax processes, augment transparency and augment compliance. When taxpayers allow them to follow their involvements, digital tools can potentially restore confidence and augment the moral tax spirit. As well, the influenceness of these initiatives depends on the appropriate infrastructure and digital literacy, particularly in areas that have not been developed. Overall, while digitalization offers promising solutions, it must be accompanied by efforts to combat corruption and augment public trust in tax systems (Schmidt et al., 2023).

LITERATURE GAPS AND PRACTICAL CHALLENGES

Ideally, a strong tax system would foster a strong sense of civic duty among citizens, leading to high levels of compliance and equitable involvement to state resources. In this ideal scenario, citizens recognize their function in depicting public goods and services, fostering a culture of trust and mutual responsibility among the administration and its constituents. The Eastern part of Africa's tax compliance problem is complex and reflects a substantial disconnect among the ideal state of tax solidarity and the realities that taxpayers face today (Rika Widianita, 2023). As well, the current situation reveals a concerning paradox: even though tax compliance is understanding to be substantial for the improvement of the country, many citizens have low tax morale and a weak sense of civic duty, which leads to substantial revenue losses and impedes the provision of public services (Sandu, 2022). Contradictory outcomes about the elements influencing tax morale in the literature now under publication exacerbate this disjunction. The influence of communal norms and community consequences on taxpayer behavior is highlighted in some investigation (Amelio et al., 2024; Greggi et al., 2024), while others stress the importance of views of corruption and faith in the administration (Guo & Gong, 2024; Sandu, 2022). These contradictory outcomes leave gaps in our understanding of the precise interactions among these factors in the Eastern part of Africa. Also, the empirical outcomes are frequently equivocal, indicating that further investigation is necessary to fully understand the association among civic responsibility, tax morality, as well tax solidarity. There are still theoretical gaps as well, especially with regard to the subtleties of the setting that influence taxpayer behavior in the Eastern part of Africa (Guyo et al., 2024). The majority of current frameworks were created in various socioeconomic circumstances, sometimes neglecting to take into consideration the distinct political and cultural dynamics that exist in the area. Also, because a large portion of the investigation is generic and does not take into account indigenous circumstances, there are substantial information gaps about the particular incentives and obstacles to compliance that taxpayers in the Eastern part of Africa confront (Schmidt et al., 2023).

The scenario is made more difficult by contextual issues. A strong feeling of civic responsibility cannot be fostered in an environment that is characterized by political instability, poor governance, pervasive informality, and a lack of influence taxpayer education (Amelio et al., 2024). These real-world obstacles jeopardize initiatives to augment tax compliance and emphasize the necessity of regional studies that may guide focused policy changes. By offering a thorough examination of the association among tax solidarity as well taxpayers' feeling of civic responsibility in the Eastern part of Africa via the lens of tax morality, this investigation seeks to close these gaps (Kant & Adula, 2025). This project will investigate the unique institutional, communal, and cultural elements that influence taxpayer behavior in the area using a mixed-methods approach that blends qualitative and quantitative investigation. As well, it will evaluate influence case studies and best practices from other settings, assimilating useful manifestations catered to the particular difficulties faced by the Eastern part of Africa (Guyo et al., 2024).

By filling up these complex gaps, our investigation will augment the scholarly conversation on tax compliance while also offering policymakers useful information. The outcomes will work as a guide for upcoming scholars and professionals, directing initiatives to augment tax structures, encourage civic engagement, and advance sustainable improvement in the Eastern part of Africa.

THEORETICAL REVIEW

Communal Contract Theory: A number of interconnected theories that offer a thorough explanation of tax compliance behaviors serve as the foundation for the investigation of tax solidarity and the taxpayer's feeling of civic obligation. One fundamental perspective is the Communal Contract perspective, which holds that in return for protection and the provision of public goods, people agree to give up part of their liberties and submit to administrational power. As per to this view, people feel a strong sense of civic obligation when they believe that their taxes support the wellbeing of society, manifesting the reciprocal link among the state and its residents. The influenceness of this communal compact may be questioned in the Eastern part of Africa, where administrational competence may be seen as poor, which might outcome in lower tax morale (Schmidt et al., 2023).
Tax Morale Theory: Tax Morale Theory is another pertinent theory that highlights people's natural incentives to fulfill their tax duties founded on moral and ethical principles rather than coercive enforcement. This approach emphasizes how societal norms, cultural consequences, and personal beliefs influence the attitudes of taxpayers. Knowing how civic duty as well tax morale interact might help augment compliance in areas like the Eastern part of Africa, where indigenous norms and community ties greatly influence behavior (Amelio et al., 2024; Schmidt et al., 2023).
Institutional Theory: Grasp tax compliance also requires a grasp of institutional theory. This theory looks at how taxpayer behavior is influenced by the procedures and structures of institutions, including political systems, legal frameworks, as well tax administrations. Institutional flaws like poor governance and corruption can damage tax systems' credibility in the Eastern part of Africa, which will ultimately make compliance more difficult (Cabelkova & Smutka, 2021).

HYPOTHESES SYNETHIS

Tax Solidarity as Well as Taxpayer's Sense of Civic Duty

Empirical investigation has focused a lot of emphasis on the association among tax solidarity and the feeling of civic responsibility that taxpayers have, especially as administrations work to augment tax compliance and advance communal wellbeing. As per to a seminal investigation by (Stetsenko & Nishcheretov, 2021), people's beliefs of tax solidarity have a substantial influence on tax morale, which is defined as the innate drive to pay taxes. (Stetsenko & Nishcheretov, 2021) discovered that high tax morale is more common among those who have a strong sense of community and shared responsibility for paying for public amenities. This emphasizes the idea that paying taxes is a communal compact that links people to their communities as well as a legal requirement. (Sottomesso, 2020) further investigation emphasizes how communal norms influence tax compliance practices. As per to their outcomes, people are more willing to confirm their conduct to communal standards when they perceive that their peers are following the law and see paying taxes as a group duty. This supports the notion that a sense of civic responsibility may be fostered via fiscal solidarity, which is the shared commitment of citizens to support the state financially. When tax compliance is seen as a civic virtue, people are driven by together ethical concerns about their involvements to the benefit of society and the potential legal repercussions.

Numerous studies have examined how tax solidarity influences civic responsibility in developing nations where issues like corruption and poor governance are prevalent (Guyo et al., 2024).

As per to a Ukraine investigation by (Stetsenko & Nishcheretov, 2021), people are more likely to feel obligated to pay taxes if they believe that administration spending benefits their community. This manifests that taxpayers have a greater moral incentive to carry out their tax obligations when they witness the concrete outcomes of their involvements, such as augmented communal services and infrastructure. Nevertheless, empirical data also manifests inconsistencies in the association among civic responsibility as well tax solidarity. For a case study, an investigation by (Sandu, 2022) manifests that widespread corruption and a lack of faith in administration institutions cause tax compliance to stay low in some areas even when there is a high degree of perceived tax solidarity. This manifests that although tax solidarity is crucial, it is not a cure-all; the institutional environment has a major influence on how influence tax morale is. Also, investigation indicates that the link among civic obligation as well tax solidarity is substantially shaped by cultural variables. As per to (Ummah, 2019), people's perceptions of their tax responsibilities are influenced by cultural attitudes on taxes, which are shaped by historical and communal settings. Strong collectivist cultures are more likely to have a greater feeling of fiscal solidarity, which is correlated with a greater sense of civic responsibility. On the other hand, the association could be weaker in more individualistic societies, which would reflect different communal expectations about tax payments.

H1: Tax solidarity has a substantial influence on the taxpayer's sense of civic duty

Tax Solidarity as Well Tax Morality

The notion of tax morality, or the innate ethical duty people feel to pay taxes, is closely related to the idea of tax solidarity. A complex interaction of communal, psychological, and institutional elements has been revealed by empirical investigation that has increasingly concentrated on how tax morality is influenced by beliefs of tax solidarity. As per to a substantial amount of data, people's tax morale tends to rise and compliance rates tend to rise when they have a strong feeling of communal togetherness (Rika Widianita, 2023). A fundamental explanation of this association may be found in (Sandu, 2022) work, which manifests that people are more likely to feel morally bound to pay if they see taxes as a collective duty. As per to his investigation, tax solidarity creates a communal climate where paying taxes is viewed as a civic obligation rather than just a legal need. This is consistent with the more general idea of communal contract theory, which holds that people voluntarily support the administration in return for the advantages that come from infrastructure and public services (Guyo et al., 2024).

This link is further supported by investigation by (Schmidt et al., 2023), which manifests that people with higher tax morale are more likely to feel that tax systems are fair and influence. This belief is frequently reinforced by a sense of tax solidarity. As per to their investigation, people are more inclined to abide by tax laws when they believe that their taxes are being used wisely for the benefit of society. This manifests that tax solidarity acts as a stimulant to augment tax ethics, especially when the advantages of paying taxes are apparent and palpable to the populace. Also, investigation from a variety of settings, including (Amelio et al., 2024) work, manifests that communal norms and community expectations are substantial mediators of the link among tax morality as well tax solidarity. As per to Wenzel's investigation, people are more likely to fulfill their tax duties when they believe that their peers do the same. Communal pressure to abide by tax regulations may greatly strengthen moral duties in communities with substantial tax solidarity, generating a optimistic feedback loop where adherence strengthens bonds within the community (Guyo et al., 2024). The link among tax morality as well tax solidarity is sometimes strained in developing nations by concerns with governance and corruption. As per to a investigation by (Greggi et al., 2024), mistrust of administrational institutions can nevertheless compromise the efficacy of tax morality in areas where residents believe there is a high degree of tax solidarity. This emphasizes the need for the institutional context to foster ethical tax compliance, even if tax solidarity alone can augment tax morality. As well, studies conducted in certain cultural situations manifest that there might be substantial variation in the influence of tax solidarity on tax morality. For a case study, investigation by (Greggi et al., 2024) indicates that tax solidarity has a substantial influence on tax morality in collectivist societies, which have strong communal and communal ties. Individualistic societies, on the other hand, may manifests weaker associations among these concepts, which would be indicative of different communal attitudes around civic duty as well taxes.

H2: Tax solidarity has a substantial influence on Tax morality

Mediation of Tax Morality, Tax Solidarity, Taxpayer's Sense of Civic Duty

Empirical investigation has focused on the association among tax solidarity, tax morality, as well taxpayers' sense of civic responsibility, especially as nations look to augment tax compliance and encourage civic involvement. One substantial mediating factor that influences how tax solidarity influences people's views of their civic duties is tax morality. This link emphasizes how crucial it is to comprehend the processes by which societal perceptions of taxes influence individual tax compliance habits (Cabelkova & Smutka, 2021). (Cabelkova & Smutka, 2021) investigation provides a fundamental framework for comprehending this mediation influence. As per to Torgler, tax morality may be greatly augmented by tax solidarity, which is the collective duty people feel to contribute to the state. Individuals are more likely to understand the ethical implications of their tax payments when they have a strong sense of community. As a outcome of this internalization, people start to see paying taxes as together a moral and legal requirement to support their community, which heightens their feeling of civic responsibility. The idea that tax morality mediates the link among tax solidarity and civic responsibility is supported by additional empirical investigation, such as that conducted by (Ummah, 2019). As per to their outcomes, people are more likely to feel morally bound to abide by tax regulations if they believe that their tax payments are benefiting society. Their feeling of civic responsibility is strengthened by this moral obligation, which raises compliance rates. This mediation manifests that by bolstering taxpayers' moral incentives, increasing tax solidarity—through community involvement and awareness campaigns—can successfully augment a culture of tax compliance (Guyo et al., 2024).

Also, Wenzel's investigation has emphasized the relevance of communal norms in this mediation process (Stetsenko & Nishcheretov, 2021). As per to Wenzel's investigation, societal expectations about tax compliance rise in societies with a high level of tax solidarity, which augments tax morality. People are more inclined to follow suit when they observe their peers actively engaging in tax compliance as a civic obligation. As a outcome, tax morality serves as a link among the commitment of an individual to pay taxes and the sense of community solidarity, demonstrating how communal dynamics may influence individual motives. Given the difficulties caused by corruption in influence administration, the mediating function of tax morality is especially substantial in developing nations. For a case study, (Cabelkova & Smutka, 2021) stress that a lack of faith in administration institutions might compromise tax morality even in situations when tax solidarity is recognized. This manifests that although tax solidarity can augment tax morality, the perceived efficacy and integrity of administrational processes determine how influence this mediation is. Therefore, increasing the beneficial influences of tax solidarity on civic responsibility through tax morality requires bolstering institutional trust.

As well, this mediation association is substantially shaped by cultural influences. As per to investigation by (Guo & Gong, 2024), the benefits of tax solidarity on civic responsibility as well tax morality are more noticeable in collectivist cultures where communal cohesiveness and community are consequence. Individualistic cultures, on the other hand, may manifests weaker ties, which would be indicative of different communal attitudes about personal and group responsibilities. This emphasizes how crucial it is to place the mediation investigation within particular cultural contexts in order to completely comprehend the ways in which fiscal solidarity influences tax morality and, in turn, civic obligation.

H3: Tax morality Play substantial Mediation function among Tax solidarity as well taxpayer's sense of civic duty

Conceptual Framework framed on base of developed hypothesis is mentioned in figure 2.

Figure 1. Conceptual Framework

METHOD AND MATERIAL

The investigation used a quantitative methodology to investigate the association among taxpayers' feeling of civic responsibility, tax morality, as well tax solidarity in the Eastern part of Africa. Samples of 390 respondents—selected using a stratified random sampling technique to guarantee representation across several demographics, such as age, gender, income level, and educational background—were given a structured questionnaire. Founded on power examination considerations, the sample size of 390 was judged sufficient to ensure reliable statistical analyses. The investigation used a number of statistical methods to evaluate the constructs' validity and reliability, starting with the Bartlett's test of sphericity and the Kaiser-Meyer-Olkin (KMO) score. The sample size was sufficient for exploratory factor examination (EFA), as manifested by the KMO consequence, which validated the suitability of factor examination. The fundamental features of the constructions pertaining to civic responsibility, tax morality, as well tax solidarity were then determined by EFA. The EFA's outcomes supported the construct validity of the investigation's scales by identifying unique constituents that fit the theoretical framework.

Using AMOS software, Structural Equation Modeling (SEM) was used to validate the factor structure obtained from the EFA and to provide further validation. Complex interactions among the variables, such as the mediating function of tax morality among tax solidarity and the taxpayer's feeling of civic responsibility, might be examined thanks to SEM. To evaluate the proposed model's goodness of fit, the model fit indices—such as the Chi-square, Root Mean Square Error of Estimate (RMSEA), and Comparative

Fit Index (CFI)—were computed. Strong support for the manifested associations among the constructs was on condition that by the outcomes, which manifested a reasonable model fit. The scale's creation adhered to recognized protocols, guaranteeing the validity and reliability of the questionnaire's items. Items that assessed civic responsibility, tax solidarity, as well tax morality were modified from existing investigation and pre-tested on a smaller sample to augment the questionnaire. The final tool was made up of validated scales, which made it possible to measure the constructs precisely and augmented the overall dependability of the investigation outcomes.

DATA EXAMINATION

Table 1. Item-Total Statistics

	Scale Mean	Scale Variance	Corrected Item-Total Correlation	Cronbach's Alpha
Tax solidarity	6.8508	1.077	.680	.710
Tax morality	6.9317	1.098	.638	.773
Taxpayer's sense of civic duty	7.0542	.974	.655	.750

Source: Authors

Table 1 summarizes the item-total data for three tax-related structures: tax solidarity, tax morality, and taxpayer sense of civic obligation. Each concept is evaluated using four essential metrics: scale mean, scale variance, corrected item-total correlation, along with Cronbach's alpha. Tax solidarity possesses a mean of 6.8508 and an average variance of 1.077, as well as a corrected item-total correlation of.680 and a Cronbach's Alpha of.710, suggesting high reliability. Tax morality has a mean of 6.9317 as well as an average variance of 1.098, with a lower correlation (.638) although a higher reliability (.773). Finally, the average taxpayer's feeling of civic responsibility is 7.0542, with a variance of.974, a correlation of.655, and a reliability of.750. These values indicate a high level of internal consistency throughout the items.

Table 2. Descriptive Statistics

	Mean	Std. Deviation	Skewness		Kurtosis	
	Statistic	Statistic	Statistic	Std. Error	Statistic	Std. Error
Tax solidarity	3.5675	.60666	-.046	.122	-.595	.243
Tax morality	3.4867	.62157	-.039	.122	-.205	.243
Taxpayer's sense of civic duty	3.3642	.68553	-.264	.122	-.507	.243

Source: Authors

Table 2 includes statistical information on three tax-related constructs: tax solidarity, revenue morality, and taxpayer feeling of civic duty. Each concept is assessed using the average, standard deviation, skewness, along with kurtosis. Tax solidarity has a mean of 3.5675, standard deviation of.60666, skewness for -.046 along with kurtosis of -.595, indicating a distribution that is roughly average. Tax morality, featuring a mean of 3.4867 and a standard deviation of.62157, has a little downward skewness of -.039

as well as a kurtosis of -.205, indicating weak normalcy. Finally, taxpayers' feeling of civic obligation has a mean of 3.3642 and a standard deviation of.68553, with a the skewness of -.264 along with kurtosis of -.507, reflecting a more pronounced tail on the left. These statistics help understand the distribution characteristics of the constructs.

Table 3. Posterior Distribution

	Posterior			95% Credible Interval	
	Mode	**Mean**	**Variance**	**Lower Bound**	**Upper Bound**
Tax solidarity	3.5675	3.5675	.001	3.5077	3.6273
Tax morality	3.4867	3.4867	.001	3.4254	3.5479
Taxpayer's sense of civic duty	3.3642	3.3642	.001	3.2966	3.4317

Source: Authors

Table 3 shows the posterior distributions of three tax-related constructs: tax solidarity, revenue morality, and taxpayer sense of civic obligation. Each concept is characterized by its mode, mean, variance, and 95% credible interval. For financial solidarity, the standard deviation and mean are the same 3.5675, alongside a variation of.001 and a credible CI of 3.5077 to 3.6273. Tax morality has a median and mean of 3.4867, a variance of.001, and a credible CI of 3.4254–3.5479. Finally, taxpayers' feeling of civic obligation has a mode and mean of 3.3642, a variance of.001, and a credible CI of 3.2966–3.4317. These statistics give information on the uncertainty along with the accuracy associated with the estimates.

Table 4. Model Summary[b]

Model	R	R Square	Adjusted R Square	Std. Error of the Estimate	Durbin-Watson
1	.758[a]	.528	.124	.64168	2.257

a. Predictors: (Constant), Tax morality, Tax solidarity
b. Dependent Variable: Taxpayer's sense of civic duty
Source: Authors

Table 4 highlights the model outcomes that examine the relationship amongst tax morality with tax solidarity as predictors of taxpayers' sense of civic responsibility. The model has a correlation score (R) of.758, showing a strong parametric connection among the predictors alongside the dependent variable. The correlation coefficient (R Square) of .528 shows that about 52.8% the overall variance in taxpayer's feeling of civic responsibility can be determined through the combined impacts of tax morality along with tax solidarity. The modified Chi Square, at .124, demonstrates a moderate adjustment for the number of variables employed, exposing some limits in the model's explanatory ability. The estimate's standard error is.64168, and the Durbin-Watson value of 2.257 indicates no substantial heterogeneity in the residuals as well as indicating a credible model.

Table 5. ANOVA[a]

Model		Sum of Squares	df	Mean Square	F	Sig.
1	Regression	24.042	2	12.021	29.195	.000[b]
	Residual	163.466	397	.412		
	Total	187.509	399			

a. Dependent Variable: Taxpayer's sense of civic duty
b. Predictors: (Constant), Tax morality, Tax solidarity
Source: Authors

Table 5 shows the ANOVA findings for a regression framework that investigates the effects of tax morality along with tax solidarity on taxpayers' feeling of civic obligation. The regression's total number of squares is 24.042 with two degrees of freedom (df), resulting in an average square of 12.021. The F-statistic of 29.195 shows a substantial overall model fit, yielding a p-value (Sig.) of.000, implying strong evidence rejecting the null hypothesis being correct and demonstrating that at least one predictor has a meaningful effect on the dependent variable. The remaining amount of squares equals 163.466, with 397 variables of freedom, giving a mean square of.412. The overall sum of squares is 187.509, which includes either regression along with residual components, indicating that the model is valid for examining prediction influence.

Figure 2. Structure equation model

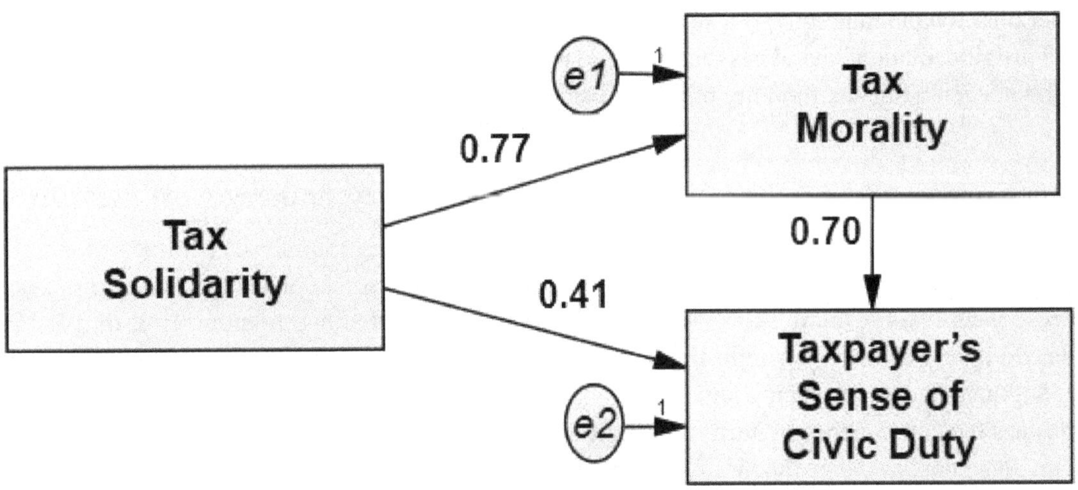

Table 6. Mediating function Influence

	Influence	worth	Path Influence
Tax solidarity → taxpayer's sense of civic duty	Direct Influence	.34	Direct influence stated
Tax solidarity → Tax morality → taxpayer's sense of civic duty	Indirect Influence	.59*.89=.54	Indirect Influence Ensued
	Whole influence	.88	Partial mediation

Source: Authors

The link among tax solidarity and the taxpayer's feeling of civic responsibility is mediated by tax morality, as manifest in Table 6. By differentiating among direct and indirect influences, the investigation offers a thorough understanding of the interactions among various constituents in the manifested model. Tax solidarity has a direct influence of 0.34 on the taxpayer's sense of civic responsibility. This consequence manifests a substantial optimistic influence, indicating that a greater feeling of civic responsibility among taxpayers is mostly correlated with higher levels of tax solidarity. This immediate influence emphasizes how crucial it is to augment communal harmony and shared accountability in order to augment civic involvement. The table also manifests how tax solidarity indirectly influences taxpayers' feeling of civic responsibility through tax morality, in addition to the direct approach. An indirect influence of 0.48 is obtained by multiplying the influence of tax morality on the taxpayer's feeling of civic responsibility (0.59) by the influence of tax solidarity on tax morality (0.89). This investigation manifests that tax solidarity influences civic obligation together directly and indirectly by augmenting tax morality, which in turn augments civic responsibility. When direct and indirect influences are included, the overall influence comes to 0.88. This substantial overall influence manifests that tax solidarity, together directly and indirectly, is a key factor in forming taxpayers' feeling of civic responsibility. The term "Partial mediation" manifests that tax solidarity is still a powerful indicator of civic responsibility on its own, even while tax morality plays a substantial function in the association.

DISCUSSION

The investigation's conclusions shed substantial light on the associations among taxpayers' sense of civic responsibility, tax morality, as well tax solidarity. As per to the investigation, civic duty is mostly influenced by tax solidarity, manifesting that a strong feeling of community and shared responsibility might augment people's participation in civic activities pertaining to tax compliance. This investigation emphasizes the consequence of nurturing a culture of solidarity, which might persuade taxpayers to see their involvements as a constituent of a larger endeavor to augment society. As well, the investigation found that a crucial mediator in this link is tax morality. Augmenting moral attitudes toward taxes can augment the benefits of solidarity, as evidenced by the indirect influence of tax solidarity on civic responsibility through tax morality. This mediating function emphasizes the necessity of programs that uphold the moral aspects of tax compliance while simultaneously fostering tax solidarity. A more responsible taxpayer base might be fostered by such activities, which could include educational programs that highlight the moral requirements and societal advantages of tax involvements. The interdependence of these constructs is further manifested by the large overall influence of 0.88, which manifests that together direct and indirect pathways are indispensable for comprehending how tax solidarity translates into civic obligation. The phrase "partial mediation" manifests that whereas tax morality strengthens the influence of tax solidarity, the latter still has a substantial independent influence. This investigation manifests that in addressing moral issues in taxes, administrations and civic leaders should give main concern to initiatives that foster tax solidarity. In summary, by clarifying the complex association among tax solidarity, tax morality, and civic responsibility, this investigation adds to the body of understanding on tax compliance. The outcomes point to practical ways that community-building programs and moral education might augment civic involvement and compliance. Stakeholders may augment a more assimilated and accountable taxpayer community by giving main concern to these constructions, which will eventually augment tax compliance and benefit society more broadly.

The results of cultural and communal influences as per to tax requirements guide influence reforms of tax policy for the Eastern part of Africa, manifesting the involvement of autism for community, cultural integrity and education. First, the involvement of indigenous and influential community leaders in tax debates can generate confidence and participation in the citizens. These leaders can protect taxes and create them not as administration requirements but as involvements to community wellbeing. Second, tax policies need to clearly link tax revenues with indigenous interests. For a case study, we can change perceptions by manifesting how tax funds support universities, healthcare and infrastructure, depicting taxation as a co-investment. This consistency with indigenous values can augment acceptance and compliance. Also, educational campaigns that meet community standards can destroy the tax process. The use of indigenous language and culturally important messages can augment understanding and participation. Demonstrations of successful tax-funded projects serve as a powerful a case study of the optimistic influence of involvements. Finally, implementation of incentive structures, such as compliant taxpayer recognition programs, can generate optimistic reinforcements. By transforming tax compliance into a communal duty recognized by peers, policymakers can foster a culture of compliance that strengthens the communal contract among citizens and the state, ultimately enhancing revenue collection and governance.

CONCLUSION

In conclusion, this investigation manifests the importance of each construct in influencing civic involvement in tax compliance by manifesting the complex linkages among tax solidarity, tax morality, and the taxpayer's feeling of civic responsibility. The outcomes highlight the implication of augmenting together community cohesiveness and moral views on taxes by manifesting that tax solidarity not only directly influences civic responsibility but also indirectly through its influence on tax morality. The substantial overall influence manifest highlights how interrelated these concepts are indicating that encouraging moral responsibility and unity among taxpayers should be the main goal of initiatives to augment tax compliance. The investigation's conclusions have substantial ramifications for civic leaders and legislators, who may use these associations to create initiatives that will augment the communal cohesion of tax payments. It is feasible to develop a more assimilated and responsible taxpayer community by putting in place programs that emphasize the moral imperatives of tax compliance and build a feeling of shared responsibility. In the end, this investigation advances our understanding of the elements that influence public participation in taxes, assimilating a means of augmenting adherence and advancing societal well-being.

IMPLICATIONS

The investigation's conclusions have a number of useful management ramifications for businesses and legislators looking to augment tax adherence and encourage public participation. First, fostering tax solidarity across communities may be a very influence way to motivate people to pay their taxes responsibly. Managers and civic leaders must to think about putting in place initiatives that foster a feeling of belonging and shared accountability about tax payments. The public's impression of tax solidarity may be augmented by initiatives like forums, seminars, and community involvement campaigns that highlight the advantages of taxes as a whole. As well, the function of tax morality as a mediator highlights the importance of ethical education in taxation. Organizations can develop training programs and informational resources that communicate the moral implications of tax compliance, helping individuals understand their civic duties in a broader societal context. By framing tax involvements as not just legal obligations but also ethical responsibilities, managers can cultivate a culture of integrity and accountability. Also, the outcomes manifest that fostering associations among taxpayers as well tax authorities can augment transparency and trust, further reinforcing together tax solidarity and morality. Managers should prioritize open communication strategies, encouraging dialogue among the public as well tax authorities to address concerns, clarify tax policies, and manifest how tax revenues are utilized for community benefits.

The investigation's conclusions have a number of applications for augmenting taxpayer civic involvement as well tax compliance. First, community-founded programs that prioritize shared responsibility may be used to operationalize the promotion of tax solidarity. Outreach initiatives that augment community participation in conversations regarding tax policy and its influences on society can be created by tax authorities and groups. These programs, which can be public forums, seminars, or events, can strengthen a feeling of togetherness and shared purpose by bringing residents together to talk about the consequence of tax involvements for community improvement. As well, there are practical methods for incorporating moral instruction into tax compliance strategies. Universities, businesses, and community organizations may all implement instructional programs to augment awareness of the moral consequences of taxation. By assimilating resources that manifest the moral obligations of taxpayers and the societal benefits of taxes, these campaigns can help people develop a sense of moral accountability and responsibility. Also, it is imperative that tax administration be made more transparent. In order to enable taxpayers to observe how their involvements are being used, tax authorities have to think about implementing user-friendly interfaces. Detailed data on public expenditure and the immediate advantages of tax income should be part of this. This transparency may be facilitated by useful tools like community meetings or online dashboards, which help taxpayers, better understand the influence of their involvements and build public-tax authority confidence.

In the Eastern part of Africa, actual tax issues are related to political instability, low management, and high level of informality in the economy. Many companies manage formal external rules that complicate influence tax costs. In addition, ongoing conflicts and ethnic tension can lead to fragmented management, which further complicates the tax management and compliance. Corruption exacerbates these problems, destroying the trust of taxpayers and compliance with the requirements. Citizens often consider tax systems as vehicles for elite enrichment rather than funding from the public service, which reduces its desire to pay. The lack of transparency in the way tax revenue is used skepticism as well tax evasion. Policy solutions must focus on strengthening governance and enhancing transparency. Establishing independent anti-corruption agencies and augmenting public financial management can help restore trust.

Also, thanks to targeted at its and education, the integration of informal sectors in the formal economy can extend the tax base. The implementation of electronic governance and mobile payment platforms can rationalize tax collection, reduce corruption opportunities and augment public responsibility. These efforts, associated with community engagement to highlight the advantages of taxation, can augment a culture of conformity and civic duty in the region.

The investigation's conclusions have substantial theoretical ramifications for our comprehension of civic involvement as well tax compliance. This investigation adds to the body of literature by manifesting the complex nature of taxpayer behavior by clarifying the associations among tax solidarity, tax morality, and the taxpayer's feeling of civic responsibility. The theoretical framework around tax compliance is expanded by the identification of tax morality as a mediator among civic duty as well tax solidarity, implying that moral concerns are a substantial factor in determining civic involvement. This investigation supports the idea that communal and moral settings have a substantial function in tax compliance, which is not just a outcome of legal requirements or financial incentives. The outcomes cast doubt on conventional tax compliance models, which frequently ignore the communal and psychological aspects of taxpayer behavior. This investigation augments a more comprehensive view of why people meet their tax obligations by fusing ideas of morality and solidarity. Future studies should examine how these dimensions interact in various cultural and socioeconomic situations, as manifest by the investigation's substantial direct and indirect influences. More complex theories that take into consideration the differences in taxpayer behavior among various demographics may outcome from this.

RECOMMENDATIONS

The investigation's conclusions allow for the formulation of a number of manifestations aimed at augmenting taxpayer civic involvement as well tax compliance. First and foremost, it is imperative that tax authorities and legislators aggressively support programs that foster tax solidarity among indigenous communities. This might entail planning talks, workshops, and community gatherings that highlight the advantages of taxes for everybody. A greater feeling of community and shared responsibility may be fostered by assimilating forums for residents to interact with one another and express their opinions about tax payments. Also, it is crucial to include ethical teaching in tax compliance plans. Campaigns for education should be created to educate taxpayers about the ethical implications of taxes, emphasizing together their civic responsibilities and the advantages that society derives from tax income. To make sure that people realize the consequence of their efforts in a larger societal context, these campaigns might target companies, universities, and community groups. Also, increasing tax administration openness is indispensable to fostering confidence among taxpayers as well tax authorities. Accountability and compliance may be augmented by putting in place user-friendly technologies that let people monitor how their taxes are being spent. Frequent public reporting on the distribution of tax money and how it influences community services may help strengthen the link among tax payments and real advantages, which will encourage taxpayers to pay their fair share. At end, it is advised that more investigation be done to examine the ways in which various socioeconomic and cultural elements influence the associations among civic responsibility, tax morality, as well tax solidarity. Comprehending these aspects can assist in customizing approaches that appeal to a range of demographics, ultimately outcompeting in more successful tax compliance programs. Stakeholders may augment overall compliance and advance societal well-being by implementing these manifestations and developing a more assimilated and accountable taxpayer community.

Cultural and communal influences play an important function in tax compliance in the Eastern part of Africa. Informal institutions such as clan loyalty and religious beliefs often determine their attitudes towards taxation. In many communities, tax respect is associated with communal solidarity. People may, in their opinion, be more likely to pay taxes that benefit their groups and communities. To augment compliance, culturally relevant political recommendations should include initiatives that involve communities using these communal structures. Involving indigenous managers in tax education campaigns, for a case study, can augment trust and encourage compliance. Also, integrity among tax policy and cultural values, such as manifesting the benefits of indigenous administrations of tax revenue, could augment acceptance. The implementation of recognition programs that celebrate civic involvements to the community can also strengthen optimistic tax behavior. By supervising taxation as a community duty rather than a administration obligation, decision-makers can cultivate a culture of conformity rooted in communal responsibility and collective well-being.

DIRECTIONS FOR FUTURE

Future studies should investigate a number of approaches to augment our comprehension of the associations among civic responsibility, tax morality, as well tax solidarity. Analyzing how socioeconomic and cultural factors influence these interactions across a range of populations is one encouraging avenue. Investigations can find differences in taxpayer behavior and attitudes by carrying out cross-cultural studies, which can outcome in more specialized and successful compliance measures that appeal to various populations. Also, longitudinal investigation may shed light on how shifting tax laws or public perceptions of taxes influence the concepts of morality as well tax solidarity over time. Gaining insight into these temporal patterns may help identify key times when actions might augment civic involvement and compliance the greatest. The investigation of how communal media and digital platforms influence taxpayer attitudes and actions is a crucial area for further investigation. As technology develops further, investigating the influences of online interaction and information exchange on moral viewpoints as well tax solidarity may offer a modern interpretation of taxpayer behavior in the digital era. At end, examining the influences of certain neighborhood-founded programs aimed at encouraging moral responsibility as well tax solidarity may provide useful information. Case studies that evaluate the success of such programs in various settings would add to the expanding corpus of investigation on the most influence ways to augment public participation in taxes.

REFERENCES

Amelio, S., Gazzola, P., Vatamanescu, M., & Dinu, E. (2024). Communal and ethical factors versus tax fraud: The function of corporate communal responsibility in the Romanian context. *Communal Responsibility Journal*, *21*(1), 1–15. DOI: 10.1108/SRJ-04-2024-0273

Cabelkova, I., & Smutka, L. (2021). The influences of solidarity, income, and reliance on the state on personal income tax preferences. The case of the czech republic. *Sustainability (Basel)*, *13*(18), 10141. Advance online publication. DOI: 10.3390/su131810141

Cascavilla, A. (2023). *What Drives the Tax Compliance Attitude of Individuals? the Function of Communal Ties, Wellbeing State and Environmental Concern in Tax Morale. February*. https://www.tdx.cat/handle/10803/688951%0Ahttps://www.tdx.cat/bitstream/handle/10803/688951/2023_Tesis_Cascavilla_Alessandro.pdf?sequence=1

Cascavilla, A., Ripollés, J., & Morone, A. (2024). Tax morale and communal capital: An empirical investigation among European citizens. *Annals of Public and Cooperative Economics*, *95*(2), 441–476. DOI: 10.1111/apce.12443

Greggi, M., Calvino, L. R., & Greyling, L. (2024). *Solidarity as well taxation: Communal Contract and the Ubuntu Approaches. May*. https://www.investigationgate.net/publication/380827401

Guo, Y., & Gong, T. (2024). The influence of tax burden on wellbeing attitudes: Micro evidence from wellbeing states. In *PLoS ONE* (Vol. 19, Issue 11 November). DOI: 10.1371/journal.pone.0311047

Guyo, D. M., Kero, C. A., & Kant, S. (2025). Is Marketing Intermediaries' Mediation Required for Livestock and Products Marketing to Improve the Economic Status of Pastoralist Communities in Ethiopia? In *AI in Agriculture for Sustainable and Economic Management* (pp. 216-234). CRC Press. DOI: 10.1201/9781003451648-16

Kant, S., & Adula, M. (2024). AI Learning and Work Attitude Mediation Between Reward and Organizational Support in Ethiopia. In Gomathi Sankar, J., & David, A. (Eds.), *Generative AI for Transformational Management* (pp. 109–136). IGI Global., DOI: 10.4018/979-8-3693-5578-7.ch005

Sandu, D. (2022). Indigenous Taxes Among Obligation and Fiscal Citizenship. *PEOPLE: International Journal of Communal Sciences*, *7*(3), 104–119. DOI: 10.20319/pijss.2022.73.104119

Schmidt, C., Matthaei, E., Schmidt, C., Matthaei, E., & Lauth, H. (2023). *Working paper. 2*.

SOTTOMESSO, P. (2020). Fo r P ee r R ev Fo r R. *Jdr*, *2001*, 3–29.

Stetsenko, T., & Nishcheretov, O. (2021). Tax Culture as well tax Morale: Influence on Tax Compliance in Ukraine. *Communal Economics*, *2*(61), 83–91. DOI: 10.26565/2524-2547-2021-61-08

KEY TERMS AND DEFINITIONS

Tax Solidarity: The collective sense of responsibility among individuals within a community regarding their involvements to the tax system, emphasizing mutual support and shared benefits derived from taxation.

Tax Morality: The ethical beliefs and attitudes that influence an individual's perception of their duty to pay taxes, encompassing notions of fairness, justice, and communal responsibility related to tax compliance.

Civic Duty: The responsibilities and obligations of citizens to participate actively in their community and society, including fulfilling legal obligations like paying taxes, contributing to the common good, and engaging in civic activities.

Tax Compliance: The act of adhering to tax laws and regulations by accurately reporting income, calculating tax liabilities, and making timely payments to tax authorities.

Community Engagement: The process by which individuals actively participate in their community, fostering associations, collaboration, and shared decision-making to address indigenous issues and augment collective well-being.

Ethical Education: Instruction aimed at enhancing individuals' understanding of moral principles and ethical behavior, particularly regarding responsibilities such as tax compliance and civic engagement.

Transparency: The degree to which tax authorities openly communicate and provide information about tax policies, revenue allocation, and the influence of tax involvements on community services, fostering trust and accountability among taxpayers.

Cultural Factors: The shared beliefs, consequences, behaviors, and norms of a specific group or society that can influence attitudes and practices related to taxation and civic engagement.

Chapter 7
Examining Creative Accounting as an Explanatory Factor of Taxpayer Behavior: Evidence From Morocco

Azzouz Elhamma
https://orcid.org/0000-0003-3382-0278
Ibn Tofaîl University, Morocco

Fatima-Ezzahra Boutafrout
Hassan II University, Morocco

ABSTRACT

Tax minimization remains a critical concern for all taxpayers, particularly for businesses. To reduce this burden, various accounting techniques can be employed within the framework of "creative accounting." While the relationship between taxation and creative accounting has been extensively studied in developed countries to better understand taxpayer behavior, such research is largely lacking in developing nations. In this context, the objective of this article is to explore the extent to which creative accounting techniques can be considered explanatory factors of taxpayer behavior in Morocco. Through a survey conducted with 50 companies, the study finds that 92% of respondents use creative accounting techniques to minimize their taxes liabilities. The most commonly employed techniques include depreciation (or amortization) and expense spreading. The findings of this study offer valuable theoretical and managerial implications for both academics and policymakers.

1. INTRODUCTION

Nowadays, taxes serve as the primary financial resource for modern states (Celikay, 2020). In Morocco, tax revenues accounted for an average of 20.7% of GDP (Gross Domestic Product) in 2019. These revenues constitute the primary source of financing for the state, covering approximately 74.5% of the general state budget (Alj and Ourahma, 2022). In France, according to the National Institute of Statistics and Economic Studies (INSEE), compulsory levies in France increased from 30.3% of GDP

DOI: 10.4018/979-8-3373-0422-9.ch007

in 1960 to 45.0% of GDP in 2018. However, on the opposite side, taxes are considered a heavy burden for taxpayers. In response to this situation, taxpayers typically engage in behaviors aimed at identifying and adopting techniques to minimize their tax burden. Among these techniques, accounting practices—particularly those commonly referred to as 'creative accounting'—are prevalent (Milesi-Ferretti, 2004; Abed et al., 2022).

In recent decades, a number of international financial scandals have highlighted the importance of the "true and fair view" provided by financial accounting. According to Esnault and Hoarau (2005, p. 3), accounting is defined as "an information system, and more precisely a formal system for identifying, measuring, classifying, and recording the transactions of organizations, intended to provide, after appropriate processing, information likely to satisfy the presumed needs of multiple users". The American Accounting Association (AAA) defined accounting as: "the process of identifying, measuring and communicating economic information to permit informed judgment and decision by users of the information" (www.aaahq.org). the American Institute of Certified Public Accountants defined accounting as "... the art of recording, classifying, and summarizing in a significant manner and in terms of money, transactions and events which are, in part at least, of a financial character, and interpreting the results thereof" (www.aicpa-cima.com).

Accounting regulations require that financial statements be transparent and reliable, accurately reflecting the company's economic, financial, and asset position. In Morocco, the General Accounting Standards Code (Code Général de la Normalisation Comptable - CGNC) stipulates that "the financial statements must provide a true and fair view of the assets and liabilities, financial position, and results of the company". However, it allows companies some discretion in modifying the presentation of their financial statements. This "legal flexibility" is often viewed as creative accounting, which managers may use for various reasons to meet the expectations of the company's stakeholders (Stolowy et al., 2003).

Creative accounting techniques are generally employed to influence stakeholders' perceptions of a company's financial situation. These techniques may involve increasing earnings to benefit shareholders or decreasing earnings to minimize tax liabilities, among other strategies. According to Stolowy (1999, p. 161), creative accounting is defined as "a set of procedures aimed at modifying the level of earnings, with a view to increasing or reducing them, or altering the presentation of financial statements, without these objectives being mutually exclusive." The detrimental effects of creative accounting are numerous. Marilena and Corina (2012) found that "creative accounting is seen as a negative creation, meant to lead to compiling financial statements that would answer managers' wishes regarding the financial position and enterprise performance". In the same sense, Akpanuko et al. (2018) found that accounting creativity is a euphemism, contributing 90% to the misleading reporting of companies' operations. Recently, Gupta and Kumar (2020 demonstrated that "creative accounting, though legal and acceptable around the world, gives in the way to loopholes provided by the acts and rules governing the preparation of financial statements and eventually leading to financial crimes and hampering the economy as a whole". In the field of taxation, creative accounting significantly influences taxpayers' behavior, particularly in efforts to minimize their tax liabilities. This is especially evident in countries where there is a strong connection between accounting and taxation, such as Morocco, for example. According to Cugova and Cug (2020), "companies are trying to underestimate their economic result in order to minimize the tax liability".

The relationship between tax objectives and the choice of creative accounting has been extensively explored in numerous studies conducted in developed countries. However, this type of research remains almost absent in some developing countries, such as Morocco, for example. In this context, this study seeks to address the following question: **To what extent can creative accounting techniques explain the behavior of Moroccan taxpayers in their efforts to minimize tax liabilities?**

To address this research question, a survey questionnaire was administered to 50 Moroccan companies. The collected data were analyzed using descriptive statistics, including the calculation of averages and the development of cross-tabulations. The main findings of this research clearly indicate that creative accounting is primarily used by Moroccan taxpayers to reduce tax expenses. More than 92% of respondents report using this accounting method for tax purposes. Additionally, the study highlights that 'depreciation' and 'expense spreading' are the two most commonly used creative accounting techniques among the companies surveyed to reduce their tax burdens. The results of this study offer significant contributions both theoretically and managerially. Theoretically, it emphasizes the role of certain creative accounting techniques in taxpayers' tax management strategies to minimize their tax liabilities. From a managerial perspective, the research provides valuable insights into the accounting methods commonly used to reduce tax burdens.

The paper is structured as follows. Section 2 presents the conceptual framework and summarizes previous literature reviews on related topics. Section 3 describes our methodological approaches. The results are presented in Section 4. Finally, Section 5 concludes the paper by synthesizing the main contributions and implications, acknowledging the study's limitations, and proposing new avenues for future research.

2. LITERATURE REVIEW

We begin by examining the concept of creative accounting and its primary objectives (2.1). Next, we will discuss the main techniques associated with creative accounting (2.2), and finally, we will examine the potential impact of creative accounting on taxpayers' behavior in efforts to minimize their tax liabilities (2.3).

2.1. What is Creative Accounting and What are Its Main Objectives?

The concept of creative accounting has its origins in the positive accounting movement, which aims to "predict and explain accounting practices" (Watts and Zimmerman, 1986). It was further developed by the founders of the Rochester School. Several authors have sought to define creative accounting. According to Colasse (1995), creative accounting refers to "the accounting information practices, often bordering on legality, of certain companies that, by flouting regulation and standardization, seek to embellish the image that accounting presents of their economic and financial situation and performance." Gillet (1998, p. 83) asserts that "creative accounting is the set of techniques, options, and areas of freedom allowed by accounting texts that, without departing from the norms and requirements of accounting, enable managers to vary the results or modify the appearance of accounting documents."

According to Raffournier (2003), creative accounting is defined as "the use of the flexibility and gaps in accounting regulations to present the financial situation of the company in a light different from that which would result from a more conventional application of existing standards." Watts and Zimmerman (1986) define creative accounting as the set of techniques employed by managers to modify their firm's accounts in a manner favorable to their expectations. Creative accounting techniques are applied at the corporate level through accounting decisions made by executives. Although they adhere to accounting standards, they simultaneously exploit "loopholes" to enhance their key performance indicators (Karim et al., 2016). Recently, according to Abed et al. (2022), "creative accounting is the practice of influencing financial indicators using accounting knowledge without explicitly violating accounting policies, rules, and the law".

Creative accounting aims to achieve several objectives. According to Stolowy (1999), this type of accounting is employed primarily to modify accounts for the purpose of improvement, but also with the intent of "deterioration." Jones (2011) identifies four categories of reasons that drive executives to engage in creative accounting:

- Personal Incentives: attainment of bonuses, salary increases, job security, personal satisfaction, etc.
- External Expectations: meeting analysts' expectations, achieving profit targets, etc.
- Particular Circumstances: new stock issuances, loan management, mergers and acquisitions, new management teams, etc.
- Covering Up Fraud.

In Greece, Baralexis (2004) demonstrated that large companies tend to overstate their profits to facilitate access to external financing, particularly bank loans, while small enterprises underreport their profits to reduce income taxes. According to Lau and Ooi (2016), the most commonly used creative accounting method in Malaysia is the overstatement of revenue through the recognition of fictitious sales to imaginary customers. The primary motive for this practice is to increase the company's equity.

Creative accounting can have a positive impact on a company in the short term; however, in the long term, it may lead to a decline in stock prices, insolvency, and even bankruptcy (Bhasin, 2016). According to Amat et al. (1999), creative accounting can help maintain or increase stock prices by artificially creating a positive trend in earnings. Similarly, Mindak et al. (2016) studied the use of creative accounting techniques to meet or exceed last year's earnings forecasts and their potential effects on market rewards. The authors demonstrated that companies that successfully surpassed their targets employed creative accounting methods to boost their profits and were rewarded by the market, thereby being perceived as "good." In contrast, companies that managed their profits with the aim of reducing them (for example, by increasing reserves) struggled to meet their established goals and, as a result, were not rewarded by the market and were not regarded as "good."

Recently, Akpanuko and Umoren (2018) demonstrated that creative accounting is a euphemism and contributes to 90% of the misrepresentation of corporate operations. Creative accounting aims to deceive the public, potential investors, and shareholders, thereby increasing the rate of corporate bankruptcy at a declining pace.

After defining the creative accounting and its primary objectives, the following sub-section will focus on the main techniques of the creative accounting, particularly those that will be examined in this study.

2.2. Main Techniques of the Creative Accounting

Generally, an accounting problem presents multiple solutions, each yielding distinct impacts on the financial position and performance of the company. This flexibility in accounting practices has led to the development of creative accounting, which employs various techniques (Marilena and Corina, 2012). Several research studies have been conducted to identify the techniques of creative accounting (Bonnet, 1995; Stolowy, 1999; etc.). Among these techniques, we highlight four that are the most widespread and will be considered in this research: inventory management, expense recognition policies, depreciation, and the accounting for provisions.

2.2.1. Creative Accounting Techniques According to Various Researchers

In his work, Bonnet (1995) classifies the techniques of creative accounting in relation to "actions":

- Income statement and accounting principles
- Income statement and accounting policies
- Income statement and management decisions
- Actions affecting the balance sheet

The key principles of this categorization are summarized in the table below.

Table 1. Categories of creative accounting techniques according to Bonnet (1995)

Categories of Creative Accounting Techniques		Some Examples
Financial Statement	**Techniques Involved**	
Income Statement	Accounting Principles	Use of external personnel, leasing, valuation of production, provisions for inventory, etc.
	Accounting Policies	Depreciation, provisions, inventory, expense recognition, investment grants, capitalization of expenses, etc.
	Management Decisions	Transfer of losses, lease-back arrangements, sales under favorable or "fictitious" conditions, etc.
Balance Sheet	-	Revaluation of assets, leasing, discounting of commercial papers, factoring, etc.

Stolowy (1995, 1999) highlights three main categories of creative accounting techniques, which are "techniques that impact the measurement of earnings, techniques that affect the presentation of the income statement, and techniques that influence the presentation of the balance sheet." The following table summarizes these major categories.

Table 2. Categories of Creative Accounting Techniques According to Stolowy (1999)

Categories of techniques	Main techniques	Account involved
Some techniques with an impact on results measurement	Incorporate financial expenses into the production cost of fixed assets	• Fixed assets • Financial expenses
	Capitalization of research and development expenses	Research and development costs
	Sale-and-leaseback: the sale of a fixed asset followed by the subsequent leasing of the same asset through a leaseback arrangement.	Fixed assets
Some techniques that impact the presentation of the income statement.	Utilization of temporary staff to decrease value added	External personnel
	Obtaining operating subsidies.	Operating subsidies

continued on following page

Table 2. Continued

Categories of techniques	Main techniques	Account involved
Some techniques that impact the presentation of the balance sheet.	Sale-and-leaseback: the sale of a fixed asset followed by the subsequent leaseback of the same asset.	Fixed assets
	Revaluation of tangible fixed assets.	Fixed assets and equity
	Use of lease financing.	Loans

Source: adapted from Stolowy (1999)

However, it should be noted that creative accounting techniques are not exhaustive, and it is not possible to identify all of them. According to Blažek (2021), in a study on models for revealing the creativity of accountants and financiers, it was confirmed that "creative accounting in the conditions of the Slovak Republic but also globally is still not possible completely to reveal".

2.2.2. Creative Accounting Techniques Selected for This Research

In this research, four techniques of creative accounting will be studied, namely: inventory management methods, depreciation, expense spreading, and provisions.

The accounting framework allows companies the right to choose the inventory valuation method that aligns with the nature of their activities, specifically the weighted average cost (WAC) method and the first-in, first-out (FIFO) method. According to the CGNC, "the weighted average cost method has two variants: the method of weighted average cost after each entry and the method of weighted average cost for the 'storage period,' while the 'first-in, first-out' method is referred to as FIFO." Companies in inflationary periods typically use the FIFO method, which allows them to delay the impact of rising prices by ensuring a minimum valuation of period costs (consumption of raw materials). The "inventory" account is affected by several creative accounting techniques. Jennings and Thompson (1996), based on a study conducted among American companies, demonstrated that the choice of inventory valuation method (FIFO or LIFO) is influenced by the desire to reduce the tax burden. Additionally, Shabou and Boulila (2002) confirmed that among the techniques that impact earnings, the choice of inventory valuation method is included.

The policy of spreading expenses over multiple accounting periods aims to avoid charging the entire amount of associated expenses to the current period's earnings. This practice particularly pertains to financial expenses and research and development costs. Shabou and Boulila (2002) consider the policy of spreading expenses as a technique that has a significant impact on earnings.

According to the CGNC, "The method of distributing depreciation over different periods should be chosen based on primarily economic considerations: it may result in constant annual depreciation (straight-line method), declining depreciation, or, less commonly, increasing depreciation." Pourquery (1991) states that depreciation allocation is "more than just an accounting technique; it is a refined art involving estimation and evaluation. It is also the art of effectively managing one's earnings."

This choice is based on the subjective assessment of a foreseeable risk or charge, or a temporary impairment of an asset. The establishment of a provision allows managers considerable flexibility in applying the principle of prudence. Additionally, any changes to the rules adopted for its establishment take the form of a change in accounting method. In practice, provisions are frequently used as a tool for creativity, as their allocations and reversals allow manipulation at various stages of earnings. According to Casta (1997), the management of provisions provides managers with a considerable degree of flexibility in shaping their accounting results. Segura (2008) notes that companies can record provisions during profitable periods to preserve earnings and subsequently utilize these reserves during loss-making periods to enhance their results.

In general, these four techniques of the creative accounting can be summarized in the following table (Table 3).

Table 3. The main creative accounting techniques

	Account involved	Mechanism	Impact on the financial statements
Inventory Valuation Method	**Inventory**	**Incorporation of financial expenses into the production cost of inventory**	**- Increase in profit in the year of charge transfer. Decrease in profit in the year of inventory write-off.**
	Inventory	**Change in inventory valuation method (FIFO, Weighted Average, etc.)**	**Change in profit based on the new method.**
Expense Spreading Policy	Expense spreading over several fiscal years or establishment costs	Change in method: Spreading of expenses through amortization, whereas these expenses were previously recorded in a single fiscal year. Or the reverse change.	Spreading of expenses or, recording expenses in a single period
Choice of depreciation method (Straight-Line vs. Accelerated)	Accumulated depreciation	At the time of preparing the depreciation schedule, there are several choices and possibilities: Determine an estimated useful life; Set a residual value; Consider usage patterns; Use physical units of production.	Modification, depending on the option chosen, of the depreciation expense amount; resulting in a change in the allocation of the depreciation charge over time.
	Accumulated depreciation	Revise the depreciation schedule, for example, by increasing (or decreasing) the residual useful life.	Reduction (or increase) of future depreciation charges over a longer (shorter) period.
provision accounting policy	Provisions and current assets	Underestimation (or overestimation) of provisions for doubtful debts. Underestimation (or overestimation) of provisions for inventory.	Increase (or decrease) in profit at the time of the provision. Reverse effect in the year of the reversal.
	Provisions for risks and charges	Non-recognition of the provision for retirement obligations is allowed.	Requirement for an evaluation to be disclosed in the notes if the amount is significant. Recognition is almost mandatory in the context of a business sale. Recognition is nearly obligatory as accrued expenses for retired employees, in the case of retirement benefits.

Source: adapted from Stolowy (1999)

In general, the techniques of the creative accounting are numerous and evolve alongside changes in the legal and accounting frameworks of different countries. In the following sub-section, we will focus on how these techniques influence taxpayers' behavior in their tax minimization strategies.

2.3. The Creative Accounting: An Explanatory Factor in Taxpayer Behavior

In Anglo-Saxon countries, such as the USA, taxation is largely disconnected from financial accounting. Taxable profit is determined based on a specific set of rules that are independent of those used in accounting. Several researchers have highlighted this divergence between accounting and taxation (Desai, 2003; Desai and Dharmapala, 2009, etc.). In contrast, in Morocco and most continental European countries, accounting and taxation are closely linked. In these countries, to increase the liquidity available to capital providers, managers often seek to minimize overall cash outflows, which include taxes paid to the tax authorities. According to Raffournier (1990), accounting choices are influenced by their impact on taxation. Jennings and Thompson (1996) also demonstrated that tax savings are a decisive factor in the selection of accounting methods. This perspective is supported by several authors (Biddle, 1980; Lee and Hsieh, 1985, etc.).

To this end, several studies have been conducted to examine the relationship between the manipulation of accounting data and the desire to reduce taxes. The main findings indicate that such accounting manipulation is more prevalent in environments characterized by high tax pressure (Jennings et al., 1996). Lacombe-Saboly (1994) demonstrated that tax minimization is the second most important motivation for accounting choices (17.67%), following accounting opportunism (37.4%). Similarly, Coppens and Peek (2005) found that "private companies operating in countries where the tax system significantly influences accounting do not attempt to avoid losses, unlike companies operating in other countries." To reduce taxes, managers exercise their discretion in making accounting choices. They may employ creative accounting techniques such as provisions, inventory management, expense spreading, depreciation, and others.

In the Tunisian context, Hamza (2012) demonstrated that companies use creative accounting to minimize their tax burden. Similarly, Daoud and Omri (2013) confirmed that "the results also show that managers choose accounting methods known to play a role in minimizing the tax burden, leading to significant discretionary divergences." In Côte d'Ivoire, Vangah Y.-C. A. (2017) indicated that tax minimization is regarded as the primary motivation for engaging in creative accounting practices. Therefore, we can formulate the following hypothesis:

Research Hypothesis: *Creative accounting is a significant factor that explains the behavior of taxpayers in minimizing their taxes.*

3. METHODOLOGY

The methodological framework will outline the characteristics of the sample (3.1) and the study variables (3.2).

3.1. The Sample of the Study

Our study is conducted among Moroccan companies. Morocco, located in North Africa, was previously under Spanish and French protectorates, which is why the management techniques employed by companies are primarily derived from French models (Elhamma and Moalla, 2015). However, in recent years, Moroccan companies have started to adopt new management tools, including the implementation of IFRS (Elhamma, 2023, 2024), and the adoption of modern management control tools in both the private sector (Elhamma, 2015, 2023, 2025) and the public sector (Elhamma and El-Moumane, 2025), etc. It is important to note that the Moroccan tax system has undergone significant development and modernization in recent years (Alj, 2019, 2024; Alj and Ourahma, 2022).

In management sciences, researchers have the option to choose between quantitative or qualitative methods (Elhamma, 2024). Given the nature of our research problem, we will adopt quantitative methods, specifically using questionnaires as the data collection tool. The questionnaire was designed for a sample of 50 companies operating in Morocco. In this study, random sampling was used, ensuring that every company operating in Morocco had an equal chance of being selected. Simple random sampling is a commonly applied method in quantitative research involving survey instruments. By selecting 50 companies randomly, we minimize bias and ensure the reliable generalization of the results.

Table 4. Sample Characteristics

Number of Employees	%	Sector of Activity	%
Less than 50 employees	50%	Industrial companies	20%
Between 50 and 100	20%	Commercial companies	28%
Between 100 and 200	14%	Construction companies	6%
More than 200 employees	16%	Service companies	46%
Total	**100%**	Total	**100%**

Half of the companies in our sample have fewer than 50 employees. Twenty percent have between 50 and 100 employees, 14% have between 100 and 200 employees, and 16% have more than 200 employees. In terms of business sector, 46% of respondents are service companies, 28% are commercial companies, 20% are industrial companies, and 6% operate in the building and civil engineering sector.

After defining our sample, the following sub-section will focus on the variables used in this study to test our research hypothesis.

3.2. Study Variables

To assess the extent of the impact of creative accounting on Moroccan taxpayers' behavior, we posed the following direct question: “How would you assess the impact of creative accounting on your behavior in minimizing taxes?” Five response options were provided, ranging from “very weak impact” to “very strong impact”. We chose this single, direct question for two main reasons. First, it is clear and simple: a direct question provides a precise and easy-to-analyze response. By offering response options from “very weak impact” to “very strong impact,” it makes data collection easier while still capturing the strength of the perceived impact. Second, it reduces bias and confusion: asking one direct question helps prevent confusion for respondents. This allows them to focus on a specific topic (the impact of creative accounting), improving the quality and relevance of their answers.

To examine the various creative accounting techniques employed by the taxpayers interviewed, we selected four commonly used techniques: provisions, inventory valuation methods, expense spreading methods, and depreciation. Four questions were thus formulated:

- Question 1: How do you use provisions to reduce tax liabilities?

- Question 2: How do you utilize inventory management methods (such as FIFO or weighted average cost) to reduce tax liabilities?
- Question 3: How do you implement expense allocation strategies to reduce tax liabilities?
- Question 4: How do you apply depreciation methods to reduce tax liabilities?

For each question, five response options were provided, ranging from "never" to "always."

For several reasons, such as simplicity and clarity, identification of trends and patterns, and reduction of statistical bias, we employed analytical methods in this research. First, we used descriptive analysis to summarize the responses to each question, providing an overview of the frequency distribution of responses. Second, we utilized cross-tabulations to examine the frequency of specific responses across the various techniques listed (provisions, inventory management, expense deferral, depreciation). This approach allows us to identify trends and patterns in the usage of these techniques. Third, we calculated the average score for each technique on a 5-point scale, where higher values indicate more frequent use. These average scores offer a quantitative assessment of the extent to which different creative accounting techniques are employed by Moroccan taxpayers.

4. RESULTS AND DISCUSSION

In this section, we first present our findings regarding the Creative Accounting as an Explanatory Factor in Taxpayers' Efforts to Reduce Tax Burdens (4.1), followed by an examination of the primary creative accounting techniques employed by the companies in our sample to minimize their tax liabilities (4.2).

4.1. The Creative Accounting as an Explanatory Factor in Taxpayers' Efforts to Reduce Tax Expenses

The results of our survey regarding the impact of creative accounting on taxpayers' behavior in relation to their tax minimization strategies are summarized in the table below (Table 5).

Table 5. Extent of Creative Accounting Practices Employed for Tax Minimization

Responses	%
Very strong	46%
Strong	36%
Moderate	10%
Weak	6%
Very weak	2%
Total	100%

Source: Authors

Figure 1. Degree of Creative Accounting Practices Used for Tax Reduction

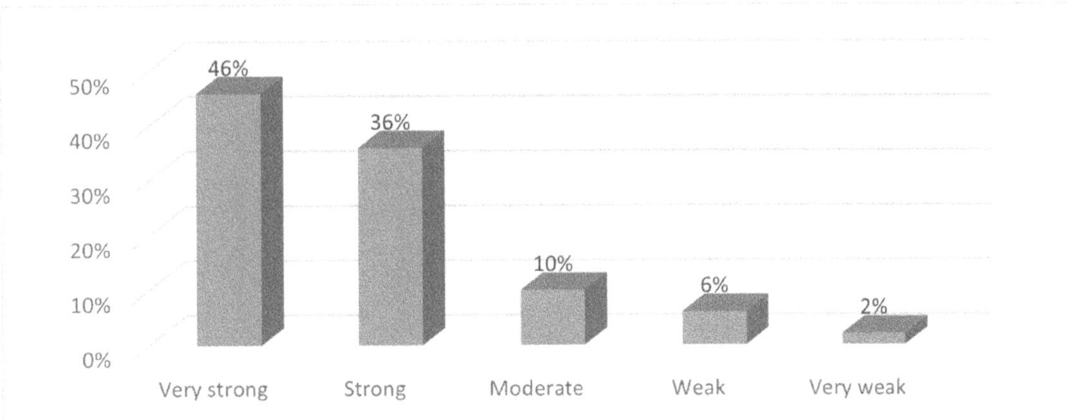

The results of our study, as presented in Table 10, demonstrate that creative accounting techniques have a significant influence on the behavior of the taxpayers surveyed. 92% of respondents reported that they frequently utilize these accounting techniques to reduce their tax liabilities. In contrast, only 8% indicated that they do not incorporate such accounting methods into their tax strategies. These findings thus support the validation of our research hypothesis, which posits that creative accounting and its associated techniques play a pivotal role in shaping taxpayers' strategies to minimize their tax burden. Despite efforts to ensure a certain degree of autonomy between accounting and taxation, the Moroccan context remains characterized by the predominance of tax rules and accounting practices shaped by tax considerations. Taxation is based on rules established by accounting, which, in turn, is influenced by tax-related considerations or constraints. This interdependence between the two disciplines compels Moroccan companies to optimize their accounting practices to meet tax requirements, particularly through creative accounting techniques. These practices have a significant impact on the behavior of Moroccan taxpayers in their efforts to reduce their tax liabilities.

The study's findings are consistent with those reported by Rossignol (2002) in the French context. According to this author, "when asked about the main purpose of preparing annual accounts, the majority of liberal accountants emphasized the tax aspect (33 out of 43 who agreed to respond, representing 76.7%)." In the Tunisian context, Hamza (2012) found that the most of the interviewees report that both small and medium-sized enterprises (SMEs) and large companies tend to reduce their profits in order to minimize taxes, which they consider their primary concern. They argue that taxes are "unfair," that the "tax rate is high," and that, in any case, "tax is a cultural problem linked to human nature.". In Romania, Lucian et al. (2016) found that more than half of the accounting professionals surveyed would employ creative accounting techniques to optimize taxation while staying within legal regulations. However, these results should be interpreted with caution. Creative accounting techniques are not solely used to minimize financial outcomes and, consequently, taxes; they can also be employed to inflate results. In this context, Blue et al. (2025), based on a study of companies listed on the Tehran Stock Exchange (TSE), found that "large Iranian companies use creative accounting to inflate profits".

After demonstrating the extent of creative accounting usage by the Moroccan taxpayers studied in this research for their tax minimization strategies, it is essential to highlight, in the following sub-section, the main creative accounting techniques employed by these taxpayers.

4.2. The Primary Creative Accounting Techniques Employed by the Surveyed Taxpayers

The table 6 presents the key findings regarding the primary creative accounting techniques employed by the companies surveyed to reduce their tax burden.

Table 6. Degree of Utilization of Creative Accounting Techniques for Tax Minimization

Responses	Provisions	Inventory management	Expense spreading	Depreciation
Always	20%	32%	26%	48%
Often	26%	18%	30%	22%
Sometimes	34%	10%	26%	12%
Rarely	14%	14%	10%	10%
Never	6%	26%	8%	8%
Total	100%	100%	100%	100%

Source: authors

Figure 2. Extent of Utilization of Each Creative Accounting Technique for Tax Minimization

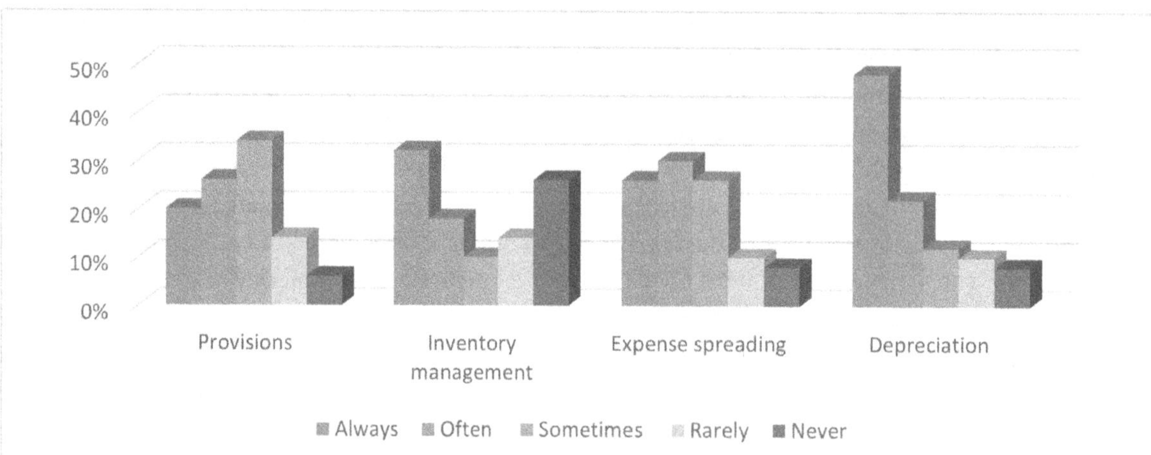

Regarding provisions, 34% of companies reported that they "sometimes" use provisions to optimize their accounting practices. Additionally, 46% of the companies in the sample indicated that they use this technique "often" or "always." Only 6% of the companies have never utilized this technique. Notably, 94% of the companies in the sample have employed this technique to varying extents. In terms of inventory management, 50% of the companies stated that they "always" or "often" use inventory management techniques to optimize their results. Conversely, 26% of these companies reported that they have never employed this technique. This finding appears reasonable, considering that nearly 50% of the companies operate in the service sector, where inventory is typically not a core aspect of their business. Regarding the expense spreading technique, 56% of Moroccan companies in the sample indicated that they "always" or "often" use this method to optimize their accounts. In contrast, only 8% of our sample reported that they have never utilized this technique. Concerning the depreciation technique, 70% of the companies in our sample stated that they "always" or "often" use it to manage earnings. Conversely, only 8% of these companies have never employed this technique to optimize their accounting practices. The utilization rate for this technique is 70%, which appears reasonable given the diverse range of accounting options available.

These results confirm those of Hamza (2012) in the Tunisian context. According to Hamza (2012), the primary method employed by Tunisian companies is the use of provisions. These provisions affect both the depreciation of asset items and the provisions for specific risks. Small and medium-sized enterprises (SMEs), which typically face tax-related concerns, often reduce their reported results by increasing provisions. Daoud and Omri (2013), based on an empirical study of 39 companies—24 of which are listed on the Tunis Stock Exchange (BVMT) and operate in various sectors, and 15 unlisted—over a period of 7 years from 2003 to 2009, demonstrated that inventory management has a significant effect on tax management.

To determine which accounting techniques are most commonly used by Moroccan companies, we coded the responses on a scale from "5: always" to "1: never" and calculated the average for each accounting technique. The results are summarized in the table and graph below.

Table 7. Average Degree of Use of Each Creative Accounting Technique in Tax Minimization

Creative accounting technique	**Average on a 5-point scale**
Provisions	3.4
Inventory management	3.16
Expense spreading	3.56
Depreciation	3.92

Source: Authors

Figure 3. Average Extent of Utilization of Each Creative Accounting Technique for Tax Minimization

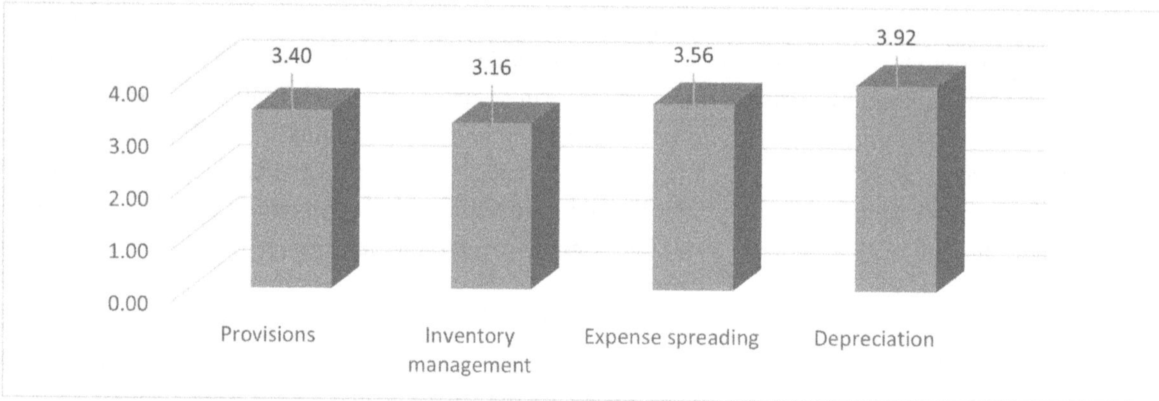

Depreciation, with the highest average of 3.92, is clearly the most commonly used creative accounting technique among the companies studied. Depreciation allows the cost of an asset to be allocated over several years, offering flexibility in adjusting accounting charges to meet the company's financial needs. A score of 3.92 suggests that this technique is widely used to adjust earnings and minimize tax liabilities. It is likely that companies apply accelerated depreciation mainly to reduce taxable income or to spread expenses over a longer period. This technique is often seen as less risky compared to others, as it is generally accepted by accounting standards and does not rely on as subjective an estimate as some alternative methods. With an average of 3.56, expense allocation appears to be a commonly used technique. This method allows expenses to be spread over multiple periods, creating a cost-smoothing effect that can positively impact the company's bottom line. The relatively high score suggests that the companies surveyed often use this technique to optimize their short-term profitability. With an average of 3.4, the use of provisions is considered moderate. Provisions are typically employed to adjust financial results based on forecasts of future expenses. A score of 3.4 indicates that while provisions are used to some degree, companies do not rely heavily on this technique. Additionally, inventory management, with an average of 3.16, appears to be less commonly used compared to the other methods. Inventory plays a key role in asset valuation, and creative accounting practices in this area may involve manipulating purchase costs or inventory valuation to influence profit margins.

Overall, the analysis of the results indicates that the companies studied tend to favor certain creative accounting techniques, particularly depreciation and expense spreading, to reduce their tax liabilities.

5. CONCLUSION

The aim of this research is to examine the extent to which creative accounting techniques can be considered explanatory factors for taxpayer behavior in Morocco, based on a sample of 50 companies, the results of the study provide important insights into the use of creative accounting techniques among Moroccan businesses. The main results indicate that 92% of respondents employ creative accounting techniques, such as "depreciation" and "expense spreading", to reduce their taxes liabilities. As a result, these creative accounting practices have a major influence on taxpayers' behavior in their tax minimization strategies.

The results of this research establish a direct connection to the modeling of taxpayer behavior, particularly in relation to tax minimization strategies employed by Moroccan companies. Specifically, the findings reveal that 92% of respondents use creative accounting techniques to reduce their tax liabilities. These practices significantly influence the tax minimization strategies of taxpayers. By modeling taxpayer behavior based on these results, it becomes possible to analyze how these techniques affect corporate tax decisions and, in turn, their role in the broader context of tax compliance dynamics.

These results offer significant contributions both theoretically and managerially. Theoretically, the study enhances the literature on creative accounting as an explanatory factor for taxpayer behavior, particularly within the Moroccan context, by identifying techniques such as depreciation and expense spreading. It also emphasizes the role of taxation as a key factor driving the use of these techniques, highlighting the relationship between tax regulations and accounting decisions. Managerially, the findings have practical implications for Moroccan businesses, suggesting that managers should be mindful of how techniques like depreciation and expense allocation affect short-term profitability and tax compliance. By aligning these methods with tax regulations, companies can optimize their performance while ensuring legal compliance.

However, the results obtained must be interpreted with caution due to certain limitations inherent to the research. First, the modest sample size (50 companies) may limit the generalizability of the findings to all Moroccan companies, particularly as the specific characteristics of the sample may not fully reflect the diversity of the country's economic landscape. Second, the use of a perceptual approach for data collection presents another significant limitation. Participants' responses are shaped by their personal perceptions and opinions, which may introduce subjective bias into the results.

Based on the limitations identified in this study, two avenues for future research can be considered. First, we suggest expanding the sample size. Future studies could use a larger and more diverse sample of Moroccan companies, covering various sizes, sectors, and geographic regions. This would improve the representativeness of the results and enhance the generalizability of the conclusions to the broader Moroccan economy. Second, we recommend adopting a mixed methodology. A study that combines both perceptual and objective approaches (e.g., using real accounting data) would allow for cross-referencing managers' perceptions with actual behaviors in creative accounting practices. This would provide a more complete and accurate understanding of the techniques used by companies.

REFERENCES

Abed, I. A., Hussin, N., Haddad, H., Almubaydeen, T. H., & Ali, M. A. (2022). Creative accounting determination and financial reporting quality: The integration of transparency and disclosure. *Journal of Open Innovation, 8*(1), 38. DOI: 10.3390/joitmc8010038

Akpanuko, E. E., & Umoren, N. J. (2018). The influence of creative accounting on the credibility of accounting reports. *Journal of Financial Reporting and Accounting, 16*(2), 292–310. DOI: 10.1108/JFRA-08-2016-0064

Alj, B. (2019). La règle fiscale: Quels risques pour l'entreprise au Maroc? *Revue Marocaine de Recherche en Management et Marketing, 19*, 134–154.

Alj, B. (2024). Défis et dynamiques de la sécurité fiscale pour le développement des affaires en Afrique: Une exploration du cas du Maroc. *Economics and Management Review, 2*(2).

Alj, B., & Ourahma, A. (2022). L'efficacité de l'impôt sur le revenu dans le système fiscal marocain. *Revue du Contrôle, de la Comptabilité et de l'Audit, 6*(4), 270-289.

Amat, O., Blake, J., & Dowds, J. (1999). The ethics of creative accounting. *Journal of Economic Literature Classification, M41.*

American Accounting Association. (n.d.). *Website of the American Accounting Association (AAA).* Retrieved March 14, 2025, from https://www.aaahq.org

American Institute of Certified Public Accountants. (n.d.). *Website of the American Institute of Certified Public Accountants (AICPA).* Retrieved March 14, 2025, from https://www.aicpa-cima.com

Baralexis, S. (2004). Creative accounting in small advancing countries: The Greek case. *Managerial Auditing Journal, 19*(3), 440–461. DOI: 10.1108/02686900410524427

Bhasin, M. L. (2016). Survey of creative accounting practices: An empirical study. *Wulfenia Journal, 23*(1), 143–162.

Biddle, G. C. (1980). Accounting methods and management decisions: The case of inventory costing and inventory policy. *Journal of Accounting Research, 18*(Supplement), 235–280. DOI: 10.2307/2490341

Blažek, R. (2021). Creative accounting as a global tool for tax optimization. *SHS Web of Conferences, 92*(1), 02007. https://doi.org/DOI: 10.1051/shsconf/20219202007

Blue, G., Chahrdahcheriki, M., Rezaee, Z., & Khotanlou, M. (2025). A model for predicting creative accounting in emerging economies. *International Journal of Accounting & Information Management, 33*(1), 1–31. DOI: 10.1108/IJAIM-09-2023-0240

Bonnet, G. F. (1995). Pièges (et délices) de la comptabilité (créative). *Economica.*

Casta, J. F. (1997). La comptabilité et ses utilisateurs. In Joffre, P., & Simon, Y. (Eds.), *Encyclopédie de gestion* (Vol. I, pp. 528–551). Economica.

Celikay, F. (2020). Dimensions of tax burden: A review on OECD countries. *Journal of Economics, Finance and Administrative Science, 25*(49), 27–43. DOI: 10.1108/JEFAS-12-2018-0138

Cernusca, L., David, D., Nicolaescu, C., & Cosmin, G. B. (2016). Empirical study on the creative accounting phenomenon. *Studia Universitatis „Vasile Goldis" Arad – Economics Series, 26*(2). https://doi.org/DOI: 10.1515/sues-2016-0010

Colasse, B. (1995). *25 ans de comptabilité générale, une nouvelle naissance d'une vieille discipline. In 25 ans de sciences d'organisation.* Masson.

Coppensa, L., & Erik, E. (2005). An analysis of earnings management by European private firms. *Journal of International Accounting, Auditing & Taxation, 14*(1), 1–17. DOI: 10.1016/j.intaccaudtax.2005.01.002

Cugova, A., & Cug, J. (2020). Motivation for the use of creative accounting techniques in the conditions of the globalized business environment. *SHS Web of Conferences, 74*(2), 01004. https://doi.org/DOI: 10.1051/shsconf/20207401004

Daoud, I. B., & Omri, M. A. (2013). Les divergences comptabilité-fiscalité en Tunisie: Quels facteurs explicatifs? *La revue des sciences de gestion, 263-264*, 179-195.

Desai, M., & Dharmapala, D. (2009). Earnings management and corporate tax shelters. *Harvard University and University of Connecticut Working Paper.*

Desai, M. A. (2003). The divergence between book and tax income. In Poterba, J. M. (Ed.), *Tax Policy and the Economy, 17, 169-206.* MIT Press. DOI: 10.1086/tpe.17.20140508

Elhamma, A. (2015). The relationship between budgetary evaluation, firm size, and performance. *Journal of Management Development, 34*(8), 973–986. DOI: 10.1108/JMD-06-2014-0053

Elhamma, A. (2023). Impact of mandatory IFRS adoption on foreign direct investment: The moderating role of conflict of interest regulation. *Journal of Financial Reporting and Accounting, ahead-of-print.* https://doi.org/DOI: 10.1108/JFRA-04-2022-0145

Elhamma, A. (2023). The relationship between organisational decentralisation, balanced scorecard, and its perceived benefits in Moroccan SMEs. *International Journal of Accounting. Auditing and Performance Evaluation, 19*(2), 185–202. DOI: 10.1504/IJAAPE.2023.132384

Elhamma, A. (2024). Determinants of national IFRS adoption: Evidence from the Middle East and North Africa region. *International Journal of Accounting. Auditing and Performance Evaluation, 20*(1-2), 69–90. DOI: 10.1504/IJAAPE.2024.135535

Elhamma, A. (2024). Participant observation as a qualitative research method in management sciences: Interests, conditions, and limitations. In Bentalha, B., & Alla, L. (Eds.), *Applying qualitative research methods to management science* (pp. 75–91). IGI Global., DOI: 10.4018/979-8-3693-5543-5.ch004

Elhamma, A. (2025). Lack of Resilience and Failure of Small and Medium-Sized Enterprises (SMEs) in Morocco: Current Situation and Key Determinants. In Dias Rouco, J. C., & Nunes Figueiredo, P. C. (Eds.), *Enhancing Resilience in Business Continuity Management* (pp. 245–266). IGI Global., DOI: 10.4018/979-8-3693-8809-9.ch008

Elhamma, A., & El-Moumane, R. (2025). The role of strategic planning in resilience and crisis management: A case study of a public organization in Morocco. In Dias Rouco, J. C., & Nunes Figueiredo, P. C. (Eds.), *Enhancing Resilience in Business Continuity Management* (pp. 433–460). IGI Global., DOI: 10.4018/979-8-3693-8809-9.ch015

Elhamma, A., & Moalla, M. (2015). Impact of uncertainty and decentralization on activity-based costing use. *International Journal of Accounting and Economics Studies, 3*(2), 148–155. DOI: 10.14419/ijaes.v3i2.4817

Esnault, E., & Hoarau, C. (2005). *Comptabilité financière*. PUF.

Gillet, P. (1998). Comptabilité créative: Le résultat comptable n'est plus ce qu'il était. *Revue française de gestion, novembre-décembre*, 83-94.

Gupta, C. M., & Kumar, D. (2020). Creative accounting: A tool for financial crime – A review of the techniques and its effects. *Journal of Financial Crime, 27*(2), 397–411. DOI: 10.1108/JFC-06-2019-0075

Hamza, S. E. (2012). Les spécificités de la gestion des résultats des entreprises tunisiennes à travers une analyse qualitative. *Comptabilité-Contrôle-Audit*, 1-28.

Jennings, R., Simko, P., & Thompson, R. (1996). Does LIFO inventory accounting improve the income statement at the expense of the balance sheet? *Journal of Accounting Research, 34*(1), 301–312. DOI: 10.2307/2491333

Jennings, R., & Thompson, R. (1996). Accounting for intangibles in the United States. *Issues in Accounting Education, 11*(2), 491–495.

Jones, M. (2011). *Creative accounting, fraud, and international accounting scandals*. Chichester, West Sussex: A John Wiley & Sons.

Karim, A. M., Shaikh, J. M., Hock, O. Y., & Islam, M. R. (2016). Solution of adapting creative accounting practices: An in-depth perception gap analysis among accountants and auditors of listed companies. *Australian Academy of Accounting and Finance Review, 2*(2), 166–188.

Lacombe-Saboly, M. (1994). Les déterminants de la qualité des produits comptables des entreprises: Le rôle du dirigeant (Thèse de doctorat, Université de Poitiers).

Lau, K. C., & Ooi, K. W. (2016). A case study on fraudulent financial reporting: Evidence from Malaysia. *Accounting Research Journal, 29*(1), 4–19. DOI: 10.1108/ARJ-11-2013-0084

Lee, C., & Hsieh, D. (1985). Choice of inventory accounting methods: Comparative analyses of alternative hypotheses. *Journal of Accounting Research, 23*(2), 468–485. DOI: 10.2307/2490821

Marilena, Z., & Corina, L. (2012). Embellishment of financial statements through creative accounting policies and options. *Procedia: Social and Behavioral Sciences, 62*, 347–351. DOI: 10.1016/j.sbspro.2012.09.055

Milesi-Ferretti, G. M. (2004). Good, bad or ugly? On the effects of fiscal rules with creative accounting. *Journal of Public Economics, 88*(1–2), 377–394. DOI: 10.1016/S0047-2727(02)00076-2

Mindak, M. P., Sen, P. K., & Stephan, J. (2016). Beating threshold targets with earnings management. *Review of Accounting and Finance*, *15*(2), 198–221. DOI: 10.1108/RAF-04-2015-0057

Pourquery, D. (1991). Les provisions ou l'art de mettre de l'argent de côté. *Science & Vie Economie*, *73*, 72–75.

Raffournier, B. (1990). La théorie positive de la comptabilité: Une revue de la littérature. *Economies et Sociétés, Série sciences de gestion, 16*.

Raffournier, B. (2003). Comptabilité créative et normalisation comptable. *Review of Finance*, *139*, 74–83.

Rossignol, J. L. (2002). La politique fiscalo-comptable des entreprises françaises: Une étude exploratoire. *Comptabilité-Contrôle-Audit*, *8*(1), 89–110. DOI: 10.3917/cca.081.0089

Segura, N. (2008). Contribution à la connaissance de la production de l'information financière: Le cas des provisions pour litiges. *Actes du 29ème congrès de l'Association Francophone de Comptabilité*, Cergy-Pontoise.

Shabou, R., & Boulila Taktak, N. (2002). Les déterminants de la comptabilité créative: Etude empirique dans le contexte des entreprises tunisiennes. *Comptabilité-Contrôle-Audit*, *8*(1), 5–24. DOI: 10.3917/cca.081.0005

Stolowy, H. (1995). Comptabilité créative. *Revue Fiduciaire Comptable*, *212*, 26–32.

Stolowy, H. (1999). Comptabilité créative. In *Encyclopédie de Comptabilité, Contrôle de Gestion et Audit* (pp. 157-178). Economica.

Stolowy, H., & Breton, G. (2003). La gestion des données comptables: Une revue de la littérature. *Comptabilité-Contrôle-Audit*, *9*(1), 125–151. DOI: 10.3917/cca.091.0125

Vangah, Y.-C. A. (2017). Les raisons de la comptabilité créative dans les entreprises ivoiriennes à travers une démarche par les entretiens. *Accountability, Responsabilités et Comptabilités*, May, Poitier, France. Available at https://hal.archives-ouvertes.fr/hal-01907530/document

Watts, R., & Zimmerman, J. (1986). *Positive accounting theory*. Prentice Hall.

Chapter 8
Moroccan Taxpayers' Perception of Tax Amnesties

Tarik Quamar
https://orcid.org/0009-0009-7989-138X
Faculty of Legal, Economic, and Social Sciences Ain Chock, Hassan II University, Casablanca, Morocco

Abderrahmane Anwar
https://orcid.org/0009-0007-6228-4407
Faculty of Legal, Economic, and Social Sciences Ain Chock, Hassan II University, Casablanca, Morocco

Aboubakr Hilali
Faculty of Legal, Economic, and Social Sciences Ain Chock, Hassan II University, Casablanca, Morocco

ABSTRACT

This chapter explores Moroccan taxpayers' perceptions of tax amnesties within a context marked by a heavy reliance on tax revenues and ongoing fiscal reforms. Based on documentary analysis and interviews with ten professionals working in taxation and in companies that have benefited from such measures, the study examines how tax amnesties influence voluntary compliance and trust in the tax administration. The findings reveal a mutually beneficial dynamic, in which amnesties serve both the interests of taxpayers and the tax authorities. The chapter also emphasizes the importance of combining incentives for compliant taxpayers with effective deterrents against non-compliant behavior to enhance the overall impact of such policies.

DOI: 10.4018/979-8-3373-0422-9.ch008

INTRODUCTION

Taxation is considered the most significant source of revenue in various countries worldwide, representing more than 50% of total public revenues (Ospina & Roser, 2020). Tax revenues expressed as a percentage of GDP (i.e., the tax-to-GDP ratio) averaged 33.9% in 2023, reflecting a slight decrease of 0.1 percentage point of GDP compared to 2022 (OECD, 2024).

In 2023, Morocco's net tax revenues reached 190.67 billion Moroccan dirhams (MMDH), recording a 6.9% increase compared to 2022, confirming their crucial role in public finances. The primary tax revenues included corporate tax (IS), which generated 65.84 MMDH (34% of net tax revenues), followed by income tax (IR) with 53.94 MMDH (28%), value-added tax (VAT) with 34.7 MMDH (18%), and registration and stamp duties amounting to 24.11 MMDH, or 12%.

However, despite these advances, the objectives of tax fairness and compliance have not been fully achieved. The National Tax Conference held in Skhirat in 2019 highlighted the need to strengthen transparency and taxpayers' right to information, harmonize tax base rules and equitable taxation, and ensure taxpayers' legal security by framing tax audit procedures.

In this context, tax amnesties are considered a means to encourage non-compliant taxpayers to regularize their status and increase tax revenues. According to Nuryanah & Gunawan (2022), a tax amnesty program provides individuals and businesses the opportunity to declare and pay previously unpaid taxes without imposing part or all of the administrative and criminal penalties typically applied when tax evasion is detected.

Kapon (2022) explains that optimal amnesties can become increasingly generous over time, which is an important element in encouraging taxpayers to wait for the best conditions. These amnesties are considered to be a tool widely used by governments to encourage taxpayers to regularise their tax situation while increasing public revenue (Alm & James, 1993).

In the Moroccan context, tax amnesties have met with increasingly mixed reactions, reflecting a paradox. Firstly, they are perceived as a factor encouraging taxpayers to regularise their irregular situation, due to the reduction in financial penalties and the simplification of administrative procedures (Alm & Beck, 1993). On the other hand. Taxpayers who are well classified and who are characterised by their compliance with tax legislation and respect for deadlines may feel a sense of injustice, perceiving amnesties as a reward for fraud (Luitel & Sobel, 2007). This can lead to a lack of confidence in the tax authorities, which can hinder taxpayers' participation in tax amnesties.

Through this research, we aim to explore how Moroccan taxpayers perceive this update of tax amnesties and what are the factors of motivation and resistance to participation.

In order to address this angle of attack, central questions are formulated as follows:

- What factors influence Moroccan taxpayers' decision to participate in tax amnesties?
- How do taxpayers express their resistance to tax amnesties?
- How do tax amnesties shape Moroccan taxpayers' perception of tax fairness?
- How do these measures impact taxpayers' confidence in the tax authorities?

First, we will look at the theoretical framework and conceptual approaches to tax amnesties. We will then analyse Moroccan taxpayers' perceptions through a qualitative study of their motivations and resistance. We will first discuss the theoretical framework and conceptual approaches related to tax amnesties. We will then analyse Moroccan taxpayers' perceptions of tax amnesties through a qualitative study of taxpayers' motivations and resistance, in line with the recommendations of Creswell (2013) and Patton (2002).

1. CONCEPTUAL FRAMEWORK

Our conceptual framework is based mainly on an analysis of concepts that are closely linked or correlated with tax amnesty and taxpayer perception. By examining the relationship between these two notions, we try to understand our target's motivations and resistances.

For the fundamental concept around which our study is centered: Tax amnesty is defined by a government program that allows taxpayers who are in arrears with their payments to the tax authorities to settle either part or all of their outstanding tax obligations without being subject to prosecution or penalties (Bayer et al. 2015)[1]. These measures are emphasized to improve tax compliance, but their use in a repetitive manner can weaken the perception of tax fairness and undermine trust in tax administration especially for taxpayers who are always up to date and respect payment deadlines.

Tax perception is the way in which taxpayers perceive the transparency, fairness and legitimacy of the tax measures implemented (Torgler, 2003). Two factors that prove to be important in determining taxpayers' perception and behavior. Firstly, we find individuals' perception of the fairness of the tax system, and secondly: the perceived quality of public services (Erdoğdu & Akar, 2022).

We can deduce that perception is strongly influenced by taxpayers' motivating or resisting factors, which manifest themselves in the reduced penalties or exemption from tax inspection offered by a tax amnesty (Langenmayr, 2017) or in the lack of trust in tax administration and fear of a lack of transparency (Zucman,2021)

It is important to weave the links between these concepts in order to understand tax behaviour, since taxpayers' motivations, such as the desire to regularise their situation or to benefit from certain advantageous conditions, can on the one hand encourage participation in amnesties, while resistance can be an obstacle to commitment.

Torgler et al (2003) explain that the granting of an amnesty can lead honest taxpayers to believe that the state cannot be relied upon because of the increased expectations of further amnesties from tax evaders. Mattiello (2005) has described the impact of tax amnesty programs. First, granting tax amnesties can increase compliance rates by allowing citizens to disclose their taxable income. Second, in the long term, tax amnesties can reduce taxpayers' willingness to meet their tax obligations to the state.

A conceptual model was developed to formalise the interactions between the different dimensions influencing Moroccan taxpayers' perception of tax amnesties. This conceptual framework is based inductively on four axes: motivations, resistance, perception of tax justice and confidence in the tax administration.

Motivations play an essential role in the compliance process, as the amnesty is often interpreted as an opportunity to comply in complete security. The perception of tax justice acts as a moral filter in the evaluation of the system, influencing taxpayers' satisfaction or frustration depending on their own level of compliance. Lastly, the level of confidence in the administration acts as a cross-cutting factor, reinforcing or weakening the effect of the previous dimensions.

These elements interact to form an overall perception of the tax amnesty, which determines taxpayers' attitude: voluntary compliance, explicit rejection or a wait-and-see strategy.

The diagram below summarises this analytical framework.

Figure 1. Diagram summarizing analytical framework

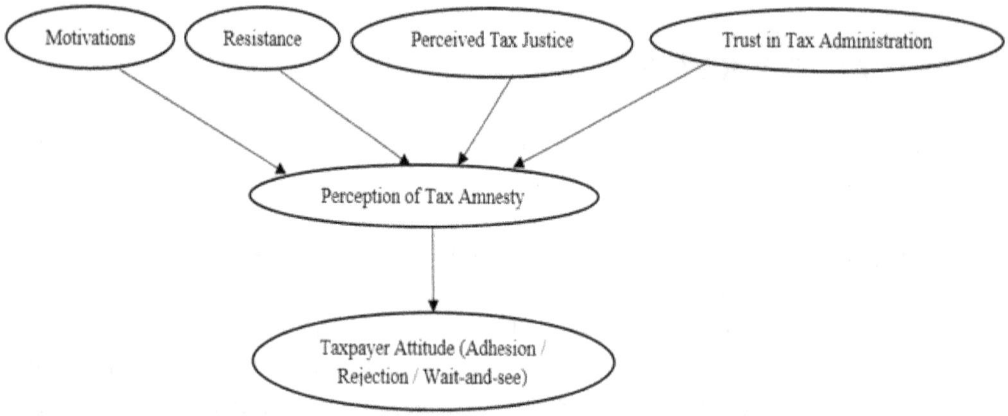

Source: Authors

This study, therefore, aims to explore the links between motivations, resistances, and perceptions of tax amnesties in Morocco to better understand taxpayers' fiscal behavior in this context.

2. THEORETICAL FRAMEWORK OF TAX AMNESTIES

Several economic theories have addressed taxpayer behavior regarding tax amnesty programs. These theories postulate that participation in a tax amnesty depends on a cost-benefit analysis conducted by the taxpayer, influenced by the risks of detection and penalties incurred, while also serving as a means to increase tax revenues.

The standard theory of tax evasion developed by Allingham & Sandmo (1972) and revisited by Alm & Beck (1991) considers participation in amnesty as a result of expected utility gains under conditions of uncertainty (Alm & Beck, 1991).

Taxpayers experience a consumption shock between the initial declaration and the tax amnesty, making them less willing to bear the risk of a tax audit (Andreoni, 1991).

Malik & Schwab (1991) assume that taxpayers are initially uncertain about their risk preferences and only discover them when an amnesty is offered. Graetz & Wilde (1993) propose a model in which taxpayers are motivated to accept amnesties because detection also results in monetary penalties for non-disclosure during non-prescribed periods.

The introduction of tax amnesties in a model where taxpayers face credit constraints and evade taxes to smooth consumption could also explain why amnesties are accepted (Andreoni, 1992).

According to Peacock and Wiseman (1961), the increase in public spending leads to higher tax collection, but there is a limit to the amount of taxes that society can tolerate. As tax revenues increase, taxpayers become increasingly reluctant to pay taxes and may resort to other means to avoid doing so. This presents a challenge for governments, particularly in developing countries like Morocco, where tax evasion and fraud are widespread. This is why the Moroccan government often implements tax amnesty programs to encourage the declaration of concealed assets and increase tax revenues. The tax amnesty program aims to encourage taxpayers to disclose and declare their hidden assets. The primary aim of a tax amnesty programs is to increase government tax revenues and then reduce tax evasion and avoidance.

Several authors, such as Alm & Beck (1993) and Baer & Le Borgne (2008), agree that the success of a tax amnesty depends on certain follow-up measures, such as strengthening implementation efforts and improving taxpayer services. Tax amnesties improve compliance while encouraging taxpayers to regularise their tax situation and appear on the tax rolls. However, they can have a negative impact on tax evaders by

By being perceived as an unfair tax break. In addition, taxpayers may delay their participation in an ongoing tax amnesty if they expect such amnesties to be repeated in the future. Frequent use of tax amnesties may indicate high levels of non-compliance and that compliance conditions are lenient.

3. LITERATURE REVIEW

Over the period from 2014 to 2024, Morocco has launched various programmes to encourage taxpayers to regularise their tax affairs. These measures are seen as incentives for taxpayers to take the step towards regularising their situation and raise questions through which to determine the impact on the perception of tax fairness, voluntary compliance and taxpayer behaviour.

For a fuller understanding of the dynamics surrounding these measures. It is important to analyse previous studies that have been undertaken by researchers interested in the field of tax amnesties. Koch & Müller (2024) explain that while tax amnesties are effective in increasing tax revenues in the short term, they can create an 'insurance effect' among taxpayers. They point out that the implementation of tax amnesties can give taxpayers a sense of tax fairness, which can be an intrinsic factor in improving tax morale.

Tax amnesty is defined by Awaeh et al. (2017), as a partial or complete abolition of taxpayers' tax obligations without subjecting them to tax or criminal penalties. Its main objective is to encourage the repatriation of undeclared assets, restructure tax obligations and minimise the likelihood of taxpayers transferring assets out of the national territory.

The research carried out in Bolivia by Canavire-Bacarreza and colleagues (2024) examined the effectiveness of tax amnesties in a study carried out in Bolivia. The aims of this study were to highlight the short- and long-term impact of these programmes. The study focused on the variety of types of amnesty that affect citizens' compliance with tax obligations.

Three types of tax amnesty were analysed: one-off amnesties, changes in the likelihood of an audit following an amnesty, and amnesties with debt cancellation.

The results indicate that one-off amnesties are more effective than extended amnesties, and that the latter are more effective when combined with measures such as debt cancellation. In addition, the effects vary according to taxpayers' level of tax compliance prior to the amnesty. Taxpayers with a compliance rate above the median are more responsive to incentives, while amnesties of any type appear to have no significant impact on taxpayers with a compliance rate below the median.

In their research, ErdoÄŸdu & Akar (2022) examined the behavioral aspects of tax amnesties and their effects in 12 countries, with a specific focus on Turkey.

The conclusion of this study is that tax amnesties should remain exceptional as their effects over a long period can be negative. As discussed and concluded, one of the disadvantages of tax amnesties is that they tend to favour tax evaders to the detriment of honest taxpayers, which has a negative impact on tax fairness and confidence in tax administration.

A study of tax amnesties in 12 countries showed that in the long term they do not increase tax revenue. In Turkey, these measures are motivated by more specifically political factors, but the results are not satisfactory enough. It can therefore be said that this study highlights the importance of improving the performance of tax systems and combating tax evasion, rather than giving greater prominence to recurrent tax amnesties.

Devano et al. (2024) found that tax amnesty significantly influences taxpayer compliance, improving taxpayer morale. It promotes tax fairness, which can serve as an intrinsic driver for enhancing taxpayer ethics. Their study showed that taxpayers' fear and guilt levels, if they did not participate in the ongoing tax amnesty program, were very high, which increased compliance.

A study conducted in Indonesia by Hajawiyah et al. (2021) analyzed the effectiveness of tax amnesty programs. The results point to a key area of focus: measures to increase tax revenues in the short term, improve compliance and broaden the tax base. Specifically, the empirical analysis revealed a positive impact of tax amnesty on the tax compliance of companies listed on the Indonesian stock exchange, suggesting that the tax policy achieved its goals of discipline and tax base expansion.

From the literature review, tax amnesty can be defined as a government policy program that provides taxpayers with the opportunity to settle past tax debts without subsequent audits, while improving compliance with the tax administration, broadening the tax base, and increasing tax revenues.

The existing literature on tax amnesty primarily focuses on international contexts, highlighting taxpayers' motivations and resistances, as well as the economic and social effects of these programs. However, studies conducted in Morocco remain scarce, particularly regarding how Moroccan taxpayers perceive tax amnesty programs. This scientific gap constitutes the starting point of the present research, which aims to analyze the motivations driving taxpayers to participate in tax amnesties and the resistances they may exhibit toward such measures, providing new insights into fiscal behavior within the Moroccan context.

4. EMPIRICAL SECTION: PERCEPTION OF TAX AMNESTIES IN MOROCCO

4.1 Research Context

Many countries have implemented tax amnesty programs, which have varying effects on the economy depending on their type, objectives, and the financial and political characteristics of the countries (Erdoğdu & Akar, 2022).

Over the past decade, the Moroccan tax administration has introduced four tax amnesties, implemented between 2014 and 2024. The first amnesty, established under the 2014 Finance Law, targeted assets and liquidity held abroad. The second, in 2018, focused on foreign residents in Morocco. The third was introduced in 2020, followed by the latest in 2024.

Among these initiatives is the exceptional measure introduced in 2014, known as the "liberatory contribution," aimed at Moroccan nationals residing in Morocco and Moroccan legal entities to regularize assets and liquidity held abroad in violation of foreign exchange regulations and tax legislation *(Report by the Foreign Exchange Office and the General Tax Directorate, 2015).*

This measure, provided under Article 4 ter of the 2014 Finance Law, was time-limited, running from January 1 to December 31, 2014 *(Circular Note, 2014).*

Subsequently, Finance Law No. 68-17 for the 2018 fiscal year established a liberatory contribution for income and profits generated by assets and liquidity held abroad by foreign nationals domiciled in Morocco who were not in compliance with tax requirements, enabling them to regularize their tax situation. Similar to the measure introduced in the 2014 Finance Law, this liberatory contribution was time-limited, offering a 12-month regularization period from January 1 to December 31, 2018.

Continuing efforts to encourage fiscal compliance, the 2020 Finance Law introduced exceptional measures aimed at encouraging the spontaneous regularization of taxpayers' fiscal situations. This included measures to incentivize newly identified taxpayers, particularly those operating in the informal sector, to integrate into Morocco's economic framework while limiting their tax obligations to income generated after their identification. Additionally, the law allowed for the spontaneous regularization of taxpayers who submitted a voluntary rectification declaration for fiscal years 2016, 2017, and 2018, enabling them to cancel penalties and, in some cases, avoid subsequent tax audits initiated by the tax administration *(Circular Note No. 730, Finance Law No. 70-19 for the 2020 fiscal year).*

The fourth and final amnesty was introduced under the 2024 Finance Law, instituting a voluntary measure to regularize undeclared income and assets before January 1, 2024. This measure, already provided under Article 7 of the 2020 Finance Law, required taxpayers to pay a 5% contribution to regularize liquid assets, non-professional properties, current account advances, and loans to third parties. Regularized amounts were excluded from audit adjustments if the taxpayer was subject to a subsequent tax audit *(Circular Note No. 735 on fiscal measures in Finance Law No. 55-23 for the 2024 fiscal year).*

The tax amnesty program aims not only to combat tax fraud but also to regularize a significant portion of the informal economy. Data published by the Foreign Exchange Office specifically regarding assets and liquidity held abroad offer insight into the scale of these regularizations. According to the official 2025 report, declarations covered a total of over 2 billion dirhams for 658 declarations. Financial assets accounted for the largest share of declared assets, amounting to 916.2 million dirhams (45% of the total), followed by real estate assets at 868.3 million dirhams (43%), and liquid assets at 244.7 million dirhams (12%). The amount paid to the Treasury under the liberatory contribution reached 231.76 million dirhams *(Foreign Exchange Office and Ministry of Economy and Finance, 2025).*

While these figures are important for understanding the scope of regularizations achieved, they do not allow for an examination of the motivations, resistances, and perceptions of tax amnesties among Moroccan taxpayers. Moreover, the Moroccan literature on taxpayer perceptions of tax amnesty programs remains limited, necessitating a study to better understand taxpayer behavior in Morocco within the framework of these measures.

4.2 Empirical Investigation Approach

4.2.1 Research Type and Methodological Approach

In this study, we aim to understand how Moroccan taxpayers perceive tax amnesties by analyzing their motivations and resistances. Our method of reasoning is inductive (from the particular to the general)., in that we formulate conceptual proposals on the basis of the documentary analysis and the interviews conducted The adopted approach is qualitative, based on document analysis and semi-structured interviews (Cherkaoui & Belgaid, 2021) as the data collection method due to their flexibility and relevance

(Cherkaoui & Oudrhough, 2024). This approach is particularly suitable for exploring the perception of Moroccan taxpayers in a sensitive context like tax amnesties.

According to Kvale (1996), semi-structured interviews allow participants to express their opinions and experiences clearly and precisely. This method is particularly suitable when studying subjects perceived as confidential, where interviewees may be reluctant to share their opinions in the presence of others, as is often the case in focus groups (Smithsonet al., 2015).

4.2.2 Sampling and Participant Profile

The sample was selected based on rigorous criteria to ensure the relevance and reliability of the data collected. The participants are exclusively professionals occupying important functions within companies, i.e. administrative and financial managers, company directors, financial directors and tax managers. This methodological choice is justified by the need to gather testimonies grounded in real-life experience with tax amnesties, thereby ensuring expertise and a comprehensive understanding of the subject under investigation.

The sampling method adopted is purposive sampling, which consists of selecting individuals on the basis of specific characteristics, in this case their important role and involvement in corporate tax management. This approach is particularly relevant in the context of this research, as it makes it possible to obtain qualitative data by targeting a homogeneous population directly concerned by tax amnesties. Unlike random sampling, this method optimises data collection by reducing the margin of error and ensuring accurate and efficient selection of respondents.

This method presents several advantages within the context of this study. It enables a detailed examination of taxpayers' perceptions, an analysis of their motivations and resistance to tax amnesties, and a deeper understanding of how such policies influence taxpayer behavior.

4.2.3 Data Analysis Methodology

We considered the diversity of interviewee profiles, setting a minimum threshold of three years of professional experience to ensure a solid professional grounding among participants. A thematic content analysis was conducted, which involves accurately and objectively reporting the interviewees' statements. The process typically includes transcribing the collected statements and then analyzing the discourse.

Challenges include gathering information that is sometimes ambiguous, approximate, imprecise, or contradictory, while leveraging the themes identified in interviews with Moroccan taxpayers.

In our study on the perception of tax amnesties by Moroccan taxpayers, most interviews were conducted via the Zoom platform to provide a flexible and convenient setting for participants. For the transcription and analysis of the collected data, the transcription software **TurboScribe** was chosen to ensure the efficiency and accuracy of processing qualitative data derived from semi-structured interviews.

The interviews with taxpayers were conducted in French, requiring a tool capable of transcribing conversations with precision. TurboScribe stood out for its performance in recognizing the French language and its ability to handle complex files while maintaining good accuracy.

Its effectiveness in processing recordings with moderate background noise was a notable advantage compared to other tools, which often present limitations when transcribing interviews conducted in French.

The questions posed to Moroccan taxpayers were divided into four main themes:

- Motivations of Moroccan taxpayers;
- Resistances and barriers of Moroccan taxpayers;
- Perception of tax fairness by Moroccan taxpayers;
- Trust in the tax administration.

Finally, we connected these themes with our research question and the collected statements to accurately interpret the responses and achieve the objectives set for this study.

Table 1. Empirical research approach

Investigative approach	Scope of the empirical investigation
Documentary Collection	• OECD Economic Outlook, Interim Report; • Recommendations from the Third National Tax Conference; • Finance Law; • General Tax Code; • Foreign Exchange Office instructions; • Circular notes; • Communications from the tax administration.
10 Interviews	10 executives.

Source: Authors

Table 2. Profiles of executives participating in the semi-structured interviews

No. Executives	Age	Seniority	Gender	Degree	Job Title
E1	31	7 years	Male	Master's	Tax Manager
E2	28	6 years	Male	Master's	Tax Manager
E3	30	8 years	Male	Master's	Business Manager
E4	26	5 years	Male	Master's	Administrative and Financial Manager
E5	37	11 years	Male	Master's	Administrative and Financial Director
E6	29	9 years	Male	Master's	Administrative and Financial Director
E7	28	8 years	Male	Master's	Administrative and Financial Manager
E8	27	5 years	Male	Master's	Administrative and Financial Manager
E9	32	8 years	Male	Master's	Business Manager
E10	29	5 years	Male	Master's	Administrative and Financial Manager

Source: Authors

The analysis of qualitative data from the semi-structured interviews with Moroccan taxpayers was analysed using an inductive thematic approach, consistent with the objective of gaining an in-depth understanding of taxpayers' perceptions, motivations and resistance to tax amnesties in Morocco.

Manual coding was preferred, due to the limited volume of interviews conducted and the desire to maintain analytical proximity with what was said. This approach made it possible to capture the richness of the often nuanced discourse and to contextualise the responses according to the tax experience of the participants.

The analysis was inspired by Grounded Theory 3rd ed, (Strauss & Corbin, 2008). Firstly, the use of open coding facilitated the identification of emergent units of meaning without prior prejudice. Subsequently, these components were grouped together using axial coding, making it possible to highlight the links between the different categories. Finally, a selective coding method was used to organise the results along the four main lines of research: taxpayers' motivations for participating in amnesties, the resistance expressed, the perception of tax justice, and the level of trust in the tax authorities.

The use of qualitative analysis software (such as NVivo or Atlas.ti) was not chosen, as manual processing would have enabled a detailed reading, anchored in the Moroccan context, of the speeches analysed. This approach helped to bring out authentic results, directly connected to the tax realities experienced by the taxpayers interviewed.

4.2.4 Identification of Emerging Trends

The identification of emerging trends during the interviews was carried out based on various analytical criteria. Among these, the repetition of comments from one interview to the next and the frequency of key expressions were major indicators of the relevance of the themes discussed. In particular, the emphasis and importance given to certain topics by participants, such as distrust of the tax administration and the perception of tax amnesty as a reward for non-compliance, were considered to be of great significance. These trends emerged when these themes appeared frequently in the interviews.

These elements were confronted with the research problem of how Moroccan taxpayers perceive tax amnesties.

The identified trends were compared with the existing literature on behavioural taxation. For example, the perception of tax amnesties as a reward for tax evasion is reminiscent of the criticisms made by Alm & Beck (1993), Dubin (2007), highlighting the negative consequences of these measures on the perception of tax fairness.

Many respondents expressed a feeling of tax injustice, believing that amnesties favour those who do not comply with the law to the detriment of regular taxpayers.

Other trends, such as persistent distrust of the tax administration or a desire to ‘turn the page’ in order to comply with the future, were interpreted in the light of the notions of trust, tax fairness and distributive justice (Kirchler et al., 2008).

This theoretical grounding helped to strengthen the validity of the results while highlighting the specific nature of the Moroccan context, particularly with regard to perceptions of tax amnesties, the relationship with the tax authorities, and the way in which these perceptions influence tax behaviour.

5. PRESENTATION OF RESULTS

5.1 Motivations of Moroccan taxpayers

Various motivations for taxpayers to participate in tax amnesties were identified throughout the conversations conducted. Their motivations primarily revolve around the desire to regularize their tax situation, start afresh with the tax administration, benefit from exemptions from tax audits, and avoid monetary penalties and forced recovery procedures.

Most participants emphasized the importance of ensuring transparency with the tax administration. One particular motivation that caught our attention was highlighted by a participant who stated:

> "Taxpayers in compliance, but with undeclared funds used for managing liquidity, take advantage of such amnesty measures to regularize their undeclared income. They do so by filing this declaration and paying a contribution at a reduced rate, thereby avoiding the higher rates applicable under normal taxation conditions."

At this stage, tax amnesties appear attractive to both evaders and compliant taxpayers, each finding a way to serve their own interests. Indeed, the rate, ranging between 3% and a maximum of 10% as in the 2018 Finance Law, played a significant role in encouraging Moroccan taxpayers to participate in these schemes.

Among the perceived advantages, taxpayers believe that tax amnesties help avoid penalties associated with non-declaration or automatic taxation procedures. A financial and administrative director of a group highlighted the benefit sought by his company through participation in the tax amnesty:

> "As you know, filing declarations that reveal anomalies, errors, or irregularities to be rectified results in surcharges and late penalties in cases of voluntary regularization. These penalties can be avoided if a corrective declaration is made. However, it is worth noting that such a declaration can also trigger a tax audit, which puts pressure on the company's cash-flow and stability."

This underscores the interest in participating in a tax amnesty, which helps avoid the increased scrutiny of the General Tax Administration while benefiting from exemptions on the origin of undeclared income in accounts.

Some participants also mentioned that clear communication from the tax administration, particularly through information campaigns such as press releases and radio broadcasts, positively influenced their decision to participate and regularize their situation. Conversely, a managerial-level participant, fully aware of the benefits offered by these tax amnesties, stated that they were not influenced by the surrounding communications about these measures.

However, some respondents expressed concerns about the regularity of amnesty programs, fearing that they might become a habit that could encourage non-compliant behaviour conducive to fraud and the continuation of fraud. Nevertheless, taxpayers generally see these measures as an opportunity to improve the relationship and mutual trust with the tax authorities, who are now committed to a more participative approach, moving away from their traditional role as mere enforcers.

> One participant asserted: "On the one hand, there is a fear that information declared under a tax amnesty will later be used to initiate tax audits. On the other hand, these measures are sometimes perceived negatively, because they can be seen as rewards for irregular taxpayers, which may discourage compliant taxpayers."

5.2 Resistance and Obstacles from Moroccan Taxpayers

Several barriers were identified by participants regarding participation in tax amnesties. The main concern is the fear that the information provided as part of the amnesty might later be used to trigger a tax audit. A taxpayer's decision to regularize their situation concerning a specific tax can result in a significant cost. Indeed, the taxpayer risks providing information to the tax administration that could lead to further audits on other types of taxes. This apprehension remains a major obstacle for many taxpayers.

Additionally, some participants noted a lack of trust in the confidentiality of the declarations, particularly in a context where the tax administration has entered into information-sharing agreements with several entities, such as banks, customs authorities, the Foreign Exchange Office, and the National Social Security Fund (CNSS).

Certain taxpayers are reluctant to participate in tax amnesty programs, arguing that they have nothing to regularize and do not see themselves as concerned by these measures. Adding to this reluctance is a crucial issue: companies with direct or indirect links through cross or reciprocal shareholdings. In this context, the General Tax Directorate may use the information declared by taxpayers benefiting from the tax amnesty to initiate accounting audits for other interlinked companies that did not participate, relying on cross-referencing techniques.

According to a discussion with a tax manager, a former inspector who worked within the tax administration, he stated:

> "Now, the General Tax Directorate, with the efficiency of its information system, is able to easily target taxpayers for verification while simultaneously examining their entire tax situation. This enables it to collect revenues it considers legitimately owed."

Another obstacle for some taxpayers is the perception of tax injustice. They consider that tax amnesties favour non-compliant taxpayers, to the detriment of those who comply with tax obligations. This perception of unfairness can dissuade compliant taxpayers from taking part in these schemes, as they feel that non-compliant taxpayers benefit from advantages without suffering any real consequences.

For example, irregular taxpayers regularise their situation at a lower cost than compliant taxpayers. Taking part in tax amnesties allows irregular taxpayers to benefit from a reduced rate of 5%, enabling them to avoid the higher rates usually applied, which vary between 10% and 28% for corporation tax. Similarly, for income tax, they escape the 37% marginal rate provided by the standard tax scale. This situation gives them an advantage in terms of optimising their tax charges, while making a tax saving equivalent to 32% on undeclared income, which is often obtained illegally.

Such scenarios raise questions of tax equity, creating a sense of tax injustice among taxpayers who comply with the tax regulations.

Indeed, the lack of clarity over participation criteria and post-amnesty monitoring is giving rise to reservations. Some taxpayers fear that the tax authorities will introduce monitoring mechanisms, which could lead to increased distrust of the tax authorities.

5.3 Perception of Tax Justice by Moroccan Taxpayers

The perception of tax fairness emerged as a critical theme in the interviews. Participants expressed mixed opinions about the fairness of tax amnesties. Some believe that these measures can restore a sense of equity by encouraging non-compliant taxpayers to regularize their situations. However, others argue that tax amnesties create a form of injustice by rewarding non-compliant taxpayers for their undeclared income, often stemming from unregistered professional activities not identified by the tax administration.

One of the executives participating in the empirical study stated:

"Initially, tax amnesty may appear unbalanced. In the short term, it seems to favor non-compliant taxpayers, allowing them to benefit at the expense of compliant taxpayers. However, another perspective reveals that after regularization, all taxpayers are placed on an equal footing regarding their contribution to the public treasury. That said, if a non-compliant taxpayer were to exploit other mechanisms of tax optimization, although no longer considered non-compliant, they could still be perceived as having taken advantage of a system loophole."

Additionally, taxpayers who comply with tax regulations may also benefit from tax amnesties, particularly in cases where they hold unexplained cash reserves. By participating in these measures, taxpayers regularize undeclared income, benefit from exemption from audits on the origin of funds, and legitimize assets acquired through non-compliant means.

Tax amnesties also appeal to taxpayers operating in the informal sector who have never been identified by the tax administration, providing an opportunity to regularize income generated from unreported professional activities. The primary objective of the tax administration is to restore tax equity among all taxpayers after regularization, evaluating each according to their fiscal behavior. For instance, through these measures, the tax administration reserves the right to impose monetary penalties on taxpayers who deliberately persist in non-compliance.

A significant portion of respondents expressed concerns about the long-term effects of tax amnesties on taxpayer behavior. They fear that these measures might encourage opportunistic behavior, with taxpayers delaying compliance in anticipation of future amnesties to regularize their situations at a lower cost.

Furthermore, it has been argued that such behaviour is sometimes encouraged by managers themselves. Managers' overconfidence (Cherkaoui & Oudrhough, 2025) may lead them to underestimate the risks associated with tax non-compliance, perceiving amnesties as strategic opportunities to regularise tax affairs at lower cost.

Nevertheless, according to some respondents, tax amnesties can have a positive impact in the short term by reducing tax evasion. However, to be effective in the long term, these measures must be accompanied by ongoing monitoring, while stressing the importance of complying with tax obligations and rules.

5.4 Trust in the Tax Administration

The impact of tax amnesties on confidence in the tax authorities is a subject of debate among tax filers. Some believe that these measures strengthen confidence by demonstrating a desire for dialogue and flexibility on the part of the tax authorities. They see the amnesties as a way of regularising undeclared income and benefiting from the exemption from a subsequent audit.

However, others believe that tax amnesties weaken confidence in the tax authorities. For some, amnesties project a negative image, reflecting a lack of credibility on the part of the tax authorities. They are often perceived as a form of tolerance of fraudulent behaviour, which risks undermining the confidence of tax-compliant citizens in the system. By offering offenders an opportunity to evade penalties, these measures can also engender a sense of injustice and impunity. They point the finger at the lack of transparency in the application of the measures and the feeling that these measures mainly benefit taxpayers in irregular and non-compliant situations.

According to a Tax Manager interviewed, *"Tax amnesty, often seen as a questionable measure, is usually allowed only in contexts marked by major events. It appears to be an opportunity for fraudsters, including those seeking to legitimize their situation by taking advantage of such measures. Every time the State aims to reduce the circulation of undeclared cash, it offers an amnesty, which can attract taxpayers to voluntarily declare their income and pay their taxes. They prefer to wait for a possible amnesty to regularize their situation by paying a minimal contribution. This allows them to reset their relationship with the tax administration, accompanied by an exemption from tax audits on the origin of declared income."*

While the opportunistic attitude of non-compliant taxpayers is highlighted, it is also important to consider the intentional and moral element, as well as the negligence of family businesses in the face of the impact of tax penalties. These businesses, often faced with situations of non-compliance, often show a willingness to regularise their situation. In fact, the introduction of a tax amnesty is an opportunity for these businesses to regularise their tax bases or seek advice in order to benefit from these measures.

However, these family businesses find themselves badly advised and assisted, and these taxpayers neglect the fact that once they have joined the tax system, they are expected to comply with the rules governing the declaration and payment of taxes and duties, such as VAT, corporation tax and personal income tax, for which they are liable.

Sometimes these business operate apply what might be called the 'dead man's theory', taking the view that a single payment made under the amnesty measures permanently exempts them from any future tax liability. However, as soon as they identify themselves to the tax authorities, they no longer remain anonymous. Their registration in the tax administration's information system makes them easily detectable and traceable, exposing them to increased risks and accountability for any irregularities committed thereafter.

In this context, the tax authorities have a great many ways of intervening. It can levy tax automatically if taxpayers fail to file their tax returns. In addition, any discrepancies or material errors identified in the returns filed will trigger a tax audit, enabling the tax bases of these companies to be corrected.

In addition, some contributors have a positive view of the effectiveness of the tax authorities in implementing amnesties, because they aim to broaden the economic fabric and increase revenue by identifying as many taxpayers as possible and then rigorously monitoring bad taxpayers who are in good standing with the tax authorities.

Others, however, consider tax amnesties ineffective, citing the administration's inability to significantly curb the circulation of undeclared funds since 2014. They argue that these measures are primarily motivated by the need to attract taxpayers to regularize their situations and comply with future tax obligations.

Such measures often benefit fraudsters who abruptly choose to end their illegal practices by regularizing undeclared liquidities. However, this practice contradicts Morocco's supreme law, the Constitution. These taxpayers remain in violation of Article 39, which states:

"All shall contribute, in proportion to their contributive capacities, to public expenses that only the law may create and allocate, in the manner stipulated by this Constitution."

One executive interviewed stated:

"Taxpayers must contribute to public expenses, each according to their ability to pay. However, this principle is not always upheld. For instance, as an employee, I pay taxes through withholding by my employer, while another taxpayer enjoying the same public services has paid no taxes. So, what kind of equity and tax justice are we talking about?"

This observation highlights an inequality in the application of the law. It is not equality before the law but rather a negative form of discrimination that tends to favor fraudsters.

These fraudsters are encouraged to regularize their situations at reduced costs despite their non-compliant behavior, thus contributing to the Treasury without fully respecting tax equity.

Banks also remain beneficiaries of the tax amnesty introduced in 2024. The banking sector benefits from this financial windfall, thanks in particular to the obligation imposed on taxpayers to deposit the regularised cash with credit institutions. This mechanism enables the banks to capture a significant proportion of these funds. These additional revenues will subsequently be used to finance credit operations, while offering advantageous conditions depending on the nature of the loans granted by the banks. This process strengthens the banks' ability to play a crucial role in financing the economy, while benefiting from the integration of this liquidity into the formal circuit.

To strengthen confidence, a number of suggestions were put forward by the participants, including the introduction of positive incentives for regular taxpayers, such as tax credits or the introduction of permanent or temporary allowances on their profits, or even the temporary taxation of declared profits at reduced rates as a reward for good behavior.

In addition, the introduction of stricter sanctions for those who continue to commit fraud after having benefited from the amnesty measures could reinforce the dissuasive effect of these measures.

These sanctions, repressive in nature, would serve as an example to deter taxpayers tempted to continue non-compliant practices. In addition, more transparent communication and rigorous monitoring of amnesties would improve taxpayers' perception of these mechanisms, thereby strengthening their legitimacy and effectiveness.

Regarding necessary changes to improve the management and perception of tax amnesties, one taxpayer suggested:

> "First, it would be wise to launch communication campaigns in the media, particularly audiovisual outlets. Audiovisual media captures more attention and conveys messages more quickly. Sometimes, even through short humorous scenes, messages are better understood. Additionally, organizing conferences could help improve understanding of tax obligations and encourage taxpayers to comply."

6. ANALYSIS OF RESULTS AND DISCUSSION

We presented Moroccan taxpayers' perception of tax amnesties. Our study shows that Moroccan taxpayers view tax amnesties ambivalently.

One of the main motivations for taxpayers to participate in tax amnesty measures is their desire to regularize their tax situation and start afresh with the tax administration. This approach also allows non-compliant taxpayers to avoid tax audits while regularizing undeclared funds. Notably, this regularization is carried out without the tax administration requiring explanations or proof regarding the origin of these incomes, which enhances the attractiveness of tax amnesties for such taxpayers.

To make tax amnesties more appealing, the tax administration offers regularization based on reduced tax rates, lower than those applied under normal taxation conditions. This approach aims to encourage taxpayers to participate in these measures while promoting a degree of tax equity among all taxpayers. Indeed, tax amnesties are not exclusively targeted at non-compliant taxpayers but are also available to compliant ones, allowing them to regularize undeclared income and illicitly held liquidity by subscribing to these declarations.

The primary objective of the General Tax Directorate through these amnesties is, on one hand, to reduce the circulation of undeclared liquidity and, on the other hand, to encourage taxpayer participation. This also helps taxpayers avoid the constraints associated with corrective declarations or automatic taxation while strengthening their compliance with the tax system.

Most taxpayers consider tax amnesty a measure that allows them to regularize their tax situation at a lower cost, thereby reducing the risks of audits and monetary penalties while improving their relationship with the tax administration.

This observation aligns with the work of Baer & Le Borgne (2008), who described amnesty as a time-limited offer by the government to a specific group of taxpayers to pay a defined amount in exchange for the cancellation of a tax debt (including penalties and surcharges) for prior tax periods, as well as immunity from prosecution.

Another factor that discourages taxpayers from taking part in tax amnesties is the perception of tax injustice. Some consider that tax amnesties favour non-compliant taxpayers to the detriment of good taxpayers. This perception of injustice may dissuade compliant taxpayers from participating in these measures, as they feel that non-compliant taxpayers benefit from the amnesties without facing sanctions for their bad behaviour in breaching the tax authorities' reporting and collection obligations.

Indeed, some respondents claim that tax amnesty schemes have become a frequent practice, encouraging non-compliant behaviour and encouraging tax evasion. This underlines the importance for tax authorities to ensure clear and transparent communication around tax amnesties. This approach would have the effect of improving the perception of these mechanisms and strengthening the relationship of trust between taxpayers and the administration.

On the other hand, our study also revealed concerns about the future use of information disclosed by taxpayers, fueling mistrust regarding confidentiality, especially in a context where the tax administration has entered into information-sharing agreements with entities such as banks, customs authorities, the Foreign Exchange Office, and the National Social Security Fund. Additionally, the exploitation of taxpayer data reinforces the sentiment that these measures primarily benefit non-compliant taxpayers at the expense of compliant ones.

These results were confirmed by the research of Alm & Torgler (2011), who conducted a study into the government's compliance and taxpayer morale strategy. The results of the study showed that, if the tax amnesty is repeated, it can lead to a decline in taxpayers' morale and level of trust in the government. The implementation of a tax amnesty can also have a negative impact on taxpayer compliance if it is too frequent (Murweni 2018).

Indeed, Castro & Scartascini, (2015) argue that tax amnesties, while effective in the short term, can encourage opportunistic behaviour in the long term if they are not accompanied by structural reforms.

Furthermore, tax amnesties can play a positive role in the short term by reducing tax evasion by taxpayers. However, their effectiveness can be compromised if there are loopholes in the tax laws that allow abusive tax optimisation. To ensure their long-term impact, these measures must be accompanied by ongoing monitoring and increased awareness of the importance of compliance with tax obligations and rules Such an approach would foster sustainable taxpayer adherence to the tax system.

James Alm & Soled (2021) highlighted that the perception of tax fairness plays a critical role in taxpayer participation. This notion resonates with participant responses, who call for greater transparency and fairness in the management of tax amnesties. The tax administration must continue to convince taxpayers that implementing tax amnesty ensures fairness for all parties (Sudarma & Darmayasa, 2017).

Similarly, the government should consistently create fairness for all taxpayers by implementing coherent and equitable tax regulations (Devano et al., 2024).

Another aspect observed in our study is that tax amnesties may weaken compliant taxpayers' trust in the tax administration. This is attributed to the perceived lack of transparency and control over fraudulent behaviors. To compliant taxpayers, this appears to be a form of tolerance toward non-compliant taxpayers, providing them with an opportunity to escape sanctions for non-declaration and non-payment. These measures also evoke feelings of injustice and inequity, as they seem to primarily benefit non-compliant taxpayers by offering advantages unavailable to those who scrupulously fulfill their tax obligations.

Conversely, some managers view the tax administration's effectiveness in implementing amnesties positively. They believe these measures contribute to broadening the economic base, thereby increasing tax revenues through the identification of more taxpayers. These managers also assert that the tax administration, through such measures, can ensure continuous monitoring of non-compliant taxpayers benefiting from amnesties while taking steps to curb persistent tax evasion.

Our study highlights a fundamental contradiction with constitutional provisions, particularly Article 39, which stipulates that all taxpayers must contribute to public expenses according to their contributive capacities. However, irregular taxpayers escape this obligation despite the wealth they generate by failing to declare their income. This situation does not reflect equality before the law but rather negative discrimination, favoring fraudsters by allowing them to regularize their situation at minimal cost despite their non-compliant behavior.

Furthermore, these measures not only replenish the Treasury but also benefit the banking sector, which emerges as a primary beneficiary of this financial windfall. The requirement to deposit regularized liquidity in banks allows them to capture significant resources, which can then be mobilized for credit operations and economic activities.

Based on the semi-structured interviews conducted with taxpayers, tax amnesties are seen as a means of regularising undeclared income and also of dispensing with tax audits. This point is supported by the work of (Soepriyanto et al., 2024), who stated that taxpayers will also be exempt from tax audits, preliminary examinations of evidence and investigations into tax offences related to the same tax obligations.

Finally, discussions with taxpayers interviewed as part of our study reveal a lack of positive incentives for regular taxpayers. They deplore the absence of mechanisms such as tax credits, allowances on their profits for the year, or temporary taxation of profits at reduced rates. In addition, they point to the lack of sufficiently dissuasive sanctions for fraudsters who persist in their practices after benefiting from amnesty measures.

In addition, there are insufficient communication campaigns in the media to facilitate the transmission of information to taxpayers with a view to complying with their tax obligations. Raising awareness of this kind is a prerequisite for the tax authorities to increase tax revenues, combat tax fraud, reduce tax evasion and re-establish trust with taxpayers.

7. LIMITATIONS AND DELIMITATIONS OF THE STUDY

As with any qualitative study, this research has methodological and contextual limitations that it is important to address in order to qualify the interpretation of the results.

Firstly, the small size of the sample (10 participants) limits the generalisation of the results to all Moroccan taxpayers. This methodological choice is part of an exploratory and interpretative approach (Maxwell, 2013; Creswell, 2014; Denzin & Lincoln, 2011).

The aim is to gain a better understanding of perceptions rather than to quantify them statistically.

Secondly, the study focused exclusively on professional players in the tax and accounting world (Tax Manager, Business Manager, Administrative and Financial Manager, Administrative and Financial Director), thereby excluding the voice of individual taxpayers, whose behaviour, understanding of the tax system and decision-making levers may differ. This limitation could be overcome in future research by broadening the scope of respondents to include a wider range of socio-professional categories.

Finally, the study is anchored in the Moroccan tax context, which has its own regulatory, historical and cultural specificities. This may limit the direct extension of the findings to other national contexts, even though some of the behavioural logics observed are consistent with more general findings in the behavioural taxation literature (Erdoğdu & Akar, 2022).

Despite these limitations, the results obtained enrich the academic literature by offering an analysis of Moroccan taxpayers' perceptions of tax amnesties. They constitute a relevant basis for future research, particularly through mixed methodologies or larger-scale quantitative surveys.

CONCLUSION

The objective of this study is to analyze the motivations and resistances of Moroccan taxpayers to tax amnesty. Morocco was chosen as a case study due to the tax amnesty programs implemented by the Moroccan government, with the most recent introduced under the 2024 Finance Law. The results of this study indicate that these measures are seen as an opportunity to regularize the tax situation at a lower cost and restore confidence with the tax administration.

The study suggests that Morocco needs to introduce tax incentives for compliant taxpayers, financial penalties for persistent tax evaders and transparent communication on the objectives and desired results of tax amnesties.

In addition, the tax administration must ensure tax equity, strengthen taxpayer confidence and encourage tax compliance by making taxpayers aware of the need to identify themselves for tax purposes, file tax returns within the legal deadlines, declare tax obligations correctly and pay taxes on time (OECD 2010). These recommendations, supported by research, underline the importance of adapting amnesty schemes by taking into account the economic, behavioural and cultural aspects of Moroccan taxpayers.

Other measures could be envisaged to make tax amnesties more effective and improve the way they are perceived by taxpayers. First of all, it seems essential to establish a clear and reassuring legal framework, in particular by means of an explicit legal clause guaranteeing that information transmitted under the amnesty will not be used for future tax reassessments, except in cases of proven fraud. The creation of an independent authority responsible for ensuring compliance with this clause would strengthen taxpayers' confidence in the tax authorities. In addition, to make it easier for taxpayers with financial constraints to sign up, it is recommended that payments of the contribution in full discharge of tax be staggered over several months, without interest, and accompanied by a digital platform for simulating the amount due and planning payments.

In the interests of sustainability, a post-amnesty follow-up system should be put in place, including personalised assistance, tax training sessions and administrative support, particularly for SMEs or new entrants from the informal sector. At the same time, the amnesty could be used as a lever to encourage the gradual integration of the informal sector, through the creation of a simplified transitional regime, with reduced rates or temporary exemptions, conditional on formal accession to the tax system. This mechanism could be reinforced by extra-tax advantages, such as access to financing, social security or public procurement, with the aim of making the regularisation procedure more attractive.

Lastly, a sectoral differentiation of the system could be envisaged, taking into account the economic and tax specificities of each business sector. Prior consultations with chartered accountants and professionals in the field would make it possible to adapt the conditions of access to the amnesty and guarantee its social acceptability. The aim of all these measures is to strengthen voluntary compliance, reduce the structural resistance observed on the ground and ensure the lasting integration of taxpayers into the national tax system.

Overall, the results of the study have an impact on the academic literature by providing an analysis of Moroccan taxpayers' perceptions of tax amnesties.

The study also makes practical contributions to tax administration by providing taxpayers' motivations and resistance to tax amnesties.

This study limits its analysis to the perception of tax amnesties by businesses, which constitutes a restriction in its scope. Consequently, this study could be extended by looking at other categories of taxpayers, such as individuals.

Finally, a comparative exploration between different countries is necessary following the recommendations of the work carried out by (Erdoğdu & Akar, 2022) by studying the behavioral aspects of tax amnesties and their effects in several countries, which may enrich the literature and offer complementary perspectives.

REFERENCES

Allingham, M. G., & Sandmo, A. (1972). Income tax evasion: A theoretical analysis. *Journal of Public Economics, 1*(3–4), 323–338. DOI: 10.1016/0047-2727(72)90010-2

Alm, J., & Beck, W. (1991). Wiping the Slate Clean: Individual Response to State Tax Amnesties. *Southern Economic Journal, 57*(4), 1043–1053. DOI: 10.2307/1060332

Alm, J., & Beck, W. (1993). Tax Amnesties and Compliance in the Long Run: A Time Series Analysis. *National Tax Journal, 47*(1), 53–60. DOI: 10.1086/NTJ41788996

Alm, J., Martinez-Vazquez, J., & Wallace, S. (2009). Do tax amnesties work? The revenue effects of tax amnesties during the transition in the Russian federation. https://doi.org/DOI: 10.1016/S0313-5926(09)50019-7

Alm, J., & Torgler, B. (2011). Is ethics important? Tax compliance and morality. *Journal of Business Ethics, 101*(4), 635–651. DOI: 10.1007/s10551-011-0761-9

Alstadsæter, A., Johannesen, N., Le Guern Herry, S., & Zucman, G. (2022). Tax evasion and tax avoidance. *Journal of Public Economics, 206*, 104587. DOI: 10.1016/j.jpubeco.2021.104587

Andreoni, J. (1991). The desirability of a permanent tax amnesty. *Journal of Public Economics, 45*(2), 143–159. DOI: 10.1016/0047-2727(91)90037-3

Andreoni, J. (1992). IRS As loan shark tax compliance with borrowing constraints. *Journal of Public Economics, 49*(1), 35–46. DOI: 10.1016/0047-2727(92)90062-K

Awaeh, M. A., Lambey, L. L. L., & Pinatik, S. (2017). Analysis of the effectiveness of the implementation of tax amnesty on tax revenues at the Bitung Pratama Tax Office. *Jurnal Riset Ekonomi, Manajemen. Bisnis Dan Akuntansi, 5*(2), 1–9. DOI: 10.35794/emba.v5i2.16529

Bayer, R.-C., Oberhofer, H., & Winner, H. (2015). The occurrence of tax amnesties: Theory and evidence. *Journal of Public Economics, 125*, 70–82. DOI: 10.1016/j.jpubeco.2015.02.006

Bose, P., & Jetter, M. (2012). Liberalization and tax amnesty in a developing economy. *Economic Modelling, 29*(3), 761–765. DOI: 10.1016/j.econmod.2012.01.017

Canavire-Bacarreza, G., Eguino, H., Heller, L., & Roman, S. (2023). When do tax amnesties work? *Journal of Economic Behavior & Organization, 207*, 350–375. DOI: 10.1016/j.jebo.2022.12.018

Castro, L., & Scartascini, C. (2015). Tax compliance and enforcement in the Pampas: Evidence from a field experiment. *Journal of Economic Behavior & Organization, 116*, 65–82. DOI: 10.1016/j.jebo.2015.04.002

Cherkaoui, A. et Belgaid, A. (2021). Les nouveaux défis des managers de proximité face à la décentralisation de la fonction RH au Maroc – Cas d'un groupe financier panafricain. Question(s) de management, n° 32(2), 43-68. https://doi.org/.DOI: 10.3917/qdm.212.0043

Cherkaoui, A., & Dembele, A. (2023). *Performances et politiques financières comparées des entreprises familiales et non familiales cotées au Maroc.* Maghreb - Machrek. *Maghreb, Machrek, N° Hors-série*(1), 73–91. DOI: 10.3917/machr.hs1.0073

Cherkaoui, A. & Oudrhough, Y. (2024). *Case Study Methodology in Business Management: A Systematic Review. In B. Bentalha & L. Alla (Eds.), Applying Qualitative Research Methods to Management Science (pp. 53-74). IGI Global Scientific Publishing.* https://doi.org/DOI: 10.4018/979-8-3693-5543-5.ch003

Cherkaoui, A. & Oudrhough, Y. (2025). *Corporate Governance and Managerial Overconfidence: A Systematic Review. In S. Ed-Dafali, F. Özsungur, & M. Mohiuddin (Eds.), Modern Corporate Governance Strategies for Sustainable Value Creation (pp. 41-60). IGI Global Scientific Publishing.* https://doi.org/DOI: 10.4018/979-8-3693-6750-6.ch003

Corbin, J., & Strauss, A. (2008). Basics of qualitative research: Techniques and procedures for developing grounded theory *(3rd ed.). SAGE Publications.*https://doi.org/DOI: 10.4135/9781452230153

Creswell, J. W. (2013). *Research design: Qualitative, quantitative, and mixed methods approaches.* Sage publications.

Denzin, N. K., & Lincoln, Y. S. (2011). *The SAGE handbook of qualitative research* (4th ed.). SAGE Publications.

Devano, S., Mulyani, S., Winarningsih, S., & Ghani, E. (2024). Tax amnesty and taxpayer morality in predicting taxpayer compliance. *International Journal of Applied Economics. Finance and Accounting, 18*(1), 98–106. DOI: 10.33094/ijaefa.v18i1.1332

Dubin, J. A. (2007). Criminal investigation enforcement activities and taxpayer noncompliance. *Public Finance Review, 35*(4), 500–529. DOI: 10.1177/1091142106295757

Erdoğdu, M. M., & Akar, S. (2022). Behavioral aspects of tax amnesties and their effects in twelve countries. *Public Finance Quarterly, 2022*(2), 270–284. DOI: 10.35551/PFQ_2022_2_7

Graetz, M. J., & Wilde, L. (1993). The decisions by strategic nonfilers to participate in income tax amnesties. *International Review of Law and Economics, 13*(3), 271–283. DOI: 10.1016/0144-8188(93)90037-6

Hajawiyah, A., Suryarini, T., Kiswanto, , & Tarmudji, T. (2021). Analysis of a tax amnesty's effectiveness in Indonesia. *Journal of International Accounting, Auditing & Taxation, 44*, 100415. DOI: 10.1016/j.intaccaudtax.2021.100415

Jakobsen, K., Jakobsen, K., Kleven, H., & Zucman, G. (2020). Wealth taxation and wealth accumulation: Theory and evidence from Denmark. *The Quarterly Journal of Economics, 135*(1), 329–388. DOI: 10.1093/qje/qjz032

Kapon, S. (2022). Dynamic Amnesty Programs. *The American Economic Review, 112*(12), 4041–4075. DOI: 10.1257/aer.20211428

Khan, M. A., & Nuryanah, S. (2023). Combating tax aggressiveness: Evidence from Indonesia's tax amnesty program. *Cogent Economics & Finance, 11*(2), 2229177. DOI: 10.1080/23322039.2023.2229177

Kirchler, E., Hoelzl, E., & Wahl, I. (2008). Enforced versus voluntary tax compliance: The "slippery slope" framework. *Journal of Economic Psychology, 29*(2), 210–225. DOI: 10.1016/j.joep.2007.05.004

Koch, C., & Müller, C. (2024). Tax amnesties and the insurance effect: An experimental study. *Journal of Behavioral and Experimental Economics, 108*, 102130. DOI: 10.1016/j.socec.2023.102130

Kvale, S. (1996). *Interview Views: An Introduction to Qualitative Research Interviewing*. Sage Publications., https://doi.org/, DOI: 10.1016/S1098-2140(99)80208-2

Langenmayr, D. (2017). Voluntary disclosure of evaded taxes — Increasing revenue, or increasing incentives to evade? *Journal of Public Economics, 151*, 110–125. DOI: 10.1016/j.jpubeco.2015.08.007

Le Borgne, M. E., & Baer, M. K. (2008). *Tax amnesties: Theory, trends, and some alternatives*. International Monetary Fund., DOI: 10.5089/9781589067363.058

Luitel, H. S., & Sobel, R. S. (2007). The Revenue Impact of Repeated Tax Amnesties. *Public Budgeting & Finance, 27*(3), 19–38. DOI: 10.1111/j.1540-5850.2007.00881.x

Malik, A. S., & Schwab, R. M. (1991). The economics of tax amnesties. *Journal of Public Economics, 46*(1), 29–49. DOI: 10.1016/0047-2727(91)90063-8

Mattiello, G. (2005). Multiple tax amnesties and tax compliance (Forgiving seventy times seven). Università Ca'Foscari, Venezia Working Paper, Maxwell, J. A. (2013). Qualitative research design: An interactive approach (3rd ed.). SAGE Publications.

Menkhoff, L., & Miethe, J. (2019). Tax evasion in new disguise? Examining tax havens' international bank deposits. *Journal of Public Economics, 176*, 53–78. DOI: 10.1016/j.jpubeco.2019.06.003

Murweni, I. (2018). Implementation of the tax amnesty program to increase tax compliance among business taxpayers. *Jurnal of Ekonomi-Bisnis, 2*(2), 53–63. DOI: 10.37339/e-bis.v2i2.84

Nuryanah, S., & Gunawan, G. (2022). Tax amnesty and taxpayers' noncompliant behaviour: Evidence from Indonesia. *Cogent Business & Management, 9*(1), 2111844. DOI: 10.1080/23311975.2022.2111844

Ortiz-Ospina, E., & Roser, M. (2020). La fiscalité. https://ourworldindata.org/taxation

Patton, M. Q. (2002). *Qualitative research and evaluation methods* (3rd ed.). Sage Publications.

Peacock, A. T., & Wiseman, J. (1973). Approaches to the analysis of government expenditure growth. *Public Finance, 7*(1), 24–45.

Shields, P. M., & Tajalli, H. (2006). Intermediate theory: The missing link in successful student scholarship. *Journal of Public Affairs Education, 12*(3), 313–334. DOI: 10.1080/15236803.2006.12001438

Smithson, A., Holmes, J., & Gillies, F. (2015). Integration, assimilation or transformation: Introducing therapists to qualitative research methods, a focus group study. *European Journal of Psychotherapy & Counselling, 17*(3), 296–313. Advance online publication. DOI: 10.1080/13642537.2015.1059868

Soepriyanto, G., Zudana, A. E., & Meiryani, M. (2024). Older and wiser? The impact of CEO age on firm's tax amnesty participation. *Cogent Business & Management, 11*(1), 2296142. DOI: 10.1080/23311975.2023.2296142

Stella, P. (1991). An economic analysis of tax amnesties. *Journal of Public Economics, 46*(3), 383–400. DOI: 10.1016/0047-2727(91)90013-R

Sudarma, I., & Darmayasa, I. N. (2017). *Does voluntary tax compliance increase after granting tax amnesty? Accounting and Finance Review* (Vol. 2). AFR.

Torgler, B. (2003). Tax morale: Theory and empirical analysis of tax compliance (Doctoral dissertation, University_of_Basel).

Chapter 9
Effective Communication and Awareness Campaigns as Tools for Enhancing Tax Compliance:
Insights and Strategies

Mohamed Bouaddi
https://orcid.org/0009-0009-0951-0203
Moulay Ismail University, Meknes, Morocco

Mohammed Beddaa
https://orcid.org/0009-0007-2342-3136
Higher School of Technology, Mohammed First University, Oujda, Morocco

Badr Bentalha
https://orcid.org/0000-0003-1339-542X
Sidi Mohammed Ben Abdellah University, Fez, Morocco

ABSTRACT

This article explores the importance of communication and tax awareness as key levers for improving tax compliance. In a context where tax compliance is essential for ensuring economic stability and funding public services, many governments face challenges in achieving high levels of compliance. The issue raised, therefore, is to understand how communication strategies can influence taxpayer behavior and encourage them to meet their tax obligations. The study aims to examine the role of communication, as well as awareness campaigns, in enhancing tax compliance. The chapter seeks to demonstrate how clear, transparent, and accessible communication, combined with awareness efforts, can help reduce tax evasion and foster a culture of respect for tax regulations. To this end, a qualitative methodology was employed, including interviews with tax experts and taxpayers. The findings reveal that tailored communication channels and targeted awareness campaigns can positively impact the understanding of tax obligations, reduce tax evasion, and build taxpayer trust in the tax system.

DOI: 10.4018/979-8-3373-0422-9.ch009

INTRODUCTION

Tax compliance ensures a country's economic stability and financing of essential public services. However, many governments find it difficult to achieve satisfactory levels of tax compliance. This situation is exacerbated by communication problems, where taxpayers often do not fully understand their tax obligations or perceive the importance of complying with them. In this context, communication and tax awareness are potential levers for improving tax compliance and performance.

Our study's central issue is understanding how communication strategies, particularly tax awareness campaigns, can influence taxpayers' favorable behavior. Indeed, although tax authorities deploy various initiatives to inform citizens, these actions sometimes seem insufficient to reduce tax evasion and promote an attitude of tax compliance. It is therefore crucial to explore the factors that make these strategies effective or ineffective, to better target communication efforts.

To analyze the impact of tax communication on taxpayers' behavior, a qualitative methodology was adopted. A series of semi-structured interviews was conducted to explore possible links between the axes of our research theme. These interviews were based on four main questions: firstly, taxpayers' general perception of the tax system and the reasons for non-compliance. Next, the evaluation of messages received concerning tax obligations, their clarity, and usefulness. Then, the impact of awareness-raising campaigns conducted by tax authorities. Finally, participants' suggestions for improving these communication strategies. Interviews were conducted with a sample of taxpayers from various social and professional groups. The data collected was transcribed and analyzed thematically.

Henceforth, the main objective of our study is to examine how clear, transparent, and accessible communication, together with appropriate awareness-raising campaigns, can improve tax compliance in a given country. The empirical study envisaged seeks to assess whether these strategies are perceived positively by taxpayers, and to what extent they can help reduce tax evasion and strengthen citizens' confidence in the tax system.

To this end, the present work will be structured around three main parts. The first part presents the conceptual and theoretical framework of our research topic. The second part is devoted to presenting the research methodology adopted for this paper. Finally, the third and last part will deal with the presentation and discussion of the results of this research.

1. THEORETICAL AND CONCEPTUAL FRAMEWORK

1.1. Tax Compliance and Communication

As part of the study of the relationship between communication and tax compliance, several concepts need to be understood: tax compliance, tax awareness, tax communication, and tax performance. Mastering these concepts will help you understand how the tax system works, and improve taxpayer compliance and performance.

1.1.1. Tax Compliance

Tax compliance refers to the legal obligation of taxpayers, whether individuals or companies, to comply with the tax laws in force in their country. This has several essential dimensions (Khomsi, 2025). Firstly, taxpayers must pay taxes due on time and according to the terms defined by tax legislation. Non-payment or late payment of taxes can result in sanctions and penalties, underlining the importance of complying with tax obligations.

In addition to paying taxes, taxpayers must declare their income accurately and completely (CGI, 2024). This includes declaring all sources of income, whether from professional activities, investments, or other forms of gain. This declaration must be made in compliance with tax procedures and within the deadlines set by the tax authorities, to avoid any form of tax evasion or avoidance.

Bookkeeping is also a crucial element of tax compliance, especially for businesses. Companies must ensure that they keep rigorous and transparent accounts of their financial operations (MEF, 2024). This not only helps to justify income and expenditure but also facilitates tax audits should the need arise. In addition, taxpayers must comply with all other tax obligations, such as declaring VAT, keeping supporting documents, or submitting specific reports, according to the requirements defined by the tax authorities.

The main objectives of tax compliance are multiple and essential to the proper functioning of a country's tax system (Machmoume, 2021). Firstly, tax compliance aims to guarantee the integrity of the tax system. Ensuring that taxpayers meet their tax obligations ensures the transparency of tax processes and strengthens the confidence of citizens and businesses in tax administration. This reduces the risk of fraud and tax evasion, which are major threats to a country's economic and social equilibrium (Karam & Berjaoui, 2021). Compliance, by guaranteeing the clarity and regularity of tax practices, contributes to the credibility of the system.

Secondly, a key objective is to ensure the efficient collection of public revenues. Compliance with tax obligations guarantees a steady inflow of financial resources into state coffers, enabling the financing of essential public services such as health, education, security, and infrastructure (Joumard & Kongsrud, 2003, Alj, 2024). Efficient collection is vital to a country's economic development and the maintenance of social programs. Non-compliance, on the other hand, can lead to a lack of funds for these services, creating imbalances in public finances (Haddouchi et al., 2021).

Finally, another crucial objective is to promote tax fairness. Compliance with tax rules helps avoid distortions and inequalities within the tax system. Strict compliance ensures that every taxpayer contributes fairly according to his or her financial capacity, thereby reinforcing tax justice. In the absence of compliance, some taxpayers could benefit from preferential tax treatment or escape their responsibilities, leading to inequality and social injustice (Khomsi & Msatfa, 2024). Tax compliance therefore makes it possible to maintain a system in which all economic players are treated fairly and equally.

Tax compliance thus plays a fundamental role in maintaining economic stability, social equity, and the transparency of public finances, all of which are essential to a country's sustainable development.

The components of tax compliance cover several aspects essential to ensuring that taxpayers meet their tax obligations. According to the French Ministry of Economy and Finance (MEF, 2024), one of the fundamental elements of tax compliance is the declaration of income. Taxpayers must submit periodic tax returns, which may be annual or quarterly, depending on the nature of their activities and status. These declarations must include complete information on income, expenses, and any other items needed to correctly assess the tax due.

Another essential component of tax compliance is the payment of taxes. After declaring their income, taxpayers are obliged to meet their tax obligations within the deadlines specified by the tax authorities. Non-payment or late payment of taxes may result in penalties and interest, as stipulated in the General Tax Code 2024 (MEF, 2024). So, meeting payment deadlines is crucial to maintaining tax compliance and avoiding financial penalties.

Finally, keeping tax records is another key component of tax compliance. Taxpayers need to keep rigorous accounting records and supporting documentation to prove the validity of their tax returns. This includes keeping invoices, bank statements, and financial reports. Good record-keeping not only facilitates tax audits but also ensures that taxpayers can justify their declarations in the event of an audit or verification by the tax authorities.

These three components - declaring income, paying taxes, and keeping tax documents - are the foundations on which tax compliance rests. They are essential for transparent and efficient tax management while reducing the risk of tax evasion and avoidance.

It is crucial to differentiate tax compliance from tax evasion because although both terms concern taxpayers' interaction with the tax authorities, they have very different meanings and implications (Bazart, 2002). Tax compliance refers to the full observance of current tax laws, which includes the correct declaration of income, the timely payment of taxes due, and compliance with other tax obligations defined by the authorities. Compliant taxpayers adhere to all the rules established by the tax authorities, thus guaranteeing the transparency and integrity of the tax system (Bazart & Blayac, 2022).

Tax evasion, on the other hand, refers to strategies used by some taxpayers to illegally reduce the amount of tax they have to pay (Boyer, 2020). This includes practices such as the manipulation of declared income, the use of false information, or the concealment of part of their assets and income to evade taxation. Tax evasion therefore involves a violation of tax rules, and can result in severe penalties, including fines and prosecution. Unlike compliance, tax evasion undermines the fairness and efficiency of the tax system, as it deprives the state of the resources needed to finance public services and infrastructure.

Thus, while tax compliance aims to strengthen confidence and transparency in the tax system, tax evasion represents an attempt to circumvent these rules to obtain personal benefits, to the detriment of the community (Bazart & Blayac, 2022).

1.1.2. Tax Awareness

Tax awareness represents a major challenge for tax administrations, as it helps to ensure taxpayer compliance while enhancing the transparency and fairness of the tax system. According to Khanfor & El Wazani (2016), tax awareness refers to the effort by tax authorities, businesses, or other relevant actors to inform and educate citizens and businesses about their tax obligations. This includes the dissemination of clear information about tax obligations, the procedures to be followed, and the consequences of non-compliance (Halimah & Juitania, 2022). Good tax awareness should enable taxpayers to better understand the importance of their tax contributions and their role in financing public services and economic development.

Moreover, tax awareness is an ongoing process that goes beyond the simple dissemination of information. It also aims to encourage voluntary and active participation by citizens and businesses in tax compliance. Sharp (2023) points out that tax awareness helps to improve understanding of tax laws, which can lead to greater acceptance of tax obligations by taxpayers. This helps reduce tax evasion and avoidance behavior, by fostering a climate of trust between tax authorities and taxpayers (Widuri et al.,

2023). Voluntary participation in tax compliance is a key objective of any awareness-raising strategy, as it relies on taxpayers' commitment and responsibility.

Tax awareness aims to achieve several key objectives that contribute to improving tax compliance and creating a more transparent and equitable tax environment. One of the main objectives of tax awareness is to educate taxpayers. This involves helping citizens and businesses to better understand the various tax laws, tax rates, as well as tax procedures (Gonidakis et al., 2024). Better understanding minimizes reporting errors and reduces the risk of non-compliance. Mascagni et al. (2024) emphasize that tax education is essential to ensure that taxpayers are well-informed and able to fulfill their tax obligations correctly.

Another key objective of tax education is to strengthen the voluntary participation of citizens and businesses in complying with tax obligations (Appiah et al., 2024). By raising taxpayers' awareness, the aim is to encourage their voluntary adherence to tax rules, which helps to reduce fraudulent behavior and strengthen the integrity of the tax system. Rguig & Guemmi (2023) argue that awareness plays a crucial role in preventing tax evasion by encouraging taxpayers to voluntarily comply with tax norms.

Finally, tax awareness aims to promote social responsibility (Oualhi, 2028). It helps develop a sense of responsibility among citizens and businesses, encouraging them to contribute fairly and equitably to the financing of public services. Mkadmi & Ben Ali (2024) explain that this promotion of social responsibility is essential to guarantee a fair distribution of the tax burden and to ensure that public services are adequately financed by those who benefit from them. In this way, these interconnected objectives help to build a relationship of trust between tax authorities and taxpayers, while strengthening the overall tax system.

Tax authorities and other stakeholders use a variety of means to raise public awareness of tax obligations and encourage compliance. Among these means, information campaigns play a key role (OECD, 2021). These include the distribution of brochures, videos, and advertisements, aimed at informing citizens about their tax obligations and the importance of complying with tax laws. These campaigns are often disseminated via the media or online platforms to reach a wide audience and reinforce understanding of tax rules.

In addition, training courses and seminars are also important tools in raising tax awareness. These events, organized for companies or individuals, aim to explain the various tax obligations and provide assistance in preparing tax returns (Nagel et al., 2019). These sessions are often led by tax experts and enable participants to ask questions and clarify specific points concerning taxation.

The use of technology has also emerged as an effective means of improving tax awareness and compliance (Okunogbe & Santoro, 2022). For example, online platforms and mobile apps can simplify the submission of tax returns, provide reminders, and even offer personalized advice on compliance. These tools enable taxpayers to easily access tax information and submit their returns quickly and securely. Finally, tax consultations and support services play a crucial role in helping taxpayers understand their rights and obligations (LeBaube & Vehorn, 1992). Tax administrations can offer assistance services, such as telephone hotlines, reception desks, or online consultations. These services can provide answers to taxpayers' questions and guide them through the administrative process.

Tax awareness-raising is essential to strengthening the tax culture among the population, as it helps to create a general awareness of each citizen's tax responsibilities (Amin et al., 2022). A well-informed public is more likely to understand the importance of complying with tax laws and to adopt compliant behavior, thus reducing non-compliance rates. According to Mohamad et al. (2022), effective awareness-raising increases understanding of tax rules and reduces misreporting.

In addition, tax awareness also contributes to transparency and accountability in the management of public finances (Cifuentes-Faura et al.,2024). When citizens are aware of their tax obligations, this creates social and moral pressure to comply more strictly with tax rules. Mebratu (2024) points out that effective educational programs have a direct impact on reducing tax evasion and encouraging voluntary participation in tax compliance.

Finally, tax awareness helps build public trust in tax authorities and the management of public funds. Capasso et al (2021) argue that improving tax transparency and tax ethics, supported by good communication, is a lever for increasing tax compliance and improving the effectiveness of tax policies. Better information on how taxes are used strengthens the sense of fairness and tax justice among taxpayers (Lestary et al., 2021).

1.1.3. Tax Communication

The socio-psychological tradition conceptualizes communication as a dynamic process of expression, interaction, and influence between individuals and groups. When applied to tax compliance, this theoretical framework provides valuable insights into how psychological factors shape taxpayer behavior. Tax authorities can leverage this understanding by developing persuasive messaging that effectively addresses taxpayers' attitudes and beliefs about compliance. This approach recognizes that taxpayers process information about tax regulations through various cognitive filters, making the credibility of the tax authority a crucial element in message acceptance. Communication strategies based on this tradition might focus on resolving cognitive dissonance that arises when taxpayers' actions conflict with their beliefs about civic responsibility. The socio-cultural tradition offers a complementary perspective by examining how communication reproduces social order and constructs shared cultural meanings around taxation. This tradition acknowledges that compliance behavior is deeply embedded within cultural norms and values that vary across different societies and communities. Tax communications must therefore navigate complex social identities and cultural narratives about the relationship between citizens and government. The socio-cultural approach emphasizes that effective tax compliance strategies must be culturally sensitive and adaptable to diverse contexts, recognizing that what works in one cultural setting may not translate effectively to another. The semiotic tradition provides yet another valuable lens by focusing on communication as a process of sign-mediation and meaning-making. In the context of tax compliance, this tradition illuminates how symbols and language choices in official communications convey implicit messages that influence taxpayer interpretations and responses. Tax authorities must carefully consider how visual elements, terminology, and linguistic structures in their campaigns create meaning across different taxpayer segments. The semiotic perspective highlights the importance of shared systems of meaning around concepts such as "fairness," "duty," and "compliance," recognizing that these terms may carry different connotations for different audiences.

Tax communication refers to the set of strategies used by tax administrations to inform taxpayers of their tax obligations and raise their awareness of the challenges of the tax system (Cotton et al., 2017). It includes actions to explain tax rules and encourage compliance, but also to strengthen citizens' trust in the tax administration. According to Bourdieu (1999), tax communication helps to legitimize public action and facilitate the relationship between the administration and taxpayers. Indeed, clear, well-structured communication is crucial to ensuring that citizens understand their tax obligations, and can fulfill them correctly. It aims to clarify tax expectations and explain the consequences of tax evasion, which in turn improves the transparency and fairness of the tax system (Purnomo, 2019). According to Bagus et al. (2011), effective tax communication plays a crucial role in preventing unintentional tax errors and reducing perceptions of unfairness.

In this sense, digital communication is increasingly used to reach a wide audience (Bouaddi et al., 2024; Boudri et al., 2025). A similar observation was made in the research work of Kleven et al. in 2009. Indeed, these authors highlighted the role of effective Internet communication campaigns in increasing transparency and taxpayer participation in the financing of public spending. Tax communication has multiple objectives. On the one hand, it seeks to inform citizens and businesses about their tax obligations and the penalties for non-compliance. This includes disseminating the information needed to ensure that every taxpayer understands the importance of his or her tax contributions and the positive repercussions for society. On the other hand, tax communication aims to promote tax compliance, notably by simplifying procedures and providing understandable information (Alm & Torgler, 2006). In addition, tax communication helps to strengthen citizens' trust in tax institutions, an essential element in guaranteeing an efficient tax system and reducing fraud (Kirchler, 2007).

Moreover, the channels and tools of tax communication have diversified considerably over time. While print media, radio, and television were historically the main means of communication, digital technology has opened up new horizons (Bouaddi et al., 2024). Interactive websites, online tax platforms, and social networks now enable direct and instant communication with taxpayers, simplifying access to tax information (Ebrill et al., 2001). These tools also offer online services such as tax simulators, helping to reduce errors and improve the accuracy of tax returns. In parallel, awareness campaigns, whether local or national, aim to reach a wide audience and make taxpayers aware of the need to comply with tax rules and procedures. These campaigns can focus on educational messages, such as the importance of taxes in financing essential public services like education and health.

1.1.4. Tax Performance

Tax performance refers to the ability of a tax system to achieve its objectives efficiently and fairly. It encompasses several dimensions, including the collection of tax revenues, the reduction of administrative costs, and the fair distribution of tax burdens among citizens. Indeed, an efficient tax system is not just about collecting taxes, but also about ensuring a fair distribution of the tax burden and combating tax evasion. According to Bird & Zolt (2005), high tax performance implies an administration that is not only efficient in collecting taxes but also transparent and fair in distributing resources. Tax performance objectives therefore include maximizing tax revenues while minimizing the costs associated with tax collection.

Tax performance also aims to reduce tax inequalities by ensuring a fair distribution of the tax burden. An efficient tax system must ensure that all taxpayers pay their fair share according to their ability to pay, while at the same time reducing tax evasion. Tax performance is thus based on criteria of fairness, efficiency, and transparency (Bird & Zolt, 2005). Among tax performance indicators, the tax collection rate is one of the most important. This rate represents the percentage of taxes collected about expected tax revenues. A high collection rate indicates good performance of the tax system. Another essential criterion is the administrative cost of tax collection. Reducing this cost, particularly by adopting digital technologies, is a sign of administrative efficiency. The use of online tax platforms, as shown by the example of several developed countries, considerably reduces the costs associated with sending documents and processing paper returns (Zodrow, 2003). Finally, the tax compliance rate is a key indicator that reflects the proportion of taxpayers who voluntarily comply with their tax obligations, without having to resort to controls or administrative sanctions. Tax performance is influenced by several external and internal factors. Tax evasion remains a major challenge, particularly in systems where tax controls are weak or poorly perceived. According to Slemrod & Yitzhaki (2002), a successful system combines effective control policies with clear communication of the risks associated with evasion. Moreover, the integrity and transparency of tax institutions play a fundamental role in maintaining taxpayers' confidence, which in turn fosters tax compliance.

In addition, technological advances, such as the introduction of digital systems and artificial intelligence, make it possible to improve the efficiency of the tax system and detect cases of fraud more quickly (Bird & Zolt, 2005; Bentalha & Boukare, 2024; Meziane et al., 2025). Finally, the international dimension of tax performance highlights significant differences from one country to another. In this sense, developing countries often face specific challenges, such as a low level of administrative capacity and a high rate of fraud. However, well-targeted tax reforms, combined with the use of modern technologies, can improve tax performance in these countries (Zodrow, 2003). Indeed, comparative experience between different tax systems shows that technological reforms and efficient tax administration are important levers for improving performance in emerging economies.

1.2. Communication, Sensitivity and Tax Compliance: A Literature Review

The issue of tax compliance and associated communication mechanisms has been the subject of numerous studies in the fields of public taxation, economic psychology and public management. This literature review examines the main theoretical frameworks and empirical research that have explored the impact of tax communication and awareness on taxpayer compliance.

Tax compliance is a complex phenomenon based on a multitude of factors. Several researchers have attempted to understand why some taxpayers comply with their tax obligations, while others choose to circumvent them. The traditional approach, represented by the work of Allingham & Sandmo (1972), is based on an economic model in which taxpayers compare the cost of tax compliance (mainly taxes payable) with the risk of being caught evading taxes. This classic model views tax compliance as a rational decision influenced by perceptions of the likelihood of detection and punishment. In this sense, tax compliance refers to taxpayers' adherence to tax requirements, namely meeting deadlines and paying taxes due (Alhempi et al., 2020). Tax compliance can be viewed in terms of formal compliance (adherence to rules) and substantive compliance (accuracy of information provided) (Muja'hidah et al., 2023). According to Torgler (2003), tax compliance is often influenced by taxpayers' perceptions of the tax system, as well as by their tax communication and trust in tax administration.

However, subsequent research has nuanced this purely economic view by introducing psychological and social factors. Torgler (2003), for example, has shown that citizens' trust in tax institutions plays a crucial role in compliance. People who perceive the tax system as fair and transparent are more inclined to comply with existing tax rules and standards. Thus, public trust and a sense of tax justice are essential elements in encouraging taxpayers' compliance (Alm, 1999). Social compliance (i.e. adherence to tax norms due to social pressure) has also been identified as a key factor by Wenzel (2005). This research suggests that taxpayers who are aware of the behavior of others and the collective impact of tax evasion are more motivated to comply with tax norms.

Tax communication therefore represents a strategic lever for improving tax compliance. According to McGee (2013), clear and accessible communication between tax authorities and taxpayers is essential to ensure that the latter understand their obligations and the benefits of voluntary compliance. Therefore, the role of tax communication is primarily to inform taxpayers about how to meet their tax obligations and to reduce misunderstandings about tax requirements.

A study by Slemrod (2007) stresses that tax communication must go beyond the mere dissemination of information, also seeking to change taxpayers' attitudes towards the tax system. The accountability dimension of Slemrod's model emphasizes the importance of tax authorities clearly demonstrating how collected revenues are utilized for public benefit. When taxpayers can see a direct connection between their contributions and tangible social outcomes, compliance rates tend to improve significantly. Furthermore, Slemrod's findings highlight the value of active engagement between tax authorities and citizens. Rather than relying exclusively on enforcement mechanisms and penalties, this approach encourages two-way communication, taxpayer education, and collaborative problem-solving. Such engagement strategies acknowledge that compliance behaviors are influenced not only by economic calculations but also by social norms and perceptions of procedural fairness. A cooperative approach to tax communication, based on transparency, accountability, and commitment, has been identified as a key factor in tax compliance. This type of communication aims to establish a dialogue with taxpayers, rather than limiting itself to unilateral messages imposed by the tax authorities (Alm, 1999). Such an approach can foster a perception of tax fairness and, consequently, a greater willingness to comply.

Tax awareness encompasses all initiatives aimed at educating citizens about the benefits of tax compliance and the consequences of tax evasion (Nguyen Thi Le et al., 2024). In this sense, well-designed awareness campaigns, such as those studied by Wenzel (2005), can influence tax behavior by instilling a sense of civic responsibility and highlighting the positive impact of taxes on society. The main aim of such campaigns is to reduce tax evasion, as highlighted by Slemrod (2007), who shows that raising awareness of the role of taxes in the provision of public services can motivate taxpayers to be more inclined to comply with existing tax rules and procedures.

Consequently, effective communication and appropriate awareness-raising are essential levers for improving compliance and tax performance. The work of Torgler (2003), McGcc (2013), Alm (1999), Kleven et al. (2016), Wenzel (2005), and Slemrod (2007) demonstrates the importance of these factors in strengthening tax compliance and reducing tax evasion, highlighting the vital role of communication strategies in the tax management process.

Digital channels are also playing an increasingly important role in tax communication (Beddaa & Bentalha, 2025). The study by Kleven et al. (2016) demonstrated that online platforms, such as tax authority websites, mobile apps, and social networks, offer effective ways of raising awareness and informing taxpayers, particularly the younger generation, who are often more comfortable with these technologies. In addition, research by Pomeranz (2015) suggests that transparency in tax communication, particularly through the publication of data on the tax behaviors of other taxpayers, can increase compliance, as this highlights the compliance behaviors of peers and makes the social impact of individual tax decisions visible.

The aim of tax communication and awareness-raising is now to promote a better understanding of the tax system and its benefits for society. Slemrod (2007) has highlighted the importance of awareness-raising campaigns in changing taxpayers' attitudes to their tax obligations. Thus, these campaigns can be directed not only at raising awareness of the harmful consequences of tax evasion but also at the collective benefits of compliance, such as the funding of essential public services.

In addition, the work of Wenzel (2005) has shown that awareness campaigns can influence taxpayers' perceptions of the legitimacy of taxation and the potential impact of tax evasion. When they highlight the benefits of compliance for the community, such as improved public infrastructure, they can encourage citizens to meet their tax obligations, even in the absence of direct controls. Research by Torgler (2003) has also suggested that tax morality - the willingness of individuals to pay taxes out of a belief that it is the right thing to do - plays a crucial role in tax compliance.

Awareness campaigns must, however, be tailored to specific groups of taxpayers. For example, small and medium-sized enterprises, as highlighted by researchers such as Di Legge et al. (2022), may need specific messages that address the particular challenges they face in their dealings with the tax authorities. In addition, campaigns need to use appropriate channels to effectively reach their targets, be they seminars for small and medium-sized businesses, information sessions for young taxpayers, or educational videos for a wider audience.

2. RESEARCH METHODOLOGY

The semi-structured interview is one of the leading methods of qualitative research in the social sciences. This survey technique lies midway between the directive interview, characterized by closed questions, and the non-directive interview, which leaves total freedom to the interviewee. Its distinctive feature lies in its ability to combine a pre-established structure with the flexibility needed to explore participants' experiences and perceptions in depth.

The epistemological foundations of the semi-structured interview are rooted in a comprehensive and interpretative approach to research (Bentalha & Alla, 2024). This method recognizes that social reality is constructed through the interactions and meanings that individuals attribute to their experiences. The interview thus becomes a space for the co-construction of meaning, where researcher and participant collaborate to bring out a deeper understanding of the phenomenon under study. To prepare for a semi-structured interview, we need to draw up an interview guide, an essential document that structures the exchange without locking it in. This guide generally consists of main themes to be addressed and open-ended questions serving as a common thread (Beddaa, 2023; Beddaa & Bachiri, 2021). It is not a rigid questionnaire, but rather a flexible framework for adapting the interview to the interviewee's discourse, while ensuring that the research objectives are met. Conducting a semi-structured interview requires specific skills on the part of the researcher. He or she must master the art of active listening, know how to bounce back on what the interviewee has to say, and maintain a delicate balance between directiveness and freedom of expression. The researcher must also be able to create a climate of trust conducive to genuine exchange, while maintaining the distance required for scientific objectivity.

The analysis of data from semi-structured interviews is part of a rigorous qualitative approach (Beddaa et al., 2020). It generally involves full transcription of the interviews, followed by a process of coding and categorizing the data (Bentalha, 2020; Beddaa, 2023). This analytical phase aims to bring out patterns, recurring themes and significant relationships between different elements of discourse, thus enabling a deeper understanding of the phenomenon under study (Beddaa & Bachiri, 2021).

Semi-structured interviews offer many advantages. This method enables us to access the richness of participants' experiences, to understand their representations and value systems, and to explore unexpected aspects that would not have been anticipated in a closed questionnaire (Beddaa et al., 2020). It also offers valuable flexibility in adapting to the particularities of each interview situation, while maintaining consistency in data collection (Beddaa & Bachiri, 2021). The limitations of this method must also be recognized. The quality of the data collected depends heavily on the interviewer's skills and ability to create a climate conducive to exchange. The subjectivity inherent in this approach requires constant reflexivity on the part of the researcher and the implementation of appropriate validation strategies. In addition, the time required to conduct and analyze interviews can be a major constraint. To guarantee the scientific validity of the results, it is essential to establish criteria of methodological rigor. This includes triangulating data with other sources of information, keeping detailed logbooks, verifying interpretations with participants and describing the research process in detail to ensure transparency and reproducibility.

This qualitative study aims to understand how communication and awareness campaigns influence taxpayers' perceptions and behavior towards tax compliance. To this end, we chose to conduct 4 semi-structured interviews, divided between 2 individual taxpayers (representing different socio-professional categories) and 2 managers of small businesses or small and medium-sized enterprises. On average, the interviews lasted between 35 and 45 minutes.

The interviews were based on an interview guide with 4 main questions: First, taxpayers' general perception of the tax system and reasons for non-compliance. Next, the evaluation of messages received concerning tax obligations, their clarity and usefulness. Then the impact of awareness-raising campaigns conducted by tax authorities, and finally, participants' suggestions for improving these communication strategies. The data collected was then transcribed and analyzed thematically to identify major trends, sticking points and possible solutions (Table 1).

Table 1. Details of interview topics

Topics	Questions	Objectives
General perception of the tax system	"How do you perceive the tax system in your country, and what do you think are the main reasons why some taxpayers fail to meet their tax obligations?"	Explore participants' overall view of taxation and reasons for non-compliance.
Receipt and understanding of tax information	What information or messages did you receive about your tax obligations? Was it clear and useful to you? Why or why not?"	Assess the effectiveness of communication messages on tax obligations. Find out whether participants find this information understandable and relevant, and what their level of satisfaction is with current communication.
Impact of awareness campaigns	"Have you ever been influenced by an awareness campaign or communication action on the part of the tax authorities? If so, how did it affect your tax compliance behavior?"	Understand whether awareness campaigns have had a direct impact on participants' behavior. This will enable us to measure the effectiveness of existing strategies.
Suggestions for improving tax communication	"In your opinion, what improvements should be made to the tax authorities' communication to encourage more taxpayers to comply with their tax obligations?"	Gather suggestions on what could be improved in communication and awareness-raising strategies. This will enable us to propose practical recommendations for strengthening tax compliance.

Source: Authors

Analysis of the interviews enabled us to identify obstacles to tax compliance, but also to measure the effectiveness of existing communication initiatives. By providing concrete recommendations for improving tax communication, such as simplifying messages, making greater use of digital channels, or intensifying tax education for taxpayers. Our study aims to provide tax authorities with avenues for boosting public confidence, reducing tax evasion and encouraging greater compliance with tax obligations.

3. RESULTS AND DISCUSSION

Analysis of the results of the qualitative study reveals several key elements concerning tax communication and its impact on taxpayer compliance. Firstly, the general perception of the tax system is largely negative, on the part of both taxpayers and managers of small and medium-sized enterprises. Indeed, participants consider the tax system to be complex, difficult to understand and lacking in transparency.

In Table 2, we present an initial analysis of the frequencies of the most repeated words in the interviews conducted during the empirical study for this paper (Table 2):

Table 2. Occurrence of the most repeated words in the interviews

Concepts	Occurrence
System	110
Information	82
Taxes	80
Businesses	74
Campaigns	71
Small	65
Help	63
Complex	52
Company	48
Online	47
Important	35
Explain	32

Source: The authors (Results of our qualitative study)

The qualitative study examined key concepts related to tax communication and compliance systems through a series of interviews. Word frequency analysis reveals several significant patterns that offer insight into stakeholders' primary concerns and perspectives regarding tax administration. With 110 occurrences, "System" emerged as the most frequently mentioned concept throughout the interviews. This overwhelming emphasis suggests that participants viewed tax administration primarily through a systemic lens, focusing on structural elements rather than individual components. This system-centric perspective indicates that reform efforts should address fundamental frameworks rather than isolated procedural adjustments. The high frequency of "Information" (82) and "Taxes" (80) demonstrates the critical relationship between information flow and tax compliance. Participants consistently highlighted information management as a cornerstone of effective taxation processes, suggesting that access to and clarity of tax-related information significantly impacts compliance behaviors. Terms like "Campaigns" (71), "Help" (63), "Complex" (52), and "Explain" (32) collectively highlight a significant theme around communication difficulties and assistance needs. The juxtaposition of complexity-related terms with help-seeking language demonstrates that participants recognize tax systems as intrinsically complicated and emphasize the necessity for enhanced explanatory support.

Figure 1, below, shows a representation of these word occurrences in the form of an image to facilitate the representation and interpretation of the most frequent concepts.

Figure 1. Word cloud of the most repeated items in the interviews

Source: The authors (Results of our qualitative study), https://www.freewordcloudgenerator.com)

The interviews conducted reveal a general perception of the complexity of the tax system, which manifests itself differently according to the profiles of the taxpayers interviewed. Indeed, young professionals in particular express difficulty in grasping and understanding tax information, pointing to a lack of support in their administrative procedures. This complexity is perceived as a major obstacle to tax compliance, with some taxpayers justifying their avoidance behavior by the opacity of the system.

The question of the efficiency of public management emerges as a central theme in the participants' discourse. Taxpayers, whether individuals or professionals, express marked skepticism about the use of public funds. This perception has a direct impact on their relationship with taxation and their willingness to comply with tax obligations. The pensioner interviewed, while having a more nuanced view of the system, shares this concern about the management of public resources. Entrepreneurs and managers of small and medium-sized businesses highlight a specific problem linked to the administrative burden. They describe a system that is "punitive" for those who seek to comply scrupulously with tax rules and standards, underlining the considerable time spent on tax obligations. The perception of infrequent controls, combined with the administrative burden, seems to encourage partial non-compliance, particularly among small businesses.

Here's a verbatim of the first question analyzed:

"I think the tax system is quite complex, especially for young people like me."

"Many feel that the state doesn't manage taxpayers' money well, which discourages them from paying."

"We have to spend an enormous amount of time on paperwork and it's hard to make sure everything is compliant. "

A generational divide emerges in the perception of the tax system. Younger taxpayers stress the need for education and simplification, while retirees, despite their criticisms, demonstrate a better understanding of the need for taxes to keep the State running. This difference in perception suggests a need to adapt tax communication approaches according to taxpayer profiles. Analysis of the interviews also reveals unanimous criticism of administrative efficiency. Participants cite the slowness of procedures and the lack of responsiveness of tax departments as discouraging factors. This perception of administrative inefficiency reinforces the feeling of disconnection between contributions paid and public services received in return. The testimonies gathered underline a pressing need for transparency in the management of public funds. Taxpayers, whatever their profile, express the desire to better understand how their taxes are used. This demand for transparency goes hand in hand with a need for greater efficiency in public management, seen as a prerequisite for improving tax acceptance.

When it comes to receiving and understanding tax information, participants' responses reveal that tax documents and messages lack clarity and are difficult to access. Both taxpayers and business managers report that they often have to call in external experts to ensure compliance, underlining the complexity of current communication. Participants suggest that simplifying documents, using more accessible language and more digestible formats, such as videos or infographics, could improve understanding.

For individuals, the complexity of administrative language is a major obstacle. Young taxpayers stress the difficulty of understanding tax jargon, forcing them to turn to outside expertise. This situation is particularly problematic, as it can generate additional costs and discourage young taxpayers from becoming actively involved in their tax obligations. Similarly, the elderly, represented by the second testimonial, express their difficulty in interpreting the documents they receive, suggesting a need for more personalized support. Among professionals, the situation is hardly any better. Managers of small and medium-sized companies are faced with an overload of insufficiently explained technical information. The first manager mentions the need to call in accountants to ensure the compliance of their declarations, representing an additional financial burden for small structures. The second testimonial reinforces this observation, highlighting the lack of practical guides tailored to the specific needs of small businesses.

As a result, this analysis reveals an urgent need to modernize and simplify tax communication. Interviewees' suggestions converge on several avenues for improvement: the need for clearer, less technical communication, the development of more accessible digital media, and the provision of personalized support, particularly for more vulnerable audiences such as the elderly and small businesses.

Awareness-raising campaigns run by tax authorities also seem to have little impact, according to respondents. The messages are considered too general and disconnected from taxpayers' real concerns. To improve this situation, several participants suggested more targeted messages, tailored to different social and professional groups, and emphasizing the direct benefits of tax compliance for both individuals and businesses. In addition, more personalized messages, especially for small businesses, could enhance the effectiveness of these campaigns.

The limited effectiveness of current campaigns is clear from the various testimonials gathered. A unanimous observation emerges: general communication efforts fail to meet the specific expectations of different categories of taxpayers.

As far as individual taxpayers are concerned, campaigns suffer from a lack of practical relevance. The young taxpayer points to the gap between traditional institutional communication (TV and online ads) and his concrete needs for assistance with his tax affairs. His suggestion to develop more practical content, notably in the form of video tutorials, reflects an expectation for more interactive and directly applicable teaching aids. The second testimonial reinforces this analysis by underlining the lack of communication on the citizen's "return on investment" in taxes paid. This lack of understanding of the practical use of tax contributions seems to undermine support for the system.

For the business sector, feedback highlights the limits of a mass communication approach. Managers of small and medium-sized businesses express a marked need for personalized support and direct expertise. The first suggests the intervention of experts in the field, while the second pleads for specific support programs. These testimonials reveal that the effectiveness of awareness campaigns could be significantly enhanced by a more targeted and interactive approach. This analysis underlines the need for a thorough overhaul of tax awareness strategies. As a result, three major areas for improvement have emerged: the development of practical, educational content tailored to different audiences; greater transparency in the use of public funds; and the provision of personalized support, particularly for professionals. The transition to more targeted and interactive communication appears to be an essential lever for boosting the effectiveness of tax awareness campaigns. Finally, suggestions for improvement converged on several axes: simplification of tax information, use of digital tools such as explanatory videos and interactive tutorials, and personalized support through local information sessions or tailored training courses. Participants believe that such an approach would make information more accessible and engaging, particularly for younger generations and small businesses, who often face specific tax difficulties.

From now on, the testimonials gathered reveal a strong demand for modernization and personalization of tax communication tools, with specific needs depending on taxpayer profiles. For the younger generation, represented by the number one taxpayer, digitalization appears to be a priority. The suggestion to create video content on social networks and interactive online guides reflects the information consumption habits of this population. This digital approach would not only reach this audience more effectively, but also offer more dynamic and engaging content.

In contrast, the testimony of the second taxpayer underlines the importance of maintaining direct human contact, particularly for the elderly. The proposal to organize local information sessions demonstrates the need for a local, educational approach. These meetings would not only explain the technical aspects, but also reinforce understanding of the link between tax contributions and public services.

On the professional side, suggestions converged on the need for more structured support. The person in charge of small and medium-sized enterprises calls for a two-pronged approach, combining simplified documentation and blended training (face-to-face and digital). This proposal reflects the need for flexibility in access to tax information. The second executive goes further, suggesting the creation of a dedicated support system for businesses, with a specialized hotline and detailed sector guides. This diversity of proposals highlights the need for a multi-channel communications strategy, combining modern digital tools with traditional approaches. The key to success seems to lie in the ability to adapt communication media and methods to the specific needs of each taxpayer segment, while maintaining overall consistency in the messages conveyed.

The results of our study reveal that the tax system is perceived as complex and lacking in transparency, a perception widely shared by respondents. This perception is in line with the classic work of Allingham & Sandmo (1972), who point out that the complexity of the tax system can discourage compliance, not least because of the costs associated with understanding tax obligations. However, more recent literature, notably that of Torgler (2003) & Wenzel (2005), adds that citizens' trust in tax institutions and social pressure also play a crucial role. Our results confirm this notion, as respondents express distrust in the use of public funds and frustration with red tape, sentiments that may indeed fuel non-compliance with tax obligations.

With regard to receiving tax information, study participants complained about the complexity of the messages received, a difficulty similar to that highlighted by the literature. The work of Slemrod (2007) and McGee (2013) highlights the need for tax communication to be clear, accessible and tailored to the target audience. This study confirms this need, as respondents, both individuals and managers of small and medium-sized businesses, emphasized the need to simplify tax messages, particularly through practical guides and instructional videos. The idea of using digital channels to disseminate information is in line with the findings of Kleven et al. (2016), who stress the importance of online platforms to effectively reach younger generations and small businesses.

The impact of awareness campaigns on tax compliance is another point of convergence between the study results and existing literature. Respondents report that current campaigns lack relevance and specificity, echoing the findings of Slemrod (2007) and Wenzel (2005), who point out that general campaigns only marginally change tax behavior. Indeed, well-targeted tax communication tailored to different groups of taxpayers is more likely to have a stronger impact on compliance, as the literature shows. In addition, the suggestion by some small and medium-sized business managers for more direct support, such as dedicated training or seminars, reinforces the idea that campaigns should be tailored to the specific needs of taxpayers, a point also raised by Di Legge et al. (2022).

Finally, respondents' recommendations for simplified messaging and greater use of digital channels overlap with suggestions in the literature, including Kleven et al. (2016), who recommend more modern, interactive approaches to improving tax communication. In addition, the demand for more personalized support, such as interactive guides or helplines, is in line with the research of Feld & Frey (2002), who advocate more personalized communication mechanisms to build taxpayer confidence and foster better compliance with existing tax rules and standards.

Overall, the results of our study largely confirm the findings of the literature review on the importance of simplifying tax communication, making information transparent and tailoring awareness campaigns to the specific needs of different taxpayer groups. Accordingly, these results suggest that improving tax communication could play a decisive role in increasing tax compliance, for both individuals and companies.

CONCLUSION

The study on the impact of tax communication and awareness on taxpayer compliance has highlighted a number of fundamental issues in the relationship between tax authorities and taxpayers. Analysis of the results of semi-structured interviews conducted with different taxpayer profiles revealed a number of major challenges hampering the effectiveness of current tax communication strategies.

The testimonies gathered demonstrate that the complexity of the tax system and the lack of clarity in communication constitute significant obstacles to tax compliance. The perception of an opaque system, combined with communication that is ill-adapted to the specific needs of different audiences, contributes to maintaining a distance between taxpayers and the tax authorities. However, the constructive suggestions put forward by participants open up encouraging prospects for improving tax communication. The emergence of a clear demand for differentiated approaches - combining modern digital tools for younger generations and personalized support for more traditional audiences - suggests the need for a multi-channel, adaptive communication strategy.

This qualitative study explored perceptions of the tax system and tax administration communication among different audiences. The results confirm a widely shared perception of the complexity of the tax system, a lack of confidence in the use of public funds, and an administrative burden that is particularly penalizing for small and medium-sized businesses. Current communication is deemed inadequate, overly technical and inaccessible, often requiring recourse to external expertise. Similarly, existing awareness-raising campaigns show limited effectiveness, underlining the need for a more targeted and interactive approach.

The study offers significant methodological advantages, in particular the qualitative approach, which provides an in-depth understanding of perceptions and needs, as well as the diversity of the profiles interviewed. It provides concrete proposals for improvement, identifying priority areas and tools adapted to each target audience. However, there are methodological limitations, notably the limited size of the sample and the focus on certain categories of taxpayers, limiting the generalizability of the results. The absence of quantitative data and a possible social desirability bias are also limitations of the present research. In addition, the study is limited to a specific geographical context and does not take into account budgetary constraints or the costs of the proposed solutions.

In the short term, the development of digital media tailored to young people, local information sessions for senior citizens and sector-specific guides for small and medium-sized enterprises, as well as the reinforcement of personalized assistance are recommended. In the medium term, the creation of a multi-channel interactive platform, the training of agents in the new tools and the introduction of monitoring indicators are necessary.

Research prospects now include extending the study to other taxpayer categories, a quantitative assessment of the impact of the new measures, an international comparative analysis and a longitudinal study. Structurally, a complete overhaul of the tax communication strategy, the adoption of a differentiated approach by target audience, investment in digital tools and enhanced training for tax agents are recommended. These recommendations aim to improve the transparency, simplicity and effectiveness of the tax system and its communication. These results corroborate our initial hypothesis on the importance of clear, targeted communication as a lever for improving tax compliance. They also underline the fact that tax awareness can only be effective if it is accompanied by genuine consideration of the specific needs of each category of taxpayer.

Ultimately, this research contributes to a better understanding of the communication levers likely to improve tax compliance, while underlining the importance of a holistic approach that takes into account the diversity of taxpayers' needs and expectations. Looking to the future, this study suggests that improving tax compliance will necessarily require an overhaul of communication strategies, integrating both new technologies and traditional proximity approaches. This transformation should be based on three essential pillars: the simplification of administrative language, the personalization of communication media, and greater transparency in the use of public funds.

REFERENCES

Alhempi, R., Ardiansyah, I., Kusumastuti, S., & Endri, E. (2020).. . *Tax Compliance in Income Tax Payments*, *13*, 356–374.

Alj, B. (2024). Defis Et Dynamiques De La Securite Fiscale Pour Le Developpement Des Affaires En Afrique: Une Exploration Du Cas Du Maroc. [Challenges and Dynamics of Tax Security for Business Development in Africa: An Exploration of the Case of Morocco]. Economics and Management Review, 2(2).

Allingham, M. G., & Sandmo, A. (1972). Income tax evasion: A theoretical analysis. *Journal of Public Economics*, *1*(3), 323–338. DOI: 10.1016/0047-2727(72)90010-2

Alm, J. (1999). Tax compliance and administration. In Bartley Hildreth, W., & Jerry, L. R. (Eds.), *The handbook of public administration* (pp. 173–193).

Alm, J., & Torgler, B. (2006). Culture differences and tax morale in the United States and in Europe. *Journal of Economic Psychology*, *27*(2), 224–246. DOI: 10.1016/j.joep.2005.09.002

Amin, S. N., Buhari, P. Z. A., Yaacob, A. S., & Iddy, Z. (2022). Exploring the influence of tax knowledge in increasing tax compliance by introducing tax education at tertiary level institutions. *Open Journal of Accounting*, *11*(02), 57–70. DOI: 10.4236/ojacct.2022.112004

Appiah, T., Domeher, D., & Agana, J. A. (2024). Tax knowledge, trust in government, and voluntary tax compliance: Insights from an emerging economy. *SAGE Open*, *14*(2), 2–13. DOI: 10.1177/21582440241234757

Bagus, P., Block, W., Eabrasu, M., Howden, D., & Rostan, J. (2011). The Ethics of Tax Evasion. *Business and Society Review*, *116*(3), 375–401. Advance online publication. DOI: 10.1111/j.1467-8594.2011.00390.x

Bazart, C. (2002). Les comportements de fraude fiscale: Le face-à-face contribuables — administration fiscale. Revue française d'économie, [Tax Fraud Behaviors: The Face-to-Face Between Taxpayers and Tax Administration. French Review of Economics]. 16(4), 171-212. https://www.persee.fr

Bazart, C., & Blayac, T. (2022). Les déterminants de la non-conformité et de la perception du fardeau fiscal en France. *Revue Économique (Paris)*, *73*(4), 605–636. DOI: 10.3917/reco.734.0605

Beddaa, M. (2023). Gestion budgétaire des ventes et performance commerciale de la firme: Exploration par étude de cas. *Revue des Études Multidisciplinaires en Sciences Économiques et Sociales*, *8*(1), 211–226.

Beddaa, M., & Bachiri, M. (2021). L'impact du potentiel touristique sur les intentions entrepreneuriales dans le tourisme durable: cas de la ville de Merzouga. Revue marocaine de recherche en management et marketing. Vol. 13, No. 1, 189-213.

Beddaa, M., & Bentalha, B. (2025). Optimizing Local Attractiveness Through Territorial Digital Communication. In Sustainable and Intelligent Territorial Marketing and Entrepreneurship (pp. 159-192). IGI Global.

Beddaa, M., Boumsiss, S., & Bachiri, M. (2020). L'impact du leadership sur la mise en place et l'amélioration du système de management intégré qualité-sécurité- environnement (QSE). *International Journal for Environment & Global Climate Change*, *8*(1), 131–151.

Bentalha, B. (2020). Big-Data et Service Supply chain management: Challenges et opportunités. *International Journal of Business and Technology Studies*, *1*(3).

Bentalha, B., & Alla, L. (2024). Revealing the subtleties: The art of qualitative studies in science and management. In *Applying qualitative research methods to management science* (pp. 1–21). IGI Global. DOI: 10.4018/979-8-3693-5543-5.ch001

Bentalha, B., & Boukare, M. (2024). AI-Driven Territorial Intelligence: An Integrated Approach to Enhancing Digital Sovereignty. In Generative AI and Implications for Ethics, Security, and Data Management (pp. 231-261). IGI Global.

Bird, R. M., & Zolt, E. M. (2005). The limited role of the personal income tax in developing countries. *Journal of Asian Economics*, *59*(1), 89–114. DOI: 10.1016/j.asieco.2005.09.001

Bouaddi, M., Beddaa, M., & El Ghalfiki, J. (2024). L'impact de la communication digitale sur la satisfaction des clients. *Revue des Études Multidisciplinaires en Sciences Économiques et Sociales*, *9*(2), 287–310.

Bouaddi, M., Lahriga, M., & Beddaa, M. (2024). Digital Transformation of Moroccan Companies and its Impact on Service Quality: A Case of the Banking Sector. *Revue Internationale du Marketing et Management Stratégique*, *6*(2), 52–79.

Boudri, R., Bentalha, B., Andaloussi, O. B., & Abbass, Z. (2025). Leveraging the "Made in Morocco" Label for Smart Marketing and Sustainable Territorial Attractiveness. In Sustainable and Intelligent Territorial Marketing and Entrepreneurship (pp. 69-94). IGI Global.

Bourdieu, P. (1990). La domination masculine. *Actes de la Recherche en Sciences Sociales*, *84*(1), 2–31. DOI: 10.3406/arss.1990.2947

Boyer, A. (2020). *Chapitre 16. L'évasion et fraude fiscale. Introduction au droit fiscal.* Ellipses., https://droit.cairn.info/introduction-au-droit-fiscal--9782340037953-page-195?lang=fr

Capasso, S., Cicatiello, L., De Simone, E., Gaeta, G. L., & Mourão, P. R. (2021). Fiscal transparency and tax ethics: Does better information lead to greater compliance? *Journal of Policy Modeling*, *43*(5), 1031–1050. DOI: 10.1016/j.jpolmod.2020.06.003

Cifuentes-Faura, J., Benito, B., & Guillamón, M.-D. (2024). The Influence of Transparency on Municipal Taxation: An Empirical Analysis. *Administration & Society*, *56*(5), 653–682. DOI: 10.1177/00953997241239024

Cotton, M., Dark, G., Menhard, P., & Ryan, J. (2017). Use of Technology in Tax Administrations 2: Core Information Technology Systems in Tax Administrations. Fiscal Affairs Department, International Monetary Fund. Authorized for distribution by Sanjeev Gupta. March 2017.

Di Legge, A., Ceccanti, D., & Hortal Foronda, F. (2022). Tax compliance costs for SMEs: An update and a complement. VVA and KPMG. European Commission, European Innovation Council and SMEs Executive Agency (EISMEA). Retrieved from EISMEA-COSME-ENQUIRIES@ec.europa.eu

Ebrill, L., Keen, M., & Summers, V. (2001). *The Modern VAT.* International Monetary Fund.

Feld, L. P., & Frey, B. S. (2002). Trust breeds trust: How taxpayers are treated. *Economics of Governance*, *3*(2), 87–99. DOI: 10.1007/s101010100032

Gonidakis, F. K., Asonitou, S., Kottara, C., & Dimitra, K.-F. (2024). The contribution of education to the creation of tax awareness and compliance. In *Strategic Innovative Marketing and Tourism* (pp. 571–583). Springer. DOI: 10.1007/978-3-031-51038-0_62

Haddouchi, A., Bouzahzah, M., & Angour, N. (2021). Fiscalité et croissance économique au Maroc. *Revue Française d'Économie et de Gestion*, *4*(10), 170–180.

Halimah, S., & Juitania, J. (2022). The effect of tax information dissemination, tax rates, and tax sanctions on compliance with annual tax return reporting of individual taxpayers (Case study at Pandeglang primary tax service office). *IDEAS Journal of Management & Technology*, *2*(1), 34–41. DOI: 10.33021/ideas.v2i1.3800

Karam, H., & Berjaoui, A. (2021). La fraude fiscale par sous-déclaration du revenu: Une décision en présence de risque, revue de littérature et états des lieux. *JSOM*, *2*, 2–21.

Khanfor, A., & Elwazani, Y. (2016). La communication fiscale au Maroc: Les obstacles à la socialisation du contribuable. Revue Marocaine de recherche en management et marketing, 14, 215-234.

Khomsi, H. (2025). La conformité fiscale des contribuables: Fondements et modèles conceptuels. Revue Internationale de la Recherche Scientifique (Revue-IRS), 3(1), 1-20.

Khomsi, H., & Msatfa, Z. (2024). La conformité fiscale des PME, un facteur clé pour le développement économique et social des pays. *American Scientific Journal*, *03*(27), 1230–1257.

Kirchler, E. (2007). The Economic Psychology of Tax Behaviour. 1-243.

Kleven, H. J., Kreiner, C., & Saez, E. (2009). Why can modern governments tax so much? An agency model of firms as fiscal intermediaries, No. 15218, NBER Working Paper. National Bureau of Economic Research, Inc. DOI: 10.3386/w15218

Kleven, H. J., Kreiner, C., & Saez, E. (2016). *Why can modern governments tax so much? An agency model of firms as fiscal intermediaries. LSE Research Online Documents on Economics*. London School of Economics and Political Science, LSE Library.

LeBaube, R. A., & Vehorn, C. L. (1992). Assisting taxpayers in meeting their obligations under the law. In Bird, R. M., & Casanegra de Jantscher, M. (Eds.), *Assisting taxpayers in meeting their obligations under the law* (pp. 311–342). International Monetary Fund.

Lestary, S. R., Sueb, M., & Yudianto, I. (2021). The effect of tax fairness, tax socialization, and tax understanding on tax compliance: A study on micro, small and medium enterprises (MSMEs). *Journal of Accounting Auditing and Business*, *4*(1), 87–98. DOI: 10.24198/jaab.v4i1.31998

Machmoune, S., & Nmili, M. (2021). Perception de l'équité fiscale et conformité du contribuable: Enquête exploratoire dans le contexte marocain. *Revue AME*, *3*(4), 433–454.

Mascagni, G., Santoro, F., & Mukama, D. (2024). Teach to comply? Evidence from a taxpayer education program in Rwanda. *International Tax and Public Finance*, •••, 45–78.

McGee, R. (2013). The Ethics of Tax Evasion: Perspectives in Theory and Practice. .DOI: 10.1007/978-1-4614-1287-8

Mebratu, A. (2024). Theoretical foundations of voluntary tax compliance: Evidence from a developing country. *Humanities & Social Sciences Communications*, *11*(1), 1–8. DOI: 10.1057/s41599-024-02903-y

Meziane, B., Alla, L., & Bentalha, B. (2025). Transformational Trends of Territorial Economic Intelligence Strategies in the Digital Era: A Systematic Theoretical Exploration. In Utilizing Technology to Manage Territories (pp. 455-490). IGI Global.

Ministère de l'Économie et des Finances. (2024). Code général des impôts 2024. https://www.finances.gov.ma/2024/CG-2024-fr

Ministère de l'Économie et des Finances. (2024). Note circulaire N° 735 relative aux mesures fiscales. https://www.finances.gov.ma/Publication/dgi

Ministère de l'Économie et des Finances. (2024). Sanctions en cas de non-respect des obligations fiscales. http://www.finances.gov.ma

Mohamad, N., Md, N., Sulaiman, S., Pengurusan, J., Sosial, S., Yayasan, K., Johor, P., & Kulai, M. (2022). Determinants of tax awareness: A systematic literature review. 303-315.

Muja'hidah, M., & Syamsuddin, A. (2023). Impact of Regulating Inadequate Local Tax Types on Fiscal Independence. Fiat Justisia. *Jurnal Ilmu Hukum*, *17*(4), 347–358. DOI: 10.25041/fiatjustisia.v17no4.3049

Nagel, H., Rosendahl Huber, L., Van Praag, M., & Goslinga, S. (2019). The effect of a tax training program on tax compliance and business outcomes of starting entrepreneurs: Evidence from a field experiment. *Journal of Business Venturing*, *34*(2), 261–283. DOI: 10.1016/j.jbusvent.2018.10.006

Nguyen Thi Le, T., Mac Thi Hai, Y., Cuong Thi, T., & Nguyen Thi Hong, M. (2024). The impact of tax awareness on tax compliance: Evidence from Vietnam. *Journal of Tax Reform*, *10*(2), 214–227. DOI: 10.15826/jtr.2024.10.2.165

OECD. (2021). *Building tax culture, compliance and citizenship: A global source book on taxpayer education* (2nd ed.).

Okunogbe, O., & Santoro, F. (2022). The promise and limitations of information technology for tax mobilization. *The World Bank Research Observer*, *38*(2), 295–324. DOI: 10.1093/wbro/lkac008

Oualhi, B. (2018). Tax awareness and social responsibility: Case study of Algeria. In *Proceedings of ISER 142nd International Conference*, Barcelona, Spain, 23rd-24th July 2018 (pp. 24-27). ISER.

Pomeranz, D. (2015). "No Taxation Without Information: Deterrence and Self-Enforcement in the Value Added Tax." American Economic Review 105, August 2015 (8), 2539-2569.

Purnomo, I. R. B. (2019). The influence of effective communication strategy on consciousness and UMKM taxpayer compliance. *Religación : Revista de Ciencias Sociales y Humanidades*, *4*(15), 125–147.

Rguig, M., & Guemmi, F. (2023). Civisme fiscal au Maroc: À la recherche du compromis. *Revue Marocaine de Gestion et de Développement*, *3*(3), 340–357.

Sharp, S. (2023). Communicating taxes: A review of the literature. ODI Literature Review, 2-29. https://www.odi.org/en/publications/communicating-taxes-a-review-of-the-literature/

Slemrod, J. (2007). Cheating ourselves: The economics of tax evasion. *The Journal of Economic Perspectives*, *21*(1), 25–48. DOI: 10.1257/jep.21.1.25

Slemrod, J., & Yitzhaki, S. (2002). Tax avoidance, evasion, and administration. In Auerbach, A. J., Chetty, R. D., Feldstein, M., & Saez, E. (Eds.), *Handbook of public economics* (Vol. 3, pp. 1423–1470). Elsevier.

Torgler, B. (2003). To evade taxes or not to evade: That is the question. *Journal of Economic Surveys*, *17*(3), 267–287.

Wenzel, M. (2005). Motivation or rationalization? Causal relations between ethical norms and tax compliance. *Journal of Economic Psychology*, *26*(4), 495–508. DOI: 10.1016/j.joep.2004.03.003

Widuri, R., Mangoting, Y., Sadjiarto, A., & Eoh, T. S. (2023). Preventing tax evasion: The moral strength of taxpayers and the power of tax authorities. Jurnal Akuntansi dan Keuangan, 25(2), 91-100.

Zaki, B. S. (2024). A conceptual framework of tax compliance for small and medium enterprises (SMEs) in emerging economies. *Global Tax Review*, *10*(4), 98–114.

Zodrow, G. (2003). Tax competition and tax coordination in the European Union. *International Tax and Public Finance*, *10*(6), 71–71. DOI: 10.1023/A:1026377819946

Chapter 10

Corporate Social Responsibility Effect on Tax Compliance by Mediation of Sense of Civic Duty in the Horn of Africa

Shashi Kant
https://orcid.org/0000-0003-4722-5736
Bule Hora University, Ethiopia

Tegene Tesfaye Degefa
https://orcid.org/0009-0008-0342-2918
Bule Hora University, Ethiopia

Aga Tuto Roba
Bule Hora University, Ethiopia

Zerihun Kinde Alemu
Ethiopian Civil Service University, Ethiopia

Gebre Sorsa Takaro
https://orcid.org/0000-0003-0846-2894
Ethiopian Civil Service University, Ethiopia

ABSTRACT

This investigation explores the complex connections that exist within business contexts among compliance for tax, civic duty, and social responsibility of corporates (CSR). The investigation's conclusions demonstrate the ability of CSR programs to influence moral behavior by manifesting a excellent optimistic correlation among them and people's feeling of social responsibility. Also, the investigation depicts a clear connection among CSR and compliance for tax, highlighting how moral company conduct encourages compliance with tax laws. It is also manifested how the Sense for Civics Duty mediates the association among CSR and compliance for tax, providing insight into the ways in which moral principles influence compliance practices. The investigation's theoretical ramifications advance knowledge of the conceptual frameworks underlying civic responsibility, social responsibility of corporates, and adherence to legal

DOI: 10.4018/979-8-3373-0422-9.ch010

obligations. Policymakers are urged to create laws that encourage moral behavior and social responsibility, and corporations are advised to incorporate CSR activities.

INTRODUCTION

In terms of the latest compliance for tax, or in the sphere of communal responsibility of corporates or CSR, a lot has been said, especially in such regions as the Horn of Africa where questions of accountability, governance and development are of immense importance (Kirui et.al, 2024). A noteworthy rationale can be provided to-analytics discussing the association among CSR activities and compliance for tax, with the moderator of people's feeling of civic responsibility. Understanding how CSR, civic responsibility, and compliance for tax interact is vital globally because it has the potential to improve tax systems' efficacy, encourage corporate responsibility, and support regional sustainable development. The idea of communal responsibility of corporates (CSR), which centers on companies operating in an ethical and communally responsible way, has become more well-known throughout time as a result of stakeholders' growing demands that firms do more than just make money (Scarpa & Signori, 2023).

Numerous facets of CSR and compliance for tax have been manifested in empirical investigation, which has depicted both favorable and unfavorable connections among corporate tax practices and CSR initiatives. However, little is known about how people's feeling of civic duty may operate as a mediator in the interaction among compliance for tax and communal responsibility of corporates (CSR) practices in the particular setting of the Horn of Africa. This information gap depicts a rare chance to investigate the fundamental processes by which CSR influences compliance for tax practices in this area (Khan et. al, 2024). The complexity of CSR initiatives, disparities in civic engagement, and the heterogeneous socioeconomic environment of the Horn of Africa are some of the practical difficulties in this field. This chapter attempts to close these gaps by examining the mediating function of civic duty and depicting insights into the ways in which CSR programs can influence people's perceptions of compliance for tax. This investigation aims to provide useful implications for regional governments and corporate corporates by illuminating these complex associations.

The investigation's backdrop on the association among compliance for tax, civic duty, and communal responsibility of corporates (CSR) in the Horn of Africa stems from the region's distinct socioeconomic environment and the growing significance of moral company conduct on a worldwide scale. CSR has been more well-known in recent years as a way for companies to satisfy their responsibilities to communal welfare and ecological sustainability while also making a optimistic contribution to society. However, there are certain obstacles that can prevent CSR projects from being implemented influence in areas like the Horn of Africa (Mkadmi et.al.2024). Lack of legal frameworks and enforcement methods to guarantee corporate responsibility is one real obstacle to putting CSR efforts into practice in the Horn of Africa. Without precise rules and supervision, businesses can find it difficult to match their CSR initiatives with community needs or provide measurable communal benefits (Kirui et.al, 2024). This may cause a discrepancy among the outcomes that stakeholders actually experience and the anticipated influence of CSR initiatives. The limited ability and resources of nearby companies to participate influence in CSR initiatives present another difficulty. Businesses in the Horn of Africa frequently struggle financially or lack the know-how to create and carry out long-term communal responsibility of corporates initiatives. As a result, the potential advantages of CSR activities may be undermined by tokenistic or superficial attempts that ignore the underlying causes of communal or ecological problems (García-Riva et. al, 2023).

Regional case studies illustrate these practical difficulties. A multinational company doing business in the Horn of Africa, for instance, would find it challenging to match its CSR plans with the various communal and cultural circumstances of the local populations. Stakeholder opposition or misunderstandings may result from this, which would hinder the company's capacity to use its CSR initiatives to have a good societal influence (Scarpa & Signori, 2023). Also, it may be more difficult to evaluate the success of these initiatives and their influence on compliance for tax practices if there is a lack of accountability and openness in reporting on CSR operations (Kumar, A.et.al, (2024). This investigation attempts to give a thorough grasp of how CSR practices intersect with compliance for tax and civic responsibility in the Horn of Africa by exploring these real-world issues through case studies and empirical investigation. The purpose of this investigation is to make suggestions as to how the augment of ethical business practice and sustainable growth in the area might be more efficiently accomplished by analyzing the factors that hinder the implementation of CSR programs and investigation the mediating influence of civic obligation among subjects' perceptions of taxes and compliance.

STATEMENT OF PROBLEM

While analyzing the theoretical connection among civic obligation, tax trajectories, and corporate communal responsiveness (CSR) in the Horn of Africa, the identification of the issue under consideration concerns a number of critical matters. A harmonious combination of CSR programs, moral compliance for tax practices, and a excellent feeling of civic duty among local individuals and corporates is the ideal state that scholars and policymakers strive to attain. The achievement of this ideal state is hampered, therefore, by conflicting information, ambiguous outcomes, theoretical, knowledge, and contextual deficiencies, as well as practical difficulties (Nabila et. al., 2024). Drawing definite and consistent conclusions on the efficacy of CSR activities in fostering moral tax behavior is made more difficult by conflicting information from previous investigation on the influence of CSR on compliance for tax behaviors. Investigations and policymakers have a fragmented understanding of the pathways via which CSR efforts may influence people's attitudes toward compliance for tax in the Horn of Africa due to inconclusive outcomes (Kirui et.al, 2024).

It is difficult to create a thorough theoretical framework that can take into consideration the intricacies of these interconnected notions because of theoretical gaps in the literature on CSR, compliance for tax, and civic obligation. Our comprehension of the fundamental mechanisms at work in this situation is further hampered by knowledge gaps about the mediating function of civic duty in the association among CSR and compliance for tax behaviors (Scarpa & Signori, 2023). The investigation of CSR and compliance for tax in the Horn of Africa is made more challenging by contextual gaps resulting from the region's distinct socioeconomic and cultural environment (Aversano et. al, 2022). The successful implementation of CSR projects that support moral taxation in the Horn of Africa is also severely hampered by practical issues like sparse legislative frameworks, resource limitations, and cultural impediments. This investigation intends to depict a thorough examination of the associations among civic duty, compliance for tax, and communal responsibility of corporates in the area by filling up these gaps and tackling these issues. This investigation aims to close the latest knowledge gaps, shed light on the mediating function of civic duty, and depict useful suggestions for future scholars and decision-makers who wish to strengthen corporate responsibility, encourage moral taxation, and support sustainable development in the Horn of Africa through empirical investigation and in-depth case studies.

DEFINITION AND ORIGIN OF TERMS

***Corporates Communal Responsibility*:** It manifests the ethics against which corporates can be measured in terms of their responsibilities to the influences of their operations on the environment and commonweal. In addition to this legislation, this concept means going further than most legislation and policies would push for and seek to augment the communal and ecological responsibility of business both internally and in their management of stakeholder associations for the sake of, and in the drive for sustainable business. CSR which was augmented with the idea that corporates owed society more than the ability to generate profits for shareholders became popular in the middle of the twentieth century when everyone came to the realization that business corporates had to consider the influence they made on the environment as well as society. Companies have over the time adopted CSR that involve charity, ecological sustainment projects, ethical labor practices, and most noteworthy participation in the community affairs as a part of the business strategy (Zaman et.al., 2022).

Tax Compliance: In order to declare their income, to pay the taxes and fulfill the taxation requirements, citizens and companies have to conform to the tax legislation. Compliance for tax plays noteworthy roles in reducing tax evasion so as to attain fairness, protect the integrity of the tax system, and provide subsidies of government development and public services. Noncompliance leads to fines, legal consequences and decreased community trust in the tax system (Boateng et.al, 2022). Ever since creation of the formal tax systems in the old empires, governments had to look for ways on how to collect incomes in a proper way. It is here that the concept of compliance for tax was thought of. Modern compliance approach provides legislation requirements and enforcement methods, on one hand, and incentives, on the other hand, in an effort to encourage voluntary compliance (Scarpa & Signori, 2023).

Civics Duty Sense: It is the inherent desire of a person to discharge his/her responsibilities as a citizen of the society; to ensure that communal order is maintained and citizens adhere to people's beliefs and standards. This idea can be however assumed from the view of that people have the right to obey the law, be involved in civil matters and work for the welfare of the society. At communal level, Communal norms, cultural values or beliefs make them develop the perceived civic duty and in relation to moral standards, perception of responsibility to the society or volunteering and participating in public processes and activities (Feitosa et.al, 2020). Historically, this concept is based on polity and philosophy where civics is noteworthy to maintain a healthy society and had an engagement of public responsibilities.

RELATED THEORIES

Communal Exchange Theory: In this theory it postulates that individuals interact with each other and behave in such manner because they expect certain gains. In compliance for tax and CSR, CSR programmes may be considered as communal exchange where through CSR, such corporates get the goodwill of the society when they fully comply with their tax obligations. By relating this theory in terms of reciprocity and mutual benefit, there is every possibility that this theory would help explicate how CSR programs alter people's perception about compliance for tax (Kirui et.al, 2024).

Institutional Theory: This theory focuses on how the culture of a society, culture in general and the structure of an corporate determine the action of corporates. In a similar vein, companies need to conform to the imperative of institutions for CSR and compliance for tax as a means of sustain institutional legitimacy and communal acceptance (Risi et.al. (2023). Learning knowledge of how various institutional aspects influence compliance for tax and/or CSR practices can go further aid one to comprehend the other general cultures that influence operations in the Horn of Africa (Scarpa & Signori, 2023).

Ethical Decision-Making Theory: This theory attempts to understand how individuals reason in their endeavors to determine what is right or wrong. The ethical decision making theory will help to understand how people's perception of their civic responsibility which in turn informs their perception of corporate responsibility and the practices used in compliance for tax within the lens of compliance for tax and CSR. Such a theory can help in defining how ethical concerns influence the perception of taxes and communal responsibility of corporates initiatives (de la Cruz et. al., 2022).

Stakeholder Theory: This theory suggests that, apart from shareholders, corporates ought to consider the best interest of the all stakeholders in their decision making processes. According to this theory, CSR and compliance for tax require engagement with a diverse array of stakeholders incorporating governments, communities and employees in the business value chain so that its operations meet with the prevailing societally acceptable standards and the business can hence contribute towards sustainable development (Scarpa & Signori, 2023). It will be possible to identify views by the various stakeholders and understand manner in which CSR programs influence perception on compliance for tax. Of these concepts, one is chosen to be our work's main theoretical perspective: Stakeholder Theory. This investigation appropriately charges understanding of how through an analysis of people's Sense for Civics Duty CSR programs influence Compliance for tax behavior In the Horn of Africa is in-line with Stakeholder theory that posits the need to be concerned with the stakeholder's interest. Stakeholder Theory is useful when approaching the complex associations of CSR, compliance for tax, and civic responsibility in the area since it dwells on company responsibilities, stakeholder demands, and appropriate and ethical taxes (Kirui et.al, 2024).

EMPIRICAL LITERATURE REVIEW

Communal Responsibility of Corporates and Compliance for Tax

In goal keeper literature and practical business environments, scholarly interest and importance of understanding the association among CSR and compliance for tax has emerged (Scarpa & Signori, 2023). The idea whereby a firm is responsible to society by balancing the necessities of the shareholders to make profits while simultaneously recognizing the needs of the society and the environment in which business is been transacted is known as communal responsibility of corporates. Since CSR programs involve noteworthy corporate influence in governance, communal wellbeing, and tax revenues collection, policymakers, corporations, and society benefit from comprehending the influences CSR programs have on Compliance for tax behaviors (Choueiri et. al., 2022). The literature review also reveals that that there is disagreement on the influence of compliance for tax on communal responsibility of corporates. From some investigation it has been seen that corporateal forms involved in CSR activities are generally more compliant to taxes due to the augmented stakeholder confidence, good reputation and communal acceptance resulting from being communally responsible. It is more trusted by stakeholders because these are believed to be moral and communal responsibility and pay taxes, if not forced to do so. CSR can also augment a company's reputation with the public and authorities through the promotion of the right corporate culture within the corporateal practices of compliance for tax (Kirui et.al, 2024).

On the opposite side, in other investigations investigators depict that CSR and compliance for tax may not always correlate. The interaction of CSR and taxation can therefore be said to be dependent on the nature of CSR programs, corporateal culture, best practices in the business world and legal requirements respectively (Scarpa & Signori, 2023). It has at times been argued that CSR programs are used in an attempt to rehabilitate managerial image or espouse corporate-green washing, except for that fact that these efforts are rarely translated into augmented compliance for tax standards. In addition, there is a possibility that the extent to which CSR influences the compliance for tax in the given enterprise, such as the complexity of the tax legislation, rivalry of stakeholders, and contradictory incentives (Amat, 2022). Further investigation should be conducted to attempt to understand the nature of the interaction among the two proxies, compliance for tax and communal responsibility of corporates while paying attention to stakeholders' perspectives and corporate characteristics and the ecological context. As a result, politicians, corporations, and regulatory bodies will all greatly benefit from the scholars' further inquiry and explanation of the processes through which CSR programmes influence moral taxation and corporate responsibility. Understanding how both CSR and compliance for tax work can help develop better arguments on how to guide firms into being communally responsible and adhere to tax obligations within a firm at the same time shall push for sound and ethical business practices.

H1: CS for corporate has a noteworthy on Compliance for tax

Communal Responsibility of Corporates and Sense for Civics Duty

One of the rather complex and interesting areas of concern is the link among personal perceptions of civic responsibility and business CSR. Apart from the economic activities of the firm, CSR is defined as a firm's commitment to balance the moral and optimistic influence it has on society (Scarpa & Signori, 2023). On the other hand, a person's pre-established internal need to perform his or her role in society, maintaining norms and values for the benefit of healthily functioning society is referred to as civic responsibility. Studies show that CSR may augment or reduce people's perception of civic responsibility through engagement in projects related to CSR (Chouaibi et. al, 2022). Using CSR, businesses can make stakeholders, comprising of staff, clients and the community, become more aware of their own responsibilities as good citizens by demonstrating a commitment to being communally and ecologically responsible. People get motivated to support community causes, be more active in civic process and or maintain a moral standing when they see businesses act communally conscious and being moral in their actions Also, people's Sense for Civics Duty can be evoked by CSR programs that address urgent communal concerns and are in line with societal ideals. Businesses can cultivate a culture of moral conduct and community involvement that transcends their corporate borders when they exhibit a sincere dedication to sustainability and communal responsibility (Jiang et. al., 2022).

Investigations have established that citizens have a civic duty and moral obligation in regard to communal responsibility and communal responsibility of corporates in particular. Through the advocacy of CSR programs relevant to all stakeholders, corporates have the potential of proactively shaping people's perception of their responsible roles within the community and guiding them to bequeath accountability on fellow businesses to improve society. More investigation in this area can assist in the augment of methods used to reinforce ethical behavior and ... civic behaviors in the individual and corporate entities, while also shed light on the ways that communal responsibility of corporates (CSR) influences a feeling of civic responsibility (Kirui et.al, 2024).

H2: An investigation depicts that communal responsibility of corporates has a pronounced influence on Sense for Civics Duty

Sense for Civics Duty and Compliance for Tax

It has established that citizens have a civic duty and moral obligation in regard to communal responsibility and communal responsibility of corporates in particular. Through the advocacy of CSR programs relevant to all stakeholders, corporates have the potential of proactively shaping people's perception of their responsible roles within the community and guiding them to bequeath accountability on fellow businesses to improve society (Scarpa & Signori, 2023). More investigation in this area can assist in the augment of methods used to reinforce ethical behavior and civic behaviors in the individual and corporate entities, while also shed light on the ways that communal responsibility of corporates (CSR) influences a feeling of civic responsibility. An investigation depicts that communal responsibility of corporates has a pronounced influence on Sense for Civics Duty. Sincere desire to support public services, contribute to the smooth operation of society, and preserve the integrity of the tax system is what motivates this adherence to tax laws. People who have a excellent sense of civic responsibility see compliance for tax as a moral requirement because they are driven by ethical considerations and a desire to respect societal norms (Jiang et. al., 2022).

Also, a excellent factor for encouraging a culture of compliance for tax in communities and businesses is the sense of civic obligation. Peer monitoring, communal pressure, and informal enforcement techniques that encourage compliance behavior among peers and coworkers are more likely to be used by those who view compliance for tax as a civic obligation. Based on a common Sense for Civics Duty, this societal norm of compliance for tax can encourage moral tax behavior, discourage tax evasion, and improve the efficacy of tax enforcement initiatives as a whole (Scarpa & Signori, 2023). It is becoming more and more vital to comprehend how people's feeling of civic responsibility influences their tax behavior as lawmakers and tax officials work to enhancement compliance for tax rates and prevent tax evasion (Kirui et.al, 2024). Policymakers can create more focused interventions, communication plans, and incentive systems that promote voluntary compliance for tax and cultivate a culture of moral tax behavior by acknowledging and utilizing people's innate incentives to carry out their civic duties. A more egalitarian and transparent tax system, enhancement societal trust, and better tax revenue collection can result from fortifying the link among compliance for tax and a sense of civic responsibility.

H3: Sense for Civics Duty has noteworthy influence on Compliance for tax

Mediation of Sense for Civics Duty

One noteworthy way that people's internal motivations and ethical considerations influence their adherence to tax laws and regulations is through the mediation of the sense of civic responsibility on compliance for tax (Jiang et. al., 2022). The process via which a sense of civic responsibility serves as an intermediary variable that manifests or transmits the association among specific elements, incorporating ethical views or communal standards, and compliance for tax behaviors is referred to in this context as mediation. To influence promote ethical tax practices and enhancement compliance rates, politicians, investigations, and tax authorities must have a thorough understanding of how the feeling of civic duty mediates the association among individual values and compliance for tax (Kirui et.al, 2024). The mediation function of civic responsibility in influencing compliance for tax habits has been clarified by empirical investigation. According to investigation, those who have a excellent Sense for Civics Duty are more likely to view paying taxes as a moral requirement and a way to fulfill their communal obligations. This innate need to uphold public services and advance the common good acts as a mediator among people's willingness to abide by tax regulations and their ethical principles. People's decisions to accurately report their income, pay taxes, and support the operation of the tax system are influenced by their sense of civic responsibility, which serves as a link among their personal values, communal norms, and compliance for tax habits (Scarpa & Signori, 2023).

Also, the association among civic duty and compliance for tax is mediated by broader societal dynamics and corporate cultures in addition to individual conduct. People are more inclined to work together to support ethical behavior, encourage compliance for tax, and preserve communal norms surrounding tax duties in communities and workplaces where a excellent sense of civic responsibility is present. The significance of peer associations, communal factors, and shared values in forming compliance for tax attitudes and behaviors within groups and corporates is further manifested by this collective mediation influence (Jiang et. al., 2022).

H4: Link among communal responsibility of corporates and compliance for tax influenced by sense for civics duty

Conceptual Framework

Figure 1. Conceptual Framework

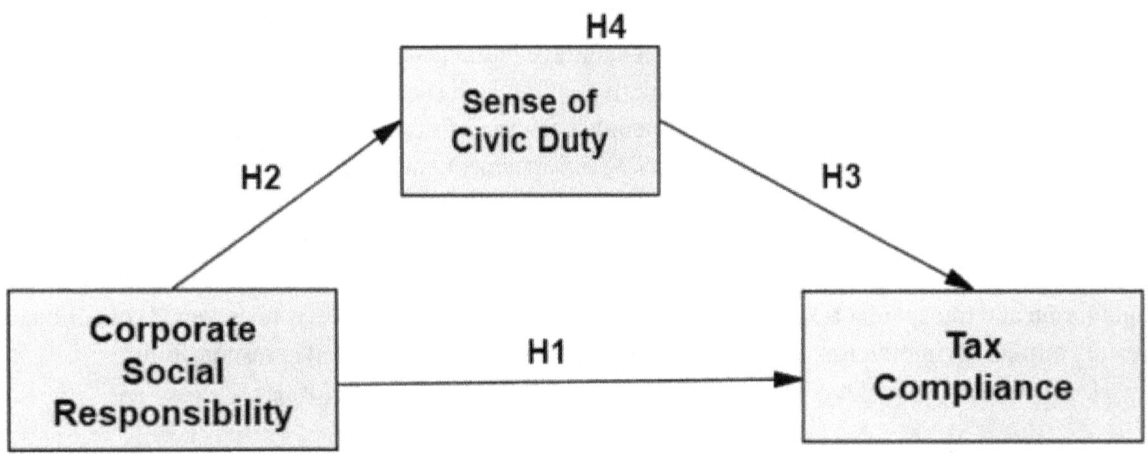

INVESTIGATION METHODOLOGY

A thorough investigation technique was used to investigate the connection among civic duty, compliance for tax, and communal responsibility of corporates (CSR). A sample size of 396 individuals was chosen for the investigation's quantitative investigation methodology in order to guarantee both statistical efficacy and demographic representativeness. Presumptuous a margin of error (5%), the Yamane (1967) formula was used to decide the size of population that was justifying a sample of 396.

396=N1+N·(0.05)2396 = \{N}{1 + N \ (0.05)^2}396=1+N·(0.05)2N

The information's appropriateness for factor analysis was assessed using the Kaiser-Meyer-Olkin (KMO) measure of sampling adequacy, which made sure the information set satisfied the requirements for additional analysis. In order to build measurement methods that would capture the concepts of civic duty, compliance for tax, and communal responsibility of corporates, the first phase of the investigation concentrated on developing a scale. The investigation team created and augmented the measurement scales to appropriately capture the multifaceted nature of these constructs by consulting latest literature and theoretical frameworks. The scales were refined through a number of expert reviews, pilot studies, and iterative refinement procedures to guarantee validity, clarity, and reliability in measuring the desired proxies.

In order to determine underlying components and evaluate the internal structure of the measuring scales, exploratory factor analysis, or EFA, was carried out after scale development. By shedding light on the connections among the latent constructs and the observed proxies, EFA assisted in identifying the unique aspects of civic duty, compliance for tax, and communal responsibility of corporates. The EFA's outcomes served as a guide for improving the measuring scales so they could better capture the subtleties of the constructs being studied. The intricate connections among CSR, compliance for tax, and civic responsibility were then manifested using Structural Equation Modeling (SEM) techniques and the AMOS program. A thorough grasp of the inter associations among these constructs was made possible by the testing of proposed linkages and pathways among the latent proxies made possible by SEM. The investigation used SEM to investigate the association among civic responsibility and compliance for tax, as well as the direct and indirect consequences of CSR. To sum up, this investigation's investigation methodology included scale development, EFA, and SEM techniques to examine the complex associations among civic duty, compliance for tax, and communal responsibility of corporates. The investigation sought to add to the body of knowledge already available on the interaction of these dimensions by employing a quantitative investigation strategy and sophisticated statistical analyses. The investigation's outcomes were validated and dependable by the strict methodological framework, which also provided insightful information about the intricacies of moral behavior in relation to compliance for tax and communal responsibility of corporates.

DATA ANALYSIS

Table 1. KMO and Bartlett's Test

Kaiser-Meyer-Olkin Measure of Sampling Adequacy.		**.825**
Bartlett's Test of Sphericity	Approx. Chi-Square	1419.513
	Df	97
	Sig.	.003

Source: Authors

In table 1, the information set's Kaiser-Meyer-Olkin (KMO) Measure of Sampling Adequacy, which was determined to be 0.825, suggested that factor analysis may be performed on the information. The KMO statistic evaluates the information set's proxies' degree of association and efficacy for using methods such as exploratory factor analysis (EFA). A KMO value of 0.825 manifests that the information set has a high degree of interrelatedness among proxies, making it appropriate for additional analysis. A KMO number above 0.6 is typically regarded as acceptable. In order to ascertain whether the proxies in the information set were associated—a need for manifests factor analysis—Bartlett's Test of Sphericity was also carried out. With 97 degrees of freedom and a significance threshold of 0.003, the test produced an approximate Chi-Square value of 1419.513. The information's eligibility for factor analysis is manifested by the statistically noteworthy result of Bartlett's Test, which depicts that the associations among the proxies in the information set were sufficiently different from zero.

These statistical tests depict vital information about the efficacy of the information set for factor analysis. The proxies in the information set were sufficiently connected and associated, according to the high KMO value and the substantial Bartlett's Test result, which satisfied the prerequisites for using methods like Exploratory Factor Analysis (EFA). These outcomes depict the information set's efficacy and set the stage for additional investigation to determine underlying causes and connections among the investigation's proxies.

Table 2. Total Variance Depicted

Component	**Initial Eigenvalues**			**Extraction Sums of Squared Loadings**			**Rotation Sums of Squared Loadings**		
	Total	**% of Variance**	**Cumulative %**	**Total**	**% of Variance**	**Cumulative %**	**Total**	**% of Variance**	**Cumulative %**
1	4.52	32.236	32.236	4.52	32.236	32.236	3.01	21.452	21.452
2	1.38	9.788	42.023	1.38	9.788	42.023	2.17	15.492	36.943
3	1.28	9.088	51.111	1.28	9.088	51.111	1.99	14.169	51.111
4	.950	6.783	57.893						
5	.872	6.224	64.116						
6	.774	5.520	69.635						

Extraction Method: Principal Component Analysis.
Source: Authors

The Principal Component Analysis (PCA) outcomes showed the variance depicted by each component as well as its eigenvalues. The components' initial Eigenvalues showed how much of the variance in the original information each component could account for. With an initial Eigenvalue of 4.52, Component 1 accounted for 32.236% of the variance. This component was essential in capturing the information's underlying structure and accounted for the largest percentage of variance. Then came Component 2, which depicted 9.788% of the variance with an Eigenvalue of 1.38, and Component 3, which depicted 9.088% of the variance with an Eigenvalue of 1.28. Component 1 remained noteworthy while taking into account the Extraction Sums of Squared Loadings, accounting for 32.236% of the variance. Components 2 and 3 continued to be noteworthy, accounting for 9.788% and 9.088% of the variation, respectively. These outcomes suggest that these three elements had the most influence in encapsulating the information and identifying the underlying trends. Following varimax rotation, the Rotation Sums of Squared Loadings had a little altered variance distribution. Even after rotation, Component 1 accounted for 21.452% of the variance, which was still the largest percentage. While Component 3 depicted 14.169% of the variation, Component 2 depicted 15.492%. By optimizing the variable loadings on one or a small number of components, the varimax rotation made it easier to understand the components and made the information's structure.

Table 3. Covariance's

Covariance			**Estimate**	**S.E.**	**C.R.**	**P**	**Hy.**
Sense for Civics Duty	**<-->**	**Corporates Communal responsibility**	**.236**	**.030**	**8.233**	**.00**	**H2**
Sense for Civics Duty	<-->	Compliance for tax	.306	.044	7.673	.00	**H3**
Corporates Communal responsibility	<-->	Compliance for tax	.263	.27	7.843	.00	**H1**

Source: Authors

Three covariance's are depict in Table 3: The first covariance, with an approximate value of 0.236 among "Sense for Civics Duty" and "Communal responsibility of corporates," is listed. A high degree of significance is indicated by the critical ratio of 8.233 and the standard error of.030 for this covariance. This covariance lends credence to assumption H2, manifesting an optimistic correlation among a person's sense of civic responsibility and their participation in CSR initiatives. A covariance value of.306 is depict among "Sense for Civics Duty" and "Compliance for tax," which is the second covariance. This covariance's critical ratio is 7.673 and its standard error is.044, both of which indicate a high degree of importance (.00). This covariance supports assumption H3, manifesting that a person's sense of civic responsibility and their adherence to tax laws are optimistically associated. "Communal responsibility of corporates" and "Compliance for tax," which have a covariance value of.263, are the third covariance display. A substantial association is suggested by the critical ratio of 7.843 and the standard error of.27 for this covariance (.00). This covariance suggests a favorable association among compliance for tax behavior and communal responsibility of corporates initiatives, manifested assumption H1.

Table 4. Validity Concern

	CR	AVE	MSV	MaxR(H)	CSR	STD	TC
CSR	0.733	0.645	0.253	0.834	**0.646**		
STD	0.763	0.660	0.137	0.767	0.175	**0.662**	
TC	0.796	0.607	0.278	0.798	0.384	0.193	**0.688**

Source: Authors

Table 4, depicts "Validity Concern,". The Composite Reliability (CR) of the first construct, Communal responsibility of corporates (CSR), is 0.733, demonstrating the internal consistency of the CSR measurement items. More over half of the variance among the items is depicted by the construct itself, as indicated by the Average Variance Extracted (AVE) for CSR of 0.645, which is higher than the suggested criterion of 0.5.

With a Maximum Shared Variance (MSV) of 0.253 for CSR, below the AVE, good discriminant validity is depicting. CSR's square root of AVE (MaxR(H)) is 0.834, manifesting that a sizable percentage of its indications may be depicted by the construct. With a Composite Reliability of 0.763, the second construct—Sense for Civics Duty (STD)—manifests that the items used to measure it have excellent internal consistency. With an Average Variance Extracted (AVE) of 0.660 for STD, it manifested the convergent validity criteria. Adequate discriminant validity is indicated by the STD's Maximum Shared Variance (MSV), which is 0.137, which is less than the AVE. The construct manifests a noteworthy amount of the variance in its indicators, as evidenced by the square root of AVE (MaxR(H)) for STD of 0.767. Excellent internal consistency among the items measuring Compliance for tax (TC), the third construct, is indicated by the Composite Reliability of 0.796. With an Average Variance Extracted (AVE) of 0.607, TC manifested the convergent validity requirement. TC has a Maximum Shared Variance (MSV) of 0.278, which is lower than the AVE and manifests high discriminant validity. The construct manifests a considerable amount of variance among its indicators, as evidenced by the square root of AVE (MaxR(H)) for TC of 0.798.

Figure 2. Structure Equation Model

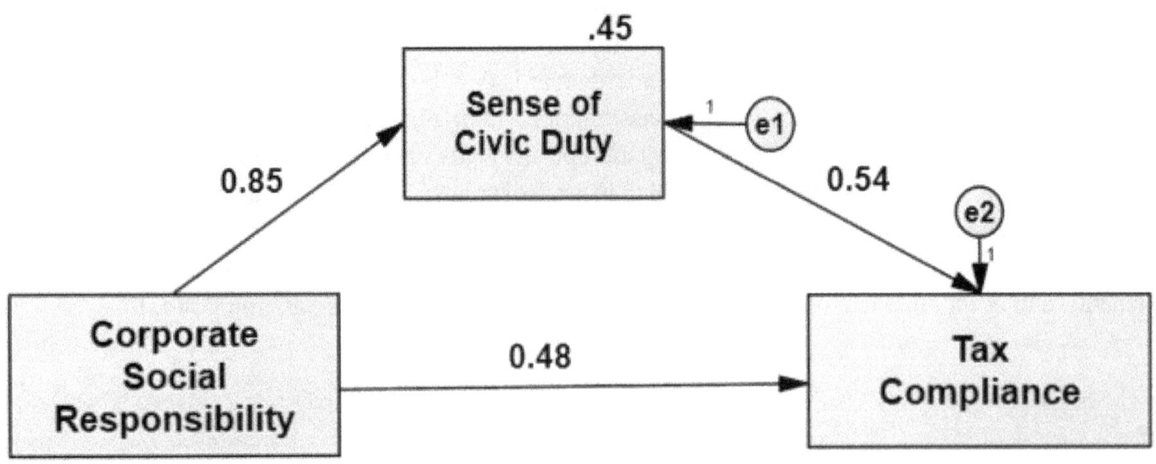

Table 5: indices for Model Fit

Sig.	Chi-Sq	RMR	Fitness Goodness	Fitness Depictatory	TLI	RMSEA
0.005	1.849	.063	0.946	0.950	0.945	.055

Source: Authors

Table 5 based on figures 2, manifested model's goodness of fit. The model fits the information well, as indicated by the significance level (Sig.) of 0.005, which manifests that the model's fit is statistically noteworthy at a p-value of 0.005. The difference among the observed and model-implied covariance matrices is measured by the Chi-Square (Chi-Sq) value, which is 1.849. A higher fit is indicated by a lower Chi-Square value, which implies that the model accurately captures the associations among the proxies The average difference among the observed and model-implied associations is represented by the Root Mean Square Residual (RMR) value of 0.063. A better fit is indicated by a lower RMR value, which depicts that the model's predictions and the observed information closely match. High levels of model fit are depict by the Fitness dedicatory value of 0.950 and the Fitness Goodness value of 0.946. These numbers usually fall among 0 and 1, where a value nearer 1 denotes a better model-to-information fit. In this instance, values near 1 indicate that the model appropriately captures the connections among the proxies and fits the information The model's fit is further manifested by the Root Mean Square Error of Estimate (RMSEA) value of 0.055 and the Tucker-Lewis Index (TLI) value of 0.945. By contrasting the target model with a baseline model, the TLI evaluates the improvement in model fit; values nearer 1 denote a better match. A better match is depict by lower values of the RMSEA, which calculates the difference among the observed information and the model.

Table 6. Regression Examination

Relative			Approx.	S.E.	C.R.	P	Ass.
Sense for Civics Duty	**<---**	**Corporates Communal responsibility**	**.864**	**.148**	**7.585**	**.00**	**H2**
Compliance for tax	<---	Sense for Civics Duty	.339	.134	2.853	.00	H3
Compliance for tax	<---	Corporates Communal responsibility	.963	.195	7.954	.00	H1

Source: Authors

The outcomes of the investigation's regression analysis are depict in Table 6. According to the regression coefficient, the Sense for Civics Duty is expected to rise by 0.864 units for every unit enhancement in Communal responsibility of corporates. With a noteworthy p-value (.00) and a high Critical Ratio (C.R.) of 7.585, this association was determined to be statistically noteworthy, depicting the investigation's second assumption (H2) On the other hand, the analysis also demonstrates a excellent optimistic correlation among communal responsibility of corporates and civic duty. According to the regression coefficient, Communal responsibility of corporates is expected to rise by 0.339 units for every unit enhancement in the Sense for Civics Duty. With a noteworthy p-value (.00) and a Critical Ratio (C.R.) of 2.853, this association was statistically noteworthy, manifested the investigation's third assumption (H3). The investigation also looked at the association among itself and communal responsibility of corporates and it depict a excellent optimistic correlation. According to the regression coefficient, for every unit rise in communal responsibility of corporates, there will be a 0.963 unit enhancement in communal responsibility of corporates. With a noteworthy p-value (.00) and a Critical Ratio (C.R.) of 7.954, this result was statistically noteworthy and manifested the investigation's first assumption (H1).

Table 7. Mediating Influence

	Influence	worth	Path Influence
Corporates Communal responsibility → Compliance for tax	Direct Influence	.48	Direct influence stated
Corporates Communal responsibility → Sense for Civics Duty → Compliance for tax	Indirect Influence	.84*.54=.45	Indirect Influence Ensued
	Whole influence	.93	Partial mediation

Source: Authors

The mediating role influence analysis of the association among Communal responsibility of corporates and Compliance for tax, as mediated by the Sense for Civics Duty, is depicting in Table 7. With a direct route coefficient of 0.48, the analysis depicts that compliance for tax is directly influenced by communal responsibility of corporates. This direct connection means that compliance for tax is predicted to rise by 0.48 units for every unit enhancement in communal responsibility of corporates. The analysis made specific reference to this direct channel influence The association among Communal responsibility of corporates and Compliance for tax was studied, incorporating the direct influence as well as the mediating function of the Sense for Civics Duty. Through the Sense for Civics Duty, the indirect influence of CSR on compliance for tax was determined to be 0.84 * 0.54 = 0.45. This suggests that the Sense for Civics Duty mediates a noteworthy amount (0.45) of the association among Communal responsibility of corporates and Compliance for tax. The complete influence of communal responsibility of corporates on compliance for tax, taking into account both direct and indirect influences, was depict to be 0.93 due to the combined influence of these two paths. According to this investigation, a considerable amount of the direct association among compliance for tax and communal responsibility of corporates is mediated by the Sense for Civics Duty The investigation depicts partial mediation since a noteworthy amount of the association among compliance for tax and communal responsibility of corporates can be depicted indirectly through the Sense for Civics Duty.

DISCUSSION

Table 7 manifests the mediation of the company's general liability regarding taxation, highlighting direct and indirect pathways. The direct impact of the business community's responsibility on compliance with tax requirements is determined quantitatively by increasing 0.48. This illustrates the important relationships when companies directly influence requirements compliance behavior. Furthermore, indirect effects emerge through mediation channels that link corporate community responsibility to a sense of civic duty, which later affects tax compliance. This path is calculated as 0.84 (the impact of community responsibility on civic duties) multiplied by 0.54 (the impact of civic duties on tax compliance), giving an indirect impact value of 0.45. In combination, the general influence reaches 0.93, which implies a strong general influence when the general responsibility of the company plays a decisive role in the increase in tax requirements both in direct and indirect channels. The analysis indicates a partial effect of mediation, emphasizing the importance of understanding this dynamic in contribution to compliance.

The investigation's outcomes provide insight into the intricate connections among compliance for tax, civic duty, and communal responsibility of corporates (CSR). The outcomes point to a excellent optimistic correlation among communal responsibility of corporates (CSR) and the Sense for Civics Duty, suggesting that companies that place a high priority on CSR programs are likely to enhancement people's Sense for Civics Duty. The significance of ethical factors in promoting communal responsibility and moral behavior in people is depicting by this mutually reinforcing association. Also, the information depicts that CSR has a noteworthy direct influence on compliance for tax. The ethical standards and values that firms uphold are highlighted by CSR's optimistic direct influence on compliance for tax, which can then influence individuals' adherence to tax laws. This clear route demonstrates the real influence that communal responsibility of corporates (CSR) initiatives have on encouraging compliance for tax in business settings. The investigation also explores how the Sense for Civics Duty mediates the association among compliance for tax and communal responsibility of corporates. The outcomes suggest that people's sense of civic responsibility mediates a noteworthy amount of the association among CSR and compliance for tax. This emphasizes how vital ingrained moral principles and a feeling of communal duty are in influencing actions like filing taxes. While CSR programs have a direct influence on compliance for tax, people's feeling of civic responsibility acts as a vital mediating mechanism in this association, according to the partial mediation depicts.

CONCLUSION

The investigation's conclusions highlight the complex connections among compliance for tax, civic duty, and communal responsibility of corporates (CSR). The investigation depict a excellent optimistic correlation among communal responsibility of corporates (CSR) and civic duty, suggesting that companies that prioritize CSR programs can have a favorable influence on people's feeling of communal obligation. This mutually reinforcing association emphasizes how vital communal values and ethical issucs arc in dctcrmining bchavior in corporatcal contcxts.

Also, the investigation showed that CSR directly and favorably influences compliance for tax, highlighting the part that moral business conduct plays in encouraging adherence to tax laws. The outcomes demonstrate the usefulness of moral conduct in financial affairs by manifesting that companies that participate in CSR initiatives are more likely to encourage compliance for tax among people. Also, the association among CSR and compliance for tax was manifested, along with the mediating function of the Sense for Civics Duty. According to the analysis, people's sense of civic responsibility mediates a sizable amount of the association among CSR and compliance for tax. This mediation emphasizes how vital internalized moral principles and a dedication to communal duty are in promoting compliance for tax.

MANAGERIAL IMPLICATIONS

The investigation's conclusions have noteworthy managerial ramifications for businesses looking to strengthen their CSR programs and encourage moral conduct, especially when it comes to compliance for tax. First and foremost, the report emphasizes how vital it is to incorporate CSR practices into the main business plan. Corporates can improve their reputation and possibly influence people's feeling of civic duty and ethical behavior by giving priority to CSR initiatives that are in line with ethical standards and communal values. Second, the direct correlation among CSR and compliance for tax emphasizes the possible advantages of cultivating a communally conscious culture within the company. Since these activities can have a good influence on employees' views about compliance for tax and ethical behavior in general, managers should think about putting in place CSR programs that promote ethical conduct and compliance with tax legislation.

Also, the investigation's discovery of the Sense for Civics Duty's mediating role implies that businesses ought to concentrate on fostering a sense of communal responsibility in their workforce. Managers can strengthen employees' dedication to moral conduct and adherence to tax regulations by fostering values like honesty, responsibility, and community involvement. A more moral corporate culture and better compliance with legal obligations can result from encouraging staff members to absorb these ideals Also, the investigation's partial mediation suggests that although CSR activities have a direct influence on compliance for tax, the Sense for Civics Duty is vital in strengthening this link. Managers could take use of this knowledge by creating incentives, communication plans, and training initiatives that highlight the value of moral behavior and communal responsibility. Corporates can enhancement employee engagement, trust, and dedication to compliance for tax by fostering a work environment that prioritizes moral conduct and civic responsibility.

PRACTICAL IMPLICATIONS

For practitioners and policymakers looking to advance Communal responsibility of corporates (CSR), foster moral behavior, and improve Compliance for tax within businesses, the investigation's practical implications provide insightful information. First and foremost, the investigation emphasizes how noteworthy it is to include CSR activities into corporate operations in order to promote an ethical and communally conscious culture. Companies can use CSR initiatives to influence employees' views on moral behavior and compliance for tax in addition to enhancing their public image Also, the investigation's discovery of the Sense for Civics Duty's mediating role emphasizes how vital it is for people to develop an excellent sense of communal duty. Practitioners can put in place communication plans, training initiatives, and recognition schemes that support moral principles and motivate staff to fulfill their civic responsibilities. Corporates can foster an atmosphere that supports moral decision-making and adherence to legal obligations by establishing a culture that emphasizes honesty, responsibility, and community involvement. CSR's direct influence on compliance for tax highlights the useful advantages of prioritizing moral company conduct in encouraging compliance with tax laws. By creating CSR strategies that put an emphasis on openness, equity, and moral leadership, practitioners can take use of this knowledge. Corporates can show their dedication to responsible corporate citizenship and support a compliance and good governance culture by incorporating ethical issues into tax-related policies and processes.

THEORETICAL IMPLICATIONS

The investigation's outcomes have theoretical ramifications that add noteworthy to the body of knowledge on compliance for tax, civic duty, and communal responsibility of corporates (CSR). First, by highlighting the interdependence of CSR, ethical conduct, and compliance for tax, the investigation clarifies the intricate connections among these concepts. The investigation augments theoretical knowledge of how ethical considerations and communal responsibility influence people's behaviors inside corporateal environments by empirically proving the beneficial associations among CSR, the Sense for Civics Duty, and Compliance for tax. Also, identifying the Sense for Civics Duty's mediation function in the association among CSR and compliance for tax provides theoretical understanding of the ways in which civic duties and ethical principles influence compliance practices. This investigation adds to theoretical frameworks that highlight how people's judgments and behaviors regarding compliance for tax are influenced by their internalized ethical norms and beliefs. The work advances theoretical perspectives on the interaction among CSR, ethical behavior, and regulatory compliance by clarifying the mediation mechanisms involved in these linkages. Also, the investigation's acknowledgment of the clear correlation among CSR and compliance for tax highlights the theoretical deportations of how communal responsibility-related corporate activities might influence people's compliance habits. This empirical information gives theoretical models that examine how corporate citizenship, ethical leadership, and corporateal values support adherence to moral and legal norms—especially when it comes to compliance for tax—more depth.

RECOMMENDATIONS

Several suggestions can be made for businesses and legislators wishing to improve Communal responsibility of corporates (CSR), foster a sense of civic responsibility, and encourage Compliance for tax based on the investigation's outcomes and theoretical ramifications. First and foremost, companies ought to give top priority to incorporating CSR activities into their strategic planning procedures, guaranteeing that communal responsibility is ingrained in their fundamental principles and operational procedures. Corporates can cultivate a culture of communal responsibility that may favorably influence employees' attitudes about compliance for tax by showcasing their dedication to moral behavior and community involvement through CSR initiatives. Second, companies can gain from putting in place communication plans and training initiatives that stress the value of moral conduct and civic responsibility among staff members.

Corporates can improve people's capacity for moral decision-making and cultivate a culture of adherence to moral and legal requirements, incorporating tax laws, by advancing values like honesty, responsibility, and integrity. Also, legislators are urged to create rules and rewards that encourage companies to follow moral principles and embrace communally conscious operations. Policymakers can encourage companies to prioritize communal responsibility of corporates (CSR) efforts and help build a more moral and legal business ecosystem by establishing a legislative framework that incentivizes ethical behavior and fosters communal responsibility.

Also, cooperation among groups, legislators, and other interested parties is necessary to advance group initiatives that support moral conduct, communal responsibility, and tax law observance. A durable framework for moral decision-making and conscientious corporate citizenship can be established by stakeholders through partnerships, knowledge-sharing, and cooperative projects.

FUTURE DIRECTIONS

Building on the investigation's conclusions and suggestions, a number of interesting directions for additional investigation can be depict to better examine the intricate associations among compliance for tax, civic duty, and communal responsibility of corporates (CSR). First, to investigate the long-term influences of CSR programs on people's feeling of civic responsibility and compliance behaviors, future investigation could focus on longitudinal studies. Investigations can better understand how corporateal practices influence moral decision-making and long-term regulatory compliance by monitoring these interactions across time. Second, there is growing interest in investigation how technology and digital platforms may support communal responsibility of corporates (CSR), encourage civic engagement, and improve compliance for tax. Examining how technology can be used to promote accountability, openness, and communication regarding tax duties and communal responsibility of corporates (CSR) initiatives could provide insightful information about creative ways to encourage moral conduct and communal responsibility in the digital era. Also, to investigate how cultural norms, beliefs, and institutional environments influence the connections among CSR, civic responsibility, and compliance for tax, future investigation could concentrate on cross-cultural comparisons.

Investigations can reveal the subtleties of moral decision-making and compliance practices in various sociocultural contexts by carrying out comparative studies across cultural boundaries, depicting insightful information to multinational corporations and politicians.

Also, an interesting direction for future investigation is to examine how multi-stakeholder collaborations and stakeholder involvement influence CSR outcomes and compliance practices. Examining how collaborations with stakeholders, such as local communities, non-governmental corporates, and government agencies, can improve the efficacy of CSR programs and encourage moral conduct may provide useful information for developing communal influence and sustainable business practices.

REFERENCES

Aversano, N., Nicolò, G., Sannino, G., & Tartaglia Polcini, P. (2022). Communal responsibility of corporates, stakeholder engagement, and universities. *Administrative Sciences*, *12*(3), 79. DOI: 10.3390/admsci12030079

Boateng, K., Omane-Antwi, K. B., & Ndori Queku, Y. (2022). Tax risk assessment, financial constraints and compliance for tax: A bibliometric analysis. *Cogent Business & Management*, *9*(1), 2150117. DOI: 10.1080/23311975.2022.2150117

Chouaibi, J., Rossi, M., & Abdessamed, N. (2022). The influence of communal responsibility of corporates practices on tax avoidance: An empirical investigation in the French context. *Competitiveness Review*, *32*(3), 326–349. DOI: 10.1108/CR-04-2021-0062

Dakhli, A. (2022). The influence of ownership structure on corporate tax avoidance with communal responsibility of corporates as mediating variable. *Journal of Financial Crime*, *29*(3), 836–852. DOI: 10.1108/JFC-07-2021-0152

de la Cruz, C. D., Fernández-Fernández, J. L., & Ferrero, I. (2022). Ethical decision-making: from practice to theory. *Ramon Llull Journal of Applied Ethics*, (13).

Feitosa, F., & Galais, C. (2020). How stable is the Sense for Civics Duty to vote? A panel investigation on the individual-level stability of the attitude. 6(5), 34-46

García-Rivas, M. I., Gálvez-Sánchez, F. J., Noguera-Vivo, J. M., & Meseguer-Sánchez, V. (2023). Communal responsibility of corporates reports: A review of the evolution, approaches and prospects. *Heliyon*. Advance online publication. DOI: 10.1016/j.heliyon.2023.e18348

Jiang, W., Zhang, C., & Si, C. (2022). The real influence of mandatory CSR disclosure: Evidence of corporate tax avoidance. *Technological Forecasting and Social Change*, *179*, 121646. DOI: 10.1016/j.techfore.2022.121646

Joel, I. C., Wisdom, E., & Bolouimbelemoere, K. P. (2023). Influence of Tax Morality and Tax Culture on Compliance for tax. *International Journal of Accounting, Management* [IJAMESC]. *Economics and Communal Sciences*, *1*(5), 500–509.

Khan, S. A. R., Sheikh, A. A., & Tahir, M. S. (2024). Communal responsibility of corporates—an antidote for sustainable business performance: Interconnecting role of digital technologies, employee eco-behavior, and tax avoidance. *Ecological Science and Pollution Investigation*, *31*(3), 4365–4383. PMID: 38102435

Kirui, D., Kapkiyai, C., & Kipruto, A. (2024). Tax Service Quality and Compliance for tax among Small and Medium Enterprises in North Rift Economic Block, Kenya: A Moderated Mediation Model of Government Trust and Communal Value Orientation. Kenya: A Moderated Mediation Model of Government Trust and Communal Value Orientation (July 20, 2024).

Kumar, A., Snehvrat, S., Kumari, P., Priyadarshani, P., & Ray, P. (2024). A communal responsibility of corporates (CSR)-led competitiveness framework through a bibliometric analysis (2001–2023). *Journal of Asia Business Studies*, *18*(3), 737–766. DOI: 10.1108/JABS-02-2023-0074

Mahajan, R., Lim, W. M., Sareen, M., Kumar, S., & Panwar, R. (2023). Stakeholder theory. *Journal of Business Investigation, 166*, 114104.

Mkadmi, J. E., & Ali, W. B. (2024). How does tax avoidance influence communal responsibility of corporates and financial ratio in emerging economies? *Journal of Economic Criminology, 5*, 100070. DOI: 10.1016/j.jeconc.2024.100070

Nabila, A. T., & Paramita, V. S. (2024). The Influence Of Communal responsibility of corporates (CSR), Growth Opportunity, And Company Characteristics On Earning Response Coefficient (Case Investigation On The Conventional Banking Sector Listed On The Indonesia Stock Exchange-IDX 2018-2022). *International Journal of Science. Technology & Management, 5*(1), 312–323.

Risi, D., Vigneau, L., Bohn, S., & Wickert, C. (2023). Institutional theory-based investigation on communal responsibility of corporates: Bringing values back in. *International Journal of Management Reviews, 25*(1), 3–23. DOI: 10.1111/ijmr.12299

Scarpa, F., & Signori, S. (2023). Understanding corporate tax responsibility: A systematic literature review. *Sustainability Accounting. Management and Policy Journal, 14*(7), 179–201.

Sulistyan, R. B. (2020). Lecturer E-learning Training: The Role of Communal Exchange Theory. *Empowerment Society, 3*(2), 50–56. DOI: 10.30741/eps.v3i2.589

Zaman, R., Jain, T., Samara, G., & Jamali, D. (2022). Corporate governance meets communal responsibility of corporates: Mapping the interface. *Business & Society, 61*(3), 690–752. DOI: 10.1177/0007650320973415

KEY TERMS AND DEFINITIONS

Corporates Communal Responsibility: It manifests the ethics against which corporates can be measured in terms of their responsibilities to the influences of their operations on the environment and commonweal. In addition to this legislation, this concept means going further than most legislation and policies would push for and seek to augment the communal and ecological responsibility of business both internally and in their management of stakeholder associations for the sake of, and in the drive for sustainable business.

Tax Compliance: In order to declare their income, to pay the taxes and fulfill the taxation requirements, citizens and companies have to conform to the tax legislation. Compliance for tax plays noteworthy roles in reducing tax evasion so as to attain fairness, protect the integrity of the tax system, and provide subsidies of government development and public services. Noncompliance leads to fines, legal consequences and decreased community trust in the tax system.

Civics Duty Sense: It is the inherent desire of a person to discharge his/her responsibilities as a citizen of the society; to ensure that communal order is maintained and citizens adhere to people's beliefs and standards. This idea can be however assumed from the view of that people have the right to obey the law, be involved in civil matters and work for the welfare of the society.

Chapter 11
Artificial Intelligence in Tax Compliance:
Transforming Taxpayer Behavior and System Efficiency

Muhammad Idreesul Islam
https://orcid.org/0000-0002-2734-8758
The University of Kashmir, North, India

Syed Immamul Ansarullah
https://orcid.org/0000-0002-0894-7595
University of Kashmir, India

Khair Ul Nisa
Bisha University, Saudi Arabia

Sheikh Ikhlaq
Deloitte, India

Sabeha Mufti
https://orcid.org/0000-0001-7341-187X
The University of Kashmir, North, India

Tyba Yousuf
SSM College of Engineering, Parihaspora, India

ABSTRACT

This chapter examines tax administration systems that utilizes artificial intelligence (AI) technologies including predictive analytics and natural language processing across multiple nations such as the United States, Europe, Australia, and India. These tools improve tax efficiency by reducing administrative costs and ensuring accurate compliance. However, the implementation of AI introduces critical ethical concerns regarding algorithmic fairness, data privacy, and equitable outcomes. These challenges can be addressed through explainable AI (XAI), ethical standards, and robust regulatory frameworks. The chapter describes the differences between AI adoption in developed nations and less developed countries alongside recommendations for local use and worldwide teamwork. Tax systems that use AI technology to serve more people become more transparent as governments learn how to handle its disadvantages. Furthermore, the chapter outlines upcoming trends like blockchain and quantum computing and presents clear steps tax authorities should take to use AI responsibly in tax operations.

DOI: 10.4018/979-8-3373-0422-9.ch011

1. INTRODUCTION

New tax administration systems work better through AI technology which adds machine learning methods and analyses written data along with predicting results (Rahman et al., 2024). These technological breakthroughs give governments unique ways to run tax operations better while making tax enforcement more effective and fairer. The automated tax checking system helps tax officials check big data and spot irregularities while seeing what taxpayers may do next with better precision. Tax authorities use these advanced tools to fight fraud better while saving money and making tax services smoother for everyone (Adelekan et al., 2024).Tax authorities worldwide use AI systems to produce better tax administration results. Predictive analytics helps tax authorities find potential risks early and use their teams more wisely. Machine learning tools work with detailed tax data to find illegal practices and prevent manual errors which make tax assessment more precise. Tax agencies that use artificial intelligence chatbots enhance taxpayer services with individualized help and guidance which boosts trust in their tax operations (Nembe et al., 2024) (Allingham, M. G., & Sandmo, A. 1972).AI technology brings fairness and openness as well as productivity improvements to tax administration. AI processing technology eliminates human bias and fraud which leads to better equal tax systems. These technologies help build taxpayer trust because they provide clear records and explain AI system decisions through XAI and blockchain solutions (Yusuf et al., 2024).

Tax compliance systems empowered by AI change how taxpayers behave through robotic automation and math-based monitoring (Botha, 2021). AI usage plays a major role in shaping taxpayer perceptions surrounding fairness, trust and voluntary compliance (Komarudin & Hermawan, 2022). While predictive analytics and chatbot integration improve system efficiency, thereby fostering greater trust, concerns about excessive monitoring can have adverse effects. Researchers like (Agu et al., 2024) emphasize that algorithmic bias stemming from non-representative datasets can result in certain taxpayer groups feeling unfairly treated, thus discouraging compliance. The integration of AI into tax compliance poses significant ethical issues, particularly algorithmic discrimination and privacy issues (Allingham, M. G., & Sandmo, A. 1972). Additionally, algorithmic biases mostly stem from historical data causing discriminatory results for minority or marginalised sections. To achieve equitable tax enforcement, Adelakun et al. (2024) call for periodic audits of AI models and holistic data collection practices. In addition, protecting taxpayer data is a primary ethical responsibility. As tax systems analyse the most extensive financial information, ensuring compliance with international data protection standards, such as the GDPR, is imperative. Transparent AI operations underpin taxpayer trust and cooperation in modern tax systems. Explainable AI (XAI) provides taxpayers clear insights into decision-making processes, reducing suspicion and uncertainty (Eghaghe et al., 2024). This type of proactive transparency engenders taxpayer confidence and helps fortify the legitimacy of the AI-fuelled compliance tools.

This chapter employs a multi-method research approach, combining qualitative analysis, case-based evidence, and review of academic and policy literature. It draws on peer-reviewed journal articles, government reports, and empirical studies to assess the current role of AI in tax administration and its associated ethical and behavioural implications. The analysis includes a comparative examination of multiple tax jurisdictions to identify effective AI strategies and highlight how contextual factors influence their success (Chacko & Mishra, 2023; Adelekan et al., 2024). Real-world case studies from selected regions illustrate how AI enhances tax compliance, improves service delivery, and reduces administrative costs. By integrating thematic insights with supporting statistical evidence, this methodology enables a comprehensive evaluation of AI's impact on tax governance. It also helps to identify existing research gaps and inform scalable, ethical policy recommendations for the development of AI-driven tax systems (Belahouaoui & Attak, 2024; Mpofu, 2024).

1.2 Research Questions

- How does AI influence taxpayer compliance decisions?
- What ethical challenges arise with AI use in tax systems?
- What lessons can be learnt from jurisdictions leveraging AI for tax compliance?

1.3 Structure of the Chapter

This chapter provides a concise and critical examination of the integration of AI in tax compliance systems, with a focus on behavioural impacts, ethical challenges, and policy implications. It begins with an introduction to the context, objectives, and methodology of the study. It then examines how AI tools are used to model taxpayer behaviour through analytics and machine learning. The literature review highlights current applications of AI in tax, including predictive analytics, chatbots, and risk models, alongside ethical and behavioural considerations. The chapter discusses the opportunities and limitations of AI in enhancing efficiency and reducing fraud, while also addressing concerns such as bias and data privacy. A comparative analysis of AI technologies is presented, followed by case studies from the United States, European Union, India, and Brazil. The ethical and behavioural implications of AI adoption are explored in terms of trust, fairness, and compliance. Long-term impacts on tax systems are assessed, and areas for future research are identified to support more transparent and inclusive AI integration. The chapter concludes with practical policy recommendations for ethical AI implementation and a summary of key insights, followed by a comprehensive list of references.

2. AI IN TAX COMPLIANCE: APPLICATIONS AND BEHAVIOURAL INSIGHTS

Artificial Intelligence plays a key role in understanding and predicting taxpayer behaviour, transforming traditional compliance processes by providing powerful insights into taxpayer decisions (Rahman et al., 2024). Using complex statistical methods and machine learning techniques, AI algorithms spot behavioural patterns that help tax agencies whether taxpayers will comply with tax laws, or if there may be a risk of avoiding compliance. These predictions draw on historical data, payment histories, income reporting behaviours, and economic variables including perceived risks of detection (Rahman et al., 2024; Dashe & Asada, 2023). AI assists authorities in efficiently organising taxpayers based on their compliance risk and allocating enforcement resources accordingly, directing large-scale scrutiny towards high-risk individuals or businesses and implementing less aggressive measures against compliant taxpayers.

It is known that supervised and unsupervised machine learning algorithms have shown good results when applied to clustering, they work particularly well for behavioural profiling (Bankole & Vara, 2023). Supervised learning algorithms (e.g. Random Forests, Neural Networks, or Gradient Boosting algorithms) utilize past audit data together with known fraudulent activities to predict future non-compliant behaviours (Nuryani et al. 2024). Unsupervised techniques, such as k-means or hierarchical clustering, detect hidden patterns of behaviour among the taxpayer without labelled data, signifying anomalous behaviour that may be suspected of fraud or evasion or (Belahouaoui & Attak, 2024).

Figure 1. AI-driven Behavioural Profiling Framework for Tax Compliance Prediction

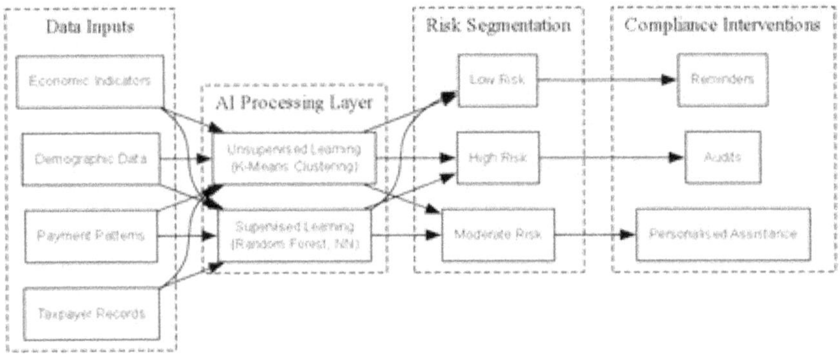

Figure 1 outlines the AI-driven taxpayer behavioural profiling framework. It starts with **Data Inputs** including taxpayer historical records, payment patterns, demographic and economic indicators. These feed into the **AI Processing Layer** involving supervised learning (Random Forest, Neural Networks) for predictive analytics and unsupervised learning (K-Means clustering) for behavioural segmentation. Results include categorisation into risk segments (**Low Risk**, **Moderate Risk**, **High Risk**), which subsequently inform compliance interventions (e.g., audits, reminders, personalised taxpayer assistance).

The United States Internal Revenue Service (IRS) has radically improved its systems for tax compliance through artificial intelligence (AI)-based behavioural profiling of taxpayers to detect and predict fraud (Adelekan et al., 2024). In this system, machine learning algorithms analyze large datasets of taxpayers, including their filing history, declared income, deductions, and demographic information (Ilori et al., 2024). Gradient Boosting algorithm was trained on historical cases of tax evasion and compliance violations to identify taxpayer attributes correlated with high fraud probability.

The IRS Model categorizes taxpayers as Low Risk, Moderate Risk, and High Risk. High-risk taxpayers are targeted for enhanced scrutiny or an audit, while lower-risk taxpayers are met with softer compliance strategies, such as reminders or positive messaging. This targeted approach has not only enhanced the precision of audit activities but also improved taxpayer behaviour by raising perceived detection risk and promoting voluntary compliance (Azmi& Daud,2024). Moreover, the model-derived behavioral insights allow the IRS for more personalized taxpayer interaction. To illustrate, AI-powered chatbots use behavioural profiles to provide personalised guidance and support to taxpayers during filing processes to prevent error and improve compliance as well as enhance trust in tax authorities (Sadovenko et al., 2024).

2.1 Predictive Analytics for Fraud Detection

Artificial intelligence enables predictive analytics systems to find and stop tax compliance fraud better (Rahman et al., 2024). Tax authorities use large datasets and artificial intelligence programs to find tax violations by people who evade taxes (Ilori et al., 2024). AI technology studies taxpayer habits and matches known patterns to find suspicious behaviour for tax authority review (Dashe & Asada, 2023). According to Nidal Zaqeeba (2024) predictive models help tax authorities fight fraud more accurately and let them act against possible risks early. Predictive analytics systems transform raw data collections from transaction history records and financial disclosures to produce valuable insights. The automated system detects hidden connections that human auditors often miss which boosts the enforcement capabilities of tax systems. According to Akinrinolaet al. (2024) predictive tools work better for tax inspection by spotting tax evasion in real time and need less person power than audit methods.

2.2 Chatbots and Natural Language Processing for Taxpayer Assistance

Tax authorities are making better taxpayer aid systems through AI chatbot technology and natural language processing (Sadovenko et al., 2024). Technology of this kind answers tax problems effectively and helps users complete their submissions while clearly explaining difficult tax terminology to all users. In India TaxBot shows how natural language processing makes tough double taxation agreements easier to understand. By enhancing tax authority services and reducing administrative work they serve taxpayers better and improve operations for the departments (Sadovenko et al., 2024). AI chatbots keep delivering non-stop assistance to users unlike normal call centre teams. Research by Adelekan et al. (2024) shows that combining chatbots with tax systems strengthens taxpayers' trust because responses come faster with precise data.

2.3 AI-Driven Risk Assessment Models

Technology-powered risk assessment tools help tax authorities better identify and control consumer compliance issues (Rane et al., 2024). Algorithms for evaluating non-compliance risk analyse complete taxpayer records together with their transaction history as well as economic factors. Tax authorities under Nembe et al.'s research (2024) use advanced AI tools to find which taxpayers face big risks first through targeted audits and save time looking at those who follow rules well. These models help organizations develop better tax policies by revealing weak spots in their tax processes. According to Dwianika et al. (2023) AI-driven risk assessment tools can show tax authorities how new policies would impact tax compliance levels before these changes take effect.

2.4 Behavioural Impacts of AI Adoption

2.4.1 Theoretical Insights into How AI Influences Taxpayer Behaviour

The use of artificial intelligence in tax compliance has greatly shifted the behaviour of taxpayers through machineries such as predictive analytics and automation systems (Kovacev, 2020). Drawing from behavioural economics and cognitive psychology, this transformation is premised on AI helping taxpayers to gain compliance by changing their perception of risks of being caught and through the simplification of procedures. Based on Snaidauf (2011), AI models assist the tax authorities in the understanding and forecasting of taxpayers' behaviour and the identification of possible infringements in the tax legislation that affects the level of compliance through the increased probability of being Identified for non-compliance by the tax authorities. Also, it helps in equality and procedural justice which are the principles of the compliance psychology. If taxpayers have the notion that the system is equitable and non-hardship, then they will be more likely to adhere to the system. Auto-generated algorithms eliminate biases and subjectivity or inefficiency in audit and assessment, thereby increasing credibility of the tax administrative system. Belahouaoui and Attak (2024) argue that the use of digital technologies including AI and blockchain has enhanced the вп impression of taxpayers regarding the tax systems. This is because using AI taxpayers' behaviour is enhanced through the delivery of personalized services such as the use of chatbots and intelligent platforms for real time assistance. These services help in the facilitation of easy compliance with tax laws, lessen mental effort required for the compliance with the tax laws and ensure voluntary compliance with the tax laws. In line with this, Nguyen (2022) has also established that enhanced quality of tax service delivery and help options enhance compliance behaviour.

2.4.2 Evidence on AI's Effectiveness in Reducing Non-Compliance and Enhancing Voluntary Compliance

The literature review provides substantial evidence of the potential of AI in decreasing non-compliance and increasing voluntary compliance (Esayas & Mahler, 2015; Wang et al., 2020). Based on the analysis of the risk scores of taxpayers, automatic risk assessment and focused control and enforcement measures are applied to prevent the non-compliance. As noted by Zaqeeba (2024) application of Artificial Intelligence in fraud detection has greatly help reduce cases of tax evasion due to early identification of trends. This type of technologies also enhances the integrity of the tax systems and in turn increase taxpayer confidence through voluntary compliance. For instance, according to Nguyen (2022), the increased confidence in the fairness and efficiency of the tax administration and the utilizing of AI, results in increased compliance through the voluntary compliance rates. The study also pointed out that through the accurate assessment of taxes, AI discourages taxpayers from falling into the wrong hands, hence encouraging voluntary compliance. Moreover, artificially intelligent self-assessment tools demystify the compliance processes and ease the access for SMEs. Belahouaoui and Attak (2024) noted that such tools foster compliance by reducing paperwork and making tax compliance easy to understand to ordinary people. Last but not the least, the integration of AI in tax systems is consistent with the compliance theories of deterrence and equity. When the perceived probability of detection is raised and taxpayers are treated fairly, AI systems promote compliance to the recommended standards, a finding that has been observed in both developed and emerging economies (Snaidauf, 2011; Nguyen, 2022). This two-pronged effect of reducing non-compliance and at the same time stepping up on voluntary compliance is a clear indication of how AI is poised at revolutionizing tax administration.

2.5 Gaps in Existing Literature

Despite major AI advancements in tax systems nobody has yet conducted studies on these technologies' lasting results. The current research focuses on quick results from AI usage in tax systems but ignores its role in these systems over longer time periods. Belahouaoui and Attak (2024) recognize that despite AI and blockchain's immediate benefits to compliance rates their research shows a need for long-term studies to understand ongoing viability and identify future problems. Tax researchers need to find out how long-term use of AI technology changes taxpayers' confidence in the system and their tax practices. As officials monitor and predict tax behaviour more intensely taxpayers may start feeling overwhelmed by rules or that their privacy rights are being violated. Wang, (2024) point out that although AI greatly transforms tax administration its long-term benefits cannot be proven without sustained research studies to understand the relationship between system efficiency and taxpayer loyalty. Research teams need to track and study AI systems continuously to see their effect on taxpayer conduct and operating expenses plus ethical challenges throughout different stages. Research efforts help us create guidelines that let AI show its full potential while stopping unwanted outcomes.

Researchers need to compare and study how various tax authorities implement AI in their operations because such analysis is inadequate today. How well AI works for tax purposes depends on national attributes which make research across different nations essential. Most studies focus on areas but ignore how developing nations face distinct problems because of missing technology infrastructure and necessary tax laws for AI systems. Belahouaoui and Attak (2024) discovered that academic research must compare AI implementation between advanced and developing economies. According to Adelekan et al. (2024) global AI tax compliance practices offer important insights but their research shows minimal understanding of adapting these methods to match different regional socio-economic and tech capacities. Research on a worldwide scale does not often consider that emerging economies deal with specific problems including technology skill shortages, weak digital systems, and insufficient tax education for citizens. Global research helps us find AI tax solutions that can work in different systems worldwide. Researchers need to study different countries simultaneously to find effective AI methods and their obstacles so that policymakers can make solutions suitable for any context.

Table 1. Summary of Literature Review

Section	Key Insights	Authors and References
2.1 Current Applications of AI in Tax Compliance		
Predictive Analytics for Fraud Detection	AI models analyze large datasets to detect irregularities, predict risks, and enhance fraud detection. Predictive analytics minimizes reliance on traditional audits.	(Ilori et al., 2024)
Chatbots and NLP for Taxpayer Assistance	AI-powered chatbots and NLP provide personalized, 24/7 assistance, reducing administrative burdens and increasing taxpayer satisfaction.	Sadovenko et al. (2024); Adelekan et al. (2024)
AI-Driven Risk Assessment Models	AI models assess compliance risks, prioritize high-risk cases for audits, and provide policy insights by identifying vulnerabilities.	(Nandan Prasad, 2024)
2.2 Behavioural Impacts of AI Adoption		
Theoretical Insights	AI increases perceived detection risk, fairness, and trust in tax systems. Simplifies compliance and influences voluntary adherence.	Snaidauf (2011); Belahouaoui & Attak (2024); Nguyen (2022)
Evidence on Effectiveness	AI tools reduce non-compliance by enhancing transparency, trust, and voluntary adherence through targeted audits and self-assessment tools.	Zaqeeba (2024); Nguyen (2022); Belahouaoui & Attak (2024)
2.3 Ethical and Legal Considerations		
Algorithmic Bias	Biases in AI systems perpetuate discriminatory practices, affecting fairness and trust. Fairness checks, audits, and explainable AI can mitigate these biases.	Eghaghe et al. (2024); Agu et al. (2024)
Data Privacy and GDPR Compliance	Tax authorities must ensure data privacy through encryption, transparency policies, and alignment with global standards such as GDPR.	Farooqi et al. (2024); Eghaghe et al. (2024)
2.4 Gaps in Existing Literature		

continued on following page

Table 1. Continued

Section	Key Insights	Authors and References
Limited Long-Term Impact Studies	Most research focuses on short-term outcomes, neglecting how AI affects tax systems, trust, and behavior over time.	Belahouaoui & Attak (2024); Wang, M. (2024)
Insufficient Comparative Analyses	Few studies examine jurisdictional differences in AI implementation, limiting insights into context-specific challenges and solutions.	Belahouaoui & Attak (2024); Rizzo& Hassan, 2024)

3. OPPORTUNITIES AND ETHICAL CHALLENGES IN AI-DRIVEN TAX SYSTEMS

3.1 Opportunities of AI in Tax Compliance

Artificial Intelligence (AI) greatly improves the speed, precision, and efficacy of tax compliance systems (Wang, 2024). Predictive analytics enables tax authorities to detect fraudulent activities in real time and allows the judicious allocation of resources, thereby reducing administrative costs (Rahman et al. 2024). As tax collection agencies strife for enhancing taxpayer satisfaction and voluntary compliance rates, Natural Language Processing (NLP)-based chatbots play their part in achieving this by enabling real-time support to taxpayers in the Digital Era (Adelekan et al., 2024). In addition, risk assessment models propelled by AI can help tax agencies manage compliance risks proactively by designating high-risk taxpayers for audits, thereby increasing the overall effectiveness of tax administration and lowering the chances of tax evasions ((Nandan Prasad, 2024; Zaqeeba, 2024). Along with these significant opportunities, however, there are also critical limitations and challenges to AI implementation.

3.2 Limitations and Risks

- **Algorithmic Bias:** By far, one of the most game-changing limitation of AI systems in tax compliance comes down to algorithmic bias risk. AI systems depend significantly on historical data for training; if such datasets include existing discrimination in society or evident practices of unfair tax enforcement, AI systems may promote or even amplify discrimination unintentionally (Eghaghe et al., 2024). For example, the data used in historical audit records may contain biases that disproportionately affect certain taxpayer groups, which can lead to unnecessary scrutiny and legal action. However, regular checks and audits of the AI algorithms can go a long way in identifying such bias and mitigating it. Standardization of the practice of collecting data that is inclusive and diverse, representing various taxpayer groups such as different genders, ethnicities, and ages, should be adopted to ensure fairness and equity (Agu et al., 2024).
- **Privacy and Trust Concerns:** The vast amounts of data required for AI systems raises serious concerns related to the privacy of taxpayers, which directly impact their trust in, and compliance behaviour towards, the AI powered tax (data) system (Ruiz, 2021). Advanced AI-based monitoring tools like real-time transaction analysis and automated profiling may be bothersome for taxpayers (Neuman& Sheu, 2022). This would be highly problematic, since if taxpayers perceive too much scrutiny, or suspect their privacy is at risk, voluntary compliance could fall, jeopardising the legitimacy and effectiveness of tax administration systems (Tan & Liu, 2016). Thererfore, tax

administrations should be transparent about the respective scope and limitations of data use to strengthen taxpayer confidence through precise privacy policies and accountability mechanisms (Deshpande, 2024).

- **Legal and Ethical Issues:** Legal and ethical challenges also pose major constraints to AI adoption in tax compliance (Schweitzer, 2024). Data protection legislation, especially the General Data Protection Regulation (GDPR) within the European Union, stipulates the strict management of taxpayer data, with corresponding obligations based on data minimisation, transparency and explicit consent (Krzysztofek, 2018). Such legal frameworks must be complied with otherwise penalties can be levied, and such damages to public trust cannot be regained easily. As a result, AI tax solutions have to ensure strong data encryption, data usage transparency and informed consent to remain compliant with GDPR and similar worldwide regulations (Farooqi et al., 2024). Also, ethical frameworks prioritizing transparency, fairness, and accountability (especially via explainable AI (XAI)) are critical to addressing taxpayers' concerns about automated decision-making (Venkatasubramanian, 2024).

3.3. Comparative Analysis of AI Technologies in Tax Compliance

In this section, we assess three main types of AI applications currently applied in tax compliance: Predictive Analytics, AI-Enabled Fraud Prevention and AI-Enabled Chatbots. Each subsection illustrates how these technologies can improve tax system efficiency, fairness, and taxpayer compliance, while also providing an overview of major advantages and limitations. At the end, I provided a comparative table summarising each technology's roles, advantages and drawbacks.

- **Machine Learning and Predicting Taxpayer Behaviour:** The advancement in Artificial Intelligence is transforming the ability of tax authorities to anticipate and influence taxpayer conduct (Saragih et al., 2023). Predictive analytics assists in identifying patterns from historical compliance data that suggests possible instances of noncompliance or fraud. Taxpayers are classified using machine learning algorithms according to their likelihood to be compliant or evade taxes, thereby drastically improving the efficiency of compliance (Rahman et al., 2024).For example, algorithms that are trained on historical observations of taxpayer behaviour can help predict future compliance, and could inform tailored intervention strategies, whether through targeted communications or audits. For instance, the European Union harnesses predictive analytics in identifying and ranking high-risk taxpayers, resulting in increased compliance rates and enhanced operational efficiency (Hadwick, 2022; Belahouaoui & Attak, 2024).
- **AI and Fraud Prevention:** The use of AI in Fraud prevention is important as it can take advantage of advanced algorithms designed to detect anomalies in large scale financial data (Ramli, 2024). These models use anomaly detection, pattern recognition, and real-time transaction monitoring to enhance the accuracy and efficiency of the auditing process (Zaqeeba, 2024; Dwianika et al., 2023).For example, AI-based fraud detection has been successfully utilized by the Australian Taxation Office (ATO), allowing detection of complex fraud schemes and leading to faster identification of potential fraud, as well as decreased operational costs (Nembe et al., 2024). But such systems are not without the potential to produce false positives, resulting in unnecessary scrutiny of taxpayers, and are may reflect algorithmic bias if the historical data used to train the system were not fairly representative (Zaqeeba, 2024).

- **AI-driven Chatbots and Taxpayer Support:** The introduction of AI-driven chatbots, enabled by Natural Language Processing (NLP), played a key role in enhancing taxpayer services through instant, customized responses (Ezeife et al., 2021). Chatbots facilitate communication between the tax authorities and taxpayers, making tax filing elaborate processes comparatively easier and enhancing voluntary compliance rates (Baliyan et al., 2024).For instance, so much that in the United States the Internal Revenue Service (IRS) uses chatbots extensively; to manage routine queries so they can focus more on more complex taxpayer issues (Adelekan et al., 2024). While this makes AI chatbots quite effective, they may still face challenges when encountering niche questions or handling ambiguity, indicating that NLP capabilities must be refined further to improve user experience (Adam et al., 2021).
- **Challenges and Prospects:** Some of the key benefits of AI in taxation systems include better efficiency; higher accuracy in fraud detection; and higher levels of taxpayer engagement. But there have been challenges, particularly algorithmic bias, privacy, and issues concerning transparency and accountability (Agu et al., 2024; Eghaghe et al., 2024).Going forward, the implementation of Explainable AI (XAI), blockchain technologies for greater transparency and continued improvement of AI tools to address ethical and practical limitations are envisioned. This poses challenges to policymakers and tax authorities who bear the responsibility of balancing innovation with regulatory oversight to promote the sustainable and equitable use of assets (Floridi et al., 2018; Yusuf et al., 2024).

Table 2. Comparative Analysis of AI Technologies in Tax Compliance

AI Technology	Role in Tax Compliance	Advantages	Drawbacks
Predictive Analytics	Predict taxpayer compliance, prioritise high-risk cases	Improved resource allocation, proactive interventions, increased efficiency	Algorithmic bias risks, potential privacy concerns, requires quality historical data
Fraud Prevention Algorithms	Real-time identification of anomalies, fraud detection	Enhanced accuracy, operational cost reduction, effective at large data scales	False positives, potential discriminatory outcomes if historical bias exists
AI-powered Chatbots (NLP)	Automated taxpayer assistance, simplified communication, increased voluntary compliance	24/7 taxpayer support, resource savings, improved taxpayer satisfaction	Limited by complexity or ambiguity of queries, potential user frustration

4. INTERNATIONAL CASE STUDIES AND COMPARATIVE PERSPECTIVES

4.1 United States: IRS's Algorithmic Fraud Detection

The Internal Revenue Service (IRS) of the United States has significantly integrated artificial intelligence into its tax administration, notably for fraud detection and taxpayer profiling. One example is the use of predictive analytics and machine learning algorithms by the Internal Revenue Service (IRS) to detect fraudulent tax filings. As an example, the IRS uses its Return Review Program (RRP), an automated AI system, to quickly review millions of tax returns and flag potential identity theft and refund fraud anomalies (Adelekan et al., 2024).In fact, using the Electronic Fraud Detection System (EFDS), the IRS uses complex algorithms to compare taxpayer-reported income to third-party data (e.g., bank statements and payroll records). When a discrepancy is detected, the system highlights those cases for a manual review or audit, greatly improving compliance rates and minimizing losses arising from fraudulent activity (Adelekan et al., 2024). This new technology approach can ensure the better optimal use of its resources by targeting its audit efforts on people/objects at higher risks and thereby improving non-compliance and efficiency of taxpayers.While effective, the IRS struggles with false positives, in which valid returns can be inappropriately flagged, which can undermine taxpayer confidence. In response to this, the IRS is constantly adjusting its algorithms and adopting explainable AI (XAI) techniques to provide more transparency to taxpayers around how these automated decisions are made (Adam et al., 2021).

4.2 European Union: AI Integration under GDPR Compliance

In the EU, applications of artificial intelligence in the domain of tax compliance are conducted under the fabric of a rigorous data protection regime that is governed by the General Data Protection Regulation (GDPR). Member states should ensure that innovative AI technologies safeguard the privacy rights of taxpayers, promote transparency and give control over the use of personal data back to individuals. EU tax authority predictive analytics systems (e.g., in Germany and France) use strong safeguards that ensure personal data minimisation, transparency, and explicit taxpayer consent (Hadwick, 2022; Deshpande, 2024).A case in point would be the use of AI-driven predictive analytics, employed by Germany's Federal Central Tax Office (BZSt) to analyse anonymised and aggregated financial data in order to assess taxpayer risk, minimising privacy risk and closely aligning their solution with the principles of the GDPR. France's tax administration likewise deploys machine learning algorithms in a highly regulated environment that demands algorithmic transparency. Data subject to automated processing: Taxpayers must be informed whenever their data are processed by automated systems and AI decisions must be explainable and contestable under GDPR Article 22 (Hadwick, 2022).This stringent regulatory approach has allowed the EU to take advantage of AI in tax administration without materially encroaching on privacy and trust. However, obstacles remain, especially concerning algorithmic fairness, demanding ongoing extrinsic assessments to prevent biased algorithmic results. As a result, routine third-party audits and stringent oversight mechanisms are now a key part of AI highways in the EU tax administration, (Deshpande, 2024)

4.3 Emerging Economies: AI Adoption in India and Brazil

Emerging economies, particularly India and Brazil, have started to harness AI as part of their tax compliance systems, albeit faced with enormous barriers including technological backlogs, low levels of taxpayer digital literacy, and relatively lax regulatory regimes.For example, India developed an AI-based tool called TaxBot, which aims to make complex tax issues easier to understand through natural language processing (NLP). TaxBot addresses queries of taxpayers immediately about tax filing procedures, double taxation agreements, and updates on regulations. This significantly enhanced voluntary compliance among taxpayers who previously thought tax procedures were difficult and scary by simplifying the process of taxation through this chatbot(Donelan, 2022).However, the leap towards AI adoption in India runs on two serious roadblocks: lack of digital infrastructure and uneven internet access, particularly in the hinterland. In response to these constraints, the government of India is investing in developing technology infrastructure and expanding digital literacy campaigns under its Digital India initiative. The recently introduced Digital Personal Data Protection Act (2023) in India is bringing some focus to privacy with respect to AI driven data collection and is setting a clearer stage for ethical and secure data management practices (Chacko & Mishra, 2023) This pivotal action towards regulation, however, is not only limited to India.

Brazil demonstrates another informative case of how AI may be adopted under adverse conditions. Brazilian Federal Revenue Service (Receita Federal) employs AI-based algorithms to identify taxpayer behaviour anomalies, placing an emphasis on VAT (ICMS) and income tax fraud. Highly sophisticated machine learning tools are used to analyse real-time transactional information against historical filing behaviour to estimate taxpayer compliance and highlight high-risk taxpayers (Faúndez-Ugalde et al., 2020).But Brazilian authorities confront obstacle course-like challenges like India's, like infrastructure limitations and taxpayer fear of data privacy and hoovering of their data. Brazil has reacted with the Brazilian General Data Protection Law (LGPD), which is similar to Europe's GDPR, which governs transparent data processing practices for AI. Moreover, Brazil has allocated an immense amount of resources to training and capacity-building programme designed to improve the digital literacy of its tax officials as well as taxpayer, which is critical for sustainable AI adoption.Nevertheless, Brazilian authorities are looking into public-private partnerships to expedite building technological capacity. Collaborations with tech companies can assist in addressing the infrastructural gap and providing innovative solutions to local problems, greatly improving the performance of AI-driven compliance systems (Faúndez-Ugalde et al., 2020).

Table 3. International AI Adoption in Tax Compliance

Country/Region	Key AI Applications	Strengths	Challenges	Regulatory Frameworks
USA	Predictive Analytics, Return Review Program, Electronic Fraud Detection System	High accuracy, efficient resource allocation, advanced fraud detection capabilities	False positives, explainability concerns	Taxpayer Bill of Rights; XAI guidelines
EU	Predictive Analytics, Risk Assessment Models	Strict GDPR compliance, transparency, high taxpayer trust	Algorithmic bias, constant audit requirement	GDPR, EU AI Act
India	NLP Chatbots (TaxBot), Fraud Detection Systems	Improved voluntary compliance, simplified taxpayer assistance	Limited digital infrastructure, digital literacy, privacy concerns	Digital Personal Data Protection Act (2023)
Brazil	Machine Learning for VAT and income tax fraud detection	Improved real-time fraud detection, increased taxpayer education	Infrastructure constraints, privacy issues	Brazilian General Data Protection Law (LGPD)

5. ETHICAL AND BEHAVIOURAL IMPLICATIONS

5.1 Changes in Taxpayer Compliance Behaviour

Artificial Intelligence (AI) plays an increasingly important role in shaping how taxpayers perceive fairness, trust, and voluntary compliance within tax systems.They present predictive analysis, chatbot integration as essential tools to improve system efficiency thus, contributing to tax-payer trust (Komarudin and Hermawan, 2022). The higher the speed, accuracy and responsiveness of systems to taxpayer needs, the more likely individuals are to voluntarily cooperate with tax authorities. But with this positive effect must be a serious caveat: anxiety over overt surveillance and monitoring. Agu et al. (2024) caution that algorithmic bias, especially driven by non-representative datasets, can lead to a situation whereby some taxpayer group feels they are treated unfairly. These perceptions of unfair treatment can deter compliance and undermine trust in tax authorities. Similarly, Eghaghe et al. (2024) find that taxpayers who believe they are being disproportionately targeted by AI systems may develop negative attitudes towards the tax system, ultimately reducing their cooperation. And so, while AI-powered systems do drive process efficiencies, they need to walk a fine line between making analytics actionable and adhering to data privacy in every aspect. It is only by doing so that they can actually reduce behavioural risks and maintain the credibility and reliability of tax compliance regimes. Thus, by ensuring that AI does not inadvertently lead to fear or resentment of honest taxpayers, this is where it becomes imperative.

5.2 An Ethical Dilemma in AI-Based Tax Systems

The main ethical concerns surrounding the use of Artificial Intelligence in tax compliance are algorithmic discrimination and data privacy (Dudu et al., 2024). AI models are typically trained on historical data and patterns, and if this data contains biases against disadvantaged taxpayer groups, it can lead to unfair targeting and increased scrutiny by tax authorities.This can result in inequitable targeting and enforcement measures that challenge the integrity and legitimacy of tax systems. Adelakun et al. (2024) suggest that regular audits of AI models and comprehensive data collection practices are critical prerequisites for equitable tax enforcement outcomes. Furthermore, Agu et al. (2024) highlight that safeguarding taxpayer data needs to be regarded as a foremost ethical obligation of tax authorities. AI systems process massive amounts of sensitive financial data, and therefore it is a critical requirement that they adhere to global data protection regulations including General Data Protection Regulation (GDPR). Taxpayer privacy must be protected by strong encryption, including clear rules about how data is accessed, and strong access control. Mechanisms of ethical accountability should also be established to ensure tax authorities are transparent and accountable for citizens' rights and data security in the impact of AI systems.

5.3 Building Trust through Transparency

Fiscal transparency lies at the core of building taxpayer trust and sustaining long-term compliance with AI-based tax regimes. Eghaghe et al. And to do this, they argue, tax should be explainable, which is best achieved with XAI (2024). Transparent communication about the capabilities and limitations of AI systems as well as how these systems operate will lessen suspicion and uncertainty among taxpayers, allowing them to participate openly in this dialogue and better understand the risks and opportunities involved. This increased transparency enhances the likelihood that taxpayers will view automated compliance decisions as fair and legitimate. Adelakun et al. (2024) also recommend setting up broad institutional oversight committees dedicated to monitoring compliance and adherence to ethical standards for AI systems. To facilitate balanced governance, these committees must have many members and be multidisciplinary in nature, including legal experts, ethicists, technologists, and taxpayer representatives. Transparency efforts, like public disclosures about AI algorithms and their impacts, enhance the legitimacy of AI-fuelled compliance tools. Implementing such measures ensures tax authorities create an atmosphere of trust where taxpayers feel valued and protected, ultimately leading to improved tax administration systems post October 2023 Transparent governance practices serve as an ethical imperative and a strategic necessity to ensure the sustainable and beneficial adoption of AI in taxation.

5.4 Long-Term Consequences and Difficulties

- **When compliance rates and administrative costs are affected:** If properly thought through, the long-term embedding of AI within tax systems presents tremendous opportunities to improve compliance rates, while simultaneously diminishing administrative costs. Tax agencies can also achieve major operational efficiency gains by allocating their managerial resources more effectively via the adoption of AI-based fraud detection systems (Belahouaoui and Attak 2024). Such systems enable thousands of compliance assessments to be carried out automatically, significantly reducing the need for manual audits. According to Nembe et al. (2024), this shift allows tax authorities to save considerable resources and make better use of their human workforce. However, there are still risks linked to relying too heavily on AI systems. If these biases, inaccuracies or errors within the system aren't regularly found and fixed, they can build into a larger systemic problem that discredits fairness and trust. Belahouaoui and Attak (2024) stress the need for a combined automated and human assessment to reduce these risks while keeping an ongoing assessment of the averages. Human oversight is still essential to identify nuanced challenges that automated systems cannot. Tax authorities can maximize the benefits of AI-powered tax compliance solutions while ensuring the integrity, fairness, and operational effectiveness long term through a combination of human judgement and technology efficiency.
- **Scalability and Adaptability Across Jurisdictions:** Although the benefits of AI are numerous, the scalability and adaptability of AI technologies across jurisdictions represent major hurdles. Shandilya et al. point out that differences in national digital infrastructures, regulatory environments, and resource economies challenge the universal adoption of AI-based tax systems ([[Borys et al. 2024]]). But countries like the USA and those in the European Union that have highly developed AI adoption-read infrastructure are struggling with the inevitable challenges of technological limitations, fragmented regulatory frameworks and funding shortages in some emerging economies. Mpofu (2024) highlights that these disparities impact the effectiveness of AI compliance systems. Adelekan et al. (2024) suggest that some of the challenges could be mitigated with the integration of emerging technologies like blockchain which not only makes it feasible to see whether a company is compliant or not in real time but also enhances data security. But for global scalability to work, tremendous investments should be put into physical development of digital infrastructure, upskilling the workforce, and reforming regulatory purposes in the developing world. But building responsible, sustainable AI systems requires collaboration at scale, an incremental approach to technological development, and policy measures designed around the

specific needs of individual jurisdictions. Without these efforts, the potential of AI to benefit tax compliance and transparency globally is at risk of being limited to a select few regions.

5.5 Areas for Future Research

- **Improving Transparency and Accountability of Algorithms:** Future research should focus on developing strategies for improving the transparency and accountability of algorithms in tax administration systems. With AI increasingly incorporated into compliance decisions, basic ethical and trust issues are raised in view of the opacity of such decision-making processes. Explainable AI (XAI) technologies offer a promising path forward, giving taxpayers and regulators the means to understand how automated decisions are made. Researchers from civil society should examine practical governance frameworks that would reconcile the complexity of advanced algorithms with a public outcry for transparency and accountability. Next, future studies are needed to study the external efficacy that independent algorithm audits could yield and whether the regular public disclosure in relation to AI operations — for example concerning algorithm behaviour and budget allocations — could enhance citizen trust in and behaviours relevant to taxpayer-stuff they typically assume they pay for. Transparency is not only a function of what technical tools can do, but also one of building and maintaining trust in tax authorities over the long term.
- **Blockchain and Quantum Computing-Backed Taxation Systems:** Further studies should investigate the implications of integrating new technologies, such as blockchain and quantum computing into tax compliance mechanisms. The secure and distributed data storage functionalities offered by Blockchain present substantial opportunities in enhancing transparency, security, and real-time compliance monitoring. On the other hand, quantum computing is still under development yet can potentially use this power of base 2 to transform data processing via rapid processing of large, complex data sets. Future work must critically evaluate the practicalities, risks and challenges associated with integrating these technologies into taxation systems. Realistic comparative case studies from some jurisdictions that are piloting early adoption of these technologies will provide invaluable lessons for broader international application. Knowing how these technologies will work with the already-existing suites of AI tools will be critical in setting up future-proof tax compliance infrastructures that are rigorous, effective, and trustworthy.

5.6 Practical Guidance for Ethical AI

- **Constructing Ethical AI Framing on Taxation:** The above discussions lay the foundation for governments/tax authorities to arrive at a strong ethical framework to ensure responsible use of Artificial Intelligence in tax compliance. They gloss over frameworks that should involve principles of fairness, transparency, privacy, and accountability that should govern everything from the research through the deployment of AI. They would need constant auditing and reviews of AI systems to keep the systems in check of ethical compliance. Ethical frameworks should exist on paper and be integrated into respective processes, such as AI development, deployment, and monitoring. This can ensure that any AI technologies are developed to align with society goals of fairness and inclusiveness in the tax domain, and minimise the risks of bias, discrimination and data misuse.

- **Policies and Regulations that Promote Transparency, Fairness, and Accountability:** Policies and regulations must be clear to instil public confidence in AI-supported tax systems. According to Russell (2019), there is a critical need for Explainable AI (XAI) based policies so that taxpayers can comprehend the decision-making process. Regulations should mandate regular independent audits of the algorithms used in tax processes to validate that they are neutrally and fairly applied across taxpayers. Moreover, governments would need to comply with international data protection guidelines like GDPR, protecting taxpayer privacy and preventing the misuse of data. Grievance mechanisms need to be established where taxpayers have the ability to dispute or appeal AI-generated decisions. Proper regulatory shields are indispensable to uphold fairness, uphold taxpayer rights, and increase the legitimacy of AI-based taxation systems.
- **Ethics: AI Implementation, Algorithmic Accountability, and Data Governance:** There must also be practical legislation from governments on the ethical use of A.I. in taxation. The elements of data use, including decision-making criteria, sources of training data, and mitigation approaches for algorithmic errors, should be documented by authorities. Such documentation should be publicly available unless otherwise restricted by confidentiality provisions. Regular independent audits should examine algorithms for biases and publicly report remedial actions taken. Equally important, strict data governance policies. These should be, at minimum, data minimisation, anonymization techniques, secure access to taxpayer data with advanced encryption and blockchain verification. Adhering to ethical principles and ensuring algorithmic accountability will enhance taxpayer confidence, have better levels of compliance and foster equity in artificial intelligence-driven taxation systems.

6. CONCLUSION

AI is transforming tax compliance systems by enabling faster fraud detection, more accurate risk assessment, and personalized taxpayer support through tools such as predictive analytics, machine learning, and natural language processing. Global case studies from the United States, the European Union, Australia, and India demonstrate how AI adoption has improved compliance rates, reduced administrative costs, and strengthened trust in tax systems.

AI has also influenced taxpayer behavior, simplifying compliance procedures, reducing error rates, and enhancing efficiency. However, full-scale implementation continues to face challenges, particularly around algorithmic bias and data privacy concerns. Addressing these issues through explainable AI and transparent decision-making processes is essential for maintaining public trust. Notably, AI adoption varies across regions, underscoring the importance of context-specific approaches—especially in emerging markets where infrastructural and policy limitations persist.

AI technologies show long-term promise due to their scalability and adaptability to evolving compliance needs. Emerging integrations with blockchain further enhance the potential for real-time, transparent, and efficient tax systems. Realizing these benefits requires sustained investment in research and development, robust ethical safeguards, and global collaboration.

The future of tax compliance lies in responsible and inclusive AI integration. Policymakers and researchers must work together to ensure that AI-driven tax systems are fair, efficient, and aligned with broader societal goals. Ethical innovation, supported by transparent governance and stakeholder engagement, will be key to shaping a more equitable and effective tax landscape.

REFERENCES

Adam, M., Wessel, M., & Benlian, A. (2021). AI-based chatbots in customer service and their effects on user compliance. *Electronic Markets*, *31*(2), 427–445. DOI: 10.1007/s12525-020-00414-7

Adelekan, O. A., Adisa, O., Ilugbusi, B. S., Obi, O. C., Awonuga, K. F., Asuzu, O. F., & Ndubuisi, N. L. (2024). Evolving tax compliance in the digital era: A comparative analysis of AI-driven models and blockchain technology in US tax administration. *Computer Science & IT Research Journal*, *5*(2), 311–335. DOI: 10.51594/csitrj.v5i2.759

Agu, E. E., Abhulimen, A. O., Obiki-Osafiele, A. N., Osundare, O. S., Adeniran, I. A., & Efunniyi, C. P. (2024). Discussing ethical considerations and solutions for ensuring fairness in AI-driven financial services. International Journal of Frontier Research in Science, 3(2), 001-009.

Akinrinola, O., Addy, W. A., Ajayi-Nifise, A. O., Odeyemi, O., & Falaiye, T. (2024). Application of machine learning in tax prediction: A review with practical approaches. *Global Journal of Engineering and Technology Advances*, *18*(02), 102–117. DOI: 10.30574/gjeta.2024.18.2.0028

Azmi, D. A. W. M., & Daud, S. A. M. M. (2024). Reconceptualizing tax compliance behavior: A theoretical matrix approach. *Accounting and Finance Research*, *13*(1), 1–67.

Baliyan, P., & Arora, B. (2024, January). TaxBot: An AI-driven Chatbot for Resolving Double Taxation Queries in India. In 2024, the IEEE 1st Karachi Section Humanitarian Technology Conference (KHI-HTC) (pp. 1-6). IEEE.

Bankole, F., & Vara, Z. (2023). A Comparison of SOM and K-Means Algorithms in Predicting Tax Compliance. In *Encyclopedia of Data Science and Machine Learning* (pp. 2573–2593). IGI Global.

Belahouaoui, R., & Attak, E. H. (2024). Digital taxation, artificial intelligence, and tax administration 3.0: Improving tax compliance behaviour—a systematic literature review using textometry (2016–2023). *Accounting Research Journal*, *37*(2), 172–191. DOI: 10.1108/ARJ-12-2023-0372

Botha, R. C. (2021). *The readiness for the 4th industrial revolution by SARS towards 2030*. Nelson Mandela University.

Chacko, M., & Mishra, S. (2023). Benchmarking the Indian Digital Personal Data Protection Act 2023 against data protection frameworks in Singapore, the EU, the US, and Australia. *Journal of Data Protection & Privacy*, *6*(2), 110–119. DOI: 10.69554/LXHZ9342

Dashe, D. N., & Asada, D. (2023). The challenges of generative artificial intelligence to administer internet taxation of online transactions in Nigeria. *NIALS Journal of Business Law*, *5*(1), 31–77.

Deshpande, A. (2024, April). Regulatory Compliance and AI: Navigating the Legal and Regulatory Challenges of AI in Finance. In *2024 International Conference on Knowledge Engineering and Communication Systems (ICKECS)* (Vol. 1, pp. 1-5). IEEE. DOI: 10.1109/ICKECS61492.2024.10616752

Donelan, E. (2022). *Regulatory governance: Policy making, legislative drafting, and law reform*. Springer Nature., DOI: 10.1007/978-3-030-96351-4

Dudu, O. F., Alao, O. B., & Alonge, E. O. (2024). Conceptual framework for AI-driven tax compliance in fintech ecosystems. *Journal of Fintech and Taxation, 12*(3), 45–60.

Dwianika, A., Sofia, I. P., & Retnaningtyas, I. (2023). Tax Compliance: Development of Artificial Intelligence on Tax Issues. KnE Social Sciences, 728-733. DOI: 10.18502/kss.v8i12.13719

Eghaghe, V. O., Osundare, O. S., Ewim, C. P. M., & Okeke, I. C. (2024). Navigating the ethical and governance challenges of AI deployment in AML practices within the financial industry. *International Journal of Scholarly Research and Reviews, 5*(2).

Esayas, S., & Mahler, T. (2015). Modelling compliance risk: A structured approach. *Artificial Intelligence and Law, 23*(3), 271–300. DOI: 10.1007/s10506-015-9174-x

Ezeife, E., Kokogho, E., Odio, P. E., & Adeyanju, M. O. (2021). The future of tax technology in the United States: A conceptual framework for AI-driven tax transformation. *Future, 2*(1).

Farooqi, M. T. K., Amanat, I., & Awan, S. M. (2024). Ethical considerations and challenges in the integration of artificial intelligence in education: A systematic review. *Journal of Excellence in Management Sciences, 3*(4), 35–50. DOI: 10.69565/jems.v3i4.314

Faúndez-Ugalde, A., Mellado-Silva, R., & Aldunate-Lizana, E. (2020). Use of artificial intelligence by tax administrations: An analysis regarding taxpayers' rights in Latin American countries. *Computer Law & Security Review, 38*, 105441. DOI: 10.1016/j.clsr.2020.105441

Floridi, L., Cowls, J., Beltrametti, M., Chatila, R., Chazerand, P., Dignum, V., Luetge, C., Madelin, R., Pagallo, U., Rossi, F., Schafer, B., Valcke, P., & Vayena, E. (2018). AI4People—an ethical framework for a good AI society: Opportunities, risks, principles, and recommendations. *Minds and Machines, 28*(4), 689–707. DOI: 10.1007/s11023-018-9482-5 PMID: 30930541

Hadwick, D. (2022). Peer Reviewed Articles: Behind the One-Way Mirror: Reviewing the Legality of EU Tax Algorithmic Governance.'. *EC Tax Review, 31*(4), 184–201. DOI: 10.54648/ECTA2022019

Ilori, O., Nwosu, N. T., & Naiho, H. N. N. (2024). Advanced data analytics in internal audits: A conceptual framework for comprehensive risk assessment and fraud detection. *Finance & Accounting Research Journal, 6*(6), 931–952. DOI: 10.51594/farj.v6i6.1213

Komarudin, & Hermawan, P. (2022). A study of trust base voluntary tax compliance through tax administration digital transformation in Indonesia. International Journal of Current Science Research and Review, 5(8), 3227-3238. DOI: 10.47191/ijcsrr/V5-i8-53

Kovacev, R. (2020). A taxing dilemma: Robot taxes and the challenges of effective taxation of AI, automation and robotics in the fourth industrial revolution. *Ohio St. Tech. LJ, 16*(2), 182. DOI: 10.31979/2381-3679.2020.090204

Krzysztofek, M. (2018). *GDPR: General Data Protection Regulation (EU) 2016/679: Post-reform Personal Data Protection in the European Union*. Kluwer Law International BV.

Mpofu, f. Y. (2024). Prospects, challenges, and implications of deploying artificial intelligence in tax administration in developing countries. *Studia universitatis babes bolyai-negotia, 69*(3), 39-78.

Nandan Prasad, A. (2024). Regulatory Compliance and Risk Management. In *Introduction to Data Governance for Machine Learning Systems: Fundamental Principles, Critical Practices, and Future Trends* (pp. 485–624). Apress. DOI: 10.1007/979-8-8688-1023-7_8

Nembe, J. K., Atadoga, J. O., Mhlongo, N. Z., Falaiye, T., Olubusola, O., Daraojimba, A. I., & Oguejiofor, B. B. (2024). The role of artificial intelligence in enhancing tax compliance and financial regulation. *Finance & Accounting Research Journal*, *6*(2), 241–251. DOI: 10.51594/farj.v6i2.822

Neuman, E. L., & Sheu, R. J. (2022). Big Data analytics in IRS audit procedures and its effects on tax compliance: A moderated mediation analysis. *The Journal of the American Taxation Association*, *44*(2), 97–113. DOI: 10.2308/JATA-2020-038

Nguyen, T. H. (2022). The impact of non-economic factors on voluntary tax compliance behaviour: A case study of small and medium enterprises in Vietnam. *Economies*, *10*(8), 179. DOI: 10.3390/economies10080179

Nuryani, N., Mutiara, A. B., Wiryana, I. M., Purnamasari, D., & Putra, S. N. W. (2024). Artificial intelligence model for detecting tax evasion involving complex network schemes. [ATT]. *Aptisi Transactions on Technopreneurship*, *6*(3), 339–356. DOI: 10.34306/att.v6i3.436

Rahman, S., Sirazy, M. R. M., Das, R., & Khan, R. S. (2024). An exploration of artificial intelligence techniques for optimizing tax compliance, fraud detection, and revenue collection in modern tax administrations. *International Journal of Business Intelligence and Big Data Analytics*, *7*(3), 56–80.

Ramli, A. I. B. (2024). Big Data and Artificial Intelligence to Develop Advanced Fraud Detection Systems for the Financial Sector. *International Journal of Advanced Cybersecurity Systems, Technologies, and Applications*, *8*(12), 31–44.

Rane, N., Choudhary, S. P., & Rane, J. (2024). Acceptance of artificial intelligence technologies in business management, finance, and e-commerce: Factors, challenges, and strategies. *Studies in Economics and Business Relations*, *5*(2), 23–44. DOI: 10.48185/sebr.v5i2.1333

Rizzo, A., & Hassan, G. (2024). Addressing the use of AI by EU tax authorities: Towards a common framework of taxpayer protection. *. *European Taxation*, *65*(1). Advance online publication. DOI: 10.59403/1avybfj

Ruiz, M. A. G. (2021). Fiscal Transformations Due to AI and Robotization: Where Do Recent Changes in Tax Administrations, Procedures and Legal Systems Lead Us? *Nw. J. Tech. & Intell. Prop.*, *19*, 325.

Ruzgas, T., Kižauskienė, L., Lukauskas, M., Sinkevičius, E., Frolovaitė, M., & Arnastauskaitė, J. (2023). Tax fraud reduction using analytics in an East European country. *Axioms*, *12*(3), 288. DOI: 10.3390/axioms12030288

Sadovenko, M., Kondratyuk, O., Suprun, N., & Tarverdiev, M. (2024). Technical engineering in the digitalization era: the role of artificial intelligence and cryptocurrency in tax systems optimizing and improving the financial efficiency of fintech businesses. Economics and technical engineering, 2(1), 64-78.DOI: 10.62911/ete.2024.02.01.06

Saragih, A. H., Reyhani, Q., Setyowati, M. S., & Hendrawan, A. (2023). The potential of an artificial intelligence (AI) application for the tax administration system's modernization: The case of Indonesia. *Artificial Intelligence and Law*, *31*(3), 491–514. DOI: 10.1007/s10506-022-09321-y

Schweitzer, B. (2024). Artificial intelligence (AI) ethics in accounting. Journal of Accounting. *Ethics & Public Policy, JAEPP*, *25*(1), 67–67.

Shandilya, S. K., Datta, A., Kartik, Y., & Nagar, A. (2024). Navigating the regulatory landscape. In *Digital Resilience: Navigating Disruption and Safeguarding Data Privacy* (pp. 127–240). Springer Nature Switzerland. DOI: 10.1007/978-3-031-53290-0_3

Snaidauf, D. (2011). Predicting Aggregate Taxpayer Compliance Behaviour. Recent Research on Tax Administration and Compliance, 73. https://www.brianerard.com/wp content/uploads/ 2015/01/predicting_aggregate_taxpayer_compliance_behavior.pdf

Tan, L. M., & Liu, X. (2016, January). SMEs tax compliance: A matter of trust? In Australian Tax Forum (Vol. 31, No. 3, pp. 527-554). Sydney, NSW: Tax Institute.

Venkatasubramanian, G. (2024). *Exploring the Impact of Internet of Things (IoT) Technologies on Tax Compliance: Opportunities, Challenges, and Policy Implications*. Edumania—An International Multidisciplinary Journal., DOI: 10.59231/edumania/9073

Wang, K., Zipperle, M., Becherer, M., Gottwalt, F., & Zhang, Y. (2020). An AI-based automated continuous compliance awareness framework (CoCAF) for procurement auditing. *Big Data and Cognitive Computing*, *4*(3), 23. DOI: 10.3390/bdcc4030023

Wang, M. (2024). AI Technologies in Modern Taxation: Applications, Challenges, and Strategic Directions. *International Journal of Finance and Investment*, *1*(1), 42–46. DOI: 10.54097/v2kgty49

Yusuf, S., Abubakar, J., Ocran, G., Owusu, P., Yusuf, P., & Paul-Adeleye, A. (2024). Exploring the impact of AI-driven and blockchain-enabled tax filing systems on SMEs in the era of technological innovation: A review of benefits, challenges, and adoption barriers. *World Journal of Advanced Research and Reviews.*, *23*(03), 1867–1878. DOI: 10.30574/wjarr.2024.23.3.2754

Zaqeeba, N. (2024). The Scope of AI Applications to Tax Evasion in Enhancing Tax Enforcement Capabilities. *Int J Digital Account Fintech Sustain*, *1*(2), 2–16. DOI: 10.70568/IJDAFS1.2

Chapter 12
The Role of E-Government in Mitigating Tax Evasion Through Behavioral Profiling of Non-Compliant Taxpayers

Muhammad Younus
https://orcid.org/0000-0001-9654-1546
Universitas Muhammadiyah Yogyakarta, Pakistan

Halimah Abdul Manaf
Universiti Utara Malaysia, Malaysia

Achmad Nurmandi
Universitas Muhammadiyah Yogyakarta, Indonesia

Dyah Mutiarin
https://orcid.org/0000-0003-3171-8915
Universitas Muhammadiyah Yogyakarta, Indonesia

Imron Sohsan
Khon Kaen University, Thailand

Abdul Rehman
Pakistan Air Force College, Pakistan

Muliany Rosa
Tourism Department Makassar, Indonesia

Rashid Minhas
Virtual University, Pakistan

ABSTRACT

Tax evasion poses significant challenges to governments, undermining revenue collection and trust in public institutions. E-Government platforms, leveraging advanced digital tools and data analytics, offer a promising solution to address this issue by enabling efficient monitoring and profiling of taxpayer behavior. This study explores the role of E-Government systems in mitigating tax evasion through the behavioral profiling of non-compliant taxpayers. By integrating machine learning algorithms and anomaly detection techniques, the research identifies patterns of non-compliance and develops predictive models for early detection of evasion risks. Furthermore, the study examines the psychological and socio-economic factors influencing taxpayer behavior, emphasizing the role of trust, transparency, and system usability in fostering voluntary compliance. The findings underscore the importance of data-driven policy interventions and ethical considerations in behavioral profiling, offering a robust framework for enhancing tax compliance and promoting fiscal transparency.

DOI: 10.4018/979-8-3373-0422-9.ch012

1 INTRODUCTION

The rapid advancement of digital technology has significantly transformed the mechanisms of public administration worldwide, marking a shift from traditional bureaucratic processes to more streamlined and transparent governance models. E-government, characterized by the use of information and communication technology (ICT) to enhance the delivery of public services, has emerged as a critical tool for fostering transparency, accountability, and efficiency in public sector management. Among its myriad applications, the role of e-government in tax administration has gained substantial attention due to the persistent challenge of tax evasion (Levaggi & Menoncin, 2024), which undermines the financial stability of nations and erodes public trust in governmental systems. Tax evasion, a deliberate underreporting or misrepresentation of taxable income, is a global issue that deprives governments of essential revenue needed for infrastructure development, social welfare, and public services. It is within this context that the integration of e-government platforms offers a transformative potential for mitigating tax non-compliance through innovative approaches such as behavioral profiling.

1.1 Problem Formulation

Historically, tax evasion has been a deeply ingrained problem, exacerbated by complex tax codes, limited oversight, and loopholes that provide opportunities for individuals and corporations to evade their tax obligations. Traditional enforcement strategies, including audits and penalties, while effective to an extent, are resource-intensive and often reactive rather than proactive (Khlif & Amara, 2019). The digitalization of tax systems, an integral aspect of e-government initiatives, has brought forth new possibilities for addressing tax evasion. Countries like Estonia and Singapore, recognized as global leaders in e-government, have successfully leveraged ICT to develop sophisticated tax systems that reduce human intervention, enhance compliance monitoring, and foster voluntary tax compliance. However, despite the widespread adoption of digital tax systems, many nations continue to grapple with high levels of tax evasion, indicating the need for more nuanced strategies that account for the behavioral tendencies of taxpayers (Baconnier, R., & Taly, R., 2005).

At the heart of the tax evasion problem lies the behavior of taxpayers, which is influenced by a myriad of factors, including economic incentives, perceptions of fairness, social norms, and the perceived likelihood of detection. Behavioral profiling, a method that involves analyzing patterns in taxpayer data to identify potential non-compliance, has emerged as a promising tool for enhancing tax enforcement efforts. By leveraging advanced analytics and machine learning algorithms, tax authorities can segment taxpayers based on their compliance behavior, allowing for targeted interventions that are both efficient and equitable (Comba, 2019). This approach aligns with the broader objectives of e-government, which seeks to harness data-driven decision-making to optimize public service delivery. Yet, the integration of behavioral profiling within e-government frameworks for tax administration remains underexplored, particularly in developing countries where data infrastructure and digital literacy may pose significant challenges (Carrero & Ribeiro, 2020).

The persistence of tax evasion as a global challenge underscores the limitations of existing enforcement mechanisms and the pressing need for innovative approaches that leverage technology and behavioral insights. Despite the growing body of literature on tax compliance, there remains a gap in understanding the interplay between e-government platforms and taxpayer behavior, particularly in the context of behavioral profiling. While studies have highlighted the effectiveness of digital tax systems in improving compliance rates (Nurunnabi, 2018), few have delved into the mechanisms through which e-government can influence taxpayer behavior at an individual level. Moreover, the ethical implications of behavioral profiling, such as privacy concerns and the potential for algorithmic bias, warrant critical examination to ensure that such approaches align with principles of fairness and transparency.

This research addresses these gaps by exploring the role of e-government in mitigating tax evasion through the lens of behavioral profiling. Specifically, it seeks to understand how digital tax systems can be designed to influence taxpayer behavior, identify the factors that drive non-compliance (Khaltar, 2024), and propose strategies for integrating behavioral profiling into e-government frameworks in an ethical and effective manner. The study is motivated by the recognition that tax compliance is not merely a function of economic incentives but is deeply rooted in behavioral dynamics that can be influenced through well-designed interventions.

1.2 Research Objective

The research objectives are threefold. First, the study aims to examine the effectiveness of existing e-government platforms in addressing tax evasion, with a focus on their ability to enhance transparency, streamline tax processes, and improve compliance monitoring. By analyzing case studies of countries that have successfully implemented digital tax systems, the research seeks to identify best practices and lessons that can inform the development of more effective e-government frameworks. Second, the study aims to explore the potential of behavioral profiling as a tool for mitigating tax non-compliance. This involves analyzing taxpayer data to identify patterns of non-compliance, understanding the behavioral factors that drive such patterns, and proposing targeted interventions that address these factors. Finally, the research aims to address the ethical and practical challenges associated with integrating behavioral profiling into e-government platforms. This includes examining issues of data privacy, algorithmic transparency, and the need for safeguards to prevent misuse or unintended consequences.

By focusing on the intersection of e-government, tax compliance, and behavioral profiling, this research contributes to the growing body of knowledge on digital governance and its potential to address complex societal challenges. It offers a novel perspective on the role of technology in shaping taxpayer behavior and highlights the importance of aligning digital innovations with principles of ethical governance. Moreover, the study provides practical insights for policymakers and tax authorities seeking to enhance tax compliance through e-government initiatives, particularly in the context of developing countries where resource constraints and systemic inefficiencies pose significant barriers.

In conclusion, the role of e-government in mitigating tax evasion represents a critical area of inquiry that holds significant implications for public finance, governance, and social equity. By examining the potential of behavioral profiling as a tool for enhancing tax compliance, this research seeks to bridge the gap between technological innovation and behavioral insights, offering a pathway toward more effective and equitable tax systems. As nations continue to navigate the complexities of digital transformation, understanding how e-government can be leveraged to address persistent challenges such as tax evasion will be essential for building resilient and inclusive governance systems.

1.3 Research Assumption

The study assumes that the use of e-government in taxation is a key factor to prevent tax evasion by shaping the behavioral tendencies of delinquent taxpayers. It is anticipated that use of electronic governance tools, such as computer-aided reporting of taxes, data examination, and real-time monitoring, ensures highest levels of transparency and minimizes the possibility of tax evasion. This assumption aligns with the hypothesis that electronic interventions, through an improvement in enforcement mechanisms, increase voluntary tax compliance by reducing bureaucratic inefficiencies and limiting human discretion in tax administration. The research also assumes that behavioral profiling of non-compliant taxpayers, informed by data-based e-government systems, enables the authorities to isolate risk factors and design targeted interventions.

It is postulated that fiscal considerations like earlier non-compliance, income streams, and age groups affect taxpayers' attitude and can be rigorously analyzed via digital profiling. The study further anticipates that e-government initiatives like digital nudges and reminders positively affect taxpayer attitudes by increasing compliance culture. The study also takes into account that the electronic image of fairness and trust of the tax administration is a determinant of compliance behavior because taxpayers are likely to comply immediately once they see the system as transparent and fair. In addition, it is assumed that the efficiency of e-government in preventing tax evasion would be dependent on taxpayers' digital literacy, the strength of data protection measures, and the degree of trust in electronic government. Finally, it is assumed that whereas e-government boosts compliance, it can also be plagued by challenges like privacy issues and possible resistance from taxpayers with no experience on digital platforms. These presuppositions form the basis for examining how e-government can serve as a strategic instrument in combating tax evasion using behavioral analysis and technological development.

2 LITERATURE REVIEW

2.1 Introduction to E-Government and Tax Compliance

The rise of e-government has revolutionized public administration, offering transformative potential in improving service delivery, transparency, and compliance in various sectors, including taxation. As governments face the persistent challenge of tax evasion, the application of digital tools has emerged as a crucial strategy (Chatzoglou et al., 2015). E-government initiatives, defined as the use of information and communication technology (ICT) to enhance public services, aim to foster trust, simplify processes, and encourage compliance (Ajzen, 1985, 1991, 2005). Tax compliance, broadly understood as the willingness of taxpayers to fulfill their tax obligations voluntarily, is influenced by myriad factors, including behavioral tendencies, perceptions of fairness, and institutional trust. Exploring the intersection of e-government and taxpayer behavior provides a promising avenue to address non-compliance (Iong & Phillips, 2022).

The adoption of e-government platforms in taxation offers unique opportunities to reduce tax evasion through increased transparency, improved data accessibility, and enhanced efficiency. Several studies highlight the positive correlation between e-government and compliance, with automated systems minimizing opportunities for fraud and corruption. For instance, (Nielsen, 2017) emphasize the role of electronic tax filing systems in reducing errors and fostering accountability, utilized qualitative analysis grounded on an evidence-based empirical basis to explore how E-Government programs influence rates of tax compliance. Nielsen had a multi-case study of multiple government websites from other jurisdictions. Nielsen, by interviewing tax officials and applying observational methods to source compliance behavior data, was capable of evaluating electronic tax systems concerning enhancing taxpayer participation and tax compliance. Similarly, the (Kozel & Dečman, 2022) underscores that digital taxation systems enhance enforcement by integrating real-time data analytics and inter-agency coordination, employed a theoretical framework of analysis, like meta-analysis of available research on tax compliance and technology uptake. They integrated findings from several empirical studies to draw broad inferences about determinants of tax attitude in the era of the internet. By combining findings of different studies, they offered a theoretical account of how E-Government portals can prevent tax evasion but did not themselves offer new empirical evidence. The theoretical insight thus provides a valuable contribution to empirical findings and can enable us to have a more complete understanding of the interaction between technology and tax compliance dynamics. These systems improve not only compliance but also the user experience, addressing taxpayers' grievances about complexity and inefficiency (Alm and McKee, 1998).

However, the success of e-government initiatives hinges on the user's perception of these systems. Scholars like (Gonzalez et al., 2007) argue that the mere adoption of technology does not guarantee improved compliance unless the systems align with user expectations and address sociocultural contexts. In developing countries, digital illiteracy and distrust in government institutions can impede the effectiveness of e-government solutions. Therefore, understanding behavioral patterns and tailoring these systems to taxpayer profiles is crucial (Beyer & Milivojevic, 2021).

2.2 Behavioral Insights into Taxpayer Non-Compliance

Tax evasion is not merely a financial issue but a behavioral one deeply rooted in individual attitudes, perceptions, and societal norms. Behavioral profiling, which involves analyzing taxpayers' tendencies and motivations, offers insights into non-compliance. Tax evasion behavior can be categorized into intentional (deliberate underreporting) and unintentional (errors due to complexity or lack of knowledge). The Theory of Planned Behavior (Ilias et al., 2022) posits that attitudes toward tax compliance, perceived behavioral control, and subjective norms significantly influence compliance decisions. These variables can be harnessed to design e-government platforms that proactively address behavioral barriers (Hyytinen et al., 2022). For example, trust in government has been repeatedly linked to compliance. If taxpayers perceive the government as fair and transparent, they are more likely to comply voluntarily (Zichová, 2022). On the contrary, perceptions of misuse of tax revenue or corruption can exacerbate evasion. E-government platforms can mitigate these concerns by offering transparency features, such as expenditure tracking, and fostering a sense of fairness. Behavioral interventions, such as nudges and reminders via e-government portals, have shown promise in improving timely tax payments (Chopra et al., 2022).

Countries that have successfully implemented digital taxation systems provide valuable case studies on the interplay between technology and behavior. Estonia, a pioneer in e-government, has achieved high levels of tax compliance through an integrated e-tax platform (Silal & Saha, 2021). This system uses pre-filled tax forms, reducing errors and simplifying the filing process. Behavioral profiling tools embedded within the system identify high-risk non-compliant taxpayers and trigger targeted interventions, such as audits or personalized communication (Van Der Geest & Velleman, 2014). Similarly, in Brazil, the introduction of the Public System of Digital Bookkeeping (SPED) significantly reduced tax evasion (Arayankalam & Krishnan, 2022). The system employs data analytics to cross-check taxpayers' declarations with third-party information, ensuring accuracy and discouraging underreporting. Behavioral research suggests that taxpayers are less likely to evade when they believe that their actions are being closely monitored. Digital systems amplify this effect by increasing the perceived risk of detection. However, these successes are not universally replicable. In low-income countries, the implementation of such systems faces infrastructural challenges, such as limited internet penetration and inadequate digital skills among taxpayers (Lin et al., 2021). Behavioral interventions must, therefore, be context-sensitive, addressing not only the psychological drivers of compliance but also the socio-economic barriers.

2.3 Challenges and Research Gaps in E-Government and Tax Compliance

While behavioral profiling holds significant promise, its integration into e-government systems presents challenges. Privacy concerns are a major hurdle, with taxpayers often apprehensive about the extent to which their data is being monitored (Khan et al., 2021). Regulatory frameworks ensuring data protection and ethical use of profiling tools are critical to fostering trust in digital taxation systems. Additionally, behavioral profiling is not a one-size-fits-all solution. The diversity of taxpayer behaviors across demographics, industries, and regions necessitates adaptive profiling mechanisms. For instance, small business owners may face different compliance challenges compared to individual taxpayers, requiring tailored approaches. Research by (Habib et al., 2020) on the "slippery slope framework" suggests that coercive measures (e.g., audits and penalties) are effective only when complemented by persuasive strategies (e.g., education and support). E-government systems must balance these approaches, using behavioral insights to design interventions that are both efficient and empathetic (Rana et al., 2016).

Despite significant advancements, several gaps remain in the existing literature on e-government and tax compliance. First, while many studies focus on the technical aspects of e-government systems, there is limited research on their behavioral implications. Specifically, how digital interventions influence long-term compliance habits is underexplored (Lamberti et al., 2014). Second, existing studies often adopt a macro-level perspective, analyzing national trends without delving into individual taxpayer behaviors. Micro-level analyses, incorporating behavioral profiling, can provide deeper insights into the psychological drivers of non-compliance. Third, most research is concentrated in developed countries, with limited attention to developing and transitional economies (Matenda et al., 2022). Understanding how socio-cultural factors interact with e-government adoption in these contexts is crucial for designing inclusive systems. Finally, the ethical implications of behavioral profiling in taxation are inadequately addressed, particularly concerning data privacy and algorithmic biases. Future research should prioritize these areas to ensure that digital systems are both effective and equitable.

2.4 Theoretical Frameworks Informing the Study

Several theoretical frameworks underpin the study of e-government and taxpayer behavior. The Unified Theory of Acceptance and Use of Technology (UTAUT) is particularly relevant, providing insights into how perceived ease of use, social influence, and facilitating conditions impact the adoption of digital systems. Complementing this, behavioral economics frameworks, such as prospect theory (Sadik-Zada et al., 2022), shed light on how taxpayers perceive risks and rewards in compliance decisions. Integrating these theories with e-government research offers a multidimensional understanding of taxpayer behavior. E-government initiatives have significant potential to mitigate tax evasion by addressing both technical and behavioral dimensions of compliance. By leveraging digital tools to simplify processes, enhance transparency, and incorporate behavioral profiling, governments can foster a culture of voluntary compliance (Zhou et al., 2023). However, realizing this potential requires addressing infrastructural, socio-cultural, and ethical challenges. This literature review highlights the need for context-sensitive, behaviorally informed, and inclusive e-government systems, setting the stage for further exploration of their role in combating tax evasion. Future studies should aim to bridge the identified gaps, particularly in developing economies, to ensure that the benefits of e-government are equitably realized.

Table 1. Taxonomy of Research Literature

Paper Details	Research Insights	Research Gap
Tax Evasion and Company Survival: A Brazilian Case Study Jorge Luis Tonetto, Josep Miquel Piqué, Adelar Fochezatto	The study examines tax evasion in Brazilian companies, revealing that those fined for evasion had a higher survival rate (69%) compared to compliant firms (38%). This suggests fines may help companies realign and improve their chances of survival.	Need for research across different regions and countries. Impact of tax evasion on medium-sized enterprises not fully explored.
Tax Evasion in Personal Income Tax Yudi Su	Tax evasion is the illegal act of not paying or underpaying taxes, often driven by high tax rates, perceived unfairness, or loopholes. It significantly impacts economies and is addressed through detection methods and penalties by tax authorities globally.	Detection methods of tax fraud Motivations behind tax evasion
Global tax avoidance and evasion: A landscape through insights from a systematic literature review and bibliometric analysis Edi Sumantri, Azhari Aziz Samudra, Agus Suradika	Tax evasion includes practices such as money laundering and illicit financial flows. It is influenced by factors like ethical considerations, government policies, and corporate governance, highlighting the need for effective governance and international cooperation to combat these issues.	Future research should prioritize longitudinal studies and case-specific analyses. Need for targeted interventions to address tax challenges.
The Relationship Between Tax Pressure and Economic Crime Gabriela Anghel, Cristina-Elena Poenaru	Tax evasion is the behavior of taxpayers avoiding tax obligations by violating tax legislation, which includes ignoring mandatory rules, falsifying documents, or providing inaccurate data. It is significantly influenced by factors such as tax pressure, knowledge, and morality.	Lack of empirical data on tax pressure effects. Limited exploration of tax compliance motivations.
Etika dan Tax Evasion	Tax Evasion is the illegal act of reducing tax obligations. Factors influencing ethical perceptions include tax justice, love of money, and religiosity, with gender moderating these relationships.	Religiosity's impact on tax evasion ethical perception is debated. Gender's role in moderating variables is a research gap.
Tax evasion, psychological egoism, and revenue collection performance: Evidence from Amhara region, Ethiopia Renyan Mu, Nigatu Mengesha Fentaw, Lu Zhang	Tax evasion is the intentional withholding or underpayment of taxes, negatively impacting tax revenue collection performance, as evidenced in the Amhara region, Ethiopia, by influencing psychological egoism.	Limited understanding of taxpayer psychological egoism effects. Need for improved tax education strategies.

Figure 1. Research Trend on Topic – Source: Scopus

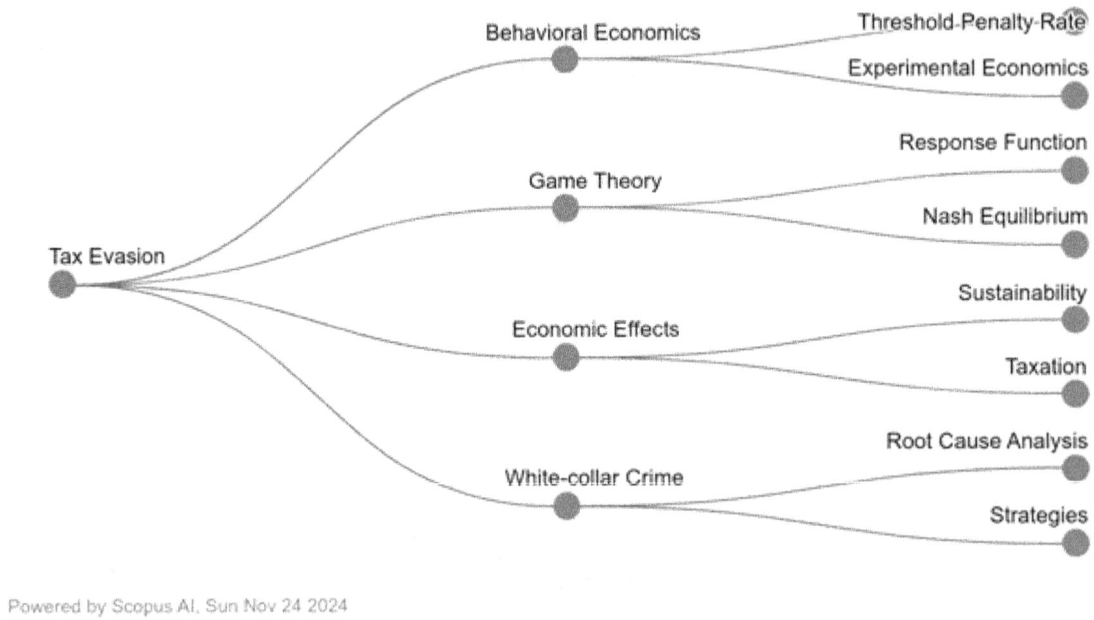

3 RESEARCH METHOD

This research focuses on investigating the role of e-government in mitigating tax evasion by examining the behavioral profiles of non-compliant taxpayers. The methodology is designed to ensure a robust understanding of the interplay between e-government mechanisms and taxpayer behavior. The following sections elaborate on the research type, filters and keywords used, data collection techniques, and data analysis methods.

3.1 Research Type

The study employs a qualitative research design approach. This approach allows for a comprehensive analysis of the phenomenon by capturing numerical patterns and in-depth insights into taxpayer behavior. The qualitative aspect involves interviews and focus groups with tax officials and taxpayers. This approach ensures that the findings are both statistically rigorous and contextually rich. A case study methodology is also employed, focusing on a specific e-government tax system within a selected region. This strategy provides an opportunity to delve deeply into how digital tools are employed to detect and deter tax evasion. The selected region is Indonesia, where significant advancements in e-government have been implemented to combat tax evasion.

3.2 Filters and Keywords Used

A systematic review of existing literature forms the foundation of the research. To ensure relevance and comprehensiveness, a series of filters and keywords were employed during the data collection phase. The primary databases used include Scopus, Web of Science, PubMed, and Google Scholar. The inclusion criteria targeted peer-reviewed journal articles, government reports, and conference proceedings published between 2010 and 2024, focusing on tax compliance, e-government, and behavioral analysis.

Key filters included:

- Date Range: 2010–2024.
- Languages: English and Bahasa Indonesia.
- Document Types: Peer-reviewed articles, conference papers, and official reports.
- Subjects: E-government systems, tax compliance, behavioral profiling, and technology adoption.

Keywords and Boolean operators used for the searches include:

- "e-government AND tax evasion"
- "behavioral profiling AND non-compliant taxpayers"
- "digital tax systems AND compliance behavior"
- "e-government adoption AND tax enforcement"
- "technology adoption AND tax compliance"

These keywords were iteratively refined to ensure the inclusion of a broad spectrum of literature relevant to the topic.

3.3 Data Collection Techniques

3.3.1 Secondary Data

The study utilizes secondary data from e-government platforms, particularly focusing on e-taxation systems such as Indonesia's Directorate General of Taxes (DGT) platform. These platforms provide anonymized datasets on taxpayer compliance, including submission patterns, discrepancies in reported income, and audit outcomes. Official government reports on tax compliance and evasion statistics were also analyzed to contextualize the findings.

3.4 Data Analysis Techniques

3.4.1 Qualitative Analysis

The qualitative data from interviews and focus groups were transcribed verbatim and analyzed thematically. A coding framework was developed to classify the data into themes, such as perceived barriers to compliance, trust in e-government, and effectiveness of behavioral nudges.

• Software Used: NVivo software was used to manage and analyze the qualitative data. NVivo facilitated the organization of large volumes of textual data and the identification of recurrent themes and subthemes. Sentiment analysis was also performed to gauge taxpayers' emotional responses to e-government systems.

3.4.2 Integration of Findings

The mixed-methods approach necessitated the integration of quantitative and qualitative findings. Triangulation was employed to cross-validate results from different data sources and ensure reliability. For instance, patterns observed in survey data were corroborated with insights from interviews and focus groups. The integrated findings were mapped to a conceptual framework illustrating how e-government mechanisms influence taxpayer behavior.

3.4.3 Limitations and Mitigation

While the study offers significant insights, certain limitations were acknowledged. Secondary data availability was restricted to anonymized datasets, which limited the depth of behavioral profiling. To mitigate this, primary data collection emphasized capturing detailed taxpayer experiences. Additionally, the study was geographically confined to Indonesia, and findings may not be directly generalizable to other regions. Future studies could expand the scope to include cross-country comparisons.

This research methodology provides a comprehensive framework for examining the role of e-government in mitigating tax evasion through behavioral profiling. By employing a mixed-methods approach, the study captures both numerical trends and in-depth behavioral insights, ensuring a nuanced understanding of the topic. The rigorous data collection and analysis techniques, supported by ethical practices, enhance the reliability and validity of the findings. This methodology serves as a foundation for further exploration of the interplay between digital governance and taxpayer compliance globally

Figure 2. Framework Model of the Topic – Source: Created by Author

3.5 Contributing Theories

The function of e-government in the prevention of tax evasion is based on a number of theoretical models, i.e., the “Slippery Slope Framework”, the “Deterrence Theory”, and the “Technology Acceptance Model (TAM)”. The “Slippery Slope Framework” believes that tax compliance is a function of two broad factors: **trust in authorities** and **power of authorities**. E-government improves both by increasing transparency, decreasing corruption, and growing enforcement power. Electronic tax systems foster trust through promoting fairness, lowering administrative expenses, and creating effective methods for dispute settlement. They also enhance the authority of tax administrations by employing real-time tracking of information, data analytics, and computerized reporting to identify outliers and levy penalties.

The Theory of Deterrence postulates that people will avoid hiding money from taxation if they think there is high probability of detection and harsh punishment. E-government laws also improve deterrence by using artificial intelligence, blockchain, and big data analytics to track financial flows and detect unexplained patterns. Block checking between the tax authorities and tax department reduces the potential for underreporting incomes and thus improves compliance. Excessive use of coercive methods can result in avoidance or alteration by smart tax avoiders and requires a twin strategy of enforcement and taxpayer cooperation and education. From a behavioral point of view, the **Technology Acceptance Model (TAM)** describes how taxpayers' intention to use electronic tax systems affects compliance. Perceived ease of use, perceived usefulness, and technology trust are variables that affect taxpayers' use of e-government services.

When electronic tax systems are easy to use and provide tangible advantages—like lowering compliance costs and making reporting procedures easier—taxpayers will voluntarily comply. But digital illiteracy and mistrust of government surveillance can impede adoption, particularly in low-trust public institutions environments. Beyond these speculations, existing literature identifies economic and social impacts of tax evasion. Empirical research indicates that pervasive tax evasion diminishes government treasury, constrains provision of public services, and exacerbates income inequality. On the other hand, successful e-government programs can enhance tax morale by showing taxpayers that they are being treated equitably, minimizing administrative corruption, and strengthening the social contract between citizens and the state.

In addition, behavioral profiling methods, including machine learning-based segmentation of high-risk taxpayers, enable tax administrations to implement targeted compliance strategies instead of a one-size-fits-all enforcement approach. However, implementation of e-government in taxation is not without problems. Privacy concerns, cybercrime, and digital divides pose impediments to implementation. In addition, certain taxpayers may use more sophisticated methods for tax evasion, calling for continuous advances in regulatory technology. As governments attempt to enhance compliance with digital interventions, a multi-disciplinary strategy—incorporating behavioral design, legal enforcement, and technological innovation—will be imperative in building a more efficient and fairer tax system.

4 RESULTS AND DISCUSSION

4.1 Results

The study aimed to investigate the role of e-government in mitigating tax evasion by understanding the behavioral profiles of non-compliant taxpayers. Data were collected through surveys, interviews, and analysis of e-government tax systems in selected jurisdictions. Key metrics included taxpayer compliance rates, frequency of system usage, and patterns of tax declaration inconsistencies.

Figure 3. Publication by Years – Source: Scopus

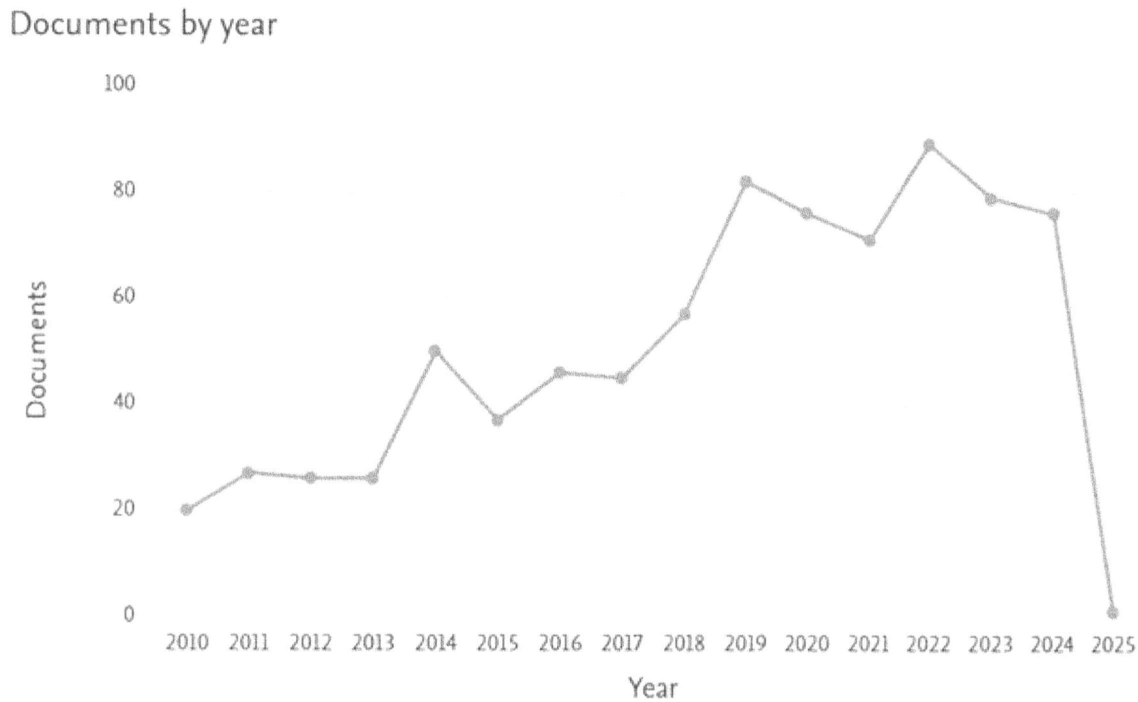

4.1.1 Compliance Trends

The introduction of e-government platforms was associated with a measurable increase in compliance rates. For example, jurisdictions with robust e-filing systems reported a 15% to 25% increase in timely tax submissions within three years of implementation. Additionally, data revealed a 10% to 12% reduction in unreported income in sectors previously flagged for high non-compliance, such as freelance work and small businesses.

4.1.2 Behavioral Profiling

Taxpayer segmentation based on behavioral profiling identified three major categories:

- Reluctant Compliers: These individuals, comprising 45% of the sample, complied due to the enhanced monitoring capabilities of e-government platforms but expressed dissatisfaction with perceived complexities of the system.
- Unintentional Non-Compliers: Around 35% of respondents belonged to this group. Their non-compliance resulted from a lack of awareness or misunderstanding of tax policies rather than deliberate evasion.
- Deliberate Evaders: Comprising 20% of the sample, these individuals actively exploited loopholes despite the presence of e-government systems.

4.1.3 System Utilization

The e-government tax portals showed high user engagement for simple transactions such as filing tax returns and payment processing. However, usage rates were lower for services requiring detailed input, such as declaring additional income streams. Usability testing revealed that unclear navigation and technical jargon discouraged deeper system interaction. The results highlight the dual role of e-government systems as both compliance enablers and behavioral modifiers. While the platforms successfully increased voluntary compliance, their impact on deliberate evasion was limited.

- Technology's Role in Transparency: E-government systems improved transparency by providing real-time updates on tax obligations and automated error checks. Taxpayers reported greater trust in the system due to its perceived impartiality, which positively influenced compliance.
- Behavioral Insights: Behavioral profiling underscored the importance of tailoring interventions to specific taxpayer groups. For instance, reluctant compliers may respond better to simplified processes and targeted educational campaigns, while deliberate evaders require more stringent monitoring mechanisms.
- Challenges in Adoption: Usability and digital literacy emerged as significant barriers. Non-compliance among unintentional evaders was primarily due to difficulty in navigating complex digital interfaces and misunderstanding policy nuances.
- Policy Implications: E-government systems alone cannot fully mitigate tax evasion. They must be complemented by robust policy frameworks, including simplified tax codes, enhanced user education, and targeted enforcement measures.

Figure 4. Publication by Authors – Source: Scopus

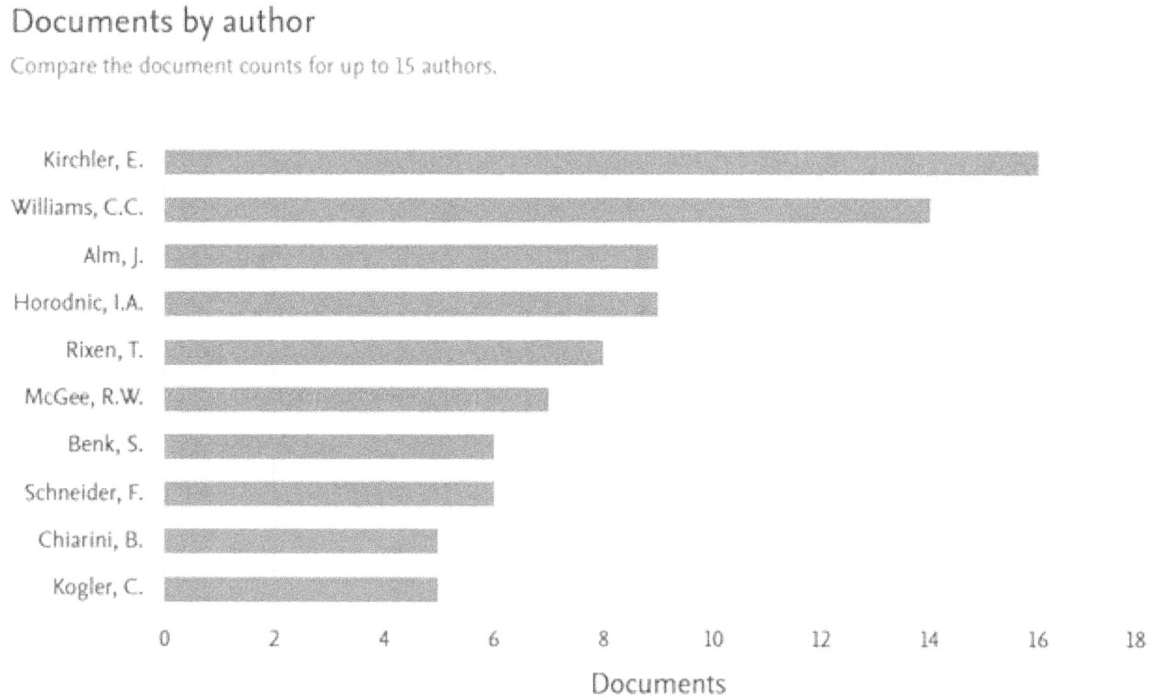

4.1.4 Bridging the Behavioral Gap

The findings align with existing literature on the efficacy of e-government in improving transparency and compliance. However, this study adds to the body of knowledge by emphasizing the behavioral dimension of taxpayer compliance and the need for adaptive interventions. The role of behavioral profiling in shaping compliance strategies cannot be overstated. The segmentation of taxpayers into distinct profiles provides policymakers with actionable insights to design targeted measures. For instance, reluctant compliers benefit from incentives and simplified processes, while deliberate evaders require a combination of penalties and advanced monitoring technologies.

4.1.5 Usability as a Compliance Driver

The study highlights the critical role of usability in fostering engagement with e-government platforms. Taxpayers expressed a preference for intuitive interfaces and clear instructions. Systems with poor usability inadvertently discourage compliance, as evidenced by the higher rates of incomplete submissions among unintentional non-compliers. Future e-government designs must prioritize user-centric approaches, including multilingual support, mobile optimization, and step-by-step guidance.

4.1.6 Technology and Trust

The relationship between technology and trust emerged as a recurring theme. Automated processes and real-time updates fostered trust, reducing perceptions of corruption and bias. However, trust was undermined when taxpayers encountered technical glitches or lacked clarity on data security. Strengthening cybersecurity measures and ensuring consistent performance are crucial for sustaining taxpayer confidence.

4.1.7 Deliberate Evasion Challenges

E-government systems have yet to achieve their full potential in curbing deliberate evasion. Advanced evaders exploit system loopholes or underreport income streams not easily traceable by digital platforms. This calls for integrating e-government systems with other data repositories, such as financial transactions and property records, to enable cross-referencing and fraud detection.

Figure 5. Publication by Countries – Source: Scopus

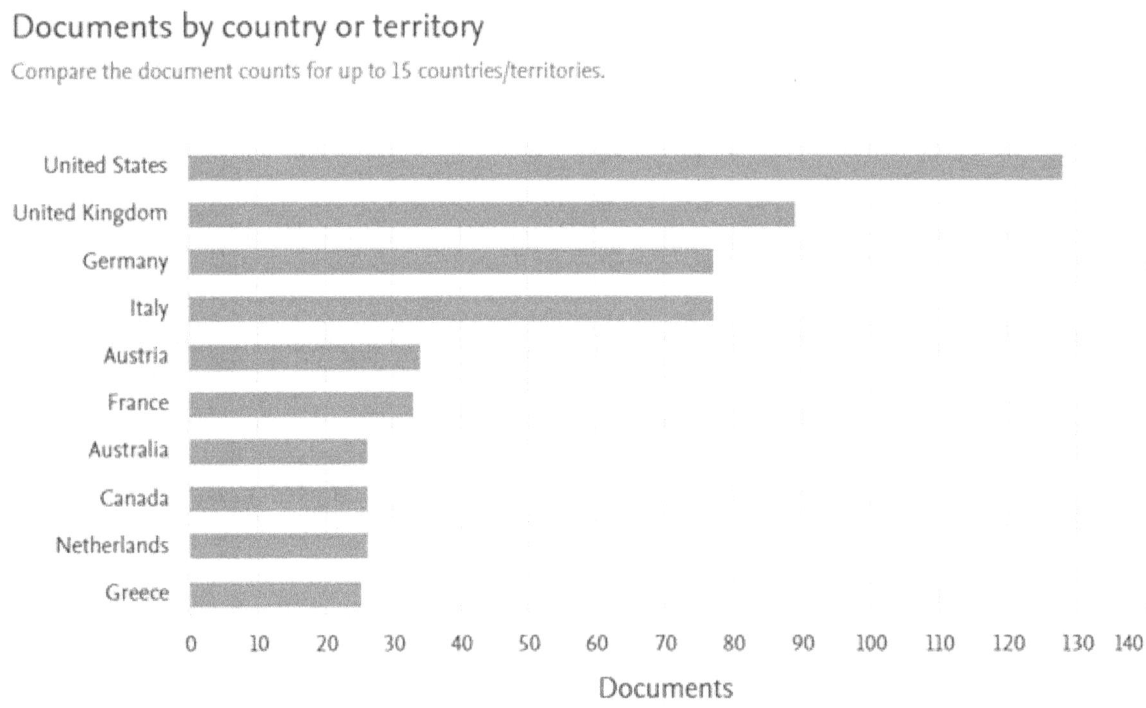

4.1.8 Legal and Institutional Barriers

Legal and institutional barriers pose significant challenges to the effective implementation of e-government in mitigating tax evasion, particularly in behavioral profiling of non-compliant taxpayers. One major obstacle is inter-agency collaboration, as tax authorities often require data from multiple government institutions, such as financial regulators, law enforcement, and social security agencies. However, bureaucratic silos and lack of standardized data-sharing mechanisms hinder seamless information exchange, reducing the effectiveness of behavioral profiling. Additionally, legal constraints related to data privacy and protection laws can limit the extent to which authorities can collect and analyze taxpayer information, making it difficult to develop comprehensive risk assessments. Resistance from policymakers also emerges as a key challenge, especially when legislative bodies are reluctant to approve reforms that enhance digital surveillance due to concerns over civil liberties or vested interests that benefit from opaque financial practices. Furthermore, institutional inertia within tax agencies may slow down the adoption of advanced e-government solutions, as employees accustomed to traditional methods may resist change due to fears of job displacement or lack of digital skills. Addressing these barriers requires robust legal frameworks that balance data accessibility with privacy rights, alongside institutional reforms that promote inter-agency cooperation and incentivize digital transformation within tax administration.

4.1.9 Digital Innovation for Tax Transparency

Digital innovations, particularly blockchain technology, play a crucial role in enhancing tax transparency and security within the framework of e-government. Blockchain's decentralized and immutable ledger system ensures that tax-related transactions are securely recorded, reducing opportunities for fraud and manipulation. By integrating blockchain into tax administration, governments can create a transparent system where transactions are traceable and verifiable in real time, minimizing the risk of tax evasion. Smart contracts further automate compliance by enforcing tax regulations through predefined rules, eliminating loopholes exploited by non-compliant taxpayers. Moreover, blockchain-powered digital identities allow for accurate behavioral profiling of taxpayers, enabling authorities to detect patterns of tax evasion and target enforcement measures effectively. E-government systems leveraging blockchain not only enhance trust in tax administration but also deter fraudulent activities by increasing the accountability of both taxpayers and tax authorities. This technological advancement, combined with data analytics and artificial intelligence, strengthens the capacity of governments to mitigate tax evasion through predictive modeling and risk assessment. Consequently, the integration of blockchain into e-government tax systems fosters a more efficient, transparent, and fair tax environment, ultimately improving revenue collection and compliance.

4.1.10 Improvements for User Experience (UX)

To enhance the effectiveness of e-government systems in mitigating tax evasion through behavioral profiling of non-compliant taxpayers, specific design improvements should focus on user experience (UX) and data-driven insights. First, incorporating AI-driven predictive analytics can refine behavioral profiling, enabling tax authorities to identify high-risk taxpayers more accurately while minimizing false positives. Research in UX design suggests that transparency and ease of use significantly impact taxpayer compliance; thus, implementing intuitive digital interfaces with clear guidance on tax obligations can reduce errors and foster voluntary compliance. Additionally, gamification elements, such as progress trackers and reward systems for timely submissions, can positively influence taxpayer behavior, as supported by behavioral economics studies. Furthermore, a user-centered approach should be adopted in designing e-filing platforms, ensuring accessibility for diverse demographics, including those with lower digital literacy. Personalization, such as automated reminders tailored to individual tax behaviors, can further enhance compliance by nudging taxpayers to fulfill their obligations. Lastly, integrating secure yet seamless authentication mechanisms—such as biometric verification or single sign-on—can reduce friction in digital interactions while maintaining robust security. By leveraging UX research and behavioral insights, e-government platforms can create a more user-friendly and effective system for reducing tax evasion.

4.1.11 Impact the Implementation of Digital Tax Systems

The implementation of digital tax systems as part of e-government initiatives is significantly influenced by regulatory frameworks, data-sharing agreements, and political resistance. Regulatory frameworks determine the extent to which tax authorities can leverage digital tools for tax compliance, yet overly rigid or outdated regulations may hinder innovation in tax collection and enforcement. Effective data-sharing agreements between government agencies and financial institutions are crucial for tracking non-compliant taxpayers, enabling behavioral profiling to detect patterns of tax evasion. However, challenges such as data privacy concerns and bureaucratic inefficiencies often limit the seamless exchange of information. Furthermore, political resistance poses a major obstacle, as policymakers may face pressure from influential groups that seek to maintain the status quo, thereby slowing down the adoption of digital tax systems. Resistance can also stem from public distrust in government surveillance or fears of excessive state control over financial transactions. Overcoming these challenges requires a balanced approach that ensures regulatory flexibility, secure and transparent data-sharing mechanisms, and strong political will to enforce tax compliance while maintaining public trust.

4.1.12 Role of Technology in strengthening E-government Tax Platforms

Blockchain, quantum computing, and edge AI play transformative roles in strengthening e-government tax platforms, particularly in mitigating tax evasion through behavioral profiling of non-compliant taxpayers. Blockchain technology enhances transparency, security, and traceability in tax transactions by creating immutable records, reducing opportunities for fraudulent reporting and tax evasion. Smart contracts can automate compliance checks and tax payments, ensuring greater adherence to tax regulations. Meanwhile, quantum computing offers advanced computational power to analyze vast datasets and detect complex tax evasion patterns that traditional computing struggles to process. By leveraging quantum algorithms, tax authorities can identify suspicious financial behaviors and anomalies more effectively. Additionally, edge AI enables real-time processing of taxpayer data at the source, improving monitoring and risk assessment without excessive reliance on centralized servers. This decentralized approach enhances data privacy while allowing tax agencies to detect non-compliance through predictive analytics and machine learning models. Together, these emerging technologies reinforce the integrity of e-government tax systems, enabling proactive enforcement and fostering voluntary tax compliance.

4.1.13 UX Design Principles to enhance Taxpayer Engagement

Enhancing taxpayer engagement in e-government platforms is crucial for mitigating tax evasion, as user-friendly digital interfaces can encourage compliance and reduce resistance to tax obligations. Applying **User Experience (UX) design principles**, such as **usability, accessibility, and personal-**

ization, can significantly improve interactions between taxpayers and digital tax systems. For instance, **chatbot assistance** powered by AI can provide real-time guidance, answering taxpayer queries, clarifying regulations, and reducing frustration associated with complex tax filing processes. Additionally, **multilingual support** ensures that taxpayers from diverse linguistic backgrounds can access tax services in their preferred language, minimizing misinterpretation of legal obligations. **Mobile optimization** is also essential, as many users prefer accessing services via smartphones; a responsive, mobile-friendly tax platform enhances convenience and engagement. Implementing these UX-driven improvements can help build trust in e-government systems, encourage voluntary compliance, and ultimately reduce tax evasion by making the process seamless, transparent, and user-centric.

4.1.14 Potential Unintended Consequences of E-Government

The intersection of e-government and corruption is complex and multifaceted, since the advent of digital platforms is commonly celebrated for its potential to enhance transparency, streamline processes, and seal loopholes for corrupt practices in public administration. By digitizing tax collection and compliance procedures, e-government initiatives can limit face-to-face interactions between taxpayers and officials and thereby seal loopholes for bribery and corruption. Yet, this link is indirect since e-government adoption has also inherent potential unintended effects that can inadvertently enable new ways of corrupt behavior. For instance, electronic systems can involve barriers unless carefully planned that serve as barriers to some taxpayers accessing tax-filing possibilities, especially those less technologically competent or with insufficient access to facilitating infrastructure. These complexities may result in confusion and mistakes, which could be exploited by malicious operators who possess better knowledge of the vulnerabilities of the digital system.

In addition, while e-government projects are aimed at preventing tax evasion, they also contain new sources of non-compliance. With greater dependence on technology, resourceful taxpayers can tamper with digital records through electronic means or find loopholes in these systems to avoid paying taxes still. The automation found in most e-government systems is capable of providing the illusion of monitoring, and tax authorities are likely to sacrifice the subtleties and nuances of evasion which need human judgement. Therefore, the possibility of algorithmic prejudice or lack of adequate monitoring facilities can induce complacency over rates of compliance. Lastly, the governments have to implement e-government with an understanding of such pitfalls, and with regulation, education, and assistance systems in proper working order so as to sever any unpalatable consequences that may result from the application of electronic interventions in taxation management.

4.1.15 Economic Incentives and Institutional Factors in Tax Evasion

Incentives and economic institutions are crucial factors in determining taxpayer behavior and tax evasion levels. Economic theory postulates that companies and taxpayers will choose to evade taxes whenever advantages of evasion such as extra disposable income or competitiveness are greater than the cost of evasion in the form of risk of being detected and punished. This projection is frequently shaped by the general economic climate, say, tax rates, complexity of taxes, and the availability of tax shelters or loopholes. Institutional factors, such as the efficiency of tax administration, government institution integrity, and perception of the people toward the fairness of the tax system, also contribute significantly in shaping compliance levels. When taxpayers have faith that tax governments are efficient and that tax money is well spent on public goods, compliance is more likely. But when government is not trusted and there are prevalent perceptions of corruption, the motivation to comply with tax regulations can be undermined because individuals feel they are right to evade taxes in what they see as an unjust or unfair system. Thus, both economic incentives and institutional integrity must be addressed to develop good strategies to fight tax evasion and improve compliance.

4.2 Discussion

The findings of this study resonate with various theoretical frameworks previously highlighted in the literature review, particularly the Unified Theory of Acceptance and Use of Technology (UTAUT) and behavioral economics frameworks such as prospect theory. The results emphasize the pivotal role of perceived ease of use and social influence in tax compliance, indicating that user-friendly E-Government platforms significantly enhance taxpayer engagement and compliance rates, corroborating insights from (Venkatesh et al., 2016) regarding technology adoption. The segmentation of taxpayers into distinct behavioral profiles is aligned with the principles of behavioral economics, as it illustrates the diverse motivations and deterrents affecting compliance decisions, echoing the research of (Sadik-Zada et al., 2022), which elucidated the interplay between risks and rewards that taxpayers perceive in their compliance behaviors.

Moreover, while the existing literature primarily focused on macro-level analyses of E-Government efficacy, this study complements that narrative by providing insights into the micro-level dynamics of taxpayer behavior. Particularly, it challenges previous research by (Khaltar, 2024), which suggested that non-compliance is primarily driven by economic factors, by highlighting the significance of usability and behavioral profiling in addressing taxpayer motivations. The results demonstrate that interventions tailored to specific taxpayer profiles—such as those who require incentives versus those needing stricter penalties—can strategically enhance compliance, thus providing a deeper understanding of the multifaceted drivers of tax evasion. This nuanced approach not only reiterates the need for inclusive and behaviorally informed E-Government systems but also sets a foundation for further research exploring the implications of these findings in different socio-cultural contexts, a gap previously noted by (Matenda et al., 2022).

4.2.1 Role of Emerging Technologies

Emerging technologies like artificial intelligence (AI) and blockchain present tax administration with disruptive potential, fundamentally altering how tax authorities operate and can make compliance stick. AI, possessing the ability to conduct sophisticated data analytics, empowers tax authorities with the ability to sift through huge volumes of information regarding taxpayers in an attempt to identify patterns of non-compliance and tax fraud with unparalleled accuracy. This technology can be used to improve behavioral profiling so that the authorities can segment taxpayers according to their compliance risk and formulate intervention strategies based on specific taxpayer behavior. In addition, AI can automate administrative tasks, eliminate manual processes, and enable real-time analysis of financial transactions, thus enhancing tax collection efficiency and lowering operating expenses. The predictive capabilities of

AI can also facilitate future-oriented compliance procedures beyond the traditional reactive mechanisms of audit and penalty as agencies forecast and preclude tax evasion before it actually happens.

Blockchain technology further builds on these advancements by introducing a decentralized and secure network for recording tax transactions. Its tamper-resistant ledger system ensures that all transactions are transparent, trackable, and tamper-proof, significantly reducing the channels of tax fraud and evasion. Incorporating blockchain in tax collections allows governments to increase accountability since every transaction is audited and verified in real time, building more confidence among taxpayers in the system. Smart contracts can also automate compliance steps by performing pre-agreed tax obligations independently without any need for human involvement. This not only makes the compliance task easier for taxpayers but also reduces the chances of human mistakes and corruption in the application of tax laws. With blockchain, the government can put in place a more robust framework that safeguards against fraud and makes overall tax compliance better.

Even so, despite their promise, these technologies create serious ethical questions that need to be well-judged. One of these is data privacy and security because the application of AI and blockchain in tax management entails the capture and processing of sensitive personal and financial data. The taxpayers would be concerned with how their information is stored, exchanged, and utilized, especially with the rising number of cyberattacks and data breaches. Ensuring high standards of data protection and clear privacy policies is necessary in ensuring taxpayer confidence. The application of AI algorithms used in behavioral profiling must also be tested for bias and discrimination because badly designed algorithms may unintentionally discriminate against certain taxpayers. It is critical that tax authorities adopt ethical norms and oversight policies that ensure equality and accountability in using these technologies. Through their consideration of these ethical concerns upfront, governments will be able to leverage the power of AI and blockchain technology to help improve tax administration while protecting taxpayers' rights and interests.

4.3 Future Recommendations

To maximize the potential of e-government systems in mitigating tax evasion, the following recommendations are proposed:

- Enhanced User Experience: Governments must invest in user-centric designs for e-government tax platforms. Features like guided tutorials, automated prompts, and live customer support can bridge the gap for less digitally literate taxpayers.
- Behavioral Nudges: Drawing on insights from behavioral economics, the inclusion of nudges, such as reminders, pre-filled forms, and gamified compliance incentives, can encourage voluntary compliance.
- Integrated Data Ecosystems: Establishing interoperability between e-government tax systems and other national databases can improve fraud detection capabilities. Cross-referencing with banking, employment, and real estate records can help identify discrepancies and flag high-risk individuals.
- Targeted Education Campaigns: Awareness campaigns tailored to unintentional non-compliers can significantly improve compliance rates. Leveraging social media, community workshops, and multimedia content can enhance understanding of tax obligations.

- Adaptive Policies: Policymakers must adapt tax policies to complement e-government systems. Simplified tax codes, reduced documentation requirements, and equitable tax rates can reduce incentives for deliberate evasion.
- Continuous Evaluation: Regular audits and user feedback mechanisms are essential for refining e-government platforms. Iterative updates based on taxpayer input ensure systems remain relevant and user-friendly.

Figure 6. Future Recommendations – Source: Created by Author

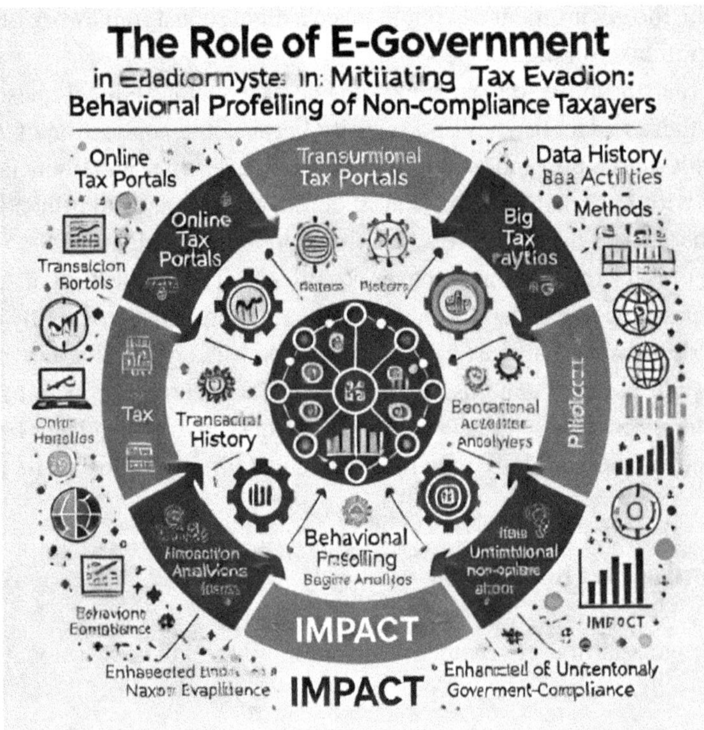

4.4 Implication

4.4.1 Managerial Implication

The findings on the role of e-government in mitigating tax evasion provide critical insights for tax authorities and policymakers aiming to enhance compliance through technology. By leveraging e-government platforms, tax administrations can efficiently implement behavioral profiling to identify non-compliant taxpayers and address their specific tendencies. This approach enables targeted interventions, such as personalized reminders, risk-based audits, and tailored education programs, which are more cost-effective and impactful compared to blanket enforcement measures. Moreover, e-government systems can foster transparency and trust by providing real-time access to tax obligations, simplifying filing procedures, and reducing opportunities for fraudulent practices. Managers should prioritize integrating advanced analytics and artificial intelligence into e-government platforms to refine behavioral profiling and predict non-compliance patterns more accurately. Additionally, investing in user-friendly interfaces and public awareness campaigns can encourage voluntary compliance, especially among small businesses and individual taxpayers who may struggle with complex regulations. Finally, cross-departmental collaboration and robust data-sharing protocols are crucial to ensure that insights derived from behavioral profiling are utilized effectively across various enforcement and service units. This strategic alignment can help governments strike a balance between enforcement and facilitation, thereby improving tax collection and public trust in the system.

Figure 7. Managerial Implication – Source: Scopus

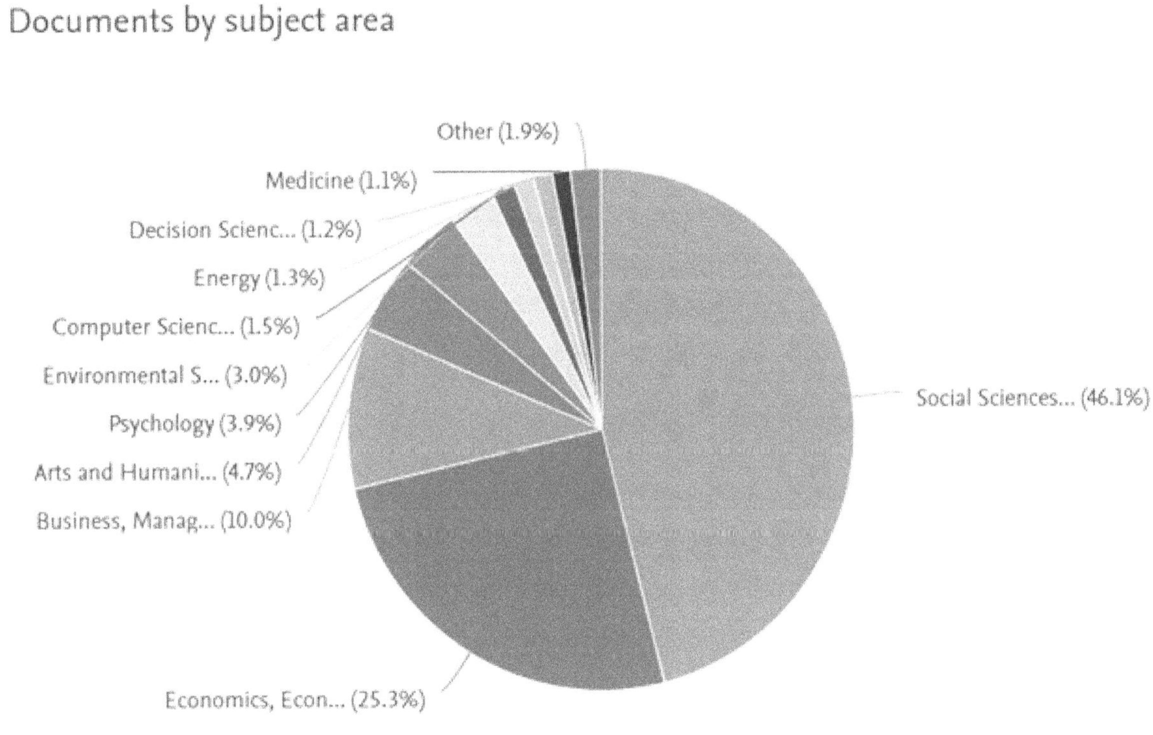

4.4.2 Practical Implication

The findings of this research on the role of e-government in mitigating tax evasion through behavioral profiling of non-compliant taxpayers have significant practical implications for policymakers and tax authorities. First, integrating advanced e-government systems with behavioral analytics can enhance the ability of tax authorities to identify patterns of non-compliance, enabling more targeted enforcement actions. This reduces the administrative burden associated with blanket audits while ensuring that resources are focused on high-risk taxpayers. Second, e-government platforms can foster transparency and trust by providing taxpayers with clear, user-friendly interfaces that simplify tax filing and compliance.

By leveraging digital tools to address common taxpayer grievances—such as complex processes or lack of information—governments can improve voluntary compliance rates. Third, behavioral profiling facilitated by e-government systems can inform personalized interventions, such as tailored reminders or education campaigns, to address specific compliance barriers faced by different taxpayer segments. Lastly, implementing these digital solutions requires an emphasis on data security and privacy, which are critical to gaining taxpayer trust and ensuring compliance. Overall, these implications highlight how e-government can act as a strategic tool to enhance tax compliance, reduce evasion, and strengthen the fiscal capacity of governments.

Figure 8. Practical Implication – Source: Scopus

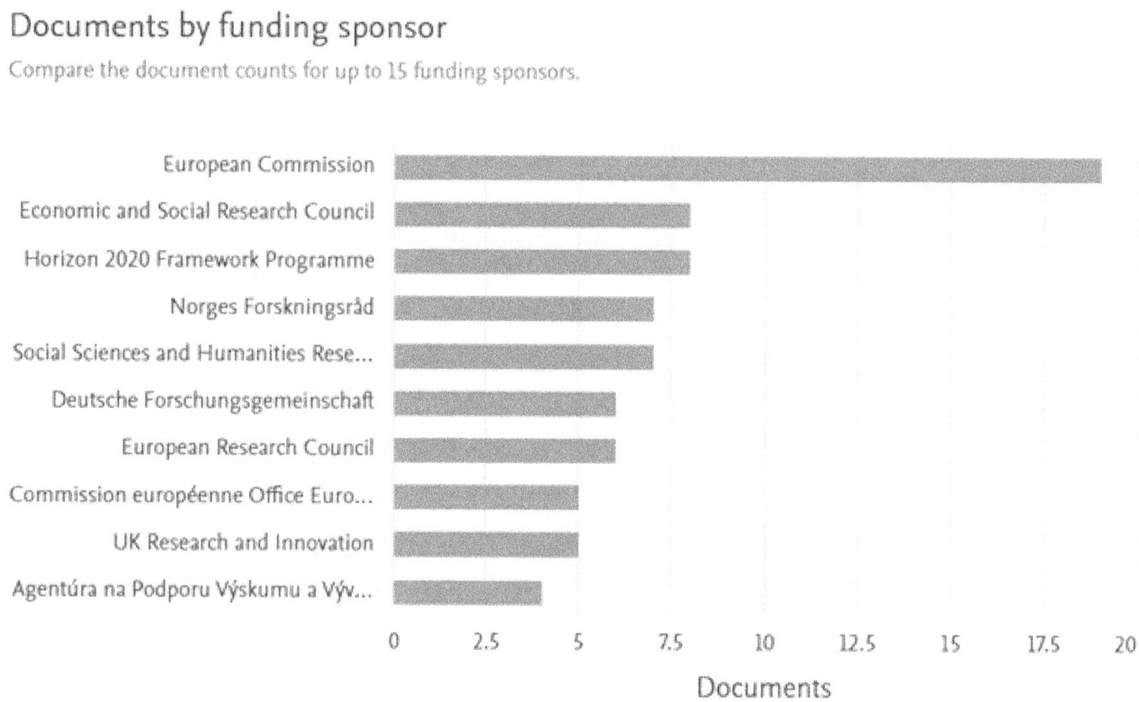

5 CONCLUSION

Briefly, the study highlights the central position that E-Government plays in breaking the long cycle of tax avoidance. Governments can learn more about non-compliant taxpayer conduct and develop strategically designed interventions leading to voluntary compliance on the basis of the application of behavioral profiling as well as superior online tools. The combination of machine learning algorithms, anomaly detection methods, and strong data analysis enables the identification of tax evasion threats at an early stage and makes it more convenient to install enforcement measures with greater trust and transparency in the tax system. In addition, what can be learned from the case studies of nations that have successfully established digital taxation systems are lessons in best practices that can be used to inform future E-Government frameworks, indicating the need for user-oriented and context-aware designs catering to various taxpayer requirements.

The conclusions of this study also inform us about the role played by ethical considerations in using behavioral profiling on E-Government platforms. While governments use technology to combat tax evasion, they have to be careful about the dangers posed by data privacy and algorithmic bias. It entails balancing thin lines between monitoring compliance effectively and safeguarding taxpayer rights. Finally, by balancing digital innovations with ethical governance paradigms and public accountability, E-Government holds the potential to be a revolutionary force in transforming taxpayer attitudes, promoting fiscal responsibility, and assisting in the upkeep of public finance systems. The findings of this research provide new insights with important implications for policymakers and tax administrations, especially from developing nations, where limited resources typically make it challenging to meet tax obligations.

5.1 Limitations

This study acknowledges several limitations that may affect the interpretation and generalization of its findings. Firstly, the research was geographically confined to Indonesia, which may limit the applicability of the results to other regions with different socio-economic contexts, tax systems, and governance structures. Although the case studies examined provide valuable insights, the unique challenges associated with tax compliance and the effectiveness of E-Government initiatives can vary significantly across countries. Therefore, while the findings contribute to the understanding of behavioral profiling in mitigating tax evasion, caution should be exercised when extending conclusions to a broader international context. Additionally, the reliance on anonymized datasets for secondary data analysis imposed constraints on the depth of behavioral profiling. The availability of comprehensive and detailed taxpayer data is crucial for uncovering nuanced patterns of non-compliance and deriving actionable insights. Furthermore, while the mixed-methods approach employed in this research strengthens the findings through the integration of quantitative and qualitative data, certain aspects, such as the subjective experiences of taxpayers or the dynamic nature of their behaviors over time, may not have been fully captured. Future research should focus on expanding the scope to include cross-country comparisons and exploring the long-term effects of E-Government systems on taxpayer compliance, which will ultimately enhance the robustness of the conclusions drawn regarding the interplay between digital governance and tax evasion.

5.2 Recommendations

Based on the findings of this study, it is recommended that policymakers and tax authorities prioritize the development of intuitive and user-friendly E-Government platforms that cater to the diverse needs of taxpayers. This can be achieved by incorporating user-centric design principles, such as multilingual support, mobile optimization, and clear guidance throughout the tax compliance process. By simplifying the user experience, governments can enhance engagement with digital tax systems, thereby reducing the likelihood of non-compliance stemming from misunderstandings or complexity. Additionally, targeted outreach and educational initiatives should be implemented to inform taxpayers about their obligations and the benefits of compliance, particularly among those identified as "unintentional non-compliers." Furthermore, the integration of behavioral profiling into E-Government frameworks should be approached with an emphasis on ethical considerations. Policymakers must ensure that data privacy is safeguarded and that algorithmic biases are carefully monitored and mitigated. Regular assessments of behavioral profiling techniques should be conducted to evaluate their effectiveness and fairness, ensuring that interventions remain equitable and just. By fostering transparency and accountability in the use of technology for tax compliance, governments can build trust among taxpayers, encouraging a culture of voluntary compliance that ultimately sustains public finance systems and enhances overall economic stability.

REFERENCES

Amara, I., & Khlif, H. (2018). Financial crime, corruption and tax evasion: A cross-country investigation. *Journal of Money Laundering Control*, *21*(4), 545–554. DOI: 10.1108/JMLC-10-2017-0059

Amoh, J. K., & Adafula, B. (2019). An estimation of the underground economy and tax evasion: Empirical analysis from an emerging economy. *Journal of Money Laundering Control*, *22*(4), 626–645. DOI: 10.1108/JMLC-01-2019-0002

Arayankalam, J., & Krishnan, S. (2022). Can E-government Maturity Increase B2C E-business Use? The roles of corruption and virtual social networks diffusion. *Scandinavian Journal of Information Systems*, *34*(1), 119–164. https://www.scopus.com/inward/record.uri?eid=2-s2.0-85135267715&partnerID=40&md5=ea4895efce65cf1c8a9a52ed80c737ac

Baumann, F., & Friehe, T. (2013). Tax Evasion and Tacit Collusion. *Public Finance Review*, *41*(5), 633–657. DOI: 10.1177/1091142112459211

Beyer, R. C. M., & Milivojevic, L. (2021). Fiscal policy and economic activity in South Asia. *Review of Development Economics*, *25*(1), 340–358. DOI: 10.1111/rode.12710

Buele, I., & Guerra, T. (2021). BIBLIOMETRIC ANALYSIS OF SCIENTIFIC PRODUCTION ON TAX EVASION IN SCIENCEDIRECT, YEARS 2010 TO 2019. *Journal of Legal, Ethical and Regulatory Issues, 24*(2), 1–15. https://www.scopus.com/inward/record.uri?eid=2-s2.0-85103728358&partnerID=40&md5=9415c00405f928c9aee188b0787617f0

Chatzoglou, P., Chatzoudes, D., & Symeonidis, S. (2015). Factors affecting the intention to use e-Government services. In P. M., M. L., G. M., & M. L. (Eds.), *Federated Conference on Computer Science and Information Systems, FedCSIS 2015* (pp. 1489–1498). Institute of Electrical and Electronics Engineers Inc. DOI: 10.15439/2015F171

Chiarini, B., Marzano, E., & Schneider, F. (2013). Tax rates and tax evasion: An empirical analysis of the long-run aspects in Italy. *European Journal of Law and Economics*, *35*(2), 273–293. DOI: 10.1007/s10657-011-9247-6

Chopra, G., Bhaskar, P., Vinay, M., & Joshi, A. (2022). E-government adoption and employees' job performance: The moderating role of age as a demographic factor. *Electronic Government*, *18*(2), 237–263. DOI: 10.1504/EG.2022.121871

Comba, A. (2019). Rural tax evasion in Argentina: An analysis of tax evasion mechanisms and social relationships in the Córdoba grain market. *International Journal for Crime. Justice and Social Democracy*, *8*(2), 68–82. DOI: 10.5204/ijcjsd.v8i2.1153

Comba, A. (2019). Rural tax evasion in Argentina: An analysis of tax evasion mechanisms and social relationships in the Córdoba grain market. *International Journal for Crime. Justice and Social Democracy*, *8*(2), 68–82. DOI: 10.5204/ijcjsd.v8i2.1153

D'Agostino, E., De Benedetto, M. A., & Sobbrio, G. (2021). Tax evasion and government size: Evidence from Italian provinces. *Economics and Politics*, *38*(3), 1149–1187. DOI: 10.1007/s40888-021-00227-7 PMID: 35422597

Dobrovič, J., Gombár, M., & Benková, E. (2017). Sustainable development activities aimed at combating tax evasion in Slovakia. *Journal of Security and Sustainability Issues*, *6*(4), 761–772. DOI: 10.9770/jssi.2017.6.4(19)

Dularif, M., Sutrisno, T., & Saraswati, E. (2019). Is deterrence approach effective in combating tax evasion? A meta-analysis. *Problems and Perspectives in Management*, *17*(2), 93–113. DOI: 10.21511/ppm.17(2).2019.07

Ermasova, N., Haumann, C., & Burke, L. (2021). The Relationship between Culture and Tax Evasion across Countries: Cases of the USA and Germany. *International Journal of Public Administration*, *44*(2), 115–131. DOI: 10.1080/01900692.2019.1672181

Fagbemi, T. O., Uadiale, O. M., & Noah, A. O. (2010). The ethics of tax evasion: Perceptual evidence from Nigeria. *European Journal of Social Sciences*, *17*(3), 360–371. https://www.scopus.com/inward/record.uri?eid=2-s2.0-78649799260&partnerID=40&md5=fd46224c6ed69ee17a2791dbe1108caa

Forteza, A., & Noboa, C. (2019). Perceptions of institutional quality and justification of tax evasion. *Constitutional Political Economy*, *30*(4), 367–382. DOI: 10.1007/s10602-019-09287-1

Gonzalez, R., Gasco, J., & Llopis, J. (2007). E-government success: Some principles from a Spanish case study. *Industrial Management & Data Systems*, *107*(6), 845–861. DOI: 10.1108/02635570710758752

Grym, J., Aspara, J., Nandy, M., & Lodh, S. (2024). A Crime by Any Other Name: Gender Differences in Moral Reasoning When Judging the Tax Evasion of Cryptocurrency Traders. *Behavioral Sciences (Basel, Switzerland)*, *14*(3), 198. Advance online publication. DOI: 10.3390/bs14030198 PMID: 38540501

Habib, A., Alsmadi, D., & Prybutok, V. R. (2020). Factors that determine residents' acceptance of smart city technologies. *Behaviour & Information Technology*, *39*(6), 610–623. DOI: 10.1080/0144929X.2019.1693629

Hemberg, E., Rosen, J., Warner, G., Wijesinghe, S., & O'Reilly, U.-M. (2016). Detecting tax evasion: A co-evolutionary approach. *Artificial Intelligence and Law*, *24*(2), 149–182. DOI: 10.1007/s10506-016-9181-6

Hyytinen, A., Tuimala, J., & Hammar, M. (2022). Enhancing the adoption of digital public services: Evidence from a large-scale field experiment. *Government Information Quarterly*, *39*(3), 101687. Advance online publication. DOI: 10.1016/j.giq.2022.101687

Ifere, E. O., Ovat, O. O., Owan, E. J., Chijioke, M. I., Ofem, L. U., Ndome, J. N., Ugbaka, M. A., & Atelhe, A. G. (2023). PERCEPTION AND CRIMINALITY OF TAX EVASION IN A DEVELOPING ECONOMY. *Corporate Law and Governance Review*, *5*(2 Special Issue), 164–173. DOI: 10.22495/clgrv5i2sip3

Ilias, A., Ghani, E. K., & Azhar, Z. (2022). The e-government of eXtensible business reporting language adoption process in Malaysia: Drivers and challenges from environmental perspective. *Electronic Government*, *18*(4), 399–423. DOI: 10.1504/EG.2022.125920

Iong, K. Y., & Phillips, J. O. L. (2022). Examining the impact of behavioral factors on the intention of adopting E-government services: An empirical study on the hard-to-reach groups in Macao SAR, China. *Technology in Society*, *71*, 102107. Advance online publication. DOI: 10.1016/j.techsoc.2022.102107

Kemsley, D., & Kemsley, S. A. (2024). Tax evasion savings versus unlawful predicate proceeds: A substance-based approach. *Journal of Money Laundering Control*, *27*(4), 647–657. DOI: 10.1108/JMLC-12-2023-0196

Kemsley, D., Kemsley, S. A., & Morgan, F. T. (2022). Tax evasion and money laundering: A complete framework. *Journal of Financial Crime*, *29*(2), 589–602. DOI: 10.1108/JFC-09-2020-0175

Kemsley, D., Kemsley, S. A., & Morgan, F. T. (2024). Tax evasion on lawful income: Is it a form of money laundering? *Journal of Financial Crime*, *31*(1), 33–43. DOI: 10.1108/JFC-11-2022-0268

Khaltar, O. (2024). Tax evasion and governance quality: The moderating role of adopting open government. *International Review of Administrative Sciences*, *90*(1), 276–294. DOI: 10.1177/00208523231197317

Khaltar, O. (2024). Tax evasion and governance quality: The moderating role of adopting open government. *International Review of Administrative Sciences*, *90*(1), 276–294. DOI: 10.1177/00208523231197317

Khan, A., Krishnan, S., & Dhir, A. (2021). Electronic government and corruption: Systematic literature review, framework, and agenda for future research. *Technological Forecasting and Social Change*, *167*, 120737. Advance online publication. DOI: 10.1016/j.techfore.2021.120737

Khlif, H., & Amara, I. (2019). Political connections, corruption and tax evasion: A cross-country investigation. *Journal of Financial Crime*, *26*(2), 401–411. DOI: 10.1108/JFC-01-2018-0004

Khlif, H., & Amara, I. (2019). Political connections, corruption and tax evasion: A cross-country investigation. *Journal of Financial Crime*, *26*(2), 401–411. DOI: 10.1108/JFC-01-2018-0004

Khlif, H., Guidara, A., & Hussainey, K. (2016). Sustainability level, corruption and tax evasion: A cross-country analysis. *Journal of Financial Crime*, *23*(2), 328–348. DOI: 10.1108/JFC-09-2014-0041

Kirchler, E., Maciejovsky, B., & Schneider, F. (2003). Everyday representations of tax avoidance, tax evasion, and tax flight: Do legal differences matter? *Journal of Economic Psychology*, *24*(4), 535–553. DOI: 10.1016/S0167-4870(02)00164-2

Korndörfer, M., Krumpal, I., & Schmukle, S. C. (2014). Measuring and explaining tax evasion: Improving self-reports using the crosswise model. *Journal of Economic Psychology*, *45*, 18–32. DOI: 10.1016/j.joep.2014.08.001

Kozel, E., & Dečman, M. (2022). The Impact of Trust in Government - Young Voters' Behavioral Intention to Use I-voting in Slovenia. *NISPAcee Journal of Public Administration and Policy*, *15*(1), 61–87. DOI: 10.2478/nispa-2022-0004

Lamberti, L., Benedetti, M., & Chen, S. (2014). Benefits sought by citizens and channel attitudes for multichannel payment services: Evidence from Italy. *Government Information Quarterly*, *31*(4), 596–609. DOI: 10.1016/j.giq.2014.03.002

Lau, T.-C., Choe, K.-L., & Tan, L.-P. (2013). The moderating effect of religiosity in the relationship between money ethics and tax evasion. *Asian Social Science*, *9*(11), 213–220. DOI: 10.5539/ass.v9n11P213

Levaggi, R. (2007). Tax evasion and the cost of public sector activities. *Public Finance Review*, *35*(5), 572–585. DOI: 10.1177/1091142107300064

Levaggi, R., & Menoncin, F. (2024). Tax evasion and debt in a dynamic general equilibrium model. *Economic and Political Studies*, *12*(2), 188–206. DOI: 10.1080/20954816.2023.2179957

Levaggi, R., & Menoncin, F. (2024). Tax evasion and debt in a dynamic general equilibrium model. *Economic and Political Studies*, *12*(2), 188–206. DOI: 10.1080/20954816.2023.2179957

Lin, J., Carter, L., & Liu, D. (2021). Privacy concerns and digital government: Exploring citizen willingness to adopt the COVIDSafe app. *European Journal of Information Systems*, *30*(4), 389–402. DOI: 10.1080/0960085X.2021.1920857

Marjit, S., Mishra, S., & Mitra, S. (2021). Tax evasion by tax deferment: Sham litigation with an informal credit market. *European Journal of Political Economy*, *69*, 102008. Advance online publication. DOI: 10.1016/j.ejpoleco.2021.102008

Marriott, L. (2017). An investigation of attitudes towards tax evasion and welfare fraud in New Zealand. *Australian and New Zealand Journal of Criminology*, *50*(1), 123–145. DOI: 10.1177/0004865815596793

Matenda, F. R., Sibanda, M., Chikodza, E., & Gumbo, V. (2022). Corporate Loan Recovery Rates under Downturn Conditions in a Developing Economy: Evidence from Zimbabwe. *Risks*, *10*(10), 198. DOI: 10.3390/risks10100198

Mazurenko, O., Tiutiunyk, I., Cherba, V., Artyukhov, A., & Yehorova, Y. (2023). Shadow tax evasion and its impact on the competitiveness of the country's tax system. *Public and Municipal Finance*, *12*(2), 129–142. DOI: 10.21511/pmf.12(2).2023.11

McGee, R. W., & Benk, S. (2019). Christian attitudes toward ethics of tax evasion: A case study. *Journal of Financial Crime*, *26*(1), 74–94. DOI: 10.1108/JFC-11-2017-0104

McGee, R. W., Ho, S. S. M., & Li, A. Y. S. (2008). A comparative study on perceived ethics of tax evasion: Hong kong vs the united states. *Journal of Business Ethics*, *77*(2), 147–158. DOI: 10.1007/s10551-006-9304-1

Mohamad, A., Zakaria, M. H., & Hamid, Z. (2016). Cash economy: Tax evasion amongst SMEs in Malaysia. *Journal of Financial Crime*, *23*(4), 974–986. DOI: 10.1108/JFC-05-2015-0025

Montenegro, T. M. (2021). Tax evasion, corporate social responsibility and national governance: A country-level study. *Sustainability (Basel)*, *13*(20), 11166. Advance online publication. DOI: 10.3390/su132011166

Nielsen, M. M. (2017). E-Governance and online service delivery in Estonia. In H. C.C. & O. A. (Eds.), *18th Annual International Conference on Digital Government Research, DG.O 2017: Vol. Part F1282* (pp. 300–309). Association for Computing Machinery. DOI: 10.1145/3085228.3085284

Nurunnabi, M. (2018). Tax evasion and religiosity in the Muslim world: The significance of Shariah regulation. *Quality & Quantity*, *52*(1), 371–394. DOI: 10.1007/s11135-017-0471-1

Nurunnabi, M. (2018). Tax evasion and religiosity in the Muslim world: The significance of Shariah regulation. *Quality & Quantity*, *52*(1), 371–394. DOI: 10.1007/s11135-017-0471-1

Nurunnabi, M. (2019). Tax Evasion and the Role of the State Actor(s) in Bangladesh. *International Journal of Public Administration*, *42*(10), 823–839. DOI: 10.1080/01900692.2018.1520245

Obadina, D. A. (2016). Confronting the problem of cross-border tax evasion in an era of greater global transparency of tax relevant information: The case of Nigeria. *Journal of Money Laundering Control*, *19*(4), 470–499. DOI: 10.1108/JMLC-10-2015-0043

Owusu, G. M. Y., Bart-Plange, M.-A., Koomson, T. A. A., & Arthur, M. (2022). The effect of personality traits and tax morale on tax evasion intention. *Journal of Financial Crime*, *29*(1), 272–292. DOI: 10.1108/JFC-02-2021-0026

Owusu, G. M. Y., Bekoe, R. A., Anokye, F. K., & Anyetei, L. (2020). What Factors Influence the Intentions of Individuals to Engage in Tax Evasion? Evidence from Ghana. *International Journal of Public Administration*, *43*(13), 1143–1155. DOI: 10.1080/01900692.2019.1665686

Ozili, P. K. (2020). Tax evasion and financial instability. *Journal of Financial Crime*, *27*(2), 531–539. DOI: 10.1108/JFC-04-2019-0051

Pereira, I. V., & Cabral de Ávila, L. A. (2022). RELATION BETWEEN SELF-DECEPTION AND TAX EVASION IN BRAZIL. *Revista de Gestao Social e Ambiental*, *16*(2), e03036. Advance online publication. DOI: 10.24857/rgsa.v16n2-027

Rana, N. P., Dwivedi, Y. K., Williams, M. D., & Weerakkody, V. (2016). Adoption of online public grievance redressal system in India: Toward developing a unified view. *Computers in Human Behavior*, *59*, 265–282. DOI: 10.1016/j.chb.2016.02.019

Rashid, M. H. U., Ahmad, A., Abdullah, M. S., Ahmmed, M., & Islam, S. (2022). Doing Business and Tax Evasion: Evidence from Asian Countries. *SAGE Open*, *12*(4), 21582440221131280. Advance online publication. DOI: 10.1177/21582440221131280

Rashid, M. H. U., Uddin, N., Haque, M. S., & Hossain, S. Z. (2022). Good governance and tax evasion: Mediating effect of socioeconomic conditions. *Asia-Pacific Journal of Regional Science*, *6*(2), 759–776. DOI: 10.1007/s41685-022-00242-x

Rizzi, D. (2017). Tax Evasion Indices and Profiles. *Public Finance Review*, *45*(6), 771–791. DOI: 10.1177/1091142117691602

Sadik-Zada, E. R., Gatto, A., & Niftiyev, I. (2022). E-government and petty corruption in public sector service delivery. *Technology Analysis and Strategic Management*. Advance online publication. DOI: 10.1080/09537325.2022.2067037

Silal, P., & Saha, D. (2021). E-Government as a Tool for Human Development: The Moderating Influence of National Culture. *Journal of Global Information Technology Management*, *24*(4), 235–258. DOI: 10.1080/1097198X.2021.1993724

Strango, C. (2021). Does digitalisation in public services reduce tax evasion? *Economic Research Guardian, 11*(2), 221–235. https://www.scopus.com/inward/record.uri?eid=2-s2.0-85122026990&partnerID=40&md5=ec809f38d1e1f7eeb8c789d6c1177b36

Sunarsih, U., Hakim, M. A. D., & Rusmanto, T. (2024). THE IMPACT OF TAX UNDERSTANDING, GENDER, AND LOVE OF MONEY ON TAX EVASION WITH RELIGIOSITY AS A MODERATING VARIABLE. *Revista de Gestao Social e Ambiental, 18*(7), e06926. Advance online publication. DOI: 10.24857/rgsa.v18n7-141

Thuneibat, N., Ali, B., Alqaraleh, M., & Thneibat, H. (2022). The Mediating Role of Innovation On the Relationship Between Information Technologies and Reducing Tax Evasion. *Information Sciences Letters, 11*(5), 1359–1370. DOI: 10.18576/isl/110505

Van Der Geest, T., & Velleman, E. (2014). Easy-to-read meets accessible web in the e-government context. *5th International Conference on Software Development and Technologies for Enhancing Accessibility and Fighting Info-Exclusion, DSAI 2013, 27*, 327–333. DOI: 10.1016/j.procs.2014.02.036

Wang, Y. (2007). Income tax evasion in the United States and China. *Frontiers of Law in China, 2*(1), 123–139. DOI: 10.1007/s11463-007-0007-z

Yamen, A. E. (2021). Tax evasion, corruption and COVID-19 health risk exposure: A cross country analysis. *Journal of Financial Crime, 28*(4), 995–1007. DOI: 10.1108/JFC-10-2020-0220

Yamen, A. E., Mersni, H., & Ramadan, A. (2023). Tax evasion and public governance before and after the European "big bang": A red flag for policymakers. *Journal of Financial Crime, 30*(2), 420–436. DOI: 10.1108/JFC-04-2020-0064

Yaniv, G. (2009). The tax compliance demand curve: A diagrammatical approach to income tax evasion. *The Journal of Economic Education, 40*(2), 213–224. DOI: 10.3200/JECE.40.2.213-224

Zhou, S., Ayandibu, A. O., Chimucheka, T., & Masuku, M. M. (2023). Government social protection and households' welfare during the Covid-19 pandemic in South Africa. *Journal of Business and Socio-Economic Development, 3*(4), 308–321. DOI: 10.1108/JBSED-04-2022-0044

Zichová, T. (2022). Visual Interface Design Innovation: Citizens' Perception of Financial Administration Applications. *Acta Informatica Pragensia, 11*(1), 1–14. DOI: 10.18267/j.aip.160

KEY TERMS AND DEFINITIONS

- Tax: Tax is a compulsory financial contribution made by a government to citizens, firms, or other entities to fund public spending. Tax is one of the major sources of revenue for governments and is utilized to fund infrastructure, public amenities, defense, and social services. Tax can be income tax, sales tax, land tax, and company tax, and normally comes under legislation and regulation drawn out by the government.

- **Taxpayer:** Taxpayer is a person or business entity legally required to pay tax to the state. Taxpayers are graded according to sources of income-earning activities and financial transactions as individuals, business enterprises, corporate entities, or institutions. The payment of tax provides economic stability as it ensures continuous fund flow for government services and schemes of infrastructural growth.

- **Tax Evasion:** Tax evasion is the criminal act of deliberately evading tax payment by falsifying income, inflating deductions, or hiding financial information. It is a criminal act in most countries because it deprives the government of revenue and results in an unfair economic benefit. Tax evasion is distinct from tax avoidance, which is legally reducing tax payment through deductions and loopholes in the tax legislation.

- **E-Government:** E-Government or electronic government is the application of digital technology, more specifically the internet and information and communication technologies (ICTs), to provide government services, enhance the administration of public affairs, and facilitate citizen participation. It allows for ease of transparency, efficiency, and accessibility since citizens can access such services as taxation, business registration, and dissemination of public information through the internet. E-Government targets the modernization of governance and the reconnection of citizens to the government.

- **Digital Transformation:** Digital transformation is the adoption of digital technologies into most or all aspects of an organization, industry, or government to propel operations, provide services more efficiently, and generate innovation. Digital transformation is the adoption of new technologies like artificial intelligence, cloud computing, and data analytics to propel efficiency and generate new value. Digital transformation goes beyond technology to organizational culture, business models, and customer experience evolution.

- **Technology Adoption:** Technology adoption is a process under which organizations, societies, or individuals embrace and use new technology in an effort to enhance efficiency, quality of life, and productivity. Technology adoption encompasses processes ranging from awareness to evaluation, trials, and ultimately full implementation. Cost, social influence, perceived benefits, and the ease of use affect the adoption of the technology. Technology adoption is influenced by government and business enterprises due to the fact that technology helps in economic growth, effective delivery of services, and digital-based competitiveness.

Chapter 13
Usability of E-Government Service for Tax Payers in Ethiopia:
The Case of E-Tax System

Lemma Lessa
https://orcid.org/0000-0002-2890-9721
Addis Ababa University, Ethiopia

Abebaw Demelash
Addis Ababa University, Ethiopia

ABSTRACT

The e-tax portal/system is a web-based tax filling and payment system designed to reduce cumbersome manual processes, cut evasion and help boost domestic revenue collection. The system is also used for payment of public services and other remittances. Usability of the e-tax portals is key for the public to find it easy to use. The heuristic evaluation (HE) method is used for the usability evaluations. The data collected were analyzed based on the ten Nielsen usability heuristics. The results showed that this method of assessment is effective in pointing out various usability issues in e-government services specifically e-tax portal interface. A usable e-tax portal decreases training cost, support, and maintenance costs. The paper also provides general recommendations on how to develop and manage more usable websites.

BACKGROUND

The integration of technology has transformed numerous facets of our daily lives, impacting government services, the economy, and social interactions (Vlachogianni & Tselios, 2023). Information technologies promote ecological innovations that support sustainable development by minimizing environmental impacts and optimizing resource use (eLAC, 2020). Globally, various government sectors are

DOI: 10.4018/979-8-3373-0422-9.ch013

adopting information technology to enhance service delivery and engage more effectively with citizens (Ruta, 2017).

Revenue generation is vital for sustainability and presents a significant challenge for both advanced and developing economies, playing a crucial role in the growth and development of countries worldwide. In Ethiopia, the government has been enacting tax reforms aimed at increasing tax revenue to meet the growing demand for public services from its citizens. A key recent initiative to enhance tax revenue has been the introduction of e-taxation systems for taxpayers, a project supported by the Investment Climate Facilitation for Africa (Nazrawit, 2022). Ministry of Revenue's e-tax system is a web-based platform designed to streamline tax filing and payment processes, thereby reducing manual operations across regional and branch offices. Since its development in February 2013 by the Ethiopian Revenue and Customs Authority (now the Ministry of Revenue), the e-tax system has provided significant benefits to both the business community and the broader economy (Ruta, 2017). E-taxation involves the electronic transfer of data between the IT systems of tax professionals and tax authorities (Baguma, 2018).

To meet the government's goals of enhancing speed and accuracy in tax administration, reducing collection costs, improving information accuracy and completeness, and ultimately fostering taxpayer satisfaction and trust, it is essential to implement efficient e-tax systems. Taxpayers have access to a variety of services offered by tax authorities, including registration, e-filing, e-tax payments, and tax return submissions, all facilitated through applications for compliance certificates (Nazrawit, 2022). The adoption of e-tax systems brings numerous advantages for both tax authorities and taxpayers, such as cost-free preparation and submission of tax returns, enhanced security, 24/7 accessibility, time savings, and the convenience of filing from any personal computer or mobile device (Barati & Bakhshayesh, 2015). Furthermore, a computerized and integrated tax system can enhance national wealth by effectively curbing tax evasion and addressing issues of injustice and inefficiency within the income tax framework.

According to Baguma (2018), usability is defined as "the extent to which a product, such as software or a website, can be used by specified users to achieve specified goals with effectiveness, efficiency, and satisfaction in a specified context of use." He notes that effectiveness pertains to "the accuracy and completeness with which specified users can achieve specified goals in particular environments," while efficiency refers to "the resources expended in relation to the accuracy and completeness of goals achieved." Satisfaction encompasses "the comfort and acceptability of the system's performance to its users and others affected by its use." E-tax systems must exhibit both effectiveness and efficiency to ensure user satisfaction, as usability plays a crucial role in the overall success and quality of software. Usability inspections of e-tax systems aim to identify and resolve issues within the current user interface design, providing recommendations for improvement (Silvis, Bothma, & Beer).

This study offers a comprehensive set of heuristics and information architecture (IA) framework for evaluating the usability of the Ministry of Revenue's head office websites, along with a practical workflow for conducting assessments. Based on the findings, the paper outlines recommendations for addressing identified usability gaps within the Ministry of Revenue's e-Tax portal. Given the public-facing nature of these portals, their usability is essential for ensuring that taxpayers find them easy to navigate, effective, efficient, and satisfying to use. The integration of technology has significantly transformed various aspects of daily life, including government services, the economy, and social interactions (Vlachogianni & Tselios, 2023). Information technologies also support sustainable development by minimizing environmental impact and optimizing resource use (eLAC, 2020). Across the globe, government sectors are increasingly adopting information technology to enhance service delivery and engage with citizens (Ruta, 2017). Revenue generation remains crucial for both advanced and developing economies, and the

Ethiopian government has been implementing tax reforms to boost revenue and meet the rising demand for public services. One key initiative is the introduction of e-tax systems, aimed at streamlining tax processes and improving revenue collection, with significant benefits to both the business community and the broader economy (Nazrawit, 2022; Ruta, 2017).

PROBLEM STATEMENT

Despite being in operation for over a decade, e-tax systems in many developing countries have proven to be inefficient and less usable than anticipated. Factors contributing to taxpayer dissatisfaction include inadequate technological readiness, slow network speeds during the filing process, and insufficient system security for protecting tax-related data (Mustapha, 2015). Additionally, the lack of significant increases in tax revenue following the introduction of online tax return services in many African nations can be attributed to serious usability challenges within these systems (Eilu et al., 2021). Usability issues are often reported through usability assessments, which provide feedback from evaluations to the system designers (Nielsen, 2014). Usability experts typically use standard user tasks to engage with the product's interface, identify existing usability problems, and assign specific heuristic violations to each issue encountered (Georgsson et al., 2014). The mere availability of e-tax system technology does not guarantee taxpayer satisfaction with its implementation and use (Mustapha, 2015). A usability problem is defined as any element of an interface that is confusing, misleading, or suboptimal (Lazar et al., 2019). Consequently, many e-tax portals are not effectively usable.

Research suggests that online tax services have not improved tax return submissions as anticipated (Eilu et al., 2021). Their study found that, out of four online tax return services assessed, only 50% of these services and 33% of various electronic payment options were utilized by taxpayers, resulting in an average usability score of just 16%. This indicates serious usability issues with these services. Furthermore, research by Omar Mohamed and Yusoff (2012) revealed critical problems in heuristic evaluations, with 57.14% of issues categorized as critical for each heuristic. To address these gaps, Meyer (2022) proposed the design and validation of a novel online platform intended to attract more taxpayers, as reliance on existing e-tax systems is costly and decreases compliance levels (Baguma, 2018). A user-friendly and efficient e-tax portal could also reduce training, support, and maintenance costs.

According to Alsanous et al., usability evaluations in e-tax systems should focus on key factors such as user satisfaction, efficiency, and effectiveness. Conducting heuristic evaluations is essential for enhancing the usability of applications and software (Ramadhanti, Budiyanto, and Yuana, 2023). Currently, the Ten Usability Heuristic Evaluation (HE) framework, developed by Nielsen and Molich, is one of the most widely referenced usability techniques (Yodihartomo, 2020). Usability refers to the extent to which a product, such as software or a website, can be used by specified users to achieve defined goals with effectiveness, efficiency, and satisfaction in a given context (Baguma, 2018).The term 'usability' is commonly understood as the capability of being used, focusing on the ease with which users can accomplish their intended tasks using a designated tool (Yodihartomo, 2020). Therefore, a comprehensive set of integrated heuristics, frameworks, and evaluation workflows for utilizing these heuristics is necessary (Silvis, Bothma, and Beer).

Literature reviews on usability provide valuable context and summarize key concepts from related studies (Silvis et al.). However, research on web usability in Africa, particularly in East Africa, remains limited (Yodihartomo, 2020). Most existing studies have focused on other aspects of e-government services rather than on the usability of online government services, specifically e-tax services. This paper presents recommendations for addressing current usability gaps to enhance the effectiveness, efficiency, and user satisfaction of the e-tax portal (Baguma, 2018). To date, there has been no comprehensive study evaluating web usability in this context. The study aims to address the following research questions: (i) To what extent do usability issues in the system services pose difficulties for both users and tax authorities? (2) What specific usability-related challenges are associated with the e-tax system in Ethiopia?

REVIEW OF RELATED WORKS

This section provides an in-depth analysis of literature and models relevant to e-government, e-taxation, user-centered design, and usability. It begins by establishing foundational concepts, offering an overview of e-government and electronic tax systems; the importance of usability in evaluating e-tax services using heuristic principles. Various scholars contribute differing perspectives on e-government. Definitions from (Takeoka, 2009; Adefris, 2018, and Avdic, 2012) collectively highlight e-government as the use of ICT, particularly the Internet, to deliver essential services to citizens and businesses, including healthcare and taxation. E-government enhances service delivery through key technologies like Electronic Data Interchange (EDI) and virtual reality, supporting both public and private sectors (Anjoga et al., 2017).

Ahmad et al. (2017) and Dian (2020) highlight e-government's ability to improve government efficiency and citizen engagement, leading to better service delivery and accountability. While definitions vary, the consensus is that e-government employs ICT to facilitate interactions between government entities and the public through various electronic platforms.

The government services can be categorized into four types: government-to-citizen (G2C), government-to-business (G2B), government-to-government (G2G), and government-to-employee (G2E). Benefits include direct service provision, reduced paperwork, and faster data processing through ICT. Efficient public services can lead to significant cost savings and the development of new services. The overarching significance of e-government lies in reducing costs, enhancing service delivery, and empowering citizens through better access to information.

Different scholars defined the electronic tax system as a trans-organizational process that facilitates the collection of taxes and data transfer between tax authorities and taxpayers using internet services. Emphasizing the need for enhanced usage of e-tax systems, the authors stress the importance of training taxpayers on tax compliance (Night and Bananuka, 2018). E-taxation encompasses the electronic calculation, collection, and management of taxes.

According to (USAID, 2013; Baguma, 2018) e-tax systems offer numerous benefits, including cost-free tax return preparation, enhanced security, round-the-clock accessibility, time savings, and the convenience of filing from any device. The integrated electronic tax administration system (ITEAS) streamlines tax collection and administration through electronic channels (Uba et al., 2021; Stella & Oboh, 2020). The electronic tax system is designed to help taxpayers meet their obligations on time, allowing for the electronic filing of returns without paper submissions (Stella & Oboh, 2020; United Nations, 2007). Both advanced and developing nations benefit from adopting e-taxation by increasing revenue, improving administrative efficiency, expediting tax refund processes, and reducing tax evasion. Awai & Oboh (2020) describe the electronic payment system as an online platform for various transactions, including e-tax payments, which simplify the process for taxpayers. The e-tax system enables taxpayers to pay their taxes quickly and conveniently from any internet-enabled location, enhancing transparency, compliance, and revenue generation (Stella & Oboh, 2020). Overall, the electronic tax system represents a significant advancement in taxation, benefiting both tax authorities and taxpayers. E-tax facilitate online filing of income and tax returns, as well as electronic payments for both individuals and corporations and processes by allowing taxpayers to file returns and make payments without needing to visit tax authorities in person (Baguma, 2018; Maisiba and Atambo, 2016). Stella and Oboh (2020) emphasize that e-tax services enable taxpayers to manage payments, receive receipts, and obtain tax clearance certificates conveniently from home or office at any time. They also reference Deloitte (2017), which outlines various e-tax services such as registration, e-stamp duty, e-filing, and e-receipts. The National Tax Agency Report (2022) underscores the need for accurate information and a seamless filing experience to improve e-tax services. Ultimately, Night and Bananuka (2018) argue that governments should visibly provide services that reflect the value of taxes paid by citizens.

Usability is the extent to which a system, product, or service can be used by specified users to achieve specified goals with effectiveness, efficiency, and satisfaction in a specified context of use" (ISO, 2010). Meanwhile, (Nielsen, 2012) defines usability as a critical quality index in the interaction of digital products, which includes five key aspects or factors such as memorability, learnability, efficiency, user satisfaction, and error frequency. How easily a user can operate a product for the first time; Efficiency: The speed at which users can perform tasks once they have learned the design; Memorability: How quickly users can regain their proficiency with the design after not using it for a period; Errors: The frequency and severity of errors, as well as the ease of recovering from them; Satisfaction: The overall contentment of users after completing tasks.

Novak (2014) views usability as a crucial concept in human-computer interaction (HCI), often described as "user friendliness" or "capability of use" in information systems. Baguma (2018) defines web usability as the clarity, simplicity, consistency, and ease of use of websites. Titania et al. (2023) emphasize that usability involves the user's awareness of the application. Stella & Oboh (2020) argue that a properly implemented and fully automated electronic tax payment system enhances transparency and simplifies the tax payment process. Globally, adopting e-taxation aims to increase revenue generation, streamline administration at all government levels, reduce bureaucracy, expedite tax refund procedures, improve tax assessment processes, and help reduce and eliminate tax evasion. In essence, usability refers to how effectively, efficiently, and satisfactorily a software or website enables specified users to achieve their goals in a given context (Baguma, 2018). 2020).

Heuristic evaluation applies usability principles through "rules of thumb" to enhance interface ease of use. The evaluation methods are further categorized into "inspection methods" (without end users) and "test methods" (with end users) (FATTA et al., 2018). Usability standards provide a framework to measure user performance and satisfaction, which is crucial for integrating systems into workflows (Novak, 2014). In developed countries, concerns such as risk and privacy breaches significantly influence the adoption of electronic tax systems (Night & Bananuka, 2018). Methods like cognitive walkthroughs and expert evaluations typically require user involvement or multiple experts (Baguma, 2018).

If taxpayers find an electronic filing system challenging, they are less likely to adopt it, negatively affecting tax compliance (Maisiba & Atambo, 2016). Trust in the security of online tax systems can positively influence user attitudes and adoption (Debei et al., 2015). Novak (2014) asserts that usability can be systematically improved and evaluated. Given the central role of websites in e-services, ongoing assessment is vital for delivering high-quality services (Shayganmehr & Ali, 2021). Regular evaluations help identify strengths and weaknesses essential for developing effective online services (Joshi & Islam, 2018). Usability evaluation can be categorized into three main approaches: expert-based evaluations, automated testing with tools, and user-based testing (Mariann et al., 2010). Expert evaluations are particularly effective for assessing information architecture, as users may excel at using interfaces but may lack the expertise to evaluate their design effectively (Lazar et al., 2010).

Heuristic evaluation is a method that allows for the automatic classification of usability issues, streamlining the evaluation process by eliminating the need for post-evaluation meetings among evaluators. According to (Granollers, 2018), citecd Masip et al., 2012), describes a comprehensive framework that facilitates a semi-automatic approach to selecting the most appropriate set of heuristics for each specific situation. While using web usability heuristics by a single expert can efficiently uncover most usability issues at a low cost and in a short time, automatic web evaluation tools are often not employed because they primarily focus on reporting the number of errors rather than providing detailed analysis. Nielsen initially proposed a set of nine heuristics for early usability inspections, which were later expanded to the ten heuristics used today (Nielsen, 1994a). Heuristic evaluations are quick and cost-effective, requiring only a few days to inspect a site and produce a report.

The heuristic principles utilized to assess the usability of the e-tax portal, with the concept presents the usability evaluation results along with recommendations for improvement (Luo, 2015). Drawing from these concepts, the research framework aims to answer the question: what types of usability issues exist in the e-tax portal?

Heuristic Evaluation is also an inspection method developed by Nielsen and Molich [1990] designed to identify usability issues in user interfaces. In this straightforward approach, a small group of evaluators independently examines the interface for compliance with established usability principles, known as "heuristics." The usability problems identified are compiled into a comprehensive report, which the development team reviews to reach a consensus on how to address and prioritize these issues.

RESEARCH DESIGN AND METHODS

The researchers used both qualitative and quantitative approach where quantitative analysis emphasizes gathering information and interpreting data from participant pool. The research commenced with the collection of quantitate data through heuristic evaluation conducted by selected experts, who will assess the e-tax system based on Nielsen's ten heuristic principles and refine usability issues. The heuristic evaluation method can provide valuable insights into the design and functional aspects that require improvement, in e-tax portal ultimately offering important information for enhancing the usability of Ethiopian e-tax system.

The researcherschecks through heuristic evaluation as the research strategy to explore usability issues within the e-tax system interface and identify usability problems which closely associated with it by applied heuristic usability principles. The researchers will conduct usability testing and heuristic evaluation to gain a deeper understanding of this underexplored concept, demonstrating its significance and examining related issues.

While there are numerous usability evaluation methods assessing software usability in the field of Human-Computer Interaction (HCI), such as heuristic evaluations, cognitive walkthroughs, expert evaluations, action analysis, user tests, and perspective-based inspections (Baguma, 2018; Holzinger, 2005). Many of these require user involvement of multiple experts focus on interface inspection, while others evaluate software performance having a single expert. In web usability heuristics can identify most usability issues more quickly and cost-effectively (Baguma, 2018). To address the challenges associated with the e-tax portal in Ethiopia, the analysis methodology incorporates elements from heuristic evaluation method based on Nielsen's usability principles, allowing evaluators to assess the software interface against essential design guidelines.

According to (Preece et al., 2002), three manual methods are commonly used to identify usability issues in user interfaces: (a) Usability Testing, which involves observers documenting usability issues as users complete tasks; (b) Questionnaires and Interviews, where users share their system experiences through structured formats, discussing missing features and overall satisfaction; and (c) Expert Inspection Methods, where usability experts review the interface and identify problems based on their expertise. These manual techniques provide deeper insights into user experiences and complement automated evaluations.

Researchers have identified several key attributes for evaluating the usability of e-tax applications, which include (a) learnability; (b) effectiveness; (c) efficiency; (d) memorability; (e) errors; and (f) user satisfaction. The experts selected for this evaluation were chosen based on Nielsen and Mack's recommendation to involve 3-5 evaluators (J. Nielsen and Mack, 1994). All selected experts have a background in e-tax systems. The researchers will conduct the Heuristic evaluation with four experts who are knowledgeable about the e-tax system and 10 users familiar with usability principles.

This study focuses on the e-tax portal of Ethiopia's Ministry of Revenue, which serves all regional and branch services and connects to national e-government services. The researchers chooses this portal due to its comprehensive service offerings. The portal is managed at the federal level by the IT directorate known as the Management Information System (MIS) directorate, which oversees nine regional and six branch service providers. To evaluate the usability of the e-tax system using Nielsen's heuristic evaluation, the study will include four usability experts and designers in e-tax system. Evaluators will have full access to all features of the e-tax system, such as filing returns, checking status, and making payments; have perceptions about Jakob Nielsen's ten usability heuristics, could have assess the system independently to gather a broad range of usability issues, rate the scale of severity ratings, and improvement suggestions. A group discussion will be conducted post-evaluation to share insights and identify common themes; Reporting Results: A comprehensive report will summarize the evaluation findings, detailing usability issues, severity ratings, and recommendations for improvement; and finally follow-up evaluation: Subsequent evaluations will be planned to assess the effectiveness of implemented changes. By incorporating these components, the study aims to effectively apply Nielsen's heuristic evaluation to assess the usability of the e-tax system, ultimately enhancing organizational experience and efficiency.

Sampling is a method of selecting individuals from population in order to estimate population characteristics. Purposive sampling is a type of sampling, select members of samples according to the purpose of the study. It is also known as judgment, selective or subjective sampling. Purposive sampling used for identify the data sources of this research technique of the case. Thus, to collect the primary data, appropriate and convenient samples were selected who have direct participation and involvement in the selected e-tax system in an organization. For this purposive sampling method, key respondents experts were selected purposely from different usability inspection groups of IT experts and as information resources for the sake of the research questions to be properly answered.

According to Baguma, (2018) with heuristic evaluation, a usability expert (s) reviews the usability of site's interface using accepted heuristic usability principles. Nielsen, (1994) recommends that three to five evaluators be used; hence four is considered to be an appropriate number. The participant involved in usability experts of e-tax portal interface had knowledge and experience. Four key respondent experts include those, who are: The first two experts are digital tax announcement support and follow-up officers, the third expert is system analyst and the fourth application server administration, from 53 IT experts in the organization. According to Titania et al, (2020) studies of usability inspection methods have discovered that many usability problems are overlooked by expert testing, but that user testing also finds problems that are overlooked by inspection. Considering more than 4 respondents probably makes the data repetitive. So, the researchers collected all the information at this stage.

During the study, the researchers need to understand the usability issue of e-tax user interface. Primary data was gathered by using checklist questionnaires. Questionnaire distribute to four e-tax usability experts. Digital tax announcement support and follow-up officers, system analyst and application server administration were used for data collection. Participants were chosen by using the purposive sampling method selected from the population of 53 IT experts in the organization. An extensive literature review was conducted to identify the concepts of usability evaluation of e-tax system. The questionnaires were developed from literature review and 10 Nelsons heuristic usability evaluation principles. The questions were designed to understand and examine the respondents' attitudes and to understand their perceptions toward the factors that affect usability evaluation of e-tax system. The Checklist questionnaires were conducted between Februarys to March 2024. Questions asked were categorized under ten Nelsons' heuristic usability evaluation principles of e-tax portal. The questionnaire was collected carefully with the voluntariness of the respondents and training was conducted by researchers thirty minutes to one hour with discussion. Phone call follow-up was also used to get further explanation. Information that is provided via phone calls was added to the original documents of the respondents.

Secondary data was collected through document analysis. These sources of evidence support the credibility and richness of the study findings and provided triangulation for the collected data. When a heuristic principle is violated, an expert assesses the severity of the issue and suggests potential solutions. Data collection involved a validated checklist based on Nielsen's principles, comprising 98 questionnaires and utilizing a severity rating scale. Four experts were selected as evaluators: two with 10 years of experience in e-tax systems, one with 12 years in application server and database management, and one master's student with a background in computer science and seven years in system analysis and trainer. All evaluators received training in heuristic evaluation from the researchers.

Qualitative thematic analysis was employed to examine the interview data. This method is both robust and adaptable, making it suitable for analyzing qualitative data across different paradigms and epistemological frameworks. Thematic analysis is particularly effective for exploring experiences, thoughts, or behaviors within a dataset. Themes represent constructed patterns or meanings that address a research question, rather than simply summarizing or categorizing codes. They can be developed through either inductive or deductive approaches. Quantitative analysis in heuristic evaluation of usability involves applying statistical methods to assess and interpret the data collected during the evaluation process. This approach enhances the objectivity and reliability of the findings. Here's a breakdown of how quantitative analysis can be implemented in a heuristic evaluation:

Usability experts will interact independently with the product's interface, performing typical user tasks to identify usability issues and assign specific heuristic violations to each problem (Georgsson et al., 2014). The heuristic evaluation method will assess the e-tax portal's usability, yielding a compilation of potential concerns. Experts will evaluate the site's interface for web usability and accessibility, guided by established principles (Buguna, 2018), which will further reinforce these principles and reference relevant studies (Silvis et al., 2020).A key element of the heuristic evaluation is aggregating issues identified by different evaluators and assessing their severity. The pilot study indicated that evaluators noted problems at varying levels of detail, sometimes duplicating issues or using different terminology.

To standardize the granularity of issues, the following steps, based on Nielsen's conditions (Jaferian et al., 2011), were implemented: problem synthesis: Compound problems were broken down into individual components, eliminating unknown issues and false positives. Aggregating Problems: experts created an initial empty aggregated problem list, adding new issues and refining existing descriptions where necessary. If the heuristics associated with a new problem differed from those of an existing one, updates were made for consistency; tagging Problems with Heuristics: each issue was reviewed and tagged with relevant heuristics without referencing the original heuristics provided by evaluators; and assigning severity ratings: A five-point severity scale was used: 0 (not a usability problem), 1 (cosmetic), 2 (minor), 3 (major), and 4 (catastrophic). Four usability and security experts, knowledgeable in heuristic evaluation, independently assessed the severity of each problem based on frequency, impact, and persistence. The mean of their ratings determined the overall severity for each issue, classifying them into major (mean severity > 2) and minor (mean severity ≤ 2) categories, as outlined by Jaferian et al. (2011).

FINDINGS AND DISCUSSION

Cloud Deployment Model Selection

Respondents Information

To address the research question, the collected data from the respondents were coded into themes for the ten Nielson's principles. To support the themes, relevant information was introduced. Questions are asked by starting with general and demographic questions and continue to the research-related questions. The questions raised were towards an individual level. During the participants' response, the researchers gather information, takes notes, and recorded answers from respondents to obtain further and detailed understandings. The concepts of the check list questions drown from 10 system usability scale with 8 tasks and 10 Nelson's heuristic principles include visibility of system status, match between system and the real word, user Control and Freedom, consistency and Standards, error Prevention, recognition Rather than Recall, flexibility and efficiency of se, aesthetic and minimalist design, and help User recognize, diagnose and recovers user, and help and documentation. Accordingly, different principles are associated with e-tax system.

There are standard questions on the Nelson's heuristic principles of of usability of e-tax system, the researchers assessed and conceptualized different principles at each dimension from literature. Then the researchers formulates the check list question and tasks at each principle of e-tax system. Before starting the actual data collection, the formulated questionnaires were evaluated by the domain experts. The data collected from the respondent's answer were manually encoded to a computer by using the Microsoft word and Microsoft excels 2010 application. Checklist questions were raised for the respondents to explain what are the principles of e-tax portal usability issues.

At this stage, the evaluation results from the four experts are summarized, focusing on the severity ratings assigned to various issues. This analysis serves as a foundation for design improvements to the UI of the e-tax interface, which is a crucial aspect of the design process. A visual representation or screenshot of the proposed final design for the Ethiopian e-tax portal will be created based on the previously analyzed severity ratings. Structured problem report: numeric identifier for each problem, brief description of the issue, potential user difficulties associated with the problem, specific context, indicating the problem's location within the interface, possible causes of the issue, highlighting design flaws and the heuristic(s) applied in the evaluation. Severity rating categorized into four levels: cosmetic, minor, major, and catastrophic.

Researchers have identified and analyzed many attributes for testing the usability of e-tax applications, which include (a) learnability; (b) effectiveness; (c) efficiency; (d) memorability; (e) errors; (f) user satisfaction; and notified recommendation

Result and Discussion

Heuristic Evaluation Results

The questionnaires were sent to experts, with ten categories derived from Nielsen's 10 usability heuristics: visibility of system status; alignment between system and real-world concepts; user control and freedom; consistency and standards; error prevention; recognition over recall; flexibility and efficiency of use; aesthetic and minimalist design; assistance in recognizing, diagnosing, and recovering from errors; and help and documentation.

The usability evaluation of e-tax portal employed Jakob Nielsen's 10 usability heuristics and uncovered a total of 189 usability problems and 272 heuristic violations. Four independent evaluators identified varying numbers of issues: Evaluator 1 found 65, Evaluator 2 identified 57, Evaluator 3 reported 42, and Evaluator 4 discovered 25. These findings included overlaps, leading to a comprehensive analysis where 35 problems were recognized by all evaluators and consolidated into 14 overarching issues.

Three evaluators identified 36 similar problems, consolidating them into 15 issues.

Two evaluators found 23 overlapping problems, resulting in 7 consolidated issues.

Another pair identified 17 similar problems, also yielding 7 issues. The remaining 78 issues were unique to individual evaluators, culminating in a final master list of 121 usability issues. Evaluators showed some agreement on the severity of issues, with 14 problems rated similarly by all four, while others had varying consensus levels. Notably, the overall percentage of agreement among evaluators was only 13.18%, and the calculated reliability score was low at 0.0815, indicating significant variability in their assessments.

In the evaluation of the Ethiopian e-tax web interface by four experts, the heuristic principle "Match between system and the real world" (H2) was found to have the fewest issues, at 4.1%. A percentage distribution chart indicated that the principles of Visibility of System Status (H1), Error Prevention (H5), Consistency and Standards (H4), and User Control and Freedom (H3) had the highest number of identified issues, each exceeding 10%. Specifically, H1 emerged as the most frequently encountered principle, accounting for 19.00% of the 121 total issues noted.

Analysis of the consolidated list confirmed that all heuristic principles were violated during the evaluation. Figure 1 illustrates the percentage of issues related to each heuristic, highlighting that H1 (Visibility of System Status), H5 (Error Prevention), H4 (Consistency and Standards), and H3 (User Control and Freedom) had the highest problem rates at 19.0%, 15.7%, 15.0%, and 14%, respectively.

Figure 1. Percentage of issues related to each heuristic

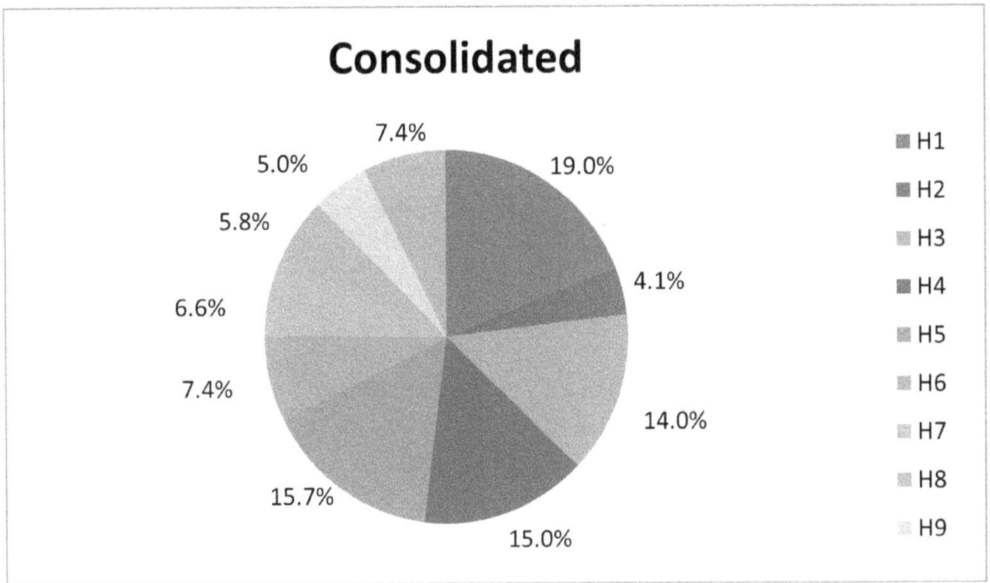

Heuristic 1: Visibility of System Status

This principle highlights the necessity of keeping users informed about ongoing processes through timely and relevant feedback. To assess the Ethiopian e-tax portal's compliance with this principle, the researchers focused on the visibility of user actions and the feedback provided during the upload and download of content, especially regarding forms. The emphasis on forms is crucial for taxpayers during registration and return submissions for various taxes. The portal includes key categories such as user registration, filing declarations, refund and clearance requests, updating taxpayer information, validating tax identification numbers (TIN), and managing the message center.

The e-tax portal offers various forms and templates for e-tax services, covering tax declarations, tax accounts, refund requests, and clearance requests. Tax declarations are categorized into different schedules, including excise tax, PAYE (Income Tax), and value-added tax (VAT), with varying levels of detail required depending on the schedule. However, several issues were identified. Firstly, the navigation under each menu tab is not straightforward, with unclear content and complicated layouts. For instance, progress indicators for processes are often inaccurate, and feedback can be delayed, leading to user frustration. Secondly, users are required to convert data sheets from formats like PDF, Word, or Excel into CSV format before uploading, as the system only accepts CSV files.

During the upload and download processes, users receive updates about their actions. For example, while downloading forms like the TIN for individual registration and the income tax return form, users see a visual progress indicator. Nevertheless, experts noted that the system struggles to load large numbers of files simultaneously. Overall, despite these challenges, the e-tax portal generally adheres to this principle by providing constructive and timely feedback, effectively responding to user actions without unexpected surprises or tedious data entry sequences.

Figure 2. Tax declaration uploads file detail

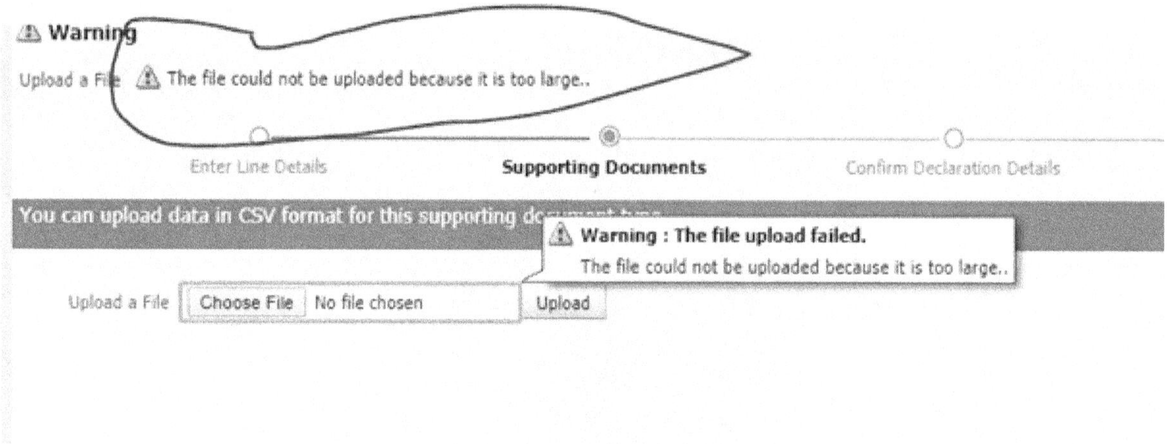

Many pages on the website do not feature clear tab names, despite the current page location being displayed. As most links open in new tabs, users must navigate through multiple pages, as illustrated in Figures 3, 4, and 5. This results in lengthy and cumbersome processes for simple tasks, such as returning to the homepage or logging into e-filing. Users often find it difficult to remember the steps required, indicating a need for improved navigation assistance to enhance their experience

Figure 3. Login page on e-filing (A)

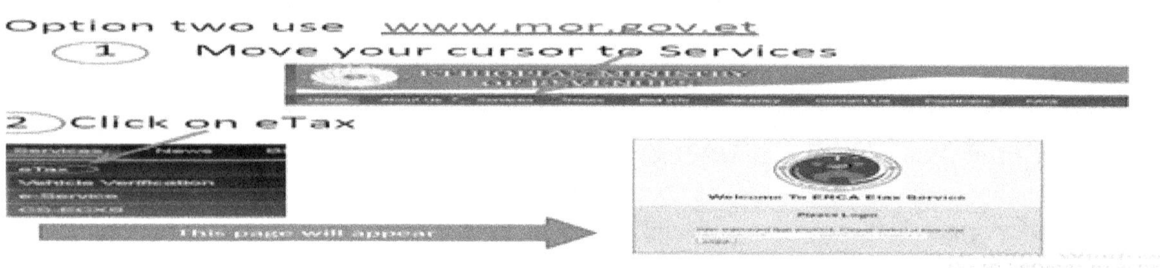

The expert emphasizes that productivity declines when users experience frustration while using the computer. This suggests a need to assess the current documentation system's user interface, as it involves lengthy and complicated steps that could be streamlined for improved efficiency.

Figure 4. Login page on e-filing (B)

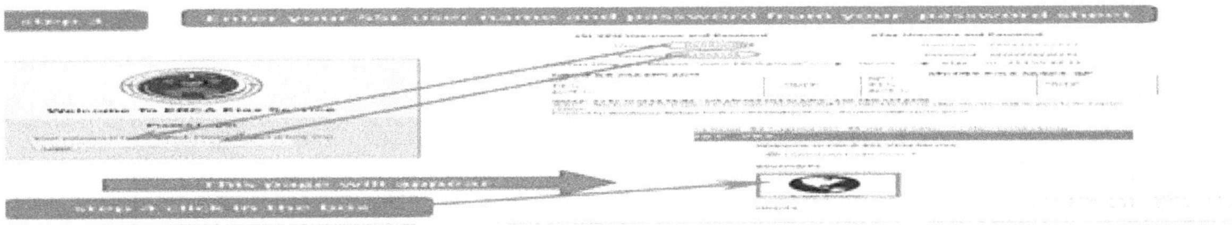

Figure 5. Login page on e-filing (C)

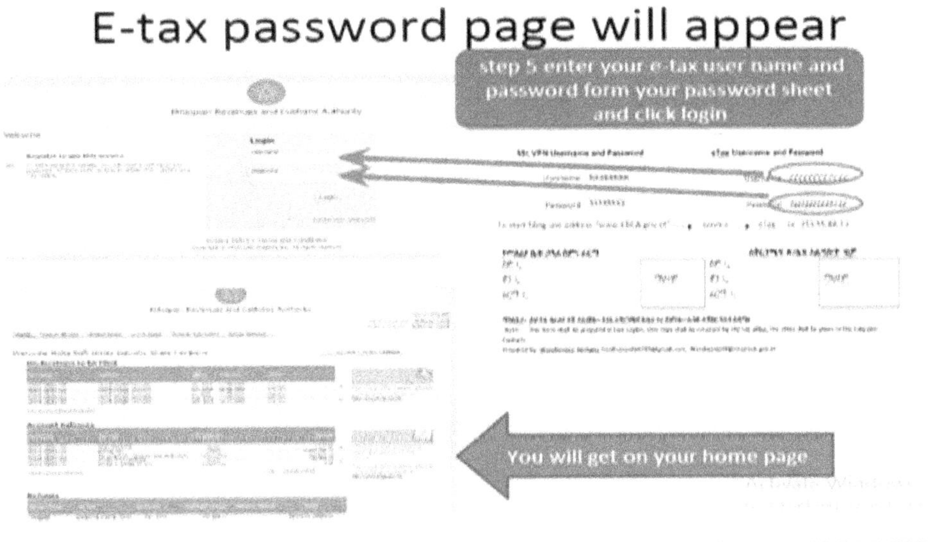

Figures 3 to 5 emphasize that users should be aware of their current capabilities within the system at all times. They need to understand which system they are in, their position within it, and how close they are to achieving their goals. Additionally, users should be clearly informed when they have completed their tasks, regardless of the outcome.

Heuristic 2: Match Between System and the Real World

This principle underscores the need for user-friendly language that resonates with users instead of relying on technical jargon. An expert reviewer, who is also a regular user of the e-tax portal, assessed the clarity and familiarity of the language throughout the site. The evaluation focused on the homepage and its subpages, revealing a well-organized layout featuring a top navigation menu, a taxpayer service section highlighting key events, and a detailed tax declaration menu on the left.

The lower section of the homepage provides updates from the Ministry of Revenue on various tax matters, including excise tax and pension contributions, while the footer includes essential links for canceling, clearing, and saving contact information. The main navigation menu comprises six items, with the e-tax service section covering intuitive categories such as tax declarations and refund requests. The dropdown menu system enhances usability by allowing users to preview sub-menu items without additional clicks. However, issues were noted by the experts: Expert 1 pointed out a lack of transparency, stating that some information leads to null outcomes. Expert 2 mentioned that the email icon is not linked to an email address, and Expert 3 observed that while the footer contains essential links, it lacks options for processing returns and clearance requests. Overall, the evaluation found the language and structure of the e-tax portal to be accessible and easy to navigate, highlighting the importance of using familiar terminology in digital platforms to improve user experience and facilitate effective interactions with the system.

Heuristic 3: User Control and Freedom

This principle highlights the importance of enabling users to easily undo and redo actions, as mistakes are common and users need straightforward recovery options. An expert reviewer, who is also a researchers, evaluated the e-tax portal's ability to help users reverse accidental actions, particularly during tasks like logging in and processing e-tax filings. Issue 1: Experts 1 and 2 noted the absence of undo and redo buttons, stating that users can only use the Ctrl + Z keys for undo actions. Issue 2: They also pointed out that transactions cannot be redone with the original tax payment date. During the login assessment, the reviewer encountered a common issue (Issue 3): forgetting the username, password, and the answer to the security question. Upon entering invalid credentials, a notification appeared. Although the portal offers a "forgot password" option, it does not function properly. Users must visit the tax center to recover their credentials, and if a password is not used within 30 days, it must be reset in person. Issue 4: Additionally, users lack the ability to exit undesirable situations, as the Ethiopian e-tax portal does not include an exit button. Overall, users should be able to undo and redo actions and understand their options within the system. Changes should be immediately reflected, and users should know why certain information is requested and how it will be used. Currently, the portal does not meet these conditions effectively.

This principle emphasizes the necessity for users to easily undo and redo actions, as mistakes are common and straightforward recovery options are essential. An expert reviewer, who is also a researchers, assessed the e-tax portal's functionality in allowing users to reverse accidental actions, particularly during login and e-tax filing processes. Issue 1: Experts 1 and 2 highlighted the lack of undo and redo buttons, noting that users can only use the Ctrl + Z keys for undoing actions. Issue 2: They also pointed out that transactions cannot be redone with the original tax payment date. During the login evaluation, the reviewer faced a common issue (Issue 3): forgetting the username, password, and the answer to the security question. When invalid credentials were entered, a notification appeared. Although a "forgot password" option is available, it does not work properly. Users are required to visit the tax center to recover their credentials, and if passwords are not used within 30 days, they must be reset in person. Issue 4: Additionally, users are unable to exit undesirable situations, as the Ethiopian e-tax portal lacks an exit button. Users should be able to undo and redo actions while understanding their options within the system. Changes should be instantly reflected, and users need clarity on why certain information is requested and how it will be used. Currently, the portal falls short in these areas.

Heuristic 4: Consistency and Standards

Users should not be left uncertain about whether different words, situations, or actions carry the same meaning. Nielsen emphasizes that adhering to standards promotes a consistent vocabulary in interface design. To evaluate this principle, the researchers assessed how well the e-tax portal aligned with common web conventions identified by Nielsen, which advocate for established standards to create a coherent design. Nielsen outlined seven key web conventions: placing the logo in the upper left corner, positioning the main navigation bar at the top, using underlined or differently colored text exclusively for links, employing buttons strictly for navigation, utilizing standard icons for recognized functions, applying visual hierarchy to highlight the importance and sequence of information, and providing clear names for navigation links.

The evaluation of the e-tax portal yielded the following findings: Placement of the Logo: The Ministry of Revenue logo was correctly displayed in the upper left corner, accompanied by the phrase "Welcome to ERCA E-Tax Service." Main Navigation Bar: While the portal featured a six-item navigation menu beneath the logo, it did not fully comply with the convention, as it contained eight or more sub-navigation options, which can overwhelm users and hinder efficient navigation. Use of Underlined or Differently Colored Text for Links: The portal fell short in this area, as some text, like "logout" and "cancel," matched the link color but did not function as links. Only the accompanying images were clickable, suggesting a lack of thorough usability testing. Using Buttons Only for Navigation Links: Although the portal generally adhered to this principle, some buttons for external sites like Facebook and Google did not link properly. Standard Icons for Common Functions: The homepage effectively used standard icons to represent commonly understood functions. Visual Hierarchy: The main content was positioned above the fold, making key information easily accessible. Nielsen's study highlighted that 77% of website visitors do not scroll, so placing crucial elements at the top is beneficial.

Clear Names for Navigation Links: All navigation link names were straightforward, employing conventional terms like "Home," "About Us," and "Contact Us." For specialized terms, the best possible wording was used, with dropdown menus displaying content upon hovering. In summary, while the e-tax portal demonstrates some adherence to Nielsen's web conventions, several areas require improvement to enhance user experience and facilitate efficient navigation.

Figure 6. Tax declaration with its sub navigation

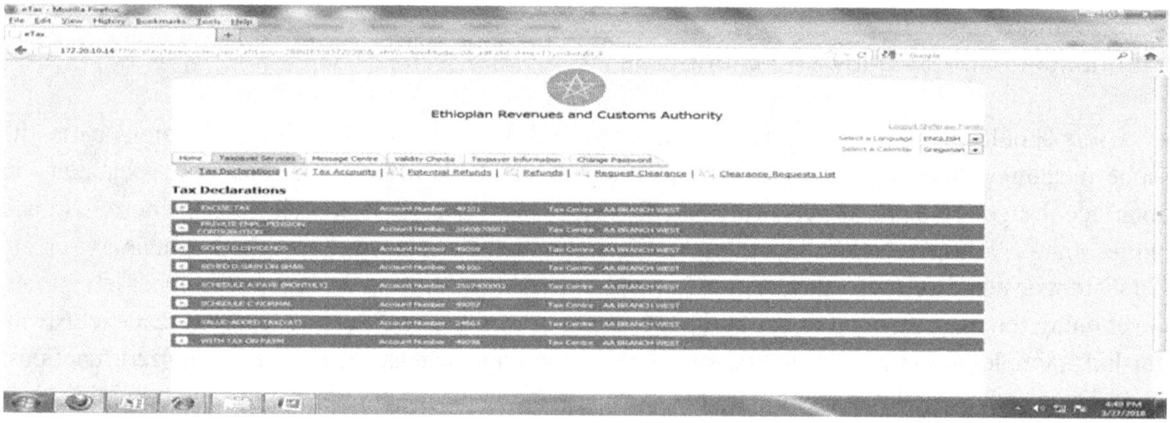

Heuristic 5: Error Prevention

This principle emphasized that it is more effective to design systems that prevent errors from occurring rather than merely providing good error messages. When users entered incorrect data types in fields such as date of birth, mobile number, maiden name, and email, the system became unresponsive, caused confusion. This highlighted that, despite implementing input constraints, the lack of clear feedback hindered user understanding and navigation, indicating a need for improved guidance and communication within the system. Additionally, the issue of inadequate to support for new taxpayers was noted, emphasizing the importance of addressing the needs of individuals unfamiliar with the tax system to ensure compliance and engagement. The research highlighted the importance of forgiving formatting as part of Laubheimer's strategies for error prevention, which include adhering to design conventions, communicating usage clearly, previewing results, displaying contextual information, confirming destructive actions, allowing undo options, and providing real-time error warnings.

The assessment of the portal's design conventions revealed that while it adhered to some common standards such as using familiar icons, and placing the main navigation menu in the upper left corner, certain elements fell short. For instance, buttons linked to functional elements lacked distinct colors or underlining for hyperlinks, failing to meet established conventions. The report included detailed evaluations of which conventions were successfully implemented and which were not. Furthermore, the usability study did not effectively demonstrate how to assess the portal's usability, highlighting a lack of pages or features for testing this aspect. This indicates a need for clearer guidance to help users navigate and utilize the portal more effectively.

However, the research identified a lack of suitable pages or functionalities to test recommendations related to confirming actions before destructive events and offering an undo option. Since the focus was on the public-facing interface, critical features likely available in the internal interface used by staff were not assessed. The issue of "inability to make corrections when the taxpayer informs" suggests that when a taxpayer alerts the relevant authority (like a tax center) about an error, the authority may be unable to implement the necessary corrections. This could indicated systemic limitations in processing such requests or a lack of responsive mechanisms to address user-reported issues.

Figure 7. Declaration details

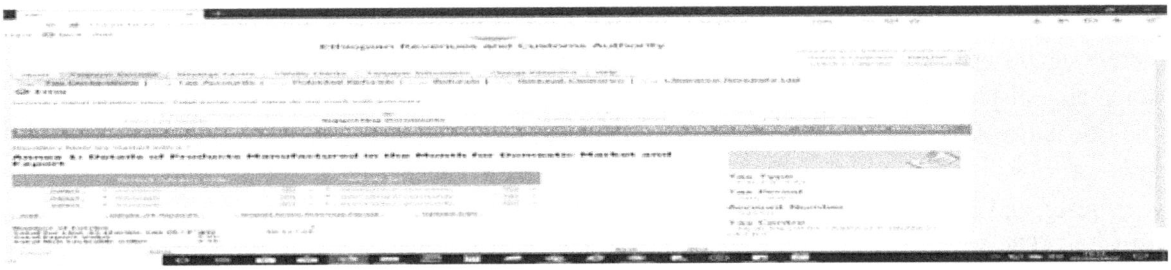

The analysis found that the forms included contextual error warnings for some fields, prompting users with messages like "please enter a proper value for the text" and "enter numeric data in this field." However, fields such as username, request summary, and request description did not have similar warnings, despite being prone to incorrect entries. This highlights the need to identify additional fields that would benefit from contextual error warnings to enhance user experience and minimize errors. Additionally, there was no distinction between the excise on summary and detail pages, yet discrepancies in the amounts were reported, indicating a potential issue that requires attention.

Heuristic 6: Recognition Rather Than Recall

According to Nielsen, users should not need to recall information from one part of the interface to another; instead, instructions for using the system should always be visible or easily retrievable when needed. This principle was assessed based on Nielsen's recommendations, which advocate for making content and interface functions visible and accessible, including providing access to recently visited pages and previous searches, as well as ensuring that interface elements such as buttons and menus are both visible and intuitive.

However, during the evaluation, the evaluators were unable to access user account, and their request for assistance through the online service desk went unanswered. Issue one according to expert three" not processing our return, example clearance request", It suggests that a request for the return of something (such as a tax return, merchandise, or documentation) or a request for clearance (possibly related to customs, security, or compliance) is not being acted upon or is being delayed indicates that a request for return or clearance is not being processed, potentially due to delays, missing information, compliance issues, or other administrative factors. The system should provide users with suggestions to make the process of remembering their needs easier i.e the system don't exactly recall but provide with suggestions.

Heuristic 7: Flexibility and Efficiency of Use

This principle suggests that interface designers should develop interfaces that cater or provide to the needs of both expert and novice users. This can be accomplished by integrating accelerators that are not visible to all users but are accessible to more experienced users, enabling them to expedite interactions and customize frequently used actions, such as adding commonly visited websites to their favorite's folder in the browser. However, the study found no evidence of such accelerators, including shortcuts or options for saving frequently visited pages in the portal's favorite's folder. The system should provide users with different ways to accomplish the same goal to accommodate different users and different situations with different paths toward accomplishing the same goal. This indicates that the information may not have been entered correctly or may have been omitted entirely during the data entry process or there could be technical issues, such as software glitches or filtering settings, preventing the information from being displayed.

Issue two as expert two assessment "Not seeing what we announced 2 years ago" suggests that there was a previous announcement made by an individual (likely a leader, executive, or public figure) two years prior, and currently, there is a lack of evidence or realization of that announcement's promises or outcomes. This phrase conveys a sense of disappointment or confusion regarding the follow-through on a past announcement, suggesting that the expected outcomes or changes have not materialized as initially communicated. Here are some potential interpretations consequently; the Ethiopian e-tax center should consider incorporating this functionality to improve the portal's usability and efficiency for regular users.

Heuristic 8: Aesthetic and Minimalist Design

This principle highlights the importance of avoiding the inclusion of irrelevant or rarely needed information in an interface, as each additional piece of information competes with essential content and diminishes its visibility. Nielson notes that interfaces should only present elements and content that is relevant to the goals and tasks of the page. This principle was assessed on the home page, which, during the study, featured only content pertinent to the portal's objectives. This included the main navigation menu (Home, user registration, filing declarations, and refund and clearance requests, updating taxpayer information, validating Tax Identification Numbers (TIN), and managing the message Centre. Additionally, the portal offers forms and templates for e-tax services, which encompass tax declarations, tax accounts, potential refunds, refund requests, and clearance request lists, and a more detailed navigation menu for services located in the middle left section of the page. The footer contained links for contacting e-tax portal downloading forms.

Overall, all content on the home page was relevant to supporting the objectives and tasks of Ethiopian taxpayers. But according to expert two "the system interface elements appear to be not in a harmony or combination of related elements, the content of the system should not organized in a way that allows the user to distinguish each related elements, it contain any unnecessary content that would distract the user or extraneous content on the system (features, icons, texts, etc.) omitted, The system contain any unnecessary content that would distract the user. The content that users need to accomplish certain goals should be clearly presented to them, and they should not need to rely on their memory to remember them.

Heuristic 9: Help Users Recognize, Diagnose, and Recover From Errors

This principle advocates for error messages to be presented in plain language, clearly identifying the issue and offering constructive solutions. Duggirala underscores the necessity of explaining errors to users in a way that is easy to understand. Most systems do not provide error-free information, leading to confusion for both taxpayers and officers. For instance issue one the system files information only after 24 hours without an error message, additionally, issue two when the bank does not utilize the document number, Issue three issuing with depositing funds into the wrong account, and issue four mistakenly deducted taxes from customers' accounts multiple times the error message did not tell whether the problem happed or not.

Furthermore, Issue five when registering for VAT, if the main TIN is not registered, it is incorrectly rejected as "not registered for VAT" during e-filing. Issue six for withholding payments, the system allows data entry up to line 40 but then generates an error that cannot be resolved. Despite attempts to remove the entered details one by one, the error persists. Lastly, tax type supporting documents often display an "unexpected error occurred." Furthermore, the guidance provided for resolving this issue was inadequate; after struggling to recall the answer to the secret question, it was unable to proceed with the recovery process. In such cases, offering options could have enabled a more effective resolution to the error. Users should be able to easily identify when an error has occurred. They should also clearly understand the nature of the error. Furthermore, the system should offer recommendations on how to resolve the issue.

Heuristic 10: Help and Documentation

This principle advises that if help and documentation is provided in a Website, it should be easy to search, focused on the user's task, list concrete steps to be carried out, and not too large. Therefore, the test was focused on establishing availability of help and documentation, ease of search, extent of focus on the user's task, list of concrete steps to be carried out and size. Issue one Evaluator three observed that "the system is complex as a help tool" and recommended that it should provide users with a clear navigation structure on a single page. Additionally, while the search results are organized by relevance, the filtering options do not deliver the expected results, making it difficult for users to find the companies' TIN in the e-tax user list."

The system should also facilitate easy access for users to contact the help team. The portal also has a service desk option on you tube where users can initiate service desk requests as well as search the status of a service request. However, it would have been better to consolidate all these forms of help and documentation in one place or link them to each other to provide one stop help and documentation centr instead of scattering them as was the case at the time of the study. Issue two Evaluator two emphasizes that "the system should provide users with sufficient resources to understand its functionalities and tackle any potential challenges. Currently, there is a lack of adequate learning materials to help users navigate the system and overcome obstacles while searching for content. Additionally, materials should be prioritized based on action frequency."

The system should offer suggestions to help users easily recall their needs. Catering to diverse users and varying situations. Additionally, the sequence of tasks within the system should be streamlined for simplicity. Evaluator four pointed out that an issue "the system does not allow users to quickly identify the most relevant resources. Additionally, there are no short video or audio tutorials available to help users consolidate all these forms of help and documentation in one place or link them to each other and learn the system and address potential challenges. Contextual documentation should be presented alongside major tasks to offer users immediate guidance. And evaluator two emphasized that "user's lack straightforward access to learning materials, effective search capabilities, and prioritized content based on action frequency, and contextual documentation for major tasks." Overall, the system needs to provide users with adequate resources to support their learning and help them navigate any challenges they may encounter. And also the content required for users to meet specific objectives should be clearly displayed, eliminating the need for them to rely on memory.

CONCLUSION

After analyzing the consolidated list of issues identified from the heuristic evaluation of the portal, it was found that some heuristics were violated with the system. Figure 1 illustrates the percentage of issues associated with each heuristic. Notably, the heuristics for (H1) Visibility of System Status, (H5) Error Prevention Consistency, and (H4) Standards, and (H4) User Control and Freedom exhibited the highest number of detected problems, with percentages of 19.0%, 15.7%, 15.0%, and 14%, respectively. Based on the issue findings in table 13, calculations were performed to determine the Heuristic principle most frequently encountered in the evaluation of the e-tax website. The code H1, which corresponds to the principle of Visibility of System Status, was found to be the most frequently identified principle, of 121 identified issues.

The evaluation results highlight both strengths and weaknesses in the usability of the e-tax portal. On the positive side, the portal has made notable progress in aligning with conventional web standards for content categorization and link naming, as evidenced by the clear labeling of most elements on the homepage. In instances where standard conventions were not applicable due to the specialized nature of the content, the portal effectively organized information to facilitate easy navigation, employing interaction styles such as dropdown menus to structure sub-content under main menu items. Additionally, a combination of commonly and less commonly used icons was generally not implemented successfully. Certain services within the portal offered adequate support for users to undo erroneous actions, and some form fields featured important contextual error warning functions. For example, support for undoing actions was inadequate in some services, highlighting issues with user control and freedom (heuristic principle number 2).

Furthermore, several text elements intended to function as links were inactive, and some buttons, such as the Twitter and Facebook buttons and user manual link for help users, did not perform as expected action. Common Web Design Conventions—like ensuring that all buttons link to relevant actions and duplicating contact information in multiple locations—were inconsistently applied, negatively affecting usability. Additionally, constraints on user data input often lacked appropriate feedback, failing to inform users about their actions or guide them through the next steps in navigation, particularly in the email and telephone fields of forms. Certain form fields, such as the user ID field, would benefit from contextual error warnings, which were absent, potentially increasing data entry errors and undermining the overall quality and value of the collected data. To address these issues, it is essential to conduct comprehensive testing of all elements and features, especially involving real users, to confirm they function as intended. Further identification of form fields that could benefit from contextual error warnings is necessary, along with providing appropriate guidance to assist users in their next steps.

This paper demonstrates a quick and cost-effective approach for evaluating the usability of e-tax or e-government services. It offers recommendations to the Ethiopia revenue authority aimed at enhancing the usability of the tax portal to attract and retain a broader user base. Additionally, it provides general guidelines for webmasters to create and maintain more user-friendly e-taxportal and web-based services. The detailed interpretation of Jakob Nielsen's 10 usability heuristics in relation to web usability objectives illustrates how these principles can be effectively applied in the usability evaluation process. Future research will focus on conducting usability tests with actual users. The Ethiopian e-tax system exhibits a mix of usability strengths and areas for improvement. While users typically find the system effective, efficient, and satisfying, significant usability challenges persist, including navigation difficulties, inconsistent design, lack of search functionality, and inadequate mechanisms for error recovery. Addressing these challenges could greatly enhance the overall usability and user experience of the system.

REFERENCES

Awai, E. S., & Oboh, T. (2020). Ease of paying taxes: The electronic tax system in Nigeria. Accounting and taxation review, 4(1), 63-73.

Baguma, R. (2018, April). Usability evaluation of the etax portal for uganda. In *Proceedings of the 11th International Conference on Theory and Practice of Electronic Governance* (pp. 449-458).

Barati, A., & Bakhshayesh, S. (2015). Electronic tax system and the facing challenges (case study: Kermanshah Province tax payers). *Indian Journal of Fundamental and Applied Life Sciences*, *5*(S1), 480–497.

Eilu, E., Walyawula, C., & Soita, R. (2021, March). An assessment of usability of online tax return services in Uganda and its influence on tax revenue. In *Proceedings of the 3rd African Human-Computer Interaction Conference: Inclusiveness and Empowerment* (pp. 113-118).

Gajjar, D. (2013). Ethical consideration in research. *Education*, *2*(7), 8–15.

Maccarthy, M. I. T., Abolo, A. P., & Ogullah Stephen Brass Ph, D. (2022). Electronic Tax System And Tax Revenue Efficiency In Nigeria 2008-2021. BW Academic Journal, 22-22.

Mulisa, F. (2023). The Use of True-Random, Quasi-Random, and Nonrandom, Vol.14, No.1.

Pilcher, N., & Cortazzi, M. (2023). across subject fields: implications for research values, assumptions, and practices.

Silvis, I. M., Bothma, T. J., & de Beer, K. J. (2018). Evaluating the usability of the information architecture of academic library websites. *Library Hi Tech*, *37*(3), 566–590.

Vlachogianni, P., & Tselios, N. (2023). Perceived usability evaluation of educational technology using the post-study system usability questionnaire (PSSUQ): A systematic review. *Sustainability*, *15*(17), 12954.

Xiong, X. (2022, July). Critical review of quantitative and qualitative research. In 2022 3rd International conference on mental health, education and human development (MHEHD 2022) (pp. 956-959). Atlantis Press.

Yoseph, R. (2017). Assessment of Electronic Tax Filing System in Selected Branch Offices of Ethiopian Revenues and Customs Authority (ERCA) (Doctoral dissertation, St. Mary's University).

Chapter 14
Utilizing 10-K Filings to Profile American Corporate Tax Conduct:
A Methodological Proposal

Georgia Beake Litle
https://orcid.org/0009-0006-8188-3651
University of Oklahoma, USA

ABSTRACT

This chapter seeks to highlight and evaluate the use of 10-K filings as a methodology to effectively measure corporate tax behavior at publicly traded, American corporations. The chapter delivers examples of how to utilize sections of the 10-K filing (including textual analyses strategy and example of application to recent presidential policy) to evaluate tax behavior in the context of federal regulation. Utilization of both qualitative narrative and quantitative metrics found in the 10-K filing leads to more substantive and meaningful analyses of the corporate tax conduct that impacts the direction of the global economy.

1. INTRODUCTION

Large, American publicly traded corporations (corporations that list and issue shares on a public exchange) are influential taxpayers that arguably dominate the course of global economic relations. Notably, the influence of these larger corporations extends beyond pure economic jurisdiction to exert political, social, and cultural influences that direct global trade relations, multi-national tax burdens and procedures, and shape national policies. In addition, internal corporate policies pertaining to employment conditions at these organizations influence the quality of life of billions of corporate employees.

From a methodological standpoint, an issue previously explored within business and accounting academic literature concerns how to evaluate, and potentially predict, taxation related decision-making from large, publicly traded entities. Key corporate decision-makers (such as the Chief Financial Officer and Chief Executive Officer) do not operate in a vacuum. Rather, in the American context, these corporate leaders make influential decisions under the observation of shareholder investors and regulatory bodies via data provided in public filings.

DOI: 10.4018/979-8-3373-0422-9.ch014

More specifically, the United States Securities and Exchange Commission (SEC) requires an annual, public 10-K filing from registered publicly traded entities. This 10-K report is circulated to shareholders before the annual corporate meeting to evaluate executive management and elect the Board of Directors. 10-K financial disclosures provide data for the Internal Revenue Service (IRS) to use in their enforcement processes and to corroborate private information provided in corporations' tax filings (Chen et al., 2021).

The issue of how publicly traded corporations "behave" in a taxation context is generally measured via pure financial metrics. Substantial accounting and business academic literature suggests that corporate firms find 10-K disclosures particularly relevant to improve transparency and alleviate investor concerns through additional narrative disclosure. The presence of a more narrative type of disclosure within the 10-K provides rich content depicting the contextualized opinions of corporate management. Accounting and business studies provide considerable analyses pertaining to how these narrative disclosure patterns relate to taxation related corporate decision-making and conduct.

In essence, this chapter will deliver an explanation and examples of how 10-K filings can describe and contextualize tax behavior of large, publicly traded, American corporations. Arguably, 10-K filings should be used in analyses of corporate taxation decision-making practices to lead to more reliable and substantive conclusions about the tax behavior and trajectory of large corporations. This subject matter is particularly impactful considering the critical influence of these large corporations on the direction of the global economy.

2. THEORETICAL FOUNDATIONS

a. Upper Echelons Theory

10-K disclosures are particularly helpful for two reasons (i) corporate managers have discretion over certain contents and length of disclosures, which allows managerial incentives and priorities to come to light and (ii) majority of prior accounting literature on the relation between risk and corporate disclosure tends to focus on more discretionary disclosures to better show managerial priorities (Bourveau & Schoenfeld, 2017). The 10-K is a publicly available filing that provides a relatively comprehensive and narrative depiction of the current state of a public company's business, including risks and relevant financial metrics. The narrative portion of the 10-K provides management's explanation of the organization's reported financial results, which includes a certification of accuracy and completeness of the 10-K filing from the chief executive officer or chief financial officer (referred to as Sections 302 and 906 certifications). According to upper echelons theory, corporate managements' experiences substantially influence corporate strategic decision-making and behavior subject to certain external limitations, such as institutional and network related pressures (Frerich et al., 2015). Thus, the key driver of the importance of the 10-K filing is analysis of upper management's discretionary disclosures to predict tax avoidance behavior and measure the impacts of tax policies.

b. Resource Dependency Theory

Resource dependency theory focuses on how shareholder dependency explains corporate relational power dynamics. Thus, scholars have extended this foundational theoretical premise to explain corporations' dependence on shareholders. A resource dependent theoretical framework (that corporations rely on shareholders for resources and thus act in their interests) provides substantial explanation of why institutionalized dependence on shareholders for capital steers corporate tax related behavior (Schnatterly et al. et al. 2018, 2413).

When it comes to tax related audit and litigation, the financial impact of litigation is not the only concern to larger corporations due to corporations' enormous revenue overshadowing most potential settlements amounts and/or regulatory fines. Reputational damage and impact to short- or long-term value for shareholders (including damage to reputation among larger, impactful institutional shareholder investors) carries substantial impact for key decision-makers at larger companies when considering whether to alter corporate tax behavior after audit or litigation. This dependency highlights the importance of the 10-K, which is a public statement to investors.

c. Corporate Networks

The idea of reputational penalties may be mitigated by assertions that impactful corporate networks collude to build legitimacy of malfeasant corporate behavior through systematic insulation from reputational backlash (Tillman, 2009). Reputational theory was revived and reformulated by proponents of the Law and Economics perspective, an offshoot of the Chicago School of Economics, that centers on philosophies of rationality and assumptions about the importance of free markets (Tillman, 2009). To summarize, such reputational theory provides that corporate actors operate in networks and markets that impose penalties (external to traditional legal penalties) on corporate actors that fail to carry out expected behaviors within the network. These penalties arise in the form of damage to the offending corporation's reputation (Tillman, 2009). The theory of reputational penalties has been commonly accepted by economists (Tillman, 2009). Utilization of 10-K filings provides context to Tillman's (2009) analysis on institutional, corporate networks. The narrative, managerial disclosures within the 10-K related to malfeasant financial acts share common characteristics within a particular corporate network and industry. Thus, 10-K filings are primed to address theoretical inquiries pertaining to the impact of corporate networks and reputation yet are underutilized in certain academic disciplines.

3. OVERVIEW OF THE 10-K FILING

American publicly traded corporations are required to annually prepare and file 10-K reports with the Securities and Exchange Commission (SEC). The purpose of the filing is to provide reliable information about a company's financial practices to help corporate shareholders make informed investment decisions. The 10-K generally overlaps with, or is the same as, the publicly traded corporation's annual report to shareholders. The annual report is used to explain the company's current position to shareholders before the annual meeting to elect the board of directors. In basic terms, the 10-K provides perspective from the corporation's management on the company's overall health and position in the market similar to the annual report. To note, a Form "10-Q" is a similar but abbreviated version of the 10-K that relates to the relevant fiscal quarter.

One of the most advantageous aspects of utilizing 10-K filings to evaluate corporate tax behavior is that the filings can provide a uniform and predictable method for evaluation. The filings have generally comparable sections across corporations and are annually (and thus reliably) reported. Correspondingly, tax analysts can utilize the most "effective" years for comparative analyses. In addition, Form 10-K requirements relate to certain tax penalties created via the American Jobs Creation Act of 2004. The American Jobs Creation Act of 2004 (AJCA) amended the Internal Revenue Code, which among other things, requires that a 10-K filer disclose any requirement to pay penalties relating to certain "reportable transactions" under Section 6707 A. Failure to report triggers penalties, as outlined in IRS Treasury Decision 9550 (Sec 13 or 15, 2025).

a. Mandatory Disclosures Relevant to Corporate Taxation and Tax Audit

The 10-K filing includes information about a company's current federal income tax strategy, including the company's best estimate of the corporate federal income tax for the year. In addition, the 10-K provides information on "uncertain tax positions" that executive management believes are less than 50% likely to be upheld by a tax authority. The 10-K also provides information relevant to tax analysis of publicly traded corporations provided below, such as legal information, management discussion of corporate strategy, and disclosure of information pertaining to relevant business operations.

The Sarbanes Oxley Act requires the SEC to review every public company's financial statements at least once every three years, including metrics relevant to taxation analyses. Although the SEC closely monitors 10-K filings and provides guidance to corporations pertaining to filing deficiencies, perhaps even more frequently than required by Sarbanes Oxley (a law intended to protect investors), the SEC does not guarantee the accuracy of the 10-K. Rather, the SEC expressly prohibits publicly traded corporations from providing materially false or misleading statements or omitting material information in the filing while providing specific requirements and topics that must be disclosed with interpretive guidelines. Furthermore, corporations must explain any unresolved comments previously received from the SEC in the corporation's current report.

The 10-K is an annual filing. Thus, a potential argument exists that the 10-K filing is not timely or frequent enough to accurately demonstrate change in corporate behavior. However, accounting and business literature provides additional support to the unique value of the 10-K filings compared to other required corporate disclosures. For a specific example, more frequent disclosures, such as voluntary 8-K corporate filings, do not mitigate a statistical relationship between external capital shock to a corporation and disclosure within the 10-K (Leuz, 2009).

Specific sections of the 10-K form include a general description of the company's dealings, what subsidiaries it owns, and an overview of market concerns (such as regulatory pressures and description of factors specific to the company's unique competitive market). In addition, corporations must disclose information pertaining to material risk factors. Other notable sections that assist in contextualization of corporate tax paying behavior include information on significant pending legal proceedings and information on equity securities (such as number of shareholders, dividends, and stock repurchases). One of the most enlightening sections pertains to management's discussion and analysis of financial conditions, also known as the Management Discussion and Analysis (MD&A) section. This 10-K section allows management to provide a story of the company's operations and financial metrics (including tax data) and how any risks may materially impact the health of the corporation. The MD&A section further allows corporate management the opportunity to explain how management views or plans to address material risks, financial shortcomings, or accounting judgements that impact the taxation metrics found in the corresponding financial documents.

Turning to the corporation's tax and financial documents, the 10-K requires disclosure of the company's audited financial statements in compliance with Generally Accepted Accounting Principles ("GAAP'), such as the income statement, balance sheet, statement of cash flows, and statement of stockholders' equity. "Non-GAAP financial measures" may be found in the 10-K that do not conform to GAAP. However, corporations must generally explain how such numbers differ from the comparable GAAP metrics. The SEC further requires that the Form provide an exhibit list of all essential and relevant documents discussed in the Form 10-K, which generally includes the company's bylaws, material contracts, and the list of subsidiaries.

These corporate financial statements are required to be audited by an independent accountant. The independent accountant provides a report on the corporation's financial reporting integrity. This auditor's report is a foundational piece of the integrity of the 10-K. An "unqualified opinion" indicates that the independent auditor opines that the corporation's financial statements provide a fair representation of the company's financial position in compliance with GAAP. In contrast, a "qualified opinion" or "disclaimer of opinion" indicates discrepancies found during the independent audit. Companies must also provide explanation of any change in its accountants or disagreement with accountants. Any uncommon changes or disagreements with auditing firms are red flags for both shareholders and regulators.

In addition, the 10-K further provides information pertaining to directors, executive management, the corporation's general corporate governance practices, the independence of the board, and the company's code of ethics. The 10-K must provide disclosure of relationships and transactions between the company and its directors, executive officers, and their family members. Also pertaining to executive management, the report includes disclosures pertaining to executive compensation programs (including equity compensation) and shares owned by members of the board of directors, larger shareholders, and executive officers. The 10-K is comparable to the Form 10-Q, which is a quarterly SEC filing that is less detailed and usually unaudited, and the Form 8-k, which is a required filing following a "significant" event as notification to investors (German, 2025).

Turning to more modern filing requirements and litigation, executive perks will likely be a prominent issue for disclosure in upcoming annual filings because, in late 2024, the SEC settled a prominent case centered on failure to disclose perks and personal benefits to shareholders in its proxy statements (Sheppard Mullin, 2025). As applies to tax regulation, the SEC asserted that the company erroneously applied a standard in which a "business purpose" was sufficient to categorize an "item" as not a perk or personal benefit for disclosure purposes (Sheppard Mullin, 2025). The litigation demonstrated the importance of disclosure controls and that categorization of an expense as "an ordinary or necessary business expense" for general taxation purposes is not the suitable test for determining whether an expense is a perk subject to disclosure in the 10-K filing (Sheppard Mullin, 2025).

As described below in the shareholder model overview section of this chapter, disclosure to investors is a primary purpose of the 10-K filing. An example court case displaying the importance of disclosure was heard before the U.S. Supreme Court in 2024 in a multibillion-dollar shareholder lawsuit that alleged that corporate giant Meta omitted key information from the risk disclosure statements in Facebook's annual 10-K filings when the corporate disclosure merely cautioned about potential exploitation of user data as a hypothetical risk that could harm the company's business and reputation (Coyne, 2025). The company did not disclose that it knew the risk had very likely already occurred (Coyne, 2025). Thus, the 10-K filing is a useful methodological tool due its intended purpose of fair disclosure and required uniform corporate compliance with SEC disclosure guidelines.

4. THE AMERICAN SHAREHOLDER MODEL OF CORPORATE GOVERNANCE AND CORPORATE TAX BEHAVIOR

A discussion of American corporate taxation practices is not properly contextualized without adequate understanding of the American shareholder model of corporate governance. An appreciation of the importance of shareholder value to corporate conduct illuminates the relationship between shareholders and corporate executive management. "The amount of corporate income tax a company pays is material to [shareholder] profitability" (Principles for Responsible Investment, 2018).

Notably, the primary source of influence on corporate operations is corporate executive management, and management is primarily responsible for drafting 10-K filings (Bavaso 2018). The concept of corporate motivation to increase shareholder value speaks to the tax specific issue of how managers strive to invest in strategies that lower corporate taxes to increase value for shareholders (Chen et al., 2021). Notably, non-tax related costs, such as consumer pricing strategy, reputational and network costs, and regulatory penalties relate to tax avoidance strategies (Chen et al., 2021).

Corporate executive managers, such as the chief executive officer, do not operate or make decisions in a vacuum but under observation of shareholder investors through public filings (Schnatterly et al., Gangloff, and Tuschke 2018, 2407). Thus, in this current shareholder dominated era of corporate governance, corporate executive management falls in line to pursue and develop interests focused on maximizing shareholder return (Pernell et al., 2017, 534). Correspondingly, literature suggests that corporate dependence on shareholders permeates both the individual and organizational levels of any public corporate entity: at the organizational level, dependence on external shareholders affects critical resources to the organization while, at the individual level, managers as individuals may engage in or encourage behavior to reap the personal benefits of successfully increasing shareholder value (Prechel & Zheng 2016, 657).

Thus, maximizing shareholder value, which is described and proven through SEC filings, is now popularly categorized as the foundational element of rational managerial behavior and decision-making (Godfrey 2005, 779). Current sociological literature provides that the shift to focus on shareholder value in the United States specifically marked a loss of independent power of corporate managers: a transition occurred in the United States in the 1980s from "managerial capitalism" to "investor capitalism" (Heilbron et al. 2014, 2-3; Useem & Gager, 1996). In summary, any communications with shareholder investors, such as the 10-K filing, are crucial indicators of corporate tax behavior in the American context.

For historical perspective, the shareholder value model of corporate governance became prominent in the United States during the 1980s and 1990s (Prechel & Zheng 2016, 657). It is commonly known that the concept of shareholder value emerged in the United States as a response to the economic crisis of the late 1970s and early 1980s when (due to two oil crises and a stagnating economy with high inflation) American corporations experienced substantial financial difficulty (Heilbron et al. 2014, 1-2; Fligstein, 2001). Moreover, in the early 1980s, corporations were confronted with globalization and increased market competition, which resulted in declining profits and acute shareholder pressure to improve rate of return (Prechel & Boies 1998, 321).

As a response to such globalization and economic hardship, a movement emerged in the context of corporate governance based on contractarian legal theories that identified the corporation as a nexus of contracts among different stakeholders with shareholders recognized as residual claimants to corporate financial value (Bavaso 2018, 255). Moreover, certain interest groups advocated for a shareholder oriented corporate governance philosophy in the 1990s; thus, a corresponding myth of the importance of shareholder value evolved and expanded through encouragement of relevant market actors (Dobbin & Zorn 2005, 181). Corporate boards, executive management, and shareholders developed governance mechanisms that focused on maximizing shareholder returns (Pernell et al., 2017). The concept of shareholder value ideology spread to become the dominant governance model for corporations in the United States.

In another attempt to increase shareholder influence, large institutional investors (such as the Council of Institutional Investors) lobbied to change regulations governing relations between investors and corporate managers in the early 1990s. In response, in 1992, the SEC and the FASB relaxed regulations pertaining to communication between managers and investors, which facilitated more opportunities for large investors to communicate their opinions to influence corporate filings, including 10-K filings (Prechel & Zheng 2016, 664). Today, the ability to generate shareholder value through filings to the SEC is essential to the definition of corporate behavior in America and is perceived as the primary defining feature of corporate firms (Heilbron et al. 2014, 18). Such focus on these SEC filings, which include annual 10-K filings, renders the filings especially impactful metrics to measure corporate conduct. In conclusion, the American shareholder model of governance provides essential background to understanding decision-making behaviors in American corporations and why executives make decisions to satisfy shareholders, including large institutional investors.

5. THE 10-K TO THE TAX AUDIT PROCESS

Tax audits are crucial tools to curb corporate tax behavior on both a domestic and international scale. The primary purpose of an audit is to reduce malfeasant behavior in the context of tax avoidance activities. "Corporate tax avoidance activities may suggest underlying legal, operational, reputational, financial and/or governance risks" (Principles for Responsible Investment, 2018). Corporations subject to higher audit risk engage in less tax avoidance behavior (Chen et al., 2021). Moreover, corporations that receive a tax-related SEC comment letter will usually reduce tax avoidance behaviors in the future (Chen et al., 2021). Thus, tax audits critically influence corporate tax planning strategy and the resulting economic ramifications (Lin, 2024). Notably, the IRS and SEC are limited in time and resources; thus, how these agencies approach the audit process is an essential issue impacting corporate tax behavior. In other words, corporate tax audits have a substantial ripple effect on national and global economies and influence key economic indicators (Suárez Serrato & Zidar, 2023). The importance of the audit process is apparent across international jurisdictions in diverse global regions, such as the Asia Pacific markets of Thailand, Malaysia, the Philippines, Indonesia, Pakistan, Bangladesh, Sri Lanka, Vietnam, and Papua New Guinea, which also require some disclosure of audit processes and fees (Institutional Shareholder Services, 2025).

Executives see the threat of audit as a crucial influence on corporate tax planning. However, tax authorities, including the IRS, generally do not divulge which corporations are subject to audit; thus, it is difficult to research the impact of formal audits on corporate tax practices (Lin, 2024). Lin (2024) provides an example of utilizing public disclosures within 10-K filings to evaluate the consequences of audit policy. 10-K filings provide a public narrative of corporate tax behavior that facilitates analysis of taxation practices at the firm level and firm level impact of audits over time for more aggregate investigation (Lin, 2024). Time series analysis utilizing 10-K filings can be used at both the aggregate and firm level (Lin, 2024).

Tax audits can signal uncertainty for firms, which curbs more egregious taxation related behavior. Tax authorities may challenge corporate tax planning strategies, and this potential challenge instigates uncertainty regarding tax settlement payouts (Lin, 2024). Moreover, Lin (2024) correspondingly found that increased operational uncertainty at the corporate level due to impending audit can also translate to stock return volatility and a corresponding cost of capital that restrains investment and new debt issuance.

Analyses of 10-K filings demonstrates that approximately three-quarters of United States firms disclosed information about audits in their annual 10-K filing and how tax audit settlements could impact future corporate earnings (Lin, 2024). Lin (2024) asserted that tax audits reduce incidents of corporate tax avoidance, even after the audits ended. Lin (2024) found that such deterrence can linger for up to three years post audit.

Furthermore, at the market level, audits may cause undesirable implications: a decrease in abnormal stock returns occurs around filing dates when corporate firms are subject to audit (Suárez Serrato & Zidar, 2023). This is likely due to the uncertainty triggered by audits and these trends in abnormal stock returns can continue for months after the audit filing dates (Suárez Serrato & Zidar, 2023). In general, more profitable corporations with foreign operations are more likely to attract IRS attention, whereas corporations with less cash holdings and capital intensity may be less subject to IRS inquiry (Chen et al., 2021).

6. CASE STUDIES

An abundance of accounting literature suggests that corporate firms find 10-K disclosures particularly relevant "to improve transparency and alleviate investor concerns" (Leuz, 2009). Moreover, a dominance of a narrative disclosure is obvious within 10- K reports (Hasan, 2020). "On average 80% of a 10-K report is devoted to the textual component of... disclosures... such qualitative information is vital in understanding firms' current performance, past results, and future outlook" (Hasan, 2020). Accounting studies provide substantial analyses of these qualitative disclosure patterns and policies to contextualize quantitative metrics related to taxation (Leuz et al., 2009).

Correspondingly, 10-K filings have historically provided unique methodological value. A major obstacle in studies of corporate behavior is the scarcity of systematic data that can be relied upon to define relevant samples. Regulation of 10-K filings by the SEC affords a natural safeguard to control data quality within the 10-K filings. "In 2013, the SEC began a comprehensive review of regulation with the intent of identifying excessive, unduly complex, and redundant disclosure" (Dyer, 2017). Furthermore, disclosures in annual filings change over time, indicating corporate and industry trends, including increases in audit concerns, globalization, regulation, and mandatory disclosures (Dyer, 2017). Attributes within the 10-K can transform in a time series evaluative pattern that explains trends in specific textual attributes (Dyer, 2017). In addition, 10-K filings provide a type of uniformity for comparison of tax behavior across corporations in a particular sector.

a. Case Study 1:

Calculating of Corporate Tax Liability During and After the First Trump Administration

The forthcoming case study provides a particularly relevant example of use of 10-K filings to evaluate specific tax policy implementation.

The first Trump administration undoubtedly marked policy transitions within the modern American political environment. More specifically, the administration substantially impacted the taxation behaviors of American public corporations. The Tax Cuts and Jobs Act (TCJA), also known as the 2017 Trump Tax Law, was created with the intent to cut corporate tax rates. The law reduced the federal top corporate tax income rate from 35% to 21% (Cleven, 2020). Relevant issues are correspondingly presented of how this law practically translated to influence corporate tax paying practices and, from a methodological standpoint, how academics and economists can empirically evaluate these changes. The related policy argument for lowering the corporate tax rate is that American corporate income places undue burden on United States corporations. This burden leads to less effective overall American economic performance. The United States has generally had one of the highest corporate income-tax rates among advanced countries (Hungerford, 2013).

Since the advent of the corporate income tax in 1909, debate has existed over whether and how taxation of large corporations impacts the American and global economies. Some, such as former President Obama, advocate more revenue-neutral corporate tax reform with reduction in the statutory corporate tax rate (Hungerford, 2013). Others argue for simple rate reduction or eradication of the corporate income tax. Currently, the United States statutory corporate income tax rate is higher than most advanced countries but generally akin to other OECD nations (Gardner et al., 2013). Arguments in favor of higher corporate income tax argue that the tax raises necessary revenue for the federal government and facilitates a more progressive American taxation system by placing burden on corporate capital accumulation (Hungerford, 2013). In addition, the argument exists that higher corporate income tax provides a safeguard against corporate taxpayers that seek to circumvent income tax because it prevents individuals from utilizing corporations as a form of tax shelter.

The 2017 Tax Cuts and Jobs Act (TCJA) undoubtedly facilitated pivotal changes in the American corporate tax code: the United States had a statutory federal corporate tax rate of 35% and American corporate profits were only subject to tax when repatriated (although the effective corporate tax rate was lower) (Siripurapu, 2021). The former system correspondingly encouraged corporations to place their profits overseas to avoid American taxation (Siripurapu, 2021). The TCJA lowered the corporate tax rate to 21%, transitioned to a more "territorial" corporate tax system, and provided deductions for licensing intellectual property to keep such assets in the United States (Siripurapu, 2021). The practical impact of the law is ripe for academic exploration. Thus, the issue is presented of how corporations behave considering current American corporate income tax policies: does increased statutory or effective corporate income tax rate cause corporations to place burden on their corporate capital, or does increase in taxation trigger other ramifications, such as reduction to the labor force? The 10-K filing can be used as a methodological tool to explore corporate income tax related behavior via time series and/or historical analyses.

Correspondingly, the non-partisan Institute on Taxation and Economic Policy (ITEP) released a report addressing corporate taxation behavior during the Trump administration (2024). Corporate 10-K reports provided the data for this analysis of key changes in taxation conduct during this political period. Per the results of the ITEP report, Trump's corporate tax policy facilitated a substantial decline in corporate tax rates for large, publicly traded corporations:

America's largest, consistently profitable corporations saw their effective tax rates fall from an average of 22.0 percent to an average of 12.8 percent after the Trump tax law went into effect in 2018 [and] [t]he 296 largest and consistently profitable United States corporations in this study paid $240 billion less in taxes from 2018 to 2021 than if they had continued to pay the effective rates they'd paid before the Trump tax law

While profits for the largest, continuously profitable United States corporations rose by 44 percent after passage of the Trump tax law, their federal tax bills dropped by 16 percent.

The number of these corporations paying tax rates of less than 10 percent increased from 56 to 95 after the Trump tax law went into effect. Many of the largest and most well-known corporations in the country — including Walmart, Verizon, Disney, and Meta — had the largest tax reductions after the Trump tax law went into effect (Gardner et al., 2024).

These results indicate considerable, potential impact for patterns in corporate taxation related behavior as well as the global economy at large. As noted above, these researchers utilized 10-K filings to arrive at these conclusions and identify specific determinants of the corporations' tax behaviors.

In their report, researchers included corporations that were profitable from 2013 through 2021 comparing "what companies paid in two four-year time periods when federal corporate tax law was stable and predictable" (Gardner et al., 2024). Moreover, in this case, the year 2017 was excluded from the analysis considering corporations reported transition tax paid on offshore profits, as required under the 2017 law (Gardner et al., 2024). This additional reporting requirement rendered accurate calculation of federal income tax on United States profits nearly impossible for that year considering it would require bifurcation from offshore profit reporting (Gardner et al., 2024).

How This Study Utilized Corporate 10-K Filings to Evaluate Corporate Taxation Behaviors:

(i) Sampling Technique

This study sought to evaluate corporate effective tax rates to address the broader issue of the health of the United States corporate income tax system (Gardner et al., 2024). The study looked at the largest American corporations utilizing a sample of 296 corporations in the Fortune 500 (ranked by revenue) and S&P 500 (ranked by market capitalization), excluding companies that reported United States pretax loss in any year addressed in the analysis or companies that did not provide sufficient information to calculate pretax income or current federal income tax (Gardner et al., 2024). Moreover, Apple Inc. was excluded based on geographic income splits that seemed flawed relative to the amount of tax expense reported: Apple reported effective United States tax rates over 40% in years after 2012, almost twice as high as the statutory tax rate, suggesting inaccuracies in the United States/foreign income split (Gardner et al., 2024).

(ii) Effective Taxation Rate Utilizing the 10-K

The study provides analysis of effective federal income taxes reported by each company on their pretax income from 2013 to 2016 and 2018 through 2021 (Gardner et al., 2024). More specifically, the report calculates current federal income tax expense as a share of pretax income as reported on the 10-K annual reports (Gardner et al., 2024). Such "effective tax rate" is the product of the company's pretax income, current federal income tax, and current state income tax (Gardner et al., 2024).

(iii) Utilizing the 10-K for a Pretax Income Calculation

Pertaining to pretax income calculation, noncontrolling interest income from a given company's subsidiaries provided for on financial statements as income may not be taxable to the corporation (Gardner et al., 2024). Such income was subtracted from calculated American and foreign pretax income (Gardner et al., 2024). Moreover, non-cash, non-taxable charges or impairments against income were occasionally taken by companies to suggest a reduced estimate of the company's future earnings (Gardner et al., 2024). When such impairments were disclosed, the researchers added these impairments back to pretax income (Gardner et al., 2024).

(iv) Utilizing the 10-K for the Federal Tax Expense Calculation

The use of current federal tax expense is significant to the analysis of effective tax rate because current taxes are those that the company is obligated to pay during the year and excludes "deferred" income taxes that are postponed until successive years (Gardner et al., 2024). Thus, the effective federal income tax rate was calculated as the current federal tax expense divided by the pretax income less current state tax (Gardner et al., 2024).

Concerning the federal income tax expense calculation, a transition tax was imposed on pre-2018 earnings by the 2017 tax law: companies were required to add the expected value of this tax to the company's tax calculation (Gardner et al., 2024). Some corporations reported the effect of the transition tax after 2017 because their fiscal year did not follow a typical calendar year or revisions were made on the estimate of the transition tax liability (Gardner et al., 2024). In this situation, the authors deducted the transition tax expense from the current tax (Gardner et al., 2024).

On the relevant 10-Ks, some corporations disclosed tax benefits from stock options before 2016. The researchers in this study chose to deduct these benefits from calculation of total tax expense (Gardner et al., 2024). Before 2016, the values of these tax breaks were reported in the corporation's consolidated statement of cash flows. Correspondingly, general accounting instructions permitted companies to report their current tax expense totals as if most stock option tax breaks did not exist (Gardner et al., 2024). In 2016, however, the Financial Accounting Standards Board (FASB) required companies to begin subtracting such stock option benefits from tax expense totals going forward but provided flexibility in the adoption date. Thus, researchers identified companies that disclosed these stock option benefits and would subtract the benefits from the corporations reported tax for years before adoption of the relevant FASB standards (Gardner et al., 2024).

(v) Determination of State Income Tax from 10-K Filings

State income tax was subtracted from pretax income to get net pretax income (Gardner et al., 2024). The Form 10-K does not require disclosure of pre-tax income. To circumvent this issue, for companies with a multinational presence that did not specify a geographic split of pretax income, the authors calculated the United States and foreign income share utilizing data on geographic operating profit or estimated foreign income generally employing reported foreign tax for these calculations (Gardner et al., 2024).

This study provides an exceptional example of how to utilize 10-K filings as a method to calculate effective tax rate and thus provides suggestion and inference regarding how changes to the statutory corporate tax rate practically influences effective corporate tax rates and corporations' taxation related behavior.

b. Case Study 2: Narrative and Textual Analyses

Textual analysis can quantify "a variety of 10-K disclosure attributes and provide initial descriptive evidence on trends in these attributes over time" (Dyer, 2017). Prior research provides substantive analysis of 10-K narrative disclosures (Brown & Caylor, 2009). For example, "[u]sing automated text analysis, Li (2010) finds that the annual [10-K] reports (including the MD&A section) of firms with lower earnings and those with positive but less-persistent earnings are more difficult to read" (Brown & Caylor, 2009). These findings demonstrate a defensible relationship between quality of text and corporate taxation integrity (Brown & Caylor, 2009).

For a first example pertaining to textual analysis, Dyer (2017) utilizes Latent Dirichlet Allocation (LDA) to track trends in 10-K disclosures from 1996–2013 for 10,452 firms examining length, boilerplate terminology, redundancy in language, specificity of content, readability, amount of hard information; the author also explores how these factors as related to 150 specific topics within the 10-K, including taxation, internal controls, and risk factor disclosure. LDA is a Bayesian computational linguistic technique that classifies the latent topics in a body of filings to enable analysis of specific topics found in a large group of lengthy documents over time (Dyer, 2017). Dyer's (2017) analysis attributes changes in SEC requirements to explain an overall increase in length in 10-K disclosures and that 3 of the 150 corporate topics (such as fair value, internal controls, and risk factor disclosures) account for virtually all of the increase in length of 10-K disclosures. Furthermore, Dyer (2017) demonstrates that these fair value/impairment, risk factor, and internal control disclosures tend to contain some redundancy and boilerplate language (Dyer, 2017).

Language used in financial disclosure analyzed via established word lists is routine to predict corporate behaviors (Frerich et al., 2015). Moreover, the purpose of most 10-K analysis is predictive in aim. Balakrishan et al. (2010) specifically investigates narrative disclosures in 10-K filings to predict market performance. Although this example pertains to market performance metrics, this study clearly demonstrates pairing narrative disclosure with financial metrics and use of text classification for predictive modeling (Balakrishan, et al., 2010).

To turn to a specific narrative coding example, Frerich et al. (2018) evaluates CEO psychological behavior via establishment of indicators in 10-K text to examine filings for an abnormally optimistic tone and predict CEO narcissistic behavior (Frerich et al., 2015). The study uses five determinants of CEO optimistic behavior (media exposure, perquisites, compensation, power, and growth) in an effort to reflect distinctive patterns (Frerich et al., 2015).

To apply this methodology to a tax specific perspective, and to predict tax avoidance behaviors, a proposed methodology could encompass five tax determinants (reported "current" federal income tax [to establish effective tax rate], noncontrolling interest income from subsidiaries [to demonstrate foreign tax avoidance strategy], auditor or accounting flag or transition, risk factor disclosure, and internal control disclosures). These predictive indicators can be analyzed via (i) extracted non-discretionary financial metrics and (ii) Loughran and McDonald's (2015) keyword list for discretionary terminology.

Words such as tax, cost, and liability, loss, unpaid, restated, litigation, and misstatement are generally coded as negative (Frerich et al., 2015). In line with majority of financial language studies, the total number of positive words found in the sample of 10-K filings can be subtracted from the total number of negative words as a percentage of the total number of words used in 10-K filings to measure "negative tone" as applied to predict taxation avoidance behavior (Frerich et al., 2015). Subsequently, a first stage regression can then decompose tone of the filing into a a more normal component, which refers to non-discretionary descriptions of tax behavior, and an abnormal component, reflecting management's choice to provide discretionary information or to manipulate a firm's corporate tax narratives via word choice to provide a net measurement of tax avoidance tone as a basis for predictive model development (Frerich et al., 2015).

c. Additional Considerations:
   (i) Utilizing eXtensible Business Reporting Language

In 2011, the SEC required small-cap corporations to file their 10-K reports utilizing eXtensible Business Reporting Language (XBRL), which renders the reports as machine readable and easier for extracting and comparing data (Chen et al., 2021). The tax related financial metrics found in this language can implicate certain strategic tax avoidance behaviors. For example, corporate firms with larger book-tax differences are subject to audit risk, and XBRL enables comparison of corporations' taxable and book incomes (Chen et al., 2021). The XBRL directive was not intended to encourage disclosure of new information; rather, the requirement was implemented to create a more user-friendly search environment (Chen et al., 2021). Correspondingly, with XBRL reporting, quantitative metrics provided in corporate financial statements are tagged in accordance with standard taxonomies common to all firms (Chen et al., 2021).

Also from a quantitative perspective, Liu (2021) utilizes content of income tax footnotes extracted from 10-K filings in eXtensible Business Reporting Language (XBRL) to "calculate the proportion of quantitative data relative to… entire footnote disclosure as the dependent variable" in a multivariate regression analysis. The study examines the proportion of qualitative data in the income tax footnotes of United States public companies to demonstrate that the proportion of quantitative data in these tax related footnotes is negatively associated level of tax aggressiveness at a publicly traded entity (Liu, 2021). Similarly, Hasan (2020) examines the association between managerial ability and the readability of narrative disclosures in 10-K reports to find that managerial ability is significantly positively associated with the readability of narrative disclosures in 10-K reports and that such association is more pronounced for firms with high levels of profitability.

Chen et al. (2021) addresses the research question of whether XBRL impacted corporate decision-making related to tax avoidance events. Chen et al. (2021) found a statistically significant increase in IRS downloads of relevant corporations' 10-K filings in the post-XBRL adoption period, which suggests that the XBRL mandate bolstered the importance of 10-K filings as a methodological tool to examine corporate decision-making and behavior (Chen et al., 2021). In addition, XBRL data generates similar data format across firms, which makes comparison between firms easier (Chen et al., 2021). Researchers found that a negative relationship was suggested between the XBRL reporting mandate and tax avoidance (Chen et al., 2021). In essence, adoption of XBRL increased the chances that the IRS would discover tax avoidance behavior via increased access to tax-related information in a more automated format and improved ability to compare tax liabilities among peer benchmarks to implement relevant tax penalties (Chen et al., 2021).

As mentioned above, Chen et al. (2021) reviews tax avoidance behaviors from 2009-2013, to assess behavior before and after adoption of XBRL at small-cap corporations (such small-cap firms may experience less financial stability and thus have more incentive for tax avoidance) (Chen et al., 2021). Previous studies investigated whether XBRL adoption influenced corporate tax strategies for large and mid-cap firms to suggest that a relationship between XBRL adoption and corporate tax avoidance was not statistically significant (Chen et al., 2021). Chen et al. (2021) extracted XBRL filings submitted to the SEC from the SEC's EDGAR database spanning diverse industries (Chen et al., 2021). Ultimately, researchers concluded, based on regression analyses (with and without a control group), that XBRL reporting led to a decrease in use of tax avoidance strategy (Chen et al., 2021). Notably, corporations that were already subject to more intense IRS scrutiny before the XBRL requirement demonstrated less impact after the required XBRL reporting on their tax avoidance strategies (Chen et al., 2021). Moreover, corporations with negative pretax income and/or significant net operating loss carry forwards have less incentive to engage in tax avoidance (Chen et al., 2021).

These results speak to the broader thematic assertion that IRS monitoring practically operates to curb tax avoidance behavior and that 10-K filings can serve as sources of information for the IRS to identify tax avoidance conduct (Chen et al., 2021). Furthermore, these research findings call to question issues pertaining to 10-K reporting in general, including whether corporate leadership can manipulate filings to obscure tax information or reporting opacity to deter detection of tax avoidance strategies (Chen et al., 2021). These findings bolster the argument in favor of the importance of 10-K filings considering that the IRS relies on 10-K financial data when performing tax examinations (Chen et al., 2021). It follows that IRS and SEC information processing costs and tax avoidance are arguably subject to the phenomenon of reverse causality in an audit context (Chen et al., 2021).

For measures of tax avoidance strategy, the authors utilized total book-tax differences (BTD), which was defined as the total difference between pre-tax book income and estimated taxable income, scaled by lagged total assets (Chen et al., 2021). This metric has been utilized in prior literature as an indicator of tax avoidance behavior, and corporations with larger BTD are more likely subject to federal audit and positively associated with tax sheltering (Chen et al., 2021). The second metric used as an identifier of tax avoidance strategy was a residual book tax difference (Chen et al., 2021). The third metric was effective tax rate differential ("ETR"), which is defined as the difference between total book-tax differences and temporary book-tax differences, scaled by lagged total assets (Chen et al., 2021). Researchers finally constructed a factor analysis to determine the common factor from the aforementioned three metrics (Chen et al., 2021). Control variables to isolate the XBRL reporting effect included firm size, research and development investment, financial leverage, book-to-market ratio, cash holdings, firm profitability, and non-current assets (Chen et al., 2021). In conclusion, XBRL is a valuable instrument in utilizing 10-K text to detect corporate taxation behavior patterns.

(ii) Litigation Disclosures

For a more specific example of utilizing 10-Ks in the dependent variable context, Bourveau & Schoenfeld (2017) utilized 10-K filings to demonstrate that implementation of universal demand laws (and the corresponding increased difficulty in filing shareholder derivative lawsuits) relate to increased firm disclosure of information, including earnings forecasts, voluntary filings, and increased MD&A

analysis within the 10-K. Similarly, Li (2023) examined litigation disclosures in the 10-K context finding that litigation disclosures are predictive of future occurrence of litigation and "complementary in providing litigation information to investors." Accordingly, established accounting literature speaks to how certain tax audit, litigious, political, and regulatory changes (and mechanisms that serve as catalysts for these potential variables) practically impact corporate behavior through analysis of 10-K filings.

(iii) Artificial Intelligence

To note, due to the narrative nature of the 10-K report, the 10-K is particularly suitable for utilization of artificial intelligence (AI). For example, Lin (2024) utilized GPT-4.0 from OpenAI to discern corporate tax behavioral practices from 10-K filings. Although tax-related disclosures may appear boilerplate or repetitive, artificial intelligence can be used to review narrative sections on a large scale to distinguish more detailed linguistic nuances in corporate reporting strategy. Consequently, utilization of the 10-K filing to research corporate tax behavior in the context of federal audit opens new research opportunities for both firm and macro level corporate research, including the economic consequences of tax audits for government policymakers. In summary, audits are a topic generally addressed in 10-K filings and are key indicators of corporate tax behavior trajectory. The use of AI is and will continue to be helpful to detect patterns in corporate reporting of audit influence in 10-K filings.

(iv) Cryptocurrency and Blockchain

Huang et al. (2024) provides evaluation of blockchain and cryptocurrency related activities provided for in 10-K filings to evaluate potential association between blockchain disclosures in 10-K reports and audit fees for corporate firms between the years of 2013 to 2020. The study demonstrated a positive association between audit fees and companies disclosing blockchain activities, which was more distinct for companies disclosing *current* blockchain implementation than those companies with future blockchain implementation plans; such findings suggest that disclosure of blockchain activities in 10-K filings are indicators for potential tax compliance behaviors that can assist regulatory evaluations (Huang et al., 2024)

(v) Length of Disclosure

Evidence suggests that length of 10-K disclosure is a "reasonable proxy for the level of value-relevant disclosure" in the 10-K filing (Bourveau & Schoenfeld, 2017). Several variables related to length of disclosure can be used to evaluate 10-K filings, including percent change in overall page count for the entire filing and percent change in page or word count for key sections within the 10-K (such as the MD&A section). Although length of the entire 10-K filing is measured in some accounting literature, length of the specific narrative sections within the 10-K is more commonly indicative of changes in corporate tax behavior. A primary example is the MD&A section: while the MD&A section is mandatory in 10-K filings, the content is both discretionary and arguably predictive of future behavior, including behavior related to tax audits (Bourveau & Schoenfeld, 2017). Publicly traded firms with larger economic changes modify MD&A sections of the 10-K filing more than those with smaller economic changes (Brown & Caylor, 2009).

The length of narrative disclosures has specifically been utilized to measure change in corporate behavior following major external events. For example, Leuz (2009) provides that the cost of capital shocks over the Enron event are associated with increased disclosure in 10-K filings, especially in the more subjectively constructed narrative sections. Such disclosure provides general evidence for the argument that firms respond to transparency concerns, in any context, with increased disclosure in 10-K filings (Leuz, 2009).

The link between external capital shocks and 10-K disclosure related to taxation behavior is well documented in accounting and business literature (Leuz, 2009). "Capital shocks" to publicly traded corporate actors can occur due to a variety of influences, including large litigation and major political or economic events (such as national security concerns, scandals within a given industry, or economic recession). Moreover, firms most impacted by capital shocks may be more likely to respond to the external event in subsequent filing narratives (Leuz, 2009). Findings suggest that additional disclosures are informative and lower cost of capital for investors (Leuz, 2009)

(vi) Mixed Methodology

A blend of quantitative and qualitative measurement is essential to paint a full picture of corporate taxation related conduct. This necessary blend that facilitates more comprehensive understanding is already established in the accounting and business literature addressing 10-K methodology. These sentiments echo the assertion that managerial preferences are highly detectable in analysis of 10-K filings, especially as applied to external events that cause corporate capital shock and certain tax related responses to those external shocks.

A division between quantitative and qualitative data has been observed in many academic traditions. Lee (2023) attempts to counter this stereotype with the use of Python with 10-K filings programming interface to analyze 10-K source data. To accomplish this, Lee (2023) uses the 10-K filing system. "The SEC uses Central Index Key (CIK) as [the] company identifier, so each company is assigned with unique 10-digit number" (Lee, 2023, 3022). The SEC uses this identifier to identify each entity's filings records (Lee, 2023).

Utilization 10-Ks to measure corporate behavior as the dependent variable provides additional context to more sterile financial metrics. For example, Prechel & Zheng (2016, 655) analyzed how the shareholder value model facilitates opportunities for corporate financial malfeasance in the context of the FIRE sector (i.e., financial, insurance, and real estate) considering historical, industry-specific contextualization (Prechel & Zheng 2016, 655). The study's findings supported the hypothesis that a lower dividend payout per share increased a firm's odds of financial malfeasance, including taxation related behaviors: hypothetically, one dollar decrease in dividend payout increased a firm's odds to violate securities laws by more than nine times (Prechel & Zheng 2016, 670). However, the relationship between change in stock price and a company's likelihood of committing a financial violation was not statistically significant. The authors correspondingly posited that this finding may occur because stock prices are affected by other macro-economic factors (Prechel & Zheng 2016, 670). Such macroeconomic dynamics are generally addressed in the text of 10-K narrative explanations. Additional contextualization with 10-K disclosures would add necessary perspective to more barren financial metrics in a large corporate context.

7. INTERNATIONAL CONTEXT, POLICY, AND ANALYSES

a. International Comparison of Taxation Rates

Turning to the issue of the perspective of American corporate taxation on a global scale, large American corporations are unquestionably moneymaking: before tax corporate profits averaged approximately 10.5% of American national income since the end of World War II (Hungerford, 2013). The impact of large corporations' tax payments on the American political and economic landscapes is extraordinary: American corporations' federal tax expense reported by a sample of 296 of the largest America companies totaled to approximately one-third of total United States federal corporate income tax collections from 2013-2021 (Gardner et al., 2024). Correspondingly, corporate taxation most certainly impacts economic development. Policymakers, both in the United States and around the globe, utilize corporate tax incentives to stimulate and manipulate global and national economies. The policy argument exists that increased corporate taxation, and more intense corporate audit practices, can disincentivize capital investment and discourage expansion of the corporate labor force. In essence, this policy argument rests on the assumption that lower corporate tax rates encourage general economic growth. The 10-K filing can be utilized to study the validity of this policy argument.

Corporate taxation as a percentage of American gross domestic product (GDP) has generally declined since World War II (Siripurapu, 2021). As mentioned herein, although the American corporate income tax rate is lower among OECD countries, the American statutory corporate tax rate remains one of the highest in the world. Arguably, statutory corporate tax rates are in sync with economic growth: higher tax rates seem consistent with higher economic growth rates (Hungerford, 2013). For example, the economic growth rate was in average 3.9% between 1950 and 1960, and the statutory corporate tax rate was over 50%; in contrast, between 2000 and 2010, the statutory tax rate was 35% and annual economic growth only averaged 1.8% (Hungerford, 2013). Moreover, some sort of positive association appears to exist between growth in American GDP and corporate tax rates. America's top corporate tax rate occurred during the Eisenhower administration at 52% (Hungerford, 2013). Corporate profits were generally high throughout the 1940s and 1950s, and then decreased until 1982 when profits reversed and then largely increased since that period (Hungerford, 2013).

These statistics, however, arguably lack necessary context: statutory tax rates and quantitative profit metrics alone are too simplistic to tell the most helpful story of the impact of corporate taxation on economic growth. These data points do not consider multifaceted decision-making circumstances inherent to tax strategy. For example, simply reviewing the statutory corporate tax rate does not account for unconnected market pressures and potential tax burdens on new investments that are considered by key decisionmakers. The effective marginal tax rate on earnings, as calculated from the 10-K, better demonstrates true burden on investment and corporate tax practices. For example, reviewing effective marginal tax rates on capital income between 1953 and 2005 indicates an overall trend downward in overall investment with substantial tax burden (Gardner et al., 2024).

Correspondingly, effective tax rate is frequently used as the most helpful summary measure of the corporation's tax strategies that investors use to evaluate corporate behavior (Chen et al., 2021). Drake et al. (2020) utilizes tax footnote data to demonstrate cross-sectional differences in effective traits for domestic and international firms. Moreover, tax policies and strategy should be analyzed over time with comparisons made within specific industries and across countries. Benchmarking effective tax rate against similar firms in a similar industry allows real assessment and evaluation of tax planning strategy in comparison to other corporate firms with similar business and market concerns (Chen et al., 2021).

b. Corporate Bonus Depreciation as an Economic Indicator and International Labor Comparisons

Policymakers in the United States and elsewhere often use tax audits and incentives to fuel economic change (NBER, 2023). A potential method to study changes in capital investment, and how these changes impact the macro level economy, is to provide analysis of corporate bonus depreciation practice as reported on the 10-K filing. Corporations can claim additional tax deductions in the year that equipment investments are made (Suárez Serrato & Zidar, 2023). These deductions lower the tax cost of investment. Such bonus depreciation policies are a global issue: these policies were expanded as part of the Tax Cuts and Jobs Act and have been generally adopted by other countries outside of the United States, such as including China, Germany, and the United Kingdom (Suárez Serrato & Zidar).

Corporations in industries that utilize assets with longer depreciation schedules benefit most from the bonus depreciation policy. Thus, the impact of this policy, and the study of this impact, must be contextualized in the framework of the corporations' specific industry. For example, a 2001 study provided evidence that the bonus depreciation policy can facilitate employment growth in geographic areas with more exposure to the policy based on industry concentration (Suárez Serrato & Zidar, 2023).

For one example, an argument exists that lowering costs of labor-reducing technology, and providing corresponding tax incentives for technological investment, accelerates automation to harm the traditional labor force (NBER, 2023). Looking at bonus depreciation, which lowers the tax cost of investment by allowing companies to claim added tax deductions in the year that equipment investments are made and have been significantly expanded as part of the TCJA, in China, Germany, and the United Kingdom (NBER, 2023). In the American context, corporations that provide for longer depreciation schedules benefit most from such regulations (NBER, 2023). Contrary to such preliminary assumptions, increasing exposure to bonus depreciation increased employment (NBER, 2023). In essence. Bonus depreciation provided for on the 10-K provides demonstration of a tax practice that substantially influence labor markets, especially in the modern age of increasing automation.

c. Competitive Analyses

Extending beyond the behavior of the American corporation alone, tax behavior assumes additional complexity when considering interactions between nations. Moreover, the global, digital nature of the modern economy calls into question issues regarding how American corporate taxes operate considering economic relations with other nations. Corporate taxation substantially alters global economic behavior. "As corporate tax regimes are reconsidered across countries to avoid revenue loss to tax avoidance, multinational companies will face increased pressure to defend their tax-related transactions and/or may see new forms of taxation applied" (Principles for Responsible Investment, 2018). Taxation policies can hinder economic growth and can work to manipulate trends in corporate investment (Siripurapu, 2021). Such factors trigger significant implications for global economic relations and competitiveness (Siripurapu, 2021).

The realm of international relations presents unique governance issues because no sole body has complete authority to govern taxation between nations. International taxation is generally governed by bilateral treaties. These treaties primarily began to impact the global economy during the existence of the predecessor to the United Nations, the League of Nations. Recently, some countries have unilaterally implemented new digital services taxes that disproportionately impact United States technological firms (Siripurapu, 2021). Large technological companies that earn billions in countries with customers, but no brick-and-mortar operations, generally do not pay taxes in those countries (Siripurapu, 2021). The recent Biden administration advocated for a global minimum corporate tax and potential redistribution of tax revenue from larger, multinational corporations. (Siripurapu, 2021). Many countries, including many in Europe, India, and Turkey implemented their own digital service taxes (Siripurapu, 2021). Some United States politicians have threatened tariffs on these nations that they argue unfairly target large American corporate actors.

Correspondingly, global corporate taxation can be generally categorized via two approaches, which are "worldwide" or "territorial" approaches (Siripurapu, 2021). Under the "territorial" system, which is the generally accepted approach for more wealthy nations, corporate profits earned domestically are subject to taxation (Siripurapu, 2021). Current international treaties usually provide taxation authority to countries in which a corporation has a physical presence, such as an office or factory (Siripurapu, 2021). Under a proposed "worldwide" system, all of a corporation's profits would be subject to corporate tax, both foreign and domestic (Siripurapu, 2021). Corporations would be credited for taxes paid to other foreign governments to prevent multiple burdens of taxation (Siripurapu, 2021).

Corporate taxation policies can encourage "profit shifting." Profit shifting occurs when multinational corporations report profits in countries with lower tax rates, such as Bermuda and Ireland (Siripurapu, 2021). Corporations can accomplish profit shifting strategy through various strategic mechanisms like relocating intellectual property and then relicensing it to its subsidiaries (Siripurapu, 2021). An estimated 40% of corporate profits are relocated annually, which reduces global tax revenue by approximately $200 billion per year (Siripurapu, 2021). Furthermore, corporations can report higher costs in countries with higher taxation rates to reduce profits and thus their tax liability (also known as the amount required by the government) in those national jurisdictions. Notably, corporate subsidiaries are generally treated as independent entities (Siripurapu, 2021). Generally speaking, transactions between subsidiaries are supposed to occur at arm's length, as if entities have no relation to one another (Siripurapu, 2021).

From a comparative perspective in respect to other nations with tax filings that attempt to promote transparency, the Australian government provides for "Voluntary Tax Transparency" to urge bigger businesses to publish reports on tax strategy and corporate governance with centralized access of these published reports (Principles for Responsible Investment, 2018). This stands in juxtaposition to US regulations for public corporations that provide more specific form and content requirements for annual reports, including GAAP reporting and requirements for disclosure of material tax strategy and risks (Principles for Responsible Investment, 2018). Akin to the United States, the UK Finance Act required all UK companies of a certain size to publish tax strategy and level of risk, which applies to any multinational and requires the entity to publish tax strategy addressing UK operations (Principles for Responsible Investment, 2018).

8. PRACTICAL INSIGHTS FROM THIS CHAPTER

- A primary purpose of the 10-K filing is disclosure. Such disclosure is intended to provide reliable information about a company's financial practices to help shareholders make investment decisions.

- The primary source of influence on corporate operations is corporate executive management, and management is primarily responsible for drafting 10-K filings.
- The disclosures required on the 10-K filing by the SEC provide an ethical foundation for tax related conduct and corporate disclosure for American corporate actors.
- One of the most advantageous aspects of utilizing 10-K filings to evaluate corporate tax behavior is that these filings can provide a uniform and predictable method for evaluation.
- Executives see the threat of audit as a crucial influence on corporate tax planning. However, tax authorities, including the IRS, generally do not divulge which corporations are subject to audit; thus, it can be difficult to research the impact of audits. 10-K filings provide a publicly available narrative of corporate tax behavior.
- Textual analysis can quantify 10-K disclosure attributes, including disclosures pertaining to new technological areas, such as blockchain and crypto related activities.
- Utilization of increasingly sophisticated artificial intelligence textual analyses techniques can detect nuances in 10-K text to develop more detailed indicators of corporate tax behavior based on language utilized in the 10-K filing.
- 10-K filing analysis can facilitate calculation of effective federal income taxes reported by each company on their pretax income.
- Pure statutory tax rates and quantitative profit metrics alone are too simplistic to tell the most helpful story of the impact of corporate taxation on economic growth. These data points do not consider multifaceted decision-making circumstances inherent to tax strategy, which can be provided for within 10-K filings.

9. LIMITATIONS

Four primary drawbacks are presented when using 10-K as a methodology. First, narrative disclosures rely on some subjective interpretation of what information, words, or financial metrics are important to extract and interpret data from the filing. Second, the 10-K is a polished document intended for mass public circulation. Consequently, the 10-K does not present "true" management opinions because it is "marketed" for public appeal. Managerial intention is inferred from a polished document. Accountants, investors, and board members need to constantly assess whether current disclosure requirements are sufficient to compel truth from management. Third, through "boilerplate" disclosures and narratives, corporations may disclose minimal information in the filing or use language not truly informative to academic or regulatory analysis. Fourth, manipulation by managerial actors in the wording of the 10-K filing is an important possibility, as demonstrated in the recent Meta litigation. Executive management can "spin" disclosures to mislead investors subject to SEC standards, monitoring, and enforcement.

10. CONCLUSION

To conclude, this chapter provides examples of how to utilize the annual 10-K filing as a mixed methodological tool to evaluate corporate taxation related conduct given current issues relevant to American federal tax law. American corporations are some of the most impactful actors in the global economy. These corporations' taxation related behaviors impact competition in the global market and substantially influence national revenues. In the American context, the 10-K filing is an essential methodological tool to evaluate corporate tax conduct over time and provides comparison to industry peers. Such methodological utility increases with additional advances in textual analysis and artificial intelligence. These advances can help researchers, policymakers, and governmental entities become more efficient in evaluation of corporate tax conduct in an effort to competently evaluate tax behaviors of major corporate actors. Academic literature already suggests that corporate firms find 10-K disclosures particularly relevant to improve transparency and alleviate shareholder concerns through the filings' narrative disclosures from corporate management. The use of narrative disclosure coupled with financial metrics provides essential content to contextualize decision-making at American corporate firms.

REFERENCES

Balakrishnan, R., Qiu, X. Y., & Srinivasan, P. (2010). On the predictive ability of narrative disclosures in annual reports. *European Journal of Operational Research, 202*(3), 789–801. DOI: 10.1016/j.ejor.2009.06.023

Bavoso, V. (2018). The corporate law dilemma and the enlightened sovereign control paradigm:in search of a new legal framework. *Brooklyn Journal of Corporate, Financial & Commercial Law, 12*(2). https://brooklynworks.brooklaw.edu/bjcfcl/vol12/iss2/1

Bourveau, T., & Schoenfeld, J. (2017). Shareholder activism and voluntary disclosure. *Review of Accounting Studies, 22*(3), 1307–1339. DOI: 10.1007/s11142-017-9408-0

Brown, L. D., & Caylor, M. (2009). Corporate governance and firm operating performance. *Review of Quantitative Finance and Accounting, 32*(2), 129–144. DOI: 10.1007/s11156-007-0082-3

Buchholz, F., Jaeschke, R., Lopatta, K., & Maas, K. (2018). The use of optimistic tone by narcissistic CEOs. *Accounting, Auditing & Accountability Journal, 31*(2), 531–562. DOI: 10.1108/AAAJ-11-2015-2292

Chen, J. Z., Hong, H. A., Kim, J.-B., & Ryou, J. W. (2021). Information processing costs and corporate tax aggressiveness: Evidence from the SEC's XBRL Mandate. *Journal of Accounting and Public Policy, 40*(2), 106822. DOI: 10.1016/j.jaccpubpol.2021.106822

Cleven, A. (2020). How did the Tax Cuts and Jobs Act change business taxes*? Tax Policy Center*. https://taxpolicycenter.org/briefing-book/how-did-tax-cuts-and-jobs-act-change-business-taxes

Coyne, R. (2025) Facebook v. Amalgamated Bank. *Georgetown Law Journal*. https://www.law.georgetown.edu/georgetown-law-journal/submit/glj-online/supreme-court-coverage-program/facebook-v-amalgamated-bank-why-did-the-supreme-court-dismiss-facebooks-writ-of-certiorari-as-improvidently-granted/

Dobbin, F., & Zorn, D. (2005). Corporate malfeasance and the myth of shareholder value. In *Political power and social theory* (Vol. 17, pp. 179–198). Emerald Group Publishing., DOI: 10.1016/S0198-8719(04)17006-3

Drake, K. D., Hamilton, R., & Lusch, S. J. (2020). Are declining effective tax rates indicative of tax avoidance? Insight from effective tax rate reconciliations. *Journal of Accounting and Economics, 70*(1), 101317. DOI: 10.1016/j.jacceco.2020.101317

Dyer, T., Lang, M., & Stice-Lawrence, L. (2017). The evolution of 10-K textual disclosure: Evidence from Latent Dirichlet allocation. *Journal of Accounting and Economics, 64*(2–3), 221–245. DOI: 10.1016/j.jacceco.2017.07.002

Fligstein, N. (2001). Social skill and the theory of fields. *Sociological Theory, 19*(2), 105–125. DOI: 10.1111/0735-2751.00132

Gardner, M., Ettlinger, M., Marasini, S., & Wamhoff, S. (2024). Corporate taxes before and after the trump tax law. *Institute on Taxation and Economic Policy, 2*.https://itep.org/corporate-taxes-before-and-after-the-trump-tax-law/

Gardner, M., Ettlinger, M., Wamhoff, S., & Marasini, S. (2024). Corporate taxes before and after the Trump Tax Law. *Institute of Taxation and Economic Policy*. https://www.epi.org/publication/ib364-corporate-tax-rates-and-economic-growth/

German, M. (2025). Securities and Exchange Commission Filings. CSU Los Angeles University Library. https://libguides.calstatela.edu/c.php?g=1072937&p=7823298

Godfrey, P. C. (2005). The relationship between corporate philanthropy and shareholder wealth: A risk management perspective. *Academy of Management Review*, *30*(4), 777–798. DOI: 10.5465/amr.2005.18378878

Hasan, M. M., & Habib, A. (2020). Readability of narrative disclosures, and corporate liquidity and payout policies. *International Review of Financial Analysis*, *68*, 101460. DOI: 10.1016/j.irfa.2020.101460

Heilbron, J., Verheul, J., & Quak, S. (2014). The origins and early diffusion of "shareholder value" in the United States. *Theory and Society*, *43*(1), 1–22. DOI: 10.1007/s11186-013-9205-0

Huang, F., Tawei, W., and Ju-Chun, Y. (2024). "Opportunities or challenges? Audit risk and blockchain disclosures in 10-K filings." *Auditing: A Journal of Practice & Theory* 43(2): 131–58. ` https://doi:DOI: 10.2308/AJPT-2021-045

Hungerford, T. L. (2013). Corporate tax rates and economic growth since 1947. *Economic Policy Institute Issue Brief, 364*. https://www.epi.org/publication/ib364-corporate-tax-rates-and-economic-growth/

Institutional Shareholder Services. (2025). Asia Pacific Region. *Proxy Voting Guidelines*. https://www.issgovernance.com/file/policy/active/asiapacific/Asia-Pacific-Regional-Voting-Guidelines.pdf?v=1

Lee, J. H., & Lee, S. J. (2023). Efficient access to qualitative data: A case of MD&A analysis from 10-K with Python via SEC's API. *Applied Economics Letters*, *30*(21), 3021–3025. DOI: 10.1080/13504851.2022.2118219

Leuz, C., & Schrand, C. M. (2009). Disclosure and the cost of capital: Evidence from firms' response to the Enron shock. SSRN *Electronic Journal*. (No. w14897). National Bureau of Economic Research. https://doi.org/DOI: 10.2139/ssrn.1319646

Li, F. (2010). The information content of forward-looking statements in corporate filings—A naïve Bayesian machine learning approach. *Journal of Accounting Research*, *48*(5), 1049–1102. DOI: 10.1111/j.1475-679X.2010.00382.x

Li, H. (2023). Litigation-disclosure modifications in the 10-K: Large-sample evidence. *Journal of Accounting, Auditing & Finance*, *38*(2), 437–452. DOI: 10.1177/0148558X211017838

Lin, S. (2024). Understanding corporate tax audits: Insights from novel firm-level data. *Duke Financial Economics Center*. https://sites.duke.edu/thefinregblog/2024/03/04/understanding-corporate-tax-audits-insights-from-novel-firm-level-data/

Liu, H. (2021). Tax aggressiveness and the proportion of quantitative information in income tax footnotes. *Journal of Financial Reporting and Accounting*, *20*(2), 352–370. DOI: 10.1108/JFRA-08-2020-0233

Loughran, T., & McDonald, B. (2015). *The use of word lists in textual analysis* (SSRN Scholarly Paper No. 2467519). DOI: 10.1080/15427560.2015.1000335

Pernell, K., Jung, J., & Dobbin, F. (2017). The hazards of expert control: Chief risk officers and risky derivatives. *American Sociological Review*, *82*(3), 511–541. DOI: 10.1177/0003122417701115

Prechel, H., & Boies, J. (1998). Capital dependence, financial risk, and change from the multidivisional to the multilayered subsidiary form. *Sociological Forum*, *13*(2), 321–362. DOI: 10.1023/A:1022197917767

Prechel, H., & Zheng, L. (2016). Do organizational and political–legal arrangements explain financial wrongdoing? *The British Journal of Sociology*, *67*(4), 655–677. DOI: 10.1111/1468-4446.12212 PMID: 27753077

Principles for Responsible Investment. (2018). Evaluating and Engaging on Corporate Tax Transparency. https://www.unpri.org/Uploads/t/r/l/PRI_Evaluating-and-engaging-on-corporate-tax-transparency_Investor-guide.pdf

Schnatterly, K., Gangloff, K. A., & Tuschke, A. (2018). CEO Wrongdoing: A review of pressure, opportunity, and rationalization. *Journal of Management*, *44*(6), 2405–2432. DOI: 10.1177/0149206318771177

Securities and Exchange Commission. Sec 13 or 15(d), 2025.

Sheppard Mullin. (2025). Things to keep in mind for your annual report on form 10-K and proxy statement. https://www.corporatesecuritieslawblog.com/wp-content/uploads/sites/46/2025/01/Things-to-Keep-in-Mind-for-Your-2025-10K-and-Proxy-Statement-Client-Alert-0125.pdf

Siripurapu, A. (2021). Corporate taxes in a globalized world. *Council on Foreign Relations*. https://www.cfr.org/backgrounder/corporate-taxes-globalized-world

Suárez Serrato, J. C., & Zidar, O. M. (2023). How do corporate taxes affect economic activity*? NBER Reporter, (3),* 8–13. https://www.nber.org/reporter/2023number3/how-do-corporate-taxes-affect-economic-activity

Tillman, R. (2009). Reputations and corporate malfeasance: Collusive networks in financial statement fraud. *Crime, Law, and Social Change*, *51*(3–4), 365–382. DOI: 10.1007/s10611-008-9161-1

Useem, M., & Gager, C. (1996). Employee shareholders or institutional investors? When corporate managers replace their stockholders. *Journal of Management Studies*, *33*(5), 613–632. DOI: 10.1111/j.1467-6486.1996.tb00811.x

Compilation of References

Abdixhiku, L., Pugh, G., & Hashi, I. (2018). Business tax evasion in transition economies: A cross-country panel investigation. *European Journal of Comparative Economics*, *15*(1), 11–36.

Abed, I. A., Hussin, N., Haddad, H., Almubaydeen, T. H., & Ali, M. A. (2022). Creative accounting determination and financial reporting quality: The integration of transparency and disclosure. *Journal of Open Innovation*, *8*(1), 38. DOI: 10.3390/joitmc8010038

Abeler, J., & Jäger, S. (2015). Complex tax incentives. *American Economic Journal. Economic Policy*, *7*(3), 1–28. DOI: 10.1257/pol.20130137

Adam, M., Wessel, M., & Benlian, A. (2021). AI-based chatbots in customer service and their effects on user compliance. *Electronic Markets*, *31*(2), 427–445. DOI: 10.1007/s12525-020-00414-7

Adams, J. S., & Freedman, S. (1976). Equity theory revisited: Comments and annotated bibliography. *Advances in Experimental Social Psychology*, *9*, 43–90. DOI: 10.1016/S0065-2601(08)60058-1

Adelakun, B. O., Nembe, J. K., Oguejiofor, B. B., Akpuokwe, C. U., & Bakare, S. S.Beatrice Oyinkansola AdelakunJoseph Kuba NembeBisola Beatrice OguejioforChidiogo Uzoamaka AkpuokweSeun Solomon Bakare. (2024). Legal frameworks and tax compliance in the digital economy: A finance perspective. *Engineering Science & Technology Journal*, *5*(3), 844–853. DOI: 10.51594/estj.v5i3.922

Adelekan, O. A., Adisa, O., Ilugbusi, B. S., Obi, O. C., Awonuga, K. F., Asuzu, O. F., & Ndubuisi, N. L. (2024). Evolving tax compliance in the digital era: A comparative analysis of AI-driven models and blockchain technology in US tax administration. *Computer Science & IT Research Journal*, *5*(2), 311–335. DOI: 10.51594/csitrj.v5i2.759

Agu, E. E., Abhulimen, A. O., Obiki-Osafiele, A. N., Osundare, O. S., Adeniran, I. A., & Efunniyi, C. P. (2024). Discussing ethical considerations and solutions for ensuring fairness in AI-driven financial services. International Journal of Frontier Research in Science, 3(2), 001-009.

Akerlof, G., & Kranton, R. (2000). Economics and identity. *The Quarterly Journal of Economics*, *115*(3), 715–753. DOI: 10.1162/003355300554881

Akhand, Z. (2018). The influence of the corporate sector on the effectiveness of tax compliance instruments. In *Advances in taxation* (Vol. 25, pp. 119–146). Emerald Publishing Limited. DOI: 10.1108/S1058-749720180000025006

Akinboade, O. A. (2015). Correlates of tax compliance of small and medium size businesses in Cameroon. *Managing global transitions, 13*(4), 389-413.

Akinrinola, O., Addy, W. A., Ajayi-Nifise, A. O., Odeyemi, O., & Falaiye, T. (2024). Application of machine learning in tax prediction: A review with practical approaches. *Global Journal of Engineering and Technology Advances*, *18*(02), 102–117. DOI: 10.30574/gjeta.2024.18.2.0028

Akpanuko, E. E., & Umoren, N. J. (2018). The influence of creative accounting on the credibility of accounting reports. *Journal of Financial Reporting and Accounting*, *16*(2), 292–310. DOI: 10.1108/JFRA-08-2016-0064

Alabede, J. O., Ariffin, Z. Z., & Idris, K. (2011). Individual taxpayers'' attitude and compliance behaviour in Nigeria: The moderating role of financial condition and risk preference. *Journal of Accounting and Taxation*, *3*(6), 91–104.

Alarcón, G., Mayor, J. M., & Ayala, E. A. (2021). La participación ciudadana y el pago voluntario de los impuestos. *Obets*, *16*(2), 227–244. DOI: 10.14198/OBETS2021.16.2.01

Alarcón, G., Mayor, J. M., & Quintanilla, C. M. (2022). Conciencia fiscal y presupuestos participativos: Un estudio exploratorio. *Revista Española de Investigaciones Sociológicas*, *177*(177), 69–88. DOI: 10.5477/cis/reis.177.69

Alarcón, G., & Tipke, K. (2007). La Conciencia Fiscal. In Serrano, F. (Ed.), *La Conciencia Fiscal y el Marketing Tributario en las Haciendas Locales* (pp. 45–66). Editorial Civitas.

Alarcón-García, G., & Ayala, E. (2013). Trust in Spanish Governments: Antecedents and Consequences. *Economic Analysis and Policy. Australian Economic Association*, *43*(2), 135–152.

Alarcón-García, G., & Ayala, E. A. (2013). Trust in Spanish Governments: Antecedents and Consequences. *Economic Analysis and Policy*, *43*(2), 177–193. DOI: 10.1016/S0313-5926(13)50017-8

Alarcón-García, G., Beyaert, A., & De Pablos, L. (2012). Fiscal awareness: a study of female versus male attitudes towards tax fraud in Spain. In Pickhardt, M., & Prinz, A. (Eds.), *Tax Evasion and the Shadow Economy* (pp. 61–86). Edward Elgar. DOI: 10.4337/9781781006740.00012

Alarcón-García, G., De Pablos, L., & Garre, E. (2009). Análisis del comportamiento de los individuos ante el fraude fiscal. Resultados obtenidos a partir de la Encuesta del Observatorio Fiscal de la Universidad de Murcia. *Revista Principios*, *13*, 55–84.

Al-Asfour, F., & McGee, R. W. (2024). Tax Evasion and Tax Compliance: What Have We Learned from the 100 Most Cited Studies? In R.W. McGee & J. Shopovski (Eds.), The Ethics of Tax Evasion, Volume 2: New Perspectives in Theory and Practice. Springer.

Al-Debei, M. M., Akroush, M. N., & Ashouri, M. I. (2015). Consumer attitudes towards online shopping: The effects of trust, perceived benefits, and perceived web quality. *Internet Research*, *25*(5), 707–733. DOI: 10.1108/IntR-05-2014-0146

Alexander, P., & Balavac-Orlic, M. (2022). Tax morale: Framing and fairness. *Economic Systems*, *46*(1), 100936. DOI: 10.1016/j.ecosys.2021.100936

Alhempi, R. R., Ardiansyah, I., Kusumastuti, S. Y., & Endri, E. (2020). Tax compliance in income tax payments. *International Journal of Innovation. Creativity and Change*, *13*(1), 356–374.

Alhempi, R., Ardiansyah, I., Kusumastuti, S., & Endri, E. (2020).. . *Tax Compliance in Income Tax Payments*, *13*, 356–374.

Ali, M. M., Cecil, H. W., & Knoblett, J. A. (2001). The Effects of Tax Rates and Enforcement Policies on Taxpayer Compliance: A Study of Self-Employed Taxpayers. *Atlantic Economic Journal*, *29*(2), 186–202. DOI: 10.1007/BF02299137

Ali, M., Fjeldstad, O. H., & Sjursen, I. H. (2014). To pay or not to pay? Citizens' attitudes toward taxation in Kenya, Tanzania, Uganda, and South Africa. *World Development*, *64*, 828–842. DOI: 10.1016/j.worlddev.2014.07.006

Alj, B. (2024). Defis Et Dynamiques De La Securite Fiscale Pour Le Developpement Des Affaires En Afrique: Une Exploration Du Cas Du Maroc. [Challenges and Dynamics of Tax Security for Business Development in Africa: An Exploration of the Case of Morocco]. Economics and Management Review, 2(2).

Alj, B. (2024). Défis et dynamiques de la sécurité fiscale pour le développement des affaires en Afrique: Une exploration du cas du Maroc. *Economics and Management Review, 2*(2).

Alj, B., & Ourahma, A. (2022). L'efficacité de l'impôt sur le revenu dans le système fiscal marocain. *Revue du Contrôle, de la Comptabilité et de l'Audit, 6*(4), 270-289.

Alj, B. (2019). La règle fiscale: Quels risques pour l'entreprise au Maroc? *Revue Marocaine de Recherche en Management et Marketing*, *19*, 134–154.

Alkhatib, A. A., Abdul-Jabbar, H., Abuamria, F., & Rahhal, A. (2019). The effects of social influence factors on income tax evasion among the Palestinian SMEs. *International Journal of Advanced Science and Technology*, *28*(17), 690–700.

Allingham, M. G., & Sandmo, A. (1972). Income tax evasion: A theoretical analysis. *Journal of Public Economics*, *1*(3–4), 323–338. DOI: 10.1016/0047-2727(72)90010-2

Alm, J. (2023). Tax Compliance Technology, Trust, and Inequality in a Post-Pandemic World. *eJTR, 21*, 152.

Alm, J., Martinez-Vazquez, J., & Wallace, S. (2009). Do tax amnesties work? The revenue effects of tax amnesties during the transition in the Russian federation. https://doi.org/DOI: 10.1016/S0313-5926(09)50019-7

Alm, J. (1991). A perspective on the experimental analysis of taxpayer reporting. *The Accounting Review*, *66*(3), 577–593.

Alm, J. (1999). Tax compliance and administration. In Bartley Hildreth, W., & Jerry, L. R. (Eds.), *The handbook of public administration* (pp. 173–193).

Alm, J. (2019). What motivates tax compliance? *Journal of Economic Surveys*, *33*(2), 353–388. DOI: 10.1111/joes.12272

Alm, J., & Beck, W. (1991). Wiping the Slate Clean: Individual Response to State Tax Amnesties. *Southern Economic Journal*, *57*(4), 1043–1053. DOI: 10.2307/1060332

Alm, J., & Beck, W. (1993). Tax Amnesties and Compliance in the Long Run: A Time Series Analysis. *National Tax Journal*, *47*(1), 53–60. DOI: 10.1086/NTJ41788996

Alm, J., Bloomquist, K., & Mckee, M. (2015). On the external validity of laboratory tax compliance experiments?*Economic Inquiry*, *53*(2), 1170–1186. DOI: 10.1111/ecin.12196

Alm, J., Cherry, T., Jones, M., & McKee, M. (2010). Taxpayer information assistance services and tax compliance behavior. *Journal of Economic Psychology*, *31*(4), 577–586. DOI: 10.1016/j.joep.2010.03.018

Alm, J., & Gomez, J. L. (2008). Social capital and tax morale in Spain. *Economic Analysis and Policy*, *38*(1), 73–87. DOI: 10.1016/S0313-5926(08)50007-5

Alm, J., Jackson, B., & Mckee, M. (1992). Estimating the determinants of taxpayer compliance with experimental data. *National Tax Journal*, *45*(1), 107–114. DOI: 10.1086/NTJ41788949

Alm, J., & Malézieux, A. (2021). 40 years of tax evasion games: A meta-analysis. *Experimental Economics*, *2021*(24), 699–750. DOI: 10.1007/s10683-020-09679-3

Alm, J., Martínez-Vázquez, J., & Torgler, B. (2006). Russian attitudes toward paying taxes before, during, and after the transition. *International Journal of Social Economics*, *33*(12), 832–857. DOI: 10.1108/03068290610714670

Alm, J., McClelland, G. H., & Schulze, W. D. (1992). Why do people pay taxes? *Journal of Public Economics*, *48*(1), 21–48. DOI: 10.1016/0047-2727(92)90040-M

Alm, J., McClelland, G. H., & Schulze, W. D. (1999). Changing the social norm of tax compliance by voting. *Kyklos*, *48*(2), 141–171. DOI: 10.1111/j.1467-6435.1999.tb01440.x

Alm, J., & McKee, M. (2004). Tax compliance as a coordination game. *Journal of Economic Behavior & Organization*, *54*(3), 297–312. DOI: 10.1016/j.jebo.2003.02.003

Alm, J., & Torgler, B. (2006). Culture differences and tax morale in the United States and in Europe. *Journal of Economic Psychology*, *27*(2), 224–246. DOI: 10.1016/j.joep.2005.09.002

Alm, J., & Torgler, B. (2011). Do ethics matter? Tax compliance and morality. *Journal of Business Ethics*, *101*(4), 635–651. DOI: 10.1007/s10551-011-0761-9

Almunia, M., & Lopez-Rodriguez, D. (2018). Under the radar: The effects of monitoring firms on tax compliance. *American Economic Journal. Economic Policy*, *10*(1), 1–38. DOI: 10.1257/pol.20160229

Alstadsæter, A., Johannesen, N., Le Guern Herry, S., & Zucman, G. (2022). Tax evasion and tax avoidance. *Journal of Public Economics*, *206*, 104587. DOI: 10.1016/j.jpubeco.2021.104587

Álvarez García, S., & Herrera Molina, P. M. (2004). *Ética Fiscal, Documentos de trabajo del Instituto de Estudios Fiscales, nº 10*. Ministerio de Economía y Hacienda.

Al-Zaqeba, M. A. A., & Al-Rashdan, M. T. (2020). Extension of the TPB in tax compliance behavior: The role of moral intensity and customs tax. *International Journal of Scientific and Technology Research*, *9*(4), 227–232.

Amara, I., & Khlif, H. (2018). Financial crime, corruption and tax evasion: A cross-country investigation. *Journal of Money Laundering Control*, *21*(4), 545–554. DOI: 10.1108/JMLC-10-2017-0059

Amat, O., Blake, J., & Dowds, J. (1999). The ethics of creative accounting. *Journal of Economic Literature Classification, M41.*

Amelio, S., Gazzola, P., Vatamanescu, M., & Dinu, E. (2024). Communal and ethical factors versus tax fraud: The function of corporate communal responsibility in the Romanian context. *Communal Responsibility Journal*, *21*(1), 1–15. DOI: 10.1108/SRJ-04-2024-0273

American Accounting Association. (n.d.). *Website of the American Accounting Association (AAA).* Retrieved March 14, 2025, from https://www.aaahq.org

American Institute of Certified Public Accountants. (n.d.). *Website of the American Institute of Certified Public Accountants (AICPA).* Retrieved March 14, 2025, from https://www.aicpa-cima.com

Amin, S. N., Buhari, P. Z. A., Yaacob, A. S., & Iddy, Z. (2022). Exploring the influence of tax knowledge in increasing tax compliance by introducing tax education at tertiary level institutions. *Open Journal of Accounting*, *11*(02), 57–70. DOI: 10.4236/ojacct.2022.112004

Amoh, J. K., & Adafula, B. (2019). An estimation of the underground economy and tax evasion: Empirical analysis from an emerging economy. *Journal of Money Laundering Control*, *22*(4), 626–645. DOI: 10.1108/JMLC-01-2019-0002

Andreoni, J. (1991). The desirability of a permanent tax amnesty. *Journal of Public Economics*, *45*(2), 143–159. DOI: 10.1016/0047-2727(91)90037-3

Andreoni, J. (1992). IRS As loan shark tax compliance with borrowing constraints. *Journal of Public Economics*, *49*(1), 35–46. DOI: 10.1016/0047-2727(92)90062-K

Andreoni, J., Erard, B., & Feinstein, J. (1998). Tax compliance. *Journal of Economic Literature*, *36*, 818–860.

Andreoni, J., Erard, B., & Feinstein, J. (1998). Tax Compliance. *Journal of Economic Literature*, *36*, 818–860.

Andreoni, J., & Vesterlund, L. (2001). Which Is the Fair Sex? Gender Differences in Altruism. *The Quarterly Journal of Economics*, *116*(1), 293–31. DOI: 10.1162/003355301556419

Annuar, H. A., Salihu, I. A., & Obid, S. N. S. (2014). Corporate ownership, governance and tax avoidance: An interactive effects. *Procedia: Social and Behavioral Sciences*, *164*, 150–160. DOI: 10.1016/j.sbspro.2014.11.063

Antequera, G., & Florensa, M. (2008). Determinantes de la Moral Tributaria en la Provincia de Buenos Aires. *Serie Anales de La Asociación de Economía Política*, (Noviembre), 1–15.

Appiah, T., Domeher, D., & Agana, J. A. (2024). Tax knowledge, trust in government, and voluntary tax compliance: Insights from an emerging economy. *SAGE Open*, *14*(2), 2–13. DOI: 10.1177/21582440241234757

Aquino, M. Á. (2008). *La evasión fiscal: Origen y medidas de acción para combatirla.* Instituto de Estudios Fiscales. DOC. N.º 13/08. Madrid.

Arayankalam, J., & Krishnan, S. (2022). Can E-government Maturity Increase B2C E-business Use? The roles of corruption and virtual social networks diffusion. *Scandinavian Journal of Information Systems, 34*(1), 119–164. https://www.scopus.com/inward/record.uri?eid=2-s2.0-85135267715&partnerID=40&md5=ea4895efce65cf1c8a9a52ed80c737ac

Arias, R. J. (2008). Comentarios sobre "Determinantes de la Moral Tributaria en la Provincia de Buenos Aires", de Germán Antequera y Marcelo Florensa. *Serie Anales de La Asociación de Economía Política*, (Noviembre), 16–20.

Aristantia, S. E., Yuniarni, R. K., & Junjunan, M. I. (2022). The Effect of Taxation Rational Attitude, Religiusity, and Ethics on Taxpayer Compliance. *Journal of Accounting* [JAEF]. *Entrepreneurship and Financial Technology, 4*(1), 1–14.

Aronmwan, E., & Eragbhe, E. (2015, May). Taxpayers income, taxpayers attributes and personal income tax compliance. *African Journal of Management Sciences, 1*, 95–111.

Ashby, J., & Webley, P. (2010). The existence of distinct occupational taxpaying cultures in Australia. *Australian Tax Forum*, 25(1), 29–55.

Aversano, N., Nicolò, G., Sannino, G., & Tartaglia Polcini, P. (2022). Communal responsibility of corporates, stakeholder engagement, and universities. *Administrative Sciences, 12*(3), 79. DOI: 10.3390/admsci12030079

Awaeh, M. A., Lambey, L. L. L., & Pinatik, S. (2017). Analysis of the effectiveness of the implementation of tax amnesty on tax revenues at the Bitung Pratama Tax Office. *Jurnal Riset Ekonomi, Manajemen. Bisnis Dan Akuntansi, 5*(2), 1–9. DOI: 10.35794/emba.v5i2.16529

Awai, E. S., & Oboh, T. (2020). Ease of paying taxes: The electronic tax system in Nigeria. Accounting and taxation review, 4(1), 63-73.

Azaka, L. (2022). Tax Knowledge, Tax Attıtude, And Perceptıon Of Tax Faırness As Predıctors Of Tax Complıance Among Tech Workers In Lagos State, Nıgerıa. *Afrıcan Journal For The Psychologıcal Studıes Of Socıal Issues, 25*(2).

Azmi, D. A. W. M., & Daud, S. A. M. M. (2024). Reconceptualizing tax compliance behavior: A theoretical matrix approach. *Accounting and Finance Research, 13*(1), 1–67.

Baguma, R. (2018, April). Usability evaluation of the etax portal for uganda. In *Proceedings of the 11th International Conference on Theory and Practice of Electronic Governance* (pp. 449-458).

Bagus, P., Block, W., Eabrasu, M., Howden, D., & Rostan, J. (2011). The Ethics of Tax Evasion. *Business and Society Review, 116*(3), 375–401. Advance online publication. DOI: 10.1111/j.1467-8594.2011.00390.x

Balakrishnan, R., Qiu, X. Y., & Srinivasan, P. (2010). On the predictive ability of narrative disclosures in annual reports. *European Journal of Operational Research, 202*(3), 789–801. DOI: 10.1016/j.ejor.2009.06.023

Baliyan, P., & Arora, B. (2024, January). TaxBot: An AI-driven Chatbot for Resolving Double Taxation Queries in India. In 2024, the IEEE 1st Karachi Section Humanitarian Technology Conference (KHI-HTC) (pp. 1-6). IEEE.

Bandura, A. (1977). *Social learning theory.* General Learning Press.

Bankole, F., & Vara, Z. (2023). A Comparison of SOM and K-Means Algorithms in Predicting Tax Compliance. In *Encyclopedia of Data Science and Machine Learning* (pp. 2573–2593). IGI Global.

Baralexis, S. (2004). Creative accounting in small advancing countries: The Greek case. *Managerial Auditing Journal, 19*(3), 440–461. DOI: 10.1108/02686900410524427

Barati, A., & Bakhshayesh, S. (2015). Electronic tax system and the facing challenges (case study: Kermanshah Province tax payers). *Indian Journal of Fundamental and Applied Life Sciences, 5*(S1), 480–497.

Bărbuţă-Mişu, N. (2011). A review of factors for tax compliance. *Annals of Dunărea de Jos University. Fascicle I: Economics and Applied Informatics.*

Bargh, J. A., & Chartrand, T. L. (1999). The unbearable automaticity of being. *The American Psychologist, 54*(7), 462–479. DOI: 10.1037/0003-066X.54.7.462

Barile, S., Saviano, M., & Polese, F. (2024). Rethinking fiscal policies: A systemic perspective. *Journal of Systemic Fiscal Studies, 5*(1), 45–63.

Barone, G., & Mocetti, S. (2011). Tax morale and public spending inefficiency. International Tax and Public Finance, 18, 724-749.Bazart, C., &Bonein, A. (2014). Reciprocal relationships in tax compliance decisions. *Journal of Economic Psychology, 40*, 83–102.

Barone, G., & Mocetti, S. (2011). With a little help from abroad: The effect of lowskilled immigration on the female labour supply. *Labour Economics, 18*(5), 664–675. DOI: 10.1016/j.labeco.2011.01.010

Barrett, L. F. (2017). The theory of constructed emotion: An active inference account of interoception and categorization. *Social Cognitive and Affective Neuroscience, 12*(1), 1–23. DOI: 10.1093/scan/nsx060 PMID: 27798257

Bătrâncea, L., & Nichita, R.-A. (2012). Tax non-compliance behavior in the light of tax law complexity and the relationship between authorities and taxpayers. *Scientific Annals of Alexandru Ioan Cuza University of Iasi - Economic Series, 59*(1), 97–106.

Batrancea, L. M., Nichita, R., & Batrancea, I. (2012). Understanding The Determinants Of Tax Compliance Behavior As A Prerequisite For Increasing Public Levies. *USV Annals of Economics and Public Administration, 12*, 201–210.

Baumann, F., & Friehe, T. (2013). Tax Evasion and Tacit Collusion. *Public Finance Review, 41*(5), 633–657. DOI: 10.1177/1091142112459211

Baumard, P. (1997). *Constructivisme et processus de la recherche: l'émergence d'une posture épistémologique chez le chercheur. Cahiers de recherche LAREGO*. Université de Versailles St Quentin.

Bavoso, V. (2018). The corporate law dilemma and the enlightened sovereign control paradigm:in search of a new legal framework. *Brooklyn Journal of Corporate, Financial & Commercial Law, 12*(2). https://brooklynworks.brooklaw.edu/bjcfcl/vol12/iss2/1

Bayer, R.-C., Oberhofer, H., & Winner, H. (2015). The occurrence of tax amnesties: Theory and evidence. *Journal of Public Economics, 125*, 70–82. DOI: 10.1016/j.jpubeco.2015.02.006

Bazart, C. (2002). Les comportements de fraude fiscale: Le face-à-face contribuables — administration fiscale. Revue française d'économie, [Tax Fraud Behaviors: The Face-to-Face Between Taxpayers and Tax Administration. French Review of Economics]. 16(4), 171-212. https://www.persee.fr

Bazart, C., & Blayac, T. (2022). Les déterminants de la non-conformité et de la perception du fardeau fiscal en France. *Revue Économique (Paris)*, *73*(4), 605–636. DOI: 10.3917/reco.734.0605

Bazart, C., & Bonein, A. (2014). Reciprocal relationships in tax compliance decisions. *Journal of Economic Psychology*, *40*, 83–102. DOI: 10.1016/j.joep.2012.10.002

Bazart, C., & Bonein, A. (2017). La force du symbole: Sommes-nous prêts à punir les fraudeurs? *Revue Économique (Paris)*, *68*(5), 829–841. DOI: 10.3917/reco.pr3.0092

Becker, G. (1968). Crime and punishment: An economic approach. *Journal of Political Economy*, *76*(2), 169–217. DOI: 10.1086/259394

Beddaa, M., & Bachiri, M. (2021). L'impact du potentiel touristique sur les intentions entrepreneuriales dans le tourisme durable: cas de la ville de Merzouga. Revue marocaine de recherche en management et marketing. Vol. 13, No. 1, 189-213.

Beddaa, M., & Bentalha, B. (2025). Optimizing Local Attractiveness Through Territorial Digital Communication. In Sustainable and Intelligent Territorial Marketing and Entrepreneurship (pp. 159-192). IGI Global.

Beddaa, M. (2023). Gestion budgétaire des ventes et performance commerciale de la firme: Exploration par étude de cas. *Revue des Études Multidisciplinaires en Sciences Économiques et Sociales*, *8*(1), 211–226.

Beddaa, M., Boumsiss, S., & Bachiri, M. (2020). L'impact du leadership sur la mise en place et l'amélioration du système de management intégré qualité-sécurité- environnement (QSE). *International Journal for Environment & Global Climate Change*, *8*(1), 131–151.

Bedoya, A., & Vásconez, B. (2010). Entendiendo la Moral Tributaria en Ecuador. *Fiscalidad.Revista Institucional Del Servicio de Rentas Internas*, *5*, 91–132.

Behavioural Insights Team, Cabinet Office, UK. (2012). *Applying behavioural insights to reduce fraud, error and debt.*

Belahouaoui, R., & Attak, E. H. (2024). Digital taxation, artificial intelligence, and tax administration 3.0: Improving tax compliance behaviour—a systematic literature review using textometry (2016–2023). *Accounting Research Journal*, *37*(2), 172–191. DOI: 10.1108/ARJ-12-2023-0372

Ben Othman, H., Hussainey, K., & Moumen, N. (2024). The influence of cultural tightness–looseness, religiosity, and the institutional environment on tax evasion behaviour: A cross-country study. *European Financial Management*, *30*(1), 346–374. DOI: 10.1111/eufm.12420

Bénabou, R., & Tirole, J. (2011). Identity, morals, and taboos: Beliefs as assets. *The Quarterly Journal of Economics*, *126*(2), 805–855. DOI: 10.1093/qje/qjr002 PMID: 22073409

Bentalha, B., & Boukare, M. (2024). AI-Driven Territorial Intelligence: An Integrated Approach to Enhancing Digital Sovereignty. In Generative AI and Implications for Ethics, Security, and Data Management (pp. 231-261). IGI Global.

Bentalha, B. (2020). Big-Data et Service Supply chain management: Challenges et opportunités. *International Journal of Business and Technology Studies*, *1*(3).

Bergolo, M., Ceni, R., Cruces, G., Giaccobasso, M., & Perez-Truglia, R. (2017). Tax audits as scarecrows: Evidence from Uruguay. *NBER Working Paper No. 23631*.

Bergolo, M. L., Leites, M., Perez-Truglia, R., & Strehl, M. (2020). *What makes a tax evader? (No. w28235)*. National Bureau of Economic Research. DOI: 10.3386/w28235

Bertrand, M., & Shafir, E. (2006). Behavioral Economics and Marketing in Aid of Decision Making Among the Poor. *Journal of Public Policy & Marketing*, *25*(1), 8–23. Advance online publication. DOI: 10.1509/jppm.25.1.8

Beuermann, D. W., & Amelina, M. (2014). Does Participatory Budgeting Improve Decentralized Public Service Delivery? *Inter-American Development Bank Working Paper Series* No. IDB-WP-547.

Beyer, R. C. M., & Milivojevic, L. (2021). Fiscal policy and economic activity in South Asia. *Review of Development Economics*, *25*(1), 340–358. DOI: 10.1111/rode.12710

Bhargava, S., & Manoli, D. (2015). Psychological frictions and the incomplete take-up of social benefits: Evidence from an IRS field experiment. *The American Economic Review*, *105*(11), 3489–3529. DOI: 10.1257/aer.20121493

Bhasin, M. L. (2016). Survey of creative accounting practices: An empirical study. *Wulfenia Journal*, *23*(1), 143–162.

Biddle, G. C. (1980). Accounting methods and management decisions: The case of inventory costing and inventory policy. *Journal of Accounting Research*, *18*(Supplement), 235–280. DOI: 10.2307/2490341

Biderman, C., & Da Silva, G. P. (2007). *Estimating the Impact of Participatory Budget on Observed Outcomes. Comunicación presentada en el 35 Encontro Nacional de Economia*. Recif.

Bidin, Z., Idris, K. M., & Shamsudin, F. M. (2009). Predicting compliance intention on zakah on employment income in Malaysia: An application of reasoned action theory. *JurnalPengurusan*, *28*(July), 85–102.

Bidin, Z., & Sinnasamy, P. (2018). Excise duty compliance behavior in Malaysia. *The International Journal of Accounting*, *3*(13), 106–116.

Bilgin, C. (2014). Determinants of tax morale in Spain and Turkey: an empirical analysis. European Journal of government and economics, 3(1), 60-74.

Bin, F. (2020). À l'ombre du positivisme: quelle place pour une doctrine de la justice fiscale propre aux juristes fiscalistes (XIXe-XXe siècle)?.

Bird, R. M., Martinez-Vazquez, J., & Torgler, B. (2008). Tax effort in developing countries and high-income countries: The impact of corruption, voice and accountability. *Economic Analysis and Policy*, *38*(1), 55–71. DOI: 10.1016/S0313-5926(08)50006-3

Bird, R. M., & Zolt, E. M. (2005). The limited role of the personal income tax in developing countries. *Journal of Asian Economics*, *59*(1), 89–114. DOI: 10.1016/j.asieco.2005.09.001

Bjork, J. M., Knutson, B., Fong, G. W., Caggiano, D. M., Bennett, S. M., & Hommer, D. W. (2004). Incentive-elicited brain activation in adolescents: Similarities and differences from young adults. *The Journal of Neuroscience : The Official Journal of the Society for Neuroscience*, *24*(8), 1793–1802. DOI: 10.1523/JNEUROSCI.4862-03.2004 PMID: 14985419

Blažek, R. (2021). Creative accounting as a global tool for tax optimization. *SHS Web of Conferences, 92*(1), 02007. https://doi.org/DOI: 10.1051/shsconf/20219202007

Blue, G., Chahrdahcheriki, M., Rezaee, Z., & Khotanlou, M. (2025). A model for predicting creative accounting in emerging economies. *International Journal of Accounting & Information Management*, *33*(1), 1–31. DOI: 10.1108/IJAIM-09-2023-0240

Blumenthal, M., & Christian, C. (2004). Tax preparers. In Aaron, H. H., & Selmrod, J. (Eds.), *The crisis in tax administration* (pp. 201–299). Brookings Institution Press.

Boateng, K., Omane-Antwi, K. B., & Ndori Queku, Y. (2022). Tax risk assessment, financial constraints and compliance for tax: A bibliometric analysis. *Cogent Business & Management*, *9*(1), 2150117. DOI: 10.1080/23311975.2022.2150117

Bobek, D. D., Hageman, A. M., & Kelliher, C. F. (2013). Analyzing the role of social norms in tax compliance behavior. *Journal of Business Ethics*, *115*(3), 451–468. DOI: 10.1007/s10551-012-1390-7

Bohnet, I. (2007). Why Women and Men Trust Others. In B. S. Frey y A. Stutzer (Eds.), *Economics and psychology: A promising new cross-disciplinary field*. London: CESifo Seminar Series. DOI: 10.7551/mitpress/2604.003.0008

Bohnet, I., Greig, F., Herrmann, B., & Zeckhauser, R. (2008). Betrayal aversion: Evidence from Brazil, China, Oman, Switzerland, Turkey, and the United States. *The American Economic Review*, *98*(1), 294–310. DOI: 10.1257/aer.98.1.294

Bohnet, I., & Zeckhauser, R. (2004). Trust, risk, and betrayal. *Journal of Economic Behavior & Organization*, *55*(4), 467–484. DOI: 10.1016/j.jebo.2003.11.004

Boly, A., Konte, M., & Shimeles, A. (2019). *Corruption and tax morale in Africa. Maastricht Economic and Social Research Institute on Innovation and Technology*. UNU-MERIT.

Boly, A., Konte, M., & Shimeles, A. (2021). Corruption perception and attitude towards taxation in Africa. *Journal of African Economies*, *30*(Supplement_1), i140–i157. DOI: 10.1093/jae/ejab024

Bonnet, G. F. (1995). Pièges (et délices) de la comptabilité (créative). *Economica*.

Bornman, M. (2015). The determinants and measurement of trust in tax authorities as a factor influencing tax compliance behaviour. *Journal of Economic and Financial Sciences*, *8*(3), 772–789. DOI: 10.4102/jef.v8i3.121

Borrego, A. C. D. C. (2015). Tax compliance and tax complexity in Portugal: essays on the perception of tax professionals.

Bosco, A., & Verney, S. (2012). Electoral Epidemic: The Political Cost of Economic Crisis in Southern Europe 2010-11. *South European Society & Politics, 17*(2), 129–154. DOI: 10.1080/13608746.2012.747272

Bosco, L., & Mittone, L. (1997). Tax evasion and moral constraints: Some experimental evidence. *Kyklos, 50*(3), 297–324. DOI: 10.1111/1467-6435.00018

Bose, P., & Jetter, M. (2012). Liberalization and tax amnesty in a developing economy. *Economic Modelling, 29*(3), 761–765. DOI: 10.1016/j.econmod.2012.01.017

Botha, R. C. (2021). *The readiness for the 4th industrial revolution by SARS towards 2030.* Nelson Mandela University.

Bott, K. M., Cappelen, A. W., Sørensen, E. Ø., & Tungodden, B. (2020). You've got mail: A randomized field experiment on tax evasion. *Management Science, 66*(7), 2801–2819. DOI: 10.1287/mnsc.2019.3390

Bouaddi, M., Beddaa, M., & El Ghalfiki, J. (2024). L'impact de la communication digitale sur la satisfaction des clients. *Revue des Études Multidisciplinaires en Sciences Économiques et Sociales, 9*(2), 287–310.

Bouaddi, M., Lahriga, M., & Beddaa, M. (2024). Digital Transformation of Moroccan Companies and its Impact on Service Quality: A Case of the Banking Sector. *Revue Internationale du Marketing et Management Stratégique, 6*(2), 52–79.

Boudri, R., Bentalha, B., Andaloussi, O. B., & Abbass, Z. (2025). Leveraging the "Made in Morocco" Label for Smart Marketing and Sustainable Territorial Attractiveness. In Sustainable and Intelligent Territorial Marketing and Entrepreneurship (pp. 69-94). IGI Global.

Bourdieu, P. (1990). La domination masculine. *Actes de la Recherche en Sciences Sociales, 84*(1), 2–31. DOI: 10.3406/arss.1990.2947

Bourdieu, P. (2001). El capital social. Apuntes provisionales. *Zona Abierta*, (94/95), 83–87.

Bourveau, T., & Schoenfeld, J. (2017). Shareholder activism and voluntary disclosure. *Review of Accounting Studies, 22*(3), 1307–1339. DOI: 10.1007/s11142-017-9408-0

Boyer, A. (2020). *Chapitre 16. L'évasion et fraude fiscale. Introduction au droit fiscal.* Ellipses., https://droit.cairn.info/introduction-au-droit-fiscal--9782340037953-page-195?lang=fr

Braithwaite, V., & Ahmed, E. (2005). A threat to tax morale: The case of Australian higher education policy. *Journal of Economic Psychology, 26*(4), 523–540. DOI: 10.1016/j.joep.2004.08.003

Brehm, J. & Rahn, W. (1997). Individual-Level Evidence for the Causes and Consequences of Social Capital. *American Journal o f Political Science, 41*(3), 999–1023.

Breiter, H. C., Aharon, I., Kahneman, D., Dale, A., & Shizgal, P. (2001). Functional imaging of neural responses to expectancy and experience of monetary gains and losses. *Neuron, 30*(2), 619–639. DOI: 10.1016/S0896-6273(01)00303-8 PMID: 11395019

Brink, W. D., & Porcano, T. M. (2016). The Impact of Culture and Economic Structure on Tax Morale and Tax Evasion: A Country-Level Analysis Using SEM. In J. Hasseldine (Ed.), *Advances in Taxation (Advances in Taxation, Volume 23)* (pp. 87–123). Emerald Group Publishing Limited. DOI: 10.1108/S1058-749720160000023004

Brizi, A., Giacomantonio, M., Schumpe, B. M., & Mannetti, L. (2015). Intention to pay taxes or to avoid them: The impact of social value orientation. *Journal of Economic Psychology*, *50*, 22–31. DOI: 10.1016/j.joep.2015.06.005

Brockmeyer, A., Hernandez, M., Kettle, S., & Smith, S. (2016). Casting the tax net wider: Experimental evidence from Costa Rica. *World Bank Policy Research Working Paper* No. 7850. https://hdl.handle.net/10986/25167

Brown, L. D., & Caylor, M. (2009). Corporate governance and firm operating performance. *Review of Quantitative Finance and Accounting*, *32*(2), 129–144. DOI: 10.1007/s11156-007-0082-3

Bruns, C., Fochmann, M., Mohr, P. N., & Torgler, B. (2023). Multidimensional tax compliance attitude. *Freie Universität Berlin, School of Business & Economics Discussion Paper*, (2023/7).

Buchholz, F., Jaeschke, R., Lopatta, K., & Maas, K. (2018). The use of optimistic tone by narcissistic CEOs. *Accounting, Auditing & Accountability Journal*, *31*(2), 531–562. DOI: 10.1108/AAAJ-11-2015-2292

Buele, I., & Guerra, T. (2021). BIBLIOMETRIC ANALYSIS OF SCIENTIFIC PRODUCTION ON TAX EVASION IN SCIENCEDIRECT, YEARS 2010 TO 2019. *Journal of Legal, Ethical and Regulatory Issues*, *24*(2), 1–15. https://www.scopus.com/inward/record.uri?eid=2-s2.0-85103728358&partnerID=40&md5=9415c00405f928c9aee188b0787617f0

Cabannes, Y. (2015). The impact of participatory budgeting on basic services: Municipal practices and evidence from the field. *Environment and Urbanization*, *27*(1), 257–284. DOI: 10.1177/0956247815572297

Cabelkova, I., & Smutka, L. (2021). The influences of solidarity, income, and reliance on the state on personal income tax preferences. The case of the czech republic. *Sustainability (Basel)*, *13*(18), 10141. Advance online publication. DOI: 10.3390/su131810141

Campbell-Meiklejohn, D. K., Bach, D. R., Roepstorff, A., Dolan, R. J., & Frith, C. D. (2010). How the opinion of others affects our valuation of objects. *Current Biology*, *20*(12), 1165–1170. DOI: 10.1016/j.cub.2010.04.055 PMID: 20619815

Canavire-Bacarreza, G., Eguino, H., Heller, L., & Roman, S. (2023). When do tax amnesties work? *Journal of Economic Behavior & Organization*, *207*, 350–375. DOI: 10.1016/j.jebo.2022.12.018

Capasso, S., Cicatiello, L., De Simone, E., Gaeta, G. L., & Mourão, P. R. (2021). Fiscal transparency and tax ethics: Does better information lead to greater compliance? *Journal of Policy Modeling*, *43*(5), 1031–1050. DOI: 10.1016/j.jpolmod.2020.06.003

Carrillo, P. E., Castro, E., & Scartascini, C. (2017, April). Do rewards work? Evidence from the randomization of public works. *Inter-American Development Bank (IDB) Working Paper Series* No. 794.

Casagrande, A., Di Cagno, D., Pandimiglio, A., & Spallone, M. (2015). The effect of competition on tax compliance: The role of audit rules and shame. *Journal of Behavioral and Experimental Economics*, *59*, 96–110. DOI: 10.1016/j.socec.2015.08.006

Cascavilla, A. (2023). *What Drives the Tax Compliance Attitude of Individuals? the Function of Communal Ties, Wellbeing State and Environmental Concern in Tax Morale. February*. https://www.tdx.cat/handle/10803/688951%0Ahttps://www.tdx.cat/bitstream/handle/10803/688951/2023_Tesis_Cascavilla_Alessandro.pdf?sequence=1

Cascavilla, A., Ripollés, J., & Morone, A. (2024). Tax morale and communal capital: An empirical investigation among European citizens. *Annals of Public and Cooperative Economics, 95*(2), 441–476. DOI: 10.1111/apce.12443

Casta, J. F. (1997). La comptabilité et ses utilisateurs. In Joffre, P., & Simon, Y. (Eds.), *Encyclopédie de gestion* (Vol. I, pp. 528–551). Economica.

Castañeda, N. (2024). Fairness and tax morale in developing countries. *Studies in Comparative International Development, 59*(1), 113–137. DOI: 10.1007/s12116-023-09394-z PMID: 37360793

Castañeda, V. M. (2015). La moral tributaria en América Latina y la corrupción como uno de sus determinantes. *Revista Mexicana de Ciencias Politicas y Sociales, 60*(224), 103–132. DOI: 10.1016/S0185-1918(15)30005-2

Castro, L., & Scartascini, C. (2015). Tax compliance and enforcement in the pampas evidence from a field experiment. *Journal of Economic Behavior & Organization, 116*, 65–82. DOI: 10.1016/j.jebo.2015.04.002

Celikay, F. (2020). Dimensions of tax burden: A review on OECD countries. *Journal of Economics, Finance and Administrative Science, 25*(49), 27–43. DOI: 10.1108/JEFAS-12-2018-0138

Cernusca, L., David, D., Nicolaescu, C., & Cosmin, G. B. (2016). Empirical study on the creative accounting phenomenon. *Studia Universitatis „Vasile Goldis" Arad – Economics Series, 26*(2). https://doi.org/DOI: 10.1515/sues-2016-0010

Chacko, M., & Mishra, S. (2023). Benchmarking the Indian Digital Personal Data Protection Act 2023 against data protection frameworks in Singapore, the EU, the US, and Australia. *Journal of Data Protection & Privacy, 6*(2), 110–119. DOI: 10.69554/LXHZ9342

Chan, H. F., Supriyadi, M. W., & Torgler, B. (2017). Trust and tax morale. In Eric M. Uslaner (ed.). *The Oxford Handbook of Social and Political Trust*. Oxford Handbooks online Oxford Academic. DOI: 10.1093/oxfordhb/9780190274801.013.23

Chan, C. W., Troutman, C. S., & O'Bryan, D. (2000). An expanded model of taxpayercompliance: Empiricalevidencefrom the United States and Hong Kong. *Journal of International Accounting, Auditing & Taxation, 9*(2), 83–103. DOI: 10.1016/S1061-9518(00)00027-6

Chan, S. H., & Song, Q. (2021). Implications of tax audit risk, consequences, aggressive behavior and ethics for compliance. *International Journal of Accounting & Information Management, 29*(5), 823–847. DOI: 10.1108/IJAIM-09-2021-0183

Chatzoglou, P., Chatzoudes, D., & Symeonidis, S. (2015). Factors affecting the intention to use e-Government services. In P. M., M. L., G. M., & M. L. (Eds.), *Federated Conference on Computer Science and Information Systems, FedCSIS 2015* (pp. 1489–1498). Institute of Electrical and Electronics Engineers Inc. DOI: 10.15439/2015F171

Chen, J. Z., Hong, H. A., Kim, J.-B., & Ryou, J. W. (2021). Information processing costs and corporate tax aggressiveness: Evidence from the SEC's XBRL Mandate. *Journal of Accounting and Public Policy, 40*(2), 106822. DOI: 10.1016/j.jaccpubpol.2021.106822

Cherkaoui, A. & Oudrhough, Y. (2024). *Case Study Methodology in Business Management: A Systematic Review. In B. Bentalha & L. Alla (Eds.), Applying Qualitative Research Methods to Management Science (pp. 53-74). IGI Global Scientific Publishing.* https://doi.org/DOI: 10.4018/979-8-3693-5543-5.ch003

Cherkaoui, A. & Oudrhough, Y. (2025). *Corporate Governance and Managerial Overconfidence: A Systematic Review. In S. Ed-Dafali, F. Özsungur, & M. Mohiuddin (Eds.), Modern Corporate Governance Strategies for Sustainable Value Creation (pp. 41-60). IGI Global Scientific Publishing.* https://doi.org/DOI: 10.4018/979-8-3693-6750-6.ch003

Cherkaoui, A. et Belgaid, A. (2021). Les nouveaux défis des managers de proximité face à la décentralisation de la fonction RH au Maroc – Cas d'un groupe financier panafricain. Question(s) de management, n° 32(2), 43-68. https://doi.org/.DOI: 10.3917/qdm.212.0043

Cherkaoui, A., & Dembele, A. (2023). *Performances et politiques financières comparées des entreprises familiales et non familiales cotées au Maroc.* Maghreb - Machrek. *Maghreb, Machrek, N° Hors-série*(1), 73–91. DOI: 10.3917/machr.hs1.0073

Chetty, R., Mobarak, M., & Singhal, M. (2014, August). Increasing tax compliance through social recognition. *International Growth Centre Policy Brief* No. 14/0658.

Chiarini, B., Marzano, E., & Schneider, F. (2013). Tax rates and tax evasion: An empirical analysis of the long-run aspects in Italy. *European Journal of Law and Economics, 35*(2), 273–293. DOI: 10.1007/s10657-011-9247-6

Chopra, G., Bhaskar, P., Vinay, M., & Joshi, A. (2022). E-government adoption and employees' job performance: The moderating role of age as a demographic factor. *Electronic Government, 18*(2), 237–263. DOI: 10.1504/EG.2022.121871

Chorvat, T. (2007). Tax Compliance and the Neuroeconomics of Intertemporal Substitution. *National Tax Journal, 60*(3). The University of Chicago Press Journals. DOI: 10.17310/ntj.2007.3.15

Chouaibi, J., Rossi, M., & Abdessamed, N. (2022). The influence of communal responsibility of corporates practices on tax avoidance: An empirical investigation in the French context. *Competitiveness Review, 32*(3), 326–349. DOI: 10.1108/CR-04-2021-0062

Cifuentes-Faura, J., Benito, B., & Guillamón, M.-D. (2024). The Influence of Transparency on Municipal Taxation: An Empirical Analysis. *Administration & Society, 56*(5), 653–682. DOI: 10.1177/00953997241239024

Ciziceno, M., & Pizzuto, P. (2022). Life satisfaction and tax morale: The role of trust in government and cultural orientation. *Journal of Behavioral and Experimental Economics, 97*, 101824. DOI: 10.1016/j.socec.2021.101824

Cleven, A. (2020). How did the Tax Cuts and Jobs Act change business taxes*? Tax Policy Center*. https://taxpolicycenter.org/briefing-book/how-did-tax-cuts-and-jobs-act-change-business-taxes

Clotfelter (1983) .Tax Evasion and Tax Rate: An Analysis of Individual Return. *The Review of Economic and Statistics*, 65 (3), 363-373.

Colasse, B. (1995). *25 ans de comptabilité générale, une nouvelle naissance d'une vieille discipline. In 25 ans de sciences d'organisation.* Masson.

Comba, A. (2019). Rural tax evasion in Argentina: An analysis of tax evasion mechanisms and social relationships in the Córdoba grain market. *International Journal for Crime. Justice and Social Democracy*, *8*(2), 68–82. DOI: 10.5204/ijcjsd.v8i2.1153

ConseilÉconomique. Social et Environnemental. (2019). Le Nouveau Modèle de Développement du Maroc: Contribution du Conseil Économique, Social et Environnemental. Rabat.

Coppensa, L., & Erik, E. (2005). An analysis of earnings management by European private firms. *Journal of International Accounting, Auditing & Taxation, 14*(1), 1–17. DOI: 10.1016/j.intaccaudtax.2005.01.002

Corbin, J., & Strauss, A. (2008). Basics of qualitative research: Techniques and procedures for developing grounded theory *(3rd ed.). SAGE Publications.*https://doi.org/DOI: 10.4135/9781452230153

Coricelli, G., Joffily, M., Montmarquette, C., & Villeval, M. C. (2010). Cheating, emotions, and rationality: An experiment on tax evasion. *Experimental Economics*, *13*(2), 226–247. DOI: 10.1007/s10683-010-9237-5

Cotton, M., Dark, G., Menhard, P., & Ryan, J. (2017). Use of Technology in Tax Administrations 2: Core Information Technology Systems in Tax Administrations. Fiscal Affairs Department, International Monetary Fund. Authorized for distribution by Sanjeev Gupta. March 2017.

Coyne, R. (2025) Facebook v. Amalgamated Bank. *Georgetown Law Journal*. https://www.law.georgetown.edu/georgetown-law-journal/submit/glj-online/supreme-court-coverage-program/facebook-v-amalgamated-bank-why-did-the-supreme-court-dismiss-facebooks-writ-of-certiorari-as-improvidently-granted/

Creswell, J. W. (2013). *Research design: Qualitative, quantitative, and mixed methods approaches.* Sage publications.

Cugova, A., & Cug, J. (2020). Motivation for the use of creative accounting techniques in the conditions of the globalized business environment. *SHS Web of Conferences, 74*(2), 01004. https://doi.org/DOI: 10.1051/shsconf/20207401004

Cummings, R. G., Martinez-Vazquez, J., McKee, M., & Torgler, B. (2009). Tax morale affects tax compliance: Evidence from surveys and an artefactual field experiment. *Journal of Economic Behavior & Organization*, *70*(3), 447–457. DOI: 10.1016/j.jebo.2008.02.010

D'Agostino, E., De Benedetto, M. A., & Sobbrio, G. (2021). Tax evasion and government size: Evidence from Italian provinces. *Economics and Politics*, *38*(3), 1149–1187. DOI: 10.1007/s40888-021-00227-7 PMID: 35422597

Dahlan, A., Chandrarin, G., & Triatmanto, B. (2024). *Understanding Tax Morale: A Critical Review of Its Impact on Compliance and Policy.* KnE Social Sciences.

Dakhli, A. (2022). The influence of ownership structure on corporate tax avoidance with communal responsibility of corporates as mediating variable. *Journal of Financial Crime*, *29*(3), 836–852. DOI: 10.1108/JFC-07-2021-0152

Dalton, A. G., Manning, L. A., Jamison, J. C., Sen, I. K., Karver, J. G., Nunez, C., Jorge, L., Guedes, L. P., Estevez, M., & Serrana, B. (2021). *Behavioral insights for tax compliance*. World Bank Group.

Damasio, A. (2009). Neuroscience and the emergence of neuroeconomics. In Glimcher, P. W., Camerer, C. F., Fehr, E., & Poldrack, R. A. (Eds.), *Neuroeconomics: Decision making and the brain* (pp. 209–217). Academic Press. DOI: 10.1016/B978-0-12-374176-9.00014-2

Damasio, A. R. (1994). *Descartes' error: Emotion, reason, and the human brain*. Putnam.

Damasio, A. R. (1996). The somatic marker hypothesis and the possible functions of the prefrontal cortex. *Philosophical Transactions of the Royal Society of London. Series B, Biological Sciences*, *351*(1346), 1413–1420. DOI: 10.1098/rstb.1996.0125 PMID: 8941953

Damayanti, T. W., & Matasik, A. L. (2021). Market competition, fairness and tax compliance: The formal sector's perspective. *Journal of International Students*, *14*(1).

Daoud, I. B., & Omri, M. A. (2013). Les divergences comptabilité-fiscalité en Tunisie: Quels facteurs explicatifs? *La revue des sciences de gestion, 263-264*, 179-195.

Dashe, D. N., & Asada, D. (2023). The challenges of generative artificial intelligence to administer internet taxation of online transactions in Nigeria. *NIALS Journal of Business Law*, *5*(1), 31–77.

De Juan, A., & Truyols, M. A. (1993). Predisposición, habilidad y oportunidad de los contribuyentes hacia el fraude fiscal. *Cuadernos de Actualidad*, (1), 27–36.

de la Cruz, C. D., Fernández-Fernández, J. L., & Ferrero, I. (2022). Ethical decision-making: from practice to theory. *Ramon Llull Journal of Applied Ethics*, (13).

De Miguel, I., & De Miguel, A. (2001). *Los españoles y los impuestos*. Centro de Investigaciones Sociológicas.

De Neve, J. E., Imbert, C., & Spinnewijn, J. (2024). How to improve tax compliance? Evidence from population-wide experiments in Belgium. *Journal of Political Economy*, *132*(1), 85–128.

Deci, E. L., & Ryan, R. M. (1980). The empirical exploration of intrinsic motivational processes. In Berkowitz, L. (Ed.), Advances in Experimental Social Psychology: Vol. 13. *Academic Press* (pp. 39–80). DOI: 10.1016/S0065-2601(08)60130-6

Delgado, M. L., Fernández-Cuartero, M., Maldonado, A., Roldán, C., & Valdenebro, M. L. (2005). *La Educación Fiscal en España*. Instituto de Estudios Fiscales. DOC. N.º 29/05. Madrid.

Denzin, N. K., & Lincoln, Y. S. (2011). *The SAGE handbook of qualitative research* (4th ed.). SAGE Publications.

Desai, M., & Dharmapala, D. (2009). Earnings management and corporate tax shelters. *Harvard University and University of Connecticut Working Paper.*

Desai, M. A. (2003). The divergence between book and tax income. In Poterba, J. M. (Ed.), *Tax Policy and the Economy, 17, 169-206*. MIT Press. DOI: 10.1086/tpe.17.20140508

Deshpande, A. (2024, April). Regulatory Compliance and AI: Navigating the Legal and Regulatory Challenges of AI in Finance. In *2024 International Conference on Knowledge Engineering and Communication Systems (ICKECS)* (Vol. 1, pp. 1-5). IEEE. DOI: 10.1109/ICKECS61492.2024.10616752

Devano, S., Mulyani, S., Winarningsih, S., & Ghani, E. (2024). Tax amnesty and taxpayer morality in predicting taxpayer compliance. *International Journal of Applied Economics. Finance and Accounting, 18*(1), 98–106.

Devos, K. (2013). *Factors influencing individual taxpayer compliance behaviour.* Springer Science & Business Media.

Dhakal, B. (2024). Impact of attitude variables, Tax rate and perceptions of government fairness on Tax Compliance.

Dhami, S., & al-Nowaihi, A. (2007). Why do people pay taxes? Prospect theory versus expected utility theory. *Journal of Economic Behavior & Organization, 64*(1), 171–192. DOI: 10.1016/j.jebo.2006.08.006

Di Legge, A., Ceccanti, D., & Hortal Foronda, F. (2022). Tax compliance costs for SMEs: An update and a complement. VVA and KPMG. European Commission, European Innovation Council and SMEs Executive Agency (EISMEA). Retrieved from EISMEA-COSME-ENQUIRIES@ec.europa.eu

Do, H. T. H., Mac, Y. T. H., Van Tran, H. T., & Nguyen, T. T. L. (2022). The impact of attitude towards an e-tax system on tax compliance of Vietnamese enterprises: Adoption of an e-tax system as a mediator.

Dobbin, F., & Zorn, D. (2005). Corporate malfeasance and the myth of shareholder value. In *Political power and social theory* (Vol. 17, pp. 179–198). Emerald Group Publishing., DOI: 10.1016/S0198-8719(04)17006-3

Dobrovič, J., Gombár, M., & Benková, E. (2017). Sustainable development activities aimed at combating tax evasion in Slovakia. *Journal of Security and Sustainability Issues, 6*(4), 761–772. DOI: 10.9770/jssi.2017.6.4(19)

Doğan, E., Tekin, A., & Çelikay, F. (2019). Mükelleflerin Vergiye Bakışında Yargı Yetisi Sorunsalı: Kant Perspektifinden Mekânsal Farklılık Temelli Bir Değerlendirme. *Mehmet Akif Ersoy Üniversitesi İktisadi ve İdari Bilimler Fakültesi Dergisi, 6*(3), 702–720. DOI: 10.30798/makuiibf.597471

Donelan, E. (2022). *Regulatory governance: Policy making, legislative drafting, and law reform.* Springer Nature., DOI: 10.1007/978-3-030-96351-4

Doran, M. (2009). Tax penalties and tax compliance. *Harvard Journal on Legislation, 46*, 111.

Drake, K. D., Hamilton, R., & Lusch, S. J. (2020). Are declining effective tax rates indicative of tax avoidance? Insight from effective tax rate reconciliations. *Journal of Accounting and Economics, 70*(1), 101317. DOI: 10.1016/j.jacceco.2020.101317

Druckman, J. N. (2001). The implications of framing effects for citizen competence. *Political Behavior, 23*(3), 225–256. DOI: 10.1023/A:1015006907312

Drumbl, M. L. (2013). Those Who Know, Those Who Don't, and Those Who Know Better: Balancing Complexity, Sophistication, and Accuracy on Tax Returns. *Pitt. Tax Rev.*, *11*(1), 113. DOI: 10.5195/taxreview.2013.23

Dubin, J. A. (2007). Criminal investigation enforcement activities and taxpayer noncompliance. *Public Finance Review*, *35*(4), 500–529. DOI: 10.1177/1091142106295757

Dudu, O. F., Alao, O. B., & Alonge, E. O. (2024). Conceptual framework for AI-driven tax compliance in fintech ecosystems. *Journal of Fintech and Taxation*, *12*(3), 45–60.

Dularif, M., Sutrisno, T., & Saraswati, E. (2019). Is deterrence approach effective in combating tax evasion? A meta-analysis. *Problems and Perspectives in Management*, *17*(2), 93–113. DOI: 10.21511/ppm.17(2).2019.07

Dulleck, U., Fooken, J., Newton, C., Ristl, A., Schaffner, M., & Torgler, B. (2016). Tax compliance and psychic costs: Behavioral experimental evidence using a physiological marker. *Journal of Public Economics*, *134*, 9–18. DOI: 10.1016/j.jpubeco.2015.12.007

Dumre, D. P., & Shrestha, L. M. (2023). Factors influencing tax compliance behavior among the industries of Butwal Industrial Estate. *The Lumbini Journal of Business and Economics*, *XI*(2), 1–20. DOI: 10.3126/ljbe.v11i2.64720

Durham, Y., Manly, T. S., & Ritsema, C. (2014). The effects of income source, context, and income level on tax compliance decisions in a dynamic experiment. *Journal of Economic Psychology*, *40*, 220–233. DOI: 10.1016/j.joep.2012.09.012

Dwenger, N., Kleven, H., Rasul, I., & Rincke, J. (2016). Extrinsic and intrinsic motivations for tax compliance: Evidence from a field experiment in Germany. *American Economic Journal. Economic Policy*, *8*(3), 203–232. DOI: 10.1257/pol.20150083

Dwianika, A., Sofia, I. P., & Retnaningtyas, I. (2023). Tax Compliance: Development of Artificial Intelligence on Tax Issues. KnE Social Sciences, 728-733. DOI: 10.18502/kss.v8i12.13719

Dyer, T., Lang, M., & Stice-Lawrence, L. (2017). The evolution of 10-K textual disclosure: Evidence from Latent Dirichlet allocation. *Journal of Accounting and Economics*, *64*(2–3), 221–245. DOI: 10.1016/j.jacceco.2017.07.002

Eaton, G.M. (1937). "Organizations for Compliance with Taxing Statutes". Tax Mag, No 15.

Ebrill, L., Keen, M., & Summers, V. (2001). *The Modern VAT*. International Monetary Fund.

Eckel, C. C., & Grossman, P. J. (2001). Chivalry and Solidarity in Ultimatum Games. *Economic Inquiry*, *39*(2), 171–188. DOI: 10.1111/j.1465-7295.2001.tb00059.x

Eghaghe, V. O., Osundare, O. S., Ewim, C. P. M., & Okeke, I. C. (2024). Navigating the ethical and governance challenges of AI deployment in AML practices within the financial industry. *International Journal of Scholarly Research and Reviews*, *5*(2).

Eilu, E., Walyawula, C., & Soita, R. (2021, March). An assessment of usability of online tax return services in Uganda and its influence on tax revenue. In *Proceedings of the 3rd African Human-Computer Interaction Conference: Inclusiveness and Empowerment* (pp. 113-118).

Eisenhauer, J. G. (2008). Ethical preferences, risk aversion, and taxpayer behavior. *Journal of Socio-Economics*, *37*(1), 45–63. DOI: 10.1016/j.socec.2007.01.030

El Ghazali, M., &Benkendil, H. (2020). Civisme fiscal: Comment peut-on instaurer un climat de confiance entre l'administration fiscale et le contribuable ? International Journal of Accounting, Finance, Auditing, Management and Economics, 1(2).

El Harchi, A., & El Bennissi, L. (2024). Réflexions autour de l'articulation des sanctions dans la répressionfiscale: uneapproche comparative entre la France et le Maroc. International Journal of Accounting, Finance, Auditing, Management and Economics.

Elena, D. A., Alberto, D. B. M., & Giuseppe, S. (n.d.). *Tax Evasion, government size and taxpayers perceptions on public goods provision, evidence from italian regions.*

Elffers, H. (2000). But taxpayers do cooperate! In A. Biel, M. Snyder, T. R. Tyler, & M. van Vugt (Eds.), *Cooperation in modern society: Promoting the welfare of communities, states, and organizations* (pp. 184–194). Taylor & Francis Group.

Elhamma, A. (2023). Impact of mandatory IFRS adoption on foreign direct investment: The moderating role of conflict of interest regulation. *Journal of Financial Reporting and Accounting, ahead-of-print.* https://doi.org/DOI: 10.1108/JFRA-04-2022-0145

Elhamma, A. (2015). The relationship between budgetary evaluation, firm size, and performance. *Journal of Management Development*, *34*(8), 973–986. DOI: 10.1108/JMD-06-2014-0053

Elhamma, A. (2023). The relationship between organisational decentralisation, balanced scorecard, and its perceived benefits in Moroccan SMEs. *International Journal of Accounting, Auditing and Performance Evaluation*, *19*(2), 185–202. DOI: 10.1504/IJAAPE.2023.132384

Elhamma, A. (2024). Determinants of national IFRS adoption: Evidence from the Middle East and North Africa region. *International Journal of Accounting. Auditing and Performance Evaluation*, *20*(1-2), 69–90. DOI: 10.1504/IJAAPE.2024.135535

Elhamma, A. (2024). Participant observation as a qualitative research method in management sciences: Interests, conditions, and limitations. In Bentalha, B., & Alla, L. (Eds.), *Applying qualitative research methods to management science* (pp. 75–91). IGI Global., DOI: 10.4018/979-8-3693-5543-5.ch004

Elhamma, A. (2025). Lack of Resilience and Failure of Small and Medium-Sized Enterprises (SMEs) in Morocco: Current Situation and Key Determinants. In Dias Rouco, J. C., & Nunes Figueiredo, P. C. (Eds.), *Enhancing Resilience in Business Continuity Management* (pp. 245–266). IGI Global., DOI: 10.4018/979-8-3693-8809-9.ch008

Elhamma, A., & Moalla, M. (2015). Impact of uncertainty and decentralization on activity-based costing use. *International Journal of Accounting and Economics Studies*, *3*(2), 148–155. DOI: 10.14419/ijaes.v3i2.4817

Elster, J. (1991). *El cemento de la sociedad. Las paradojas del orden social*. Gedisa Editorial.

Enachescu, J., Olsen, J., Kogler, C., Zeelenberg, M., Breugelmans, S. M., & Kirchler, E. (2019). The role of emotions in tax compliance behavior: A mixed-methods approach. *Journal of Economic Psychology, 74*, 102194. Advance online publication. DOI: 10.1016/j.joep.2019.102194

Engida, T. G., & Baisa, G. A. (2014). Factors influencing taxpayers' compliance with the tax system: An empirical study in Mekelle City, Ethiopia. *eJournal of Tax Research, 12*(2), 433–452.

Engida, T. G., & Baisa, G. A. (2014). Factors Influencing t axpayers" compliance with the tax system: An empirical study in Mekelle City, Ethiopia. *Journal of Tax Research, 12*(2), 433–453.

Engström, P., Nordblom, K., Ohlsson, H., & Persson, A. (2015). Tax compliance and loss aversion. *American Economic Journal. Economic Policy, 7*(4), 132–164. DOI: 10.1257/pol.20130134

Erard, B., & Feinstein, J. (1994). Honesty and evasion in the tax compliance game. *The RAND Journal of Economics, 25*(1), 1–19. DOI: 10.2307/2555850

Erdoğdu, M. M., & Akar, S. (2022). Behavioral aspects of tax amnesties and their effects in twelve countries. *Public Finance Quarterly, 2022*(2), 270–284. DOI: 10.35551/PFQ_2022_2_7

Ermasova, N., Haumann, C., & Burke, L. (2021). The Relationship between Culture and Tax Evasion across Countries: Cases of the USA and Germany. *International Journal of Public Administration, 44*(2), 115–131. DOI: 10.1080/01900692.2019.1672181

Esayas, S., & Mahler, T. (2015). Modelling compliance risk: A structured approach. *Artificial Intelligence and Law, 23*(3), 271–300. DOI: 10.1007/s10506-015-9174-x

Esnault, E., & Hoarau, C. (2005). *Comptabilité financière*. PUF.

Ezeife, E., Kokogho, E., Odio, P. E., & Adeyanju, M. O. (2021). The future of tax technology in the United States: A conceptual framework for AI-driven tax transformation. *Future, 2*(1).

Fagbemi, T. O., Uadiale, O. M., & Noah, A. O. (2010). The ethics of tax evasion: Perceptual evidence from Nigeria. *European Journal of Social Sciences, 17*(3), 360–371. https://www.scopus.com/inward/record.uri?eid=2-s2.0-78649799260&partnerID=40&md5=fd46224c6ed69ee17a2791dbe1108caa

Faizal, S., Palil, M., Maelah, R., & Ramli, R. (2017). Power and trust as factors influencing tax compliance behavior in Malaysia. *Asian Journal of Accounting and Governance, 8*, 79–85. DOI: 10.17576/AJAG-2017-08-07

Fajriana, N., Irianto, G., & Andayani, W. (2023). The role of tax fairness and taxpayer trust in building voluntary compliance in MSME taxpayers. *International Journal of Business and Society, 24*(1), 478–487. DOI: 10.33736/ijbs.5629.2023

Falkinger, J. (1988). Tax Evasion and Equity: A Theoretical Analysis. *Public Finance, 43*, 388–395.

Farooqi, M. T. K., Amanat, I., & Awan, S. M. (2024). Ethical considerations and challenges in the integration of artificial intelligence in education: A systematic review. *Journal of Excellence in Management Sciences, 3*(4), 35–50. DOI: 10.69565/jems.v3i4.314

Faúndez-Ugalde, A., Mellado-Silva, R., & Aldunate-Lizana, E. (2020). Use of artificial intelligence by tax administrations: An analysis regarding taxpayers' rights in Latin American countries. *Computer Law & Security Review*, *38*, 105441. DOI: 10.1016/j.clsr.2020.105441

Fauziati, P., & Kassim, A. A. M. (2018). The effect of business characteristics on tax compliance costs. *Advanced Science Letters*, *24*(6), 4377–4379. DOI: 10.1166/asl.2018.11608

Febrian, Y. B., & Islami, I. N. (2020). Gender, trust, and tax compliance: The mediating effect of fairness perception. [Journal of Applied Accounting and Finance]. *JAAF*, *4*(2), 131–145. DOI: 10.33021/jaaf.v4i2.1244

Fehr, E., Fischbacher, U., & Gächter, S. (2002). Strong reciprocity, human cooperation and the Enforcement of Social Norms. *Human Nature (Hawthorne, N.Y.)*, *13*(1), 1–25. DOI: 10.1007/s12110-002-1012-7 PMID: 26192593

Fehr, E., & Gächter, S. (2002). Altruistic punishment in humans. *Nature*, *415*(6868), 137–140. DOI: 10.1038/415137a PMID: 11805825

Feingold, A. (1983). Happiness, unselfishness, and popularity. *The Journal of Psychology*, *115*(1), 3–5. DOI: 10.1080/00223980.1983.9923590

Feinstein, J. S. (1991). An econometric analysis of income tax evasion and its detection. *The RAND Journal of Economics*, *22*(1), 22–50. DOI: 10.2307/2601005

Feitosa, F., & Galais, C. (2020). How stable is the Sense for Civics Duty to vote? A panel investigation on the individual-level stability of the attitude. 6(5), 34-46

Feld, L. P. ve Frey, B.S. (2002), "Trust Breeds Trust: How Taxpayers are Treated", Cesifo Working Paper Series, 2-18.

Feld, L. P., & Frey, B. S. (2010). Tax evasion and the psychological tax contract. Developing alternative frameworks for explaining tax compliance, 59, 74.

Feld, L. P., & Frey, B. S. (2002). Trust breeds trust: How taxpayers are treated. *Economics of Governance*, *3*(2), 87–99. DOI: 10.1007/s101010100032

Feld, L. P., & Frey, B. S. (2007). Tax compliance as the result of a psychological tax contract: The role of incentives and responsive regulation. *Law & Policy*, *29*(1), 102–120. DOI: 10.1111/j.1467-9930.2007.00248.x

Feld, L. P., & Kirchgässner, G. (2000). Direct Democracy, Political Culture, and the Outcome of Economic Policy: A Report on the Swiss Experience. *European Journal of Political Economy*, *16*(2), 287–306. DOI: 10.1016/S0176-2680(00)00003-3

Feld, L. P., & Larsen, C. (2012). Self-perceptions, government policies and tax compliance in Germany. *International Tax and Public Finance*, *19*(1), 78–103. DOI: 10.1007/s10797-011-9196-6

Feld, L., & Tyran, J. R. (2002). Tax evasion and voting: An experimental analysis. *Kyklos*, *55*(2), 197–222. DOI: 10.1111/1467-6435.00183

Fernández-Espejo, E. (2000). Cómo funciona el nucleus accumbens? [How does the nucleus accumbens function?]. *Revista de Neurología, 30*(9), 845–849. DOI: 10.33588/rn.3009.99617 PMID: 10870199

Fernández, J. J. (2006). *Sociología de la Hacienda Pública.* Ministerio de Economía y Hacienda. Instituto de Estudios Fiscales.

Fligstein, N. (2001). Social skill and the theory of fields. *Sociological Theory, 19*(2), 105–125. DOI: 10.1111/0735-2751.00132

Flores-Macías, G. A. (2018). Building support for taxation in developing countries: Experimental evidence from Mexico. *World Development, 105*, 13–24. DOI: 10.1016/j.worlddev.2017.12.014

Floridi, L., Cowls, J., Beltrametti, M., Chatila, R., Chazerand, P., Dignum, V., Luetge, C., Madelin, R., Pagallo, U., Rossi, F., Schafer, B., Valcke, P., & Vayena, E. (2018). AI4People—an ethical framework for a good AI society: Opportunities, risks, principles, and recommendations. *Minds and Machines, 28*(4), 689–707. DOI: 10.1007/s11023-018-9482-5 PMID: 30930541

Fonseca Corona, F. J. (2024). Tax morale: A global scopingreviewfrom the cultural approach to economics. *International Review of Economics, 71*(2), 343–365. DOI: 10.1007/s12232-024-00446-x

Fonseca, M. A., & Grimshaw, S. B. (2017). Do behavioral nudges in prepopulated tax forms affect compliance? Experimental evidence with real taxpayers. *Journal of Public Policy & Marketing, 36*(2), 213–226. DOI: 10.1509/jppm.15.128

Forteza, A., & Noboa, C. (2019). Perceptions of institutional quality and justification of tax evasion. *Constitutional Political Economy, 30*(4), 367–382. DOI: 10.1007/s10602-019-09287-1

Fortin, B., Lacroix, G., & Villeval, M. C. (2007). Tax evasion and social interactions. *Journal of Public Economics, 91*(11-12), 2089–2112. DOI: 10.1016/j.jpubeco.2007.03.005

Freire-Serén, M. J., & Panadés, J. (2013). Do higher tax rates encourage/discourage tax compliance? *Modern Economy, 4*(12), 809–817. DOI: 10.4236/me.2013.412086

Frey, B. (1997). A constitution for knaves crowds out civic virtues. *Economic Journal (London), 107*(443), 1043–1053. DOI: 10.1111/j.1468-0297.1997.tb00006.x

Frey, B. S., & Meier, S. (2004). Pro-social behavior in a natural setting. *Journal of Economic Behavior & Organization, 54*(1), 65–88. DOI: 10.1016/j.jebo.2003.10.001

Frey, B. S., & Weck-Hanneman, H. (1984). The hidden economy as an unobserved variable. *European Economic Review, 26*(1-2), 33–53. DOI: 10.1016/0014-2921(84)90020-5

Frey, B., & Meier, S. (2004). Social comparisons and pro-social behaviour. Testing conditional cooperation in a field experiment. *The American Economic Review, 94*(5), 1717–1722. DOI: 10.1257/0002828043052187

Frey, B., & Torgler, B. (2007). Tax Morale and Conditional Cooperation. *Journal of Comparative Economics, 35*(1), 136–159. DOI: 10.1016/j.jce.2006.10.006

Fullerton, D., & Metcalf, G. E. (2002). Tax incidence. *Handbook of public economics, 4*, 1787-1872.

Gächter, S. (2007). Conditional Cooperation: Behavioral Regularities from the Lab and the Field and Their Policy Implications. In B. S. Frey y A. Stutzer (Eds.), *Economics and psychology: A promising new cross-disciplinary field* (pp. 19–50). London: CESifo Seminar Series.

Gajjar, D. (2013). Ethical consideration in research. *Education, 2*(7), 8–15.

Gangl, K., Hofmann, E., & Kirchler, E. (2015). Tax authorities' interaction with taxpayers: A conception of compliance in social dilemmas by power and trust. *New Ideas in Psychology, 37*, 13–23. DOI: 10.1016/j.newideapsych.2014.12.001 PMID: 25859096

Gangl, K., & Torgler, B. (2020). How to achieve tax compliance by the wealthy: A review of the literature and agenda for policy. *Social Issues and Policy Review, 14*(1), 108–151. DOI: 10.1111/sipr.12065

García, A. G. Beyaert Stevens, A & De Pablos Escobar, L. (2012) 'Fiscal Awareness: a study of the female attitude towards fraud in Spain' in Michael Pickhardt, and Aloys Prinz (ed.) Tax Evasion and the Shadow Economy, Publisher (if book): Edward Elgar, pp. 61-86.

García, A. G., Buendía Azorín, J. D., & Sánchez de la Vega, M. M. (2020): Shadow Economy and National Culture: A Spatial Approach, Hacienda Pública Española / Review of Public Economics, 232-(1/2020), pp. 53-74 DOI: 10.7866/HPE-RPE.20.1.3

García, A. G., Quiñones, E., & Sánchez-Meca, J. (2015). How can being a housewife influence women's fiscal awareness? The case of Spain. Anales de Psicología/Annals of Psychology, 31(3), 952-961. ISSN 0212-9728.

García, J. (1975). Crítica popular al sistema tributario español. *Hacienda Pública Española*, (34), 55–99.

García-Rivas, M. I., Gálvez-Sánchez, F. J., Noguera-Vivo, J. M., & Meseguer-Sánchez, V. (2023). Communal responsibility of corporates reports: A review of the evolution, approaches and prospects. *Heliyon*. Advance online publication. DOI: 10.1016/j.heliyon.2023.e18348

Gardner, M., Ettlinger, M., Marasini, S., & Wamhoff, S. (2024). Corporate taxes before and after the trump tax law. *Institute on Taxation and Economic Policy, 2*.https://itep.org/corporate-taxes-before-and-after-the-trump-tax-law/

Gardner, M., Ettlinger, M., Wamhoff, S., & Marasini, S. (2024). Corporate taxes before and after the Trump Tax Law. *Institute of Taxation and Economic Policy*. https://www.epi.org/publication/ib364-corporate-tax-rates-and-economic-growth/

Gayathri P, Jayakumar K (2016) A Study on Tax Payer's Perception Towards EFiling of Income Tax Returns. International Journal of Trend in Research and Development 32-38.

Geetha, R., & Sekar, M. (2012). E-Filing of Income Tax: Awareness and Satisfaction level of individual tax payer. *Research Journal of Management Science, 1*, 6–11.

Gemmell, N. (2016). *An Allingham-Sandmo Tax Compliance Model with Imperfect Enforcement. Chair in Public Finance*. Victoria Business School.

German, M. (2025). Securities and Exchange Commission Filings. CSU Los Angeles University Library. https://libguides.calstatela.edu/c.php?g=1072937&p=7823298

Gillet, P. (1998). Comptabilité créative: Le résultat comptable n'est plus ce qu'il était. *Revue française de gestion, novembre-décembre*, 83-94.

Gitaru, K. (2017). The effect of taxpayer education on tax compliance in Kenya. Munich Personal RePEc Archive, 2(80344), 12–23. https://mpra.ub.unimuenchen.de/id/eprint/80344

Glimcher, P., Camerer, C., Fehr, E., & Poldrack, R. (2009). *Neuroeconomics: Decision making and The Brain*. Academic Press., DOI: 10.1016/B978-0-12-374176-9.00016-6

Gobena, L. B., & Van Dijke, M. (2017). Fear and caring: Procedural justice, trust, and collective identification as antecedents of voluntary tax compliance. *Journal of Economic Psychology*, *62*, 1–16. DOI: 10.1016/j.joep.2017.05.005

Godfrey, P. C. (2005). The relationship between corporate philanthropy and shareholder wealth: A risk management perspective. *Academy of Management Review*, *30*(4), 777–798. DOI: 10.5465/amr.2005.18378878

Goksu, G. G., & Sahpaz, K. I. (2015). Comparison of Tax Morale of Turkish and Spanish Higher Education Students: The Samples of Sakarya University and the University of Zaragoza. *Procedia: Social and Behavioral Sciences*, *186*, 222–230. DOI: 10.1016/j.sbspro.2015.04.027

Gomà, R., & Font, J. (2001). La democracia local: Un mapa de experiencias participativas. En J. Font (Ed.), *Ciudadanos y decisiones públicas* (pp. 61–91). Barcelona: Editorial Ariel, S.A.

Gonidakis, F. K., Asonitou, S., Kottara, C., & Dimitra, K.-F. (2024). The contribution of education to the creation of tax awareness and compliance. In *Strategic Innovative Marketing and Tourism* (pp. 571–583). Springer. DOI: 10.1007/978-3-031-51038-0_62

Gonzalez, R., Gasco, J., & Llopis, J. (2007). E-government success: Some principles from a Spanish case study. *Industrial Management & Data Systems*, *107*(6), 845–861. DOI: 10.1108/02635570710758752

Gordon, J. (1989). Individual morality and reputation costs as deterrents to tax evasion. *European Economic Review*, *33*(4), 797–805. DOI: 10.1016/0014-2921(89)90026-3

Górecki, M. A., & Letki, N. (2021). Social norms moderate the effect of tax system on tax evasion: Evidence from a large-scale survey experiment. *Journal of Business Ethics*, *172*(4), 727–746. DOI: 10.1007/s10551-020-04502-8

Graetz, M. J., & Wilde, L. (1993). The decisions by strategic nonfilers to participate in income tax amnesties. *International Review of Law and Economics*, *13*(3), 271–283. DOI: 10.1016/0144-8188(93)90037-6

Greggi, M., Calvino, L. R., & Greyling, L. (2024). *Solidarity as well taxation: Communal Contract and the Ubuntu Approaches. May*. https://www.investigationgate.net/publication/380827401

Grinstein-Weiss, M., Cryder, C., Despard, M. R., Perantie, D. C., Oliphant, J. E., & Ariely, D. (2017, October 1). The Role of Choice Architecture in Promoting Saving at Tax Time: Evidence from a Large–Scale Field Experiment. *Behavioral Science & Policy*, *3*(2), 21-38. Sage Journals. DOI: 10.1177/237946151700300203

Grym, J., Aspara, J., Nandy, M., & Lodh, S. (2024). A Crime by Any Other Name: Gender Differences in Moral Reasoning When Judging the Tax Evasion of Cryptocurrency Traders. *Behavioral Sciences (Basel, Switzerland)*, *14*(3), 198. Advance online publication. DOI: 10.3390/bs14030198 PMID: 38540501

Guo, Y., & Gong, T. (2024). The influence of tax burden on wellbeing attitudes: Micro evidence from wellbeing states. In *PLoS ONE* (Vol. 19, Issue 11 November). DOI: 10.1371/journal.pone.0311047

Gupta, S., & Keen, M. (2024). Digital transformation and tax administration. IMF Working Paper Series, WP/24/15.

Gupta, C. M., & Kumar, D. (2020). Creative accounting: A tool for financial crime – A review of the techniques and its effects. *Journal of Financial Crime*, *27*(2), 397–411. DOI: 10.1108/JFC-06-2019-0075

Guyo, D. M., Kero, C. A., & Kant, S. (2025). Is Marketing Intermediaries' Mediation Required for Livestock and Products Marketing to Improve the Economic Status of Pastoralist Communities in Ethiopia? In *AI in Agriculture for Sustainable and Economic Management* (pp. 216-234). CRC Press. DOI: 10.1201/9781003451648-16

Habib, A., Alsmadi, D., & Prybutok, V. R. (2020). Factors that determine residents' acceptance of smart city technologies. *Behaviour & Information Technology*, *39*(6), 610–623. DOI: 10.1080/0144929X.2019.1693629

Haddouchi, A., Bouzahzah, M., & Angour, N. (2021). Fiscalité et croissance économique au Maroc. *Revue Française d'Économie et de Gestion*, *4*(10), 170–180.

Hadwick, D. (2022). Peer Reviewed Articles: Behind the One-Way Mirror: Reviewing the Legality of EU Tax Algorithmic Governance.'. *EC Tax Review*, *31*(4), 184–201. DOI: 10.54648/ECTA2022019

Hajawiyah, A., Suryarini, T., Kiswanto, , & Tarmudji, T. (2021). Analysis of a tax amnesty's effectiveness in Indonesia. *Journal of International Accounting, Auditing & Taxation*, *44*, 100415. DOI: 10.1016/j.intaccaudtax.2021.100415

Hakki, T. W., Simanungkalit, J., & Siat, M. (2023). The Antecedents Of Tax Evasion Perception With A Religiousity As Moderation. *Kajian Akuntansi*, *24*(2), 325–335. DOI: 10.29313/kajian_akuntansi.v24i2.2526

Halimah, S., & Juitania, J. (2022). The effect of tax information dissemination, tax rates, and tax sanctions on compliance with annual tax return reporting of individual taxpayers (Case study at Pandeglang primary tax service office). *IDEAS Journal of Management & Technology*, *2*(1), 34–41. DOI: 10.33021/ideas.v2i1.3800

Hallsworth, M. (2014). The use of field experiments to increase tax compliance. *Oxford Review of Economic Policy*, *30*(4), 658–679. DOI: 10.1093/oxrep/gru034

Hammar, H., Jagers, S. C., & Nordblom, K. (2009). Perceived tax evasion and the importance of trust. *Journal of Socio-Economics*, *38*(2), 238–245. DOI: 10.1016/j.socec.2008.07.003

Hamza, S. E. (2012). Les spécificités de la gestion des résultats des entreprises tunisiennes à travers une analyse qualitative. *Comptabilité-Contrôle-Audit*, 1-28.

Haruna, H. T., Ibrahim, A. S., Yusuf, A. U., & Ardo, A. M. (2023). The impact of forensic accounting on tax payer attitude and compliance towards tax evasion within smes in the north east nigeria. *Journal of Business Management and Accounting*, *13*(1), 79–105. DOI: 10.32890/jbma2023.13.1.4

Hasan, I., Hoi, C. K., Wu, Q., & Zhang, H. (2017). Does social capital matter in corporate decisions? Evidence from corporate tax avoidance. *Journal of Accounting Research*, *55*(3), 629–668. DOI: 10.1111/1475-679X.12159

Hasan, M. M., & Habib, A. (2020). Readability of narrative disclosures, and corporate liquidity and payout policies. *International Review of Financial Analysis*, *68*, 101460. DOI: 10.1016/j.irfa.2020.101460

Hashimzade, N., & Myles, G. D. (2023). A comparative analysis of tax compliance across OECD countries. *International Tax and Public Finance*, *30*(2), 367–396.

Hashimzade, N., Myles, G. D., & Tran-Nam, B. (2013). Applications of behavioural economics to tax evasion. *Journal of Economic Surveys*, *27*(5), 941–977. DOI: 10.1111/j.1467-6419.2012.00733.x

Heilbron, J., Verheul, J., & Quak, S. (2014). The origins and early diffusion of "shareholder value" in the United States. *Theory and Society*, *43*(1), 1–22. DOI: 10.1007/s11186-013-9205-0

Heldt, T. (2005) Conditional Cooperation in the Field: Cross-Country Skiers? Behaviour in Sweden, unpublished manuscript, Uppsala University.

Hemberg, E., Rosen, J., Warner, G., Wijesinghe, S., & O'Reilly, U.-M. (2016). Detecting tax evasion: A co-evolutionary approach. *Artificial Intelligence and Law*, *24*(2), 149–182. DOI: 10.1007/s10506-016-9181-6

Herreros, F., & De Francisco, A. (2001). Introducción: El capital social como programa de investigación. *Zona Abierta*, (94/95), 1–46.

Hidayat, K., Utama, M. S., Nimran, U., & Prasetya, A. (2022). The effect of attitude and religiosity on tax compliant intention moderated by the utilization of e-Filing. *Journal of Financial Services Marketing*, •••, 1.

Higueras Udía, G. (1982). *Ética fiscal* (Biblioteca de Autores, C., Ed.).

Hoffmann, H., Hoelzl, E., & Kirchler, E. (2008). Preconditions of Voluntary Tax Compliance: Knowledge and Evaluation of Taxation, Norms, Fairness, and Motivation to Cooperate. *Zeitschrift für Psychologie*, *216*(4), 209–217. DOI: 10.1027/0044-3409.216.4.209 PMID: 22428111

Hofmann, E., Voracek, M., Bock, C., & Kirchler, E. (2017). Tax compliance across socio demographic categories: Meta-analyses of survey studies in 111 countries. *Journal of Economic Psychology*, *62*, 63–71. DOI: 10.1016/j.joep.2017.06.005

Horodnic, I. A. (2018). Tax morale and institutional theory: a systematic review IJSSP 38,9/10 www.emeraldinsight.com/0144-333X.htm

Horodnic, I. A. (2018). Tax morale and institutional theory: A systematic review. *The International Journal of Sociology and Social Policy*, *38*(9/10), 868–886. DOI: 10.1108/IJSSP-03-2018-0039

Huang, F., Tawei, W., and Ju-Chun, Y. (2024). "Opportunities or challenges? Audit risk and blockchain disclosures in 10-K filings." *Auditing: A Journal of Practice & Theory* 43(2): 131–58.` https://doi:DOI: 10.2308/AJPT-2021-045

Huettel, S., Stowe, C., Gordon, E., Warner, B., & Platt, M. (2006). Neural signatures of economic preferences for risk and ambiguity. *Neuron, 49*(5), 765–775. DOI: 10.1016/j.neuron.2006.01.024 PMID: 16504951

Hungerford, T. L. (2013). Corporate tax rates and economic growth since 1947. *Economic Policy Institute Issue Brief, 364*. https://www.epi.org/publication/ib364-corporate-tax-rates-and-economic-growth/

Hyytinen, A., Tuimala, J., & Hammar, M. (2022). Enhancing the adoption of digital public services: Evidence from a large-scale field experiment. *Government Information Quarterly, 39*(3), 101687. Advance online publication. DOI: 10.1016/j.giq.2022.101687

Ifere, E. O., Ovat, O. O., Owan, E. J., Chijioke, M. I., Ofem, L. U., Ndome, J. N., Ugbaka, M. A., & Atelhe, A. G. (2023). PERCEPTION AND CRIMINALITY OF TAX EVASION IN A DEVELOPING ECONOMY. *Corporate Law and Governance Review, 5*(2 Special Issue), 164–173. DOI: 10.22495/clgrv5i2sip3

Ilias, A., Ghani, E. K., & Azhar, Z. (2022). The e-government of eXtensible business reporting language adoption process in Malaysia: Drivers and challenges from environmental perspective. *Electronic Government, 18*(4), 399–423. DOI: 10.1504/EG.2022.125920

Ilori, O., Nwosu, N. T., & Naiho, H. N. N. (2024). Advanced data analytics in internal audits: A conceptual framework for comprehensive risk assessment and fraud detection. *Finance & Accounting Research Journal, 6*(6), 931–952. DOI: 10.51594/farj.v6i6.1213

Inasius, F. (2019). Factors influencing SME tax compliance: Evidence from Indonesia. *International Journal of Public Administration, 42*(5), 367–379. DOI: 10.1080/01900692.2018.1464578

Institutional Shareholder Services. (2025). Asia Pacific Region. *Proxy Voting Guidelines*. https://www.issgovernance.com/file/policy/active/asiapacific/Asia-Pacific-Regional-Voting-Guidelines.pdf?v=1

Iong, K. Y., & Phillips, J. O. L. (2022). Examining the impact of behavioral factors on the intention of adopting E-government services: An empirical study on the hard-to-reach groups in Macao SAR, China. *Technology in Society, 71*, 102107. Advance online publication. DOI: 10.1016/j.techsoc.2022.102107

Jackson, B. R., & Milliron, V. C. (1986). Tax compliance research: Findings, problems, and prospects. *Journal of Accounting Literature, 5*(1), 125–165.

Jacquemet, N., Luchini, S., Malézieux, A., & Shogren, J. F. (2017). L'évasion fiscale est-elle un trait de personnalité? Une évaluation empirique des déterminants psychologiques de la «morale fiscale». *Revue Économique (Paris), 68*(5), 809–828. DOI: 10.3917/reco.pr3.0091

Jahnke, B., & Weisser, R. A. (2019). How does petty corruption affect tax morale in Sub-Saharan Africa? *European Journal of Political Economy, 60*, 101751. DOI: 10.1016/j.ejpoleco.2018.09.003

Jaime-Castillo, A. M., & Sáez-Lozano, J. L. (2016). Preferences for tax schemes in OECD countries, self-interest and ideology. *International Political Science Review*, *37*(1), 81–98. DOI: 10.1177/0192512114539716

Jakobsen, K., Jakobsen, K., Kleven, H., & Zucman, G. (2020). Wealth taxation and wealth accumulation: Theory and evidence from Denmark. *The Quarterly Journal of Economics*, *135*(1), 329–388. DOI: 10.1093/qje/qjz032

James, S. (2016). The Importance of Fairness in Tax Policy: Behavioral Economics and the UK Experience. [IJABE]. *International Journal of Applied Behavioral Economics*, *3*(1), 1–12. DOI: 10.4018/ijabe.2014010101

Jayawardane, D. (2015). Psychological factors affect tax compliance. A review paper. *International Journal of Arts and Commerce*, *4*(6), 131–141.

Jennings, R., Simko, P., & Thompson, R. (1996). Does LIFO inventory accounting improve the income statement at the expense of the balance sheet? *Journal of Accounting Research*, *34*(1), 301–312. DOI: 10.2307/2491333

Jennings, R., & Thompson, R. (1996). Accounting for intangibles in the United States. *Issues in Accounting Education*, *11*(2), 491–495.

Jestin, K. (2020). De la perception du concept de Responsabilité Sociétale de l'Entreprise (RSE) a sa transposition dans le domaine fiscal. Revue européenne et internationale de droit fiscal, (1), 129-144.

Jiang, W., Zhang, C., & Si, C. (2022). The real influence of mandatory CSR disclosure: Evidence of corporate tax avoidance. *Technological Forecasting and Social Change*, *179*, 121646. DOI: 10.1016/j.techfore.2022.121646

Jiang, Y. (2024). A theory of the neural mechanisms underlying negative cognitive bias in major depression. *Frontiers in Psychiatry*, *15*, 1348474. DOI: 10.3389/fpsyt.2024.1348474 PMID: 38532986

Jimenez, P., & Iyer, G. S. (2016). Tax compliance in a social setting: The influence of social norms, trust in government, and perceived fairness on taxpayer compliance. *Advances in Accounting*, *34*, 17–26. DOI: 10.1016/j.adiac.2016.07.001

Job, J., & Reinhart, M. (2003). Trusting the tax office: Does Putnam.s thesis relate to tax., *Australian Journal of Social Issues*, 38(3), 307-334.

Joel, I. C., Wisdom, E., & Bolouimbelemoere, K. P. (2023). Influence of Tax Morality and Tax Culture on Compliance for tax. *International Journal of Accounting, Management* [IJAMESC]. *Economics and Communal Sciences*, *1*(5), 500–509.

Jones, M. (2011). *Creative accounting, fraud, and international accounting scandals*. Chichester, West Sussex: A John Wiley & Sons.

Judd, H. W., McGuire, S. T., Weaver, C. D., & Xia, J. (2023). Check Your Attitude: An Examination of Companies' Attitude Toward Tax Enforcement. *Available atSSRN* 4322643. DOI: 10.2139/ssrn.4322643

Kahneman, D. (2011). *Thinking, fast and slow*. Farrar, Straus and Giroux.

Kahneman, D., & Tversky, A. (1979). Prospect Theory: An Analysis of Decision under Risk. *Econometrica*, *47*(2), 263–291. DOI: 10.2307/1914185

Kant, S., & Adula, M. (2024). AI Learning and Work Attitude Mediation Between Reward and Organizational Support in Ethiopia. In Gomathi Sankar, J., & David, A. (Eds.), *Generative AI for Transformational Management* (pp. 109–136). IGI Global., DOI: 10.4018/979-8-3693-5578-7.ch005

Kaplanoglou, G., Rapanos, V. T., & Daskalakis, N. (2016). Tax compliance behaviour during the crisis : The case of Greek SMEs. *European Journal of Law and Economics*, *42*(3), 405–444. DOI: 10.1007/s10657-016-9547-y

Kaplan, S. E., & Reckers, P. M. J. (1985). A Study of Tax Evasion Judgments. *National Tax Journal*, *38*(1), 97–102. DOI: 10.1086/NTJ41791998

Kapon, S. (2022). Dynamic Amnesty Programs. *The American Economic Review*, *112*(12), 4041–4075. DOI: 10.1257/aer.20211428

Karam, H., & Berjaoui, A. (2021). La fraude fiscale par sous-déclaration du revenu: Une décision en présence de risque, revue de littérature et états des lieux. *JSOM*, *2*, 2–21.

Karim, A. M., Shaikh, J. M., Hock, O. Y., & Islam, M. R. (2016). Solution of adapting creative accounting practices: An in-depth perception gap analysis among accountants and auditors of listed companies. *Australian Academy of Accounting and Finance Review*, *2*(2), 166–188.

Kasper, M., & Alm, J. (2022). Audits, audit effectiveness, and post-audit tax compliance. *Journal of Economic Behavior & Organization*, *195*, 87–102. DOI: 10.1016/j.jebo.2022.01.003

Kastlunger, B., Dressler, S. G., Kirchler, E., Mittone, L., & Voracek, M. (2010). Sex differences in tax compliance: Differentiating between demographic sex, gender-role orientation, and prenatal masculinization (2D:4D). *Journal of Economic Psychology*, *31*(4), 542–552. DOI: 10.1016/j.joep.2010.03.015

Kastlunger, B., Lozza, E., Kirchler, E., & Schabmann, A. (2013). Powerful authorities and trusting citizens: The Slippery Slope Framework and tax compliance in Italy. *Journal of Economic Psychology*, *34*, 36–45. DOI: 10.1016/j.joep.2012.11.007

Kelman, H. C. (1958). Compliance, identification, and internalization three processes of attitude change. *The Journal of Conflict Resolution*, *2*(1), 51–60. DOI: 10.1177/002200275800200106

Kemsley, D., & Kemsley, S. A. (2024). Tax evasion savings versus unlawful predicate proceeds: A substance-based approach. *Journal of Money Laundering Control*, *27*(4), 647–657. DOI: 10.1108/JMLC-12-2023-0196

Kemsley, D., Kemsley, S. A., & Morgan, F. T. (2022). Tax evasion and money laundering: A complete framework. *Journal of Financial Crime*, *29*(2), 589–602. DOI: 10.1108/JFC-09-2020-0175

Kemsley, D., Kemsley, S. A., & Morgan, F. T. (2024). Tax evasion on lawful income: Is it a form of money laundering? *Journal of Financial Crime*, *31*(1), 33–43. DOI: 10.1108/JFC-11-2022-0268

Keppler, S., & Nagin, D. (1989). The anatomy of tax evasion. *Journal o f Law. Economics and Organization*, *5*(1), 1–24.

Khaerunnisa, I., Wiratno, A., & Luthan, E. (2016). The effect of tax morality, tax culture, and good governance to taxpayers compliance. *The Accounting Journal of BINANIAGA, 1*(1), 267759.

Khaltar, O. (2024). Tax evasion and governance quality: The moderating role of adopting open government. *International Review of Administrative Sciences, 90*(1), 276–294. DOI: 10.1177/00208523231197317

Khan, A., Krishnan, S., & Dhir, A. (2021). Electronic government and corruption: Systematic literature review, framework, and agenda for future research. *Technological Forecasting and Social Change, 167*, 120737. Advance online publication. DOI: 10.1016/j.techfore.2021.120737

Khanfor, A., & Elwazani, Y. (2016). La communication fiscale au Maroc: Les obstacles à la socialisation du contribuable. Revue Marocaine de recherche en management et marketing, 14, 215-234.

Khan, M. A., & Nuryanah, S. (2023). Combating tax aggressiveness: Evidence from Indonesia's tax amnesty program. *Cogent Economics & Finance, 11*(2), 2229177. DOI: 10.1080/23322039.2023.2229177

Khan, S. A. R., Sheikh, A. A., & Tahir, M. S. (2024). Communal responsibility of corporates—an antidote for sustainable business performance: Interconnecting role of digital technologies, employee eco-behavior, and tax avoidance. *Ecological Science and Pollution Investigation, 31*(3), 4365–4383. PMID: 38102435

Khlif, H., & Amara, I. (2019). Political connections, corruption and tax evasion: A cross-country investigation. *Journal of Financial Crime, 26*(2), 401–411. DOI: 10.1108/JFC-01-2018-0004

Khlif, H., Guidara, A., & Hussainey, K. (2016). Sustainability level, corruption and tax evasion: A cross-country analysis. *Journal of Financial Crime, 23*(2), 328–348. DOI: 10.1108/JFC-09-2014-0041

Khodamipour, A., & Pourheydari, O. (2024). Investigating the effect of attitude, risk aversion and loss aversion of tax payers on tax compliance considering the moderating role of personality type (case study of tax payers of Kerman city). *Journal of Tax Research, 32*(61), 87–132. DOI: 10.61186/taxjournal.32.61.87

Khomsi, H. (2025). La conformité fiscale des contribuables: Fondements et modèles conceptuels. Revue Internationale de la Recherche Scientifique (Revue-IRS), 3(1), 1-20.

Khomsi, H., & Msatfa, Z. (2024). La conformité fiscale des PME, un facteur clé pour le développement économique et social des pays. *American Scientific Journal, 03*(27), 1230–1257.

Kijjambu, F. N., & Mwesigye, B. (2024). Taxpayer Perception and Income Tax Filing Compliance among Small Taxpayers in Mbarara City. *American Journal of Finance, 10*(1), 89–110. DOI: 10.47672/ajf.1896

Kim, B. R., Liss, A., Rao, M., Singer, Z., & Compton, R. J. (2012). Social deviance activates the brain's error-monitoring system. *Cognitive, Affective & Behavioral Neuroscience, 12*(1), 65–73. DOI: 10.3758/s13415-011-0067-5 PMID: 22038705

Kirchgässner, G. (2011). Tax morale, tax evasion and the shadow economy. In *Handbook on the shadow economy*. Edward Elgar Publishing. DOI: 10.4337/9780857930880.00019

Kirchler, E. (2007). The Economic Psychology of Tax Behaviour. 1-243.

Kirchler, E., Muehlbacher, S., Kastlunger, B., & Wahl, I. (2010). Why pay taxes? A review of tax compliance decisions. *Developing alternative frameworks for explaining tax compliance, 59.*

Kirchler, E. (1997). The burden of new taxes: Acceptance of taxes as a function of affectedness and egoistic versus altruistic orientation. *Journal of Socio-Economics*, *26*(4), 421–437. DOI: 10.1016/S1053-5357(97)90005-6

Kirchler, E. (1998). Differential representations of taxes: Analysis of free associations and judgments of five employment groups. *Journal of Socio-Economics*, *27*(1), 117–131. DOI: 10.1016/S1053-5357(99)80080-8

Kirchler, E. (2007). *The economic psychology of tax behavior*. Cambridge University Press. DOI: 10.1017/CBO9780511628238

Kirchler, E., & Gangl, K. (2023). Future trends in tax compliance: A prospective analysis. *Behavioural Public Policy*, *7*(2), 252–276.

Kirchler, E., Hoelzl, E., & Wahl, I. (2008). Enforced versus voluntary tax compliance: The "slippery slope" framework. *Journal of Economic Psychology*, *29*(2), 210–225. DOI: 10.1016/j.joep.2007.05.004

Kirchler, E., Maciejovsky, B., & Schneider, F. (2003). Everyday representations of tax avoidance, tax evasion, and tax flight: Do legal differences matter? *Journal of Economic Psychology*, *24*(4), 535–553. DOI: 10.1016/S0167-4870(02)00164-2

Kirchler, E., & Wahl, I. (2010). Tax Compliance Inventory: TAX-I Voluntary tax compliance, enforced tax compliance, tax avoidance, and tax evasión. *Journal of Economic Psychology*, *31*(3), 331–346. DOI: 10.1016/j.joep.2010.01.002 PMID: 20502612

Kiring'a, S.E., Jagongo, A., Kiio, J.M., Njuguna, I.M., Muguongo, G.K., Nganyi, M.S., & Sei, M.J., KaraniGichimu, C., Macharia, I., Mwangi, M. and Qiao, Y. (2017). Impact of online tax filing on tax compliance among small and medium enterprises (MSE) in Kibwezi Sub-County in Kenya. *International Journal of Current Research*, *9*(4), 45196–45206.

Kirsch, P., Esslinger, C., Chen, Q., Mier, D., Lis, S., Siddhanti, S., Gruppe, H., Mattay, V. S., Gallhofer, B., & Meyer-Lindenberg, A. (2005). Oxytocin modulates neural circuitry for social cognition and fear in humans. *The Journal of Neuroscience : The Official Journal of the Society for Neuroscience*, *25*(49), 11489–11493. DOI: 10.1523/JNEUROSCI.3984-05.2005 PMID: 16339042

Kirui, D., Kapkiyai, C., & Kipruto, A. (2024). Tax Service Quality and Compliance for tax among Small and Medium Enterprises in North Rift Economic Block, Kenya: A Moderated Mediation Model of Government Trust and Communal Value Orientation. Kenya: A Moderated Mediation Model of Government Trust and Communal Value Orientation (July 20, 2024).

Kleven, H. J., Kreiner, C., & Saez, E. (2009). Why can modern governments tax so much? An agency model of firms as fiscal intermediaries, No. 15218, NBER Working Paper. National Bureau of Economic Research, Inc. DOI: 10.3386/w15218

Kleven, H. J., Knudsen, M. B., Kreiner, C. T., Pedersen, S., & Saez, E. (2011). Unwilling or unable to cheat? Evidence from a tax audit experiment in Denmark. *Econometrica*, *79*(3), 651–692. DOI: 10.3982/ECTA9113

Kleven, H. J., Kreiner, C., & Saez, E. (2016). *Why can modern governments tax so much? An agency model of firms as fiscal intermediaries. LSE Research Online Documents on Economics*. London School of Economics and Political Science, LSE Library.

Klucharev, V., Hytönen, K., Rijpkema, M., Smidts, A., & Fernández, G. (2009). Reinforcement learning signal predicts social conformity. *Neuron, 61*(1), 140–151. DOI: 10.1016/j.neuron.2008.11.027 PMID: 19146819

Knoch, D., Nitsche, M. A., Fischbacher, U., Eisenegger, C., Pascual-Leone, A., & Fehr, E. (2008). Studying the neurobiology of social interaction with transcranial direct current stimulation: The example of punishing unfairness. *Cerebral Cortex (New York, N.Y.), 18*(9), 1987–1990. DOI: 10.1093/cercor/bhm237 PMID: 18158325

Knutson, B., Adams, C. M., Fong, G. W., & Hommer, D. (2001). Anticipation of increasing monetary reward selectively recruits nucleus accumbens. *The Journal of Neuroscience : The Official Journal of the Society for Neuroscience, 21*(16), RC159. Advance online publication. DOI: 10.1523/JNEUROSCI.21-16-j0002.2001 PMID: 11459880

Knutson, B., & Greer, S. M. (2008). Anticipatory affect: Neural correlates and consequences for choice. *Philosophical Transactions of the Royal Society of London. Series B, Biological Sciences, 363*(1511), 3771–3786. DOI: 10.1098/rstb.2008.0155 PMID: 18829428

Knutson, B., Taylor, J., Kaufman, M., Peterson, R., & Glover, G. (2005). Distributed neural representation of expected value. *The Journal of Neuroscience : The Official Journal of the Society for Neuroscience, 25*(19), 4806–4812. DOI: 10.1523/JNEUROSCI.0642-05.2005 PMID: 15888656

Koch, C., & Müller, C. (2024). Tax amnesties and the insurance effect: An experimental study. *Journal of Behavioral and Experimental Economics, 108*, 102130. DOI: 10.1016/j.socec.2023.102130

Koenigs, M., Young, L., Adolphs, R., Tranel, D., Cushman, F., Hauser, M., & Damasio, A. (2007). Damage to the prefrontal cortex increases utilitarian moral judgements. *Nature, 446*(7138), 908–911. DOI: 10.1038/nature05631 PMID: 17377536

Komarudin, & Hermawan, P. (2022). A study of trust base voluntary tax compliance through tax administration digital transformation in Indonesia. International Journal of Current Science Research and Review, 5(8), 3227-3238. DOI: 10.47191/ijcsrr/V5-i8-53

Konrad, K. A., & Qari, S. (2012). The last refuge of a scoundrel? patriotism and tax compliance. *Economica, 79*(315), 516–533. DOI: 10.1111/j.1468-0335.2011.00900.x

Korndörfer, M., Krumpal, I., & Schmukle, S. C. (2014). Measuring and explaining tax evasion: Improving self-reports using the crosswise model. *Journal of Economic Psychology, 45*, 18–32. DOI: 10.1016/j.joep.2014.08.001

Korteling, J. E., Brouwer, A. M., & Toet, A. (2018). A Neural Network Framework for Cognitive Bias. *Frontiers in Psychology, 9*, 1561. DOI: 10.3389/fpsyg.2018.01561 PMID: 30233451

Kovacev, R. (2020). A taxing dilemma: Robot taxes and the challenges of effective taxation of AI, automation and robotics in the fourth industrial revolution. *Ohio St. Tech. LJ*, *16*(2), 182. DOI: 10.31979/2381-3679.2020.090204

Kozel, E., & Dečman, M. (2022). The Impact of Trust in Government - Young Voters' Behavioral Intention to Use I-voting in Slovenia. *NISPAcee Journal of Public Administration and Policy*, *15*(1), 61–87. DOI: 10.2478/nispa-2022-0004

Krueger, F., McCabe, K., Moll, J., Kriegeskorte, N., Zahn, R., Strenziok, M., Heinecke, A., & Grafman, J. (2007). Neural correlates of trust. *Proceedings of the National Academy of Sciences of the United States of America*, *104*(50), 20084–20089. DOI: 10.1073/pnas.0710103104 PMID: 18056800

Krzysztofek, M. (2018). *GDPR: General Data Protection Regulation (EU) 2016/679: Post-reform Personal Data Protection in the European Union*. Kluwer Law International BV.

Kubick, T. R., Lockhart, G. B., Mills, L. F., & Robinson, J. R. (2017). IRS and corporate taxpayer effects of geographic proximity. *Journal of Accounting and Economics*, *63*(2-3), 428–453. DOI: 10.1016/j.jacceco.2016.09.005

Kucirkova, N., Landoni, M., Murgia, E., & Pera, M. S. (2019). Theo Huibers University of Twente Enschede, The Netherlands twc huibers@ utwente. Nl.

Kuhnen, C. M., & Knutson, B. (2005). The neural basis of financial risk taking. *Neuron*, *47*(5), 763–770. DOI: 10.1016/j.neuron.2005.08.008 PMID: 16129404

Kumar, A., Snehvrat, S., Kumari, P., Priyadarshani, P., & Ray, P. (2024). A communal responsibility of corporates (CSR)-led competitiveness framework through a bibliometric analysis (2001–2023). *Journal of Asia Business Studies*, *18*(3), 737–766. DOI: 10.1108/JABS-02-2023-0074

Kumar, S., & Gupta, S. (2017). A study on income tax payers perception towards electronic filing. *Journal of Internet Banking and Commerce*, *22*(S7), 1.

Kvale, S. (1996). *Interview Views: An Introduction to Qualitative Research Interviewing*. Sage Publications., https://doi.org/, DOI: 10.1016/S1098-2140(99)80208-2

Kwok, B. Y. S., & Yip, R. W. Y. (2018). Is Tax Education Good or Evil for Boosting Tax Compliance? Evidence from Hong Kong. *Asian Economic Journal*, *32*(4), 359–386. DOI: 10.1111/asej.12163

Lacombe-Saboly, M. (1994). Les déterminants de la qualité des produits comptables des entreprises: Le rôle du dirigeant (Thèse de doctorat, Université de Poitiers).

Lagares, M. J. (1991). Fraude fiscal y aceptación social del sistema tributario. *Moneda y Crédito*, *192*, 127–162.

Lago-Peñas, I., & Lago-Peñas, S. (2010). The determinants of tax morale in comparative perspective: Evidence from European countries. *european. European Journal of Political Economy*, *26*(4), 441–453. DOI: 10.1016/j.ejpoleco.2010.06.003

Lamberti, L., Benedetti, M., & Chen, S. (2014). Benefits sought by citizens and channel attitudes for multichannel payment services: Evidence from Italy. *Government Information Quarterly, 31*(4), 596–609. DOI: 10.1016/j.giq.2014.03.002

Lambert, T. (Ed.). (2007). *Les sanctions pénales fiscales* (p. 173). L'Harmattan.

Langenmayr, D. (2017). Voluntary disclosure of evaded taxes — Increasing revenue, or increasing incentives to evade? *Journal of Public Economics, 151*, 110–125. DOI: 10.1016/j.jpubeco.2015.08.007

Latif, F., Jabeen, M., & Jabeen, M. (2023). The Impact of Tax Knowledge, Tax System Complexity and Tax Fairness Perception on Compliance Behavior of a Taxpayer in KPK:-. *International Journal of Business and Management Sciences, 4*(4), 19–40.

Lau, K. C., & Ooi, K. W. (2016). A case study on fraudulent financial reporting: Evidence from Malaysia. *Accounting Research Journal, 29*(1), 4–19. DOI: 10.1108/ARJ-11-2013-0084

Lau, T.-C., Choe, K.-L., & Tan, L.-P. (2013). The moderating effect of religiosity in the relationship between money ethics and tax evasion. *Asian Social Science, 9*(11), 213–220. DOI: 10.5539/ass.v9n11P213

Lavery, T. J., Mahieu, V., Emmer de Albuequerque Green, C., Bol, E., Nohlen, H., Zafiroglu, A., Perriam, J., & Varazzani, C. (2024). Neuro-Nudging and Predictive Models:Adaptive Ethics for Behavioural Science in a Changing World. In Samson, A. (Ed.), *The Behavioral Economics Guide 2024* (pp. 100–108).

Le Borgne, M. E., & Baer, M. K. (2008). *Tax amnesties: Theory, trends, and some alternatives*. International Monetary Fund., DOI: 10.5089/9781589067363.058

LE, H. T. D., BUI, M. T., & NGUYEN, G. T. C. (2021). Factors affecting electronic tax compliance of small and medium enterprises in Vietnam. *The Journal of Asian Finance, Economics and Business, 8*(1), 823–832.

LeBaube, R. A., & Vehorn, C. L. (1992). Assisting taxpayers in meeting their obligations under the law. In Bird, R. M., & Casanegra de Jantscher, M. (Eds.), *Assisting taxpayers in meeting their obligations under the law* (pp. 311–342). International Monetary Fund.

Lecourt, B. (2022). Transparence fiscale: Directive no 2021/2101 du 24 novembre 2021 sur la publication d'informations relatives à l'impôt sur les revenus des sociétés. [Journal des Sociétés]. *Revue des Sociétés*, (02), 119.

LeDoux, J. (1996). Emotional networks and motor control: A fearful view. *Progress in Brain Research, 107*, 437–446. DOI: 10.1016/S0079-6123(08)61880-4 PMID: 8782535

Lee, C., & Hsieh, D. (1985). Choice of inventory accounting methods: Comparative analyses of alternative hypotheses. *Journal of Accounting Research, 23*(2), 468–485. DOI: 10.2307/2490821

Lee, J. H., & Lee, S. J. (2023). Efficient access to qualitative data: A case of MD&A analysis from 10-K with Python via SEC's API. *Applied Economics Letters, 30*(21), 3021–3025. DOI: 10.1080/13504851.2022.2118219

Lestary, S. R., Sueb, M., & Yudianto, I. (2021). The effect of tax fairness, tax socialization, and tax understanding on tax compliance: A study on micro, small and medium enterprises (MSMEs). *Journal of Accounting Auditing and Business*, *4*(1), 87–98. DOI: 10.24198/jaab.v4i1.31998

Leuz, C., & Schrand, C. M. (2009). Disclosure and the cost of capital: Evidence from firms' response to the Enron shock. SSRN *Electronic Journal*. (No. w14897). National Bureau of Economic Research. https://doi.org/DOI: 10.2139/ssrn.1319646

Levaggi, R. (2007). Tax evasion and the cost of public sector activities. *Public Finance Review*, *35*(5), 572–585. DOI: 10.1177/1091142107300064

Levaggi, R., & Menoncin, F. (2024). Tax evasion and debt in a dynamic general equilibrium model. *Economic and Political Studies*, *12*(2), 188–206. DOI: 10.1080/20954816.2023.2179957

Levin, M., & Satarov, G. (2000). Corruption and institutions in Russia. *European Journal of Political Economy*, *16*(1), 113–132. DOI: 10.1016/S0176-2680(99)00050-6

Lewis, A. (1982). *The Psychology of Taxation*. Martin Robertson.

Li, F. (2010). The information content of forward-looking statements in corporate filings—A naïve Bayesian machine learning approach. *Journal of Accounting Research*, *48*(5), 1049–1102. DOI: 10.1111/j.1475-679X.2010.00382.x

Lignier, P., & Evans, C. (2012). The rise and rise of tax compliance costs for the small business sector in Australia. In *Australian Tax Forum* (Vol. 27, No. 3, pp. 615-672). Sydney, NSW: Tax Institute.

Lignier, P., Evans, C., & Tran-Nam, B. (2014). Tangled up in tape: The continuing tax compliance plight of the small and medium enterprise business sector. *Austl.SSRN*, *29*, 217. DOI: 10.2139/ssrn.2479153

Li, H. (2023). Litigation-disclosure modifications in the 10-K: Large-sample evidence. *Journal of Accounting, Auditing & Finance*, *38*(2), 437–452. DOI: 10.1177/0148558X211017838

Lin, S. (2024). Understanding corporate tax audits: Insights from novel firm-level data. *Duke Financial Economics Center*. https://sites.duke.edu/thefinregblog/2024/03/04/understanding-corporate-tax-audits-insights-from-novel-firm-level-data/

Lin, J., Carter, L., & Liu, D. (2021). Privacy concerns and digital government: Exploring citizen willingness to adopt the COVIDSafe app. *European Journal of Information Systems*, *30*(4), 389–402. DOI: 10.1080/0960085X.2021.1920857

Lisi, G. (2015). Tax morale, tax compliance and the optimal tax policy. *Economic Analysis and Policy*, *45*, 27–32. DOI: 10.1016/j.eap.2014.12.004

Litina, A., & Palivos, T. (2016). Corruption, tax evasion and social values. *Journal of Economic Behavior & Organization*, *124*, 164–177. DOI: 10.1016/j.jebo.2015.09.017

Liu, H. (2021). Tax aggressiveness and the proportion of quantitative information in income tax footnotes. *Journal of Financial Reporting and Accounting*, *20*(2), 352–370. DOI: 10.1108/JFRA-08-2020-0233

Lo, A., Repin, D., & Steenbarger, B. (2005). Fear and Greed in Financial Markets: A Clinical Study of Day-Traders. *The American Economic Review*, *95*(2), 352–359. DOI: 10.1257/000282805774670095

López-Laborda, J., & Rodrigo, F. (2023). Tax compliance in developing countries: Evidence and policy implications. *World Development, 161*, 106089.

López-Lozano, M. A., & Pérez-López, C. (2023). Tax compliance determinants: A systematic literature review using bibliometric analysis. *Economic Analysis and Policy, 77*, 584–601.

López-Luzuriaga, A., & Scartascini, C. (2023) Willing but Unable to Pay? The Role of Gender in Tax Compliance, IDB Working Paper Series; 1330.

Loughran, T., & McDonald, B. (2015). *The use of word lists in textual analysis* (SSRN Scholarly Paper No. 2467519). DOI: 10.1080/15427560.2015.1000335

Lozza, E., Kastlunger, B., Tagliabue, S., & Kirchler, E. (2013). The relationship between political ideology and attitudes toward tax compliance: The case of Italian taxpayers. *Journal of Social and Political Psychology, 1*(1), 51–73. DOI: 10.5964/jspp.v1i1.108

Luitel, H. S., & Sobel, R. S. (2007). The Revenue Impact of Repeated Tax Amnesties. *Public Budgeting & Finance, 27*(3), 19–38. DOI: 10.1111/j.1540-5850.2007.00881.x

Luttmer, E. F., & Singhal, M. (2014). Tax morale. *The Journal of Economic Perspectives, 28*(4), 149–168. DOI: 10.1257/jep.28.4.149

Maccarthy, M. I. T., Abolo, A. P., & Ogullah Stephen Brass Ph, D. (2022). Electronic Tax System And Tax Revenue Efficiency In Nigeria 2008-2021. BW Academic Journal, 22-22.

Machmoune, S., & Nmili, M. (2021). Perception de l'équité fiscale et conformité du contribuable: Enquête exploratoire dans le contexte marocain. *Revue AME, 3*(4), 433–454.

Macintyre, A., &Torgler, B. (2024). Neuroscience and Tax Compliance. The Ethics of Tax Evasion, 2.

Macintyre, A., Chan, H. F., Schaffner, M., & Torgler, B. (2023). National pride and tax compliance: A laboratory experiment using a physiological marker (No. 2021-07). *CREMA Working Paper.*

Mahajan, R., Lim, W. M., Sareen, M., Kumar, S., & Panwar, R. (2023). Stakeholder theory. *Journal of Business Investigation, 166*, 114104.

Maisiba, J. G., & Atambo, W. (2016). Effects of electronic tax system on the revenue collection efficiency of Kenya Revenue Authority. *Imperial Journal of Interdisciplinary Research*, 2(4), 815–827.

Malik, A. S., & Schwab, R. M. (1991). The economics of tax amnesties. *Journal of Public Economics, 46*(1), 29–49. DOI: 10.1016/0047-2727(91)90063-8

Mamta, B. (2012). Taxpayers' perception of E-File adoption: An empirical investigation. *Journal of Management Research, 5*, 1–16.

Manan, S. (2021). The Influence of Nationalism Attitude, Institutional Perception, and Trust in Willing to Pay Tax. *Golden Ratio of Taxation Studies, 1*(2).

Marandu, E. E., Mbekomize, C. J., & Ifezue, A. N. (2015). Determinants of tax compliance: A review of factors and conceptualizations. *International Journal of Economics and Finance*, 7(9), 207–218. DOI: 10.5539/ijef.v7n9p207

Marcelo Leonardo, G. (2011). *Politics, and tax morale. The rol of trust, values and beliefs, in shaping individual attitudes towards tax compliance*. Georgia State University.

María-Dolores, R., Alarcón, G., & Garre, M. E. (2010). Tax morale in Spain: A study into some of its principal determinants. *Journal of Economic Issues*, *44*(4), 855–876. DOI: 10.2753/JEI0021-3624440401

Marilena, Z., & Corina, L. (2012). Embellishment of financial statements through creative accounting policies and options. *Procedia: Social and Behavioral Sciences*, *62*, 347–351. DOI: 10.1016/j.sbspro.2012.09.055

Marjit, S., Mishra, S., & Mitra, S. (2021). Tax evasion by tax deferment: Sham litigation with an informal credit market. *European Journal of Political Economy*, *69*, 102008. Advance online publication. DOI: 10.1016/j.ejpoleco.2021.102008

Marriott, L. (2017). An investigation of attitudes towards tax evasion and welfare fraud in New Zealand. *Australian and New Zealand Journal of Criminology*, *50*(1), 123–145. DOI: 10.1177/0004865815596793

Martínez-Vázquez, J., & Torgler, B. (2009). The evolution of tax morale in modern Spain. *Journal of Economic Issues*, *43*(1), 1–28. DOI: 10.2753/JEI0021-3624430101

Martin, W. J. (1944). Costs of Tax Administration: Expenses of Compliance. *The Bulletin of the National Tax Association*, *29*(6), 162–167. DOI: 10.1086/bullnattax41787304

Mas'ud, A., Aliyu, A. A., Gambo, E. M. J., Al-Qudah, A. A., & Al Sharari, N. (2014). Tax rate and tax compliance in Africa. *European Journal of Accounting Auditing and Finance Research*, *2*(3), 22–30.

Mascagni, G., & Santoro, F. (2018). ICTD Research in Brief: Why is tax education important for compliance?: Summary of African Tax Administration. ICTD Working Papers, 23.

Mascagni, G., Nell, C., & Monkam, N. (2017). *One Size Does Not Fit All: A Field Experiment on the Drivers of Tax Compliance and Delivery Methods in Rwanda*. ICTD Working Paper 58.https://www.ictd.ac/publication/ictd-wp58/

Mascagni, G., Santoro, F., & Mukama, D. (2024). Teach to comply? Evidence from a taxpayer education program in Rwanda. *International Tax and Public Finance*, •••, 45–78.

Matenda, F. R., Sibanda, M., Chikodza, E., & Gumbo, V. (2022). Corporate Loan Recovery Rates under Downturn Conditions in a Developing Economy: Evidence from Zimbabwe. *Risks*, *10*(10), 198. DOI: 10.3390/risks10100198

Mattiello, G. (2005). Multiple tax amnesties and tax compliance (Forgiving seventy times seven). Università Ca'Foscari, Venezia Working Paper, Maxwell, J. A. (2013). Qualitative research design: An interactive approach (3rd ed.). SAGE Publications.

Mazurenko, O., Tiutiunyk, I., Cherba, V., Artyukhov, A., & Yehorova, Y. (2023). Shadow tax evasion and its impact on the competitiveness of the country's tax system. *Public and Municipal Finance*, *12*(2), 129–142. DOI: 10.21511/pmf.12(2).2023.11

Mbilla, A. S. E., Abiire, M. A., Atindaana, P. A., & Ayimpoya, R. N. (2020). Tax Education and Tax Compliance In Ghana. Researchjournali's. *Journal of Accountancy*, *28*(1), 1–22.

McGee, R. (2013). The Ethics of Tax Evasion: Perspectives in Theory and Practice. .DOI: 10.1007/978-1-4614-1287-8

McGee, R. W., & Benk, S. (2019). Christian attitudes toward ethics of tax evasion: A case study. *Journal of Financial Crime*, *26*(1), 74–94. DOI: 10.1108/JFC-11-2017-0104

McGee, R. W., Ho, S. S. M., & Li, A. Y. S. (2008). A comparative study on perceived ethics of tax evasion: Hong kong vs the united states. *Journal of Business Ethics*, *77*(2), 147–158. DOI: 10.1007/s10551-006-9304-1

McGee, R. W., Petrides, Y., & Zhou, J. (2022). Attitude toward tax evasion in Brazil, Russia, India and China (BRIC). *Philosophy. Economics and Law Review*, *2*(2), 70–84.

McKerchar, M., Bloomquist, K., & Pope, J. (2013). Indicators of tax morale: an exploratory study. eJTR, 11, 5.

Mebratu, A. (2024). Theoretical foundations of voluntary tax compliance: Evidence from a developing country. *Humanities & Social Sciences Communications*, *11*(1), 1–8. DOI: 10.1057/s41599-024-02903-y

Megías E. (2006). El discurso de los jóvenes sobre la política. *Temas para el debate,* 138 (6), 29-32.

Mei Tan, L., & Chin-Fatt, C. (2000). The impact of tax knowledge on the perceptions of tax fairness and attitudes towards compliance. *Asian Review of Accounting*, *8*(1), 44–58. DOI: 10.1108/eb060720

Meiselman, B. (2018). Ghostbusting in Detroit: Evidence on nonfilers from a controlled field experiment. *Journal of Public Economics*, *158*, 180–193. DOI: 10.1016/j.jpubeco.2018.01.005

Menkhoff, L., & Miethe, J. (2019). Tax evasion in new disguise? Examining tax havens' international bank deposits. *Journal of Public Economics*, *176*, 53–78. DOI: 10.1016/j.jpubeco.2019.06.003

Meziane, B., Alla, L., & Bentalha, B. (2025). Transformational Trends of Territorial Economic Intelligence Strategies in the Digital Era: A Systematic Theoretical Exploration. In Utilizing Technology to Manage Territories (pp. 455-490). IGI Global.

Miendlarzewska, E. A., Kometer, M., & Preuschoff, K. (2019). Neurofinance. *Organizational Research Methods*, *22*(1), 196–222. DOI: 10.1177/1094428117730891

Milesi-Ferretti, G. M. (2004). Good, bad or ugly? On the effects of fiscal rules with creative accounting. *Journal of Public Economics*, *88*(1–2), 377–394. DOI: 10.1016/S0047-2727(02)00076-2

Milesi, P., & Alberici, A. I. (2018). Pluralistic morality and collective action: The role of moral foundations. *Group Processes & Intergroup Relations*, *21*(2), 235–256. DOI: 10.1177/1368430216675707

Mindak, M. P., Sen, P. K., & Stephan, J. (2016). Beating threshold targets with earnings management. *Review of Accounting and Finance*, *15*(2), 198–221. DOI: 10.1108/RAF-04-2015-0057

Ministère de l'Économie et des Finances. (2024). Code général des impôts 2024. https://www.finances.gov.ma/2024/CG-2024-fr

Ministère de l'Économie et des Finances. (2024). Note circulaire N° 735 relative aux mesures fiscales. https://www.finances.gov.ma/Publication/dgi

Ministère de l'Économie et des Finances. (2024). Sanctions en cas de non-respect des obligations fiscales. http://www.finances.gov.ma

Mkadmi, J. E., & Ali, W. B. (2024). How does tax avoidance influence communal responsibility of corporates and financial ratio in emerging economies? *Journal of Economic Criminology*, *5*, 100070. DOI: 10.1016/j.jeconc.2024.100070

Mohamad, N., Md, N., Sulaiman, S., Pengurusan, J., Sosial, S., Yayasan, K., Johor, P., & Kulai, M. (2022). Determinants of tax awareness: A systematic literature review. 303-315.

Mohamad, A., Zakaria, M. H., & Hamid, Z. (2016). Cash economy: Tax evasion amongst SMEs in Malaysia. *Journal of Financial Crime*, *23*(4), 974–986. DOI: 10.1108/JFC-05-2015-0025

Molero, J. C., & Pujol, F. (2012). Walking inside the potential tax evader's mind: Tax morale does matter. *Journal of Business Ethics*, *105*(2), 151–162. DOI: 10.1007/s10551-011-0955-1

Montague, P. R., Dayan, P., & Sejnowski, T. J. (1996). A framework for mesencephalic dopamine systems based on predictive Hebbian learning. *The Journal of Neuroscience : The Official Journal of the Society for Neuroscience*, *16*(5), 1936–1947. DOI: 10.1523/JNEUROSCI.16-05-01936.1996 PMID: 8774460

Montenegro, T. M. (2021). Tax evasion, corporate social responsibility and national governance: A country-level study. *Sustainability (Basel)*, *13*(20), 11166. Advance online publication. DOI: 10.3390/su132011166

Mpofu, f. Y. (2024). Prospects, challenges, and implications of deploying artificial intelligence in tax administration in developing countries. *Studia universitatis babes bolyai-negotia, 69*(3), 39-78.

Muehlbacher, S., & Hartl, B. (2023). The role of artificial intelligence in tax compliance: Opportunities and challenges. *Journal of Tax Administration*, *9*(1), 22–45.

Muehlbacher, S., Kirchler, E., & Schwarzenberger, H. (2011). Voluntary versus enforced tax compliance: Empirical evidence for the "slippery slope" framework. *European Journal of Law and Economics*, *32*(1), 89–97. DOI: 10.1007/s10657-011-9236-9

Muja'hidah, M., & Syamsuddin, A. (2023). Impact of Regulating Inadequate Local Tax Types on Fiscal Independence. Fiat Justisia. *Jurnal Ilmu Hukum*, *17*(4), 347–358. DOI: 10.25041/fiatjustisia.v17no4.3049

Mulisa, F. (2023). The Use of True-Random, Quasi-Random, and Nonrandom, Vol.14, No.1.

Murphy, K. (2003). Procedural justice and tax compliance. [Australian Council of Social Service]. *The Australian Journal of Social Issues*, *38*(3). Advance online publication. DOI: 10.1002/j.1839-4655.2003.tb01151.x

Murphy, K. (2004). The role of trust in nurturing compliance: A study of accused tax avoiders. *Law and Human Behavior*, *28*(2), 187–209. DOI: 10.1023/B:LAHU.0000022322.94776.ca PMID: 15141778

Murweni, I. (2018). Implementation of the tax amnesty program to increase tax compliance among business taxpayers. *Jurnal of Ekonomi-Bisnis*, *2*(2), 53–63. DOI: 10.37339/e-bis.v2i2.84

Mustapha, B. (2013). The impact of perceived ease of use and perceived usefulness on an online tax system. *International Journal of Advanced Research*, *1*(4), 1–18.

Nabila, A. T., & Paramita, V. S. (2024). The Influence Of Communal responsibility of corporates (CSR), Growth Opportunity, And Company Characteristics On Earning Response Coefficient (Case Investigation On The Conventional Banking Sector Listed On The Indonesia Stock Exchange-IDX 2018-2022). *International Journal of Science. Technology & Management*, *5*(1), 312–323.

Nagel, H., Rosendahl Huber, L., Van Praag, M., & Goslinga, S. (2019). The effect of a tax training program on tax compliance and business outcomes of starting entrepreneurs: Evidence from a field experiment. *Journal of Business Venturing*, *34*(2), 261–283. DOI: 10.1016/j.jbusvent.2018.10.006

Nandan Prasad, A. (2024). Regulatory Compliance and Risk Management. In *Introduction to Data Governance for Machine Learning Systems: Fundamental Principles, Critical Practices, and Future Trends* (pp. 485–624). Apress. DOI: 10.1007/979-8-8688-1023-7_8

Nembe, J. K., Atadoga, J. O., Mhlongo, N. Z., Falaiye, T., Olubusola, O., Daraojimba, A. I., & Oguejiofor, B. B. (2024). The role of artificial intelligence in enhancing tax compliance and financial regulation. *Finance & Accounting Research Journal*, *6*(2), 241–251. DOI: 10.51594/farj.v6i2.822

Neuman, E. L., & Sheu, R. J. (2022). Big Data analytics in IRS audit procedures and its effects on tax compliance: A moderated mediation analysis. *The Journal of the American Taxation Association*, *44*(2), 97–113. DOI: 10.2308/JATA-2020-038

Newton, K. (1997). Social Capital and Democracy. *The American Behavioral Scientist*, *40*(5), 575–586. DOI: 10.1177/0002764297040005004

Nguyen Thi Le, T., Mac Thi Hai, Y., Cuong Thi, T., & Nguyen Thi Hong, M. (2024). The impact of tax awareness on tax compliance: Evidence from Vietnam. *Journal of Tax Reform*, *10*(2), 214–227. DOI: 10.15826/jtr.2024.10.2.165

Nguyen, T. H. (2022). The impact of non-economic factors on voluntary tax compliance behaviour: A case study of small and medium enterprises in Vietnam. *Economies*, *10*(8), 179. DOI: 10.3390/economies10080179

Nguyen, V. M. H., Nguyen, V. T. B., Nguyen-Cuu, D., Nguyen, V. T. T., Ngoc, P. L., Ngoc Ngo, T. T., & Tran-Nam, B. (2021). The effects of emotion, trust and perception on tax compliance: empirical evidence from vietnam. In *Advances in Taxation* (pp. 111–134). Emerald Publishing Limited. DOI: 10.1108/S1058-749720210000029010

Nielsen, M. M. (2017). E-Governance and online service delivery in Estonia. In H. C.C. & O. A. (Eds.), *18th Annual International Conference on Digital Government Research, DG.O 2017: Vol. Part F1282* (pp. 300–309). Association for Computing Machinery. DOI: 10.1145/3085228.3085284

Night, S., & Bananuka, J. (2020). The mediating role of adoption of an electronic tax system in the relationship between attitude towards electronic tax system and tax compliance. *Journal of Economics, Finance and Administrative Science*, *25*(49), 73–88. DOI: 10.1108/JEFAS-07-2018-0066

Nurunnabi, M. (2018). Tax evasion and religiosity in the Muslim world: The significance of Shariah regulation. *Quality & Quantity*, *52*(1), 371–394. DOI: 10.1007/s11135-017-0471-1

Nurunnabi, M. (2019). Tax Evasion and the Role of the State Actor(s) in Bangladesh. *International Journal of Public Administration*, *42*(10), 823–839. DOI: 10.1080/01900692.2018.1520245

Nuryanah, S., & Gunawan, G. (2022). Tax amnesty and taxpayers' noncompliant behaviour: Evidence from Indonesia. *Cogent Business & Management*, *9*(1), 2111844. DOI: 10.1080/23311975.2022.2111844

Nuryani, N., Mutiara, A. B., Wiryana, I. M., Purnamasari, D., & Putra, S. N. W. (2024). Artificial intelligence model for detecting tax evasion involving complex network schemes. [ATT]. *Aptisi Transactions on Technopreneurship*, *6*(3), 339–356. DOI: 10.34306/att.v6i3.436

Oanh, T. T. K., LE THUY, N. T., VAN SONG, N. G. U. Y. E. N., MAC THI HAI, Y. E. N., HANG, N. T., & HUONG, N. T. T. (2021). Assessing perception and attitude of supporting of enterprises regarding the continued application of E-Tax In Vietnam. *Journal of Contemporary Issues in Business and Government*, *27*(3), 216–227.

Obadina, D. A. (2016). Confronting the problem of cross-border tax evasion in an era of greater global transparency of tax relevant information: The case of Nigeria. *Journal of Money Laundering Control*, *19*(4), 470–499. DOI: 10.1108/JMLC-10-2015-0043

Oberholzer, R. (2008). Attitudes of South African taxpayers towards taxation: A pilot study. *Account. Bus. Public Interest*, *7*(1), 46–52.

OECD data. (2024). Tax on Personel Income Indicators. https://www.oecd.org/en/data/indicators/tax-on-personal-income.html?oecdcontrol-3422f520c2-var8=PC_GDP&oecdcontrol-38c744bfa4-var1=OAVG%7COECD%7CAUT%7CBEL%7CDEU%7CFRA%7CNLD%7CTUR

OECD. (2020), Tax Administration 3.0: The Digital Transformation of Tax Administration, OECD, Paris. https://www.oecd.org/tax/forum-on-tax-administration/publications-and-products/tax-administration-3-0-the-digital-transformation-of-tax-administration.htm

OECD. (2021). *Building tax culture, compliance and citizenship: A global source book on taxpayer education* (2nd ed.).

OECD. (2022), Digital Transformation Maturity Model, OECD, Paris. www.oecd.org/tax/forum-on-tax-administration/publications-and-products/digital-transformation-maturity-model.htm

OECD. (2022). *Tax Morale II: Building Trust between Tax Administrations and Large Businesses*. OECD Publishing., DOI: 10.1787/7587f25c-

OECD. (2024). *Tax Administration 3.0: The Digital Transformation of Tax Administration*. OECD Publishing.

Ogungbade, O. I., Enitan, A., & Adekoya, A. C. (2021). Tax Awareness, Taxpayers" Perceptions and Attitudes and Tax Evasion in Informal Sector of Ekiti State, Nigeria. *International Journal of Financial Research*, *12*(5), 24–40. DOI: 10.5430/ijfr.v12n5p24

Okunogbe, O., & Santoro, F. (2022). The promise and limitations of information technology for tax mobilization. *The World Bank Research Observer*, *38*(2), 295–324. DOI: 10.1093/wbro/lkac008

Oladipo, O. A., Nwanji, T. I., Eluyela, F. D., Godo, B., & Adegboyegun, A. E. (2022). Impact of tax fairness and tax knowledge on tax compliance behavior of listed manufacturing companies in Nigeria. *Problems and Perspectives in Management, 20*(1), 41–48. DOI: 10.21511/ppm.20(1).2022.04

Olatunji, O. C., & Ayodele, K. B. (2017). *Impact of information technology on tax administration in the southwest.* DOI: 10.14738/abr.59.3549

Ondara, T. G., Kimani, M., & Kwasira, J. (2016). Influence of online tax filing on tax compliance among small and medium enterprises in Nakuru town, Kenya. *IOSR Journal of Business and Management, 18*(10), 82–92. DOI: 10.9790/487X-1810028292

Ortega, D., & Scartascini, C. (2015, November). Don't Blame the Messenger: A Field Experiment on Delivery Methods for Increasing Tax Compliance. IDB Working Paper No. IDB-WP-627. DOI: 10.18235/0000204

Ortega, D., Ronconi, L., & Sanguinetti, P. (2016). Reciprocity and Willingness to Pay Taxes: Evidence from a Survey Experiment in Latin America. *Economía (Washington, D.C.), 16*(2), 55–88. DOI: 10.31389/eco.78

Ortiz-Ospina, E., & Roser, M. (2020). La fiscalité. https://ourworldindata.org/taxation

O'shaughnessy, D. B. (2014). Tax compliance determinants: A proposed model for cross-country analysis.

Ostrom, E. (2010). Beyond markets and states: Polycentric governance of complex economic systems. *The American Economic Review, 100*(3), 641–672. DOI: 10.1257/aer.100.3.641

Otekunrin, A. O., Nwanji, T. I., Eluyela, D. F., Inegbedion, H., & Eleda, T. (2021). E-tax system effectiveness in reducing tax evasion in Nigeria. *Problems and Perspectives in Management, 19*(4), 175–185. DOI: 10.21511/ppm.19(4).2021.15

Oualhi, B. (2018). Tax awareness and social responsibility: Case study of Algeria. In *Proceedings of ISER 142nd International Conference*, Barcelona, Spain, 23rd-24th July 2018 (pp. 24-27). ISER.

Owusu, G. M. Y., Bart-Plange, M.-A., Koomson, T. A. A., & Arthur, M. (2022). The effect of personality traits and tax morale on tax evasion intention. *Journal of Financial Crime, 29*(1), 272–292. DOI: 10.1108/JFC-02-2021-0026

Owusu, G. M. Y., Bekoe, R. A., Anokye, F. K., & Anyetei, L. (2020). What Factors Influence the Intentions of Individuals to Engage in Tax Evasion? Evidence from Ghana. *International Journal of Public Administration, 43*(13), 1143–1155. DOI: 10.1080/01900692.2019.1665686

Ozgen, F. B., & Turan, A. H. (2007). Usage and adoption of online tax filing and payment system in tax management: An empirical assessment with Technology Acceptance Model (TAM) in Turkey. *9th International Scientific Conference, Management Horizons: Visions and Challenges*, Vytautas Magnus University, Kaunas, September 27-28, 2007, Lithuania. DOI: 10.1057/ejis.2010.63

Ozili, P. K. (2020). Tax evasion and financial instability. *Journal of Financial Crime, 27*(2), 531–539. DOI: 10.1108/JFC-04-2019-0051

Pampel, F., Andrighetto, G., & Steinmo, S. (2019). How institutions and attitudes shape tax compliance: A cross-national experiment and survey. *Social Forces*, *97*(3), 1337–1364. DOI: 10.1093/sf/soy083

Pardisi, A., & McGee, R. W. (2020, October). The Relationship between Income Level and Attitude toward Tax Evasion: An Empirical Study. In *International Academy of Business and Public Administration Disciplines Fall Conference* (Vol. 17, No. 4, pp. 128-138).

Patton, M. Q. (2002). *Qualitative research and evaluation methods* (3rd ed.). Sage Publications.

Paulus, M., Rogalsky, C., Simmons, A., Feinstein, J., & Stein, M. B. (2003). Increased activation in the right insula during risk-taking decision making is related to harm avoidance and neuroticism. *NeuroImage*, *19*(4), 1439–1448. DOI: 10.1016/S1053-8119(03)00251-9

Peacock, A. T., & Wiseman, J. (1973). Approaches to the analysis of government expenditure growth. *Public Finance*, *7*(1), 24–45.

Pereira, I. V., & Cabral de Ávila, L. A. (2022). RELATION BETWEEN SELF-DECEPTION AND TAX EVASION IN BRAZIL. *Revista de Gestao Social e Ambiental*, *16*(2), e03036. Advance online publication. DOI: 10.24857/rgsa.v16n2-027

Pernell, K., Jung, J., & Dobbin, F. (2017). The hazards of expert control: Chief risk officers and risky derivatives. *American Sociological Review*, *82*(3), 511–541. DOI: 10.1177/0003122417701115

Phelps, E. (2009). The study of emotion in Neuroeconomics.

Pickhardt, M., & Prinz, A. (2014). Behavioral dynamics of tax evasion–A survey. *Journal of Economic Psychology*, *40*, 1–19. DOI: 10.1016/j.joep.2013.08.006

Piketty, T. (2014). *Capital in the twenty-first century*. Trans. Arthur Goldhammer/Belknap. DOI: 10.4159/9780674369542

Pilcher, N., & Cortazzi, M. (2023). across subject fields: implications for research values, assumptions, and practices.

Pine, A., Shiner, T., Seymour, B., & Dolan, R. J. (2010). Dopamine, time, and impulsivity in humans. *The Journal of Neuroscience : The Official Journal of the Society for Neuroscience*, *30*(26), 8888–8896. DOI: 10.1523/JNEUROSCI.6028-09.2010

Pomeranz, D. (2015). "No Taxation Without Information: Deterrence and Self-Enforcement in the Value Added Tax." American Economic Review 105, August 2015 (8), 2539-2569.

Pomeranz, D. (2015). No Taxation without Information: Deterrence and Self-Enforcement in the Value Added Tax. *The American Economic Review*, *105*(8), 2539–2569. https://www.nber.org/papers/w19199 DOI: 10.1257/aer.20130393

Pommerehne, W., & Weck-Hannemann, H. (1996). Tax rates, tax administration and income tax evasion in Switzerland. *Public Choice*, *88*(1-2), 161–170. DOI: 10.1007/BF00130416

Porcano, T. M. (1988). Correlates of tax evasion. *Journal of Economic Psychology*, *9*(1), 47–67. DOI: 10.1016/0167-4870(88)90031-1

Pourquery, D. (1991). Les provisions ou l'art de mettre de l'argent de côté. *Science & Vie Economie, 73*, 72–75.

Prechel, H., & Boies, J. (1998). Capital dependence, financial risk, and change from the multidivisional to the multilayered subsidiary form. *Sociological Forum, 13*(2), 321–362. DOI: 10.1023/A:1022197917767

Prechel, H., & Zheng, L. (2016). Do organizational and political–legal arrangements explain financial wrongdoing? *The British Journal of Sociology, 67*(4), 655–677. DOI: 10.1111/1468-4446.12212 PMID: 27753077

Prieto, J., Sanzo, M. J., & Suárez, J. (2006). Análisis económico de la actitud hacia el fraude fiscal en España. *Hacienda Pública Española, 177*, 107–128.

Principles for Responsible Investment. (2018). Evaluating and Engaging on Corporate Tax Transparency. https://www.unpri.org/Uploads/t/r/l/PRI_Evaluating-and-engaging-on-corporate-tax-transparency_Investor-guide.pdf

Pui, Y. C., Moorthy, K., & Choo, K. S. W. (2017). Taxpayers" perceptions on tax evasion behaviour: An empirical study in Malaysia. *Journal of Law and Management, 59*(3), 413–429. DOI: 10.1108/IJLMA-02-2016-0022

Purnomo, I. R. B. (2019). The influence of effective communication strategy on consciousness and UMKM taxpayer compliance. *Religación : Revista de Ciencias Sociales y Humanidades, 4*(15), 125–147.

Putnam, R. D. (2001). La comunidad próspera. El capital social y la vida pública. *Zona Abierta*, (94/95), 89–104.

Putnam, R. D. (2011). *Para que la democracia funcione: las tradiciones cívicas en la Italia moderna*. Centro de Investigaciones Sociológicas.

Rabin, M., & Thaler, R. H. (2001). Anomalies: Risk Aversion. *The Journal of Economic Perspectives, 15*(1), 219–232. DOI: 10.1257/jep.15.1.219

Raffournier, B. (1990). La théorie positive de la comptabilité: Une revue de la littérature. *Economies et Sociétés, Série sciences de gestion, 16*.

Raffournier, B. (2003). Comptabilité créative et normalisation comptable. *Review of Finance, 139*, 74–83.

Rahman, S., Sirazy, M. R. M., Das, R., & Khan, R. S. (2024). An exploration of artificial intelligence techniques for optimizing tax compliance, fraud detection, and revenue collection in modern tax administrations. *International Journal of Business Intelligence and Big Data Analytics, 7*(3), 56–80.

Rahmayanti, N. P., & Prihatiningtias, Y. W. (2020). Effect of tax penalties, tax audit, and taxpayers awareness on corporate taxpayers' compliance moderated by compliance intentions. *International Journal of Research in Business and Social Science (2147-4478), 9*(2), 118-124.

Rakayana, W., Sudarma, M., & Rosidi, R. (2021). The structure of company ownership and tax avoidance in Indonesia. *International Research Journal of Management. IT and Social Sciences, 8*(3), 296–305.

Ramkumar, G., Kalimuthu, L. P., Selvaraj, A. P., Shankarii, S., & Rajasekaran, K. K. (2023). A structural equation modelling approach towards taxpayers' perceptions on goods and services tax in India. *International Journal of Professional Business Review*, *8*(4), e02166–e02166. DOI: 10.26668/business-review/2023.v8i4.2166

Ramli, A. I. B. (2024). Big Data and Artificial Intelligence to Develop Advanced Fraud Detection Systems for the Financial Sector. *International Journal of Advanced Cybersecurity Systems, Technologies, and Applications*, *8*(12), 31–44.

Rana, N. P., Dwivedi, Y. K., Williams, M. D., & Weerakkody, V. (2016). Adoption of online public grievance redressal system in India: Toward developing a unified view. *Computers in Human Behavior*, *59*, 265–282. DOI: 10.1016/j.chb.2016.02.019

Randlane, K. (2015). Tax Compliance as a System: Mapping the Field. *International Journal of Public Administration*, *39*(7), 515–525. DOI: 10.1080/01900692.2015.1028636

Rane, N., Choudhary, S. P., & Rane, J. (2024). Acceptance of artificial intelligence technologies in business management, finance, and e-commerce: Factors, challenges, and strategies. *Studies in Economics and Business Relations*, *5*(2), 23–44. DOI: 10.48185/sebr.v5i2.1333

Rangel, A., Camerer, C., & Montague, P. (2008). A framework for studying the neurobiology of value-based decision making. *Nature Reviews. Neuroscience*, *9*(7), 545–556. DOI: 10.1038/nrn2357

Rashid, M. H. U., Ahmad, A., Abdullah, M. S., Ahmmed, M., & Islam, S. (2022). Doing Business and Tax Evasion: Evidence from Asian Countries. *SAGE Open*, *12*(4), 21582440221131280. Advance online publication. DOI: 10.1177/21582440221131280

Rashid, M. H. U., Uddin, N., Haque, M. S., & Hossain, S. Z. (2022). Good governance and tax evasion: Mediating effect of socioeconomic conditions. *Asia-Pacific Journal of Regional Science*, *6*(2), 759–776. DOI: 10.1007/s41685-022-00242-x

Rashid, S. F. A., Ramli, R., Palil, M. R., & Amir, A. M. (2022). The influence of power of tax administrator on cognitive and affective tax attitude in Malaysia. *Asian Journal of Accounting and Governance*, *17*, 59–74.

Ratnawati, A. T., & Darmanto, S. (2023). Role of attitude and intention on the relationship between perceived ease of use, perceived usefulness, trust, and e-tax system behavior. [GBFR]. *Global Business & Finance Review*, *28*(7), 89–104. DOI: 10.17549/gbfr.2023.28.7.89

Razak, A. A., & Adafula, C. J. (2013, September). Evaluating taxpayers " attitude and its influ ence on tax compliance decisions in Tamale, Ghana. *Journal of Accounting and Taxation*, *5*(3), 48–57. DOI: 10.5897/JAT2013.0120

Reck, D., & Bomare, J. (2022). Different from you and me: Tax enforcement and sophisticated tax evasion by the wealthy. *LSE Public Policy Review*, *2*(4), 6. DOI: 10.31389/lseppr.71

Reddy, D., Moodley, A., & Olugbara, O. (2024). Factors informing tax compliance: A meta-analytical study. *Suid-Afrikaanse Tydskrif vir Ekonomiese en Bestuurswetenskappe*, *27*(1), 11. DOI: 10.4102/sajems.v27i1.5738

Reese, H. W., & Fremouw, W. J. (1984). Normal and normative ethics in behavioral sciences. *The American Psychologist*, *39*(8), 863–876. DOI: 10.1037/0003-066X.39.8.863

Rguig, M., & Guemmi, F. (2023). Civisme fiscal au Maroc: À la recherche du compromis. *Revue Marocaine de Gestion et de Développement*, *3*(3), 340–357.

Richardson, G. (2008). The Relationship between Culture and Tax Evasion across Countries: Additional Evidence and Extensions. *Journal of International Accounting, Auditing & Taxation*, *17*(2), 67–78. DOI: 10.1016/j.intaccaudtax.2008.07.002

Rilling, J., Gutman, D., Zeh, T., Pagnoni, G., Berns, G., & Kilts, C. (2002). A neural basis for social cooperation. *Neuron*, *35*(2), 395–405. DOI: 10.1016/S0896-6273(02)00755-9

Risi, D., Vigneau, L., Bohn, S., & Wickert, C. (2023). Institutional theory-based investigation on communal responsibility of corporates: Bringing values back in. *International Journal of Management Reviews*, *25*(1), 3–23. DOI: 10.1111/ijmr.12299

Ritov, I., & Baron, J. (1990). Reluctance to vaccinate: Omission bias and ambiguity. [Wiley Online Library.]. *Journal of Behavioral Decision Making*, *3*(4), 263–277.DOI: 10.1002/bdm.3960030404

Ritsatos, T. (2014). Tax evasion and compliance; from the neo classical paradigm to behavioural economics, a review. *Journal of Accounting & Organizational Change*, *10*(2), 244–262. DOI: 10.1108/JAOC-07-2012-0059

Rizzi, D. (2017). Tax Evasion Indices and Profiles. *Public Finance Review*, *45*(6), 771–791. DOI: 10.1177/1091142117691602

Rizzo, A., & Hassan, G. (2024). Addressing the use of AI by EU tax authorities: Towards a common framework of taxpayer protection. *. *European Taxation*, *65*(1). Advance online publication. DOI: 10.59403/1avybfj

Roberts, M. L., Hite, P. A., & Bradley, C. F. (1994). Understanding attitudes toward progressive taxation. *Public Opinion Quarterly*, *58*(2), 165–190. DOI: 10.1086/269417

Rodríguez Duplà, L. (2001). *Ética* (Biblioteca de Autores, C., Ed.).

Rosa, A. (2024). *Civisme fiscal vs éthique fiscale: Quel (s) devoir (s) du contribuable? Saad, N. (2011). Fairness perceptions and compliance behavior: Taxpayers' judgments in self-assessment environments.* University of Canterbury.

Rossignol, J. L. (2002). La politique fiscalo-comptable des entreprises françaises: Une étude exploratoire. *Comptabilité-Contrôle-Audit*, *8*(1), 89–110. DOI: 10.3917/cca.081.0089

Rothenhoefer, K., Costa, V., Bartolo, R., Vicario-Feliciano, R., Murray, E., & Averbeck, B. (2017). Effects of Ventral Striatum Lesions on Stimulus-Based versus Action-Based Reinforcement Learning. *The Journal of Neuroscience : The Official Journal of the Society for Neuroscience*, *37*(29), 6902–6914. DOI: 10.1523/JNEUROSCI.0631-17.2017

Ruiz, M. A. G. (2021). Fiscal Transformations Due to AI and Robotization: Where Do Recent Changes in Tax Administrations, Procedures and Legal Systems Lead Us? *Nw. J. Tech. & Intell. Prop.*, *19*, 325.

Ruzgas, T., Kižauskienė, L., Lukauskas, M., Sinkevičius, E., Frolovaitė, M., & Arnastauskaitė, J. (2023). Tax fraud reduction using analytics in an East European country. *Axioms*, *12*(3), 288. DOI: 10.3390/axioms12030288

Saad, N. (2012). Perceptions of tax fairness and tax compliance behavior: A comparative study. [UKM Journal of Management]. *Jurnal Pengurusan*, *36*, 89–100.

Saberi Moghadam, S., Samsami Khodadad, F., & Khazaeinezhad, V. (2019). An Algorithmic Model of Decision Making in the Human Brain. *Basic and Clinical Neuroscience*, *10*(5), 443–449. DOI: 10.32598/bcn.9.10.395

Sadik-Zada, E. R., Gatto, A., & Niftiyev, I. (2022). E-government and petty corruption in public sector service delivery. *Technology Analysis and Strategic Management*. Advance online publication. DOI: 10.1080/09537325.2022.2067037

Sadovenko, M., Kondratyuk, O., Suprun, N., & Tarverdiev, M. (2024). Technical engineering in the digitalization era: the role of artificial intelligence and cryptocurrency in tax systems optimizing and improving the financial efficiency of fintech businesses. Economics and technical engineering, 2(1), 64-78.DOI: 10.62911/ete.2024.02.01.06

Safian, N., & Ngah, N. (2020, October). The Influence Of Attıtude Towards Tax Complıance Behavıour Among Cıvıl Servants In Selangor. In *Proceedıng: 3rd Internatıonal Conference On Global Busıness And Socıal Scıence 2020 (3RD ICGBSS 2020)* (p. 44).

Samanez-Larkin, G., Gibbs, S., Khanna, K., Nielsen, L., Carstensen, L., & Knutson, B. (2007). Anticipation of monetary gain but not loss in healthy older adults. *Nature Neuroscience*, *10*(6), 787–791. DOI: 10.1038/nn1894

Sandu, D. (2022). Indigenous Taxes Among Obligation and Fiscal Citizenship. *PEOPLE: International Journal of Communal Sciences*, *7*(3), 104–119. DOI: 10.20319/pijss.2022.73.104119

Saragih, A. H., Reyhani, Q., Setyowati, M. S., & Hendrawan, A. (2023). The potential of an artificial intelligence (AI) application for the tax administration system's modernization: The case of Indonesia. *Artificial Intelligence and Law*, *31*(3), 491–514. DOI: 10.1007/s10506-022-09321-y

Scarpa, F., & Signori, S. (2023). Understanding corporate tax responsibility: A systematic literature review. *Sustainability Accounting. Management and Policy Journal*, *14*(7), 179–201.

Schmidt, C., Matthaei, E., Schmidt, C., Matthaei, E., & Lauth, H. (2023). *Working paper. 2*.

Schmölders, G. (1959). Fiscal psychology: A new branch of public finance. *National Tax Journal*, *12*(4), 340–345. DOI: 10.1086/NTJ41790780

Schmölders, G. (1960). Survey Research in Public Finance: A Behavioural Approach to Fiscal Theory. *Public Finance*, *25*, 300–306.

Schmölders, G. (1965). Lo Irracional en la Hacienda Pública. In *Problemas de Psicología Financiera* (pp. 3–149). Editorial de Derecho Financiero.

Schmölders, G. (1970). Survey research in public finance: A behavioral approach to fiscal theory. *Public Finance*, *25*(2), 300–306.

Schnatterly, K., Gangloff, K. A., & Tuschke, A. (2018). CEO Wrongdoing: A review of pressure, opportunity, and rationalization. *Journal of Management*, *44*(6), 2405–2432. DOI: 10.1177/0149206318771177

Schneider, F., & Torgler, B. (2007). *The impact of tax morale and institutional quality on the shadow economy* (No. 0702). Working Paper.

Scholz, J. T., & Lubell, M. (1998). Trust and taxpaying: Testing the heuristic approach to collective action. *American Journal of Political Science*, *42*(2), 398–417. DOI: 10.2307/2991764

Schweitzer, B. (2024). Artificial intelligence (AI) ethics in accounting. Journal of Accounting. *Ethics & Public Policy, JAEPP*, *25*(1), 67–67.

Securities and Exchange Commission. Sec 13 or 15(d), 2025.

Segura, N. (2008). Contribution à la connaissance de la production de l'information financière: Le cas des provisions pour litiges. *Actes du 29ème congrès de l'Association Francophone de Comptabilité,* Cergy-Pontoise.

Shabou, R., & Boulila Taktak, N. (2002). Les déterminants de la comptabilité créative: Etude empirique dans le contexte des entreprises tunisiennes. *Comptabilité-Contrôle-Audit*, *8*(1), 5–24. DOI: 10.3917/cca.081.0005

Shafir, E., & LeBoeuf, R. (2002). Rationality. *Annual Review of Psychology*, *53*(1), 491–517. DOI: 10.1146/annurev.psych.53.100901.135213

Shaharuddin, N. S., Palil, M. R., Ramli, R., & Maelah, R. (2012). Sole Proprietorship and Tax Compliance Intention in Self-Assessment System: A Theory of Planned Behavior Approach. *International Journal of Business. Economics and Law*, *1*(6), 34–42.

Shandilya, S. K., Datta, A., Kartik, Y., & Nagar, A. (2024). Navigating the regulatory landscape. In *Digital Resilience: Navigating Disruption and Safeguarding Data Privacy* (pp. 127–240). Springer Nature Switzerland. DOI: 10.1007/978-3-031-53290-0_3

Shang, J., & Croson, R. (2005). *Field experiment in charitable contribution: The impact of social influence on the voluntary provision of public goods*. University of Pennsylvania.

Sharp, S. (2023). Communicating taxes: A review of the literature. ODI Literature Review, 2-29. https://www.odi.org/en/publications/communicating-taxes-a-review-of-the-literature/

Sheppard Mullin. (2025). Things to keep in mind for your annual report on form 10-K and proxy statement. https://www.corporatesecuritieslawblog.com/wp-content/uploads/sites/46/2025/01/Things-to-Keep-in-Mind-for-Your-2025-10K-and-Proxy-Statement-Client-Alert-0125.pdf

Shestakova, A., Rieskamp, J., Tugin, S., Ossadtchi, A., Krutitskaya, J., & Klucharev, V. (2013). Electrophysiological precursors of social conformity. *Social Cognitive and Affective Neuroscience*, *8*(7), 756–763. DOI: 10.1093/scan/nss064

Shields, P. M., & Tajalli, H. (2006). Intermediate theory: The missing link in successful student scholarship. *Journal of Public Affairs Education, 12*(3), 313–334. DOI: 10.1080/15236803.2006.12001438

Sikayu, S. H., Rahmat, M., & Chan, A. N. (2022). Fairness, transparency and attitude towards tax evasion amongst owners of SMEs [IJSMS]. *International Journal of Service Management and Sustainability, 7*(1), 185–206. DOI: 10.24191/ijsms.v7i1.17786

Silal, P., & Saha, D. (2021). E-Government as a Tool for Human Development: The Moderating Influence of National Culture. *Journal of Global Information Technology Management, 24*(4), 235–258. DOI: 10.1080/1097198X.2021.1993724

Silvis, I. M., Bothma, T. J., & de Beer, K. J. (2018). Evaluating the usability of the information architecture of academic library websites. *Library Hi Tech, 37*(3), 566–590.

Simuyu, K. E., & Jagongo, A. (2019). Impact of online tax filing on tax compliance among small and medium enterprises in Kibwezi Sub-county in Kenya. *International Journal of Current Research, 9*(1), 45196–45206.

Siripurapu, A. (2021). Corporate taxes in a globalized world. *Council on Foreign Relations.* https://www.cfr.org/backgrounder/corporate-taxes-globalized-world

Sjoberg, F., Mellon, J., Peixoto, T., Hemker, J., & Tsai, L. (2019, May). Voice and Punishment: A Global Survey Experiment on Tax Morale. Policy Research Working Paper; No. 8855, World Bank. https://hdl.handle.net/10986/31713

Slemrod, J., & Yitzhaki, S. (2023). Tax avoidance, evasion, and administration. In *Handbook of Public Economics* (Vol. 3, pp. 1423-1470).

Slemrod, J. (2007). Cheating ourselves: The economics of tax evasion. *The Journal of Economic Perspectives, 21*(1), 25–48. DOI: 10.1257/jep.21.1.25

Slemrod, J. (2019). Tax compliance and enforcement. *Journal of Economic Literature, 57*(4), 904–954. DOI: 10.1257/jel.20181437

Slemrod, J. (2024). What taxpayers, governments and tax economists do–and what they should do. *Fiscal Studies, 45*(1), 7–19. DOI: 10.1111/1475-5890.12324

Slemrod, J. B. (1985). An empirical test for tax evasion. *The Review of Economics and Statistics, 67*(2), 232–267. DOI: 10.2307/1924722

Slemrod, J., Collins, B., Hoopes, J. L., Reck, D., & Sebastiani, M. (2017). Does credit-card information reporting improve small-business tax compliance? *Journal of Public Economics, 149*, 1–19. DOI: 10.1016/j.jpubeco.2017.02.010

Slemrod, J., & Yitzhaki, S. (2002). Tax avoidance, evasion, and administration. In Auerbach, A. J., Chetty, R. D., Feldstein, M., & Saez, E. (Eds.), *Handbook of public economics* (Vol. 3, pp. 1423–1470). Elsevier.

Smart, M. (2012). The application of the theory of planned behaviour and structural equation modelling in tax compliance behaviour: a New Zealand study.

Smithson, A., Holmes, J., & Gillies, F. (2015). Integration, assimilation or transformation: Introducing therapists to qualitative research methods, a focus group study. *European Journal of Psychotherapy & Counselling*, *17*(3), 296–313. Advance online publication. DOI: 10.1080/13642537.2015.1059868

Snaidauf, D. (2011). Predicting Aggregate Taxpayer Compliance Behaviour. Recent Research on Tax Administration and Compliance, 73. https://www.brianerard.com/wp content/uploads/ 2015/01/predicting_aggregate_taxpayer_compliance_behavior.pdf

Sniderman, P. M., & Theriault, S. M. (1999). The Dynamics of Political Argument and the Logic of Issue Framing. Paper presented at the annual meeting of the Midwest Political Science Association, Chicago, IL, 15-17.

Soepriyanto, G., Zudana, A. E., & Meiryani, M. (2024). Older and wiser? The impact of CEO age on firm's tax amnesty participation. *Cogent Business & Management*, *11*(1), 2296142. DOI: 10.1080/23311975.2023.2296142

Song, Y., & Yarbrough, T. E. (1978). Tax Ethics and Taxpayer Attitudes: A Survey. *Public Administration Review*, *38*(5), 442–452. DOI: 10.2307/975503

SOTTOMESSO, P. (2020). Fo r P ee r R ev Fo r R. *Jdr*, *2001*, 3–29.

Spicer, M. W., & Lundstedt, S. B. (1976). Understanding tax evasion. *Public Finance*, *31*, 295–305.

Spitzer, M., Fischbacher, U., Herrnberger, B., Grön, G., & Fehr, E. (2007). The neural signature of social norm compliance. *Neuron*, *56*(1), 185–196. DOI: 10.1016/j.neuron.2007.09.011

Sritharan, N., & Salawati, S. (2019). Economic factors impact on individual taxpayers" tax compliance behaviour in Malaysia. Nternational Journal of Academic Research in Accounting. *Finance and Management Sciences*, *9*(2), 172–182. DOI: 10.6007/IJARAFMS/v9-i2/6166

Stella, P. (1991). An economic analysis of tax amnesties. *Journal of Public Economics*, *46*(3), 383–400. DOI: 10.1016/0047-2727(91)90013-R

Stetsenko, T., & Nishcheretov, O. (2021). Tax Culture as well tax Morale: Influence on Tax Compliance in Ukraine. *Communal Economics*, *2*(61), 83–91. DOI: 10.26565/2524-2547-2021-61-08

Stolowy, H. (1999). Comptabilité créative. In *Encyclopédie de Comptabilité, Contrôle de Gestion et Audit* (pp. 157-178). Economica.

Stolowy, H. (1995). Comptabilité créative. *Revue Fiduciaire Comptable*, *212*, 26–32.

Stolowy, H., & Breton, G. (2003). La gestion des données comptables: Une revue de la littérature. *Comptabilité-Contrôle-Audit*, *9*(1), 125–151. DOI: 10.3917/cca.091.0125

Strango, C. (2021). Does digitalisation in public services reduce tax evasion? *Economic Research Guardian, 11*(2), 221–235. https://www.scopus.com/inward/record.uri?eid=2-s2.0-85122026990&partnerID =40&md5=ec809f38d1e1f7eeb8c789d6c1177b36

Strümpel, B. (1969). The Contribution of Survey Research to Public Finance. In Peacock, A. T. (Ed.), *Quantitative Analysis in Public Finance* (pp. 13–32). Praeger.

Suárez Serrato, J. C., & Zidar, O. M. (2023). How do corporate taxes affect economic activity*? NBER Reporter, (3),* 8–13. https://www.nber.org/reporter/2023number3/how-do-corporate-taxes-affect-economic-activity

Sudarma, I., & Darmayasa, I. N. (2017). *Does voluntary tax compliance increase after granting tax amnesty? Accounting and Finance Review* (Vol. 2). AFR.

Suharnoko, B., Castaneda, N., Jorge, L., Chairunissa, T., Farid, M., Poerwanto, J., & Wirapati, B. (2020). *Applying Behavioral Insights to Promote SME Tax Compliance in Indonesia: Activity Report.* World Bank Documents and Reports.

Sulistyan, R. B. (2020). Lecturer E-learning Training: The Role of Communal Exchange Theory. *Empowerment Society*, *3*(2), 50–56. DOI: 10.30741/eps.v3i2.589

Sunarsih, U., Hakim, M. A. D., & Rusmanto, T. (2024). THE IMPACT OF TAX UNDERSTANDING, GENDER, AND LOVE OF MONEY ON TAX EVASION WITH RELIGIOSITY AS A MODERATING VARIABLE. *Revista de Gestao Social e Ambiental*, *18*(7), e06926. Advance online publication. DOI: 10.24857/rgsa.v18n7-141

Surugiu, M. R., Vasile, V., Surugiu, C., Mazilescu, C. R., Panait, M. C., & Bunduchi, E. (2025). Tax Compliance Pattern Analysis: A Survey-Based Approach. *International Journal of Financial Studies*, *13*(1), 14. DOI: 10.3390/ijfs13010014

Sussman, R., & Gifford, R. (2013). Be the change you want to see: Modeling food composting in public places. *Environment and Behavior*, *45*(3), 323–343. DOI: 10.1177/0013916511431274

Svanoe, H. T. (1944). "Cost to Life Insurance Companies of Tax Compliance in Information at the Source". *Proceedings of the Annual Conference on Taxation under the Auspices of the National Tax Association 37.*

Tabibnia, G., & Lieberman, M. (2007). Fairness and cooperation are rewarding: Evidence from social cognitive neuroscience. *Annals of the New York Academy of Sciences*, *1118*(1), 90–101. DOI: 10.1196/annals.1412.001

Tan, L. M., & Liu, X. (2016, January). SMEs tax compliance: A matter of trust? In Australian Tax Forum (Vol. 31, No. 3, pp. 527-554). Sydney, NSW: Tax Institute.

Teega, S. (2008). The Effect of Tax Education on Tax Compliance in Uganda: A Case Study of Kampala Central Tax District. Uganda Martyrs University. https://ir.umu.ac.ug/xmlui/handle/20.500.12280/972

Tehulu, T. A., & Dinberu, Y. D. (2014). Determinants of tax compliance behavior in Ethiopia: The case of Bahir Dar city taxpayers. *Journal of Economics and Sustainable Development*, *5*(15), 268–280.

Tekin, A., Doğan, E., & Çelikay, F. (2018). Vergi Ahlakı Kavramsallaştırmasına Yönelik Bir Değerlendirme: Eskişehir-Kütahya Örneği. *Maliye Dergisi*, *175*, 228–252.

Thaler, R. (1990). Anomalies: Saving, Fungibility, and Mental Accounts. *The Journal of Economic Perspectives*, *4*(1), 193–205. DOI: 10.1257/jep.4.1.193

Thuneibat, N., Ali, B., Alqaraleh, M., & Thneibat, H. (2022). The Mediating Role of Innovation On the Relationship Between Information Technologies and Reducing Tax Evasion. *Information Sciences Letters, 11*(5), 1359–1370. DOI: 10.18576/isl/110505

Tillman, R. (2009). Reputations and corporate malfeasance: Collusive networks in financial statement fraud. *Crime, Law, and Social Change, 51*(3–4), 365–382. DOI: 10.1007/s10611-008-9161-1

Timmons, J. F., & Garfias, F. (2015). Revealed corruption, taxation, and fiscal accountability: Evidence from Brazil. *World Development, 70*, 13–27. DOI: 10.1016/j.worlddev.2014.12.011

Tipke, K. (2002). *Moral tributaria del Estado y de los contribuyentes* (Pons, M., Ed.).

Tittle, C. (1980). *Sanctions and Social Deviance: The Question of Deterrence*. Praeger Publishers.

Tom, S., Fox, C., Trepel, C., & Poldrack, R. (2007). The neural basis of loss aversion in decision-making under risk. *Science, 315*(5811), 515–518. DOI: 10.1126/science.1134239

Torgler, B. (2002b). *Preaching Matters: Tax Morale and Religiosity*. WWZ-Discussion Paper 02/03, Basel: WWZ.

Torgler, B. (2002c). Vertical and Exchange Equity in a Tax Morale Experiment. WWZ-Discussion Paper 02/02, Basel: WWZ.

Torgler, B. (2003). Tax morale: Theory and empirical analysis of tax compliance (Doctoral dissertation, University_of_Basel).

Torgler, B. (2003c). Tax morale: theory and empirical analysis of tax compliance, PhD Thesis, University of Basel, Faculty of Business and Economics.

Torgler, B. (2011). Tax morale and compliance.Review of evidence and case studies for Europe. World Bank policy research working paper series, 5922.

Torgler, B., & Schneider, F. (2007). Shadow Economy, Tax Morale, Governance and Institutional Quality: A Panel Analysis. QUT School of Economics and Finance Working/Discussion Paper 210, February 2007.

Torgler, B., & Valev, N. (2006). Women and Illegal Activities: Gender Differences and Women.s Willingness to Comply over Time. *CREMA Working Paper* 15.

Torgler, B. (2001). Is tax evasion never justifiable? *Journal of Public Finance and Public Choice, 19*(2-3), 143–167. DOI: 10.1332/251569201X15668905707203

Torgler, B. (2002a). Direct Democracy Matters: Tax Morale and Political Participation. *Proceedings. Annual Conference on Taxation and Minutes of the Annual Meeting of the National Tax Association, 95*, 50–59.

Torgler, B. (2003). Tax Morale in Transition Countries. *Post-Communist Economies, 15*(3), 357–381. DOI: 10.1080/1463137032000139052

Torgler, B. (2003). To evade or not: That is the question. *Journal of Socio-Economics, 32*(3), 283–302. DOI: 10.1016/S1053-5357(03)00040-4

Torgler, B. (2003). To evade taxes or not to evade: That is the question. *Journal of Economic Surveys*, *17*(3), 267–287.

Torgler, B. (2003a). Direct Democracy Matters: Tax Morale and Political Participation. *National Tax Association Papers and Proceedings*, *95*, 50–59.

Torgler, B. (2003b). Does culture matter? Tax morale in an east–west German comparison. *Finanz-Archiv*, *59*(4), 504–528. DOI: 10.1628/0015221032500856

Torgler, B. (2004). Cross-Culture Comparison of Tax Morale and Tax Compliance: Evidence from Costa Rica and Switzerland. [Sage Journals.]. *International Journal of Comparative Sociology*, *45*(1-2), 17–43. DOI: 10.1177/0020715204048309

Torgler, B. (2004). Moral suasion: An alternative tax policy strategy? Evidence from a controlled field experiment in Switzerland. *Economics of Governance*, *5*(3), 235–253. DOI: 10.1007/s10101-004-0077-7

Torgler, B. (2005a). Tax morale and direct democracy. *European Journal of Political Economy*, *21*(2), 525–531. DOI: 10.1016/j.ejpoleco.2004.08.002

Torgler, B. (2005b). Tax Morale in Latin America. *Public Choice*, *122*(1-2), 133–157. DOI: 10.1007/s11127-005-5790-4

Torgler, B., & Murphy, K. (2004). Tax Morale in Australia: What Factors Shape It and Has It Changed Over Time? *Journal of Australian Taxation*, *7*, 298–335.

Torgler, B., Schaffner, M., & Macintyre, A. (2010). Tax compliance, tax morale, and governance quality. In Alm, J., Martinez-Vazquez, J., & Torgler, B. (Eds.), *Developing Alternative Frameworks for Explaining Tax Compliance* (pp. 56–73). Routledge.

Torgler, B., & Schneider, F. (2005). Attitudes Towards Paying Taxes in Austria: An Empirical Analysis. *Empirica*, *32*(2), 231–250. DOI: 10.1007/s10663-004-8328-y

Torgler, B., & Schneider, F. (2009). The Impact of Tax Morale and Institutional Quality on the Shadow Economy. *Journal of Economic Psychology*, *30*(2), 228–245. DOI: 10.1016/j.joep.2008.08.004

Trawule, A. Y., Gadzo, S. G., Kportorgbi, H. K., & Sam-Quarm, R. (2022). Tax education and fear-appealing messages: A grease or sand in the wheels of tax compliance? *Cogent Business & Management*, *9*(1), 2049436. Advance online publication. DOI: 10.1080/23311975.2022.2049436

Traxler, C. (2010). Social norms and conditional cooperative taxpayers. *European Journal of Political Economy*, *26*(1), 89–103. DOI: 10.1016/j.ejpoleco.2009.11.001

Trepel, C., Fox, C., & Poldrack, R. (2005). Prospect theory on the brain? Toward a cognitive neuroscience of decision under risk. *Brain Research. Cognitive Brain Research*, *23*(1), 34–50. DOI: 10.1016/j.cogbrainres.2005.01.016

Tversky, A., & Thaler, R. (1990). Anomalies: Preference Reversals. *The Journal of Economic Perspectives*, *4*(2), 201–211. DOI: 10.1257/jep.4.2.201

Tyler, T. R. (2001). Public trust and confidence in legal authorities: What do majority and minority group members want from the law and legal institutions? *Behavioral Sciences & the Law*, *19*(2), 215–235. DOI: 10.1002/bsl.438 PMID: 11385699

Useem, M., & Gager, C. (1996). Employee shareholders or institutional investors? When corporate managers replace their stockholders. *Journal of Management Studies*, *33*(5), 613–632. DOI: 10.1111/j.1467-6486.1996.tb00811.x

Usunier, J. C., Easterby-Smith, M., & Thorpe, R. (1993). *Introduction à la recherche en gestion*. Economica.

Utama, M. S., Nimran, U., Hidayat, K., & Prasetya, A. (2022). Effect of religiosity, perceived risk, and attitude on tax compliant intention moderated by e-filing. *International Journal of Financial Studies*, *10*(1), 8. DOI: 10.3390/ijfs10010008

Valentin, V., & O'Doherty, J. (2009). Overlapping prediction errors in dorsal striatum during instrumental learning with juice and money reward in the human brain. *Journal of Neurophysiology*, *102*(6), 3384–3391. DOI: 10.1152/jn.91195.2008

Van Der Geest, T., & Velleman, E. (2014). Easy-to-read meets accessible web in the e-government context. *5th International Conference on Software Development and Technologies for Enhancing Accessibility and Fighting Info-Exclusion, DSAI 2013, 27*, 327–333. DOI: 10.1016/j.procs.2014.02.036

van Dijk, W. W., Goslinga, S., Terwel, B. W., & van Dijk, E. (2020). How choice architecture can promote and undermine tax compliance: Testing the effects of prepopulated tax returns and accuracy confirmation. *Journal of Behavioral and Experimental Economics*, *87*, 101574. Advance online publication. DOI: 10.1016/j.socec.2020.101574

Vangah, Y.-C. A. (2017). Les raisons de la comptabilité créative dans les entreprises ivoiriennes à travers une démarche par les entretiens. *Accountability, Responsabilités et Comptabilités*, May, Poitier, France. Available at https://hal.archives-ouvertes.fr/hal-01907530/document

Venkatasubramanian, G. (2024). *Exploring the Impact of Internet of Things (IoT) Technologies on Tax Compliance: Opportunities, Challenges, and Policy Implications*. Edumania—An International Multidisciplinary Journal., DOI: 10.59231/edumania/9073

Vera, P., & Grijalva, D. (2014). Motivación Intrínseca y Cooperación Condicional en el Pago de Impuestos: Una perspectiva Experimental. *Fiscalidad.Revista Institucional Del Servicio de Rentas Internas*, *9*, 52–94.

Vincent, O. (2021). Assessing SMEs tax non-compliance behaviour in Sub-Saharan Africa (SSA): An insight from Nigeria. *Cogent Business & Management*, *8*(1), 1938930. DOI: 10.1080/23311975.2021.1938930

Vlachogianni, P., & Tselios, N. (2023). Perceived usability evaluation of educational technology using the post-study system usability questionnaire (PSSUQ): A systematic review. *Sustainability*, *15*(17), 12954.

Vogel, J. (1974). Taxation and public opinion in Sweden: An interpretation of recent survey data. *National Tax Journal*, *27*(4), 499–513. DOI: 10.1086/NTJ41861983

Wahl, I., Kastlunger, B., & Kirchler, E. (2010). Trust in authorities and power to enforce tax compliance: An empirical analysis of the "slippery slope framework". *Law & Policy*, *32*(4), 383–406. DOI: 10.1111/j.1467-9930.2010.00327.x

Wahlund, R. (1992). Tax changes and economic behavior: The case of tax evasion. *Journal of Economic Psychology*, *13*(4), 657–677. DOI: 10.1016/0167-4870(92)90017-2

Wang, J., & Cui, S. (2018). Associative memory cells and their working principle in the brain. *F1000 Research*, *7*, 108. DOI: 10.12688/f1000research.13665.1

Wang, K., Zipperle, M., Becherer, M., Gottwalt, F., & Zhang, Y. (2020). An AI-based automated continuous compliance awareness framework (CoCAF) for procurement auditing. *Big Data and Cognitive Computing*, *4*(3), 23. DOI: 10.3390/bdcc4030023

Wang, M. (2024). AI Technologies in Modern Taxation: Applications, Challenges, and Strategic Directions. *International Journal of Finance and Investment*, *1*(1), 42–46. DOI: 10.54097/v2kgty49

Wang, X. (2008). Decision making in recurrent neuronal circuits. *Neuron*, *60*(2), 215–234. DOI: 10.1016/j.neuron.2008.09.034

Wang, Y. (2007). Income tax evasion in the United States and China. *Frontiers of Law in China*, *2*(1), 123–139. DOI: 10.1007/s11463-007-0007-z

Watts, R., & Zimmerman, J. (1986). *Positive accounting theory*. Prentice Hall.

Weber, E., & Johnson, E. (2009). *Decisions under uncertainty: Psychological, Economic and Neuroeconomic explanations of Risk Preference. Glimcher, P., Camerer, C., Fehr, E., Poldrack, Rl. (2009). Neuroeconomics: Decision making and The Brain*. Academic Press.

Webley, P. (2004). Tax compliance by businesses. *New perspectives on economic crime*, 95-126.

Weck, H., Pommerehne, W. W., & Frey, B. S. (1984). *Schattenwirtschaft*. Franz Vahlen.

Weigel, J. (2018). Building State and Citizen: How Tax Collection in Congo Engenders Citizen Engagement with the State. Working Paper.

Wenzel, M. (2004). An analysis of norm processes in tax compliance. *Journal of Economic Psychology*, *25*(2), 213–228. DOI: 10.1016/S0167-4870(02)00168-X

Wenzel, M. (2005). Misperceptions of social norms about tax compliance: From theory to intervention. *Journal of Economic Psychology*, *26*(6), 862–883. DOI: 10.1016/j.joep.2005.02.002

Wenzel, M. (2005). Motivation or rationalization? Causal relations between ethical norms and tax compliance. *Journal of Economic Psychology*, *26*(4), 495–508. DOI: 10.1016/j.joep.2004.03.003

Wenzel, M. (2006). A letter from the tax office: Compliance effects of informational and interpersonal justice. *Social Justice Research*, *19*(3), 345–364. DOI: 10.1007/s11211-006-0011-y

Widuri, R., Mangoting, Y., Sadjiarto, A., & Eoh, T. S. (2023). Preventing tax evasion: The moral strength of taxpayers and the power of tax authorities. Jurnal Akuntansi dan Keuangan, 25(2), 91-100.

Williams, C. (2020). Evaluating public administration approaches towards tax non-compliance in Europe. *Administrative Sciences*, *10*(3), 43. DOI: 10.3390/admsci10030043

Xiong, X. (2022, July). Critical review of quantitative and qualitative research. In 2022 3rd International conference on mental health, education and human development (MHEHD 2022) (pp. 956-959). Atlantis Press.

Yamen, A. E. (2021). Tax evasion, corruption and COVID-19 health risk exposure: A cross country analysis. *Journal of Financial Crime*, *28*(4), 995–1007. DOI: 10.1108/JFC-10-2020-0220

Yamen, A. E., Mersni, H., & Ramadan, A. (2023). Tax evasion and public governance before and after the European "big bang": A red flag for policymakers. *Journal of Financial Crime*, *30*(2), 420–436. DOI: 10.1108/JFC-04-2020-0064

Yaniv, G. (1999). Tax Compliance and Advance Tax Payments: A Prospect Theory Analysis. [University of Chicago Press.]. *National Tax Journal*, *52*(4), 753–764.DOI: 10.1086/NTJ41789428

Yaniv, G. (2009). The tax compliance demand curve: A diagrammatical approach to income tax evasion. *The Journal of Economic Education*, *40*(2), 213–224. DOI: 10.3200/JECE.40.2.213-224

Yepes-López, G. A., & Gergerlioğlu, U. (2022). Tax Education and the Attitude of University Students Towards Tax Consciousness: The Case of University of Externado (Colombia). *Journal of Tax Reform*, *8*(1), 69–87. DOI: 10.15826/jtr.2022.8.1.109

Yimam, S., Asmare, F., & Moore, M. (2023). *Does Competition from the Informal Sector Reduce Tax Compliance in the Formal Sector?* Evidence from Ethiopia.

Yitzhaki, S. (1974). A note on income tax evasion: A theoretical analysis. *Journal of Public Economics*, *3*(2), 201–202. DOI: 10.1016/0047-2727(74)90037-1

Yong, S., & Martin, F. (2017). Tax compliance of ethnic minority immigrant entrepreneurs: A social capital perspective. *eJTR, 15*, 51.

Yoo, C., & Jang, W. (2019). Social empathy for society beyond the social work profession: A contextual understanding of poverty and attitudes towards government interventions. *Sociétés*, *145*(3), 25–36. DOI: 10.3917/soc.145.0025

Yoo, J., Zell, V., Gutierrez-Reed, N., Wu, J., Ressler, R., Shenasa, M., Johnson, A., Fife, K., Faget, L., & Hnasko, T. (2016). Ventral tegmental area glutamate neurons co-release GABA and promote positive reinforcement. *Nature Communications*, *7*(1), 13697. DOI: 10.1038/ncomms13697

Yoseph, R. (2017). Assessment of Electronic Tax Filing System in Selected Branch Offices of Ethiopian Revenues and Customs Authority (ERCA) (Doctoral dissertation, St. Mary's University).

Young, A., Lei, L., Wong, B., & Kwok, B. (2016). Individual tax compliance in China: a review. International Journal of Law and management, 58(5), 562-574.

Yusuf, S., Abubakar, J., Ocran, G., Owusu, P., Yusuf, P., & Paul-Adeleye, A. (2024). Exploring the impact of AI-driven and blockchain-enabled tax filing systems on SMEs in the era of technological innovation: A review of benefits, challenges, and adoption barriers. *World Journal of Advanced Research and Reviews.*, *23*(03), 1867–1878. DOI: 10.30574/wjarr.2024.23.3.2754

Zakaria, Z., Hussin, Z. H., Zakaria, Z., Noordin, N. B., Sawal, M. Z. H. B. M., Saad, S. F. B. M., & Kamil, S. B. O. (2009). E-Filing System Practiced by Inland Revenue Board (IRB): Perception towards Malaysian Taxpayers/Systeme De Depot Electronique Applique Par Inland Revenue Board (Irb): Perception Des Contribuables De Malaisie. *Cross-Cultural Communication*, *5*(4), 10.

Zaki, B. S. (2024). A conceptual framework of tax compliance for small and medium enterprises (SMEs) in emerging economies. *Global Tax Review*, *10*(4), 98–114.

Zak, P. (2017). The neuroscience of trust. *Harvard Business Review*, *95*(1), 84–90.

Zaman, R., Jain, T., Samara, G., & Jamali, D. (2022). Corporate governance meets communal responsibility of corporates: Mapping the interface. *Business & Society*, *61*(3), 690–752. DOI: 10.1177/0007650320973415

Zaqeeba, N. (2024). The Scope of AI Applications to Tax Evasion in Enhancing Tax Enforcement Capabilities. *Int J Digital Account Fintech Sustain*, *1*(2), 2–16. DOI: 10.70568/IJDAFS1.2

Zhou, S., Ayandibu, A. O., Chimucheka, T., & Masuku, M. M. (2023). Government social protection and households' welfare during the Covid-19 pandemic in South Africa. *Journal of Business and Socio-Economic Development*, *3*(4), 308–321. DOI: 10.1108/JBSED-04-2022-0044

Zichová, T. (2022). Visual Interface Design Innovation: Citizens' Perception of Financial Administration Applications. *Acta Informatica Pragensia*, *11*(1), 1–14. DOI: 10.18267/j.aip.160

Zodrow, G. (2003). Tax competition and tax coordination in the European Union. *International Tax and Public Finance*, *10*(6), 71–71. DOI: 10.1023/A:1026377819946

About the Contributors

Bouchra Alj is a professor and researcher specialising in the field of management sciences, with over two decades of experience. She has gained international recognition for her contributions to the fields of organisational management, public finance and taxation. Subsequently, she obtained her PhD at Mohammed V University, Faculty of Legal, Economic and Social Sciences (FSJES) in Rabat-Agdal, after which she was appointed to the faculty at Cadi Ayyad University in Marrakesh. She subsequently accepted a position at Hassan II University in Casablanca, where she is currently based at the FSJES in Mohammedia. In this capacity, she is responsible for the coordination of the Accounting, Finance and Taxation course, and for the delivery of specialised modules at the bachelor's, master's and PhD levels. These include organisational management, corporate taxation, tax auditing, entrepreneurship and management science research methodology. Moreover, Prof. Bouchra ALJ serves as the head of a research team at the Laboratoire de Recherche en Économie, Management et Stratégies des Organisations (LAREMSO). In this role, she is responsible for leading pioneering research initiatives and for overseeing doctoral dissertations, in addition to undergraduate and postgraduate projects. She guides the team in investigating a range of subjects related to finance, economics, management, and econometrics, employing an interdisciplinary approach to address urgent and relevant issues. In addition to her academic responsibilities, Prof. Bouchra ALJ has authored several books, including works on income taxation in Morocco and organizational management. Additionally, she serves as the co-editor of several forthcoming collective works with IGI Global, which focus on the utilisation of technology in territorial management and sustainable marketing. In her capacity as editor of The Economics & Management Review, a journal included in the IMIST index, she plays an active role in the dissemination of original research, thereby reinforcing the connections between Moroccan researchers and the international scientific community. She is also a member of several scientific and editorial boards for leading academic journals. Her role as a consultant in the private sector enables her to integrate the latest developments in management and taxation within an international context, thereby facilitating the alignment of theoretical and practical approaches. Professor Bouchra ALJ is a prolific contributor to both national and international academic journals, and her research is presented at a number of highly regarded conferences around the globe. Her research interests lie in the fields of management, public finance and taxation, with a particular focus on the psychology of taxation and tax justice. She has also co-authored articles published in English and French, thereby broadening the scope of her contributions. Professor Bouchra ALJ is a highly active member of the national and international academic community. She has been invited to serve on juries and panels at national and international conferences and plays a pivotal role in the organization and leadership of seminars, colloquia and study days, fostering collaboration among dedicated researchers. She regularly contributes to the scientific and evaluation committees of research projects, thereby enhancing her influence in the field of management sciences.

Lhoussaine Alla is a professor in management sciences at the National School of Applied Sciences, a researcher at the LAREMEF laboratory, Sidi Mohamed Ben Abdellah University, Fez, Morocco. He is a permanent professor of various marketing management modules at Sidi Mohamed Ben Abdellah University in Fez (Morocco) and in several public and private business graduate schools. He is an accredited professional expert in the fields of Training Engineering, Professional Coaching and Mentoring young entrepreneurs. After a PhD thesis on creating value for the customer and its impact on the overall performance of companies, Prof. Lhoussaine Alla invested more in scientific research in marketing, through various scientific contributions in the form of participation in international conferences and symposia and scientific publications, in various themes inherent to Marketing (customer value creation, customer behaviour, e-marketing, customer experience, sales performance, Marketing Data Analytics, territorial marketing, territorial attractiveness, territorial economic intelligence, ...), finance (stock market performance, financial analysts, financing package,...), entrepreneurship (entrepreneur profile, startups, entrepreneurial resilience,...), tourism (tourist attractiveness, visitor behaviour, tourism, performance of tourist destinations,...), logistics (SC, SCM, SSCM, Green SCM, logistics performance,...). Prof. Lhoussaine ALLA is also (co)editor of the e-book "Integrating Intelligence and sustainability into supply chains. IGI Global. DOI: 10.4018/979-8-3693-0225-5" and Publication Director of the scientific journal "Managerial and Economic Alternatives - AME", indexed on the IMIST portal, . Prof. Lhoussaine ALLA is also (co)coordinator of many scientific events devoted to marketing research. As much scientific and educational accumulation, the publisher aims to mobilize the potential to bring together researchers and imminent experts to share the fruits of their relevant and innovative research in the implementation, supervision, evaluation, Mastery and reinvention of innovative solutions developed through Data Engineering and AI in Marketing. He is now co-editor of two collective works that will be published via IGI Global: 1. Applying Qualitative Research Methods to Science and Management. 2. Utilizing Technology to Manage Territories. Prof Lhoussaine is the coordinator of a young researchers team, very dynamic and talented, with complementary profiles, creating a friendly space for high-level scientific research.

Badr Bentalha teaches Supply Chain and Operations Management at National School Of Business and Management – Fez, Sidi Mohamed Ben Abdellah University – Morocco. Dr. Bentalha investigates the structural dynamics and control of complex networks, applying his findings to supply chain management, Industry 4.0, risk analysis, and digital supply chains. His pioneering research has established seminal academic and practical approaches for sustainable and intelligent supply chain optimization. Using optimization, simulation, control theory, and AI, he tackles real-world supply chain and operations challenges. His work emphasizes the intersection of supply chain management, operations research, industrial engineering, and digital technology. As a professor, he teaches undergraduate, graduate, and, doctoral courses in operations management, supply chain management, logistics, management information systems, and strategic management. Through guest lectures, webinars, and scholarly presentations, he engages students and fosters an active learning environment. He aims to equip future industry leaders with the management knowledge and technological skills to build more resilient, adaptable, and sustainable supply chain operations. Dr. Bentalha's academic background includes management and economics, operations research, and supply chain management. He studied management operations and supply chain management, graduating with honors. He earned PhD degrees and completed an aggregation in economics and management. Before entering academia, he primarily worked in industry and consulting, focusing on process optimization in manufacturing, logistics, and ERP systems. His practical experience includes numerous operations research and process optimization projects for operations design, logistics, scheduling, and supply chain management. Before joining the Fez National School of Business and Management, he was a professor of economics and management preparatory classes since 2009. Dr. Bentalha's influential research is cited in supply chain management and logistics. His publication record includes over 60 papers in prestigious academic journals such as the International Journal of Logistics Systems and Management, International Journal of Business Performance Management, International Journal of Business and Technology Studies, Journal of Environmental Issues and Climate Change, and Economical Managerial Alternatives. He is also the author of three books: Netnography: Principles, Method, and Ethics, Internal Audit of Treasury and Cash Management: Report on the Audit of Treasury and Integrating Intelligence and Sustainability in Supply Chains. Professor Bentalha specializes in supply chain and operations management, operations research, and service management. He is passionate about integrating knowledge across disciplines to solve real-world problems. He has delivered numerous invited plenary talks, keynotes, and panel discussions at conferences and global webinars. He serves as Associate Editor of the Economical Managerial Alternatives journal and is on the editorial boards and advisory committees of several other publications. He regularly presents his research and has chaired organized program committees, and served on advisory boards for over 60 international conferences in supply chain management, operations, management studies, control theory, and information science. He is a member of numerous scientific committees of international journals and conferences. Since 2009, Mr. Bentalha has helped sundry companies implement an audit system, resolve issues, and improve performance.

***

Syed Immamul Ansarullah is a distinguished academic with a strong educational background. He completed his BCA from the University of Kashmir, followed by an MCA from Baba Ghulam Shah Badshah University. He also completed a B.Ed. and M. Phil, culminating in a Ph.D. in AI and Machine Learning. Since 2019, he has contributed to esteemed colleges and has an impressive research portfolio, including books, patents, and articles. He also reviews for reputable journals.

Abderrahmane Anwar is a PhD candidate in management sciences at the Laboratory of Applied Economics and Finance, University Hassan II of Casablanca. He teaches accounting, taxation, and auditing at the Faculty of Legal, Economic, and Social Sciences, Ain Chock, Hassan II University, Casablanca, Morocco. His research focuses on accounting, taxation, auditing, and corporate finance.

Mohammed Beddaa obtained his doctorate in Marketing and Territorial Management from Mohammed V University in Rabat, Morocco. He is a professor of marketing, entrepreneurship, accounting and management. He has written several articles and participated in various international conferences. He is a member of numerous scientific committees of international journals and conferences. Since 2009, Mr BEDDAA has helped various companies to set up a management system, solve management problems and improve their performance.

Badr Bentalha teaches Supply Chain and Operations Management at National School Of Business and Management – Fez, Sidi Mohamed Ben Abdellah University – Morocco. Dr. Bentalha investigates the structural dynamics and control of complex networks, applying his findings to supply chain management, Industry 4.0, risk analysis, and digital supply chains. His pioneering research has established seminal academic and practical approaches for sustainable and intelligent supply chain optimization. Using optimization, simulation, control theory, and AI, he tackles real-world supply chain and operations challenges. His work emphasizes the intersection of supply chain management, operations research, industrial engineering, and digital technology. As a professor, he teaches undergraduate, graduate, and, doctoral courses in operations management, supply chain management, logistics, management information systems, and strategic management.

Naoual Bouhtati is a doctoral student in Business Management at the Ecole Nationale de Commerce et Gestion de Fès, Sidi Mohamed ben Abdellah University (Morocco), and a researcher at the LAREMEF Laboratory. Preparing a thesis in logistics management, the researcher has explored numerous questions on the subject, particularly in terms of determinants, measurement and management indicators, as well as studying numerous contexts such as mass retailing, small shops, hospitals and local produce.

Esra Doğan received her Bachelor's Degree and PhD in public finance from Ankara University and her Economics master's degree from the University of Essex. She works as a lecturer in Eskisehir Osmangazi University Department of Public Finance. She has studies on theoretical and empirical studies on public finance, and is academically interested in logic and statistics-based empirical studies. She, who has published in national and international journals, has publications on local governments as well as the publications on budget and tax theory.

Gloria Garcia, PhD in Law and Professor of Applied Economics at the University of Murcia (since 1996). She holds a Master's in Equality and Gender in the Private and Public Spheres (2007-2008) and leads the research group "Tax Observatory: Public Policy Analysis" and the "Network on Public Policies and Gender." Her teaching and research focus on fiscal awareness, tax compliance and gender, taxation and gender equality, gender budgeting, and gender well-being through the Capability Approach. She has published extensively on these topics and worked on national and international projects analyzing public budgets with a gender perspective. Dr. Alarcón has collaborated with Professor Klaus Tipke on tax fraud and supported governments in enhancing fiscal awareness and reducing tax fraud. She is a member of the European Gender Budgeting Network, the International Network on Leave Policies and Research, and the Scientific Committee of The Shadow Economy, Tax Evasion and Public Finances (2020-2023)

Georgia Beake Litle, J.D., is a former practicing attorney and current PhD student in Political Science at the University of Oklahoma. Her legal and professional practice areas include work in corporate compliance at a large international proxy advisory firm, experience with corporate financial audits, practice in complex estate planning, and evaluation of corporate anti-trust litigations. Georgia currently works as a Graduate Teaching Fellow for American Federal Government at the University of Oklahoma. Her research interests relate to the fields of public policy analysis, public law, corporate malfeasance, and comparative politics.

Alicia Martinez Serrano, Full University Lecturer at the Department of Political Science, Social Anthropology and Public Finance of the University of Murcia since 2004. PhD in Economics and Business Administration. Doctor with European mention. Lecturer of Taxation in the Degree in Business Administration and the Double Degree in Business Administration and Law. Researcher in Fiscal Systems, researcher at the Fiscal Observatory of the University of Murcia. Author of several publications of the

European Parliament's Directorate-General for Research and author of numerous research papers on taxation. Main research lines are: Taxation in the European Union, Tax Reforms, Tax competition and tax co-ordination in the European Union, Corporate Tax, Tax morale and Fiscal awareness.

Achmad Nurmandi is a Professor at the Department of Government Affairs and Administration, Jusuf Kalla School of Government, Universitas Muhammadiyah Yogyakarta, Indonesia. His research interests are on e-government, urban governance and strategic management in the public sector and published in many international journal and Book Chapter, such as International Journal of Public Sector Management, Transforming Government: People, Policy and Process, Jamba Journal of Disaster Studies, Asian Review of Political Science, Journal of Human Behavior in the Social Environment, Public Policy and Administration, Global Encyclopedia of Public Administration, Public Policy, and Governance, Springer. He is currently the Secretary of the Asia Pacific Society for Public Affairs (APSPA). He is also the Editor-in-Chief of Jurnal Studi Pemerintahan (Journal of Government and Politics) and a Guest Editor of International Journal of Public Sector Performance Management and International Journal of Sustainable Society.

Muhammad Idrees ul Islam is a dedicated researcher at the North Campus of the University of Kashmir, examining the intersections of artificial intelligence, entrepreneurship, e-commerce, and marketing. His published works investigate subjects such as sustainable tourism, digital commerce, and the socio-political influences that shape business outcomes. Notably, he has explored the transformative potential of AI and machine learning within financial analysis, identifying promising opportunities as well as challenges in technology-driven markets. Through collaborations with fellow scholars, he aims to address emerging issues in mobile payment systems, conflict-affected management activities, and open network platforms. His research is anchored by a commitment to practical impact, evident in his focus on the sustainable development of tourism enterprises and other industries. Driven by intellectual curiosity, he continues to push disciplinary boundaries, contributing novel insights to both local and global discussions on innovation and entrepreneurship. His work exemplifies a devotion to meaningful progress and sustainability.

Maithilee Umranikar, holds an M.Sc. Economics degree from Symbiosis School of Economics, Pune. Contributed to various research projects in Behavioral Economics, including studies on investor biases and the relationship between lifestyle choices and the preference for immediate gratification. Deeply passionate about teaching. Believes that human behavior is the fundamental element shaping cultures, societies, and driving global developments.

Muhammad Younus graduated in 2019 from the Karachi Institute of Economics and Technology University in Karachi, Pakistan, and got a Bachelor's degree in Computer Science. The four-year undergraduate program in Computer Science formed the basis of Younus's perseverance towards achieving an in-depth knowledge in the field. After graduation, Younus worked for the past few years as a business IT analyst in the product and research development of a logistics startup in Pakistan called TPL Logistics. They aim to Digitize Logistics Operations in Pakistan from the First Mile to the Last Mile. After this, Younus graduated in 2024 from the Universitas Muhammadiyah Yogyakarta in Yogyakarta, Indonesia, and got a Master's Degree in Government Science. Younus's research interest is transforming governance and the public sector through technology. This experience has given Younus the confidence and also kindled a desire to do research. The interdisciplinary nature has convinced Younus in taking this decision as it is the ideal choice for an exciting research career. At the same time, I am confident of contributing originally to the ongoing work. By working under the guidance of distinguished Team, Younus shall certainly be able to exploit my potential to the fullest.

Index

L

M

N

P

R

S

T

U

www.ingramcontent.com/pod-product-compliance
Lightning Source LLC
LaVergne TN
LVHW060400300926
849162LV00006B/1314
* 9 7 9 8 3 3 7 3 0 4 2 2 9 *